ALSO BY NEIL HANSON

The Custom of the Sea

The Great Fire of London

The Confident Hope
of a Miracle

The Confident Hope of a Miracle

The True History of the Spanish Armada

NEIL HANSON

ALFRED A. KNOPF   NEW YORK   2005

Originally published in Great Britain by Doubleday,
a division of Transworld Publishers, London, in 2003.

Library of Congress Cataloging-in-Publication Data
Hanson, Neil.
The confident hope of a miracle : the true history of the
Spanish Armada / Neil Hanson.—1st American ed.
p. cm.
Includes bibliographical references and index.
ISBN 1-4000-4294-1
1. Armada, 1588.   2. Great Britain—History, Naval—Tudors, 1485–1603.
3. Spain—History, Naval—16th century.   I. Title.

DA360.H34 2005
942.05'5—DC22   2004048378

Printed in the United States of America
First American Edition

For Lynn, Jack and Drew

Contents

PART III

Aftermath

Illustrations

FIRST PICTURE SECTION

Royaux des Beaux-Arts de Belgique, Brussels. Photo Institut Amatller d'Art Hispànic-Arxiu Mas, Barcelona; *Pope Sixtus V*, c. 1588–90, Venetian School. The Vatican Museums; *Justin of Nassau*, studio of Jan Anthonisz. van Ravesteyn. Rijksmuseum, Amsterdam; *Henri III*, French School, sixteenth century. Musée de Tessé, Le Mans. © The Bridgeman Art Library; *Henri IV*, French School, sixteenth century. Château de Versailles. © The Bridgeman Art Library.

Map of the south-west coast, 1539. By permission of the British Library, Department of Manuscripts, Cotton Augustus li. 38–39; anonymous portrait of Charles Howard, Lord Effingham and Earl of Nottingham, 1602. © The National Portrait Gallery Picture Library; anonymous portrait of Sir Francis Drake, c. 1580. © The National Portrait Gallery Picture Library; *Sir John Hawkins*, English School, sixteenth century. © National Maritime Museum; *Sir Martin Frobisher* by Cornelius Ketel, 1577. The Curators of the Bodleian Library, Oxford.

Three pages from "Fragments of Ancient English Shipwrightry" by Matthew Baker, c. 1586. Pepysian Library MS 2820. By permission of the Master and Fellows of Magdalene College, Cambridge; mariner's astrolabe, 1588. © National Maritime Museum; frontispiece by Theodor de Bry to *The Mariner's Mirror*, Lucas Jansz. Waghenaer, 1588. © National Maritime Museum.

Robert Dudley, Earl of Leicester, English School, sixteenth century. The Collection at Parham Park, West Sussex. © Mark Fiennes; *Sir Francis Walsingham* by John de Critz the Elder. © The National Portrait Gallery Picture Library; *William Cecil, 1st Baron Burghley*, English School, 1586. The Collection at Parham Park, West Sussex. © The Bridgeman Art Library; title page of the pamphlet "A Pack of Spanish Lies...," 1588.

SECOND PICTURE SECTION

Sixteenth-century map of Portland Bill and Weymouth Bay. By permission of the British Library, Department of Manuscripts, Cotton Augustus li. 31 and 33; beacon hut, Higher Manhay, Cornwall. Author's photo.

Details of the Armada charts from *Expeditionis Hispanorum in Angliam vera description Anno Do:MDLXXXVIII*, 1590, by Augustin Ryther after Robert Adams: 30–31 July (top left); 31 July–1 August (bottom left);

2–3 August (top right); 8 August (bottom right). © National Maritime Museum.

Detail of *The Launch of the English Fireships against the Armada, 7 August 1588*, Netherlandish School, sixteenth century. © National Maritime Museum.

A shipwreck, sixteenth-century manuscript illumination. Glasgow University Library. © The Bridgeman Art Library; anonymous portrait of Sir Richard Bingham, 1564. © The National Portrait Gallery Picture Library; resolution to pursue the Armada. By permission of the British Library, Department of Manuscripts, Add. MSS. 33740 f. 5; map showing the route of the Armada fleet from *Expeditionis Hispanorum . . .* as above. © National Maritime Museum; salamander pendant from the *Girona*, sixteenth century, gold with rubies. Photograph © Ulster Museum, Belfast. Reproduced with the kind permission of the Trustees of the National Museums & Galleries of Northern Ireland; Lacada Point, Northern Ireland. Bates Littlehales © National Geographic Society.

Elizabeth I, the Armada Portrait, attributed to George Gower, c. 1588. Woburn Abbey, Bedfordshire. © The Bridgeman Art Library; a rich man spurns a beggar, from *A Christall Glass of Christian Reformation* by Stephen Bateman, 1569. Private collection. © The Bridgeman Art Library; list of executed Armada survivors, December 1588. The National Archives (SP63/139).

Endpapers (hardcover edition): *The English and Spanish Fleets off Berry Head . . .* : one of the series of engravings by John Pine after the House of Lords Armada tapestries, 1739. © The Bridgeman Art Library.

Acknowledgements

Among the tens of thousands of documents on the Armada held primarily, but not exclusively, in archives in England, France, Italy, Spain and The Netherlands, I have concentrated much of my original researches on the fate of the survivors of the fleets after they came ashore. Like countless other writers and historians, I have also consulted the Calendars and printed versions of contemporary documents, offering silent prayers for the dedication of those, usually Victorian, scholars who performed the difficult task of transcribing the often tattered and near-illegible originals for the benefit of writers and researchers as yet unborn, and I am also indebted to the painstaking research work in the Spanish archives undertaken by historians from Duro and Laughton in the nineteenth century to Geoffrey Parker towards the end of the twentieth.

Eugene L. Rasor's bibliography of the Armada sources and literature is the starting point for any researcher, and of the innumerable previous accounts of the Armada, I would single out four. Garrett Mattingly's, written as long ago as 1959, remains the definitive account of the diplomatic background to the launching of the Armada, though he perhaps made less of the Spanish attempts to create a second front in Scotland and Ireland than their importance merited. Geoffrey Parker and Colin Martin combined their respective expert knowledge of Spanish archives and marine archaeology and Armada wrecks to correct many prior misapprehensions, Alexander McKee constructed a vivid account from primary sources, and David Howarth wrote one of the more elegant and intelligent analyses of the campaign. Other significant sources include *Boteler's Dialogues*, written within thirty years of the Armada and invaluable on the day-to-day running of ships of the era and their conduct in battle, Peter Kemp's excellent exploration of

life on the lower deck, *The British Sailor*, Kenneth R. Andrews's absorbing study of Elizabethan privateering, Leon van der Essen's massive
biography of Alexander Farnese, Duke of Parma, and Peter Pierson's
definitive biography of the Duke of Medina-Sidonia. The many other
writers upon whose work I have drawn are listed in the bibliography.
Direct quotations have been converted into modern English—"doth"
and "hath" have been replaced by "does" and "has," for example, but
no other changes have been made to the contemporary texts.

All dates in this book use the Gregorian calendar introduced by
Pope Gregory XIII in 1582 and still in use today. Because of its "papist"
origins, England refused to adopt the system and stubbornly adhered
to the old Julian calendar for over a century after it had disappeared
from the rest of Europe. As a result, all events mentioned in contemporary English documents on the Armada appear to have occurred ten
days earlier than in Spanish ones. To avoid confusion, they have been
rendered into the equivalent "New Style" date. The first sighting of
the Armada off the Lizard therefore occurred on 30 July 1588, not
20 July.

As always, my thanks go to the knowledgeable and helpful staff at
the London Library, the Bodleian Library in Oxford, the British
Library in London and its outstation at Wetherby, the Public Record
Office, the Historic Manuscripts Commission, the National Maritime
Museum, and all the many regional libraries, museums, archives,
record offices and historical societies who responded so positively to
my requests for help and information. I'm grateful also to the fishermen, yachtsmen, coastguards, naval officers and many other people
with expertise in a variety of fields whom I encountered during my
researches, and who, without exception, gave freely of their time in
answering my queries.

My thanks also to my New York agent Kim Witherspoon and
David Forrer; to Mark Lucas and his assistant Alice Saunders in London; and to the magnificent team at Knopf Publishing including,
among many others, Ashbel Green, Sonny Mehta, Andrew Miller,
Luba Ostashevsky, Gabriele Wilson, Maria Massey, Lydia Buechler,
Katherine Hourigan, Eric Bliss, Soonyoung Kwon, and Tracy Cabanis;
to the proofreader, Kate Norris; and to Christine Casaccio, the publi-
cist for this book, and to all the people in sales and marketing who promoted this book.

My personal thanks also go to Peter Metcalf for his help with the
research from regional sources, to Didy Metcalf, who drew my attention to some interesting documents in Ireland and Yorkshire, and most
of all to Lynn, Jack and Drew, whose love and support over the last

three years have sustained me through the mammoth task of researching and writing this book. Lastly, I'm grateful to Chris Harper, who pointed me in the direction of this incredible story, so familiar to us all in half-remembered myth and legend, and yet so utterly unfamiliar in its true details.

Neil Hanson
JUNE 2004

Glossary

ARQUEBUS: matchlock weapon of variable barrel length, bore and weight

BEAR ROOM: pull away

CABLE: thick rope attached to the anchor

CALIVER: standardized version of the arquebus with a consistent bore and barrel length

CANNON: heavy gun delivering a large projectile over short ranges

CARAVEL: lighter and more manoeuvrable three-masted version of the carrack

CAREEN: scrape the hull of a ship to remove weed, barnacles, etc. Also came to mean sailing at a list, from the angle which ships assumed when beached for careening

CARRACK: Mediterranean merchant ship readily converted to a warship. Often with three decks, deep holds and high fore- and sterncastles

CULVERIN: longer-range version of the cannon

DOWNS: sea area between the East Kent coast and the Goodwin Sands

DUCAT: Spanish gold coin weighing approximately one-eighth of an ounce

EMBARGO: impound, seize

FATHOM: measurement of depth, six feet

FLOTA: Spanish treasure fleet from the New World

FLYBOAT: light, shallow-draught vessel, capable of operating in water too shallow for conventional warships

GALLEASS: ship fitted with oars and sails in an attempt to combine the speed of a galley with the seaworthiness and firepower of a galleon

GALLEON: large ocean-going fighting ship of two or more decks with gun batteries in broadsides. Spanish galleons had fighting castles fore and aft; English ships were sleeker and lower.

GALLEY: oared warship with banks of oars five metres long, weighing 300 kilograms and each powered by five men. In combat they could achieve speeds of four knots, rowing at 22 to 26 strokes per minute.

GREAT SHIP: armed merchantman, usually over 300 tons. The great ships of the Levant Company were heavily armed to fight off corsairs.

HULK: either a sailing ship stripped of its masts and rigging and used as a store, hospital, prison, guardship, barracks, etc. or a northern European sailing ship used in the Baltic trade. Lacking a keel, the flat-bottomed hulks were capacious, but slow and clumsy.

LAST: measure of gunpowder, approximately equal to 2,400 pounds weight

MORION: visorless helmet

MUSKET: long-barrelled weapon firing a shot capable of penetrating personal armour, and fired using a wooden rest to support the barrel

PAPER ROYAL: strong paper used in cartridges

PINNACE: smaller, faster version of a galleon, used mainly for scouting, communications and shallow-water fighting

PRESS GANG: group carrying out forced recruitment of seamen

PRIVATEER: state-sponsored pirate

RUMMAGE: clean the gravel ballast in the bilges

RUTTER: route map used by navigators, showing headlands and other prominent features

SCONCE: fortress

SPRING TIDE: high tide produced when the sun and moon are directly aligned with the earth, combining their gravitational pulls

WARP: pull clear of harbour into a contrary wind by hauling in anchor cables or ropes at fixed points along the shore

WEATHER GAUGE, HAVING THE: being to windward

ZABRA: fast pinnace

Philip of Spain wept when his armada went down.
Was he the only one to weep?

BERTOLT BRECHT,
Questions from a Worker Who Reads

PART I

The Enterprise of England

CHAPTER ONE

King of Spain consults the
enlarging his Empire by the
Conquest of England.

God's Obvious Design

A little after ten o'clock on the morning of Wednesday, 18 February 1587, Mary Stuart, Queen of Scots, entered the great hall of Fotheringay, preceded by the Sheriff, bearing the white wand of his office, and escorted by the Earls of Kent and Shrewsbury. Her retinue of six followed behind. She had already kept her audience waiting for three hours as she made her prayers, read her will aloud to her servants, gave them final instructions, and finished last letters to be smuggled with her "principal notes and papers" to her cousin the Duc de Guise and to Henri of France. "I must die like a criminal at seven in the morning," she wrote, but even on the day of her execution none had dared to hurry the preparations of a queen, until at last soldiers were ordered to break down the door to her quarters if she delayed any longer. Over two hundred knights and gentlemen were present, hastily summoned to witness her end. Some had ridden all night; their boots were mud-splashed and the smell of damp wool from their rain-soaked cloaks hung in the air, for the logs blazing in the great stone hearth did little to lessen the chill of a bitter winter's day. A much larger crowd had gathered outside the castle, some holding placards depicting Mary as a mermaid—the symbol of a prostitute. They were watched over by a troop of cavalry, and musicians assembled in the courtyard played a dirge, "an air commonly played at the execution of witches."[1]

The crowd stirred, men jostling and craning their necks to see the most notorious woman in Europe, tall, beautiful and sexually voracious, but also a constant treacherous conspirator against their own queen and, if rumour were true, a murderess twice over. Many must have been disappointed; there was no hint of such scandals in the modest demeanour of the woman in front of them that cold morning. Mary's gait was slow and measured, and her eyes downcast "like a devout woman going to her prayers." A chain of scented beads with a golden cross hung around her neck, she had a rosary at her waist, and she carried an ivory crucifix in her hand. Age had dimmed her beauty but her eyes, in a face almost as pale as the white lace at her throat, remained clear and keen. The auburn hair showing beneath her kerchief was the only flash of colour in the room. She was clad from head to foot in black velvet, echoing the drapes on the dais in front of her. Hurriedly constructed after the arrival of the death warrant signed by Queen Elizabeth on Sunday evening, the platform was twenty feet by twelve and little more than three feet high, topped by a rail like a picket fence, low enough to allow the spectators an uninterrupted view. It was a modest stage for the last act of a drama that had been played out for almost thirty years.

The murmur of voices died away and a silence fell on the room as Mary mounted the steps of the platform and walked slowly towards the single high-backed, black-draped chair at the far end. In front of it was a kneeling cushion and then the scalloped shape of the executioner's block, both also draped in black serge. As she sank into the chair, Mary raised her eyes, dark as the velvet she wore, and surveyed her audience. The firelight reflected from the breastplates and helmets of the row of guards facing her, sheriff's men, each holding a halberd in his right hand. Her expression betrayed no emotion as her gaze moved from them to two powerfully built, masked and black-clad figures, one of them resting his hands on the haft of his double-headed axe, "like those with which they cut wood." Robert Beale, the Clerk to the Privy Council and brother-in-law to the principal Secretary of State, Sir Francis Walsingham, unrolled the parchment bearing the Queen's seal and began to read from it. The warrant cited Mary's "stubborn disobedience and incitement to insurrection against the life and person of Her Sacred Majesty." The crime was high treason and the sentence was death.

Mary was nine years younger than Elizabeth—"the Virgin Queen" or "the English Jezebel," depending on the observer's religious persuasion. Daughter of James V of Scotland and Marie de Guise of France, she had become Queen of the Scots in 1542 at just one week old, following the death of her father, who collapsed and died after hearing that his invading army had been slaughtered by Henry VIII's troops at Solway Moss. At the age of six, she was betrothed to the Dauphin of France, the future Francis II of the royal house of Valois, and became a ward of Catherine de' Medici at the French court. She duly married at the age of fifteen and within a year was Queen of France, but she soon showed her talent for intrigue by passing secret information to her uncles the de Guises, the enemies of the Valois kings.

The granddaughter of Henry VIII's sister, Mary felt herself, not Elizabeth, to be the rightful heir to his throne. Monarchs were not constrained by the same laws as their subjects in civil or ecclesiastical matters; many inconvenient marriages had been dissolved with the compliance of the Vatican, and many bastard offspring, including the Emperor Charles V's son, Don Juan of Austria, and daughter, Margaret, Duchess of Parma, had been declared legitimate. But Henry VIII had gone too far ever to be forgiven, even posthumously. He had not only divorced a woman of the imperial blood—Catherine of Aragon was Charles V's aunt—he had also wrenched his populace from the Church of Rome, and confiscated its assets. There was no possibility that Elizabeth would ever be seen in Paris, Madrid or Rome as anything but the bastard daughter of Henry's bigamous marriage to Anne Boleyn, and moreover one whose self-proclaimed virginity hid a score of scandals: "Wife to many and to many daughter-in-law, oh foul queen, nay no queen, but lustful, beastly whore." Even among Englishmen, the title the "Virgin Queen" may well have been entirely ironic when first bestowed.[2]

After Mary Tudor's death in 1558, Francis II declared himself and his wife to be "rulers of France, Scotland, England and Ireland" and quartered the English coat of arms with his own, but following Mary's bloody reign of terror few Englishmen could stomach the idea of another Catholic monarch, and Elizabeth began to consolidate her hold on power. The immediate threat to her throne was removed when Francis died suddenly on 6 December 1560, having reigned for only sixteen months, leaving Mary, Queen of Scots, a widow at just eighteen. She accepted the Scottish crown, but scandal surrounded her from the first. She took a string of lovers, was implicated in the murder of David Rizzio, her secretary, and of her second husband, Lord Darnley, and then compounded the outrage by marrying her husband's murderer, the Earl of Bothwell. Imprisoned and forced to abdicate, she escaped from her captivity and rallied forces loyal to her, but they were defeated at the battle of Langside in 1568 and she then fled to England, seeking the protection of Elizabeth. She spent the remainder of her life under confinement, but it was a gilded cage—she was allowed a retinue of forty and was permitted to hunt and visit spas to take the waters—and she was the constant focus and sometimes the wellspring of intrigues and plots.

Mary's son, the future James VI of Scotland and James I of England, "a sickly, backward lad, shambling, awkward and unattractive," had been taken from his mother at the age of ten months and raised as a Protestant, and by her will of 1577 Mary made plain her intention to bequeath her rights to the English throne not to her son but to Philip II of Spain. The former husband of Mary Tudor, Philip had also once been a suitor of Elizabeth, albeit for purely pragmatic and dynastic reasons: "Nothing would make me do this except the clear knowledge that it might gain the kingdom." He had constructed a tenuous claim to the English throne in his own right through his descent from Constanza of Castile's marriage to John of Gaunt, son of Edward III. Some saw Mary's gesture as an invitation for Philip to invade and place her on the throne, though it might equally have been a calculated attempt to stay Elizabeth's hand, for fear of unleashing an even greater danger.

Elizabeth had dithered over the fate of Mary since she took up the crown. Her father, Henry VIII, would not have hesitated for a moment; he would have had Mary executed as soon as she came into his hands and defied all of Europe's popes and princes to do their worst. He had done as much by divorcing Catherine of Aragon and breaking with Rome, and had built the most powerful navy in Europe to defend his shores against his enemies. Elizabeth had already been given ample grounds for executing Mary. In 1569, the Rising of the North, a rebellion led by the northern Catholic earls, was an immediate reminder of the dangers posed by a rival for the throne. It was crushed with great brutality, but no action was taken against Mary, even when she was then implicated in a plot against Elizabeth in 1572. Funded by the Florentine banker Roberto di Ridolfi, the conspirators included the Spanish ambassador, the Pope, the Duke of Norfolk and the privateer John Hawkins. Hawkins sent a message to Philip professing to be weary of Elizabeth's "fickle and tyrannical rule," and when asked for proof, he sent a letter "cunningly procured" from Mary, Queen of Scots. Philip then sent gold "to be used by him in making traitors of other Englishmen and in preparing some English ships for Spanish service." Hawkins pocketed the money, but passed information on every move that the plotters made to Elizabeth's spymaster, Sir Francis Walsingham, who ran a chain of 500 agents operating as far afield as Constantinople. He liked to remark that "knowledge is never too dear" and "might well have been compared to him in the Gospel that sowed his tares in the night; so did [he sow his] seeds in division, in the dark."[3]

Hawkins was certainly a consummate double agent, Ridolfi may well have been, and Elizabeth's ministers were so well informed about the plot that all the chief conspirators were arrested. Under interrogation that would certainly have included torture, the Bishop of Ross, Mary's confessor, implicated her not only in the plot to depose Elizabeth but also in the murder of her second husband, Lord Darnley, and, less plausibly, her first, Francis II. The Duke of Norfolk, who was to have married Mary on her assumption of the throne, was convicted of treason on 16 January 1572, and executed after much hesitation by Elizabeth on 2 June, but she stayed her hand from administering the same punishment to Mary herself. She vetoed a bill of attainder in favour of her own bill making Mary "unable to enjoy the Crown of this realm" and then vetoed that bill too. "A law to make the Scottish Queen unable and unworthy of succession to the Crown was by Her Majesty neither assented to nor rejected, but deferred." After the St. Bartholomew's Day Massacre of French Protestants the same year, Bishop Sandes advised Elizabeth's Lord Treasurer, William Cecil, Lord Burghley, "forthwith to cut off the Scottish Queen's head." His advice was ignored and Mary remained alive, closely confined, but still the focus of a succession of plots and intrigues against Elizabeth.[4]

In 1582, Walsingham, an expert linguist and cryptographer, had deciphered the codes used in secret messages passing between Mary and the French and Spanish courts. From then on, everything that Mary wrote was intercepted and read. The first fruit of it came that same year, when Walsingham revealed a plot involving Mary and her kinsmen the de Guises, the Pope, the Jesuits, Don Bernardino de Mendoza, then Spanish ambassador in London, and Philip II himself to restore Scotland to the old faith and then invade England. In the winter of 1583 Walsingham exposed the Throckmorton Plot, again involving Mendoza. The leading conspirators, including Francis Throckmorton, were arrested and tortured, and Mendoza was expelled in January 1584; no Spanish ambassador replaced him for the remainder of Elizabeth's reign, but Philip continued to intrigue against her and fund the Queen of Scots.

Several Spanish plots against the Dutch leader William the Silent, of the House of Orange, had also failed, but his assassination in 1584, coupled with the exposure of a plan by John Somerville to shoot Elizabeth, caused terror in England, where it seemed all too likely that she might suffer a similar fate. Her crown was "not like to fall to the ground for want of heads that claim to wear it." As a result, access to her wardrobe, laundry and kitchens was rigidly controlled and in October 1584 Burghley and Walsingham drew up a Bond of Association. Members swore to defend Elizabeth's life with their own and "pursue as well by force of arms as by all other means of revenge all manner of persons of what estate so ever they shall be . . . that shall attempt . . . the harm of Her Majesty's royal person . . . [and] never desist from all manner of forcible pursuit against such persons to the uttermost extermination of them . . . No pretended successor by whom or for whom any such detestable act shall be attempted or committed" would be allowed to take the throne.[5]

The implication was clear: if a plot in which Mary, Queen of Scots, was either a co-conspirator or even the innocent beneficiary should succeed, the members of the Association swore to strike her down before she could claim the throne. This could also apply to James VI, Elizabeth's putative heir, if the members of the Association so chose, a clear warning to him not to involve himself in plots and conspiracies in order to bring forward the time of his accession. As soon as Parliament reassembled in November, an "Act for the Queen's Safety" was proposed and passed, including a provision that any attempt on the Queen's life with the aim of advancing a claimant to the throne rendered any then supporting that claimant guilty of treason. However, the claimant's heirs were exempted from any penalty unless they were "privy" to the crime, making it clear that the Act's target was Mary, not her son James. The Act also authorized the persecution of Jesuits and Catholic priests, and laid down that Englishmen studying at Catholic seminaries abroad were to return home within six months or be found guilty in absentia of treason.

The legislation had no visible effect on the frequency of plots against Elizabeth. The Parry Plot—William Parry, MP for Queensborough, plotted to murder the Queen—was exposed in 1585, causing fresh panic over the succession, but Elizabeth still stayed her hand, more scared of French and Habsburg hostility than of the threat that Mary represented to her throne. The memory of the beheading of her own mother, Anne Boleyn, on Tower Green no doubt weighed heavily with her, and she perhaps feared even more the dangerous precedent she would set by implying that any "prince" anointed by God could be subject to mere mortal justice at the hands of man; "absolute princes ought not to be accountable for their actions to any other than to God alone."[6]

Yet though she professed to find the idea of a judicial execution "utterly repugnant," she also went out of her way to encourage her subordinates to find means to dispose of Mary without recourse to the executioner's block. She both hated and was jealous of Mary and missed few opportunities to humiliate her. When Mary fled to England without even a change of raiment, Elizabeth sent her a gift of clothing— "two torn shifts, two pieces of black velvet, two pairs of shoes and nothing else"—and then bought Mary's jewels from the Scottish regent. When a diplomat remarked that Mary was very beautiful, Elizabeth haughtily announced that she herself was far "superior to the Queen of Scotland." In the early 1570s, Elizabeth had sent Sir Henry Killigrew to offer three successive Scottish regents—Moray, Lennox and Mar—a lavish bribe in return for their agreement that if Mary were released and returned to Scotland, she would be immediately executed, "so as neither that realm nor this should be endangered by her hereafter."[7] Each regent perished of natural causes before any deal could be concluded and the next one, the Earl of Morton, though no better disposed to Mary than his predecessors, was also "too old a cat to draw such a straw as that after him," knowing that whatever the financial rewards, he would either be a scapegoat for the killing or the target of assassins seeking revenge. However, as England's long-simmering conflict with Spain grew more open, Mary's presence became an ever greater threat, and her involvement in yet another conspiracy sealed her fate.[8]

After the Throckmorton Plot, Mary had been placed in the custody of the puritan Sir Amyas Paulet and kept isolated, but a secret channel of communication was set up between her and the French ambassador using a watertight box hidden inside an ale barrel. Unknown to Mary, Walsingham had devised the method and was monitoring the correspondence. The Babington Plot to murder Elizabeth, endorsed by Mary in a secret letter dictated by her on 17 July 1586 and at once intercepted by Walsingham, was her death sentence. The evidence was overwhelming; Anthony Babington was so enamoured of the fame that would be his if the plot succeeded that he even had his portrait painted with the six chosen assassins.

The Earl of Leicester, always a fierce opponent of Mary, even though he had once been dispatched as a reluctant suitor for her hand, saw the chance to put an end to the plots and conspiracies that had bedevilled Elizabeth's reign. "If the matter be well handled, it will break the neck of all dangerous practices during Her Majesty's reign." Mary was incarcerated at Fotheringay, a safe distance from both London and her potential supporters in the north, and her trial began on 14 October 1586, by which time her fellow conspirators had already been tried and hanged. After hearing of the tortures that had been inflicted on the assassin of William the Silent, Elizabeth demanded that the Privy Council should find similar means to execute Anthony Babington and his co-conspirators, so that they should suffer a more terrible end than "mere" hanging, drawing and quartering. Only when Burghley had convinced her of the terrible pain and duration of the latter punishment did she relent. Typically she then changed her mind after hearing of the torments Babington had suffered and ordered that the other conspirators should be hung without drawing or quartering.[9]

Mary at first refused to attend her trial, claiming the court had no jurisdiction over her, but when Elizabeth gave her a "veiled hint of clemency" she defended herself for two days with such "vigour and ability" that proceedings were suspended and then reconvened in the closed Star Chamber. The guilty verdict was pronounced on 25 October but, as her Private Secretary William Davison complained, Elizabeth still hesitated to take her rival's life "unless extreme fear compels her." Parliament sent her a petition to execute Mary, "whilst the Queen of Scotland lived she would never be free from such conspiracies," and backed it up by a threat to withdraw the funds they had just voted for Crown expenditure if their wishes were not heeded. Elizabeth delivered her response on 24 November: "If I should say I would not do what you request, it might peradventure be more than I thought; and to say I would do it, might perhaps breed peril of that you labour to preserve." She described this as an "answer answerless" but even those unskilled in deciphering Elizabeth's meaning would not have been troubled to decide that she wanted Mary dead, but also wanted to appear blameless in the deed.[10]

William Cecil, Lord Burghley, prepared the death warrant in early December, but it remained unsigned by Elizabeth for two months, during which time Mary was permitted to write to the Pope, Philip of Spain, Mendoza, Henri III and the Duc de Guise in France and other Catholic leaders, appealing for support and confirming her bequest of her claim to the throne of England to His Most Catholic Majesty Philip II. Elizabeth's procrastination at last came to an end on 11 February, when, as Davison had predicted, terrified by rumours that Spanish troops had landed in Wales and that Mary had escaped from her confinement at Fotheringay, she ordered him to bring the document, called for pen and ink and signed it. She then gave Davison contradictory verbal orders—to have the royal seal fixed to the warrant, and not to do so until so ordered. Davison, "a terrible heretic and an enemy of the queen of Scotland," acted on the first instruction. A meeting of eleven Privy Counsellors arranged for the sentence to be carried out with all possible speed but, fearing yet another royal change of mind, they did not inform Her Majesty of this "before the execution were past."[11]

As Mr. Beale finished reading the warrant and fell silent, George Talbot, Earl of Shrewsbury, addressed the Queen of Scots. "Madam, you hear what we are commanded to do?"

"Do your duty," she said. "I was born a queen and sovereign princess, not subject to laws, a near relative of the Queen of England and her legitimate heir. After having been long and unlawfully imprisoned in this country, where I have endured many pains and evils . . . I thank my God that He has permitted that in this hour, I die for my religion." Anxious to stem the heretical discourse, the earl signalled to Dr. Fletcher, the dean of Peterborough, who stood up and tried to speak, but his nerves were so great that three times he began and each time he stumbled to a halt after a few words. Mary raised a hand to silence him. "Mr. Dean, trouble me not. I am settled and persuaded in the Catholic Roman faith and mean to shed my blood in defence of it." As he continued to try to speak, she "began with tears and loud voice to pray in Latin." Her voice drowned his and still rang out long after the dean abandoned his prepared speech and resumed his seat. She raised her crucifix over her head so that it glinted in the firelight and, switching to English, offered prayers for "the conversion of England to the true faith, the perseverance of Catholics in their creed and their constancy in martyrdom." It was a powerful performance, and one aimed at an audience that extended far beyond those assembled at Fotheringay.[12]

Following an old tradition, the executioner, "one Bulle, the hangman of London," and his assistant knelt before her and "desired her Grace to forgive them her death." She answered, "I forgive you with all my heart, for now, I hope, you shall make an end of all my troubles." As she fell silent, Bulle made to remove her gown. Mary stopped him and even managed a joke, though it drew not a smile. "Let me do this, I understand this business better than you. I never had such a groom of the chamber." As her ladies in waiting helped to remove it, she added that she had "never put off her clothes before such a company." Beneath the black gown she was wearing a bodice and petticoat of crimson satin—the martyr's colour—vivid as fire in that sombre, monochrome hall. Even the most dour Puritan must now have been craning his neck, the better to see the scene unfolding on the platform. Mary "helped to make ready herself . . . with some haste as if she had longed to be gone." She took the gold cross from her neck and asked the executioner to allow her maid to keep it. In return he would be paid "more than its value in money." Bulle refused, claiming the traditional right of the executioner to the personal effects of the victim, and "put it in his shoe."[13]

She had earlier told the Earl of Kent that "he is not worthy of the joys of heaven, whose body cannot suffer the stroke of the executioner," and she knelt on the cushion "most resolutely and without any token of fear of death . . . she laid down her head, putting her chin over the block with both hands." The Earl of Shrewsbury had already raised his hand ready to signal the execution, when Bulle's assistant noticed that Mary's hands were still under her chin and would have been "cut off had they not [been] espied." The assistant moved her hands and Bulle stepped forward and raised his axe. Mary, Queen of Scotland, Dowager Queen of France, heir to the English throne and the lawful Queen of England in the eyes of all adherents to the old religion, stretched out her arms in the pose of Christ crucified and offered her final prayer in Latin, consigning herself into the hands of her God. [14]

"She cried, 'In manus tuas, Domine,' etc., three or four times," then lay motionless, held "slightly" by the executioner's assistant, as the axe fell once, twice, the dull thud of the blade on wood echoing through the room, "she making very small noise or none at all, and not stirring any part of her from the place where she lay. And so the executioner cut off her head, saving one little gristle, which being cut asunder," Bulle stooped to complete the final, preordained part of the ritual. He straightened, raising his right arm and crying out "God save the Queen," to an answering chorus of "Amen." But all he held was the kerchief and an auburn wig. The shaved head, stubbled with grey, rolled across the platform. "It appeared as grey as one of three score years and ten, polled [cropped] very short, her face in a moment being so much altered from the form she had when she was alive, as few could remember her by her dead face."[15]

The Earl of Kent pronounced the final words over her lifeless body: "May it please God that all the Queen's enemies be brought into this condition. This be the end of all who hate the Gospel and Her Majesty's government." Bulle then "placed her head on a salver" and showed it from the window to the crowd in the courtyard, holding it up three times. The castle gates had been closed and barred before the axe had fallen so that none could leave until the official messenger, Shrewsbury's third son, Henry Talbot, had been dispatched to carry the news of Mary's death to the Court in London. Her servants who had witnessed her end were hustled away, "lest some of them with speeches would . . . disquiet the company . . . or seek to wipe their napkins in some of her blood," and, "every man being commanded out of the hall," the head and body were at once gathered up and taken to a side-room. There the lifeless body was stripped, placed in a coffin and removed to the chapel. The gold cross was taken from the executioners and they were sent away empty-handed save for their fee, "not having any one thing that belonged to her." Mary's rosary was thrown into the fire blazing in the great hearth, while her robes, the black serge fabric that had covered the executioner's block and everything stained with her blood were consigned to the flames of a bonfire in the courtyard; no holy relics of the martyr were to be preserved. The blaze set off a chain of beacons in every town and village, for as Henry Talbot passed by with his escort, shouting the news as they rode hell for leather towards London, bonfires were "lit for joy all over the countryside" and church bells rung in celebration.[16]

Talbot reached the Royal Palace at Greenwich within twenty-four hours of Mary's death, but the Queen, mounting her horse to go hunting, did not see him arrive and instead Lord Burghley was the first to hear the news. By the time Elizabeth returned from the hunt, the palace and half of London were abuzz with it. A mob gathered outside the home of the French ambassador and forced him to provide the fuel for "a very large fire opposite his door . . . a piece of insolent intolerance such as [had] never been practised . . . on the ambassador of so great a King." According to a witness, the Queen took the news with equanimity at first, displaying no visible sign of emotion, but reports carried to Mary's son, James VI, claimed that Elizabeth had been so astonished and heartbroken over the execution that she had burst into torrents of weeping and taken to her bed. Some historians, as besotted with the Queen as her courtiers affected to be, have taken this as a sign of genuine grief on the part of Elizabeth. They cite the tongue-lashing she gave to her Privy Council, abusing them with such force and vehemence that even Burghley was reduced to helpless silence. In all her reign, one counsellor said afterwards, he had never seen her "so much moved." She refused to see Burghley for a month, but reserved her particular vitriol for her Secretary, Sir William Davison, who was arrested, tried by the Lords and sentenced to a fine of 10,000 marks and confinement in the Tower at the Queen's pleasure, infuriating the Commons, which refused to "vote any of the supplies requested until he was liberated."[17]

The Queen at once eased the conditions under which Davison was being held, and he was quietly released eighteen months later. Although her fury with him may have been genuine enough, it was not over the death of Mary but the means by which it was achieved. She had not the slightest trace of affection for Mary, who had been a constant thorn in her side and a threat to her throne and her life throughout her reign. But in disposing of her rival, Elizabeth had executed a foreign national, a former Queen of France and Scotland and a woman with connections to some of the greatest families of Europe, not only mother of James VI of Scotland but sister-in-law to Philip of Spain and Henri III of France, and the cousin of Henri, Duc de Guise, leader of the Catholic League, a shadowy Spanish-funded organization, dedicated to the extirpation of Protestantism in France and throughout Europe.

Even in the act of signing the death warrant, she had indicated to Davison that there were more seemly ways for a queen to die than by the headsman's axe. When such hints failed to bear fruit, she made her meaning absolutely explicit: she wanted Mary to be assassinated. At her direction, Davison then wrote to Sir Amyas Paulet, who had been given the task of keeping Mary confined, asking him to kill her without warrant according to the Bond of Association he had signed. Paulet refused even to consider the idea, saying "God forbid that I should make so foul a shipwreck of my conscience." Elizabeth, furious at his "daintiness," then spoke of "one Wingfield" instead, who might be persuaded to do the deed. However, none was willing to assassinate Mary, knowing that the inevitable consequence would be the sacrifice of a scapegoat to appease the Scots and Mary's Catholic allies in France and Spain.

Frustrated in her schemes, Elizabeth then signed the death warrant, well knowing what would ensue, but she took steps to distance herself from the act as much as she could by her floods of tears, her abuse of her Privy Counsellors and the imprisonment of Secretary Davison. She also laid on a lavish funeral for Mary at Peterborough Cathedral, albeit "without bells or chanting," though she did not attend in person; it was further north than she cared to venture. Mary was interred in a vault directly opposite the tomb of Catherine of

Aragon; "the same grave-digger, Scarlet, prepared both vaults." As was the custom, a wax figure of the dead Queen of Scots presided over a "most royal feast" held at the Bishop's Palace after the funeral, but Mary's grave remained unmarked until her son, James VI and I, succeeded to the throne.[18]

Elizabeth's performance was highly effective, sufficient to placate James and at least some of the Scottish lords, despite an earlier warning from one of his ambassadors that the King would "exact satisfaction from any person who assailed her [Mary's] honour or her safety and with that object would appeal for help to all Christian princes," including Philip of Spain. James himself had written a warning letter to Elizabeth a fortnight before his mother's execution. "What thing, Madam, can greater touch me in honour both as a king and a son, than that my nearest neighbour, being in straight friendship with me, shall rigorously put to death a free sovereign prince and my natural mother?" Fearing a Scots invasion of the North of England, and knowing that Spanish bribes and subsidies were being paid to Scottish lords to foment a rebellion, Walsingham had been urging Elizabeth to award the Scottish king a substantial increase in his annual pension of £4,000, a bribe to buy his acquiescence in Mary's death. Elizabeth's tears, and a copy of the intercepted letter from his mother leaving her rights in the English throne not to him but to Philip of Spain—Elizabeth had burned the original on Burghley's advice—achieved the same result at no additional cost, though James was also shrewd enough to realize that his own prospects of succeeding Elizabeth would be best served by remaining loyal to her. "The old enmities between the countries would be aroused by a war and the English would then never accept a Scotsman for their King . . . and neither France nor Spain will help him except for their own ends," while Philip's own "ambition and claims will make him a dangerous ally." "How fond and inconstant I were, if I should prefer my mother to my title," James argued, with chilling logic.[19]

The diplomatic offensive mounted by Elizabeth and Walsingham extended across Europe. The Venetian ambassador reported that the Queen bitterly regretted that, having signed the warrant only as a gesture in the hope of satisfying the demands of her counsellors and subjects, her officers had then greatly exceeded their brief. English diplomats spread similar stories in the other European Courts, and even Mendoza, now the Spanish ambassador in Paris and one of Elizabeth's most implacable enemies, was sufficiently convinced to write to his master that she was so grief-stricken at Mary's death that she had taken to her bed. Philip was not so easily fooled. "It is very fine for the

Queen of England now to want to give out that it was done without her wish, the contrary being so clearly the case."

Elizabeth also wrote, expressing her shock, fury and sorrow, to Mary's brother-in-law Henri III, King of France, last of the Valois line and one of "les trois Henris" locked in an increasingly bloody struggle with the Protestant and Catholic aspirants to his throne. The French Court had gone into official mourning at the news of Mary's death and a Requiem Mass was held in Notre Dame, but the sincerity of such gestures was open to question. Despite the comment of Believre, the French ambassador, that Elizabeth "must think that monarchs' heads were laced on, to have done such a knavish thing to the Queen of Scotland," Mendoza claimed that while Henri had ostensibly sent his ambassador to London to plead for Mary's life, he had actually been charged with ensuring that the axe would fall by promising France's tacit support. "The way in which the King of France is behaving towards the Englishwoman, it might be thought that they would fall out in real earnest, but I can assure you nothing is further from their thoughts." Whatever the true feelings of the French monarch, there was no doubting the popular outrage at Mary's execution. Preachers and demagogues throughout Catholic Europe poured out a stream of invective against Elizabeth, lauding the martyred Mary and urging retribution for the crime.[20]

The most potent internal threat to Elizabeth's throne had now been eliminated, but through her death Mary might yet fulfil the words of her cryptic motto, "My end is my beginning," and achieve the aim that had eluded her in life, for the execution had also removed the most significant obstacle to Spanish intervention. Philip II was a Habsburg and the prime aim of Habsburg diplomacy was always to prevent an alliance between England and France, the greatest threat to Spanish hegemony in Europe. While Mary remained alive, Philip had stayed his hand, hesitating to topple Elizabeth lest it prove a Pyrrhic victory, restoring England to the true faith only by placing a French queen upon the throne. With Mary dead, that was no longer a fear and his appetite for fresh crowns and kingdoms could now be safely assuaged.

The commander of Philip's forces in The Netherlands, Alexander Farnese, Duke of Parma, the most ruthless and brilliantly effective military leader of his age, was strident in his calls for vengeance for Mary's death. "This cruel act must be the last of many which she of England has performed . . . our Lord will be served if she receives the punishment she has deserved for so many years . . . Above all I beg Your Majesty that neither on this nor on other occasions will you relax in any way in regard to your preparations for the prosecution of the war and the Enterprise [the invasion of England] which was conceived in Your Majesty's heart." Mendoza was equally emphatic. "As God has so willed that these accursed people, for His ends, should . . . commit such an act as this . . . I pray that Your Majesty will hasten the Enterprise of England to the earliest possible date, for it would seem to be God's obvious design to bestow upon Your Majesty the crowns of these two kingdoms."[21]

CHAPTER TWO

The Pope and Traiterous
English Fugitives confult
the Conqueſt of England .

In the Cause of God

The last of the winter snows blocking the passes through the Pyrenees and the storms battering shipping on the open seas delayed the messengers bringing news of Mary Stuart's execution to Spain, and it was 23 March before the first reports reached Philip II. For some days they may have lain unregarded among the endless streams of papers, reports and pleas received daily from his ambassadors, spies and informers at every court and seat of government, and from all his sprawling dominions—Spain, Portugal, Sicily, Sardinia, Naples, Milan, Franche-Comté and The Netherlands; Guinea, Angola and Mozambique in Africa; Sri Lanka, Goa, Malacca, the Philippines and Macao in Asia; the Azores, Canaries and Cape Verde Islands, the West Indies, Florida and the South and Central American mainlands in the New World—but in any event, it was not Philip's custom to take hasty action.

His father, the brilliant soldier, statesman and diplomat the Emperor Charles V, was a formidable example to follow, and from his earliest childhood Philip had been schooled in the responsibilities he would one day assume. The size of the known world had doubled in less than a century and Philip was to become ruler of by far the greater part of it. At sixteen years old he was made Regent of Spain and he became the King of Naples and King-Consort of England at the age of twenty-seven. Within a month of her taking the English throne, Mary Tudor and Charles V had sealed an alliance by arranging her marriage to Philip, even though she was eleven years older than he. A lean, ascetic, deeply religious man, the sword of the Counter-Reformation, he had already buried one wife and had few illusions about the purpose of his second wedding. He told one of his retainers, "I am going to a crusade, not a marriage feast," but the birth of a Catholic heir would seal the succession in England and cement the alliance between England and Spain that their fathers had fostered. Philip was brought to Southampton by a peaceful armada of 130 ships on 18 July 1554; England was reconciled with the Catholic Church before the end of the year and the first of a long succession of Protestant martyrs went to the stake that winter.

While in England, Philip also met Elizabeth. He had persuaded Mary to spare Elizabeth's life in the aftermath of Wyatt's rebellion in 1554 and, according to the accounts of the French and Venetian ambassadors in London, Philip secretly visited her in 1555, while Mary was confined with the first of two phantom pregnancies, and saw her again on a number of occasions, both in Mary's company and alone. The Venetian ambassador, Giovanni Michieli, reported that "at the time of the Queen's pregnancy, Lady Elizabeth contrived so to ingratiate herself with all the Spaniards and especially the King, that ever since, no one has favoured her more than he does . . . the King had some particular design towards her."[1]

At the end of August 1555 Philip returned to Spain to succeed his ailing father, who abdicated in October and divided his great but unwieldy European kingdom in two. His surviving brother, Ferdinand I, took the title of Emperor and ruled over the Habsburg dominions in Central Europe, while Philip was crowned King of Spain and ruler of a global empire. In June 1557 he persuaded Mary to join his war on France, but her army was defeated and England lost its last foothold in Europe, the city of Calais. Philip made only one more brief visit to England before Mary's cruel death in November 1558, her second "pregnancy" being the cancerous tumour that killed her.

Philip's affection for Elizabeth led his ambassador, the Count de Feria, to tell the Privy Council that, despite her Protestant faith and her assertion to Feria that she would "acknowledge no obligations" to Philip, Spain would support her claim to the throne. Philip then proposed marriage to the newly crowned Elizabeth but, as was to be her habit throughout her reign, she procrastinated over a decision. After waiting in vain for a reply, Philip instead married the fourteen-year-old Elizabeth of Valois, daughter of Henri II of France, prompting Elizabeth of England to complain to the Spanish ambassador, "Your master must have been much in love with me not to be able to wait four months." It was said that she kept Philip's portrait in her private cabinet for many years afterwards, but, as with so much about Elizabeth, that may have been more propaganda for overseas consumption than a statement of fact; the cabinet also contained a picture of her Court favourite, Robert Dudley, the Earl of Leicester.

Philip's choice of bride offers an insight into the ruthless side of his character, for Elizabeth of Valois was already betrothed to Crown Prince Don Carlos, Philip's deformed and mentally unstable son by his first wife. He made an unsuccessful attempt to find his son an alternative partner by foisting him on Mary, Queen of Scots—a bizarre coupling of one of the most desired and desirable women in Europe with one of its least attractive princes—and then went ahead with his own wedding. The marriage provoked Don Carlos to an understandable fit of jealous, violent fury and Philip ordered him restrained within his apartments and then imprisoned. His subsequent death has never been adequately explained.

Isolated by circumstance and geographical distance from his siblings, Philip, "the least talkative of our kings," had a long, lonely and often tragic reign. He married four times, always for dynastic reasons, "conquest by marriage" as he himself described it, but all of the four—Maria of Portugal, Mary Tudor, Elizabeth of Valois and his cousin, Anne of Austria, daughter of the Emperor Maximilian II—died young. Apart from Don Carlos, who died in 1568, only one of his other sons, the future Philip III, survived infancy; in all, seventeen members of his close family died well before their natural term. Always devout, he was driven to seek even more consolation in his religion, and his convictions hardened as he grew older and the physical decline of his body became a constant reminder of his own mortality.[2]

His vast library was dominated by religious books, he attended Mass daily and spent hours at his prayers, and in his later years he shunned the Court for the spartan simplicity of San Lorenzo de Escorial, the vast, forbidding complex of buildings, more monastery than palace and in appearance more fortress than either, that he had built in the Guadarrama mountains thirty miles from Madrid. It took twenty-one years to construct and swallowed over three and a half million ducats. Dedicated to St. Lawrence, the great building was designed to resemble the gridiron upon which the saint met his death, and was conceived on an epic scale with seven towers and 12,000 windows piercing the granite walls like the firing slits in a medieval castle. The interior was richly decorated with frescoes, paintings, sculpture, alabaster, marble, jasper, rose coral, rich hardwoods, precious metals and jewels from the Indies and the New World, but for all their opulence the rooms remained cold and austere. Save for the priests and the cowled, murmuring monks in the long, echoing corridors, the Escorial could have been a mausoleum.

Fed by intermarriage and inbreeding, a strain of insanity ran through the Habsburgs—Philip's grandmother "Joanna the Mad" and his son, Don Carlos, had fallen prey to it—and if he himself showed no outward sign of it, the Escorial was certainly the palace of an obsessive. At its heart was a great church—only St. Peter's in Rome was larger—and Philip used his power and wealth to acquire over seven thousand relics of the saints for his reliquary within the Royal Basilica, to the great profit of those who furnished the suitably authenticated bone fragments, heads and even whole bodies, encased in golden caskets mimicking the body parts contained within them. With so many relics, their keeper could boast that there were only "three saints of whom we do not have some part or other here." The Escorial was also a shrine to the Habsburgs and one by one the disinterred bodies of his forebears and relatives were brought there for reburial. His father Charles V, his mother Isabella, his brothers Don Juan and Don Fernando who both died in infancy, his half-brother Don Juan of Austria, his first wife Maria, his grandmother and his aunts, all were buried in the Escorial, and the tomb that would one day be his own last resting place had already been constructed.

A concealed doorway next to the altar of the great church led to his modest suite of private rooms. There he worked ceaselessly in his tiny office, at a long narrow table facing a blank wall, as if even the view of a barren mountainside would be too much of a distraction from his duties as king. Plagued by arthritis in his later years—he was sixty-one in the year of the Armada—he spent his days and much of his long, sleepless nights at that table, scrawling annotations and terse orders on the endless stream of papers and documents that passed before him, unable to delegate even the most minute decisions to others. He found personal contact difficult and even distasteful, and preferred to receive the reports of his subordinates in writing rather than in audience—not for nothing has he been called "the Bureaucrat King"—but the ensuing mountains of papers flooding in from every part of his empire ruined his eyesight and his health. He was also christened "Philip the Prudent" by his people, but others might have chosen a less flattering sobriquet, and he shared one trait with Elizabeth of England: a tendency to defer difficult or painful decisions, sometimes for years, only to reach an abrupt and often capricious and illogical solution. "As often happens with irresolute men when they have been forced to a decision, they are as too hasty as before they were too slow." Even in the baking heat of high summer, as the cicadas raised their dry choruses from the branches of the stunted trees, Philip remained deep within the Escorial, shielded by layer upon layer of cold stone, poring over his state papers or on his knees praying for the success of his enterprises.[3]

Philip took pride in his title of "Most Catholic Majesty." He had established the Inquisition to root out heresy at home and believed it was his divine mission to extirpate Protestantism from Europe by any means necessary—when attending a royal auto-da-fé at Valladolid he had even announced, "If my own son was a heretic, I would carry wood to burn him myself"—but he was also shrewd enough to balance his crusading zeal with the requirements of the broader interests of the Habsburgs and Spain. By far the most powerful ruler in Europe, he was a meticulous planner and skilled manipulator of events, using Spain's vast wealth to bribe or suborn others to his will. At the time of the Armada he had been ruler of his country for more than thirty years. Few of his advisers could match his experience and knowledge, and fewer still would have dared to query the wisdom of an absolute, divinely appointed ruler. His marriage to Mary Tudor and the brief periods in the 1550s when he had been resident in England also made him feel uniquely well qualified to comment on the country. "I can give better information and advice on that kingdom and on its affairs and people than anyone else."

Whether his decisions were right or wrong, Philip's courtiers, officials and military commanders were soon made to realize that the King "did not welcome initiative, even when it succeeded, and he never excused failure to carry out his orders, even when they were impossible."[4] His belief in the rightness of his causes also bordered on the pathological. "You are engaged in God's service and in mine; which is the same thing," he wrote to Don Luis de Requescens, and though he often turned his powerful intellect to the smallest detail, time and again in his most extravagant and far-reaching campaigns—not least in that of the Armada—he chose to rely on God to provide the miracle that would guarantee success. Despite his faith, and the daily hours he spent bending his arthritic knees—"his old disease, aches in the bones"—in prayer upon the cold stone floors of the Escorial, God did not always deliver the victories he sought.[5]

In a portrait painted around ten years before the Armada, Philip chose to be depicted in the austere black clothes appropriate to a priest or a monk, holding a rosary in his left hand. His grey eyes give his gaze a cold and penetrating look, and the only sign of luxury is the lace at his throat and cuffs, and the emblem of the order of the Golden Fleece on his chest. He rarely dressed in any other way, ate plain, simple food, and shunned much of the pageantry and ceremony of a royal court. It was a mark both of his seriousness and of his dislike of ostentation, and there could not have been a greater contrast with the extravagant ceremonial, opulent dress, lavish banquets and grandiose royal progresses of Elizabeth of England.

Relations between Spain and England had been steadily deteriorating ever since Mary Tudor's death. England's merchants and traders had a festering grievance with Spain dating back to a decree of Pope Alexander VI in 1493 and confirmed in the Treaty of Tordesillas the following year, granting to Spain all lands, discovered and unknown, "west and south" of the forty-second meridian west of Greenwich, creating a Spanish monopoly of the trade and mineral wealth of the New World just discovered by Columbus. Portugal received lands to the east of the meridian (later adjusted to a point 370 leagues west of the Azores after Portugal's discovery of Brazil), allowing it to exploit Africa and the spice trade of the Far East.

The annexation of Portugal in 1580 thus gave Spain a theoretical monopoly on the trade of the whole world beyond Europe. In practice England had been breaching it ever since John Cabot landed in Newfoundland in 1496, within three years of Pope Alexander's pronouncement, and when Henry VIII broke with the Church of Rome over his divorce from Catherine of Aragon, Englishmen no longer saw any need to pay even the slightest heed to papal pronouncements. Henry's alliance with Charles V had ensured that there were few disputes with Spain during his reign, but relations soured almost from the moment of Elizabeth's accession and English breaches of Spain's God-given trading rights grew in magnitude and frequency.

The Hawkins family had been overseas traders since the time of

Henry VIII, and John Hawkins made the first of several voyages to the New World in 1562, establishing the "triangular trade" by carrying English goods, principally cloth, to Guinea in West Africa, then filling his ship with 500 African slaves—some captured by his men but most prisoners bought from native chiefs—and selling them to Spanish colonists in the Caribbean, in exchange for trade goods, sugar, hides and pearls, which were then sold back in England. That voyage and the next in 1564–65, financed by unlicensed joint-stock companies, each returned a profit of 1,000 per cent and others were soon following in his wake, setting a pattern of English mercantile and colonial development that was to continue for centuries.[6]

Hawkins grew rich on the trade, and was so unashamed of the prime source of his wealth that his coat of arms included the figure of a chained slave. The English slavers were far from unique; Spain enslaved Muslim prisoners captured in the Mediterranean and North Africa, the Turks and Moors did the same with Christian prisoners, and the galleys of Portugal, France, Venice and the Papacy were also full of slaves and convicts, but the activities of the English slavers and traders further heightened tensions with Spain. In the absence of any coherent and consistent strategy from the Crown, speculative syndicates of London merchant adventurers, courtiers, ship-owners, sea-captains and often the Queen herself became the prime and sometimes the only arm of English foreign policy. They carried out three-quarters of English trade—smugglers contributed a significant proportion of the remainder—but also undertook privateering and piracy, reconnaissance and exploration, and colonization and acts of war.

Spain both resented and depended on these foreign merchants, traders and smugglers; it was incapable of supplying its New World colonies from its own resources. The "colonial and quasi-colonial goods" imported from the New World and the East were cheap to buy and commanded very high prices in Europe, and the profits to be made attracted more and more English traders. Some even settled in Seville and San Lucar and made at least an outward show of adopting the Catholic faith, but it was inevitable that they would seek ways of securing their own lines of supply in Africa, Asia and the New World rather than paying inflated prices to Spanish middlemen, and their constant attempts to expand their trade were a potent source of friction.[7]

Philip took furious reprisals against attempts to breach the Spanish monopolies. A party of French Huguenots who had settled in Florida, hoping both to escape religious persecution in their homeland and to profit from trade and piracy against the treasure ships whose homeward course to Spain lay just offshore, were confronted in 1565 by a powerful Spanish force, officered by, among others, Don Diego Flores de Valdes and his cousin Don Pedro de Valdes. The Huguenots were persuaded to surrender on the promise of fair treatment and were then slaughtered. But to Philip's impotent fury, English privateers such as Hawkins, Martin Frobisher and Francis Drake—"the master thief of the unknown world"—continued to create havoc by plundering Spanish treasure ships and possessions on the high seas, in the Caribbean and on the coast of South America. Their activities had the tacit support of the Queen, who took the lion's share of the spoils in return. Drake's plundering caused the Spanish treasure fleet to remain cowering in port and, deprived for a year of his wealth from the New World, Philip was unable to pay his Army of Flanders. The soldiers mutinied and rumours spread that the King might even be forced into bankruptcy. Spain was also heavily dependent on imported grain and timber, pitch and cordage from northern Europe, the Baltic and Scandinavia, and the pay and supplies for the Army of Flanders could only be carried by sea. In the face of the depredations of English, Dutch and Huguenot privateers, most ships from the Baltic and Scandinavia had to take the long route around the north of Scotland rather than the direct route through the Channel, and shipping plying between Spain and Flanders was vulnerable to interception and seizure.

Although Spanish hostility towards England had thus far stopped short of open war, Philip supported intrigues and plots against Elizabeth, and she in turn aided the Dutch rebels in the Spanish Netherlands and the besieged Huguenots fighting Spain's clients in the Catholic League in France. Now war between England and Spain could no longer be avoided. It would be a battle between Reformation and Counter-Reformation, but the motives of the champions of the Protestant and Catholic religions were secular as well as spiritual. Philip's appetite for fresh thrones showed no sign of being satiated; his motto *Non sufficit orbis*—the world is not enough—was an accurate statement of his ambitions. His religious duty to restore the heretics of England to the true faith would also fulfil his political and dynastic ambitions, opening the way to the complete reconquest of The Netherlands and perhaps to the eventual rout of Protestantism in Germany, Switzerland and Scandinavia. His dream of a Spanish Atlantic empire stretching from the Baltic to the New World would then become a reality, and with the wealth and military might of Europe under his domination even the Turks might finally be defeated and brought into the Holy Catholic Church. The long victory march, begun with the expulsion of the Moors from Spain, would at last be complete.

Elizabeth's faith was pragmatic; she had stated that she did not want to "make windows into men's hearts and secret thoughts" and early in her reign she had remarked that there was only one Jesus Christ and one faith, and the rest—the schism that had divided the Christian world—was a mere "dispute over trifles." She settled an argument over whether the bones of a Catholic or a Protestant divine should be reinterred in Oxford Cathedral—one had been dug up and thrown out by Protestant bigots under Edward VI and the other by Catholic bigots under Mary Tudor—by ordering the canons to bury both sets of remains together, and she would never have gone to war in the name of religion. She hesitated for a long time over military aid to the Dutch rebels, and her reluctant support of them and the Huguenots in France was born out of realpolitik, not conviction. Her policy—insofar as she had one—was "characterised by Protestant ideology and religious terminology, but she was primarily interested in commerce and national security."

She also despised those who sought to break the sacred union between ruler and subject, lest it set an example that Englishmen might follow. "We will not maintain any subject in any disobedience against the prince, for we know that Almighty God might justly recompense us with the like trouble in our own realm." Even when they opposed her, Elizabeth's first instinctive loyalty was to monarchs like Philip, not their rebellious subjects. She banned pageants in London attacking and ridiculing Philip, and even when relations had deteriorated to the point of open war, she still forbade any personal abuse of Philip; attacks on any monarch weakened all of them. But defeat for Spain and victory for England in the coming conflict would not only secure Elizabeth's throne and yield huge economic and political dividends by throwing open the new worlds of the Americas, South Africa and Asia to British ships and traders, it would safeguard the Protestant religion in its north European heartlands and embolden Philip's opponents, even in Catholic countries, to flex their own muscles against Spanish hegemony.[8]

An invasion of England was first mooted by the Duke of Alba after the English seizure of a shipment of Spanish gold in transit to Flanders in December 1568. Five ships, carrying 160,000 ducats in pay for the Spanish Army of Flanders, were pursued and scattered by French Huguenot privateers and sought shelter in Plymouth, Fowey and Southampton. From a Spanish point of view, their arrival could hardly have been worse timed, for on the third of that month the mayor of Plymouth, William Hawkins, had received news of a Spanish attack on his brother John's trading fleet, including two of the Queen's galleons.

After his fleet was damaged in a storm, John Hawkins had put in for repairs to San Juan de Ulua in modern Mexico, a "wretched makeshift" harbour, shielded from storms only by a shingle bank, but one of Spain's principal ports for the shipment of silver. Although foreign shipping was officially barred from all Spain's territories in the New World, Hawkins was always careful to pay the taxes and saw no reason for alarm when a fleet led by the Spanish viceroy, Don Martin Enriquez, entered the harbour. Enriquez proclaimed peaceful intent, but then launched a treacherous surprise attack. Hawkins, Francis Drake and a handful of men escaped in two small ships, but the remainder of the fleet was captured and most of those left behind were tortured and killed, some in an auto-da-fé. Two of the handful of survivors, Miles Philips and Job Hortop, later described how the Spaniards had whipped and flogged them and "hung them up by the arms upon high posts, until the blood burst out of their finger ends."

Hawkins returned to England in a battered, leaking ship crewed by just fifteen men—eighty-five starved to death on the voyage home—and his brother at once applied for redress from Philip's treasure. In fact Lord Burghley had already taken steps to seize it, sending orders to the Vice-Admiral of Devon, Arthur Champernoune, "under colour of friendship . . . use all policy to acquire the treasure for the Queen." Champernoune, who had three privateers at sea himself, was only too happy to oblige: "Anything taken from that wicked nation is both necessary and profitable." The bullion, supplied by Genoese bankers, was brought ashore "for greater safety." Elizabeth then ordered it to be transferred to the Tower of London under the feeble pretext that the money remained the property of Genoa, not Spain, until it was landed in Flanders. English property in Spain and The Netherlands was embargoed in retaliation; Elizabeth countered by embargoing Spanish ships in English ports, and from that moment legitimate trade between the countries entered a steep decline.

Soon afterwards Philip wrote to Alba demanding a plan to "damage" Elizabeth sufficiently to force her, at the least, to seek an accommodation with him. He also claimed a higher motive: "God has already granted by my intervention and my hand that kingdom has previously been restored to the Catholic church once," at the time of his marriage to Mary Tudor. He now proposed to restore Catholicism a second time. In furtherance of this, he gave Alba a letter of credit for 300,000 ducats to provide arms and money for those seeking Elizabeth's overthrow. Philip was content to rely on God to remove the "many inconveniences and difficulties" such a plan would entail, but, in a reply bordering on insubordination, Alba remarked that "since He normally works through the resources He gives to humans, it seems necessary to examine what human resources would be needed."[9]

Philip first used the phrase "the Enterprise of England" about the Ridolfi Plot against Elizabeth in 1571. Elizabeth was to be assassinated during her annual summer "progress" and the Duke of Alba would at once invade with part of the Army of Flanders to place Mary, Queen of Scots, on the throne. Even if the assassination did not take place, Philip insisted that Alba was still to invade. Once more God was to make up for any deficiencies in the plan or the force assembled: "I have such confidence that God our Lord, to whose service it is dedicated . . . will guide and direct it." But his confidence was misplaced; the plot was exposed and the invasion never took place.

In the face of these Spanish-backed threats to her throne, Elizabeth encouraged the activities of English privateers against Spanish shipping and possessions in the New World, from which she often profited handsomely. As relations deteriorated, Philip expelled Elizabeth's ambassador to Spain, Dr. John Man, after he described the Pope as a "canting little monk," though it may have been as much in retaliation for English privateering. Elizabeth was also persuaded to be less discreet in her support of Dutch and Huguenot rebels, causing Philip in turn to accelerate his plans for the Enterprise of England. In 1575 he began to assemble an armada of over 200 ships at Santander, but epidemics decimated the crews and delays in provisioning caused many of the ships to disperse. Only thirty-eight ships, many of them of modest size, eventually set out for Dunkirk. Five ran aground on the shoals there, three were driven back to Spain by storms, and the remainder, under the joint commanders Juan Martinez de Recalde and Don Pedro de Valdes, were forced to shelter in the Solent before fleeing for home.

A planned invasion of Ireland in 1578 was also aborted, but the following July, infuriated by the "notorious" activities of Sir John "Black Jack" Norris and his English volunteers against Spanish troops in the Low Countries, Philip backed a fresh enterprise, seeking to establish a bridgehead in Ireland from which the eventual invasion of England could take place. The preparations were noted by an English spy, Thomas Cely, who sent Elizabeth warnings of "great store of fireworks made, great store of scaling ladders, great provision of yokes to draw ordnance by mules and horses, and terrible cannons and many, with all other provision for war." A small armada led by an exiled Irishman, James Fitzmaurice Fitzgerald, funded and blessed by Pope Gregory XIII but equipped and organized by Spain, duly landed at Smerwick in County Kerry and established a base, the Castello del Oro (the Golden Fort). In 1580 Philip answered their appeals for reinforcements by sending another 800 to 1,000 Italian and Spanish troops in a fleet commanded by Juan Martinez de Recalde, but the hoped-for wholesale Irish uprising never occurred, and a squadron of English ships led by Sir William Wynter used their cannons to pound the Golden Fort into ruins. The defenders surrendered on the promise of fair treatment; all but fifteen were then killed in cold blood. Sir Walter Ralegh "helped in the slaughter." For the second time Juan Martinez de Recalde had been involved in the failure of an armada from Spain. It was not to be the last.[10]

If the execution of Mary, Queen of Scots, was the catalyst for the launching of the Armada, Philip's annexation of Portugal in 1580 had been the essential prerequisite. His nephew, King Sebastian of Portugal, had died in 1578 while fighting the Moors in a campaign in which Philip fatefully refused to come to his aid, having already agreed to a secret treaty with the ruler of Fez, Abd-el-Malek. Some even suggested that Philip had connived at his nephew's death, since it furthered his own territorial ambitions. Sebastian's successor, his ailing great-uncle, Cardinal Henry, was the last legitimate male in the line of Portuguese succession and after his death, Philip, son of a Portuguese princess, claimed the throne. The Duke of Medina-Sidonia led a force to occupy the Algarve, while the commander of Philip's navy, the Marquis of Santa Cruz, launched an amphibious attack on Lisbon, in concert with a thrust by the main army led by the Duke of Alba. There was little organized resistance to Philip's troops, who plundered, raped and slaughtered as they advanced on a scale that made the infamies of the blood-drenched Army of Flanders pale into insignificance, and left even the notorious Alba complaining that the indiscipline and atrocities were "such that I never imagined I would see them, nor that soldiers were capable of them." His second-in-command reported that "I have hanged or beheaded many of them on a scale I never did in my life."

The Portuguese capital, site of the finest and most strongly defended harbour in Europe, fell on 25 August 1580, leaving the colony of the Azores, 1,000 miles into the Atlantic, as the only remaining centre of Portuguese resistance, led by Dom Antonio of Crato, an illegitimate nephew of the former king. The following year, a first assault led by Don Pedro de Valdes on Salga on the island of Terceira was a humiliating failure. A Portuguese priest cajoled the islanders into stampeding herds of wild bulls towards the invaders, and as the Spaniards turned and ran they were cut apart by the guns of the defenders. Only 60 out of 600 men survived.

In 1582, Santa Cruz led a much stronger armada of 60 ships and 8,000 men to the attack. Dom Antonio's fleet, commanded by Filippo Strozzi, a former officer in the French Guards, was larger and more heavily armed, including over 40 French ships and eleven English privateers. On 26 July the two fleets met in the naval battle of Villa Franca. The cannon of Strozzi's fleet inflicted serious damage on the Spanish flagship, the San Martin, and several of the other vessels, but Strozzi's "ill-judged and suicidal manoeuvre" of closing with Santa Cruz's fleet played into Spanish hands, since their preferred tactics were to engage the enemy at close range, and grapple and board them at the first opportunity. Santa Cruz captured the enemy flagship and Strozzi was killed along with thousands of his men. Seeing the battle lost, the English privateers shook out their sails and departed, leaving their allies to their fate. It was a cold, commercial calculation; the hopes of prizes and trading or territorial concessions having evaporated, there was no profit—in any sense—in the English ships remaining to share in the inevitable defeat. But seeing his vaunted enemies cutting and running, Santa Cruz was moved to assure Philip that he would take on the whole might of the English navy at the King's command, and the flight of the English ships also had a strong influence on Philip's advisers.[11]

The following spring, Santa Cruz assembled a huge amphibious force of 100 ships and 15,000 men to complete the destruction of Dom Antonio's last redoubt, the island fortress of Terceira. Using his galleys as seaborne gun platforms, Santa Cruz landed his invasion force in barges and, after bloody fighting, they overran the Portuguese defences. Dom Antonio survived and fled, but his cause was lost. Spanish officers crowed, "Now that we have all of Portugal, England is ours." The annexation of Portugal had delivered the Lisbon dockyards, arms foundries and the great Atlantic fleet of royal galleons into Philip's hands. These fighting ships had been the defenders of Portuguese trade and possessions in the Atlantic and Indian Oceans, defeating the Turks in the east and repelling Spanish, French and English attempts to break the Portuguese monopoly of African and Brazilian trade. Several of them were reaching the end of their lives but, combined with Spain's own Indian Guard, Philip felt that he now had a fleet of galleons to match those of Elizabeth.

Honoured by Philip with the title Captain General of the Ocean Seas, Alvaro de Bazan, first Marquis of Santa Cruz, Knight of Santiago, Mayor for life of Gibraltar and one of the heroes of the great battle of Lepanto against the Turks, where he had commanded the Spanish reserve fleet and, by committing them at a crucial moment, had helped

to swing the battle in Spain's favour, added even more lustre to his reputation with the victory at Terceira. His father had also been Captain
General of the Spanish fleet and Santa Cruz had spent his life at sea,
seeing his first action off Galicia when he was just sixteen. More than
forty years had passed since then, but the ageing Santa Cruz remained
Spain's foremost admiral. The amphibious landing at Terceira was
almost a dress rehearsal for an invasion of the English coast, and in the
wake of his victory Philip asked his advisers to prepare summaries of
the potential means of conquering England and the record of success
of previous invasions.

An exiled English Jesuit, Robert Parsons, obliged him with a catalogue that included the conquest by Julius Caesar in 55 B.C. and the
Norman invasion of A.D. 1066. The Tudor era had begun with another
invasion. On 7 August 1483, Henry VII, a man "without money, without power, without reputation, and without right," led his army of
3,000 French, Breton and Scots troops ashore at Milford Haven, and
on to eventual victory over Richard III at Bosworth Field. The Pretender Perkin Warbeck twice made landings with foreign troops, the
French burned Brighton in 1514 and Seaford in 1545, there were other
invasion scares in 1539 and 1545, and the Scots had also invaded in
1497, 1513 and 1542. "Sixteen times England has been invaded. Twice
only the native race have repelled the attacking force. They have been
defeated on every other occasion and with a cause so holy and just as
ours, we need not fear to fail." In his enthusiasm, Parsons may have
been guilty of exaggeration, but there were certainly precedents
enough. Far from being an impregnable island fortress, England had
proved remarkably easy to invade; ten seaborne invasions had been at
least partially successful.[12]

The combined merchant fleet of Spain and Portugal was by far the
largest in the world—the great majority of all trans-oceanic trade was
conducted by their vessels—and Philip could also draw on several fleets
of galleys, but when asked for his estimate of the forces needed for the
Enterprise of England, Santa Cruz warned, "If we fall to considering
the difficulties of the task, nothing will be done . . . It will be necessary
to mobilise and to concentrate in the English Channel, the whole naval
power of Your Majesty's dominions, together with land forces." In all
he required over 500 ships: 150 great ships, including armed merchantmen and every available galleon, 40 galleys and six galleasses—huge
hybrids four times the size and weight of galleys, and regarded as the
equal of five of them in battle. They carried the sails and armaments of
ocean-going galleons in addition to 25 to 30 oars per side, each
manned by five to eight convicts, slaves or *buenaboya*—"volunteer"

oarsmen, press-ganged into service and chained to their oars just like the rest. There would also be 40 hulks (cargo ships) to carry the expedition's munitions and stores, 80 auxiliary craft including fast pinnaces to carry despatches, scout ahead of the main fleet and maintain picket lines, and 240 landing craft, carried to England on the decks of the transport ships. This vast armada was to be crewed by 30,000 seamen and would carry 64,000 fighting troops, allowing for the loss of 10,000 men to disease, desertions and battlefield casualties. The provisions would include 373,337 hundredweight of biscuits, 22,800 of bacon, 21,500 of cheese, 23,200 barrels of tunny fish, 16,040 of salt-beef, 11,200 of vinegar, a quarter of a million gallons of water and 46,800 of wine. He estimated the total cost of equipping, arming, provisioning and maintaining this expeditionary force over a period of eight months at almost four million ducats.[13]

Santa Cruz was a vastly experienced and battle-hardened commander and his estimate of his requirements was no doubt a shrewd one, but such a fleet would have emptied Spain's Atlantic and Mediterranean ports of almost every available craft and the cost would have drained the Royal Treasury dry. A plan proposed by Philip's other great military strategist, the Duke of Parma, Captain General of the Army of Flanders, was altogether more modest in scale and cost. He insisted that the operation should be self-sustaining without assuming any initial involvement or support from English Catholics, and saw that the twin foreign threats to the enterprise—the intervention of the Dutch or French—must be neutralized in advance. But, given favourable conditions, he believed that just 30,000 infantry and a company of horsemen could bring England to its knees, and that the invasion force could be shipped across the Channel in flat-bottomed barges in the course of a single night. In 1513 Henry VIII's armada of 300 ships had crossed from Dover to Calais to invade France in just three hours. Under cover of darkness, with favourable winds and a spring tide to carry them, Parma's forces could certainly cross from Dunkirk and Nieuport to Kent in one night. A mere 25 great ships, Parma estimated, would be enough to safeguard them as they crossed the Channel. With the element of surprise they could establish a strong bridgehead before the English even knew they were there. A thousand men would be left to fortify and hold the beachhead; the rest would march on London.

Forced to defend hundreds of miles of coastline, the English would be unable to mass troops quickly enough to repulse a determined thrust by the invaders. The countryside through which they would pass was easy for infantry to negotiate and rich and fertile enough to yield plentiful supplies of food to foraging parties, and Parma expected his forces to have taken the capital in no more than eight days. Having seized London and captured the Queen or forced her to flee, he would await the Catholic risings in the north and in Ireland that would inevitably follow, to help cement his victory. However, more than 700 barges would be required to transport this invasion force and such a vast concentration of ships and men could scarcely escape the notice of Elizabeth's agents in The Netherlands, depriving him of the crucial element of surprise. In that event 25 ships would be completely inadequate to protect the invasion force from English attacks. Philip himself wrote "Nonsense!" in the margin of Parma's letter.

Philip had only ever experienced battle once. It unnerved him sufficiently never to repeat the experience, but an absolute ruler of thirty years' standing did not lack confidence in his own abilities, even in areas in which he possessed minimal expertise. From the plans of his two commanders he produced a synthesis of his own. An armada commanded by Santa Cruz would set sail from Spain carrying a siege train and several thousand fighting troops. Strong enough to hold off the English navy, it would be far larger than the fleet of 25 ships that Parma had envisaged, but much smaller than the 500-ship fleet that Santa Cruz had originally specified. The necessary prelude to the invasion of England would be a diversionary landing on the coast of Ireland or west Wales, drawing off much of Elizabeth's land forces and naval strength, before striking the decisive blow. Parma's forces, reinforced by fresh troops from Italy, would assemble on the Flanders coast in their invasion barges and the Armada would then escort them across the Channel. If the English fleet sought a battle, Santa Cruz would give them one, but his main instruction was simply to protect the landing force. The experience of the battle for the Azores had taught Philip the dangers of naval battles; Santa Cruz had triumphed over Strozzi's fleet, but his own ships had been so damaged in the process that a further year had elapsed before he was able to complete the task of taking Terceira. That experience was crucial in shaping Philip's determination that the Armada should be a purely defensive formation, holding the English fleet at bay while the invasion force was convoyed to England.

Once the English coast was reached, the tactics of Terceira would be repeated, albeit on a much larger scale. The shallow-draught galleys and galleasses would act as mobile firing platforms, reducing coastal defences and laying down covering fire under which the landing barges could come safely to shore and the invasion forces and their siege train be unloaded. The troops remaining in Flanders would also be reinforced to prevent adventures by the Dutch and to stop the French from using the moment of Spanish weakness while Parma's main force was occupied overseas to seize the southern territories of Flanders that they had long coveted. The Armada would remain offshore to secure Parma's supply lines until Elizabeth had been overthrown. The original plan was that she would be replaced by Mary, Queen of Scots, with a suitably pliant Catholic consort to ensure that her ties with the French did not lead her astray—Parma was suggested as one possible partner. Should the battle against Elizabeth's forces prove inconclusive, the Spanish troops were to fortify and hold their positions until concessions had been exacted from her.

On 29 December 1585 Philip began drawing up plans and collating intelligence on the state of English defences, and on 2 April 1586 he authorized Santa Cruz to begin assembling an armada in Lisbon. Don Juan Martinez de Recalde, the veteran of two previous failed armadas, was to form a northern squadron based in the Cantabrian port of Santander, while the Duke of Medina-Sidonia was to assemble troops and supply vessels in Cadiz and the other Andalusian ports. Medina-Sidonia and Santa Cruz had collaborated during the annexation of Portugal in 1580 but they had barely been on speaking terms since then, and the Venetian ambassador remarked that Medina-Sidonia's presence in the Armada was "incompatible with that of the Marquis of Santa Cruz."

New companies of foot soldiers were formed and the older ones strengthened with new recruits, while experienced troops were recalled from the garrisons of Naples and Sicily and replaced with pressed men. Every armoury was ransacked for weapons; the Secretary of State for War claimed that "not a single arquebus, pike or musket is left in all Spain." Thousands of picks, shovels and gabions (wicker or metal baskets filled with stones as fortifications or gun emplacements) were stockpiled, and tents, packs, leather canteens and 12,000 pairs of shoes were bought from Seville. The King's agents began scouring Europe for cannons, culverins, powder and shot, sailcloth and rigging, oil, wine, ship's biscuit and dried fish and salt meat. The Lisbon shipyards were set to work repairing the old galleons and constructing new ones, and, as was routinely done in time of war, merchantmen were converted to fighting ships by the addition of extra armaments and complements of fighting soldiers. Yet even this large fleet was still well below the required strength. The deficiency was made up by "embargoing"—impounding—ships of every nationality that could be found in Spanish ports.

Dozens of English, Dutch, German, French, Genoese, Neapolitan, Venetian, Danish and Ragusan (from modern Dubrovnik) galleons and hulks were impounded, 23 from Ragusa alone, to carry the men, munitions and equipment for the great invasion force. The viceroy of Sicily seized a number of ships including the Genoese *La Rata Santa Maria Encoronada* and two Ragusan ships, the *San Juan de Sicilia* and the *Anunciada*, and, to the helpless fury of the Venetians, two of their huge armed merchant ships, the *Trinidad Valencera* and the *Juliana*, were also seized when they docked at Lisbon to unload cargo. "These ships were the finest, the best armed and manned of all that lay in Lisbon and on no account should His Majesty let them go." A number of Baltic hulks, including the *Gran Grifon* of Rostock, were impounded at Lisbon, the English ship *Charity* was seized at Gibraltar and a Scottish trading vessel, the *St. Andrew*, was taken in Malaga.[14]

The Grand Duke of Tuscany also lost his most prized possession, the galleon *Florencia*, in a similar manner. The war in the Spanish Netherlands had severely disrupted the spice trade centred on Antwerp, and the Duke saw the chance to make Florence the new fulcrum of the trade. Such was the value of the cargo that only the most heavily armed ship would deter pirates and corsairs and, after reaching satisfactory agreements with Philip, the Duke sent his prized new galleon to transport the spices from the New World stored in the warehouses of Lisbon. But the captain found his loading date postponed again and again while Spanish sea-captains and admirals, including the Marquis of Santa Cruz, made admiring visits to the *Florencia*. After delays stretching into months, the Duke, now thoroughly alarmed, ordered his captain to set sail for home. The Spaniards refused him permission to leave and warned him that the shore batteries had orders to sink his ship if he attempted to make a clandestine departure. The next time the *Florencia* left harbour, it had been renamed the *San Francisco* and was sailing as part of the Armada, the finest and most heavily armed ship in the fleet. The Grand Duke of Tuscany never saw his ship again.

The scale of Spanish preparations for war did not escape the notice of the spies, agents and ambassadors of the European powers. But there was as yet no complete consensus on what it portended. Despite the mounting clamour for action from the Pope in Rome, Mendoza in Paris and the colonies of English exiles who had fled the persecution and confiscation of Catholic estates after the failure of the Rising of the North, Philip continued his unshakeable habit of moving at snail's pace, believing that "in so great an Enterprise as that of England it is fitting to move with feet of lead." By an irony that must have haunted him, Philip himself had urged the strengthening of the English navy when he was married to Mary Tudor: "The kingdom of England is and must always remain strong at sea since on this, the safety of the realm depends." Now his Armada would have to face it in battle.

The ruinous expense also terrified him. The fleet assembled for the Battle of Lepanto had emptied Spain's coffers, even though the costs had been shared between Spain, Venice and the Papacy. This enterprise was on an even larger scale and of infinitely greater duration and, barring a putative contribution from Pope Sixtus V, the cost was to be borne by Spain alone. Philip's Treasury was merely a way-station for the vast wealth plundered from his imperial territories in the New World and the Indies. Although in English eyes "his treasure comes to him as our salads to us," Spanish cynics referred to the fabulous cargoes as "rain-drops," for as fast as they were brought to Spain they vanished like rain falling on the parched earth of the Andalusian plains. Each year's *flota*, or treasure fleet, was mortgaged before it had even put to sea, and its revenues were dispensed throughout Europe as soon as they were received, to pay bankers, traders and manufacturers, and meet the costs of maintaining Philip's huge armies and the sprawling networks of paid spies, informers, agents provocateurs and foreign clients.[15]

When Ferdinand and Isabella drove the Moors from Granada in 1492, their troops included large contingents from England, Italy, France and Germany and their weapons were imported from Flanders, Venice and Milan. Spanish dependence on foreign supplies of everything from foodstuffs to military manpower had grown still greater over the following century. Spanish noblemen found no honour in commerce, trade or industry, and Spain produced only a fraction of the goods it needed and even those were often of poor quality. As a result, almost everything—ships, cannon and the articles of war, basic commodities like grain, iron and textiles, and the luxuries sought by the rich—was manufactured abroad and imported at vast expense. A French economist noted that in the thirty-five years since the Spanish conquest of Peru, "more than a hundred million of gold and twice as much silver" had been shipped to Spain and yet "the Spaniard, being compelled by unavoidable necessity to come here for wheat, cloths, stuffs, dyestuffs, paper, books, even joinery and all handicraft products, goes to the ends of the earth to seek gold and silver and spices to pay us." The continual creation of vast quantities of new gold and silver coins also fuelled ferocious inflation throughout Europe, driving up the prices that Spain had to pay and forcing the destitute to the brink of starvation.

Fearing war "as a burnt child dreads the fire," every cautious instinct had held Philip back as his allies and officials were urging him forward, but a week after receiving the news of Mary, Queen of Scots', death, he at last took the final, irrevocable decision to launch the Enterprise of England. The execution of Mary should have altered nothing but the identity of Elizabeth's successor on the throne, but in the two years between the formation of the plan and the sailing of the Armada, Philip made one other crucial change to the strategy he had laid down. The King of Poland was among those cautioning Philip to secure a base for the Armada before proceeding with the main invasion, "first seizing Ireland and the Isle of Wight as both of them will afford ports for the fleet . . . It would be better to take no steps at all than to take them insufficient to secure a victory," but Philip ignored the advice. Far from making a feint or establishing any kind of toehold on Irish, Welsh or English territory, the Armada was now to head immediately for the Straits of Dover and a rendezvous with Parma's invasion force. How that was to be achieved was almost the only aspect of the entire operation that Philip did not lay down in advance; it was simply assumed that as soon as the Armada hove into view, Parma's invasion force would put to sea to meet it. "He [Santa Cruz] will sail up the Channel and anchor off Margate Point [the North Foreland on the Kent coast] . . . When you [Parma] see the passage assured by the arrival of the fleet . . . you will, if the weather permits, immediately cross with the whole army in the boats that you will have ready." One of the most basic of military tenets is that no forces should ever attempt to effect a rendezvous within sight of the enemy. Philip's plan for the commanders of his land and sea forces to "join hands off the Cape of Margate" violated this principle, but no attempt was ever made to bring them together to co-ordinate their tactics before the Armada sailed, or even to brief them about this crucial facet of the Enterprise. Philip and his officials made many mistakes in the preparation of the Armada, but none was to have more catastrophic consequences than this.[16]

His invasion plan required a spring tide—a particularly high tide— and a south-easterly wind set fair for the coast of England, yet a night calm enough to allow the flat-bottomed boats to make the crossing. It also required the thousands of troops to embark at breakneck speed and to do so either in such complete secrecy that the English and Dutch fleets would not be able to impede the crossing, or after the Armada had completely destroyed them. It was a combination of events that even a person with the most unquestioning faith in the power of the Almighty would have regarded as optimistic. However, preparations now began in earnest. A flurry of orders issued from the Escorial. Santa Cruz was to make ready to sail that spring. The galleys based at

Barcelona were to join him at Lisbon and all available ships' stores and "warlike provisions" were to be sent there at once. His agents were to redouble their efforts to find armaments, powder and shot, and food. Ship's biscuit was procured from Alicante, Cartagena, Lisbon and Malaga—forty new ovens were built in Malaga to cope with the demand—and huge quantities of foodstuffs, masts, timbers, sailcloth, cordage and Stockholm tar (pitch) were brought to Spain from Scandinavia and the Baltic.

The goods were shipped by the long route around the north of Scotland to avoid interception by the privateers and Queen's galleons patrolling the Channel, and Elizabeth made furious complaint to the King of Denmark at this furtive trading with the Catholic enemy: "How cunningly the merchants of Danzig, Lubeck and other ports . . . have this summer time made great provision of grain and other victual and of all things belonging to shipping and carried the same to Spain by passing the north of Scotland and west of Ireland." Rice was imported from Milan, cheese from the Baltic, and "1,000 pecks of corn and half a score horses" were shipped from Waterford to Lisbon for the use of the Armada; but the harvest throughout Europe had been poor and the Spanish demand drove the price of grain to unprecedented levels. Dried and salted fish, bacon, beans and lentils, wine, vinegar and olive oil also had to be acquired by purchase or compulsion from a Spanish population that was already suffering hardship. In the poorest regions, such as Estremadura, grain was so scarce that men were forced to supplement their diet with flour ground from acorns.[17]

Among those charged with obtaining supplies was Miguel de Cervantes Saavedra, an old campaigner who had fought at the battle of Lepanto in 1570, where he was wounded in the head and lost his left hand. He was captured by Moorish corsairs as he sailed for home and imprisoned for five years in Algiers, "fettered and manacled and threatened with death by impalement," until a ransom of 500 gold ducats was paid. Cervantes' travels over the searing high plains of Andalusia and Cordoba, requisitioning wheat and olive oil for the Armada, helped to inspire his greatest work, *Don Quixote*. He carried out his requisitioning duties with such enthusiasm that he was excommunicated twice by the Vicars General of Ecija and Cordoba for depleting the ecclesiastical granaries, but the opacity of the accounts he presented for his purchases led to his incarceration for a time in a Lisbon jail. He was still imprisoned there when the Armada sailed.

Philip's preparations were not confined to the logistics of manning, arming and equipping the fleet. Parma's Army of Flanders was reinforced: 2,000 Spanish troops arrived in 1586 and a further 13,500—two thirds from Naples, the remainder from Spain—the following year, marching overland along "the Spanish Road," the military corridor stretching 600 miles from Milan and Franche-Comté to Flanders. The Archduke Ferdinand of Austria also sent a regiment of troops, commanded by his son the Marquis of Burgholt. Spanish agents and ambassadors also began a diplomatic offensive to enlist support, further isolate England and protect Spain's vulnerable flank in Flanders.

Philip had to reconcile two incompatible aims. The Pope, the Emperor and the other Catholic sovereigns could be expected to support a Spanish invasion of England only if it was done in the name of a Holy Crusade to restore the country to Catholicism. Yet to avoid alarming the Protestant princedoms and kingdoms of Germany and Scandinavia (particularly the King of Denmark, who had a powerful fleet) and provoking them into forming a defensive alliance with Elizabeth, Philip had to give them the impression that the Enterprise of England was merely European war as usual—a dispute over trade and interference in Spain's "domestic" affairs in The Netherlands, not a crusade.

The Spanish ambassador in Paris, Don Bernardino de Mendoza, was a key figure in Philip's plans, and he urged him to complete secrecy about the Enterprise of England, "in order not to awaken the evil action which would be exerted in all parts from France." Mendoza had been expelled from England in January 1584 because his plots and intrigues against Elizabeth had "disturbed the realm." As he boarded the ship taking him out of London, he turned to the Privy Counsellors who were escorting him. "Tell your Mistress that Bernardino de Mendoza was born not to disturb kingdoms but to conquer them." He was determined to return in triumph and was one of the most active and strong proponents of the Enterprise of England. Given his head by Philip, he at once began to issue a stream of disinformation to keep Elizabeth and her Council off balance, while putting into operation long-planned strategies to foment insurrection in France, Ireland and Scotland, denying Elizabeth French support and threatening her with a war on two or even three fronts.[18]

One of the few surviving portraits of Mendoza, in the collection of a Madrid museum, shows that, like his master, he favoured plain, black clothes, with no more decoration than a small ruff of fine lace at his neck. He had fine features and the high forehead of an intellectual, and covered his receding hair with a black velvet cap. His dark eyes stare out from the painting, directing a keen and penetrating gaze, not at the viewer, but at something hidden from our sight, and his mouth is slightly pursed as if in disapproval of the sinful world in which he finds himself. There is no visible warmth in his expression, only a cold and calculating air.

No one in Europe, not even the Venetians, had more contacts and sources of information than Mendoza, and as the representative of the richest and most powerful nation on earth, the guardian of Catholic orthodoxy, he had access to people and areas barred to all other ambassadors. Ministers of the Crown sought him out and King Henri III of France often summoned him to discourse on policy. Henri's comments were usually tailored with an eye to their ultimate audience at the Escorial in Spain, but Mendoza was shrewd enough to discern at least some of his true intent. The French King's mother, Catherine de' Medici, also sought Mendoza's help and advice, and released titbits of gossip and information to him. She was his equal in guile and intrigue and he believed little of what she told him, but Spanish gold bought him many additional informants. The Duc de Guise and his brothers in the Catholic League, lavishly funded by Spain, yielded much valuable information and had the ability to destabilize the French Crown by force of arms. Mendoza was also closely allied with the Society of Jesus—the Jesuits—and maintained a link with the Paris Committee of Sixteen, a shadowy body ready to bring the Paris mob onto the streets.

In addition, English, Scottish and Irish exiles brought Mendoza their information and sought his support for intrigues against Elizabeth. Even the English ambassador in Paris, Sir Edward Stafford, unpaid by the Queen and burdened by gambling debts, let it be known that he was eager to serve the King of Spain providing it was "not against the interest of his Mistress the Queen." He did not elaborate on how betraying state secrets to the Spaniards could fail to be against the Queen's interest. His treachery should not have been unexpected, for his brother had been involved in a plot to murder Elizabeth, and in January 1587, Stafford duly became Mendoza's most valued informant, identified only as "Julio" or "the new confidant" in even the most secret dispatches. So valuable was he that, until a suitable go-between could be found, Mendoza even took "the risk of going to his house at night" to obtain his information. In recognition of his services, Stafford received ever greater amounts of Philip's largesse, beginning with "2,000 crowns" on 28 February 1587, which he earned by relaying the news of the execution just ten days earlier of Mary, Queen of Scots, and he fed Mendoza a stream of information about the state of England's military preparations and the comings and goings of the fleets of Francis Drake and the Lord Admiral, Charles Howard.[19]

The ambassador in Rome, Henriquez de Guzman, Count of Oli-vares, was meanwhile ordered to seek an immediate audience with Pope Sixtus V, Felice Peretti. Sixtus's preference had been for Mary to be queen with an English Catholic prince or lord as her successor, and there was considerable acrimony between Rome and Madrid over the vexed question of who should now inherit Elizabeth's throne. One of the Queen of Scots' last acts had been to send a letter, smuggled out by her apothecary, urging Philip, "notwithstanding her death, [to] perse-vere in the English Enterprise as the quarrel was in the cause of God and was worthy of being maintained by so Catholic a King." Philip needed no urging and was already taking steps to secure the documents that would bolster his flimsy claim to the thrones of England and Scot-land. He ordered Mendoza to keep the letter "with great care," together with the previous letter Mary had written detailing the bequest of her rights in the throne, and told him to take steps to "secure"—to keep under his control, by force if necessary—the wit-nesses to her wishes and actions. "If the other two [the apothecary and Mary's secretary] have any inkling of it . . . they also may be treated in the same way."

Philip hated Sixtus and resented any papal intrusion into his own affairs or those of his subjects, but he needed his support and forced himself to write a personal letter to the Pope in which he was at pains to stress that he was taking up the burden of the Enterprise of England with the greatest reluctance. "I am extremely grieved . . . as she [Mary] would have been so appropriate an instrument for converting those countries to our holy Catholic faith. Since God, however, has ordained otherwise . . . He will provide in other ways for the success of His cause." Olivares was now to show Sixtus a genealogical study commis-sioned by Mendoza and prepared by two prominent English Catholic exiles, "proving" that Philip was the most legitimate claimant to the English throne by virtue of his descent from John of Gaunt. This required the claims of all the surviving descendants of the dozen mon-archs who had ruled England since Edward III to be set aside. Feeble though Philip's pretensions to the English throne were, they were certainly more substantial and legitimate than those of Henry VII, and he had successfully invaded England in 1485, seized the throne and founded the Tudor dynasty that Philip now hoped to end. "Right of conquest" remained a powerful and widely recognized basis for legitimacy.[20]

Olivares was to press Sixtus to confirm Philip as the true heir to the English throne, "his claim being a more valid one than that of any other claimant . . . besides the double disqualification of bastardy and heresy under which they all suffer." "You will impress upon his Holiness that I cannot undertake a war in England for the purpose merely of placing upon that throne a young heretic like the King of Scotland"—but with thrones enough, Philip would immediately cede the kingdom to his twenty-one-year-old daughter, the Infanta Isabella, though that concession was qualified in a way that suggested Philip might change his mind at some later point. "The only scruple which assails him is whether he is justified in depriving the Prince, his son, of a kingdom which not only has descended to him by right, but for the recovery of which, revenues of the Crown of Spain will have been alienated to a rather greater value than the worth of the acquisition."

When an agreement with Sixtus was eventually reached, the artful Olivares had been able to blur the question of the succession. The Pope failed to realize the significance of a bland but crucial clause inserted in the middle of the rambling document, and "the matter . . . was so wrapped up that he passed over it without cavil or difficulty . . . In the end it was left to Your Majesty and the clause was so worded that Your Majesty might appoint the Prince or the Infanta." Olivares was also to draw the Pontiff's attention to "the well-known fact" that Mary had made a will that "left His Majesty heir to the Crown, this being the reason of her death and of the approval of it by the King of France." He then requested a papal contribution of one million ducats in gold towards the cost of equipping an invasion force for the Enterprise of England, citing the cost to Philip of the "Holy War" to restore The Netherlands to Catholicism (and to Spanish rule) as one of the reasons why Sixtus should underwrite a substantial part of the cost of invading England. Philip certainly needed the contribution; the cost of the Armada and the enlarged Army of Flanders—approaching 50,000 ducats a day in total—was emptying his treasury, and had already forced him to veto plans to strengthen the defences of Spanish possessions in Africa and the New World against further raids by English privateers. However, Olivares warned Philip that "Your Majesty must give up all hope of secrecy from the moment the Pope signs the warrants for the money, however much he may swear to say nothing. Other Popes might drop hints but he simply reveals everything."[21]

The garrulous Sixtus took care to nurture his image as an unsophisticated man of peasant stock, uncouth in manners and speech, and prone to violent outbursts, "throwing the crockery about furiously," but his lack of education and boorish manner concealed a shrewd and calculating mind, and the unguarded look he directs out of a surviving portrait in the Vatican suggests a man of vulpine cunning. He was occasionally lavish in his praise of Elizabeth's courage and independence, and often caustic and disparaging about Philip's habitual caution, taunting his ambassador that "The King of Spain is the greatest prince in Christendom, yet he is negotiating for peace with a woman who insults him and will never give up Holland and Zeeland." He also told the Venetian ambassador, Giovanni Gritti, that "the King goes trifling with this Armada of his, but the Queen acts in earnest. We are sorry to say but we have a poor opinion of this Armada and fear some disaster." But he was also implacably dedicated to the recovery of heretic individuals and nations to the Catholic faith—he had been Inquisitor General at Venice from 1557 to 1560, and had pursued his task with such fervour and ferocity that the Venetians had requested his withdrawal. In his new and greater mission, only Philip had the military power to aid him. There was no more stubborn barrier to the success of the Counter-Reformation than England. English money funded the Dutch rebels and the Huguenots in France, and was also the guarantor of the safety of the Protestant princedoms of Scandinavia and Germany. If England was restored to the fold, the rest of Protestant Europe might follow.

Sixtus had continually prompted Philip to intervene against Elizabeth. In August 1587 he urged him "not to delay" and the following month sent him a golden sword, just as Pope Pius had done to the Duke of Alba fifteen years earlier. It was a symbol of the crusade in God's name that Philip was about to undertake but, in the face of appeals for financial support for the Armada, Sixtus also showed a parsimony that even the English Queen would have envied. He begrudged every penny he spent, even though he stood to recoup a handsome return on his investment if the Enterprise of England succeeded. If Elizabeth was deposed and the old religion restored, Sixtus's million ducats would be a mere trifle against the torrents that would once more begin flowing into the Vatican coffers from England, yet he displayed even more than his usual ill-temper at having to part-fund Philip's attempts to add yet another dominion to his already overpowering array. He sought to make his support conditional on Philip's agreement that the new sovereign of England would be neither a Spaniard nor a Spanish puppet, but, whatever may have been said to reassure him on that account, it was inconceivable that Philip would take the massive risk of attacking England without claiming the throne as part of the spoils of victory.[22]

Sixtus also made an implicit attack on Philip's hubris in claiming to act as God's instrument. "No sin is as heinous in the eyes of the Lord as the usurpation of the divine jurisdiction." At first he promised nothing towards the cost of the Armada, arguing that it served Philip's own vested interests more than God's, and when he at length made the pledge of a million ducats in gold, the terms were composed with typical cunning. The sum would be payable only when the first Spanish boots trod English soil; "until the men are landed it will be impossible to get anything out of his Holiness."

Defeat or failure for the Armada would therefore cost him nothing, but if the outcome of a battle between the English and Spanish fleets was unpredictable, there was almost no one in the whole of Europe who doubted the result of a clash between the crack Spanish Army of Flanders and the raggle-taggle militias and Trained Bands who "would sooner kill one another than annoy the enemy" but who were all that Elizabeth could put in the field. If Parma succeeded in landing his battle-hardened, professional soldiers on English soil, most observers, including many Englishmen, expected the invasion to become a rout. The only delays to the remorseless advance of the Army of Flanders on London would be occasioned by the attendant slaughter, raping and pillaging. Lord Howard wrote to Burghley, "God send us the happiness to meet with them before our men on the land discover them, for I fear me a little sight of the enemy will fear the land men much."[23]

Philip's suspicion of the Vatican made him require an undertaking from every cardinal that Sixtus's pledge would be honoured even if the Pontiff died before the invasion had taken place, lest their suspicions that he was "forwarding the enterprise mainly out of regard to his individual advantage" rather than his Christian zeal should lead them to refuse. He was right to be concerned. The cardinals echoed Sixtus's hostility towards Spain to such an extent that the Venetian ambassador remarked on the absence of any "sign of that fervent zeal for the extirpation of heresy and the salvation of souls" that he would have expected on the eve of a crusade against Protestant England.

However, the million ducats was duly transferred to a bank— Olivares forwarded the warrant to Philip on 30 July 1587—where it was held in escrow against notification that the invasion of England had begun, but the involvement of so many loose-tongued cardinals in the decision-making process removed the last hope of keeping the Armada's target a secret. When the Dutch captured and interrogated the nephew of one of those cardinals, he disclosed the full details of the papal contribution and the Armada's timetable and destination. The information was at once passed to Sir Francis Walsingham in London, but it was disregarded for several crucial months because it was flatly contradicted by the English ambassador in Paris, Sir Edward Stafford, who continued to supply Philip with English secrets and Elizabeth with Spanish disinformation: "The Queen had not decided anything about sending out the fleet as the intelligence sent by her ambassador here has cooled her." Even when the Armada had already been sighted off the English coast, Stafford's dispatches from Paris continued to insist that it had never left harbour.[24]

CHAPTER THREE

The Master of the Sea

During her lifetime, with her own active encouragement, a cult of the Virgin had developed around Elizabeth I. She remained unmarried, claiming that she was wedded to her people, and many of her subjects—though inevitably fewer than her courtiers claimed or she herself believed—worshipped her with a similar fervour to that devoted to the Virgin Mary before the breach with the Church of Rome. Her concern to promote and control her public image has an undoubted resonance today, and the cult of Elizabeth has gained many new adherents in modern times, when she has been hailed as England's

greatest monarch ever, an omniscient blend of patriotism, statesmanship, diplomacy, high principle and low cunning.

Like her father, she was pragmatic in matters of religion, and science and literature benefited from her tolerance, but her Court was a
snake-pit of favourites and sycophants—"a glittering misery, full of
malice and spite," "it glows and shines like rotten wood"—and her government was venal and corrupt. "Her vanity was notorious, her tongue
sharp, and, despite her declared intention to 'live and die a virgin,' sex-
ual jealousy soured many of her personal relationships." She was also
intemperate in the extreme, and regularly slapped and punched her
advisers and ladies in waiting. "When she smiled it was pure sunshine
that everyone did choose to bask in if they could; but anon came a
storm from a sudden gathering of clouds and the thunder fell in won-
drous manner on all alike." So monumental was her vanity that any
artist aspiring to paint her portrait had to base it on a standard template
issued by Court officials. Artists' studios were liable to be searched and
any unauthorized portrayals were "by her own commandment knocked
in pieces and cast into the fire." Our best idea of what she really looked
like comes not from the scores of official portraits but from the
descriptions written by foreign visitors to England.

The French King, Henri III, complained that "The Queen of England always thinks that everyone must be in love with her," and
courtiers were expected to be so dazzled by her beauty, even when
withered by age, that they would have eyes for no other woman. It was
a pretence that must have been harder and harder to maintain, for in
later years she was an alarming prospect. Her balding pate was concealed beneath a lurid red wig and her face showed the ravages of age
and smallpox beneath a thick mask of death-white make-up. Her
cheeks were sunken, her skin "wrinkled, her nose a little hooked, her
lips narrow and her teeth black (a defect the English seem subject to,
for their too great use of sugar)." She used mouthwashes to try to conceal her foul breath and when she spoke quickly, covering her gap-
toothed mouth with her hand, her speech was so slurred that her
courtiers had difficulty in understanding her.[1]

Despite all this, Elizabeth continued to demand the flattery and
flirtatiousness she regarded as her due. Her courtiers obliged with ful-
some and increasingly ludicrous compliments to "youthful, beautiful,
virginal Gloriana," and those who allowed themselves to be distracted
by other women felt the lash of Elizabeth's rage. Sir Walter Ralegh for-
feited the leadership of an expedition to the Indies that he himself had
largely funded and was also imprisoned for a dalliance with one of Elizabeth's maids of honour. Women other than her ladies-in-waiting were

excluded from the Court—Elizabeth wanted the undivided attention of her courtiers, who, if they had the temerity to marry at all, were forced to banish their wives to the country, while they fawned upon and flattered Elizabeth. She required unquestioning devotion and obedience from the cradle to the grave—even on her deathbed, her oldest lady-in-waiting, Kat Carey, was forced to remain at Court, separated from her husband, because Elizabeth would not allow her to leave. Her need for favourites and sycophants may help to explain why she retained traitors such as the Staffords, Sir James Croft and Lord Henry Howard in her inner circles for years, and entrusted Sir Edward Stafford and Croft with two of the most crucial posts in the Armada years, when she must have known that all were at least sympathetic to Spanish aims and at worst—as was in fact the case—in Spanish pay.

Elizabeth was certainly a remarkable woman, talented and well educated, fluent in several languages, but she was also grotesquely vain, mean of purse and spirit, capricious, choleric and fundamentally incapable of taking difficult, and sometimes any, decisions. Some—male—historians have attempted to attribute Elizabeth's chronic indecision in the 1580s to the onset of the menopause and her emotional turmoil over her failure to marry and have children to secure the succession. But Elizabeth was nothing if not consistent; she had been showing the same vacillation and prevarication throughout her reign. She spent twenty years agonizing over the fate of Mary, Queen of Scots, and "her hesitations about her marriage may have been chiefly due to her inability to make up her mind, which she carried to extraordinary lengths." Elizabeth had learned to dissimulate young, as a vulnerable rival at the Court of Mary Tudor, and she continued the habit even when circumstances did not require it. Her foreign policy was one of "procrastination, evasion and simulated innocence," and she continually "vacillated when faced by important decisions: unless panicked, she could delay for years."[2]

Arguing backwards from results to supposed causes, some of Elizabeth's modern admirers have argued that despite her limited means, she maintained consistent, clever strategies in domestic and foreign affairs, alternately wooing and rebuffing foreign monarchs and diplomats, playing one off against another and employing her talent for obfuscation to conceal her true intents. Yet there is no real evidence that Elizabeth ever conceived such a strategy at home or abroad, and it is equally easy to argue that everything she did throughout her reign was simply a knee-jerk reaction to events as she floundered from crisis to crisis with no clear destination in mind. As with all expenditure not directed towards her own aggrandizement, she spent as little as she could, as late as she could; and to turn her cheese-paring into acts of brilliant statesmanship requires too great a leap of faith for many to make.

Throughout the period of covert hostilities between Spain and England, two factions had been competing for Elizabeth's ear. The group led by her Lord Treasurer, Burghley, always a conservative voice in her Council, had little appetite for an aggressive policy of expensive military interventions and argued that Spain could be held at bay purely by diplomacy and defensive alliances and by strengthening England's land and sea defences. "So would England become impregnable and she on every side be secure at home and a terror to her enemies."

Leicester and Walsingham, two of "the principal devils that rule the Court," led the interventionist faction, urging an aggressive policy to expand England's overseas trading and privateering activities at Spain's expense, and arguing that to allow the seemingly inevitable Spanish reconquest of The Netherlands to proceed undisturbed was to guarantee the same fate for England. They believed that an aggressive alliance of Protestant states supporting the Dutch rebels and the French Huguenots offered the best guarantee of security, but Elizabeth was reluctant to intervene militarily in Europe, partly because of fear of the costs and partly, perhaps, after her humiliation in France in 1562. She had sent troops and money to support the Huguenots in return for the right to garrison the ports of Le Havre and Dieppe, until Calais—lost to the French under Mary Tudor—could be restored to the English Crown. Her troops had been roundly defeated, and at the Treaty of Troyes she had been forced to abandon for ever and without compensation the English claim to Calais. Any territorial ambitions she might have harboured in Europe had been ended there and then, and instead of direct intervention, her policy, "if the defensive expediency of 1572–85 can be dignified with that term, attempted to reconcile conflicting strategic, commercial and religious interests at minimum cost."[3]

The Treaty of Blois, signed on 19 April 1572, had united the historic enemies, France and England, against Spain. "If Spain will now threaten . . . it will be afraid hereafter, seeing such a wall adjoined." However, four months later, on 24 August, Catherine de' Medici conspired with her son Henri and the young Duc de Guise to arrange the shooting of the Huguenot Admiral de Coligny, and then covered her tracks by persuading her feeble-minded elder son, King Charles IX, to sanction the St. Bartholomew's Day Massacre to save his own throne from a fictitious Protestant plot. Some 8,000 Huguenots were slaughtered in Paris and perhaps twice as many in the country as a whole. The political consequences were disastrous for France, leaving the Treaty of Blois in tatters and fomenting civil war at home, but when Philip of Spain received news of the massacre, he "began to laugh" and in high good humour sent congratulations to Catherine de' Medici on having such a son and to Charles on having such a mother. Pope Gregory called the massacre a hundred times more welcome than the outcome of the battle of Lepanto, and ordered fireworks and the striking of a commemorative medal in celebration.

The carnival atmosphere in Rome, Spain and other Catholic realms caused a wave of revulsion, hatred and panic throughout Protestant Europe, uniting the Dutch rebels under William of Orange, and pushing the Protestant states and princedoms into closer alliance. Walsingham now saw "less peril to live with them [the French] as enemies than friends," but after Charles IX died on 30 May 1574, Elizabeth renewed the Treaty of Blois with the new king, Henri III, and dabbled in marriage negotiations with his younger brother, François of Valois, Duke of Anjou, while simultaneously sending money, munitions and mercenaries to the embattled Huguenot leader Henri Bourbon of Navarre. When she delayed paying part of the money, Walsingham complained, "The whole course of Her Majesty's proceedings shows that she has no power to do things in season as may work her security and therefore we must prepare ourselves for the cross." Sir Walter Ralegh was equally dismissive, albeit in retrospect: "Her Majesty did all by halves."[4]

Her attitude to the Portuguese pretender Dom Antonio was also confused. She welcomed him to her Court, subsidized him and issued regular promises that "she would miss no opportunity of ruining his enemy and hers" by installing him on the Portuguese throne, but Mendoza and Philip, in a direct letter to Elizabeth, made clear how any military support for the Pretender would be interpreted. "If Dom Antonio leaves her country for any of my dominions or to injure any of my subjects, I shall understand it to be a declaration of war." "When peace, so often shaken by you, has been quickly broken, I shall not lack force to meet the consequences." Dom Antonio was also the target of Spanish assassination attempts. Philip offered a reward of "25,000 ducats, or even up to 30,000 . . . Get it done at once . . . If he can do it by giving him a mouthful of something it would be less dangerous to the people concerned than if it were done by steel," but none of the attempts succeeded.

On receipt of Philip's letters, Elizabeth had dropped any thought of direct support for the Pretender. When his French-backed fleet was defeated by Santa Cruz, Dom Antonio, having sold the Portuguese crown jewels to raise funds, was forced to resume an impoverished exile in England, where Elizabeth kept him short of money and a virtual prisoner. She made vague promises to him but essayed no action on his behalf and merely retained him as a potential threat to Philip and a possible bargaining counter. Fearing that the peace negotiations Elizabeth was conducting with the Duke of Parma would lead to his being handed over to Philip, Dom Antonio tried to escape England with the aid of London merchants sweetened with grants of future trading privileges, but his ship was intercepted by the Lord Admiral, who reportedly realized the identity of his prisoner only when he recognized his pet dog. Dom Antonio was sent back to London and closely watched to prevent a further escape. Even when it became obvious that England was to be attacked by Spain, Elizabeth still prevaricated over open support for him. In January 1587 Leicester, Walsingham and Howard persuaded her that she should advance Dom Antonio "three years of his pension of £2,000 a year" and provide him with ships and soldiers, so as "on no account [to] miss such an opportunity of troubling" Philip by provoking an insurrection in Portugal, but Elizabeth changed her mind once more and vetoed the plan.[5]

In October 1584, the Privy Council had considered methods of defence against what was now seen as an inevitable Spanish attack. As usual, her advisers were split between intervention and purely defensive actions and Elizabeth wavered between the two, avoiding direct military action but sanctioning deniable raids on Spanish shipping and possessions by English privateers. These conferred the triple benefit of hampering Spanish military preparations, depleting Philip's Treasury and filling Elizabeth's own coffers. By November 1584 Sir Francis Drake was ready to put to sea with a fleet of fifteen great ships and twenty pinnaces, but by then Elizabeth had yet again changed her mind and Drake was left to cool his heels for nine months. Meanwhile her half-hearted attempts to form defensive alliances were hampered by the inadequacy of the people she chose to represent her. She "often delighted to send out second-rate chamber gentlemen who, compared with the representatives of the Spanish, French and Imperial Crowns, or the Papal and Venetian courts . . . were inadequately equipped with languages and social graces."

Philip had already considered and dismissed the possibility of an English-led coalition of hostile states. Although William Harborne, an envoy of Elizabeth to the Ottoman Empire, had persuaded Sultan Murad III that no material benefit would accrue to him from renewing his armistice with Spain, he also had nothing to gain from further hostilities when the Turks were already fighting a war with the Persians.

Even if Murad did attack Spain while the Armada was at sea, Philip's Mediterranean galley fleets remained intact to face the threat. France was riven by civil war and "in no condition to help, owing to their internal feuds; the rebels in Holland and Zeeland care more for their own interests. The German Protestants are at most able to create some slight diversion which cannot avert the blows which the Armada will deliver. The Danish king . . . who could have reinforced the English fleet, is dead." "That news," Philip noted with satisfaction, "has caused hope to fade in England of receiving help from that quarter." "As for the King of Scotland, no help can be looked for from him, for the blood of his beheaded mother is not yet congealed. One might rather expect that the Scottish forces would themselves move to attack the English from their side. Thus there appears to be no possibility of considerable reinforcements or help reaching the enemy from any source whatsoever."[6]

In her desperate search for allies, Elizabeth had even tried to woo the Duc de Guise from Spain's embrace, but her attempt was an embarrassing failure. He replied to her overtures that his aim was to see her "ruined and hanged, and if a hangman could not be found, he himself would willingly put the rope around her neck." He added that any further messenger from Elizabeth would be thrown from the highest window of his castle. There were few other potential allies, even among the Protestant states. The death of the King of Denmark was a particular blow, for he was sympathetic to Elizabeth and commanded a powerful fleet. He "was to have been present at the meeting of Protestant Princes in Germany," but his death left his young son on the throne and he and his advisers had no appetite for foreign adventures until the succession had been assured.

The Swiss had already reached an accommodation with Philip and would not be lending or hiring their fierce fighters to Elizabeth, and though many of the princedoms of Germany were Protestant, most of them, led by the conservative Elector of Saxony, preferred to co-exist with the Austrian Habsburgs and avoid provocations to the other Catholic powers. Many of their subjects were mercenaries, offering themselves at the spring Frankfurt hiring fair, but it was a purely commercial transaction, and they were as likely to sign for a Catholic as a Protestant employer. The men of the Palatinate, under their militant, proselytizing Calvinist leader John Casimir, were the exceptions and pursued an aggressive anti-Catholic policy, but the Palatinate and the Dutch rebels were Elizabeth's only certain allies. Casimir had no navy and could offer little aid against the Armada, but the Dutch fleet of heavily armed, shallow-draught "flyboats" might yet prove invaluable assets in the maze of shallows and shoals off the coast of Flanders through which Parma's invasion force would have to pass.[7]

The prospect of open war with Spain moved closer in 1585. On the last day of the previous year Philip of Spain and Henri, Duc de Guise, had signed the secret Treaty of Joinville, giving de Guise 500,000 Spanish ducats a year, in return for a pledge to use the forces of the Catholic League to subvert Henri III and prevent Henri of Navarre from ever succeeding to the French throne. News of the treaty reached the ears of Walsingham and Elizabeth by March 1585. Such a development threatened to confront England with a wall of Spanish-ruled or -dominated territories stretching from the Rhine to the Adriatic. As a result, she was persuaded to cement her loose bonds with the Dutch rebels into a formal alliance and suspend all trade with the Spanish Netherlands.

Spanish retaliation was swift. In May 1585 Philip issued an appeal for wheat to make up the deficiencies of the previous year's poor harvest. Scenting large profits, English merchants were among those to comply, only to find that all foreign ships in Spanish ports were being seized and their cargoes confiscated. The attempt to embargo one English ship, the *Primrose*, in Bilbao was a fiasco. The captain and crew overpowered the soldiers sent to impound the ship and put to sea with the Spanish official himself on board, still carrying Philip's written instructions to welcome English crews to allay their suspicions and then imprison them and requisition their ships, armaments and victuals for the Armada.

Philip's actions turned the screw of escalation again. Even those English courtiers, ship-owners and merchants who had previously opposed hostilities with Spain—there were rich profits to be made in trading with the wealthiest but also one of the least productive nations on earth—were now roused to call for reprisals, and for once Elizabeth acted without prevarication or delay. On 7 July she authorized the issue of "letters of marque, mart or reprisal" to "merchants and others" who claimed to have incurred losses of "ships, goods and merchandises in Spain, Portugal or elsewhere in the King of Spain's dominions." Any holder of letters of marque was authorized to "set upon by force of arms and take and apprehend upon the seas any of the ships or goods of the subjects of the King of Spain" to the value of the losses suffered at Spanish hands. English soldiers were also sent to The Netherlands to stiffen Dutch resistance to Parma's armies, and Walsingham drew up a plan "for the annoyance of the King of Spain," in which Bernard Drake was dispatched to sink or seize the Spanish fishing fleet on the Grand Banks off Newfoundland, further breaching Spanish claims of sovereignty of the Western Seas, while his brother Francis was to be set loose upon the coast of Spain.

Francis Drake was born in Devon, the son of Edmund Drake, a poor, Puritan "hedge preacher" who had been forced to flee his home during Mary Tudor's religious purges. He went into hiding on St. Nicholas' Island [now Drake's Island] in Plymouth Sound and eventually made his way to the Medway in Kent where he eked out a bare existence living "in one of the hulks on the river, in considerable poverty and no little danger, since he read prayers and preached religious sedition to the seamen in the Queen's ships on the Medway." As a young boy, Drake sailed in cargo boats operating between the Medway and Antwerp, but in time he became one of a number of young men serving in the Plymouth house of his kinsman William Hawkins, a prosperous merchant and seafarer with a profitable sideline in piracy. When still in his teens, Drake was sailing the oceans in company with his older cousin, John Hawkins.

His father's faith and a burning sense of injustice and hatred for Catholics stayed with Drake throughout his life, and he was also fuelled by an equally potent desire for revenge against Spain. In 1568, he had been in command of the *Judith*, part of John Hawkins's fleet, when it was attacked at San Juan de Ulua. Hawkins later reported that "the barque *Judith*, the same night forsook us in our great misery," and though there was no other public criticism of Drake's actions, his honour was tarnished, and "in Sir Francis was an insatiable desire of honour, indeed beyond reason." His purse was also emptied, for he had invested all his money in the voyage. "All is lost, save only honour," he wrote to the Queen, who had also lost her investment and her ships.[8]

Drake returned to the Caribbean in search of plunder in 1570, 1571 and 1572, and in those raids and several more during the following decade he rebuilt his reputation and revenged himself many times for the indignities he had suffered, but his hatred of Philip of Spain and the treacherous Spaniards who had attacked him at San Juan de Ulua burned as bright at the end of his life as it had done in his youth. In his eyes, the campaign against Philip, "the wolf with the privy paw," was God's battle against the forces of Rome, but it was also the means by which Drake's self-aggrandizement could continue. He had already taken a rich harvest of plunder from Spanish treasure ships and possessions, but his appetite was far from sated. He often carried letters of marque from the Crown, authorizing him to carry out reprisal raids on Spanish shipping, but he was always likely to take every prize he could find, whether or not English losses merited it. The gifts he made to the Queen and the cash dividends she received on the sale of the plunder he brought home were almost invariably sufficient to overcome any objections that he had exceeded his brief.

He first forced himself upon the attention of Elizabeth—and of Philip—in 1573. On Sunday 9 August, "about sermon time," he and his tiny crew returned to Plymouth in triumph with a captured Spanish frigate and a hold full of silver, the result of a raid in which, in concert with French Huguenots and a group of *cimarrones* (black slaves who had escaped from their Spanish masters in Panama), he had seized a mule train carrying silver near Nombre de Dios. He had been wounded in the leg during the raid and walked with a limp for the rest of his life, but his exploits made his fortune and his reputation, and he secured financial backing for his next voyage from a prominent group of courtiers, led by Walsingham.

All nations, including Spain, saw reprisals as a legitimate means of obtaining redress for wrongs done to them, and English privateers were following in the footsteps of the French and Scots who had pioneered raids on Spain's New World territories and shipping as far back as the 1520s. The first significant English attack on Spanish shipping for profit was by Robert Reneger, who plundered the treasure ship the *San Salvador* off Cape St. Vincent in 1545. Spain impounded English ships in Andalusian ports in retaliation and Henry VIII then welcomed Reneger at Court, putting an official seal of approval on his piracy and signalling the end of the Anglo-Spanish alliance. Henry also hired out his "great ships" to merchant adventurers and privateers, and though His Majesty's Shipkeeper sailed with them, the merchants supplied their own captains and crew. Mary Tudor's accession and Spanish marriage brought a temporary halt to attacks on Spanish shipping, but as relations deteriorated during Elizabeth's reign the privateers became more and more active. John Hawkins, "the most respectable of pirates," led the way, but his privateering and piracy was a way of making extra profits from his semi-legitimate trading voyages, not an end in itself. Like many of the later generation of privateers, Hawkins's young cousin was uninterested in trade. Ever since his first voyage to the Spanish Main, Drake's main purpose had been to seize Spanish ships and raid settlements for the prizes, plunder and ransoms that they could yield.

Drake began his greatest voyage on 15 November 1577, leading a flotilla of five small ships carrying a total of just 164 men. Even his flagship, the *Pelican*, was of only 100 tons burthen. He had let it be known that he was planning to make for Guinea or the Mediterranean, but instead sailed for Brazil and Cape Horn on a voyage that was partly a reconnaissance mission for a future colonization attempt and partly a privateering raid. After being battered by storms, one ship turned for home and another foundered even before they entered the Straits of Magellan, but Drake carried on in the *Pelican,* renaming it the *Golden Hind,* and raided the shipping and the Spanish colonies on the virtually undefended Pacific coast of South America. At Tarapaza he "found by the seaside a Spaniard lying asleep, who had lying by him 13 bars of silver . . . we took the silver and left the man." Further north he took a far richer prize, a ship carrying 26 tons of silver bars, "so much silver as did ballast the *Golden Hind."*

He crossed the Pacific, made landfall at Java and filled the remaining space in his holds with spices from the Moluccas, including six tons of cloves, half of which had to be thrown overboard along with eight cannon after he ran aground on a reef off the coast of Celebes (in modern Indonesia). He then returned home by the Indian Ocean and the Cape of Good Hope, arriving back in Plymouth on 26 September 1580. Only 57 of his original crew had survived and Drake's wife had given him up for dead, but he brought home £600,000 in gold, silver, jewels, silks, cloves, ginger and pepper. The investors received £47 for each pound they had speculated, a dividend of almost 5,000 per cent. The Queen's share—over £160,000, almost as much as her total annual income—was enough to clear her foreign debt and leave a surplus of £42,000, which she invested in the newly formed Levant Company. He also gave her the pick of the treasures he had stolen, including five enormous emeralds that she incorporated into a new crown.[9]

The low-born Drake rose rapidly in Tudor society and enjoyed flaunting his new-found wealth. Even aboard ship he was "served on silver dishes with gold borders and gilded garlands . . . he carries all possible dainties and perfumed waters . . . dines and sups to the music of viols." He bought a substantial estate, Buckland Abbey, and after his first wife, Mary, died in 1582 or 1583, he married a well-born and much younger woman, Elizabeth Sydenham, on whom he lavished almost as many jewels as in the tribute he paid to the Queen. A portrait painted at the time of their wedding shows a beautiful and poised woman, dressed in the height of court fashion and richly arrayed with the spoils of Drake's voyages: ruby and emerald rings on her fingers, a belt of gold filigree and precious stones, pearls decorating her headdress and full sleeves, two huge pearl earrings and a four-stranded necklace containing around 800 matching pearls, reaching to below her waist.

If Drake had grown rich from his voyages, the Crown had profited even more handsomely. Privateers carried out attacks on enemy shipping without any charge to the Treasury at all; only six of the 26 ships that attacked Cadiz in 1587 were supplied by the Queen, and 192 of the 226 ships that played some part in the Armada campaign were privately owned, 83 of them commandeered without compensation. The Crown also took a handsome share of the prizes those privateers secured. Within two years of the Admiralty Court being charged with assessing the value of such prizes, a judge of the court estimated that "Her Majesty has got and saved by these reprisals since they began above two hundred thousand pounds." "Instead of controlling and taxing its subjects, the Crown entered with them into a race for private profit," and the Queen lent her ships to Drake's voyages and eagerly sought her substantial share of the proceeds. Her typical reaction to the return to port of one of her privateers was: "Her Majesty may be duly informed what profit may be looked for by that voyage." She also often used her position to force through a grossly unequal division of the spoils. When the carrack the *Madre de Dios* was taken, laden with a fabulous cargo, Elizabeth offered each seaman £1 as his share of a prize valued at several hundred thousand pounds. Her greed received its due reward when the infuriated seamen stole vast quantities of pearls and precious stones, removing as much as three-quarters of the ship's cargo. A single seaman sold 1,800 diamonds and 300 rubies to a dealer for £130. Even so the Queen still recouped a return of 3,000 per cent on her £3,000 investment.[10]

Despite the riches she garnered, Elizabeth always denied any prior knowledge of or responsibility for the privateers. In any case, attempts to regulate privateering were "a striking example of late Elizabethan administration at its worst—feeble and corrupt"—and the Admiralty was "at once a department of state under the authority of the Crown and a private province or liberty of the Lord Admiral." In theory, letters of marque were issued in exchange for undertakings that privateers would sail directly to enemy waters, attack only enemy ships and possessions, and return any prizes garnered to an English port where they could be inventoried and valued, with a tenth of the value being paid to the Lord Admiral, Lord Charles Howard. In practice, neutral ships were often attacked, part or all of the prize cargoes would often be sold abroad or on the black market, and "tenths" and customs duties were evaded. Such was the power and influence of those involved in privateering—Lord Charles Howard himself, Sir Walter Ralegh, Sir George Carey and Thomas Myddleton, one of the richest London merchants, and, of course, the Queen were just a few of those with a vested interest—that blind eyes were routinely turned to corrupt practices, and neutral merchants and ship-owners had very little hope of any restitution for stolen cargoes. Attempts to control such piracy were perfunctory at best, and Elizabeth further undermined them by her characteristic insistence that ships to patrol against pirates should be hired at local expense and their men paid only out of whatever prizes they could take. In effect those regulating piracy were being encouraged to take up piracy themselves, and not a single pirate was ever apprehended at sea.

After 1585, the open but undeclared war with Spain was marked by a period of "general reprisal" in which any Spanish ship was fair game for any English privateer, whether or not he had suffered alleged losses at Spanish hands, but even in less troubled times Lord Howard complained that Letters of Reprisal were "disorderly handled, bought and sold for money" and the names of ships and owners erased and replaced by others. His complaints would have carried more force had he not been so eager to profit from such activities himself. The real essence of his complaint was that in bypassing the Admiralty they were depriving him of his "tenths," but he himself frequently sold commissions for cash without even bothering to notify the Admiralty Court. The Queen and her senior courtiers also took bribes—what else were the caskets of jewels that Sir Francis Drake was always careful to donate to her?—from privateers and merchant adventurers, originally established as the sole exporters of woollen cloth from England but now combining privateering with trade in a huge range of goods in Europe, Asia, Africa and the Americas. One wrote to Burghley, "having full authority *without account* [my italics] to appear thankful, I have thought it my duty in regard to your most honourable favours to us . . . to promise and assure to pay or deliver to your use . . . the full sum of 1,000 pounds." [11]

English privateers not only accepted letters of marque from Elizabeth, they were equally happy to accept them from William of Orange, Henri of Navarre, Dom Antonio or indeed anyone else who would provide a legal pretext, no matter how flimsy, for attacks on Spanish ships and possessions. Without such authority they were mere pirates, but timing was often everything; what was piracy one day might be patriotism the next. When three Devonian captains, including Sir Walter Ralegh's father, seized two Scottish ships in 1557, the Privy Council ordered the seizure of their own ships and goods as punishment, but when the Scots army crossed the border into England shortly afterwards, the ships and goods were restored and the men hailed as heroes.

Martin Frobisher was "a most valorous man, and one that is to be reckoned among the famousest men of the age for counsel and glory gotten at sea," but he was also one of the most lawless of all privateers. Practically illiterate, he was sent to sea as a boy in 1553, left as a hostage to a chief in Guinea and then captured by the Portuguese, and did not return to England until 1559. He became a successful privateer and explorer, and made three voyages in search of the North-West Passage, but after the failure of the third in 1578 he fell out of favour at Court— Elizabeth was never slow to punish those who failed to produce a profit for the Crown—and made no further official voyages until he became Drake's Vice-Admiral on a privateering voyage in 1585–86. In the intervening years he had lived by piracy, and even Elizabeth's allies, the Dutch, were moved to complain about his depredations of their ships in the Channel. He was far from unique—"home waters [were] alive with felons, traitors, malefactors, depredations, robbers, trespassers and even debtors"—and the Hanseatic merchants, Denmark and Poland also made formal complaints to Elizabeth about the lawless actions of her privateers, without noticeable effect. [12]

As legitimate avenues of commerce were closed by hostilities with Spain—by the summer of 1588 "trade came to a virtual standstill"— more and more merchants turned to privateering, sometimes in combination with their normal trade, sometimes in place of it. They also possessed the warehousing, transport and contacts to dispose of their prize goods at the optimum price, a facility denied to common seamen, who were forced to accept a fraction of the true value of the goods they sold. In the late 1580s and early 1590s a minimum of one hundred privateering voyages a year were being undertaken by English ships, and the true figure may well have been much higher—documentation of a trade that operated at the margins of legality was always scant. Even those who had lost no goods or ships to the Spaniards had no difficulty in obtaining letters of marque on payment of a suitable fee to the Lord Admiral, and one man claimed that there were "never less than 200 sail of voluntaries" off the coasts of Spain and her overseas possessions. Even an official list, which, given the number of ships sailing under forged, stolen or unofficial letters of marque, must have considerably understated the true figure, showed 236 privateers at sea in a period of just three years, and many of them must have made multiple voyages in that time.

Many ports also flourished on the trade, fitting out the privateering ships and establishing markets where goods of any sort, in any quantity, could be traded without questions about ownership or provenance. Torbay and the Isle of Wight were well-known havens of privateers, and several Irish ports, Milford Haven in Wales and Mead Holes on the Isle of Wight also housed flourishing black markets, where "such as make sale there are suspected to have some evil by the goods they there sell." Much of the trade was not in treasure and precious metals but in basic materials and foodstuffs: hardwoods, hides, sugar, salt, iron, corn, Spanish and Gascon wines, salt-fish, nuts and olives. Prize goods may have accounted for as much as 15 per cent of the value of England's total imports at the time, and "nothing is thought to have enriched the English most, nor done so much to allow many individuals to amass the wealth they are known to possess as the wars with the Spaniards."[13]

The press gang was never needed for privateers; the reputation of a commander such as Drake and the prospect of plunder and prize money were enough to fill a ship with crew. Privateers were always heavily overmanned at their departure. They carried three men for every five tons burthen, triple the rate of a merchant ship, ensuring both a large boarding force and sufficient men to form prize crews to sail captured ships home. They also invariably sailed with a large complement of officers to guard against mutinies. Overmanning allowed for the inevitable wastage of men through casualties and disease, but by causing a more rapid depletion of water and provisions and even worse overcrowding and hygiene than the already appalling norm, it also ensured that scurvy, "the bloody flux" (dysentery) and ship's fever (typhus) would strike the crew earlier and with even more virulence.

Despite the hardships and the low life expectancy, the lure of pillage and prize money continued to ensure that privateers were never short-handed. Some affected not to understand the reasons. "It is strange what misery such men will choose to endure in small ships of reprisal, though they be hopeless of gain, rather than serve Her Majesty, where their pay is certain, their diet plentiful and their labour not so great . . . The ships these men covet to go in are neither of service nor strength to the State or annoyance to the enemy. Their owners are men of as base condition as themselves . . . Thus have more seamen been consumed than in all other actions or enterprises against Spain. And no man dares reprove it, because the Lord Admiral is interested in all such prizes as these unprofitable ships take."

Others found the attractions of privateers over the Queen's service less hard to fathom. A prime cause for disaffection with the Queen's ships was "the wages being so small," which, as John Hawkins pointed out, caused "men to run away, to bribe and make means to be cleared from the service, and insufficient, unable and unskilful persons supply the place." Even worse were "the procrastinations which they have met with in point of pay at the end of the service." The crewmen of the English Grand Fleet would have ample evidence of that when the threat from the Armada had passed. On a privateer or merchant ship they could profit from "secret trading" on their own account and enjoy "the loose liberty and undisciplined life," but the greatest attraction was "the promising hopes that they flatter themselves with when they go upon their thirds" (the one-third value of captured prizes allocated as the crew's share) and the prospect of pillage: "there is nothing that more bewitches them" and "once entered into that trade, they are hardly reclaimed." The right of pillage extended to anything that was not part of the captured ship's fixtures, fittings and cargo, including the personal property of the crew and officers, and anything above decks or lying loose. In theory the items of pillage were brought to the mainmast and distributed according to the customary shares of the officers and crew; in practice such items were considered fair game for anyone who could seize them, and disputes often led to brawls and even deaths among the victorious privateers. The captain and officers of one ship "were all that day until evening on board their prize pacifying of brawls."[14]

Many gentlemen adventurers in search of excitement, glory and quick profit also sailed with the privateers or, like George Clifford, Earl of Cumberland, became privateers themselves. His ship, the *Red Dragon*, was as fast and as heavily armed as the Queen's galleons. In previous centuries such men had amassed fortunes through plunder and ransom in war. William of Windsor was only one "active and valorous knight, rich in great wealth which he had acquired by his martial prowess," and many castles were "partly built by spoils gotten in France." By the late sixteenth century, the private armies of retainers had been brought more under the control of an increasingly powerful monarch, and war—at least on land—was no longer the means to wealth and fortune. Influence at court, whether as minister or Crown favourite, was now the key to riches, but at sea fortunes were still to be made by men whose stock in trade was the cannon, the musket and the sword. Few held on to the fortunes they made, for almost all the privateers were also spendthrifts; wealth easily acquired was just as easily squandered. Despite the riches he had garnered on his earlier voyages, Drake still thirsted for more. Lord Howard was one of the noblest lords in the realm but one of the poorest; John Hawkins dressed in the height of fashion and maintained a style of living that consumed much of even his substantial income, and the Earl of Cumberland lost one fortune in reckless extravagance and "expensive sports," and another in funding ten privateering expeditions to regain his lost wealth. By 1600 he reckoned to have spent £100,000 on fitting out ships for privateering and he died penniless.

Privateering remained a risky business, for all except the Queen, who would hire out her royal galleons to privateers in return for a substantial share of the anticipated rewards. The merchant adventurers were required to arrange and pay for a complete refit of each Queen's ship before they sailed, and meet all the costs of equipping, crewing and supplying them, in addition to the hire charge that was payable even if the voyage returned no profit whatsoever. They nominated their own commander, but the Queen had the right to appoint the second-in-command, and the merchant adventurers would pay his wages. By operating at one remove, the Queen was able to claim a lack of foreknowledge of any acts of piracy committed during these voyages, while still collecting a handsome dividend from them. She was thus able to conclude the Treaty of Conciliation with the Duke of Alba in 1573 while pocketing her share of Drake's raid on the Spanish Main in the same year, and right up to the eve of the launching of the Armada she continued to benefit from privateering while still protesting her innocence to Philip of Spain.

She showed her gratitude to Drake for his success in these enterprises by knighting him aboard his own ship at Deptford in 1581, and he gave her another series of lavish presents in return, including "a salt of gold, like a globe," with the oceans picked out in green enamel. So many spectators watched the pageant that a bridge collapsed under their weight. "The Queen's Majesty came aboard his weather-beaten barque; where being as highly graced as his heart could wish with knightly honour . . . his name and fame became admirable in all places"—except in the corridors of the Royal Court in Spain, where by 1582 Philip was offering a reward of 20,000 ducats to anyone who brought him Drake's head or proof that he had been permanently prevented from carrying out any more of his "terrible handiwork."[15]

Utterly fearless, shrewd and intuitive, Drake wreaked havoc among Spanish shipping and raided the coast of the New World and Spain itself with equal impunity, and his vaulting ambition even embraced the aim of taking Panama and Havana or the Azores as permanent bases from which to raid Spanish possessions and intercept the *flota*. The Venetian ambassador to Spain believed it to be entirely possible, for Drake was "Master of the Sea, and finds no hindrance to the development of his designs," and even Burghley, no admirer of provocations to Philip, was forced to admit that "Sir Francis Drake is a fearful man to the King of Spain." Mendoza had warned Elizabeth not to "offend a king who had so strong an arm and so long a sword," but after knighting Drake, Elizabeth had made it clear that his activities would continue: "The use of the sea and air is common to all and neither Nature nor custom permit any possession thereof," though having made her ringing public proclamation, Elizabeth kept Drake at Court for some time to avoid further antagonizing Spain.

Philip regarded Drake and his ilk as nothing but common pirates, and any captured English privateers were treated accordingly. The captains, ships' officers and pilots were beheaded in front of their crews, who were then sent as slaves to the galleys. Drake saw himself not as a pirate but as the King's rival and chief opponent, a view reflected in many European capitals, where such was his fame that "many princes of Italy, Germany and elsewhere, enemies as well as friends, desired his picture," and when his portrait was displayed in a shop in Ferrara crowds gathered to view "the great English corsair." He also provided the Protestant population of northern Europe with almost the only successes they could celebrate against the seemingly irresistible tide of victories by the forces of the Counter-Reformation.[16]

All spoke of Drake as if he embodied the English navy and such was his success that Spaniards came to regard him as in league with the devil, possessed of supernatural powers, and keeping in his cabin "a familiar spirit with whom he talks," or "a magic crystal in which he could discern the most secret movements of his enemies" far away across the sea. Strangely, the latter belief may have had some foundation in fact. Robert Recorde in 1551 and Leonard Digges in 1571 had both described using a lens and a mirror to "make distant objects larger," and Thomas Harriot, a scientist sent by Sir Walter Ralegh to the fledgling colony of Roanoke in Virginia in 1585, took with him what he described as "a perspective glass." In the same year William Bourne claimed to have discovered a way of using two lenses to view distant objects, though he did not produce a working device in support of his claim.

The telescope was patented by a Dutch inventor in 1608, but the earlier experiments of Recorde, Digges, Bourne and Harriot at least raise the intriguing possibility that the "perspective glass" might have been the first telescope. The ability to see enemies at long range, well before they were visible to the naked eye, would have conferred a huge military advantage, and such scientific knowledge—if it had existed at that time—would have been the most closely guarded of state secrets. As well as supporting Roanoke, Ralegh was also a backer of Drake's privateering expeditions, and in his restless and relentless search for means to improve the performance of his ships, Drake would certainly have grasped the significance of the telescope, had it been shown to him.[17]

Drake had "inflamed the whole country with a desire to adventure unto the seas . . . every place where any profit might be had," but not everyone who sailed with him was equally enamoured of him. Short, stocky, bearded and florid-faced, he had a spark in his eye suggesting a quick humour, but he was also a man of ferocious temper and black moods, and often suspicious to the point of paranoia of other men's motives and intentions. He could be abrupt, "boastful of himself as a mariner and a man of learning," and "a willing hearer of every man's opinion, but commonly a follower of his own." Sir Richard Grenville, "a gentleman who has always sailed with pirates[,] . . . would not serve under Drake"; Martin Frobisher bore him a deep antipathy after serving under him in 1585–86, and Richard Madox, a ship's chaplain who sailed with him in 1582, showed his own enmity in his sarcastic description of Drake as "that golden knight of ours."

Others, even among his enemies, formed a more balanced view. He was "forceful . . . feared and obeyed by his men . . . firm in punishing, alert, restless, well-spoken, ambitious, vainglorious, but generous and liberal; not a cruel man," and he inspired loyalty and affection among most of his men, and not merely because he made them rich. Even his detractors were forced to admit to his brilliance as a naval commander; if Parma was the greatest land commander of his age, Drake had no peers at sea: "one of the greatest mariners that sail the sea, both as a navigator and as a commander." "He was more skilful in all points of navigation than any that ever was before his time, in his time or since his death," and his attention to detail included having careful paintings of uncharted coasts and harbours made by his brother John, Francis Fletcher and other skilled members of his ships' companies, to form "rutters" (route maps) that would allow himself and others to navigate those coasts in the future. Captured Spanish charts were almost as highly prized by Drake as the plunder that could be obtained, and his pursuit of efficiency on his ships extended to the search for plunder and prizes. He was a master of subterfuge and planned and prepared his operations with meticulous thoroughness, then struck with lightning speed, daring and savage force, but he also treated captives, indigenous peoples and runaway slaves with exemplary fairness, and in return gleaned much valuable intelligence and sometimes military assistance from them.[18]

He was the first to "recognise that the ship was the fighting unit, not the soldiers on board," and he made sure that his ship and its equipment and crew were the best available. One Spanish nobleman captured by him recorded that Drake's galleon was "a perfect sailer . . . as well mounted with artillery as any I have seen in my life, [carrying] about thirty heavy pieces of artillery and a great quantity of firearms with the requisite ammunition and lead . . . manned with a hundred men all of service and of an age for warfare, and all are as practised therein as old soldiers from Italy could be . . . He treats them with affection and they treat him with respect." The discipline Drake imposed on his men extended to the spoil and plunder they took—"no man dared take anything without his orders"—but his own ascent from humble origins also strengthened his revolutionary belief in his oft-stated maxim that a ship's crew must be "of a company," under the command of a single captain, and that the gentlemen and officers must "haul and draw" alongside their seamen. It was inconceivable that any Spanish nobleman would have soiled his hands with such manual work but, initiated by Drake, it had become common practice aboard English ships by the time of the Armada.

Even the Lord Admiral, Lord Charles Howard of Effingham, Earl of Nottingham—one of the few members of his mainly Catholic family not to carry the taint of treachery—was at pains to familiarize himself with the work of his ship and the men who crewed it, and the increase in efficiency and morale that this generated played no small part in English naval success. Howard had been an admiral since 1570 and was made Lord Admiral of the Fleet in 1585, like three of his ancestors before him—his father had commanded the English escort that brought Philip of Spain into Southampton for his wedding to Mary Tudor—but he had no experience of active service at sea, and owed his position to his social rank. He and his wife, Catherine Carey, daughter of the Earl of Hunsdon and a favourite lady-in-waiting of Elizabeth, were both closely related to the Queen and linked by birth or marriage to almost all the great families of England. He had held a series of glittering posts ever since Elizabeth had made him her ambassador to France at the tender age of twenty-three, and if he owed his rapid early advancement as much to his youthful good looks as to any innate abilities, he was industrious and effective enough to retain the royal favour long after a succession of younger men had caught the Queen's eye. He was a Knight of the Garter and Lord Chamberlain of the Household, and as General of Horse had played a leading role in putting down the Rising of the North in 1569. A commissioner at the trial of Mary, Queen of Scots, he was one of the loudest voices calling for her execution. Fifty-two at the time of the Armada, Howard was "no deep seaman but he had skill enough to know those who had more skill than himself and to follow their instructions . . . the Queen having a navy of oak and an admiral of osier."[19]

Drake, his Vice-Admiral, would not have been human if he had not resented being outranked by a man who, in naval if not social terms, was his clear inferior, and his lowly birth also made him insecure and aggressive, particularly when his authority was challenged by men of more noble origins. He had no public disputes with Howard during the

Armada campaign, though the fact that the two men were hostile to each other ever afterwards suggests that matters were different in private, but others felt the lash of Drake's refusal to allow any man aboard his ships to question his actions. Drake regarded seamen as "the most envious people of the world and so unruly without government" and he demonstrated the firmness of his own rule during his voyage of circumnavigation. In July 1578, as the *Pelican* reached St. Julian's Bay in the far south of South America, Thomas Doughty made strong objections to the course of action Drake proposed. "This gentleman must have sustained this opinion with more vigour than appeared proper to the General [Drake]. His answer was that he had the gentleman carried below deck and put in irons. On another day, at the same hour, he ordered him to be taken out and to be beheaded in presence of all" for incitement to mutiny. On another voyage, Drake also sentenced Sir William Borough to death for treason, though he was later reprieved. Drake was undoubtedly a solitary figure; there is no evidence of a long-term friendship with any man, and his wife was routinely left alone for months and even years while he was away at sea. Even aboard ship, among those to whom he perhaps felt closest, he was isolated by his position; the lengthy, wide-ranging conversations he held with captives aboard his ships may hint at the loneliness of this driven, friendless but brilliantly successful man.

In his mid-forties, Drake was at the peak of his powers and reputation. On 24 September 1585, after twelve months kicking his heels while awaiting the Queen's permission to sail, he began his latest voyage of reprisal. He had prepared with all speed and sailed at the head of twenty-one great ships, two of them, the *Bonaventure* and the *Aid*, the Queen's own galleons. Among the captains sailing with him were Thomas Fenner, Frobisher and Wynter. Drake told them that if storm damage or other calamity should force them to put in to port early in the voyage, they should do so in France or Ireland rather than on the English coast, in case the Queen had yet again changed her mind and issued orders to recall them. In the event, the voyage to Spain proceeded without incident and Drake first put in at Vigo, terrorizing the town, rescuing the crews of the embargoed English ships from jail and allowing them to sail for home, and helping himself to provisions for his ships. For ten days he wreaked further destruction on the coast of Galicia, sacking villages, looting, burning and desecrating Catholic churches, and capturing twenty-six ships.

Drake then sailed for the New World, arriving in Hispaniola on 26 November, and for the next six months he terrorized Spanish shipping and settlements. On New Year's Day, 1586, he captured Santo

Domingo, the capital of the western empire, and then sacked Cartagena, the richest city in the New World and the embarkation point of the treasure brought from the silver mines of the interior. Unfortunately for Drake, he missed the *flota* by a hair's breadth: "It escaped us but twelve hours the whole treasure which the King of Spain had out of the Indies this last year." With scurvy, typhus and dysentery wreaking havoc among his crew, he was forced to sail for home. The voyage was a financial failure, returning only fifteen shillings in the pound to the Queen and the merchant adventurers who had backed it, and Elizabeth was furious at the lack of profit, but Drake had done considerable damage to Spanish possessions and struck an even more telling psychological blow. The mere mention of his name was enough to strike fear into Spanish ships and settlements on both sides of the Atlantic, and such was his renown that even the knowledge that he was at sea was enough to prevent the treasure fleet from sailing. No silver from the New World reached Spain throughout the rest of 1586, and as a result many Spanish merchants were brought to the brink of ruin and the Spanish treasury was bare. The King's Principal Secretary tried to put a brave face on it—"The English sting us much, perhaps God permits it thus for something better"—but it was "such a cooling to King Philip as never happened to him since he was King of Spain."[20]

Despite the constant English raids on Spanish possessions, Elizabeth's support in money and men for the Dutch rebels defying Spanish rule, and Philip's support for plots and insurrections against her and his well-advanced preparations for invasion, the two rulers had always played out a charade of innocence. Like a schoolteacher bemoaning her inability to control her charges beyond the school gates, Elizabeth claimed that, even when utilizing the Queen's galleons, her mariners were outside her direct control, mere private citizens exacting due reparations for previous losses rather than instruments of state policy, but Drake's voyage from 1585 to 1586 ended the charade for ever. Within a week of receiving the news of Drake's latest depredations, Philip had recalled his envoy, Count de Feria, informed Pope Sixtus that he was planning the invasion of England, and begun urgent preparations for war.

The trigger was only partly Drake's raids on the New World, even though the vast wealth of precious metals mined and shipped to Spain was the financial underpinning of Philip's entire empire. Gold production had entered a steep decline as early as the 1570s, but the output of silver, particularly from the great Potosi mine high in the Andes, doubled in value between 1570 and the time of the Armada. Between a fifth and a third of the silver shipped back to Spain in each year's *flota* was the property of the Crown, and part of the fortunes earned by other Spaniards from this bonanza also found its way to Philip's coffers in taxes. His annual revenues exceeded the combined total of all the other European states and princedoms, but he could not sustain the Armada, the Army of Flanders or any of his other imperial ambitions if the flow of wealth from the treasure fleets was interrupted. It was also increasingly difficult for Philip to obtain credit from his bankers, since he could not guarantee that the treasure fleet would arrive intact. Drake had now disrupted the annual voyage of the *flota* on two occasions, but his raids were an irritation rather than a disaster for Spain and English dreams of capturing the entire treasure fleet were never realized. From the mid-sixteenth to the mid-seventeenth century, no more than one treasure ship in forty was lost and fewer than one in five even of those losses was caused by the attacks of privateers or warships.

If raids on the *flota* and the New World colonies were a considerable provocation to Philip, attacks on the Spanish mainland, whether Elizabeth willed them or not, were a different matter entirely. They amounted to a declaration of war on Spain, and it was a challenge that Philip was bound to accept. There could be no further pretence, for even more than the Dutch rebellion, Drake's impudent raids threatened to shake the whole precarious edifice of Philip's sprawling empire. If the all-powerful sovereign could be so taunted and humiliated on his own coastline, how could he hope to defend or maintain control of dominions thousands of miles away? "With this pirate at sea in such strength, we cannot defend any island or coast, nor predict where his next attacks may come, so it is uncertain what we can do to prevent them." Spain had been attacked, the King's forts had been destroyed, his warships sunk, his merchantmen captured and their cargoes plundered. Philip's reputation in Europe and his honour within his own country required the insult to be avenged.[21]

CHAPTER FOUR

The 4 Gallies of Portugall
under the Comand of Don
Diego de Medrana w.th 220
Souldiers, 2J2 Mariners, 200
Slaves, J00 Canons.

Smoking the Wasps from Their Nests

In late 1586, Francis Drake heard reports of the strength of the fleet being assembled in the harbours of Spain and Portugal, and burned to be at sea once more, attacking Spanish ships and settlements and securing a few more fat prizes. As winter turned to spring, he urged the Queen to let him "smoke the wasps out of their nests," certain that if he could only strike hard and early, before the Armada had even set sail, he could deal it a blow from which it might never recover. But Elizabeth was distracted, maintaining her public display of grief at the execution of Mary, Queen of Scots, and Drake was also in temporary disfavour, excluded for the moment from the inner circles of the Court, in punishment for the losses she had sustained from his last voyage. Elizabeth, as was her invariable custom, also hesitated and prevaricated. Early in her reign, she had taken the decision to send her navy to help defeat the French forces in Scotland and establish a Protestant state there only after changing her mind three times in a fortnight. On this occasion she exceeded even that indecision, sending Drake no fewer than four contradictory orders in a matter of days. "Give me five vessels and I will go out and sink them all [the Spanish fishing fleet off Newfoundland] and the galleons shall rot in Cadiz harbour for want of hands to sail them. But decide, Madam, and decide quickly. Time flies and will not return," Drake wrote, but for crucial weeks and then months Drake and the rest of her pirate admirals were kept cooling their heels.

Still fearful of provoking too open a breach with Philip, when Elizabeth at last gave Drake her permission for a new voyage, her commitment was discreet and hedged around with restrictions, and she exercised her right to appoint the second-in-command by sending Sir William Borough with him "for the express purpose of tempering his rashness." The Royal Letters Patent permitted him to set sail "for the honour and safety of our realms and dominions. We do of our authority Royal and of our certain knowledge, give full power and jurisdiction to you to punish and correct." His squadron was to cruise the oceans looking for prizes, but the Queen's commission also allowed him to "impeach the purpose of the Spanish fleet and stop their meeting at Lisbon" even if that meant "distressing their ships within their haven." She authorized him to take six of her ships, four front-line galleons and two fast pinnaces, and to negotiate with London merchants for as many more ships as they were willing to offer him. The Lord Admiral, Charles Howard, offered his own galleon and pinnace, and Drake also had four ships of his own waiting at Plymouth. His commission was dated 25 March 1587, but a few days before this Mendoza had already heard through his network of agents that Drake was equipping the Queen's ships.[1]

On 28 March, Drake signed agreements with the London merchants and the Queen's ships sailed from Gravesend to rendezvous with his own at Plymouth. Alongside his flagship, the *Elizabeth Bonaventure*, were three other galleons—the *Golden Lion*, the *Dreadnought* and the *Rainbow*—and three ships of the Levant Company. The risks from pirates and corsairs on the Barbary Coast during their normal trading voyages meant that the Levant ships were almost as heavily armed as the galleons. There were also seven smaller men-of-war and a dozen frigates and pinnaces. Drake led them into Plymouth Sound on 4 April, but remained there only a week, completing the equipping and provisioning of the ships "in a furious hurry," driven partly by the pressing need to strike the Spanish fleet while it still lay unprepared at anchor, but also by the fear that Elizabeth would once more change her mind and issue orders cancelling his commission. An ordinary traveller would take at least a week to cover the 215 miles from London to Plymouth, but a courier with a royal dispatch, travelling "by post" using a series of horses stabled at inns and post-houses roughly ten miles apart, could make the journey in as little as thirty-six hours.

Drake had let it be known that he was once more making for the riches of the New World, but as rumours began to circulate about his true destination, recruitment of seamen ground to a virtual halt and the ones already aboard deserted in droves. "When Drake announced last summer that he was going to attack the Indian flotillas men flocked to him eagerly and he could have armed 200 ships . . . but now they come very reluctantly and almost by force." It was one thing to risk your life for the chance of a fortune attacking treasure ships on the Spanish Main; it was quite another to beard Philip's ships in their own harbours, braving the guns of the forts and shore batteries. The same rumours had inevitably reached Mendoza. "With the exception of Drake himself, not a soul on the fleet knows what the object of it is, but various surmises are afloat, one to the effect that they are going to prevent the junction of His Majesty's fleet in Spain, destroying a portion of it as it will have to be fitted out in various ports." By 26 February he had reports that an English fleet "would shortly sail for the Straits of Gibraltar" and he at once sent word to Spain that Drake's target was probably Cadiz or Lisbon.[2]

As desertions increased, Drake suspected treachery, as he was always prone to do, and appealed to the local authorities to apprehend the deserters. He also wrote to Lord Howard that actions "so injurious to the Queen's service" required the most draconian punishment. He replaced the missing men with soldiers from the local garrison, and when the five remaining ships of the London contingent sailed into Plymouth on 11 April he at once made preparations to put to sea. Mendoza was again informed by "the Fleming I have there [in Plymouth] and from other quarters." "No living soul knew what the design was to be. The Queen would not have even the Lord Admiral informed, as she considers him a frank-spoken man, but judging from general indications and the haste in sending Drake off, it would seem as if the intention was to try to prevent the junction of Your Majesty's fleet . . . to this end they had let out a few words to Drake about Cadiz being a good port to burn the shipping in." Mendoza's prediction proved remarkably accurate but Philip received the dispatch only when Drake was already entering Cadiz. Yet even without inside information, his choice of target should not have been a complete surprise. Lisbon, the Armada's principal assembly point, was approached by a long, difficult and well-defended channel that even Drake might have jibbed at entering, but Cadiz, the main port of assembly after Lisbon, though guarded by shore batteries, was easy of access and egress and commanded a crucial position near the juncture of the Atlantic and the Mediterranean.

Drake wrote to Walsingham the next morning as his flagship, the *Elizabeth Bonaventure*, was about to make sail. "I thank God I find no man but as all members of one body to stand for our gracious Queen and our country against anti-Christ and his members . . . If your Honour did now see the fleet under sail and knew with what resolution men's minds do enter into this action as your Honour could rejoice to see them, so you would judge a small force would not divide them." Even as he sailed, Drake showed his fear that those who advocated peace with Spain, whether through altruism, financial prudence or more sinister motives, might yet influence the Queen. "It is a hard measure to be reported ill by those which will either keep their finger out of the fire, or too well affect to the alteration of our government, which I hope in God that they shall never live to see . . . The wind commands me away, our ships are under sail. God grant we may so live in His fear that the enemy may have course to say that God fights for Her Majesty as well abroad as at home. Haste."[3]

He was right to fear a change of heart by the Queen for, following the receipt of yet more disinformation from Stafford in Paris and fresh peace overtures from Parma in The Netherlands, she had already sent a courier riding hard for Plymouth with new instructions. In his previous orders Drake had been "particularly directed to distress the ships within the havens themselves." The one unambiguous comment in the new message was a reminder that the Queen still expected her full share of any prizes, but Drake was also ordered to "forbear to enter forcibly into any of the said King's [Philip's] ports or havens, or to offer violence to any of his towns or shipping within harbour, or to do any act of hostility upon the land. And yet, not withstanding this direction, Her pleasure is that both you and such of Her subjects that serve there under you, should do your best endeavour (avoiding as much as may lie in you the effusion of Christian blood) to get into your possession such shipping of the said King or his subjects as you shall find at sea."

Elizabeth wanted Spanish prizes, Spanish silver and gold, and the Armada hampered and damaged, but she also wanted to protest her innocence to Philip, just as she had done over the execution of Mary. Burghley was able to swear on his honour to Parma's representative, de Looe, that the Queen had forbidden Drake to carry out any warlike act against the King of Spain—"So unwitting, yea unwilling to Her Majesty were those actions committed by Sir Francis Drake, for the which Her Majesty is as yet greatly offended with him"—and Walsingham could write to Stafford in Paris that Elizabeth had forbidden Drake even to enter any Spanish harbour, but there was no real hindrance on him. The pinnace bearing Elizabeth's new orders did not leave Plymouth until nine days after Drake's squadron had set course for Spain. A storm blew it back into the Channel and the captain, a distant relative of Drake, then abandoned all attempts to overhaul him, contenting himself instead with taking a Portuguese merchant ship laden with £5,000 worth of sugar and Brazilian hardwood as a prize. Meanwhile Drake was free to follow his instincts and his inclinations and make whatever attacks he chose.[4]

His squadron had been scattered by a storm off Finisterre but reassembled with the loss of only one pinnace. It claimed several prizes, including a Portuguese caravel. "Two ships of Middleborough" [Middleburg in The Netherlands] were intercepted off the Rock of Lisbon and their captains reported a great number of ships at Cadiz, preparing to join the Armada. By Wednesday, 29 April, Drake's ships had rounded Cape St. Vincent and, with a south-westerly driving them on, were racing past the coastal salt marshes towards the long, rocky spit of land screening the great harbour of Cadiz. English naval standing orders stated that an admiral could not "take in hand any exploit to land or enter into any harbour of the enemy, but he shall call a council and make his captains privy to his device," and Drake accordingly held a council of war aboard his flagship at four o'clock that afternoon. He asked his vice-admiral, William Borough, captain of the *Golden Lion*, whether they should enter the harbour at once or wait until the morning. Borough's fence-straddling reply was that there was some argument for waiting but that the wind might fail in the meantime and there would still be daylight enough to reach the outer harbour that night.

A gentleman and a long-serving officer, expert navigator and cartographer, Borough had sailed with Sir Hugh Willoughby to the Arctic in 1553 and served on the ships of the Muscovy Company for twenty years. Prior to Drake's voyage of circumnavigation, Borough had been regarded as the highest English authority on maritime affairs, and he had seen combat, commanding a fleet that fought and captured a notorious Baltic pirate, Hans Snarke. He must have expected the respect due to his experience and to his position as the Queen's representative aboard the fleet, but Drake had fought twenty battles for every one that Borough had seen, and cared little for officers of gentle birth and even less for those who tried to restrict his freedom of action. It was Borough's first experience of Drake's leadership and he was rapidly made to realize that his commander had no time for prevarication, niceties or formalities, or indeed for opinions other than his own. "There are some would have us stay till morning; we shall not stay at all," he said. That was the end of the council of war.

Drake immediately set sail for Cadiz, leaving the rest of his ships to form what order of battle they could as they followed him in. It was "in such confused order as was never heard of in such an action," according to Borough, but they did have the element of surprise. The population of Cadiz was blissfully unaware of the looming threat, for who would dare to challenge the power and might of imperial Spain in one of its greatest harbours? Many of the citizens and nobles were in the town square, watching some strolling players and tumblers, and the crews of many of the ships at anchor were also ashore. Even when word was brought that a line of ships was passing the Pillar of Hercules guarding the entrance to the harbour, there was no alarm at first; they were assumed to be more Spanish ships, perhaps the Biscayans of Juan Martinez de Recalde, arriving to reinforce the Armada. But as they bore down on the harbour, "an hour before sun setting," the realization began to dawn that these were not Spanish but English ships, undoubtedly led by the notorious El Draque (The Dragon) and advancing "with more speed and arrogance than any pirate has ever shown."[5]

Further attempts at subterfuge were now useless and Drake and his captains broke out their English colours while his trumpets sounded a call to arms from the quarterdecks. Six Spanish galleys and a galliot commanded by Don Pedro de Acuna, newly arrived from Gibraltar, were sufficiently manned and prepared to cast off almost at once and form a defensive line across the entrance to the lower bay, and one galley was detached to challenge the enemy. It moved rapidly ahead, its banks of oars flashing in the light of the setting sun and its great bronze ram glinting, but, met at once by a hail of cannon fire, it was forced to turn tail and flee. The sight of the ships, the sound of gunfire and the mere whisper of Drake's name were enough to throw the townsfolk into panic. Women, children, the old and the sick were ordered to take refuge in the old castle of Matagorda but, caught up in the general terror, the commandant shut his gates against them. In the panic and confusion twenty-five women and children were killed, trampled underfoot or forced off the path to fall into the sea. Such foot soldiers and cavalry as could be mustered in haste were stationed throughout the town and sent to guard Puental, a rough, rocky area outside the city walls that seemed to offer the English the best prospect of making a landing.

Having put the attacking galley to flight, Drake's fleet was already engaging the defensive screen barring the way to the lower bay. In the summer of the previous year, five "tall and stout ships" of the Levant Company "intending only a merchant's voyage" had fought and defeated eleven Spanish galleys of the Sicilian Guard after a battle lasting five hours. Three of those Levant ships were with Drake now and the Spanish galleys were even more disadvantaged. The galleys were fast and manoeuvrable—they could turn 360 degrees in their own length—but their rams, boarding troops and relatively light armaments were of minimal use against heavily gunned English galleons that could destroy the galleys before their own weapons were even within range. The English cannon fire caused carnage among the banks of slaves and convict oarsmen chained to their benches. As de Acuna's battered squadron fled, two galleys were so badly damaged that Drake was convinced they were sinking and the upperworks of the others were strewn with dead and wounded.

The galleys' shallow draught allowed them to cross the sandbars and shoals guarding Puerta de Santa Maria, four miles from Cadiz on the other side of the lower bay, and there they were safe from further attacks, but the myth of the supremacy and invincibility of galleys, built up during a century of conflict in the Mediterranean, had been exploded. Never again would they dominate a naval battle. "Twelve of Her Majesty's ships will not make account of [will not be troubled by] all his [Philip's] galleys in Spain, Portugal and all his dominions within the Straits [of Gibraltar] although they are 150 in number. If it be to their advantage in a calm, we have made such trial of their fights that we perfectly see into the depth thereof." So completely had the galleys' once-fearsome reputation been demolished that when Sir Walter Ralegh led another raid on Cadiz nine years later, "the English fleet replied to the fire of the Spanish galleys with blasts of discordant derision from a band of trumpeters."

The captains of the mass of vessels in the anchorage beyond the promontory of Puntales, fifty or sixty ships in total, were thrown into even greater panic by the flight of their defenders. There were five huge hulks—transport ships—laden with wine and ship's biscuit for the Armada and several Dutch hulks embargoed by the Spanish for the same purpose. There were also Indies ships and merchantmen from northern Europe and the Mediterranean, some loading wine from

Jerez, some laden with Mediterranean goods and merely waiting for a change in the wind to carry them north towards their destination. Those with crew and sea-room enough to manoeuvre made attempts to escape, either seeking shelter in water too shallow for the great English ships or making a run for the sanctuary of the upper bay, but the majority were trapped and helpless.

Only one offered armed resistance, a huge Genoese ship of 700 tons (though the English took her to be a Ragusan from her lines) laden with wood, hides, wool and cochineal, and heavily armed to protect her from corsairs. The captain's defiance was a brave but futile gesture, denying Drake a valuable prize but only because, when his guns had finished their work, the ship, her cargo and her forty brass cannon lay at the bottom of the harbour. There is no record of any member of the crew surviving. They died "tumbling into the sea, heaps of soldiers so thick as if coals had been poured out of a sack in many ports at once; some drowned and some sticking in the mud . . . The spectacle was very lamentable on their side, for many drowned themselves, many, half-burnt, leapt into the water, very many hanging by the ropes' ends by the ship's side, under the water even to the lips, many swimming with grievous wounds, stricken under water and put out of their pain, and with so huge a fire and such of the ordnance in the great [ship] and the rest when the fire came to them, as if any man had a desire to see Hell itself, it was there most lively figured."[6]

There was no further resistance. Drake's squadron came to anchor and at once his men began to work their way methodically through the captured ships. The most valuable cargoes were transferred to his holds, the better ships added to his squadron and the remaining vessels towed off their moorings, set on fire and cast loose on the flood tide, "the sight of which terrible fires were to us very pleasant, and mitigated the burden of our constant travail." The burning vessels swept in on the tide, causing fresh panic and havoc among the small ships still cowering in the inner harbour. In the gathering darkness, the glow from the burning ships cast a baleful light onto the white walls of the town. The cannon of the old fort and a battery of guns on the harbourside kept up a sporadic fire, but the range was too great and the weapons too inaccurate to threaten the English ships. However, under cover of the night the galleys crept from their sanctuary and, before Drake and his fleet were even aware that the attack was under way, they had isolated the captured Portuguese caravel at the rear of the English squadron, manned only by a small prize crew. The Spaniards riddled it with small-arms fire and when they boarded it only five men remained alive, all of whom were wounded. The recaptured caravel was towed to safety in shallow water beyond Drake's reach, but it proved to be the only Spanish success.

The night was cold and dark and the smouldering wrecks of the burned ships and the barrels of pitch ignited along the waterfront gave only a fitful, smoky light for the watchmen lining the shore and peering into the darkness to detect the first sign of the expected landing by Drake's men. The polyglot mixture of nationalities in the port heightened fears and suspicions of treachery, and every foreign or unfamiliar face was suspect. Around midnight the thunder of drums signalled an alarm that caused fresh panic in the streets, but the vessel that had caused it was not an English craft but a galley running aground on the shore. Drake sent two small boats to test the defences of the bridge over the San Pedro river—the only means of access for troops seeking to reinforce the town—but they were repulsed by two galleys that had taken refuge there.

There were no further attempts at a landing, but by dawn of the following morning, Thursday 30 April, the looting and destruction of the ships in the harbour was complete and, "with music, artillery and flags and pennants" flying, Drake led his squadron to anchor off Puental, guarding the entrance to the upper bay. Under interrogation, captured seamen and officers had revealed that the Marquis of Santa Cruz's own fine galleon had just anchored there to take on board her guns and fighting troops. Intended as the flagship of the Armada, she was the greatest prize of all. Leaving his own flagship at anchor, Drake transferred to the *Merchant Royal,* one of the shallower-draught ships of the Levant Company, and led a force of frigates and pinnaces into the upper bay. Drake himself supervised the burning of Santa Cruz's galleon while his pinnaces captured and burned many of the smaller craft that had escaped destruction the previous night. The smoke and flames were so thick and the heat so intense that it seemed to the people of Puental as if "a great volcano" were erupting before their eyes.[7]

A further forty ships lay at the furthest end of the bay, guarded by the gun batteries of Puerto Real. The inhabitants still feared an invasion but, alerted by messengers, reinforcements were now arriving from Jerez. A company of infantry and horsemen had marched through the night to reach Cadiz and there was word that the Duke of Medina-Sidonia, the commander of the land forces on this coast, was on his way with all the troops he could assemble. He entered the town towards noon with 3,000 foot soldiers and 300 cavalry. The town's defenders were also manoeuvring two huge bronze culverins, eighteen feet long and weighing several tons, into a position from where they could fire on the English ships anchored off Puental. The nearest, the *Golden*

Lion, was barely a mile away, well within range, and William Borough grew increasingly alarmed. There had been no word from Drake since that first perfunctory council of war and Borough went in search of him first on the *Elizabeth Bonaventure*, then in the upper bay, but did not overhaul him until Drake had returned to his own ship. Borough was then dismissed, his pleas that the fleet should sail at once ignored. When he returned to the *Golden Lion*, he found it under fire from the culverins on the headland. One shot had already pierced the hull and severed the leg of the Master Gunner.

In Borough's absence the Master had already made preparation to warp out of range. Seeing a further chance to attack an isolated ship, the galleys made another foray, but the *Golden Lion* manoeuvred to give them its broadside and when Drake saw its danger he sent the *Rainbow*, six merchantmen and his own pinnace to its defence. With the advantage of numbers now with him, Borough cut off the galleys and forced them to seek the shelter of the Las Puertas reef in the outer channel. He then anchored his ship midway between the old fort and the shore batteries guarding Puerta de Santa Maria, threatening the galleys if they left their shelter, but also leaving himself well placed for a swift escape from the bay if danger loomed.

Drake and his triumphant captains were now ready to put to sea, but they were betrayed for the moment by the wind. It died away and for twelve hours his ships lay almost motionless, completely becalmed, but still displaying their banners and sounding their defiance of the town and its feeble cannonade with their battle trumpets. The culverins and the most powerful cannons continued to fire on the fleet at extreme range and a few of the small ships in the shallows close to the castle walls were loaded with combustibles, set on fire and cast loose on the receding tide to drift towards Drake's fleet. As night came on, more and more fireships were launched, once more illuminating the harbour and the town. Some of the galleys, at an advantage now using their oars against the becalmed fleet, towed the fireships into better positions and did their best to cover them with their guns. But by warping the ships—hauling in and releasing their anchor cables—the English galleons kept themselves broadside on to any menacing galleys, and their ships' boats and pinnaces intercepted the blazing fireships and towed them away to burn out harmlessly on the shore. Unperturbed, Drake remarked that, by burning their own ships, the Spaniards were doing the Englishmen's work for them, and his joke was shouted from ship to ship across the harbour.

Soon after midnight the wind at last got up, a land breeze aiding the fleet's escape through the channel. The galleys and the galliot gave pursuit and as the dawn broke they opened fire. Drake at once cut sail, dropped anchor and invited the attack. It would have been suicide for the Spanish ships to have obliged him and instead Don Pedro de Acuna, harking back to a more courtly era of warfare, sent complimentary messages and a gift of wine and sweetmeats. An exchange of prisoners was also proposed but, before it could be effected, the wind again strengthened and Drake upped anchor and led his fleet west towards Cape St. Vincent. He left behind the wreckage of a large number of great ships. Spanish reports claimed that twenty-four had been lost, with a total value of 172,000 ducats. "The damage it committed there was not great," Philip said on hearing the news, "but the daring of the attempt was so." English estimates of the number of great ships captured or sunk were higher. Robert Leng, a gentleman volunteer with Drake's fleet, reckoned the Spanish losses at "about thirty," and Drake himself claimed to have sunk, burned or captured thirty-seven. In addition he had deprived the Armada of a substantial quantity of supplies. He had indeed "singed the King of Spain's beard," but he knew the blow he had dealt was far from a fatal one. As he wrote to Walsingham, "I assure your Honour, the like preparation was never heard of nor known as the King of Spain has and daily makes to invade England . . . which, if they be not impeached before they join, will be very perilous . . . This service which by God's sufferance we have done will breed some alterations . . . [but] all possible preparations for defence are very expedient . . . I dare not almost write of the great forces we hear the King of Spain has. Prepare in England strongly and most by sea."

By 13 May Elizabeth had received the news and was pleased enough to tell the French ambassador. When he remarked that it was hard to believe that Drake's fleet had "burnt the ships in Cadiz and sacked the country," she snapped, "Then you do not believe what is possible." As calm returned to Cadiz, the populace were already turning a humiliation into a victory. A procession wound its way from the cathedral to the monastery of San Francisco to give thanks for the salvation of the city, and almost at once the myth began to spread that the invaders had been driven off with heavy casualties and losses of ships. In fact the only English loss was the captured Portuguese caravel, and the only casualty was the gunner on the *Golden Lion*.[8]

Drake had meanwhile gone in search of the Biscayan squadron of Juan Martinez de Recalde, then at sea with half a dozen ships and five pinnaces and daily expected in Cadiz, but the closest Drake came to him was the capture of a dispatch boat carrying orders for de Recalde to change course and make for Lisbon at once to avoid Drake's numerically stronger squadron. On 9 May, Drake broke off the search, sum-moned a council of war and told his captains that they were returning to Cape St. Vincent to capture the castle of Sagres, "being moved . . . in his Prince's service with his courageous company to aggravate the honour of his fame." Sagres was a shrewd choice, the point where all homecoming Spanish ships from the East and West Indies sought their landfall. It was even said that seamen could find it in darkness, mist or low cloud, for they had only to reach the 37th parallel of latitude out in the Atlantic and then sail due east until the scent of pine resin from the tree-clad slopes around Sagres told them that they had reached their destination.

Not venturing to argue with Drake face to face, Borough returned to his ship after the council of war, but then sent an immediate letter protesting the decision. "There is no watering place nearer than half a mile, which is but a pool, to the which the way is bad . . . If you should achieve your purpose what have you of it? No matter of substance. Neither shall any man be better by it but a satisfying of your mind that you may say 'What have I done upon the King of Spain's land?'" He told Drake that his proper course was to cruise off the Cape and inter-cept Spanish shipping, rather than make a dangerous and superfluous landing on the coast. Whatever his motives, Borough's advice was fool-ish. Galleons and men-of-war could not long remain at sea before foul food, tainted water and disease laid waste the crew. The slim, sleek lines of English galleons made them very fast and manoeuvrable but once the armaments, munitions and crew had been accommodated, little storage space was left belowdecks, and Drake and his men would far rather have filled their holds with Spanish gold than provisions and barrels of water, salt-beef and ship's biscuit.

The uncertainty about the duration of voyages also made supply-ing them a matter of luck. The rule of thumb adopted by the English navy was that the salted meat from one bullock's carcass would feed one man for four months at sea, but on every voyage Drake always took pains to secure bases in which his ships could be repaired and careened, and his men rested and provisioned. On his voyage to Panama in 1573 he established a base on "Slaughter Island (because so many of our men died there)," hauling a prize he had captured ashore to serve as "a storehouse for ourselves and a prison for our enemies." He had already been at sea a month. If he was to remain off the Spanish coast for per-haps two or even three more months a base was essential. Drake had once had his ship's chaplain chained and manacled for what he per-ceived to be a disrespectful sermon, and to be lectured by Borough on the custom and practice of the navy, and told that he had exceeded the

Queen's instructions, was insufferable to him. In his eyes, Borough was at best insubordinate and at worst a traitor, sabotaging the morale of his men. Drake at once summoned a group of his captains to the *Elizabeth Bonaventure* and presided over a drumhead court martial, reading excerpts from Borough's letter to make his case. Captain Marchant, sergeant major of the land forces, then took command of the *Golden Lion* and placed Borough in his cabin under arrest.[9]

Drake's plan to seize Sagres went ahead without further demur. He first landed his men at Lagos, fifteen miles down the coast, and a column of 1,100 men marched towards the town, either to test its defences or, more probably, as a diversion to conceal their true target. They made no attempt to breach the city walls but merely patrolled past them, exchanging fire with the defenders, and then returned to their ships. The diversionary raid complete, Drake's fleet upped anchor and sailed up the coast to Sagres, where his troops made an immediate assault on the castle. It was "a place of such natural and ingenious strength as is a very miraculous matter," occupying a forbidding site, high above the rocks at the very tip of Cape St. Vincent, and protected on three sides by the sheer cliffs and the sea. On its landward, northern side was a massive stone wall, forty feet high and ten feet thick. Four round towers protected the gatehouse, each mounted with a large brass portingale sling—a breech-loading, swivel-mounted gun with a killing range of up to a quarter of a mile.

In the fifteenth century Henry the Navigator had established the castle as a formidable base where navigators, chart-makers, ship-designers, sailors, adventurers and explorers from all over Europe came together to pool their knowledge and expertise in a common goal: the exploration and conquest of new worlds. There they mastered the arts of navigation, studied maps bought, copied or purloined from as far away as Arabia and China, and then set out for southern Africa, Asia and the Americas, the first Europeans to sail there. Drake gave no sign that he recognized the history and significance of the site; it was simply a target to be attacked, conquered and then destroyed. He first offered the commander the chance to surrender. When this was declined, the attackers kept up a storm of musket and arquebus fire against the garrison at the firing slits and on the ramparts, while Drake himself laboured alongside his men to pile a mountain of pitch-soaked log-wood and faggots against the great wooden gates. Within two hours they had been reduced to ashes, and as the English musket fire caused carnage among the defenders, the commander—already wounded twice—finally agreed to surrender.

Drake allowed all the soldiers and civilians within the fort to escape with their personal property, leaving only their weapons behind, and by mid-afternoon his forces controlled the castle. Having conquered Sagres, Drake at once destroyed it. Heavy guns—the portingale slings, a demi-cannon, a culverin and a demi-culverin—were lowered over the cliffs to the shore and loaded aboard his ship. His own armaments were already more than adequate but such heavy weapons, cast from bronze, were hugely expensive and rich prizes to add to his haul from Cadiz. Provisions and other items of value were stripped from the fort and it was then put to the torch. The terrified inhabitants and soldiery fled the other fortifications in the area without a fight and all four "castles at the Capes" were razed, "a matter of great importance respecting all shipping that comes out of the Straits for Lisbon."

Drake spent the next five days reprovisioning and resting his men, and beaching, rummaging (cleaning the gravel ballast) and careening each of his ships in turn, hauling them onto their sides with cables attached to the mainmast, allowing the ship's hull to be scraped clean of barnacles and weed, and coated with grease or tallow, brimstone and tar. At the same time, the water butts were hauled out of the hold, scoured with sand and then refilled with sweet water. He could carry out these tasks with perfect impunity because even the fastest messenger, using relays of horses, would take days to carry the news of his attack on Sagres to Lisbon and Madrid. Even if troops were dispatched at once, it would take several days' march over the rugged terrain and dismal roads before they could reach Sagres, and by then Drake would have completed his repairs and reprovisioning and put to sea. In any event, his onslaught and his reputation had put "the country in such awe that no man comes near us."[10]

He next set sail for Lisbon. Santa Cruz was in port with his twelve galleons of Portugal but they were poorly armed, for the guns that had been promised had not yet appeared, and he had neither gunners nor soldiers and no more than skeleton crews aboard. Lisbon was the most secure and formidably defended harbour in the world and even if Drake succeeded in passing the castles guarding the approaches, he still had to run the gauntlet of the fortress of Belém, a series of shore batteries and the guns of Lisbon Castle. Yet such was his reputation that an attack was widely expected. As word spread of his approach, troops from Recalde's ships and the arquebusiers from Lisbon Castle were sent to Sesimbra—felt to be the likeliest point for an English attack—and seven galleys of the Lisbon Harbour Guard, under the command of Santa Cruz's brother, Don Alonso de Bazan, put to sea to keep watch. However, Drake ignored Sesimbra and instead came to anchor in Cascais Bay, midway between the guns of Cascais Castle, protecting the fishing village at the westward end, and Castle St. Julian, an even more formidable fortress at the other tip of the bay, guarding the North Channel, one of the two difficult and dangerous approaches to Lisbon. The South Channel was guarded by the less intimidating guns of the Torre Viejo, but it was even more tortuous, so difficult that there were different specialist pilots for each section of the river as ships sailed upstream.

Santa Cruz rushed more men and guns to defend Castle St. Julian and had his galleys ready to attack the small boats in the shallow waters if the English attempted a landing, but Drake had no intention of doing so. While his pinnaces wreaked havoc among the coastal shipping, seizing them, sinking them or driving them onto the rocks, he first tried to lure the galleys into a deep-water battle, but "the Marquis of Santa Cruz, seeing us chase his ships ashore, was content to suffer us quietly to tarry and never charged us with one shot." Drake then offered an exchange of his prisoners for Englishmen held in Lisbon. "The Marquis sent word that, as a gentleman, he had none." It was a lie; Drake knew from English agents that there were several Englishmen languishing in the galleys and prisons of Lisbon. He therefore resolved "that all such Spaniards as it shall please God to send under our hands, shall be sold unto the Moors, and the money reserved for the redeeming of our countrymen." He also issued a challenge to Santa Cruz to bring his ships out to do battle, but as the wind freshened northerly he broke off negotiations and sailed south again, back to the Cape.

For the next ten days he remained at Sagres, once more replenishing provisions and water, pumping the bilges and careening his ships. The sick men were put ashore to rest and recover. Meanwhile Drake's pinnaces—fast, manoeuvrable and sufficiently heavily armed for the task—patrolled the coast, sinking or capturing every ship that crossed their path. Well over a hundred were sunk or burned at sea, in harbour or on the beaches flanking the Cape. More than half were tunny-fishing boats and Drake's men destroyed not only the boats but even the nets drying on the beaches. The Spanish fishing fleets in the North Sea and on the Grand Banks off Newfoundland had already been destroyed or driven off by English ships and this assault sorely depleted the other prime source of salt-fish for the Armada. The remainder of Drake's prizes were barques and caravels bearing stores and provisions along the coast and into Lisbon. Some were laden with barrel staves—"hoops and pipe staithes, above sixteen or seventeen hundred ton in weight, which cannot be less than 25 or 30,000 ton [of supplies] if it had been made in cask ready for liquor, all of which I commanded to be consumed into smoke and ashes by fire, which will be unto the King no small waste of his provision beside the want of his barques." The bonfires of barrel staves represented a serious loss to the Armada; barrels made of seasoned oak were essential for the storage of wine, water, salt-fish, salt-beef, oil and ship's biscuit, the provisions upon which it would depend when at sea. Drake's men also "brought away and burnt seven hundred tons of bread [ship's biscuit]."[11]

While he remained at Cape St. Vincent, Drake also paralysed the movement of Spanish supply and warships. Four great galleasses from Naples, the Sicilian galleys and the armed merchantmen of the Levant squadron all made port at Malaga, Cartagena or Gibraltar, and a few even ventured as far as Cadiz, but none dared sail further. With them were merchantmen, barques and caravels carrying the battle-hardened soldiers of the Naples regiment, ships' crews scoured from a score of Mediterranean ports, and the foodstuffs, wine and warlike provisions for the Armada. Helpless in Lisbon, Santa Cruz could only wait, lacking both the men and the armaments with which to put to sea. Philip received daily communications about Drake's movements and bombarded his commanders with fresh instructions, often contradicting those he had issued the day before. His galleys were ordered out of port, then summoned back; his battle troops told to embark, then to disembark and march overland. Drake "merely had to shift his position now and again, and to every centre orders came tripping up each other's heels till the whole system of the enemy was in tangled confusion." Philip also sent panic-stricken dispatches to the governors of his New World territories ordering the *flota* to keep as far south as possible on its easterly voyage to Spain, avoiding the waters habitually used by Drake. His ships bearing these orders were instructed to carry false dispatches to mislead Drake if they fell into his hands.

Captain Fenner, Drake's second-in-command, was well aware of the value of the position they had seized. "We hold this Cape so greatly to our benefit and so much to their disadvantage, as a great blessing was the attaining thereof, for the rendezvous is at Lisbon, where we understand of some 25 ships and seven galleys. The rest, we lie between home and them, so as the body is without the members and they cannot come together by reason that they are unfurnished of their provisions in every degree . . . As there has been a happy beginning, so we doubt not that God will have the sequel . . . that it is not the multitude that shall prevail when it pleases him to stretch out his hand." On the same day, 24 May, Drake wrote to Walsingham, "As long as it shall please God to give us provisions to eat and drink, and that our ships and wind and weather will permit us, you shall surely hear of us near this Cape of St. Vincent where we do and will expect daily what Her Majesty and Your Honours will further command. God make us all thankful that Her Majesty sent out these few ships in time. If there were six more of Her Majesty's good ships of the second sort, we should be the better able to keep their forces from joining and happily take or impeach his fleets from all places in the next month or so, after which is the chiefest time of their returns home [i.e., the end of the good sailing weather] . . . There must be a beginning of any good matter, but the continuing to the end until it be fully finished yields of the true glory . . . God made us all thankful again and again that we have, although it be little, made a beginning on the coast of Spain."[12]

Although the destruction of Spanish fishing boats and barrel staves and the disruption of Spanish shipping making for Lisbon was valuable in strategic terms, it earned no profit for Drake's fleet of privateers and armed merchantmen, and there must have been discontented rumblings from captains whose first priority was always the profit of themselves and their backers, not the interests of their country. Drake may have seemed the absolute ruler of his fleet, as William Borough could testify, but in fact he required the support or at least the acquiescence of his other commanders, and they were free to desert him and make for home if they felt his chosen course was unlikely to bring them rewards. Drake himself faced commercial pressures, not least from the Queen, whose insistence on receiving a return on her investment was unshakeable, even when her ships were engaged in the protection of her throne.

Perhaps as a result of these pressures, on 1 June Drake sent home a few prize ships and others carrying the sick and wounded, and the loot from Cadiz and the raids along the coast. He also sent a further note to Walsingham, suggesting that the ship he had sent with his dispatch should be returned to him with other reinforcements. As a result of this appeal, "four of Her Majesty's ships with six sail of the merchants" were duly readied to join Drake at Cape St. Vincent, but by then he had already changed his plans. His fleet escorted the homeward-bound vessels well to the west of the Cape, but as they shifted course to the north, he held on due west into the Atlantic, setting a course for the Azores on the track of the *San Felipe*, a carrack reported to be returning from Goa with a rich cargo of goods and spices.

On 3 June his fleet was hit by a violent storm. It raged for forty-eight hours and when at last it cleared and the fleet re-formed, only seven galleons and their pinnaces remained. Drake claimed that the London ships had simply deserted him in mid-ocean. The perennial shipboard malaises—scurvy, dysentery and typhus—were beginning to affect the fleet and some captains would have harboured serious concerns about shortages of food and water if the voyage was further prolonged, but it seems implausible that, had they known of it, they would have turned their back on the prospect of a prize as rich as the *San Felipe*. The captains of the London ships had no idea of Drake's objective and no rendezvous point where the fleet could reassemble; if they lost touch with him, they had no alternative but to make for home. On the next day one of the missing ships was sighted and the *Golden Lion* and the pinnace *Spy* were sent in pursuit of it. Some time later the *Spy* returned alone, with Captain Marchant of the *Golden Lion* aboard. His crew had mutinied, reinstated William Borough as captain and set sail for home. A furious Drake at once convened a court martial and passed a sentence of death for high treason on Borough in his absence, but the sentence was never carried out. A Court of Inquiry sitting in London later exonerated him, and Borough and his crew claimed their full share of pay and prize money from the expedition.

On 18 June the *San Felipe* was duly sighted near São Miguel in the Azores. It repeatedly dipped the flag at the masthead, inviting the unknown ships to show their colours, but Drake's fleet "would put out no flag until we were within shot of her, when we hanged out flags, streamers and pennants that she might be out of doubt what we were. Which done, we hailed her with cannon shot and shot her through several times." Owned by Philip and trading in the East Indies for his sole benefit, the *San Felipe* was a huge ship, towering above the English galleons and outweighing any three of them together, but its crew was weakened and depleted by the privations of the long sea voyage from Goa. In addition to its own goods, it was also bringing home the cargo from another Spanish carrack "which was not fit to proceed on the voyage" and was so heavy laden that its gun-ports could not even be used. Its bow and stern chasers were the only guns that could be fired and they were no match for the English cannons and culverins. Drake's six galleons and accompanying pinnaces were amply strong enough to overpower the *San Felipe* and after a brief resistance, "six of her men being slain and several sore hurt, they yielded unto us."[13]

Drake gave the captain and his crew a boat with which to make for São Miguel and he also released 240 Africans "whom they had taken to make slaves in Spain and Portugal." He gave them a boat, allowing them to sail "whither they list, and further dealt most favourably with them." He then set sail for Plymouth with his prize, "the greatest ship in all Portugal," laden with precious metals, jewels, ivory, silks, taffetas, velvets, calico, carpets, porcelain, ebony, gum, indigo, cinnamon, cloves, ginger, mace and pepper. Such was its value that the cargo was almost literally worth its weight in gold, "so richly loaded that every man in the fleet counted his fortune made." It would have been folly for Drake to have returned to Cape St. Vincent and risked such a prize being recaptured by a Spanish fleet lying in wait for his return, and in any event he had already caused enough disruption to ensure that the Spanish Armada would not sail in 1587.

Even before Drake's raid, a crucial hiatus had occurred in the Spanish preparations because of the illness of the King. Philip complained of a cold in early February 1587, and, exacerbated by his spartan living conditions in his cold stone palace and by the stresses of his self-imposed work regime, it worsened and developed into an illness, possibly pneumonia, that lasted well into the summer. His insistence that all business of the state should still be transacted by him alone threw the Spanish government into near-paralysis for most of that time. His secretary Don Juan de Idiaquez did what he could to keep the Armada preparations moving forward and had canvassed the Duke of Medina-Sidonia for his opinions on augmenting the Armada by keeping that year's outward-bound Indies fleet and the escorts of the treasure fleet in Spanish waters. Medina-Sidonia dismissed the idea. "On the communication between the two worlds depends the wealth and power we need here ... Rather than halt the sailing of the *flota*, its prompt dispatch should be encouraged."[14]

On the question of Drake's latest raids, Idiaquez had consulted his master who, even in the depths of his illness, left him in no doubt as to the right response. "Defensive measures will no longer suffice. He [Philip] must set fire to their house ... to draw them home." By so doing, he would solve the problem not only of England, but of The Netherlands too, "that voracious monster that devours the men and treasure of Spain." Uncertainties about Drake's whereabouts and intentions and fears that he would again return to ravage Spanish harbours and shipping or intercept the *flota*, carrying "more than sixteen million, the greatest treasure that has ever entered these kingdoms in one sum from the Indies," now caused further delays to the Armada preparations. Many great ships and galleys skulked in port and Philip was forced to divert troops to defend the coast. Meanwhile, having at last received troops and armaments for his ships, Santa Cruz departed for the Azores with thirty-seven of the Armada's best fighting ships "to ensure the safety of the Indian flotillas [the treasure fleet] and sweep the corsairs from the seas, and if God should allow him to encounter Drake, I trust he will give him what he deserves." Santa Cruz sailed on 16 July 1587 and rendezvoused with the treasure fleet on 26 August, bringing it safely to the Guadalquivir River, where it was towed upstream to Seville, beyond the reach of even the most adventurous corsair. As soon as he received word of its arrival, Philip sent an envoy to Seville to levy an immediate tax of 5 per cent of the value to subsidize the Enterprise of England, but his joy at the receipt of his treasure was marred by his knowledge that the Armada would once more be delayed.

Don Alonso de Leiva had led a fleet of ships into Lisbon in early August to reinforce the Armada and such a volley was fired in celebration that the gun smoke lay like fog across the entire harbour. The crews remained aboard, ready to sail for England as soon as Santa Cruz and the remainder of the Armada's great ships returned from escorting the *flota*, but he did not drop anchor back in Lisbon until the end of September. He then announced that he could not possibly depart before November at the earliest. The ships needed careening and refitting, the men were sick and in need of rest and food, and the autumn storms were already breaking. De Leiva dismissed Santa Cruz's comments and claimed that the Armada was ready to sail at once, but when asked his opinion, Medina-Sidonia sided with Santa Cruz, arguing that to set sail so late in the year was a recipe for disaster. Once more the departure was postponed.

The source of many of Philip's problems had already set his course for home. A pinnace sailed ahead, carrying news of the prize he had captured, and when Drake himself made harbour in Plymouth, people dressed in their Sunday clothes streamed into the town from many miles around to see the *San Felipe* and join the celebrations of their countrymen's good fortune. So many guns were fired in salute that the town accounts included an "item paid for powder spent at the coming in of Sir Francis Drake." The *San Felipe* and its cargo raised a total of £114,000 when sold. The riches obtained from this single ship, coupled with the plunder that Drake had brought back from his circumnavigation in the previous decade, awakened English merchant adventurers to the phenomenal value of trade with the East Indies, and led directly to attempts by the Muscovy Company to develop trade with the Far East and to the foundation of the East India Company. Even after the London investors had received their handsome dividend and the crews had taken their share of the prize money, Drake still received £17,000 and the Queen £40,000, in addition to the chest of gold and jewels that he was careful to donate to her in an attempt to defuse any criticism of his provocations to Philip of Spain. The Queen's stupendous share was enough to build twenty galleons from scratch. Mendoza warned Philip that "this would set all the mariners in England agog to go out and plunder. For this reason he [Stafford] says it is important that . . . the armaments might be pushed forward and the Queen of England attacked, which would end it all."[15]

Drake must have expected a rapturous welcome at Court, but in his absence the unpredictable Elizabeth had lurched back towards the faction—some of whom were in receipt of covert payments from Spain—arguing for an accommodation with Philip. Despite her share of the proceeds of Drake's voyage and the casket of jewels "garnished with gold" that he had "taken charge to deliver to her Majesty with his own hands," Elizabeth spurned him. Dismissed from Court, he returned to Plymouth to await a further royal change of mind, while Elizabeth made proposals for an end to hostilities and conducted negotiations with the Duke of Parma through a ransomed prisoner of Sir Walter Ralegh. She also found more money to reassure her Dutch allies, sent additional funds to Henri of Navarre in France and raised a further £100,000 to recruit German mercenaries to strengthen his embattled forces.

As with the money lavished on Elizabeth's summer progresses through the southern counties, Drake and her other admirals and sea-captains could only look in horror at this vast expenditure on questionable military adventures on the continent when even a fraction of those huge sums would have yielded far greater dividends had it been used to arm, supply and provision her fleet, immeasurably strengthening her first, indeed her only realistic line of defence against Spain. But "in her handling of the navy she showed the same hesitation, indecision and fitfulness that she displayed in the wider field of general politics . . . to her the fleet was . . . a personal property to be preserved as a family possession or a trading capital which was not to be hazarded, but all the same was to produce great profits."

Sir Walter Ralegh had long argued that England's best defence was its ships. "An army transported over the sea and the landing place left to the choice of the invader, cannot be resisted on the coast of England without a fleet to impeach it; except that every creek, port or sandy bay had a powerful army in them . . . I take it to be the wisest way, to employ good ships upon the sea, and not trust to any entrenchment upon the shore." Even Burghley, no supporter of expenditure on the navy, called the fleet "the wall of England," but "from first to last, she [Elizabeth] never understood that the sea was her sole salvation," nor "what the fleets could or could not do . . . [She] never recognised that she was especially fortunate in being able to fight Spain where it was weakest, and chose, in preference, to make her greatest efforts where it was strongest—on land. On her navy and her naval expeditions between 1585 and 1603 she may have expended £1 million; her wars by land cost £4.5 million and the proportions fairly represent the confidence she placed in the two arms respectively, for she spent most where she hoped most."[16]

The English fear of a Spanish alliance with France against England was as great if not greater than Philip's fear of his two historic enemies uniting against him. With de Guise and the Catholic League in the ascendant in France, the English nightmare seemed a strong possibility. Coupled with the danger of a Spanish reconquest of The Netherlands, it would have left England facing a uniformly hostile coastline, punctuated by half a dozen deep-water ports from any of which an invasion force might emerge. Whether Elizabeth truly believed that negotiations with Parma could achieve peace or whether, like the Spaniards, she was content to use talks as a diversion from her true purpose, she sent peace commissioners to The Netherlands to begin formal negotiations with Parma's representatives. Her commissioners were led by the most prominent advocate of peace with Spain, the Controller of the Household, Sir James Croft, "a long grey beard, with a white head witless," and a man who was in Philip of Spain's pay. As he awaited a wind to carry his ship to Flanders, Croft wrote to warn Elizabeth that "those that recommend war, recommend it for sundry respects; some for war's sake, as I should do perhaps if I were young and a soldier; others for religion; others for spoil and robbery, whereof Your Majesty feels too much. They are all inclined to their particular interests, caring nothing for the Prince's treasure."

The professional soldier, Sir John Norris, hardly a young man himself, was at once prompted to give Elizabeth "in writing many reasons against entering into peace negotiations," and the Lord Admiral to state that "there was never, since England was England, such a stratagem and mask made to deceive England as this treaty of peace." Sir John Hawkins was even more emphatic. "We might have peace, but not with God." If the Queen would give him a dozen ships, he promised to sail for the coast of Spain and "distress anything that goes through the seas." The cost would be no more than "£2,700 a month for wages and victuals and it will be a very bad and unlucky month that will not bring in treble that charge." Elizabeth ignored the advice, leading Sir Walter Ralegh to complain that if the Queen had "believed her men of war as she did her scribes, we had in her time beaten that great empire [of Philip's] in pieces and made their kings kings of figs and oranges as in old times."[17]

Horatio Palavacino, a Genoese banker resident in England, wrote to Mendoza that Elizabeth was "so sick of the war in The Netherlands that to judge from the hurry she is in to send the peace commissioners to Holland, if the Duke of Parma was willing to come to terms, she would refuse no conditions that were not absolutely degrading." But her position was not entirely supine, for "John Herbert, one of the commissioners," was charged with "the secret mission of saying to the Duke of Parma that he ought to recollect who it was that allowed his grandfather to be murdered and that your Majesty [Philip] was now usurping the throne of Portugal from his [Parma's] son, which was not a thing lightly to be forgotten." If Parma were to break with Philip, "win the favour of the people of the country and garrison the towns with men entirely devoted to him," Elizabeth would surrender the deep-water ports of Brill and Flushing [now Brielle and Vlissingen] to him and "both the Queen and France would help him with all their strength." She even held out the possibility that Parma's son might succeed her on the English throne—"it would be better for his son to possess the throne" than Philip—but Parma knew enough of Elizabeth's fickle nature, and the long and deadly reach of Philip's assassins, not to entertain her proposals for a moment.

Throughout the winter and spring Elizabeth continued to show a stubborn faith in the peace negotiations with Parma that was not shared by a single member of her council. Parma himself reported that "the Intelligence which I receive from all quarters seems to prove that the Queen of England really desires to conclude peace . . . her alarm and the expense she is incurring are grieving her greatly. But after all, it cannot be believed that she is turning except under the stress of necessity." The price of war was undoubtedly huge, for apart from the direct costs of maintaining ships at sea and training and equipping troops on land, the cloth trade, England's prime source of wealth, had already been crippled by the simmering hostilities with Spain, and open warfare might be its death knell. As a result, Elizabeth was apparently prepared to be persuaded that if she handed Brill and Flushing to Philip's forces—she said she would only be restoring them to their rightful owner—and allowed English Catholics some measure of freedom of worship, he would be willing to conclude a lasting peace with her.

Philip needed a resolution to the Dutch conflict and, despite his claim that "I would sacrifice all my lands and lose 100 lives, if I had them, rather than be a sovereign of heretics," it was easy for Elizabeth to persuade herself that he might accept a settlement rather than face the unpredictability of war. But Philip's correspondence shows that he gave not the slightest thought to any compromise. He could have had peace in The Netherlands on several occasions, but every attempt at mediation foundered on the rock of his insistence that toleration of the Protestant religion was inconceivable. "With regard to Holland and

Zealand or any other province or towns, the first step must be for them to receive and maintain alone the exercise of the Catholic religion and to subject themselves to the Roman church, without tolerating the exercise of any other religion . . . There is to be no flaw, no change, no concession by convention or otherwise of liberty of conscience or religious peace, or anything of that sort. They are all to embrace the Catholic religion, and the exercise of that alone is to be permitted." The Dutch rebels would either have to accept the mother church, or choose exile or death; there were no other alternatives. The Enterprise of England must be seen in the same dogmatic light. It was partly about money—an attempt to end raids by English privateers on Spain's fleets and possessions—partly about political and dynastic imperatives, and partly about the loss of face that Philip had suffered through attacks on his own coast, but it was also genuinely driven by religious fundamentalism and Philip's obsession with leading the restoration of Europe to the Catholic faith. A flexible and pragmatic ruler in his youth, he was now a stubborn and dogmatic old man, brooding alone in the Escorial. The only solution that would satisfy him would be the overthrow of Elizabeth and the total destruction of the Dutch rebellion.[18]

Had the decision been Parma's to make, Elizabeth's trust might have been justified, at least until he had completed the subjugation of The Netherlands, for as late as 20 March 1588 he was urging Philip to "conclude peace . . . by this means we should end the misery and calamity of these afflicted States, the Catholic religion would be established in them and your ancient dominion restored, besides which we should not jeopardise the Armada . . . and we should escape the danger of some disaster, causing you to fail to conquer England whilst losing your hold here." It was wise, even prescient advice, but Philip had no intention of being turned aside from his chosen path, even when Parma pointed out that the Enterprise of England could still proceed, with much greater ease, once The Netherlands had been returned to his control. Philip's reply closed the door on any possibility of peace. "To you only I declare that my intention is that these negotiations shall never lead to any result, whatever conditions the English may offer. On the contrary, the only object is to deceive them and to cool them in their preparations for defence, by making them believe such preparations will not be necessary." Philip had many other advisers, and they warned him that English Catholics feared that "if peace be made, they will be totally ruined." The faction led by Leicester and Walsingham at Court had "only one objective, namely to disperse the forces gathered in Flanders," and Philip was warned that Walsingham's agents were actively seeking the leading English exiles abroad. "Let the Cardinal [the English exile William Allen] and Sir William Stanley take care that they are not poisoned, as I can assure you that the matter is being arranged."

Elizabeth's commanders remained equally sceptical of Spanish intentions. Drake warned that "the promise of peace from the Prince of Parma and these mighty preparations in Spain agree not well together," and Lord Howard found a diplomatic form of words in which to express his own profound unease. "If the Commissioners bring peace it is the happiest thing that can be; but if they come without it, look for great matters to ensue . . . for the charge is so great that the King is at, both in Spain and here in the Low Countries, that it cannot continue long, if he had five times the treasure he has."[19]

Elizabeth did not respond to the warnings. Only in late June 1588, when one of Walsingham's agents intercepted letters from Count de Olivares to Philip, "by which the Queen had learnt that his Holiness had granted the investiture of England to whomsoever might be the consort of the Infanta Isabella," did Elizabeth realize the futility of the peace negotiations. It "quite banished any hope she had of peace and greatly angered her." Ten days later, the Lord Treasurer and the Lord Chancellor were sent to Westminster to claim to the assembled lords that the Queen had been well aware of the charade being played by Parma, but had "dissembled as she then lacked many things with which she was now well supplied. Conditions had [now] been submitted to her so injurious to her dignity" that she hoped "with the help of God and the co-operation of her subjects to overthrow her enemies." Her argument that she was fully aware of the true situation and was herself using the peace negotiations to buy time for further defensive preparations would have carried more weight if there had been greater evidence of an increased urgency in such preparations or any sign that, for example, she had tried to replenish her supplies of gunpowder, which had been allowed to fall to critical levels. However, the evidence suggests that her belief in the peace process was genuine, even though her optimism was not shared by the vast majority of her courtiers and officials.

None of these developments interfered with her continued efforts to "spare her purse" from the cost of defending her realm, by attempting to make individual towns and seaports liable for fitting out and supplying the ships requisitioned to fight the Armada. The cost of supplying and training the militia was also placed upon the counties rather than the Exchequer, and since the army to defend the Queen was drawn mainly from the retinues of courtiers and nobles—at their expense—another huge saving to the Treasury was achieved. Even

Elizabeth's chief ally in this frugality, her Lord Treasurer Burghley, recognized that the huge burden of "ship money" on the towns and the "unsupportable charges towards musters, powder and new weapons" in the counties, particularly when "demanded of the poor in towns," would lead to "a general murmur of peevish, malcontented people [and] increase the ill-feeling, to the comfort of the enemy."

War was popular with the people, taxes much less so, but monarchs could ask for a "voluntary contribution" in time of war, and failure to pay could have severe consequences. One London alderman refused to contribute to Henry VIII's war with the Scots in 1542. He was immediately conscripted into the army and the orders from the Privy Council required his commanders to place him in the most exposed and perilous situations during battles. Elizabeth's Counsellors were ordered to demand such "voluntary contributions," but her attempts to persuade or compel her citizens to assume even more of the financial burden of fighting the Armada than their taxes had already met were often unsuccessful. The Council's suggestion that those merchants who had gained by reprisal raids against Spanish shipping should contribute most to the cost of supplying ships to Her Majesty's fleet was met by affirmations from the merchants "that they have thereby rather sustained loss than gain," and refusals to contribute. A request, unsanctioned by Parliament, that all the major seaports and coastal towns should supply at their own expense one or more "warlike ship and pinnace, fit and able for service, furnished for two months with victuals, mariners, munitions and other necessary provisions," was often met with evasion or flat refusal. It was unsurprising that this should be so; local taxation had increased fourfold in some towns as a result of the Queen's relentless demands upon them.[20]

"Some principal justices and men of the best living" in Cambridgeshire were reported to Walsingham for using every possible means to evade their obligations, and the Privy Council issued an order for the "best and wealthiest men" of Aldeburgh, Orford, Dunwich and Southwold to pay their share of the cost of fitting out a ship "according to their estates and wealth, no longer leaving the burden to several mean men of small wealth," nor indeed to the Crown. The Mayor of Exeter was more obliging than most of his peers, embargoing two ships "bound for Newfoundland which . . . are now stayed for this purpose," but the Mayor of Poole bemoaned "the great decay and disability of this poor town by reason of embargoes, loss at sea and by pirates," the Captain of the Isle of Wight cited the "great poverty of the merchants of Newport," and the Mayor of Southampton bemoaned "the disability and poverty of the town." All claimed that they could not meet their sovereign's demands. The Mayor of Hull promised to be more oblig-ing, but only once the town's ships had returned to port. "All the best ships . . . belonging to this port be abroad beyond the seas or at Lon-don and the town destitute of mariners." The Mayor of Lyme Regis also pleaded poverty. He furnished a pinnace for the fleet, the *Revenge of Lyme*, but failed to produce a larger ship, and the Mayor of King's Lynn reported that his town was "unwilling to be at any charge near the furnishing of a ship," and that Wells, though "well furnished with shipping, within which there be many rich men inhabiting, but they have denied altogether to contribute to our charge."

Philip commanded far greater wealth and income than Elizabeth. English trade had been hard hit by hostilities with Spain, and the dis-ruption to the banking system based on Antwerp, coupled with the widespread belief that England was doomed to defeat against the Armada, made it hard for her to borrow money except at the most penal rates of interest. Yet she continued to ignore the most effective means of raising additional money. War was never formally declared with Spain. Had she done so and summoned Parliament, an extraordi-nary grant in aid could have been raised to subsidize the cost of the fleet, but Elizabeth had no intention of allowing her Parliament any voice in the conduct of foreign affairs, any more than she would in the other areas that she considered the sole prerogative of the Crown. Matters of "diplomacy and sensitive issues such as dynastic marriage negotiations and the succession were *arcana imperii*—mysteries of state—reserved for Elizabeth's own decision—or more often indeci-sion," and whatever decisions she eventually reached, however capri-cious or illogical they may have been, were never accompanied by any word of explanation; any public justification of the Royal will was taken as a sign of weakness. She also reacted with ferocity to any attempts at interference. In 1579, the author and the publisher of a pamphlet criti-cizing her proposed marriage to the Duke of Anjou both had their right hands cut off.

Parliament was not summoned until 22 November, long after the Armada campaign was over, but the Queen's close-fistedness also ensured that the gap in funding of the navy left by the absence of sub-sidy from Parliament was not met from her own or any other resources. Had Philip been able to launch the Armada early in the New Year, as he had planned, England's coast would have been barely defended. In her insatiable drive to save money whenever and wherever she could, "never had a Queen of England brought herself and her country so near to ruin."[21]

CHAPTER FIVE

The 4 Galleasses of Naples
Comanded by D: Vgo de
Mencado cariying 800
Souldiers, 468 Mariners
1200 Slaves, 200 Canons.

The Floating Forest

While Elizabeth's actions—or lack of them—suggested that she at least adhered resolutely to Philip's famous dictum of moving with leaden feet, he had now become frantic with impatience. As soon as Santa Cruz returned from the Azores, the King, now restored to full health, was urging him to action. "Success depends mostly upon speed. Be quick." Ignoring the unanimous advice of his council of war, he ordered Santa Cruz to put to sea with the Armada and whatever forces he had assembled as soon as the victuallers from Andalusia had arrived, and make directly for "the Cape of Margate." He was to do this even in the worst of the winter weather, with the attendant risks that either the Armada would be unable to reach its destination or the invasion force would be cut off and left without resupply. In the winter of 1559, French forces in Scotland had been stranded and forced to surrender after reinforcements came within sight of the coast but were then driven back by storms to France. An attacking English fleet under William Wynter also took twenty-seven days to make the short voyage to Edinburgh from the Medway and lost three of its fourteen ships in the process. Citing such precedents, Parma questioned Philip's determination to launch the Armada at that time of year, but the King replied that he was well aware of the dangers of sending out a fleet in winter but "since it is all for His cause, God will send good weather." In an acid reply, Parma warned Philip, "God will tire of working miracles for us."

Only when Santa Cruz outlined the damage his ships had suffered on the voyage to the Azores was Philip persuaded to grant a delay, but so desperate was he for the attack on England to begin that he even suggested to Parma that, if opportunity presented itself, he should seize the chance to launch a surprise attack across the Channel without waiting for the Armada to arrive. Having sent the order, he was stricken with fear of the consequences if Parma's forces were trapped on the wrong side of the Channel, leaving The Netherlands undefended, and he then became even more frenzied in his demands that the Armada should sail without further delay. The old admiral won extensions week by grudging week until by late December Philip had so lost patience that he insisted that the fleet, even if it numbered no more than thirty-five ships, should at once put to sea under Santa Cruz's command or that of another officer.

Having earlier boasted of his readiness to comply with Philip's request for an unaided surprise attack on England, Parma was also now back-pedalling, even going so far as to berate the King for urging "what Your Majesty emphatically ordered me not to do until the arrival of . . . the Armada." Shaken by the ferocity of his complaints, Philip's resolve was then further weakened by disturbing intelligence collected by Mendoza on English naval strength. As a result he changed his mind again; Parma was now to await the rendezvous with the Armada and make no attempt to invade England before it arrived. But Philip's impatience with Santa Cruz had not been allayed. Fuming at the delays and the spiralling costs of maintaining his huge fleet, he now set a new deadline of 15 February for the Armada's departure and sent a brusque young soldier, the Count of Fuentes, to Lisbon to reinforce his orders. Fuentes' instructions were to sack Santa Cruz if he showed the least unwillingness to comply and he treated the ailing war hero with undisguised contempt. The Venetian ambassador, Hieronimo Lippomano, expressed his astonishment that Philip should so wilfully ignore the advice and opinions of his most experienced commander, and blamed Philip's mule-headed nature and his naive faith that acts performed in the name of God would be rewarded with success. Now sixty years old and in failing health, Philip was desperate to resolve the problems with England and The Netherlands that were blighting his reign and clouding the future of his nine-year-old heir. His desperation to see the Armada at sea reflects his belief that it offered him the chance to settle both problems at one stroke.[1]

News received from Paris in early February can only have increased Philip's impatience. Elizabeth and Henri III were conducting secret negotiations, with Henri urging her to use her influence with Henri of Navarre to persuade him to adopt Catholicism and submit to the King's authority, cutting the ground from under the Catholic League. Elizabeth countered by offering her financial support if the King would publicly disown the League and arrest de Guise and his leading supporters as traitors, but both courses of action were equally implausible. Navarre would have lost his leadership of the Huguenots, his only power base, and probably also his life if he abjured his religion and, much as he hated de Guise, the King was far too wary of the power of the League and the fury of the Paris mob to consider such extreme action against him yet. The "secret" negotiations came to nothing and, since they were conducted through Sir Edward Stafford, full details of them were immediately passed to Mendoza and Philip.

Faced with Philip's implacable, almost frenzied demands, Santa Cruz, victor of Lepanto and Terceira, and once famous for his ruthless speed and decisiveness, had become more and more mired in the task of preparing the Armada. He was an old and sick man, and his dispatches reflect his weariness and despair at ever readying his battle fleet for its task. He had made what efforts he could to obey the King's commands, but the Armada he had managed to assemble looked woefully unequal to the task it had been set. When the Enterprise of England had first been proposed, Santa Cruz had requested 50 galleons, another 100 great ships, six galleasses, 40 galleys, 40 hulks and 150 other craft. By February 1588 he had only 13 galleons, one so decrepit that he doubted it could even put to sea, four galleasses and 60 or 70 other ships. Many of them were embargoed foreign merchantmen, armed and provisioned in chaos, confusion and frantic haste, and even the finest galleons were under-armed and under-manned. Men had fallen ill or deserted in droves—they had not been paid for three months—

and replacement crewmen and soldiers had to be pressed from fields and villages for miles around Lisbon, while the prisons and hospitals were emptied to provide further unwilling recruits.

On 9 February, less than a week before the final deadline Philip had given him, Don Alvaro de Bazan, Marquis de Santa Cruz and Captain-General for the Ocean Seas, "thunderbolt in war, father of his troops, the unconquered," gave up the struggle and died aged sixty-two, his end undoubtedly hastened by the relentless demands of his monarch. If much feared, he was little loved—it was reported that only four men accompanied his coffin to its final resting place—but as a commander on the high seas, he had no equal anywhere in the Spanish dominions. "The loss to Spain was incalculable, for he was the only man who by birth was entitled, and by experience was competent, to command such an expedition." Within days, Santa Cruz's vice-admiral, the Duke of Paliano, had also died, but the loss of his most experienced naval commanders did not deter Philip, who even contrived to see it as further evidence of divine encouragement for the Enterprise of England. "God has shown me a favour by removing the Marquis now, rather than when the Armada is at sea."

The same day that the King heard the news, he sent instructions, prepared three days earlier, appointing as Santa Cruz's replacement Philip's thirty-seven-year-old cousin, Don Alonso Perez de Guzman, Seventh Duke of Medina-Sidonia, Count of Niebla, Marquis of Cazaza in Africa, Lord of the City of St. Lucar de Barrameda, Captain General of Andalusia and Knight of the Honourable Order of the Golden Fleece. "I am sure you will know how to serve me well in it, as you have done in all things." At first sight it was a quixotic choice ahead of experienced commanders like Don Juan Martinez de Recalde, Don Hugo de Moncada and Don Alonso Martinez de Leiva, who all put themselves forward as soon as they heard the news of Santa Cruz's death. Medina-Sidonia's duchy was the oldest in Spain and he was one of the greatest landowners in Europe. His vast estates stretching from the Algarve to the Mediterranean coast yielded rich crops of grain, citrus fruits, olives, figs and the grapes for the wines of Jerez that were blended and shipped from the port of San Lucar. There Medina-Sidonia's white-walled palace stood near the heart of the town, looking out over the estuary of the Guadalquivir and the Gulf of Cadiz. His wealth had been further increased by the monopoly of tunny-fishing granted to him by the Crown, and by the trade that had flowed through San Lucar, much of it with English ships and merchants, before it was stifled by the growing hostilities between the countries.[2]

Medina-Sidonia had inherited the family estates as a boy and at the age of twenty-one he was married in a dynastic alliance to the ten-year-old daughter of the Princess of Eboli, rumoured to be the illegitimate daughter of Philip II. Her tender age necessitated a special dispensation from the Pope before the marriage could take place. At what point it was consummated is perhaps mercifully undocumented, but she bore him a total of sixteen children over the ensuing years. Medina-Sidonia appears to have cared little for the traditional pastimes of rich noblemen; he was not a courtier, a warrior or a huntsman, but he was bound by an unshakeable sense of duty to his family, his estates, his religion and his King.

The King had previously given him command of the forces defending the Andalusian coastline against pirates and corsairs, and the supervision of the transatlantic supply convoys to the New World. Medina-Sidonia had performed these largely administrative tasks with efficiency and Philip had already entrusted him with assembling the second fleet that would sail from Cadiz with supplies and reinforcements after the Armada had invaded England. Medina-Sidonia had also given Philip sagacious advice on a number of occasions, proposing the establishment of a permanent fleet to guard against English raids—"when that is known in England it will put a brake on them so that . . . its fleet dare not go far away"—and suggesting the use of a fleet of a dozen specially built *gallizabras* (fast, oared pinnaces) instead of the ponderous carracks and galleons used to transport the New World treasure to Spain. The *gallizabras* were only sixty tons in burthen and, if cornered, would have succumbed in minutes to the heavy armaments of English privateers, but they were fast enough to outrun even the swiftest English galleon. They brought the bullion through in safety and it flowed into Philip's treasury in unprecedented and ever-increasing amounts throughout the later years of Elizabeth's reign.

Medina-Sidonia was also widely credited with having saved Cadiz from being sacked by Drake the previous year. The King had praised his conduct and the Venetian ambassador remarked that he was the only man not to dissolve into panic. But that aside, his military qualifications were far from outstanding and he had no experience whatsoever of naval warfare; indeed, he could not even put to sea without falling sick. Nor was he likely to be a forceful commander. His forebears were ferocious fighters who won the family estates on the field of battle—the family honorific El Bueno was accorded because of a Guzman's value as an ally in conflict, not as a mark of his kindly disposition—but if the hollow, watery eyes and diffident, gloomy expression that look out from the only surviving portraits of the Seventh Duke may mislead a little, for they were painted in the later years of his life, the impression they convey cannot be wholly inaccurate.

However, in Philip's eyes at least, these defects were outweighed by several crucial advantages: Medina-Sidonia's unimpeachable lineage gave him precedence over all the other nobles of the Armada fleet, ensuring that none could feel slighted by his promotion; "so many dukes, marquesses and earls, voluntarily going, would have repined [refused] to have been commanded by a man of less Quality than themselves." Unlike Santa Cruz, he was also a devout, phlegmatic and mild personality, unlikely to lock horns with a headstrong commander such as Parma. His administrative abilities would bring some order to the chaos of the Armada preparations, and he was also hugely wealthy; despite his protestations of poverty, he was to contribute a vast sum towards the costs of the Armada, around a million pounds at twenty-first-century prices.[3]

Medina-Sidonia at once attempted to dissuade the King from his choice. "I have not the health for the sea, for I know by the small experience that I have had afloat that I soon become seasick . . . My family owes 900,000 ducats, and I am therefore quite unable to accept the command. I have not a single real to spend in the King's service . . . The undertaking is so important that it would not be right for a person like myself, possessing no experience of seafaring or of war[,] to take charge of it. I cannot attempt a task of which I have no doubt I should give a bad account . . . and should have to be guided by others, of whose good or bad qualities I know nothing." Medina-Sidonia instead recommended Don Martin de Padilla, a group commander at Lepanto and Captain General of the galleys of Spain, who had "great knowledge of the sea and has seen naval warfare and naval matters." He was also "a very good Christian."

Medina-Sidonia's protestations seem to have been genuine and not the ritual self-deprecation of a noble and self-effacing man, but the King rejected his plea out of hand, attributing it to "an excess of modesty . . . It is I who must judge of your capabilities and parts and I am fully satisfied . . . Prepare and steel yourself to the performance of this service in the manner I expect from you." If anything, Medina-Sidonia's self-effacement increased his value in the King's eyes. Philip did not want another brilliant but temperamental military commander—another Parma or Santa Cruz—but a man who would follow his orders without question. As the instrument of God's design, Philip had no need of earthly counsel; he alone would lay down the course that his commander was to follow without deviation.

A year before Santa Cruz's death, Medina-Sidonia had told Secretary Idiaquez that the Armada's only prospect of success was if it was "very much superior" to the forces the English could range against it. He now wrote a further letter, arguing that the whole Enterprise of England was fatally flawed and whatever improvements he could make before sailing, the Armada would not be superior to the English fleet. His letter never reached Philip. His advisers, Idiaquez and Don Juan de Zuniga, took it upon themselves to withhold it from the King and berated Medina-Sidonia for writing in such negative terms about an enterprise so obviously blessed by God. They also added the threat that he would be exposed as a coward and lose his hard-won "reputation and opinion which today the world has of your valour and prudence, which would all be hazarded if it were known what you wrote." Refused an audience with the King where he might have argued his case directly, Medina-Sidonia gave in to their blackmail and took up his post without further demur.[4]

Had Philip himself gone to Lisbon to take personal charge of the most complex, important and expensive project of his entire reign, he might have been able to resolve some of the problems that had faced the dying Santa Cruz and his unwilling successor. As it was, despite his insistence on overseeing even the tiniest details of the Enterprise of England, Philip remained in the Escorial, a fortnight's hard ride for any courier travelling from Lisbon and then returning there after consulting the King. Such delays inevitably bred further problems.

Medina-Sidonia arrived in Lisbon to find the Armada in something approaching chaos. Supplies were still being loaded, but mainly on the basis of the whims, seniority or nobility of the commanders rather than the needs of their ships, and Medina-Sidonia at once set himself the task of bringing order to this confusion. In a move that no doubt pleased his bureaucratic monarch, one of Medina-Sidonia's first actions was to commandeer a printing press and produce printed forms to bear his orders with blank spaces for specific details to be added. The soldiers and seamen who had been ordered to remain on board their ships despite lacking proper provisions, armaments and even clothing were at once sent ashore and Medina-Sidonia then took stock of his fleet. Some merchantmen had already been converted to warships and the shipwrights were still at work on others, raising fore- and sterncastles, cutting additional gunports into their hulls and fitting the waistcloths or removable wooden screens pierced by firing slits that were used to hide musketeers and boarding troops in the waist of the ship from the sight of the enemy. Despite this work, there were few enough warships and most of them were either grossly overloaded or virtually empty. Some had almost no armaments, others so many that some of them could not even be deployed. Some had powder but no shot, others a mountain of cannonballs but no powder.

After the shock of his initial inspection, the new Captain General devoted himself to preparing his fleet for sea. By an urgent appeal to the King, Medina-Sidonia succeeded in securing Santa Cruz's plans and papers before his private secretary could remove them. He then put together a group of advisers, led by Don Diego Flores de Valdes and including two vastly experienced seamen, Don Diego de Maldonado and Captain Marolin de Juan, three squadron commanders, Don Pedro de Valdes, Don Miguel de Oquendo and Don Juan Martinez de Recalde, and an Italian expert on naval gunnery. The prime complaint of his commanders was that there were insufficient heavy guns. Even the royal galleons and galleasses were under-gunned, and most of the embargoed and requisitioned ships carried little ordnance beyond the guns that were on board them when they were seized, and those tended to be small, cast- or wrought-iron guns firing projectiles of no more than four pounds in weight. They might damage rigging or cause casualties at close range, but they were almost useless in an artillery duel.

The existing weaponry and ordnance was redistributed, though if there was logic in the way it was done, it was artfully concealed. The greatest nobles still managed to obtain a disproportionate share on account of their rank, not their abilities or tactical requirements, and rather than concentrating the most powerful weapons in the warships that would bear the brunt of the fighting, the rest of the heavy guns seem to have been shared equally throughout the fleet. Allowances of powder and shot were also made on a pro-rata basis rather than being weighted towards the main fighting ships. Additional guns were sought but there were few available anywhere. Under Santa Cruz's entreaties, the arsenal of Madrid had promised 36 new bronze cannon, demi-cannon, culverins and demi-culverins, and the Lisbon arsenal another 30, while a further 60 or 70 guns had been bought or impounded from foreign ships in Spanish harbours, though most of these were of modest size. Others were purchased or smuggled from abroad. The finest cannon came from the foundries of Venice, The Netherlands and England, but the master craftsmen of the Venetian Arsenal could not or would not meet the demand and, notionally at least, the export of English and Dutch cannon to Spain was prohibited by law. However, in such nations of smugglers, pirates and privateers, there were always those willing to seek the rich profits of contraband cargoes, whatever the national interest.

Ralph Hogge, the Queen's "gunstone maker and gunfounder of

iron" and one of the first men in England to cast an iron gun, complained to Walsingham as early as 1574 about "the shipping and selling of ordnance and cast iron to strangers to carry over the seas, they say in such numbers that your enemy is better furnished with them than the ships of our own country are . . . under colour of carrying them along the coast they carry them where they wish." No licence was required to move guns from port to port along the South Coast, and many ships loaded cannons from the Weald of Sussex and Kent that were ostensibly destined for delivery to Portsmouth or Plymouth and then sold them overseas, often to England's bitter enemies.

In January 1588 "two Spaniards in Flanders were asking for delivery of 20,000 crowns worth of iron ordnance" and during the two years before the Armada sailed, one Sussex iron founder sold over 100 cannons to Spain. Bristol merchants also supplied nine shiploads of culverins from foundries in the Forest of Dean, together with powder, muskets and shot, shipping them via Naples, even though all these items were in great demand in England. Either the guns smuggled to Spain commanded a high premium, or they knew that the Spaniards would pay for the guns in cash, whereas Elizabeth of England was notorious for her "forgetfulness" in matters of money. Guns of small calibre could also be legally exported and iron founders and smugglers showed great ingenuity in casting guns of small enough calibre to meet the regulations, but with such hugely thick barrels that foreign purchasers could then safely drill out the bore to a much greater calibre.[5]

These smuggled weapons, and the ordnance transferred from captured prizes, even including a huge and unwieldy Turkish siege cannon taken at the battle of Lepanto, were but a fraction of the Armada's requirements. Medina-Sidonia made desperate efforts to obtain still more large cannons and culverins, but the few he found were well below the number his commanders had hoped for. When the fleets came to face each other in the Channel, the Armada still had only 21 culverins and 151 demi-culverins, against the 153 culverins and 344 demi-culverins of the English fleet. Despite the efforts to obtain more heavy guns, only Miguel de Oquendo and Pedro de Valdes seemed to be fully aware of how comprehensively outgunned the Armada would be, and even then Oquendo chose to augment his ship's weaponry with short-barrelled, heavy-shotted weapons that could only be used at close range.

Attempts to obtain more cannons were also hampered by shortages of iron and copper, and a "great shortage of craftsmen" such as foundrymen, blacksmiths and metal polishers. As a result, production was even slower and more expensive; there were complaints that guns produced in Lisbon cost two-thirds more and took twice as long to make as those manufactured in Malaga, and had numerous faults. Guns hastily turned out by the Spanish and Portuguese foundries were often so poorly manufactured, with the bore cast off-centre or the metal flawed, that they were more dangerous to their crews than to their targets; a number exploded when fired. "Some of their pieces (and not a few) are bored awry . . . some are crooked . . . other of unequal bores . . . or full of honeycombs and flaws . . . [They] will either break, split, or blowingly spring their metals and (besides that mischief they do) will be utterly unserviceable ever after." Spanish iron was often of poor quality, riddled with impurities, excess carbon and iron oxides, and so lacking in strength that the flukes of anchors often sheered off under the stress of weather. To speed production, foundries were also cooling newly cast cannonballs in water, making them brittle and prone to disintegration when fired. Yet despite all the efforts to buy or manufacture new ordnance, well under 5 per cent of the guns carried by Armada ships were newly manufactured.

Even when guns and shot functioned properly, there were no side scales to aid accuracy of fire and the variations in the bore of weapons and the weight and diameter of the cannonballs they used caused chaos—the *Señora del Rosario* alone was carrying seventeen different calibres of shot—and rendered even the most experienced gunner incapable of predicting whether his next round would hit the target, overshoot or fall short. The pound weight in Milan or Naples was lighter than the one used in Spain and, with no standard calibre or measure, the individual variations in ordnance and munitions from different regions and countries caused massive problems to the quartermasters of the Armada. Many cannonballs were the wrong size for the guns they had been issued to feed and gunners were forced to carry a set of wooden calibrating rings to ensure that the shot they had been allocated would fit the muzzle of their weapons. Even so, shot was often an inch or an inch and a half less in diameter than the bore of the cannon. It ricocheted its way down the barrel and left the mouth of the gun at differing angles, making accurate gunnery as much luck as science. There was also little incentive for a gunner to practise his skills. "The cannon was held by the Spaniards to be an ignoble arm; well enough for the beginning of the fray, and to pass away the time till the moment of engaging hand to hand, that is of boarding. Actuated by such notions, the gunners were recommended to aim high, so as to dismantle [dismast] the enemy and prevent his escape; but as a vertical stick is a difficult thing to hit, the result was that shot were expended harmlessly in the sea or, at best, made some holes in the sails, or cut a few ropes of no great consequence."[6]

Medina-Sidonia had more success in locating supplies of gunpowder, and the amount carried by the fleet had almost doubled since Santa Cruz's death. Virtually all of it was fine-corned musket powder, 20 per cent more powerful than the "cannon corn" or "serpentine" powder formerly used for cannon; however, given the brittle nature of Spanish iron and the poor casting of many guns, this was not necessarily an advantage. The new cannons had been tested only with serpentine powder and the additional explosive force of the higher grade of powder was enough to cause some poorly cast guns to shatter when fired, with disastrous consequences for the gun-crews. Medina-Sidonia had also managed to obtain more shot; there were fifty cannonballs for each gun, compared to the thirty per gun that the King's Captain-General of Artillery had specified, but it was still not enough. The Armada's most experienced military commander, Don Francisco de Bobadilla, the *Maestre Campo General* (senior army general), later claimed to have made the prophetic complaint that "there was great scarcity of cannon balls . . . if the enemy did not allow us to board them and if the artillery fight lasted four days what might [we] do on the fifth day if we carried so few rounds?" Greater supplies of pikes, half-pikes, armoured morions, corselets, muskets, arquebuses and calivers had also been obtained. The muskets, so long and cumbersome that the weight of the four-foot barrel had to be supported on a long U-shaped rest propped against the deck, fired a ball of about 40 grams. The lighter arquebuses and calivers, braced against the firer's chest or shoulder, delivered a ball of one-third that weight.

The attempt to requisition all these mountains of equipment for the Armada had created desperate shortages of almost every warlike supply. One Spaniard complained that "there is no musket left in the whole of Spain," and Spanish agents scoured Europe for gunpowder, cannonballs, helmets, breastplates, guns, pitch, ropes, sails, cables and every kind of foodstuff, but the greatest weakness of the fleet remained provisions. In January Elizabeth had "advices from Lisbon that the victuals there had gone bad," and the information proved to be correct. The supplies of salt-fish, salt-meat and ship's biscuit packed the previous October and held in readiness over the winter often proved to be inedible, either through sharp practice by the victuallers, faults in the store-barrels or overlong storage before use. Although the Armada remained miraculously free of an epidemic of ship's fever, the long periods on board during the winter months, subsisting on a poor diet, had steadily depleted the crews; many more took any chance to desert. Peasants could be impressed from the surrounding area to replace the losses—"they commanded 2000 Portingals [Portuguese] to go aboard upon pain of death"—but the shortage of trained seamen and gunners was growing more and more acute. Three more gunners were lost— two killed and one mutilated—when another of the poorly cast cannons exploded while being test-fired.[7]

Over the course of three months, Medina-Sidonia had brought some order to the chaos of preparations. By the end of April the worst of the Armada ships had been repaired and most had been careened and tallowed. The fleet had also grown greatly in size, with 134 ships instead of the 104 that Santa Cruz had mustered, in eight broad classes, including twenty galleons, four galleys and four giant galleasses of Naples. Philip had also been persuaded to detach the eight first-line galleons of the "Indian Guard" from their normal duties of escorting the *flota* and patrolling the sea lanes between Spain and the Spanish Main, and they appeared at the end of March from Cadiz. The galleons of Portugal were older and less well built but still formidable, and the renamed *San Francisco* embargoed from the Duke of Tuscany was the strongest and most powerful ship in the Armada. The front-line fighting ships were divided into three squadrons: the galleons of Portugal and the galleons of Castile, with ten great ships in each squadron, and the four galleasses of Naples. The second line comprised four squadrons, again of ten ships each: the Biscayans, the Guipuzcoans (from the province surrounding San Sebastian), the Andalusians and the Levant squadron of ships from Ragusa, Genoa, Sicily, Venice and Barcelona. Many of them were large and heavily armed merchantmen converted into floating fortresses; the Levant ships were mainly grain carriers. Their sheer size and the numbers of heavy weapons and fighting troops they carried led Spanish optimists to believe they would provide a decisive advantage in close-quarter combat.

There were also four oar-driven galleys, linear descendants of the triremes of ancient Greece and Rome, and devastating fighters in shallow or sheltered waters but vulnerable in the great swells and storms of the open sea. Even though they had been reinforced for Atlantic use, they drew no more than four feet of water and were prone to swamping in heavy seas. If they could be brought safely to the Channel they would provide invaluable close support for the invasion force as it landed—Santa Cruz and Medina-Sidonia had both requested that substantially more galleys be added to the Armada to perform this role— but in storms their poor sailing qualities made them more of a liability than an asset. A squadron of thirty-four fast pinnaces—the Spanish called them *zabras, fregatas* and *pataches*—were available for scouting, carrying dispatches and inshore and shallow-water work. Bringing up the rear were twenty-three hulks, slow and ponderous freight-carriers, transporting provisions, munitions and horses. The *Trinidad de Valencera* and the other hulks carried the enormous siege cannon and the mountain of supplies needed for the siege train of the invasion force: gunpowder and great iron shot, gun carriages with huge iron-shod wheels as tall as a man, heavy timbers to construct gun platforms, palisades and fortifications, pointed stakes and pine trees with sharpened branches, used as later generations would use barbed-wire entanglements, and all the multiplicity of weapons and tools that the soldiers, gun-crews and engineers would need.

While the English fleet had recently been reconstructed on leaner, faster lines, the naval traditionalists had the ear of Medina-Sidonia and even the few Spanish ships that had been built on clean lines now had new fore- and sterncastles added. The ponderous merchantmen and hulks had also been fitted with fighting castles. They were invaluable in close-quarter combat and boarding actions, but severely compromised the ships' speed and handling, especially to windward. The drag of the wind on the forecastle made it near impossible to keep a ship's head to wind, and at anything approaching broadside on to the wind the surface area of the upperworks was so large that it negated most and sometimes all of the forward momentum the sails could generate. Some ships made modest progress to windward, some could only keep station and some were actually driven back on each tack; most hulks simply dropped anchor in a headwind and waited for a change in wind direction. Only when sailing downwind did the Spanish ships function with full efficiency, and even then they were far slower than the sleeker English galleons. The fastest progress the Armada made at any stage of its voyage was barely four knots, and much of the time it managed no more than half that—a slow walking pace, or even less.

This huge array of ships, drawn from all over Europe, also carried crewmen and soldiers speaking a dozen different tongues. There were Castilians, Basques, Sicilians, Italians, Portuguese, Dutchmen and Germans from the Hanseatic League, many pressed to serve against their will and all regarding each other with suspicion. "Among the artillery, it had been absolutely decided by the English that all should be of one nationality, one language and therefore one constant disposition to serve well, and we cannot consider that this was at all so among the enemy." The division between soldiers and sailors—the captain and crew of every ship were under the overall command of the officers of the land forces and were in every respect regarded as the inferiors of the soldiers aboard—was another potential source of discord and division. "They brawl and fight commonly aboard their ships as if they were ashore," and some soldiers in the Guipuzcoan ships turned the seamen out of their quarters, leaving them to find what shelter they could on the open deck.

In his painstaking, methodical way Medina-Sidonia drew up a report on the state of the Armada, listing each ship, its tonnage, guns, seamen and soldiers, the nobles and gentlemen adventurers on each ship and their "competent servants," the priests and friars, the officers and strengths of the fighting soldiers, the siege train and all the great ordnance and small arms, cannonballs and gunpowder, right down to the bullets and match-cord. It was a formidable inventory: 130 ships carrying well over 30,000 men, including 19,295 soldiers—9,000 more than Santa Cruz had been able to assemble—8,450 mariners, 2,088 galley slaves and around 3,000 noblemen, gentlemen volunteers, priests, physicians, paymasters and officials, all with servants and retinues; Medina-Sidonia alone had 60 servants, Prince Ascoli 39 and Don Alonso de Leiva 36. There were 2,830 cannon, 123,790 cannonballs, 22,000 pounds of "great shot" and 2,000 tons of gunpowder. Medina-Sidonia also listed the provisions that the fleet carried—salt-fish, salt-meat, ship's biscuit, rice, beans, wine, vinegar and water—and even the shoes and sandals that the soldiers would wear.[8]

Ten thousand of the Armada troops were trained and seasoned fighting men, unmatched throughout Europe, but the remainder were less impressive, no more than "vine-growers, shepherds and the like." The mass of combat troops aboard the ships of the Armada reflected the preferred battle tactics of grappling, boarding and hand-to-hand combat as much as the eventual aim of landing an invasion force and, even before the Armada embarked a further 16,000 combat soldiers from Flanders, it was the most powerful fleet ever assembled, "a greater force than ever was known to be made . . . by any Christian prince within the memory of man." The Spanish soldiers and seamen were divided into groups of eight *camaradas* who drew their own rations and prepared their own food. Allied to the vast numbers of landsmen unused to the sea, the chaos and confusion caused by this multiplicity of cooks fighting for space in the galley, and the waste and dirt that ensued, are among the reasons for the scathing comments made by English mariners—themselves no strangers to dirt and disease—about the conditions aboard the Armada ships. "Their ships are kept foul and beastly, like hog-ties and sheep-cots in comparison with ours."

However, at the start of their voyage, the soldiers and crewmen were healthier than they had been at the time of Santa Cruz's death and in better heart for the task that faced them. They had been paid and were better equipped with supplies and munitions—the King had ordered Medina-Sidonia not to leave himself "open to reproach as far as [the wages of] the crews are concerned since in that matter it is not merely a question of expense, but often at times, of victory. Do not therefore omit to pay great attention to the quality of the food." For the first time, all the ships' captains had been issued with rudimentary charts showing them the seas and coastlines they expected to be navigating. English navigators had the benefit of a "Waggoner"—an English corruption of the Dutch Lucas Janszoon Wagenaer, whose volume of charts covering northern Europe from the Baltic to Cadiz had been published in Holland in 1584 and 1585 and translated into English early in the Armada year of 1588. Every captain in the English fleet had a copy, but most of the Armada commanders had only the most limited charts. They had maps of the English coast from Land's End to the approaches to the Thames, but their knowledge of the remainder of the coasts of England and Scotland was minimal and the charts of the little-known west coast of Ireland were dangerously misleading, placing parts of it as much as forty miles to the east of its actual position and failing to show the huge promontory of Mayo, Connaught and Galway at all. The Spanish captains remained unconcerned; their destination was the Channel, not those rocky shores.

The fleet was christened the "*Felicissima Armada*"—the most fortunate fleet—but it was soon being described as "*La Invencible*"—the Invincible Armada—and some felt the mere sight of it would be enough to make Elizabeth capitulate. As he prepared to sail for England, the greatest fear of a captain of infantry, Antonio de Taso Aquereis, was that there would be no chance for him to obtain the spoils of war. "Pray to God that he gives me a house of some very rich merchant where I may place my ensign, but I do fear that they will instantly yield and agree to all that the King will demand of them, for that the King's force is marvellous great, as well by sea as by land." So strong was Spanish confidence that Medina-Sidonia's detailed inventory of the fleet, including its order of battle, was circulated throughout Europe. The propaganda purpose was presumably to impress the Vatican and neutral countries and terrify Spain's opponents with the weight and power of the forces ranged against them, but it also provided the English fleet with invaluable strategic and tactical information; a copy was in Walsingham's hands well before the Armada had been sighted off England. Not all were convinced of the Armada's invincibility. As it prepared to sail, the Venetian ambassador in Madrid sent a dispatch to his masters, warning that "the Englishmen are of a different quality from the Spaniards, bearing a name above all the West for being expert and enterprising in maritime affairs, and the finest fighters upon the sea. A battle will in any case be very bloody; for the English never yield; and although they be put to flight and broken, they ever return athirst for revenge, to renew the attack so long as they have breath."[9]

Medina-Sidonia had done what he could to ready the Armada and the King's patience would now stretch no further. In the early hours of 25 April 1588, the Feast of St. Mark the Evangelist, 650 arquebusiers were assembled in front of the Royal Palace in Lisbon, their armour and weapons polished and uniforms immaculate. As dawn broke they snapped to attention, the oak gates were thrown open and the Duke of Medina-Sidonia rode out alongside his most Catholic Majesty's viceroy, the Cardinal Archduke, representing the King. Even on this day of destiny, Philip could not be lured from his cold stone palace to preside in person. Behind them snaked a long procession of great nobles, officers and gentlemen, each man's position determined by the precedence due to his family titles or his rank, and every great house of Spain was represented. Almost without exception, the Portuguese nobility was absent, uninvited. A face-saving formula had been found—there was not room enough in the cathedral for all who wished to be accommodated—but the truth was that this was not a day that any but the most collaborationist of Portuguese would have wished to legitimize with his presence, an imperial march-past in Spain's most recently conquered territory. Their absence was barely noticeable among the ranks of Spanish grandees; even this great and historic city had rarely seen such an array of noblemen.

Silent and near-deserted moments before, the air so still that the last tendrils of night mist clung motionless to the river, the city came alive in colour and sound. The grandees rode three, four, six abreast, the outside horses in each rank brushing past the guards of the Lisbon garrison, filling the air with the jingle of harness, the creak of leather and the warm smell of the stables. Groomed till their coats gleamed and richly caparisoned in the family colours of their riders, they wheeled into the Plaza Major, their clattering hooves striking sparks from the cobbles as they passed. As they emerged from the shadows, the first rays of the sun rising over the low hills of Évora to the east glinted from helmets and breastplates and lit up the crimsons and golds of the robes of the noblemen like fire. Behind them, bringing up the rear, trudged 180 priests and friars in habits of dark homespun, eyes fixed on eternity, God's foot soldiers embarking with the Armada on its Holy Crusade. The Archbishop of Lisbon greeted Medina-Sidonia and the Cardinal Archduke on the steps of the cathedral, and celebrated

Mass and gave his blessing to the Enterprise of England, then Medina-Sidonia knelt before the High Altar and took from it the sacred standard of the Armada, "woven by the ladies of Portugal."

As he emerged once more from the cathedral at the head of the great procession, a guard of arquebusiers fired a volley in the air. Three hundred guns of the Armada ships moored in the Tagus and the guns of the Castillo San Jorge on the hill above the town boomed in echo. Small crowds had now gathered beyond the ranks of soldiers but they watched in silence and there were far fewer than might have been expected for such a momentous event, even at this early hour of the day. For the Portuguese commoners, like their lords, the memories of the last Armada that had sailed up the Tagus to complete Philip's crushing annexation of Portugal were still too fresh and too bitter for them to join the celebrations, though most were more than happy to see the Armada on the brink of departure. For those who stood to gain financially—shipyards and ships' chandlers, foundries and shot-mills, provision merchants, bar-owners, pickpockets and whores—the presence of the Armada and its sprawling, brawling mass of 30,000 men had been a blessing from God; for everyone else it had been a constant waking nightmare. Every kind of foodstuff was in desperately short supply and so expensive that it was beyond the reach of the poor. The streets were filthy, stinking and crime-ridden, and as soldiers and seamen fell sick or deserted, more and more Portuguese were pressed to replace them. Small wonder, then, that this was a day for the Spaniards to celebrate and for the Portuguese to keep behind their shutters.

The sacred standard was paraded across the Plaza Major to the Dominican Convent where Medina-Sidonia laid it on the altar in a personal dedication. It was then borne between lines of kneeling soldiers and sailors, as ranks of friars read the Papal Absolution and Indulgence granted to all those setting sail with the Armada. Medina-Sidonia embarked in his barge to another thunderous salute from the guns of his fleet, and was rowed out to his flagship, the *San Martin*—another scourge for the Portuguese, for the ship had once been the pride of their own royal fleet. It now rode at anchor at the head of an armada that filled the Tagus from bank to bank and for over a mile up-and downstream. A court poet was at hand to record the majesty of the Armada and the sanctity of its cause: "Oh floating forest, pleasing to our eyes, which the sheer faith of the Christian Ulysses draws away from Spanish shores against the falseness of a siren." As Medina-Sidonia came aboard the *San Martin*, the standard was raised to the tip of the mainmast. It unfurled and stiffened in the breeze, revealing the royal arms of Spain flanked by images of the Virgin Mary and Christ crucified, above the Latin motto *Exerge Domine et Vindica Causum Tuam*—Arise O Lord and Vindicate Thy Cause.

The Armada's destination had been known in every bar and back-street of Lisbon since the first ship had come to anchor there well over a year before, but the official silence had been maintained right up to the moment of embarkation. The captains now called their companies together and told them their objective, and the ships' priests conducted prayers and preached sermons cataloguing the crimes and mortal sins of Elizabeth I, ruler of a nation of true Catholics waiting only for the Armada to liberate them from rule by a heretical clique. "God, in whose sacred cause we go, will lead us. With such a Captain we need not fear. The saints of heaven will go in our company . . . the holy patrons of Spain and those of England itself who are persecuted by the heretics and cry aloud to God for vengeance . . . With us too will be the blessed and innocent Mary Queen of Scotland who, still fresh from her sacrifice, bears copious and abounding witness to the cruelty and impiety of this Elizabeth." The "groans of countless imprisoned Catholics, the tears of widows . . . the sobs of maidens . . . and the tender children who, suckled upon the poison of heresy are doomed to perdition" were also invoked in the Armada's cause. Every soldier and seaman in the fleet had been "confessed and absolved, with due contrition of their sins," and their bureaucratic King had even insisted that each man be issued with a form to certify that he had indeed been shriven. To emphasize the sacred nature of the Armada's mission, there were even Christian watchwords for each day of the week, beginning with Jesus on Sundays and progressing through the Holy Ghost, Most Holy Trinity, St. James, the Angels, All Saints and Our Lady. Every day, on every ship of the Armada, the ship's boys were to gather around the mainmast at dawn and dusk to sing Matins and the Ave Maria. The Salve with the Litany was to be recited "some days and at least every Saturday," while priests of the monastic orders celebrated Mass.[10]

The King had instructed his Captain General that "as all victories are the gift of God Almighty, and the cause we champion is so exclusively His, we may look for His aid and favour, unless by our sins we render ourselves unworthy." As further assurance of the necessary purity in thought and deed, Medina-Sidonia's General Orders to the Fleet forbade any man to carry a dagger, or engage in fighting or feuds. "The order holds good with all disputes, even those of long standing . . . this truce shall on no account be violated under pain of death for treason." There were also strict prohibitions on gambling, swearing, blasphemy and that "nefarious sin" sodomy; infractions were to be met with "very severe punishment to be inflicted at our discretion." All the ships were also searched to make sure no wives or whores had been hidden aboard, save on the *Santiago, la urca de las mujeres*—"the ship of the women"—a hulk that carried the wives of a number of married officers. They were the only women permitted to sail with the fleet, though one "Allemain" (German) somehow managed to smuggle his wife aboard the *San Salvador*, presumably disguised as a man, and "a lady and children" sailed with Oquendo's second-in-command. Soldiers were to remain on deck or in their quarters to await the distribution of rations and not take them by force, and all food had to be consumed and cooking fires doused before nightfall, when the priests once more led the assembled ship's company in prayers. The priests were aboard the Armada not only to ensure the spiritual well-being of the men. Once the invasion had succeeded, they were to begin the process of saving heretic souls and laying claim to the monastic property seized by Henry VIII at the Dissolution of the Monasteries. Medina-Sidonia's own chaplain carried a letter authorizing him to repossess all the confiscated properties of the Dominican order.[11]

If the Armada's voyage was dedicated to God, its officers, soldiers and crewmen also sailed with some hope of monetary as well as spiritual reward, for "proclamation was made with the sound of three drums in every ship . . . at the commandment of the King" that any of the Queen's ships that were captured would be the property of the King, but that all others would be the prize of their captors. Many Spanish nobles and English exiles were so sure of victory that they sailed with treasure chests and household effects aboard their ships, ready to take possession of the English properties that would soon be theirs. Around a thousand gentleman adventurers—300 in service with the King's bastard son, the Prince Antonio Luis de Leiva Ascoli—joined the Armada seeking profit, adventure, excitement or merely escape from their stifling round of court duties and family obligations. The vastly experienced Juan Martinez de Recalde was scathing of commands being conferred upon them merely "because they are gentlemen. Very few of them, therefore, are soldiers or know what to do." Undeterred by their lack of martial skills, they boarded ship with their servants and retinues, and "carrying with them their finest wear and innumerable jewels." Even the common soldiers were "richly appointed"; credit was easy to obtain as bankers, tailors and shopkeepers shared the expectation that the Armada would return weighed down with plunder. All men of any substance also carried a store of gold ducats and many had them sewn into their clothes, a heavy burden at all times and a fatal one if their ship sank and they were cast into the sea, not that such thoughts can have crossed many minds; the over-confidence was so widespread that medals showing Philip crowned with a victor's laurel wreath were struck before the Armada had even departed.

The servants and retainers were at once at work erecting partitions to screen off areas of the deck and give their masters a semblance of privacy, and many soldiers had brought truckle beds aboard and set them up, further constricting the space available to the rest. The partitions and mounds of personal effects were another cause of friction between the men, and were damaging to the efficiency of the ships and a potentially lethal hazard in battle. Cannonballs smashing through the ship's hull and striking the thin wood partitions would shower the decks with hails of dagger-like splinters. Before the Armada left Spanish waters, Medina-Sidonia ordered "all cabins, partitions, bunks, bedsteads and other erections between decks that may hamper the movements of the crew or the working of the artillery" to be torn down and stowed in the holds or thrown overboard.

Among the crews and officers there were around two hundred Englishmen, including "seven or eight" in the *Nuestra Señora del Rosario* alone. Some were exiles hoping to reclaim estates or fortunes, some were priests eager to claim their livings and begin the work of converting the heretics, some were laymen motivated by religious fervour to join the crusade, but others were mercenaries and coastal pilots, indifferently selling their expertise to the highest bidder. The treacherous William Stanley, who had betrayed the city of Deventer in The Netherlands to the Duke of Parma, was reported to be aboard Medina-Sidonia's flagship—"There was aboard an Englishman called Don William, a man of a reasonable stature, bald, and very like Sir William Stanley"—though he was also said to be in Dunkirk, commanding a contingent of the troops in Parma's invasion force. And there were other, less fortunate Englishmen among the slaves at the oars of the galleys and galleasses. Like their peers, they rowed while seated on straw-filled cushions, and were watched over by physicians and fed a special diet of pulses, grains, bread and water, since meat and wine were thought to spoil their condition, though the concern for their welfare related solely to the need to keep them strong and healthy enough to work the oars. They wore fetters and were chained to their benches, and slept, and often urinated and defecated, at their oars. The conditions in which they were kept were so filthy that the stench of galleys and galleasses notoriously carried for miles on the wind. If their ships sank or ran aground the slaves were dependent on the presence of mind of their officers to order their release from their fetters before they drowned.[12]

The consecration of the Armada's standard did not herald the immediate departure of the fleet. For a further fortnight the waters of the Tagus were alive with small craft as provisions, munitions and men continued to be brought aboard. Only on 9 May did Medina-Sidonia give the order to depart. As the vast Armada set sail on the afternoon tide, the Pope's special emissary to Lisbon sent a report to the Vatican of a conversation he had held with one of the highest officers in the Spanish fleet. "If you meet the English Armada in the Channel do you expect to win the battle?"

"Of course."

"How can you be sure?"

"It's very simple. It is well known that we fight in God's cause, so when we meet the English, God will surely arrange matters so that we can grapple and board them, either by sending some strange freak of weather or, more likely, just by depriving the English of their wits. If we can come to close quarters, Spanish valour and Spanish steel (and the great masses of soldiers we shall have on board) will make our victory certain. But unless God helps us by a miracle, the English, who have faster and handier ships than ours and many more long-range guns, and who know their advantage just as well as we do, will never close with us at all but stand aloof and knock us to pieces with their culverins without our being able to do them any serious hurt. So, we are sailing against England in the confident hope of a miracle." Never can such a vast enterprise have been launched on such a flimsy basis.[13]

CHAPTER SIX

So Violent a Sea and Wind

O n 11 May, the Armada "took advantage of a light easterly wind" and at last moved downstream but, although Miguel de Oquendo's squadron passed over the bar at the mouth of the Tagus and anchored off the fort of São João de Estoril in Cascais Bay, the rest of the Armada, including the flagship, got no further than the turreted tower of Belém, a fortress right at the water's edge, near the mouth of the Tagus. There they were forced to drop anchor again, unable to proceed into the teeth of a strengthening wind, backing westerly and blowing directly into the passage to the sea. For almost three weeks, wild weather continued all around the coastlines of western Europe. English ships off Flanders were battered by storms, the Dutch flyboats ran for the shelter of Flushing harbour, certain that Parma's invasion force would not dare to set out in such seas, and the Armada remained pinned off Belém, less than ten miles from its starting point and unable to make sail. Thousands of men aboard had never put to sea and as their ships rolled before the wind, many of them, even in the short, tidal chop of the estuary, must have succumbed to their first bouts of seasickness.

All the time he remained there, Medina-Sidonia received a constant stream of communications, intelligence reports and commands. There were dispatches from Mendoza on the strength and likely disposition of the English fleet, and orders from the King covering almost every possible eventuality and every aspect of the conduct of the Armada, from its broad strategic objectives to the minutiae of the means by which the sins and baser instincts of the men herded aboard the ships of the fleet might be curbed. However, he was much less explicit about two crucial tactical considerations—how the rendezvous with Parma was to be effected and how the English fleet was to be engaged and defeated. All Philip offered were repeated warnings—also given to Medina-Sidonia by almost every commander—that the English ships were faster, more weatherly and had more long-range guns, and would endeavour to fight the Armada at long range. "There is little to say with regard to the mode of fighting and the handling of the Armada on the day of battle . . . it must be borne in mind that the enemy's object will be to fight at long distance, in consequence of his advantage in artillery and the large number of artificial fires with which he will be furnished. The aim of our men, on the contrary, must be to bring him to close quarters and grapple with him, and you will have to be very careful to have this carried out . . . The enemy employs his artillery to deliver his fire low and sink his opponent's ships, and you will have to take such precautions as you consider necessary."

Medina-Sidonia would have to try to gain the weather gauge—the desirable position upwind of his enemies—and force them to fight at close quarters. However, the King also gave clear instructions that, while the Armada was not to avoid fighting the English fleet if an opportunity presented itself, it was not to seek a confrontation. "Even if Drake should have sailed for these waters . . . you should not turn back but continue on your course, not seeking out the enemy even if he should remain here. If, however, he should pursue and overtake you, you may attack him, as you should also do if you meet Drake with his fleet at the entrance to the Channel . . . It is understood that you will fight only if you cannot otherwise make secure the passage across to England of the Duke of Parma."

As the Armada waited at Belém for the wind to take them to sea, Medina-Sidonia wrote to the King seeking to clarify his orders. "The opinions of those whom I have consulted here is that the best course would be to break up the enemy's sea-forces first. When this is done . . . the rest will be safe and easy." Philip undoubtedly expected that the Armada would have to defeat the British fleet in battle; it was, he said, "the essence of the business," but in his view reaching the Cape of Margate would guarantee such a battle, for the English fleet could not allow the Armada to control the Straits of Dover. There were to be no distractions or diversions from the Armada's prime task, and no attempts to secure a safe haven to repair and reprovision his ships and rest his men, as Drake always sought to do on his voyages. Philip, the man who had once said, "I and time are one," would now brook no delays whatsoever. The Armada must meet its destiny and make its rendezvous with Parma, relying for success on God's grace and the confident hope of a miracle. Philip had also stressed to Parma the need to be ready "to do your share without delay . . . for until your passage is effected he [Medina-Sidonia] will have no harbour for shelter . . . he will be at the mercy of the weather." Only if the attempt to land Parma's forces had already failed was Medina-Sidonia to be permitted to "capture the Isle of Wight, which is not so strongly defended as to appear able to resist you . . . On no account should you try to capture the island on your journey eastwards without first having made a supreme effort to achieve success in the main task."[1]

On 28 May, the weather at last moderated and the wind shifted enough for the Armada to begin making its way out of the Tagus. Medina-Sidonia's flagship, the *San Martin,* led the great fleet, the sun glinting from its gilding and new paintwork, pennants streaming from every masthead. As each ship in turn passed Castle St. Julian, the rolling thunder of guns fired in salute sounded over the water. The process of forming up the vast Armada was a lengthy one and it was dawn the next morning before the last ship had cleared the bar at the mouth of the river to reach the open sea. Forced to govern "our progress by the speed of the most miserable tub among us," the Armada could then make only fitful, "inchworm progress" against a north-north-west breeze. Some of the more cumbersome ships made no headway to windward at all. Beating into the wind, the captain of a Hamburg merchantman returning from Cadiz recorded that it took him an entire day to sail past the Armada as it made its slow way north, strung out for miles over the ocean.

By 1 June, after two further days' sailing, the Armada was still south of the Rock of Lisbon, and it took a further thirteen days to reach Finisterre, a mere 160 sea miles to the north. That rate of progress must have been dispiriting enough for Medina-Sidonia without the other news he was given; just two weeks into a voyage of several months, provisions were already becoming a problem, for there was "great corruption and loss" of supplies. The corruption of the suppliers and provision merchants was partly to blame for that. Philip had ordered that "the fleet should be victualled for six months, but Luis Hezar and Francisco Duarte of Cadiz did victual them but for four months, and with that which was nought and rotten . . . The King commanded them to be apprehended and they remained prisoners in Portugal at our coming away."

Much of the Armada's food had been in store or in barrel since the previous autumn, and large parts of it were already foul and contaminated. The effects of Drake's raid on Cadiz the previous year were also still being felt. The destruction of over a hundred tunny-fishing boats had contributed to a shortage of salt-fish and the huge quantities of "hoops and pipe staves and such like" burned in bonfires on the foreshore had proved very difficult to replace. There was insufficient seasoned oak to be had at any price and the wood of many casks shipped with the Armada was either so green that it had warped or so old that it was rotten. Perhaps as many as half of the barrels proved to be neither air- nor watertight, and poor rotation of stocks during the fleet's chaotic and prolonged preparations had further exacerbated the problems, leaving the ship's biscuit, rice and other dry foods mouldy and crawling with maggots and worms, much of the salt-beef and salt-fish putrescent, the wine sour and the water foul and undrinkable. Many men refused to eat the food, and many of those who did were laid low with food poisoning, further fouling their quarters belowdecks.

Medina-Sidonia sent frequent appeals to Philip for more funds and supplies, and ordered the whole of Portugal to be scoured for fresh provisions to be sent after the Armada without delay, together with whatever could be loaded at the northern ports they would pass. For four days he waited off Finisterre for the promised victualling ships to appear, while ever more alarming reports came in from every squadron of shortages of food and water. Large numbers of seamen and soldiers were falling ill with "the flux" and barrels of sardines, salt-fish and meat, cheese and bacon were "so rotten and stinking that many have been thrown overboard to save the men from pestilence." The shortage of water was an even more serious problem. Medina-Sidonia wrote to Parma, "What I fear most is lack of water . . . I do not see where we can obtain any more. It will be necessary . . . to have all the butts that can be obtained, got ready and filled with water to send to the Armada as soon as it arrives."²

On Sunday 19 June, almost three weeks after the Armada had set sail and still only 300 miles north of Lisbon, Medina-Sidonia ordered a signal gun fired and a flag flown "at the poop, near the lantern" to summon a council of war. The system of guns, flags and lights during the hours of darkness was also used to indicate when the flagship was shortening sail, lowering an anchor or going about onto a new tack, and "a great gun" and "a beacon signal" were used to warn the fleet that a ship was in distress. Pinnaces soon surrounded the *San Martin* as the senior officers were ferried to the flagship. Medina-Sidonia stood on the poop deck to greet them as they came aboard, flanked by Don Diego Flores de Valdes, his chief of staff, and Don Francisco de Bobadilla, the commander of the land forces. De Valdes, much older than Medina-Sidonia, was the commander of the galleons of Castile. Vastly experienced, he had sailed to England with the fleet carrying Philip to his marriage with Mary Tudor in 1554 and had been commanding the Indian Guard, the fleet that guarded the treasure ships from the New World, since 1567. In 1581 he had also sailed with 23 ships and 3,500 men to expel all foreigners from South and Central America and establish a fortress to bar the Straits of Magellan to foreign traders and privateers, but the expedition was a failure and he was accused of abandoning part of his fleet to its fate. For all his experience, he was one of the least popular men in the fleet, quarrelling continuously with his brother officers and nurturing a bitter feud with his cousin Don Pedro de Valdes, commander of the Andalusian squadron. Don Pedro had seen service against the French and Portuguese and survived a serious wound in an engagement with English ships off Ferrol in 1580, but he had been disgraced and briefly imprisoned by Philip because of the heavy losses of soldiers during his impetuous and unsuccessful attempt to capture the Azores in 1581. Now restored to a position of command, he was eager to remove the stain on his honour.

The sixty-two-year-old Don Juan Martinez de Recalde, Knight of Santiago and a former commander of the Indian Guard, was Captain General of the Biscayan squadron, but sailed in the *San Juan de Portugal*, the vice-flagship of Medina-Sidonia's squadron. He was the oldest and most experienced officer in the fleet, and though infirm and suffering from sciatica, he remained a proud and bold commander, albeit one with an indifferent record of success, having failed to defeat the Dutch Sea Beggars off Zeeland in 1572, commanded a squadron in the disastrous landing at Smerwick in Ireland in 1580, and arrived too late to take part in the victory at Terceira in 1582. Miguel de Oquendo, fifty-nine at the time of the Armada, was Captain General of the Guipuz-coan squadron and another proud and fierce old officer, nicknamed "The Glory of the Fleet." At the battle of Terceira, he had saved Santa Cruz's flagship by sailing his own ship between two enemy vessels and then boarding and capturing the French flagship.

Don Martin Jiminez de Bertendona, forty-nine, was Captain General of the Levant squadron. His father, also a distinguished officer, had captained the ship that carried Philip to England for his marriage with Mary Tudor. Don Hugo de Moncada, commander of the galleasses of Naples, was another fiercely proud officer, who stood heavily upon his dignity. Don Diego Medrano, commander of the four galleys, and Don Alonso Martinez de Leiva, the youngest of the officers, completed Medina-Sidonia's inner council. Although only twenty-four, the "tall, slim and handsome, dashing and hot-headed" de Leiva, Knight of the Order of Santiago, was a former Captain General of the Sicilian galleys and of the Light Cavalry of Milan, though he had purchased the latter title from the Count of Fuentes with the sole aim of outranking the other Armada squadron commanders. His ploy was entirely successful; Philip had appointed him commander of the invasion force and he also carried secret dispatches from the King, authorizing him to assume command of the Armada if anything befell Medina-Sidonia.

They were not the only secret instructions being carried. Philip had entrusted sealed orders to Medina-Sidonia that were to be handed to Parma only "if (which God forbid) the result be not so prosperous as our arms shall be able to settle matters, nor . . . so contrary that the enemy shall be relieved of anxiety on our account (which God surely will not permit)." In the event of outright victory or defeat, the orders were to be returned to Philip unopened. They contained the terms upon which Philip would be willing to settle his differences with Eliza-beth: freedom of worship for all English Catholics and the return of the towns in The Netherlands garrisoned by English forces to Spanish control. Parma was also to seek financial compensation "for the injury they have done to me, my dominions and my subjects," but Philip gave him discretion to waive this requirement in order to win acceptance of the other terms. Philip had only one other, chilling instruction. "If per-chance the Duke . . . should be successful in capturing [the Portuguese pretender] Dom Antonio . . . or if [he] should chance to fall into your hands, guard him closely and see that he does not escape, so that his restlessness may no longer be a source of trouble."

Philip's reasons for wishing to conceal his orders from Parma are obvious. The terms he was willing to agree were those that Parma had already been urging upon him, in order to avoid "the danger of some disaster, causing you to fail to conquer England whilst losing your hold here [in The Netherlands]." Such was Philip's stubborn faith in the outcome of actions taken in God's cause that he preferred to take the gambler's chance of risking everything on an outright victory, but had Parma known in advance what the King was willing to agree to, he might have taken steps to secure such an agreement on his own initiative. Had he not always argued that, with English support neutralized, the Dutch could readily be defeated? Once that was achieved, Philip could then renounce the treaty with Elizabeth and launch the Enterprise of England not from far-off Lisbon but from Flushing or Antwerp, less than one day's sailing from the mouth of the Thames.[3]

Medina-Sidonia's General Orders to the Armada before its departure from Lisbon had forbidden captains to return to Spain under any circumstances: "any infraction of this shall be punished by death and forfeiture." If ships became separated from the fleet by storms, they were to proceed to a point to the south of the Scilly Isles and there await the remainder of the Armada. Beyond the Scillies, the next rendezvous was to be Mount's Bay in Cornwall. Now, faced with this desperate shortage of supplies before they had even left Spanish waters, the Armada commanders agreed without dissent to put in to Corunna (now La Coruña), and take on whatever water and provisions could be found. By the time the leading ships of the fleet had come to anchor in the harbour, guarded by the walled city on its rocky peninsula, the sun was already setting and nearly half the fleet—over fifty ships, including almost all of the hulks, guarded by Recalde's squadron and the four galleasses—were left out at sea, waiting for daylight. Just after midnight, a south-west gale blew up, so fierce that even in the harbour one ship cast its anchor and a pinnace was driven into a galleon. "So violent a sea and wind, accompanied by fog and tempest have never been seen." Those ships still at sea had no option but to turn and run before the storm. One of Recalde's galleons broke its mainmast and one of the galleys "had thrown her rudder overboard as the sea was so heavy."

By the afternoon of 21 June, the gale had blown itself out and Medina-Sidonia sent out pinnaces to search for his scattered fleet. Word began to come in from up the coast that de Leiva had managed to reach the port of Vivero with ten ships, and two of the galleasses had sheltered in Gijón. On the following day, Juan Martinez de Recalde led another ten ships into harbour, but by 24 June thirty ships, including a Florentine galleon, a Castilian galleon, two galleasses and Recalde's two best galleons, were still missing. Even those ships that had ridden out the storm in harbour were damaged. Many had lost spars or even masts and dragged their anchors, and many were leaking, "strained, it was said, by the heavy weather, but really from being overmasted." An alarming number of crew and soldiers were also falling ill with scurvy and dysentery. "I am afraid this trouble may spread and become past remedy . . . God be praised for all he may ordain," Medina-Sidonia wrote to the King, without apparent irony.[4]

He couched the rest of his grim tidings in the most tactful terms he could muster. It was scarcely credible, he suggested, that such foul weather should have hit the fleet in the best sailing month of the year. The storm "would be remarkable at the end of June, but being as it is on so great an occasion in the service of Our Lord, it is even more extraordinary, considering how fervently the enterprise has been commended and devoted to Him. We must therefore conclude that what has happened has been for some good and just reason." He was fearful that at least some of the missing ships might have been sunk or captured by English or French privateers. He listed the ships missing and the damage to those still with him, and described the state of his crews and provisions, and the dismal rate of progress necessitated by the lumbering hulks and ships of the Levant squadron not built for rough Atlantic waters. "To undertake so great a task with equal forces to those of the enemy would be inadvisable, but to do so with an inferior force . . . would be still more unwise . . . I recall the great force Your Majesty collected for the conquest of Portugal, although that country was within our own boundaries and many of the people were in your favour. Well Sire, how do you think we can attack so great a country as England with such a force as ours is now?" He concluded by urging Philip, in the strongest terms possible for a subject writing to his omnipotent sovereign, to consider abandoning the invasion of England for a further year and seeking some form of accommodation with Elizabeth in the meantime. The problems the Armada was facing made it "essential that the enterprise we are engaged in should be given the closest scrutiny."

On 27 June, as he awaited Philip's reply, Medina-Sidonia summoned another council of war to seek the support of his commanders for the course he had urged upon their King. Medina-Sidonia asked them whether it was wiser to remain in Corunna and wait for the missing ships to rejoin them, to put to sea to search for them, or to set sail immediately for England without them. Nine of the ten most senior officers supported his preference for remaining in Corunna, taking on fresh supplies and waiting for the missing ships to appear. Only Pedro de Valdes of the Andalusian squadron argued for putting to sea at once and launching a surprise attack on the English fleet with whatever ships the Armada could muster, and even he did so not from any overwhelming desire for immediate action but on the rather more prosaic grounds that there was little opportunity or likelihood of obtaining fresh supplies and to linger in Corunna would merely make their situation worse. Astonishingly, despite the harsh lessons of Cadiz in 1587, there is not the slightest sign that Medina-Sidonia and his commanders made any defensive preparations against the possibility of a raid on Corunna by the English fleet. Had Drake been able to enter the broad bay at the head of a line of galleons, he would have found the Armada disorganized and in little condition to repel an attack.

Philip's reply to Medina-Sidonia, written on 1 July and received in Corunna five days later, brushed aside all his reservations and recommendations. "From what I know of you, I believe that your bringing all these matters to my attention arises solely from your zeal to serve me and a desire to succeed in your command. The certainty that this is so prompts me to be franker with you than I should be with another . . . I see plainly the truth of what you say, that the Levant ships are less free and staunch in heavy seas than the vessels built here, and that the hulks cannot sail to windward; but it is still the case that Levant ships sail constantly to England, and the hulks hardly go anywhere else but up the Channel. Indeed it is quite an exception for them to leave it to go to other seas. It is true that, if we could have things exactly as we wished, we would rather have other vessels, but under the present circumstances, the expedition must not be abandoned on account of this difficulty." The Enterprise of England was the only means by which the stubborn English Queen could be forced to negotiate, and by lying at anchor in Corunna they were merely inviting an attack by El Draque and the rest of Elizabeth's pirates.

Medina-Sidonia was ordered to make what repairs he could and take on what stores were available—"but you must take great care that the stores are really preserved and not allow yourself to be deceived as you were before"—and even if he were obliged to sail with a depleted force, he was to do so at the first opportunity. His orders remained unchanged: to rendezvous with Parma off "the Cape of Margate." Philip once more invoked the sacred nature of the enterprise on which they were embarked. "If this were an unjust war, the storm might be taken as a sign of God's will that we should cease from our offence. As, however, it is so just, it is not to be believed that God will withhold His aid, but that He will rather favour that cause even to the utmost of our desires . . . Every great enterprise is beset with difficulties, and the merit lies in overcoming them. I have dedicated this enterprise to

God . . . Stir yourself then, to do your duty." Medina-Sidonia replied like a dutiful subject. "I am consoled to the idea that He who has this expedition in His hand deigns to take this course with it in order to infuse even more zeal in Your Majesty and more care in your officers . . . Your Majesty may rest assured that no efforts of mine shall be spared."[5]

However, in case his exhortations were not enough to hold Medina-Sidonia to his purpose, Philip also sent a minister, Andres de Alba, from Madrid to remind him of his duty, and, because it was "important to have near his person others who are highly experienced and skilled both in the art of sailing and that of war," the King also appointed Diego Flores de Valdes to serve as Medina-Sidonia's "naval adviser" aboard the *San Martin*. This only increased the jealousy and suspicion felt by the other commanders for both de Valdes and de Bobadilla, who was also sailing aboard Medina-Sidonia's flagship. Both men had ready access to the Captain General and powerful influence over him, and there were those who believed that the two were not so much advisers as watchdogs, there to ensure that the untested Medina-Sidonia would not waver from the strategy that Philip himself had laid down.

In a dispatch to Parma on 10 June, Medina-Sidonia had expressed his wish that "the coast [between Calais and Dunkirk] were capable of sheltering so great a fleet as this so that we might take some safe port to have at our backs," and while the Armada was still labouring up the Portuguese coast he had "consulted the pilots and other experts aboard this fleet who are familiar with the whole coast of England," seeking their advice on a port that the Armada might seize and use as a base until Parma signalled his readiness to launch the invasion. Informed by Parma of this proposed deviation from his masterplan, Philip at once wrote a further letter to Medina-Sidonia: "The main point was to go on until you could join hands with the Duke." There was no need of a safe haven on the English coast and, though Elizabeth's fleet was to be engaged and destroyed if it attempted to hamper the Armada's progress towards its rendezvous, there were to be no other deviations from the prescribed plan. Medina-Sidonia would arrive in the Narrow Seas with all possible speed and Parma would then emerge with his invasion force. Yet given Philip's chronic shortage of cash, it was all the stranger that his instructions to Medina-Sidonia should so specifically have excluded the possibility of capturing an English port as a base when Pope Sixtus's pledge of one million ducats would fall due as soon as the first Spanish boot touched English soil.

His equally strong insistence that Medina-Sidonia should avoid confrontation with the English fleet unless forced to it also made his orders to keep clear of the treacherous "shoals and sandbanks" off the French coast, keeping "more to the English side," seem curious. In fact, with the exception of the Bay of Boulogne, there are no dangerous shoals and sandbanks off the French coast until the approaches to Dunkirk, and it would have been perfectly possible for the Armada to have kept to that side of the Channel; a later Spanish Armada did precisely that in 1598. Whether such a vast fleet, occupying several square miles of sea, could have remained undetected even if it had been hugging the French shore is a moot point, though again the Armada of 1598 did so, but at the least it would have made the English logistics and communications more difficult and forced them to meet the Armada in waters that were less familiar to them than their own coastlines. Perhaps Philip was misinformed or perhaps he wished the English to be intimidated by the sight of his great Armada defiantly cruising past their shores, but whatever the reason, that was the course he had dictated and Medina-Sidonia would have to obey.[6]

Another month elapsed before the Armada was deemed ready to put to sea, and by then it was back to its full strength. "God . . . has been pleased to reunite the entire fleet, without the loss of a single ship . . . I hold this to be a great miracle." Even more remarkable, according to Medina-Sidonia, who hailed it as another "authentic miracle," was the survival of the Levant ship *Trinidad de Scala*, which had somehow reached Gijón despite her planks' having gaped up to four inches apart after her battering from the seas. Two of the later groups of returning ships had even been driven as far as the approaches to the Channel, and had returned, according to Recalde, "smelling of England." One had caught glimpses of what might have been Drake's fleet before sailing back on a north wind to Corunna. The other group had cruised the coast between the Scilly Isles and the Lizard, waiting in vain for the rest of the Armada to appear, and had taken a couple of prizes, capturing two Irish priests and a number of sailors. Under interrogation the latter revealed that the English fleet was divided between Plymouth and the Narrow Seas—the Straits of Dover.

The last missing ship had returned to Corunna by 15 July, but several further days elapsed before all were provisioned and ready to set sail. While in port some of Medina-Sidonia's principal ships of war had been repaired, the seams caulked and the sides tallowed, and one had even had a new mainmast stepped. Some "beef, water, fish, oils and vinegar" had been found and his men had also been able to eat a little fresh food. Morale had been improved by the stay in port and, if not greatly better, the physical condition of Medina-Sidonia's men was certainly no worse.

Reinforcements had arrived to replace some of the sickest and most injured men, but Medina-Sidonia rejected most of the forced recruits as worse than those he already had; "not a soul of them knows what an arquebus is, or any other weapon, and already they are more dead than alive." Many were so decrepit or diseased that he gave in to "the lamentation of their wives" and sailed without them. "They will only eat up the victuals and be in the way." Some men, including a few gentleman adventurers, whose taste of life at sea had already proved more than enough for them, had taken the opportunity afforded by a brief shore leave to abscond, and from then on Medina-Sidonia ensured that "a company of infantry of the country" was permanently stationed on the quay to prevent desertions. His men were landed only in groups, under guard, on the island of San Anton in the middle of the harbour. There, isolated from the normal sinful pleasures of the shore, they were confessed by priests and given a blessing and a pewter medallion of Christ and the Virgin to wear into battle. Medina-Sidonia claimed to find his medallion "such an inestimable treasure, that I esteem it more highly than the most precious jewel I carry on the fleet."[7]

On 19 July Medina-Sidonia again summoned his commanders to a council of war, at which all ten voted to sail for England on the next favourable conjunction of wind and tide, but the following day arguments continued between those advocating making sail immediately and those, including Diego Flores de Valdes, urging a wait for the new moon, in the belief that it would presage a change in the weather. In the end it was agreed that if the wind stood fair, they should sail at dawn the next morning. By that afternoon the last provision boats had returned to shore and the squadrons of Miguel de Oquendo, Diego Flores de Valdes and Pedro de Valdes had already been warped clear of the inner harbour by their ships' boats. The rest of the great ships now followed, waiting at one anchor for the wind. There was little sleep for officers or men that night. At midnight Medina-Sidonia ordered the firing of a gun, the signal to make ready, and as the first light of dawn broke, another gun sounded, ordering the fleet to sea.

It was a true summer's morning, hot and almost still with only the stirrings of a south-west breeze. The crews clustered at the rails took their last sight of Spain and the sunlight already gilding the summits of the mountains, though the vineyards and pastures cladding the lower slopes and the whitewashed houses clustered around the harbour were still in purple shadow. It must have been a bittersweet moment, familiar to all mariners taking their last sight of their homeland, for all knew that whether the Armada fared well or ill, many of those lining the rails would never see their homes again. The endless procession of ships decked with flags and pennants, their sails emblazoned with blood-red crosses, passed beyond the shelter of the bay and formed up offshore. By mid-afternoon the entire fleet was assembled, but before it had made three leagues out to sea the wind dropped to a flat calm. For the rest of that day they rode the Atlantic swell at anchor, but in the middle of the night watch a land breeze sprang up and the Armada was once more under way, passing out of sight of Spain before the next dawn broke.

CHAPTER SEVEN

Five Regiments of old Spanish Soldiers.

The Sea Beggars

The launching of the Armada was the greatest but by no means the only part of Philip's masterplan for the subjugation of England. His diplomats, military commanders, spies, agents provocateurs, foreign clients and puppets had also been set to work in a dozen different states, each attempting to bring his part of the great enterprise to fruition at the right time to influence the course of events in England. Philip's envoy in Constantinople was endeavouring to ensure that the Turks did not seek to take advantage of his military preoccupation with northern Europe by launching a surprise attack on Spain's Mediterranean coast. The Doge of Venice was also wooed to ensure his support or, at the least, his neutrality, and Philip's ambassador in Prague was tasked with securing military and financial support from the Emperor, Rudolf II. His mission was only partially successful; Rudolf sent a contingent of troops to aid Parma, but no money to defray the costs of the Armada. Agents among the German princedoms and the Swiss cantons worked to spread disinformation and sow divisions that would hamper any move against Flanders from the east.

Philip's agents and clients were also active in Ireland, Scotland and France, but their efforts in those countries were not directed towards diplomacy; their aim was nothing less than to foment rebellion and insurrection. The native population of Ireland was both Catholic and pro-Spanish, and despite the brutal English reprisals that had followed the failure of the Hispano-Papal invasion in 1580, rebel chieftains such as O'Rourke, O'Doherty and McDoe were still willing to rise against the hated English at the first sign of wholehearted support from Philip, but it had to take tangible form, for they had been let down by his promises before. If they were armed, funded and reinforced with Spanish troops, there seemed no reason why they could not sweep the Protestant settlers and their English defenders into the sea. The English garrison, mostly based in Dublin and the Pale (the fortified area around Dublin controlled by the English), was very modest in size, under 2,000 soldiers, and apart from a handful of castles and strongpoints the entire west of the country was hostile territory. But when Philip abandoned his original plan for the Armada to make a diversionary landing in Ireland, he seems also to have ceased to encourage the Irish rebel chieftains to begin an insurrection. Whether that was through oversight, a shortage of funds or troops, or a reluctance to involve himself in too many arenas at once, the result was to remove a great deal of the pressure to divide her forces that Elizabeth would otherwise have faced.

However, if Ireland was largely left to its own devices, much greater efforts were expended on Scotland. The defeat and expulsion of Mary, Queen of Scots, and her French troops in 1568 had established Scotland as a Protestant kingdom, but it was more a loose federation of warring nobles and clans than a coherent state, and the writ of its king, James VI, did not extend far into the highlands and islands of his realm. Scotland was "not like other States, solid and stable, where no changes can be brought about except after great preparations. In Scotland any accident will bring about a change, as the realm is so divided and dismembered and anyone attacking it with force is assured of victory as there are no strong towns and but few fortresses." A group of powerful

Catholic lords had never accepted the Protestant regime imposed upon them and, supported by Spain, were willing to take up arms to overthrow it. Catholics still formed a majority of the population and, as the threat from Spain grew, Elizabeth had tried to secure "the realm's postern gate" by binding James ever closer to her. She would not grant the one thing that would have bound him closest—public acknowledgement as her chosen heir, for she continued to refuse to name her successor—but as she grew older and the prospect of her ever having a child diminished from remote to literally inconceivable, James was given private assurances that he would succeed to the throne.

In July 1586, in confirmation of an informal agreement reached the previous summer, Elizabeth and James signed the Treaty of Berwick, guaranteeing to maintain the current religion of their countries, not to enter into any treaty prejudicial to the other party and to provide armed intervention in the event of an attack upon either. The twenty-one-year-old James received £4,000 in cash, a pension of £4,000 a year and an assurance that "nothing would be done that imperilled his title to the English Crown," and in return he promised to control his perennially troublesome Catholic lords and acquiesce in the continuing imprisonment of his mother. Although James infuriated Elizabeth "by refusing to listen to her increasingly hectoring advice," as he realized and regretted almost as soon as he had put his signature to the treaty, it gave her everything she sought at a very modest price; "after all the golden mountains offered, [he] received only a fiddler's wage." It is even arguable that the treaty removed the last obstacle to the execution of his mother, by driving a wedge between James and his Catholic subjects and forcing him into ever greater dependence on England, but his own long-term interests were best served by supporting Elizabeth. If she lived out her reign, he would then inherit her crown; if she was deposed by Spain, Philip would place his daughter on the throne.

Despite the Treaty of Berwick, continuing rumours and reports reached Elizabeth of "plots at [the Scottish] court," "Spanish gold" and "offers from the Duke of Parma." Since January 1587 Mendoza had been urging that she "should be assailed on the Scottish side," to compel her to divide her forces and fight on two fronts at once. "It would upset the Englishwoman to find herself attacked on that side, besides being a great thing to get a footing and a free port in the island in view of eventualities"—by which he can only have meant the landing of Spanish troops. Robert Bruce, the intermediary between Mendoza and Parma and the Scottish Catholic lords, even claimed that "the easiest means" for invading England "[was] the entrance from Scotland. This would divide the English forces . . . No less advantage may be looked for from the conquest and conversion of England by the Catholic Lords than from the [Catholic] League in France, which at first did not possess so much force. The country was never in so favourable a condition for being conquered as at present, owing to the disputes that exist."[1]

Philip responded by ordering that three Catholic lords on the Spanish payroll, the Earls of Huntly and Morton and Lord Claud Hamilton, were to be "kept in hand and encouraged to expect the aid they require." After the execution of Mary he gave them further encouragement, promising weapons, Spanish troops and "150,000 crowns three or four months after they have taken up arms and liberated their King [from Elizabeth's influence]." They were ready to revolt at once, but Philip wanted them held back until the Armada was approaching England: "It will be well to consult the Duke of Parma as to the best time for the earls to rise." But the delays in launching the Armada thoroughly alarmed Bruce, for the preparations for rebellion could not be wholly hidden from the spies of James and Elizabeth. On 18 February 1588, Bruce complained that "if the support agreed upon does not arrive quickly, the Catholic Lords will be obliged to defend themselves prematurely under overwhelming difficulties and to the great risk of the cause." Philip responded in March, authorizing Bruce to "pay the Catholic Lords the 10,000 crowns" he had been given as soon as the exiled Earl of Morton and Colonel William Semple, the traitor of Lierre in The Netherlands, had returned to Scotland to prepare the ground for the planned insurrection. Parma at once made arrangements for the two men to "embark at night from Dunkirk." Meanwhile the Scots were to be "urgently shown the importance of securing the port of Little Leith [on the Firth of Forth]." Philip voiced his optimism about the prospects of success for Morton and Semple. They were "going on an excellent mission . . . some good effect may be produced." "It is well that they should make what effort they can to see whether the blood of his mother will not arouse him [James VI] to vengeance." But whatever urge for vengeance had been aroused in James's heart, he would not have forgotten that the Spanish King had encouraged Mary to disinherit her son and name Philip as her chosen heir. Philip continued, "Even if the King will not declare himself, it will be most advantageous for Morton to cross the English border at the time the main blow is struck."[2]

Morton and Semple had fair weather and made a clandestine landing in Scotland only four days after they departed from Dunkirk, but the plan began to go badly wrong soon afterwards. The Armada's one-month halt at Corunna, following the delays in leaving Lisbon, left it well behind the agreed schedule, and as it absorbed ever more of Philip's attention and his treasure no further military or financial support for the Scottish Catholic lords was forthcoming. James had also been alerted to the presence of the traitors on his soil and on 7 July Mendoza reported that the Scots King had "declared himself much more openly than before against the Catholics . . . The English faction are desirous that the King should arrest Morton," who had "retired further into the North and raised troops. Morton, Huntly and Claud Hamilton were in close union and had collected a large force in case the King should attempt to attack them." Ten days later it was reported that as James was "trying to seize him, the Earl of Morton had therefore been obliged to embark and had gone in search of the Spanish fleet . . . After his embarkation, the Earl fell ill and was obliged by contrary weather and his illness to land secretly and obtain medical help. He was then captured by an enemy of his and the King now has him in his hands under guard. The Queen in consequence of this has sent a Secretary of the Council to Scotland with £4,000 in cash and great efforts were being made to have Morton executed."

It is probable that Morton was betrayed by another Spanish client, Henri, Duc de Guise. Catherine de' Medici had tried to ease the pressure on her son, Henri III, and stop the fighting in France by persuading de Guise to use his forces to "assist the King of Scotland in his English enterprise, since he now shows signs of turning Catholic." Mendoza was scathing. "In the face of the fact that the Duc de Guise, Cardinal Bourbon and the other confederate princes are in arms to extirpate heretics, it is a fine idea to persuade them to help to the throne of England the King of Scotland, who has been a heretic from his cradle." Spain's interests required that de Guise continue his destabilizing campaign in France. Despite de Guise's claim that his loyalty to Philip "outweighs all other considerations . . . if the King of Scots is his cousin, he looks upon the King of Spain as the father of all Catholics and especially of him," Mendoza had not kept him informed of the plans to stir revolt in Scotland, and when he discovered them the furious de Guise passed the information to James. "This was mainly instrumental in rendering it abortive."[3]

William Ashley, Elizabeth's new ambassador in Scotland, had his first meeting with James on 3 August. The King told him that his continued loyalty required something more tangible than "fair promises," and he hinted at the offers being made to him by Spanish emissaries. Elizabeth was well aware of the threat that a revolt in Scotland could pose, and as the Armada approached she took further steps to assure herself of James's loyalty. Five thousand pounds was handed by Robert

Bowes "to the Laird of Carmichael for the King of Scots," and when the news of the sighting of the Armada reached Edinburgh on 8 August, Ashley offered James enough "to satisfy His Majesty for the time and to qualify the minds of the nobility to keep all in quiet." James was to receive the Duchy of Lancaster and its revenues, an increased pension, a royal guard of 50 gentlemen, and a company of 100 cavalry and 100 foot, all maintained at Elizabeth's expense. He was also left with the clear impression that he would at last be publicly proclaimed as her chosen successor. Elizabeth wrote to him giving oblique references to the succession. "If by leaving them [the Spaniards] unhelped, you may increase the English hearts unto you, you shall not do the worst deed for your behalf."

As a result James wrote to Elizabeth expressing his undying loyalty, offering "unto you my forces, my person and all that I command . . . I promise to behave myself not as a stranger and foreign prince, but as your natural son and compatriot . . . I with honour and all my good subjects with a fervent goodwill may embrace this, your Godly and honest cause, whereby your adversaries may have ado, not with England, but with the whole island of Britain." James was also reported to be "willing to hazard his Crown and life in defence of Her Majesty," and gave Elizabeth further reassurance by arresting Lord Maxwell, another prominent Scottish Catholic, who had intrigued on Spain's and Mary, Queen of Scots', behalf on numerous occasions, and since April 1588 had been assembling followers to secure a base to assist an invasion of either Scotland or England. James had a proclamation read at every market cross in Scotland, ordering his people to repel any attempted Spanish landing on their shores.

Without a direct intervention by Spanish troops, Philip's hopes of a rebellion and a second front in Scotland now looked as doomed as his plans for Ireland, but, aided by Mendoza's intrigues, Spanish plans in France were much closer to fruition. Lord Charles Howard's reading of the European situation was remarkably acute. "This abusing [of] the treaty of peace does plainly show how the King of Spain will have all things perfect [as] his plot is laid, before he will proceed to execute. I am persuaded he will see the Duke of Guise bring the French [King] to his purpose before he will act." As Howard had predicted, de Guise and his supporters in the Catholic League were indeed active on their own and Philip's behalf.[4]

Under relentless pressure from Spain and the League, the weak and vacillating Henri III had agreed to revoke the royal edicts of toleration of Protestants and outlaw the Reformed Church. Henri, the last of the Valois line since the death of his brother François, Duc d'Anjou, in 1584, had no children—his penchant for women's clothing and the company of handsome young men suggested that none would ever be born to him—and his heir apparent was the Huguenot leader Henri Bourbon of Navarre. In September 1585 Pope Sixtus had issued a Bull denouncing Navarre as a heretic, absolving his vassals of allegiance to him, depriving him of his estates and declaring him unfit to succeed to the throne of France. The Catholic League demanded that he should be replaced as heir by the geriatric Cardinal Charles of Bourbon, as much a Spanish stalking horse as Cardinal Henry had been in Portugal. The subsequent "Guerre des Trois Henris"—Valois, de Guise and Navarre, who battled over the crown and the succession—led to a fresh slaughter of Protestants by Catholics, and Catholics by Protestants.

Navarre's forces had waged a guerrilla campaign but had been defeated in almost every open battle until Coutras in October 1587, where they overwhelmed the forces of the Duc de Joyeuse, one of the King's favourites. Instead of exploiting his victory by linking up with a force of Swiss and German mercenaries recruited with Elizabeth's money and marching on Paris, Navarre sent an emissary offering his support to the King in return for concessions. His armies then disbanded and returned home, leaving the mercenaries to fight alone against the forces of de Guise. The King had hoped that the two forces would exhaust each other in battle in Lorraine, but the mercenaries had only the most minor skirmishes with de Guise's men before marching into the heart of France, to the fury of the King's secretary Pinart. "The devil take them, why could they not have stayed in Lorraine where they could have done what was required?" Increasingly impoverished and disillusioned, and abandoned by both Navarre and Elizabeth, who was unwilling to invest further money, they lost their stomach for a fight and remained in France only in the hope of exacting a ransom from the King. Despite being outnumbered by six to one, de Guise's forces then launched a surprise attack and slaughtered thousands. Those left alive were allowed to return home under a safe conduct from the King, who then tried to claim credit for the victory at such minimal loss of French life. However, it was de Guise's name that echoed from every pulpit in Paris.

Mendoza was delighted with the success of Spain's clients and wrote to Philip from Paris, "On the whole, in spite of the victory of the King of Navarre . . . events here could hardly have gone the more happily for Your Majesty's affairs. The people of Paris can be relied on at any time; they are more deeply than ever in obedience to the Duc de Guise." Their obedience would soon be put to good use. The Parisian supporters of the Catholic League had established secret caches of arms, cobblestones and barrels filled with earth and stones, as barricades proof even against musket fire. With the confidence of a puppetmaster, Mendoza reported that Paris would be ready to revolt at any time after Martinmas [11 November] 1587 but he would need some weeks' notice of the launching of the Armada to bring matters to a head at the appropriate time. When word came from Philip that Santa Cruz would sail not later than 15 February, Mendoza and the League set events in train for that date. De Guise issued a manifesto early that month, demanding the removal of suspected heretics from the King's entourage and a declaration of his unequivocal support for the Catholic League. Chambers of the Inquisition were to be established in every province, Huguenot property confiscated and all prisoners who refused to recant their heresy put to death. It was—deliberately—an impossible manifesto for the King to accept, and he announced instead that he would raise an army against the League.[5]

At this crucial stage, Mendoza received the news of Santa Cruz's death and the postponement of the Armada. The next morning the French Queen Mother, Catherine de' Medici, as adept at manipulation and dissimulation as Mendoza himself, persuaded her son to enter negotiations with de Guise rather than confront him on the battlefield. However, Henri did not intend to sit on his hands while Spain crushed the English and the Dutch, completing the encirclement of his country, and he also feared that the Armada might be targeted not at England but at France. He "found it hard to believe that they were going to attack England because, as the Catholic King [Philip] had no ports to protect his ships from the furious storms of those seas . . . it would be rash to send a powerful fleet." He had reason to fear that the allies of de Guise might help the Armada to capture one or more Channel ports, or that the Army of Flanders might storm into France and seize Calais, threatening Henri and England alike. Henri's latest favourite, the Duc d'Epernon, prepared to launch a campaign to secure the Channel ports. He would then join forces with the English fleet or, if the Armada had already triumphed, invade Flanders and Artois before Parma's troops could return from England.

However, probably alerted by Stafford, Mendoza informed his master and the Catholic League of Epernon's plans, and in March 1587 the Duc de Guise's cousin, the Duc d'Aumale, launched a pre-emptive attack and occupied three towns in Picardy in north-east France, though crucially he failed to take Boulogne, which locked its gates against him. Aumale continued to occupy the towns throughout the summer, the prime season for an invasion of England, and withdrew only in October at the onset of winter. Had the Armada been launched in 1587 as Philip had planned, Aumale would have been in position to launch a fresh assault upon Boulogne as the Spanish fleet approached. It seems unlikely that this was a coincidence rather than a planned strategy, but the delays to the Armada and the failure to take Boulogne left Philip, for all his considerable investment in the League, still without the one thing he most needed for the success of the Enterprise of England—a deep-water port on the Channel coast. Mendoza felt that he had extracted a promise from Henri that his Channel ports would be open to any Spanish ships seeking shelter and supplies, but Henri had no reason to aid Philip in an endeavour so damaging to French interests. If he had indeed made that promise, it was a diplomatic fiction and one that was not communicated to the governors of his Channel ports.

To Mendoza's horror Henri had also begun to bargain with Elizabeth, citing his refusal to take up arms in a Catholic crusade against her and asking her in return to pressure Navarre to renounce his Protestant faith, depriving de Guise and the Catholic League of the pretext for their actions. Henri pointed out that "the Queen did not allow any other religion in her own country and it was only reasonable that the King of France should endeavour to do the same in his dominions," and warned her that if she made peace with Philip "it would not last three months." Philip would employ all his forces "to ruin him [Henri] and she might well imagine what would happen to her afterwards." Taking a leaf from Mendoza's black book, the French King also had his ministers spreading the rumour that Philip "had gone mad and in future the Infanta Isabella would sign all papers."

On 15 April Philip had assured Mendoza that the Armada would sail before the end of the month, and the priests and clerics in every church in Paris were at once prompted to begin a fresh onslaught on the King, lauding the Duc de Guise's achievements and accusing Henri of conspiring with the heretics to murder the good Catholics of Paris. Open calls were made from almost every Parisian pulpit for de Guise to defend the citizens against the King, and on 9 May he duly entered Paris. A coup d'état three years in the planning was now under way, but for reasons known only to himself, instead of going to his headquarters where he would have been protected by his supporters, de Guise made his way to the home of Catherine de' Medici. When her dwarf told her that de Guise was approaching, she called him mad, but when she herself saw him in the street below, surrounded by a crowd of admirers, she blanched and an observer heard a tremor in her voice as she issued orders. As de Guise entered, he told her in a voice loud enough to reach every ear that he had come to clear his name of slander and to offer his services to the King, trusting in the help and advice of the Queen

izabeth I in a portrait based
a template supplied by her
ficials and vetted to ensure
depiction was sufficiently
ttering, contrasted with one of the
ry few unapproved portraits to
cape destruction by them.

ght: The execution of Mary,
ueen of Scots. Outside is the
nfire on which her robes and
other relics of the "martyred"
ary were burned.

D FlAVNDERS REPRESENTE
N WHOSE BACKE KINGE PHILIP RODE
BEING MALECONTNT.

WHEARE ON THE COW DID FEEDE
A ONE THAT WAS HER GREATEST HELPE,
IN HER DISTRESSE AND NEEDE.

THE PRINCE OF ORAN
AND MADE HIS PVRSE
THE COW DID SHYT IN
WHILE HIE DID HOLD.

An English painting depicting The Netherlands as a milch cow and
showing Elizabeth as its only true friend. Philip II is trying to ride it, William of
Orange is draining its milk—its wealth—into his purse, and the cow "did shyt" on
the unpopular French Duc d'Anjou at its tail.

Below left: Philip II portrayed in his customary austere dress,
and displaying an air of cold certainty.

Below right: The reluctant and hapless commander of the Armada,
the Duke of Medina-Sidonia.

Background: A ceramic mural depicting Miguel de Oquendo (left) and Pedro de Valdes (right).

Right, from top: An unguarded look from Felice Peretti, Pope Sixtus V, suggests his peasant cunning.

Justin of Nassau, the commander of the Dutch Sea Beggars, whose naval blockade penned Parma's troops in Dunkirk.

The effete, doomed Henri III, last of the Valois kings, and his Protestant opponent and successor, Henri of Navarre, later Henri IV.

Below: Alexander Farnese, Duke of Parma, the greatest military commander of his age.

A sixteenth-century map of the coast around Plymouth.

Right, from top: England's
inexperienced Lord High Admiral,
Charles Howard.

Sir Francis Drake—"The
Dragon upon the Coast."

Sir John Hawkins, whose
redesign of the Queen's galleons on
race-built lines conferred a huge
technological advantage.

The choleric but formidable Martin
Frobisher played a key role in the
battles off Portland and the Isle of
Wight.

Above: Matthew Baker (right), the first
master shipwright to make
accurate blueprints, allowing
successful designs to be replicated.

Right and below: A race-built galleon and
pinnace, showing the clean lines, heavy
armaments and lowered fore- and sterncastles that gave the English
fleet a decisive advantage.

Right: A mariner's astrolabe from
an Armada wreck in Blasket
Sound, in the west of Ireland.

Opposite: Lucas Waghenaer's *The
Mariner's Mirror* contained the first
accurate charts, sailing directions and
navigational tables. The English captains all possessed a copy; the
Spaniards did not.

THE MARINERS MIRROVR

Wherin may playnly be seen the courses, heights, distances, depths, soundings, flouds and ebs, risings of lands, rocks, sands and shoalds, with the marks for the entrings of the Harbouroughs, Havens and Ports of the greatest part of Europe: their seueral traficks and commodities: Together with the Rules and instrumēts of NAVIGATION.

First made & set fourth in diuers exact Sea-Charts, by that famous Nauigator LVKE WAGENAR of Enchuisen. And now fitted with necessarie additions for the vse of Englishmen by ANTHONY ASHLEY.

Herein also may be vnderstood the exploits lately atchiued by the right Honorable the L. Admiral of England with her Ma.ᵗⁱᵉ Nauie and some former seruices don by that worthy Knight Sᵗ FRA: DRAKE,

HONI SOIT QVI MAL Y PENSE

Left, from top: Robert Dudley, Earl of Leicester, Elizabeth's court favourite but a military commander of doubtful competence.

The Queen's spymaster, Sir Francis Walsingham, obtained the evidence that ensured the execution of Mary, Queen of Scots.

Elizabeth's Lord Treasurer, William Cecil, Lord Burghley, whose parsimony matched her own.

Below: A pamphlet rebutting the false claims of the Armada's success that Don Bernardino de Mendoza was disseminating.

A PACKE

OF SPANISH LYES,

SENT ABROAD
THE WORLD: FIRST
printed in SPAINE in the Spanish tongue, and translated out
of the *Originall.*

Now ripped vp, vnfolded, and by iust exa
nation condemned, *as conteyning false, corrupt
and detestable wares, worthy to be dam-
ned and burned.*

PSAL. 5. VERS. 6.
Thou shalt destroy them that speake lyes, the Lord wil
abhorre the bloodie and deceitfull man.

Imprinted at London by the Deputie
of Christopher Barker, Printer to the
Queenes most excellent Maiestie.

Mother. She then drew him aside and they carried on a whispered conversation, out of earshot of all witnesses, though the same observer noted that Catherine looked frightened and de Guise embarrassed.

Dr. Cavriana, Catherine de' Medici's physician and an informant of the Grand Duke of Tuscany, told his master that Mendoza was the man "who arranged the dance and leads it," but this move by de Guise had not been choreographed and Mendoza's first intimation of the unexpected turn of events came when a roar from outside his house greeted the sight of the Queen's sedan chair being carried through the streets towards the Louvre Palace, with de Guise walking alongside it, bowing to the crowds as they strewed his path with flowers. When the Pope was informed, his reaction was rather different: "The fool! He is going to his death." When Alfonse d'Ornano, Captain of the Corsicans, was told that de Guise had arrived in Paris, he told the King, "Just give the order, Sire, and I will lay his head at your feet." Henri balked at that extreme action and the intervention of Catherine de' Medici saved de Guise from imprisonment and probably death. It was to be the last time that she was able to bend her son to her will.[6]

There were now up to 2,000 League soldiers in Paris, and they no longer took much care to conceal themselves. Arms were also handed to the mob, many wearing white crosses on their hats in an echo of the St. Bartholomew's Day Massacre, but before first light on Thursday 12 May, the King's Swiss and French Guards marched into Paris ahead of several columns of horse, flying their colours, pikes at the ready and muskets loaded. They stationed themselves at strongpoints throughout the city, but the King had issued them with strict orders not to injure any citizen of Paris, and as the realization dawned on the mob that the Guards would not resist them, they built barricades in every street. The soldiers had no food and no water and increasingly anxious messages reached the King, who finally ordered them to make an orderly withdrawal to the Louvre. As they did so, shots were fired in the Place Maubert. Alarm bells began to ring, church towers right across the city picked up the refrain and firing started to echo from every quarter. The Guards breached the first barricades without trouble but then found themselves trapped in the narrow streets under a hail of musket-fire, cobblestones, rocks and tiles from the roofs above them. "They threw down on us great stones and blocks of wood and all manner of furniture . . . and an infinite number of people armed with arquebuses fired on us as if we had been enemies of the King. All this time, very strange monks cried out, inciting the people against us as if we had been Huguenots and desecrators of sacred objects." Most of the Guards threw down their arms and surrendered, praying for mercy and showing crucifixes and rosaries to prove they were good Catholics. Bonfires blazed in the streets all night in celebration of de Guise's triumph and he wrote to one of his commanders, "This victory is so great that it will be remembered for ever."

That evening, Henri sent his mother to ask what terms de Guise wished to impose. The answer was brutal; if the King dismissed his friends and his guards, debarred Henri of Navarre from the succession, named de Guise as his rightful heir and surrendered all power to him and his allies, he would be allowed to continue as King of France, but in name only. De Guise's demands were reinforced by the growing size and menace of the mob surrounding the Louvre, but whether through accident or design, the Porte Neuve had been left unguarded. Henri again sent his mother to de Guise, asking him to control the mob, and then fled with a small group of retainers and advisers. They rode out of Paris, "some without boots, some without spurs," but Henri could not resist one final rhetorical flourish as he abandoned his capital. "Farewell Paris. I have honoured you above any place in my kingdom. I have done more for your wealth and glory than any ten of my predecessors and I have loved you better than ever I loved wife or friend. Now you have repaid my love with treachery, insult and rebellion, but I shall be revenged on you. When next I enter you it shall be through a breach in your walls." By the following day he had reached the safety of Chartres.

When reports of the events in Paris reached Parma, he remarked that "the Duc de Guise has never heard our Italian proverb: 'He who draws his sword against his prince should throw away the scabbard,'" but the news was "rejoiced at" in London, since it now appeared certain that Henri would not find common cause with the Catholic League and might even be tempted into alliance with Elizabeth and Navarre. The Queen at once summoned the French ambassador and promised that she would "place all her forces by sea and land in the struggle and promised him [Henri] mountains and fountains if he would join her." The reply must have disappointed her: Henri "had sufficient forces to punish those who were disobedient to him," and was already in negotiation with the Catholic League in an attempt to settle their differences. On 21 July an agreement was duly signed, though neither of the principals appeared to regard it as more than a holding operation. One of its terms was that Henri would "renounce his alliance and friendship with the Queen of England," but when told the Armada had been forced to put into Corunna by bad weather, Henri remained sufficiently unabashed to remark, "That is a fine story. It was only because they had seen the English fleet and were frightened."[7]

Mendoza had tried to time the "Day of the Barricades" in Paris to coincide with the Armada's approach to the Channel, but although the endless delays had rendered that aim impossible, he remained content with the outcome of his schemes, if scornful of de Guise's failure to eliminate Henri. Whatever fate befell France, most of the Spanish aims had now been achieved. Mendoza's intrigues and Philip's gold had ensured that the Enterprise of England could now proceed without the danger of a French attack on the Armada or the thinly defended Spanish Netherlands. However, in one crucial area Philip's French clients had failed to fulfil their promises to him. Although Le Havre declared for the League, the key ports of north-eastern France—Calais, Dieppe and Boulogne—remained in the control of forces loyal to the King . . . at least until they saw which way the political wind was likely to blow. As a result, the Armada still lacked a Channel port where it could resupply or take refuge. If Medina-Sidonia hoped to find one, he would have to fight for it.

The final figure in Philip's Europe-wide strategy, the Duke of Parma, Captain General of the Army of Flanders, had by far the most important role. The seventeen provinces of The Netherlands had only been brought together as Habsburg dominions by Philip's father, Charles V, and the Dutch had grown accustomed to a measure of religious freedom. When Philip made attempts to extirpate Protestant heresies from the provinces, he inflamed the existing discontent over rising food prices and failing harvests into a full-scale rebellion under the leadership of William of Nassau, Prince of Orange. Philip's response was to crush the revolt with overwhelming force. In August 1567 the Duke of Alba led 8,000 hardened Spanish troops, augmented by over 30,000 levies from Italy, Germany and Flanders, into The Netherlands and his "Council of Blood" brutally suppressed the fledgling revolt, slaughtering and burning heretics in every town and driving the remnants of the rebels into exile.

Those events presaged a sea change in English foreign policy. Until that point, England's principal continental antagonist had always been France and the main aim of Elizabeth's foreign policy was to prevent France and Scotland from combining to depose her and place Mary, Queen of Scots, on the throne. Once Alba began his reign of terror, Spain and its imperial designs became England's dominant preoccupation. The presence of this huge standing army within striking distance of England, France and the Protestant princedoms of Germany was a threat that none of them could ignore, and both Elizabeth of England and Henri III of France began to give covert assistance to the Dutch. Elizabeth's support was reluctant, but if she had refused the Dutch they would have been forced further into the arms of France, confronting England with the equally distasteful prospect of a French-controlled seaboard stretching from Biarritz to the Baltic.

After Alba had crushed the rebellion, Elizabeth allowed the "Sea Beggars," the exiled Dutch navy, to operate out of Dover and gave her tacit approval for attacks on Spanish shipping. The Sea Beggars were mostly former fishermen from the Dutch provinces of Friesland, Holland and Zeeland, and had been given their sobriquet because of their lawless behaviour and the shabby appearance of their ships, but they were fine seamen and brave and resourceful fighters. Elizabeth eventually expelled them in March 1572 as part of an attempted rapprochement with Spain, but the Sea Beggars at once seized the ports of Brill and Flushing, depriving Spain of its only deep-water anchorage on the Dutch coast and inspiring a renewed rebellion in Holland and Zeeland, "the great bog of Europe . . . an universal quagmire. Indeed, it is the buttock of the world: full of veins and blood, but no bones in it." Within this coastal warren of meres, salt marshes, shallows and shoals, the Dutch fleet of shallow-draught flyboats operated with impunity, threatening and blockading ports in Spanish-held territory and defeating any seaborne force sent against them. A Spanish fleet ran aground there in 1572, and when another was repulsed two years later, Philip abandoned attempts to defeat the rebels by sea and poured fresh resources into a land campaign.

The Duke of Alba's Army of Flanders, now swollen to 60,000 men, captured and sacked several Dutch-held cities, treating the occupants with terrible ferocity and bringing the revolt to the brink of collapse, but the cost of maintaining the army and fighting the war crippled Spain. In September 1575 the Spanish Treasury declared itself bankrupt and Philip's continuing difficulties in finding the money to pay his armies led to mutinies by the Army of Flanders in July and November 1576. Unlike Alba's earlier massacres, the resultant sacking and pillaging of Aalst and the "Spanish Fury" at Antwerp—an orgy of killing, raping and looting in which 8,000 were slaughtered by soldiers "executing all such as they overtook . . . great numbers of young children, but many more women" while their "lackeys and pages followed with firebrands and wild fire, setting the houses on fire"—were not deliberate acts of policy, but the result of the bloodlust of his mutinous soldiers. They dealt a grievous blow to their King as well as to their Dutch victims, for much of Antwerp was left in ruins, slashing Philip's tax revenues, and the city never recovered its former importance as a mercantile centre.

William of Orange became de facto leader of the entire Netherlands, but his demands for recognition, freedom of worship for his people and a right of veto over the appointment of Crown officials were more than Philip could stomach, and he at once ordered a campaign of reconquest under a new commander, his illegitimate half-brother, Don Juan of Austria. He had commanded the Spanish fleet at the battle of Lepanto, which had been fought by galleys and decided by vicious hand-to-hand fighting after he ordered his troops to hold their fire "until near enough to be splashed with the blood of an enemy." Don Juan believed that the solution to the Dutch problem lay elsewhere: "Everyone believes that the only remedy for the disorders of The Netherlands is that England should be ruled by someone devoted to Your Majesty. If the contrary case prevails, it will mean the ruin of these countries and their loss to your crown." Don Juan proposed a lightning raid across the Channel to depose Elizabeth in favour of Mary, Queen of Scots, and restore England to the old faith. His price for performing this service was to be the hand of Mary in marriage and a share of the throne. Philip originally gave a cautious blessing to the idea, but Don Juan fell out of favour and died in 1578 with his ambitions unfulfilled, and the King then gave command of his forces in Flanders to his illegitimate nephew, Alexander Farnese, Prince (later Duke) of Parma, another hero of Lepanto. As a boy Parma had visited England and become one of the many European princes touted as a possible future husband for Elizabeth; now he was to play a key role in the attempt to bring about her downfall.[8]

Parma was born in August 1545, one of twin sons—his brother died at birth—to Ottavio Farnese, Duke of Parma, and Margaret, the illegitimate daughter of Emperor Charles V. He was a power in his own right, maintaining a Court of 1,500, but for all the wealth he would inherit from his duchy and his blood connections to the royal houses of Catholic Europe, Alexander Farnese bore the stigma of his inherited illegitimacy throughout his life, and it undoubtedly shaped his chosen career. Illegitimate siblings and close relatives were always a danger to monarchs, a focus for the intrigues of disaffected factions at Court. They often fell prey to the knife or the poisoner's art, as the King or his advisers sought to secure his position, and one of the few safe ways in which they could channel their personal ambitions was through a military career far from Court intrigues. Both Philip's half-brother, Don Juan of Austria, and his nephew, Parma, were to choose that route and achieve renown throughout the known world.

After Philip was crowned King of Spain, he summoned Margaret of Parma and her eleven-year-old son to his Court, and when Philip returned to England to persuade Mary Tudor to commit the English army to his war on France, Parma and his mother went with him. Even at this tender age, Alexander's grasp of realpolitik was already apparent; after talking with him, Cardinal Pole remarked that the boy should study more religion and morals and less Julius Caesar. When the old Emperor died in 1558, Philip installed Margaret of Parma as Regent of The Netherlands, and had her son brought to Madrid to serve as guarantor of the continuing loyalty of his parents. At Court, in the company of Don Juan—a year younger, despite being his uncle—Farnese devoted himself to horsemanship and martial arts. He was a natural athlete, a brilliant swordsman and an eager and adept student of the theory and practice of warfare, but he was vain and often arrogant and his demands for the full respect and deference due to a prince of the royal blood led to friction. Philip dispatched him to Parma in 1566, where he adopted the style and outward trappings befitting a man who on the death of his father would be the absolute ruler of a rich and powerful duchy, albeit one severely constrained by the presence of a Spanish garrison. Parma continued to improve his warlike skills, by day seeking out every captain and soldier who could add to his theoretical knowledge, and by night venturing with a hand-picked group of companions into the meanest streets of his capital to test their fists and swords against any thieves and cut-throats who crossed their path.

In 1570, at the age of twenty-four, came his moment of destiny. The forces of Spain and the Vatican came to the aid of Venice in a Christian alliance against the Turks, under the overall command of Don Juan. After desperate appeals to Philip, Parma was allowed to leave his duchy and join Don Juan. The fiery and impetuous commander so fell out with his allies that he threatened to use his Spanish troops against the Venetians rather than the Turks, but Parma intervened to calm the dispute, summoned the Council of War that launched an immediate assault on the Turks and was credited by many with prompting Don Juan to his decisive intervention in the battle. The victory at Lepanto, the greatest sea-battle that had ever been seen, cemented the military reputation of Don Juan, Parma and the naval commander Santa Cruz, but it also made Parma an even greater potential threat to Philip's imperial ambitions.

After the death of Sebastian of Portugal in 1578, anti-Spanish factions in Lisbon were desperate to find a means of preventing Philip from adding yet another realm to his dominions, and Parma's son by his marriage to Princess Maria of Portugal, daughter of Prince Dom Duarte, arguably had a stronger claim to the Portuguese throne. The Dutch rebellion was also growing in strength and Mary, Queen of Scots, imprisoned in England, was still plotting to seize Elizabeth's throne. Parma's royal blood and military genius would have made him invaluable to any of them as a military commander, a regent, a king-consort or even a king, and while Don Juan replaced the Duke of Alba in The Netherlands, charged with quelling the Dutch, Philip ordered Parma back to his duchy. There he stayed for two years, while Don Juan, hampered by lack of funds and his own abrasive nature, saw the rebellion in The Netherlands rage out of control. Summoned at last in the depths of winter, Parma and three companions rode out of Parma in the dead of night, leaving his wife and his two sons behind. It was the last time he would ever see them, for Philip never permitted him to return during the remaining fifteen years of his life. He and his men rode through the snowbound Alps and north to Flanders at breakneck speed, arriving after twelve continuous days in the saddle. Within days, he wrote to Philip that no compromise was possible with William of Orange and the Estates-General. The only solution was to crush those in rebellion against their God and King.

Parma chose his first battles with care—a small cavalry action in which the Dutch were routed and then a siege of the small town of Sichem. Sieges sometimes ended with the defenders surrendering and marching out with "honours of war"—taking their weapons and horses with them—but a victorious attacker could enforce a surrender "at mercy," leaving him free to decide their fate; a number equal to his own casualties might be killed, or the entire garrison might be slaughtered. Parma surrounded the castle and reduced its walls but, seeking to make an example that would send a message throughout The Netherlands, he refused to accept its surrender and after overrunning the defences he ordered the commander hanged from the highest tower of the castle. The man wrestled free of his guards and threw himself off the battlements to escape his fate, but the fall failed to kill him and Parma had his broken body dragged up the tower a second time and hanged. All the other officers and men were then hung by their feet from every window and tree, or marched through the castle hall between lines of Spanish soldiers and clubbed to death.

Parma's success sealed his own reputation and his uncle's fate. Don Juan was recalled to Madrid—he died en route, before Philip could exact punishment for his failures—while Parma was appointed as supreme commander in his place. The Spanish Army of Flanders that Parma had inherited had always been feared for its brutality, but it was poorly paid, ill-equipped and in low morale. Having persuaded Philip to increase his funding, Parma raised his soldiers' wages and improved their equipment, while their morale was greatly restored by the looting and rapine that followed the victory at Sichem. He now began to weld them into a cohesive and fearsomely effective force. The core of hard-bitten Spanish fighting troops was augmented by German, Walloon and Italian mercenaries, and they became a professional army, paid and fully trained, and provided with medical care, welfare payments and even marriage allowances. The English career soldier Sir Roger Williams, who fought against them in The Netherlands for many years, had no doubt about their capabilities. "No army that ever I saw passes that of the Duke of Parma for discipline and good order." It contained few "raw recruits. They were powerful men, well armed and of martial aspect, highly trained and always ready . . . to fight," and there was only unending, implacable slaughter and destruction for those who continued to oppose them.

A portrait of the era shows Parma arrayed with a ruff of the finest jewel-encrusted lace and a heavy gold chain around his neck. He stares out in three-quarter profile, emphasizing his high forehead and aquiline nose. His mouth is hidden beneath his waxed moustache, and he could be any Court dandy of his age but for the piercing look in his eye and the glint of the steel breastplate beneath his finery. This was a man born to martial action, a dedicated student of military strategy and tactics, an able administrator and a veteran of many campaigns, and he brought a cold and formidable intellect to bear on the task that Philip had set him. He could act with ruthless speed when necessary, but he also had the patience to play a long game if required. Before any fighting even began, Parma's engineers had often done the crucial ground-work, building new canals, bridging dykes, constructing earthworks and mining defences—digging tunnels under fortifications that would then collapse or be demolished by explosions. Inscrutable as the sphinx, he also deployed other weapons alongside his military power: diplomacy, persuasion, espionage, bribery, treachery and murder.

Three southern provinces were won back without a fight, and "Spain's golden bullets made a greater breach in the heart of the trai-tor" than their guns did in some city walls, but where bribery failed he would use assassination, a semi-legitimate arm of state policy and widely practised. In 1582 the first attempt was made on the life of the Dutch leader, William the Silent. The assassin's gun was fired so close to his head that the powder-flash set fire to his hair, but somehow, though severely wounded, he survived. Four further unsuccessful attempts on his life were made the following year, but on 10 July 1584 another hired killer, Balthasar Gerard, at last shot dead the Dutch leader on the stairs of his house in Delft. In revenge, Gerard was captured by the Dutch, horribly tortured and executed. Philip had offered a reward of 25,000 crowns for William's death, and he showed his gratitude for the actions of their dead son by granting Gerard's parents lands and titles in Franche-Comté.[9]

Parma next led another savage onslaught on Maastricht, leaving 1,700 women and thousands of men butchered in the streets when the city fell, and when the town of Lierre was betrayed to him by its Scottish Catholic commander, Colonel William Semple, it was then reduced to rubble. Ypres prepared itself for a siege by sending out of its gates all those inhabitants too young, old or infirm to fight. Parma refused to allow them through his lines and, trapped without shelter, food or water, they remained encamped in no-man's-land, dying by hundreds, until the final storming of the town, when those who had survived were slaughtered like their menfolk.

The relentless tide of Spanish successes caused consternation in England. The Earl of Leicester had long urged Elizabeth to allow him to lead an English expeditionary force to The Netherlands, and she was briefly persuaded, but at the brink she hesitated and changed her mind, reverting to discreet financial support and offers of mediation between the Dutch and Philip. In default of stronger action from the Crown, Thomas Morgan, Sir Humphrey Gilbert and Sir John Norris led forces of several thousand volunteers to the aid of the rebels. The Dutch had offered Elizabeth the hereditary sovereignty of the United Provinces in 1576 and been rebuffed since she was reluctant both to add to her financial burdens and to further antagonize Philip. Casting around for support, they now turned instead to France. In 1581 they declared Philip to have been deposed and the Dutch leader William of Orange offered sovereignty and the title "Defender of the Liberties of the Low Countries" to the heir to the French throne, François, Duc d'Anjou. Backed by 10,000 French troops and subsidized by Elizabeth, he took up residence in his new domain, but he proved to be both arrogant and incompetent, and rapidly alienated his Dutch and English allies alike. The last of his support evaporated when his troops attempted to take control by force of Antwerp and several other towns and cities—the "French Fury" as it was christened by the Dutch in an echo of the Spanish Fury of Alba's troops—and he left the country in disgrace in June 1583. He died the following year.

Parma wasted no time in exploiting the dissension in the enemy camp. Dunkirk, Nieuport and Ostend all fell to his troops and, as the relentless advances continued, he began to temper the worst of his troops' brutal excesses, winning fresh victories as much by the promise of peace and security after long years of war as by his military power. Bruges was allowed to surrender, Ghent followed in 1584 and Brussels, the city of the Emperor Charles V's court, fell in spring 1585, by which time Parma's troops had already encircled the great port of Antwerp, the richest city in northern Europe. Parma had a massive timber bridge half a mile in length constructed to block the Scheldt river, cutting off supplies of food and the trade on which the city's wealth depended, and after a bloody year-long siege the starving city surrendered on 17 August 1585.

The conquest of the rest of The Netherlands now seemed as inevitable as time itself, but the murder of William the Silent had already thoroughly alarmed Elizabeth—the assassination of a Protestant ruler by a hired killer, paid in Spanish gold, could not have failed to concentrate her mind—and the fall of Antwerp, threatening a further loss of allies and markets for English goods now forced her always hesitant hand. Even before the city's fall, on 7 July 1585, English pro-interventionists had given Elizabeth a formal statement of the case for action to secure "protection from Spain," outlining the weakness and vulnerability of England, the unrelenting hostility of the Spanish Crown and the papacy in Rome, and the prospect that Spain and France under the leadership of de Guise might unite in a Catholic crusade throughout Europe. To counter this, Elizabeth was urged to form a citizens' militia modelled on that of ancient Rome, to improve the navy and to create a Protestant coalition to oppose Spain.

In June of that year the Dutch had again offered Elizabeth sovereignty over the United Provinces, but once more she had turned it down; now she was at last persuaded to make a direct intervention in the conflict in The Netherlands, believing that if the Dutch were beaten, Philip would at once launch an attack on England. On 10 August 1585, with Antwerp already doomed, she signed a treaty at Nonsuch Palace that was as good as a declaration of war on Spain. It committed an army of 4,000 foot and 400 horse (later increased to 5,000 foot and 1,000 cavalry) to the defence of the Dutch United Provinces, together with £126,000 a year for their support. The "cautionary towns" of Flushing and Brill, the two deep-water ports that could serve as embarkation points for a Spanish invasion force, were to be garrisoned by a further 700 troops, but purely as security for England's interests rather than as conquest by stealth. She was also to appoint a nobleman, Robert Dudley, Earl of Leicester, to command the forces and, with two others, serve as an adviser to the Dutch States General. His military qualifications were obscure. He had not seen action since serving in Mary Tudor's army in France thirty years previously, and owed his command entirely to his position as one of Elizabeth's oldest Court favourites and his enthusiastic championing of the Dutch cause.

A veteran of the English volunteers in The Netherlands, Sir John "Black Jack" Norris, led the first 2,000 infantry ashore at Middelburg at the end of August 1585, but Leicester did not arrive at Flushing to take command until 10 December. By the end of that year, some 8,000 Englishmen were stationed in The Netherlands, but yet again the Queen had changed her mind and, having committed her troops, she ordered them to restrict themselves to defensive operations. Norris was even rebuked for attacking Parma's forces and Leicester was ordered to avoid "the hazard of a battle" but to embargo Dutch trade with Spain—one of the ways the Dutch funded their own resistance was to continue to trade with their Spanish oppressors—suggesting that her bolstering of them was only to encourage them to seek a settlement with Spain. But whether or not their sovereign wished it, her forces were inevitably drawn into confrontations with the Army of Flanders. The English troops ranged against Parma's battle-hardened veterans were poorly armed and ill-trained, and many were barely clad. One captain remarked that there were "not three whole shirts" in his company and another contingent was armed only with bows and arrows. Yet though the Dutch were sometimes scathing about their worth, the English forces showed their value in that summer's campaign. The infantry resisted a Spanish advance at the Meuse and the English heavy cavalry repeatedly broke through enemy lines at Warnsfeld. For the first time in years, Parma made few gains during the fighting season. He had still reconquered only ten of the seventeen rebel provinces during a war that had laid waste the whole country.

If Leicester's troops had fought bravely enough, their commander, "greatly hated by everyone," had showed himself to be as incompetent as Anjou before him. In January 1586, without consulting Elizabeth, he accepted a Dutch offer of "the absolute government of the whole provinces of Holland, Zeeland, Friesland and Utrecht," and assumed the title of Governor-General that had been in the gift of Philip of Spain. It was a flagrant provocation of the Catholic King, and an attempt to secure de facto recognition of Elizabeth as the Dutch sovereign, when she herself had refused to consider the idea. She sent a coruscating letter to him to signal her displeasure at a move "sufficient to make me infamous to all princes . . . We could never have imagined, had we not seen it fall out in experience, that a man raised up by our-selves and extraordinarily favoured by us above any subject of this land, would have in so contemptible a sort, broken a commandment." She forced him to make a public retraction and went on to threaten him that the hand that had raised him could also "beat him to the dust."[10]

Leicester also grossly overspent the budget she had allocated to him, yet left his troops unpaid and ill-equipped. He banished to En-gland Sir John Norris, his most effective subordinate, quarrelled with Count Hohenlo, a bold commander with a fearsome temper, alienated Maurice of Nassau, and provoked discord and unrest among his own troops and his allies. The furious Dutch sent emissaries to Elizabeth to lambast Leicester's folly and cowardice, and complain that, far from aiding them, he had succeeded only in provoking rival factions to the point of near civil war. "He had more of Mercury than he had of Mars . . . his device might have been without prejudice to the great Caesar, *veni, vidi, redivi*." They sought further help from Elizabeth, but instead were harangued by her; she might criticize her favourite, but no others would be allowed such liberties. "She swears by the living God it is terrible and she does not believe such ungrateful people as they live upon the earth; if she had accepted for herself the title they had offered her, by God they would have found she would not put up with such treatment." She told them that "it was for the Queen to advise them, and not for them to advise the Queen," and they were summarily dis-missed with a scornful promise that whatever peace she agreed with Spain would include them. The Dutch declared themselves perfectly willing to fight on alone, "requesting the Queen to surrender the fortresses she held as they themselves will defend them," but their words must have rung hollow even in their own ears, for their one strength was at sea, where the fleet under William of Orange's illegiti-mate son, Justin of Nassau, maintained its blockade of the coast of Flanders and the western Scheldt.[11]

Had they known the lengths to which Elizabeth was willing to go to achieve peace, they would have been even more alarmed. Elizabeth continued to show an unwarranted faith in the possibility of peace, but if it came to open war, she could not realistically expect to inflict a total defeat on Spain, and nor would she have wished to do so. England's long-term strategic aim was to use the two European great powers, France and Spain, as checks and counter-weights to each other. French weakness in the 1570s and 1580s had invited Spanish domination of the continent, but a weak Spain was equally and possibly even more dan-gerous to England, for France had long coveted Flanders and the French history of alliances with Scotland would then threaten England with complete encirclement. Elizabeth never stated her war aims and perhaps never formulated them even to herself, but they may have been as modest as a promise of non-interference by direct or indirect means in England, and a fig leaf of religious tolerance and freedom of trade in The Netherlands.

She would have accepted, even welcomed, a return to Spanish rule of the rebellious Dutch provinces, and her peace commissioners negotiating with Parma were told that Spain only had to concede religious toleration for the Dutch for two years after regaining control. After that, it would be an internal matter for a government that would, of course, be appointed by Philip. Whether the Dutch would accept such modest gains from their long years of suffering and struggle did not concern her; the terms would be imposed on them and if they refused to accept them, she could abandon them to fight alone and face certain defeat. However, even such modest terms were never likely to be acceptable to Philip; the father of the Inquisition would tolerate no heresy in his own kingdom nor in any of the possessions he ruled. Those who opposed him, in The Netherlands and in England, would submit to his will or be crushed.

Although she had dismissed the Dutch complaints about him, Elizabeth remained privately furious with Leicester. Disgraced, he submitted his resignation in September 1586 and returned to England in early December to placate the Queen and restore his fortunes, accompanied by some near-mutinous troops "so poor and dissatisfied that the Queen, out of fear they might raise sedition, has ordered that no more than twenty of them may enter any village." His estrangement from Elizabeth did not last long and he had soon reclaimed his former power and influence at Court. However, through arrogance or stupidity he had left two Catholic captains, Sir William Stanley and Rowland York, in command of vital links in the chain of Dutch defences: the newly captured city of Deventer and the Sconce of Zutphen, a fortress constructed to threaten the Spanish garrison in the town.

Leicester had personally knighted Stanley during the campaign, and replied to the violent protests of the Dutch by saying that he would stake his life on the loyalty of his officers. The value of that pledge was demonstrated on 28 January 1587, when Stanley opened the gates of Deventer and defected to the Spaniards with 1,200 soldiers under his command, and York surrendered the Sconce of Zutphen. Both men had succumbed to Spanish bribes, though Stanley claimed to have acted only for the sake of his religion and his conscience: "Before I served the Devil, now I serve God." Parma wrote in triumph to Philip that Zutphen and Deventer "are thus Your Majesty's at a trifling cost, but what is better, the effect of this treason must be to sow great suspicion between the English and the rebels so that hereafter no-one will know whom to trust." When York died the following year, the Lord High Admiral Charles Howard commented, "Rowland York is dead of the smallpox. I would Stanley were with him."

Parma was willing enough to contemplate the invasion of England but the notion that he had once entertained, of a sudden attack across the Channel by troops carried in barges and operating under cover of darkness, was no longer remotely feasible. There was no possibility of surprise, and the Dutch were masters of the inshore coastal waters and the English of the Channel. Only with the protection of the Armada could a safe crossing be made, and unless Flushing or Brill could be conquered there was no deep-water port in which it could shelter. Many in Spain urged Philip to conquer England as the means of retaking The Netherlands, but Parma was of the opposite view. His preference was still to settle with England, for purely strategic reasons. With English financial and military support for the rebels removed and Spanish resources and troops concentrated on The Netherlands, he was confident that he could subjugate the Dutch rebels, using only a modest proportion of the money and materiel that Philip was raising for the Enterprise of England. With the deep-water ports of The Netherlands and the Dutch fleet added to the already formidable Armada, the conquest of England would be a formality.

After the fall of Deventer and Zutphen, he might have been expected to press on to the east, taking Utrecht and threatening Holland, but, realizing that his sovereign was implacably set on the Enterprise of England, Parma issued orders in March 1587 redirecting his troops away from the north-east and towards the western ports of Ostend and Sluys (Sluis)—ample proof, if any was needed, that England and not the Dutch rebels was now to be the principal target. At the same time he carried on the peace negotiations with Elizabeth, but in case he still had any lingering doubts he was given unequivocal orders by Philip: no peace was to be made on any terms whatsoever. The negotiations would continue to keep Elizabeth off her guard, but they had no other purpose. "By the common judgement of the world the same was done but to abuse Her Majesty and to win time whilst his preparations might be made complete." Parma followed his instructions to the letter. After the arrival in Ostend of the five commissioners sent by Elizabeth, weeks were spent in a morass of discussions about alternative venues for the peace conference, what items should be on the agenda and what powers they and Parma's representatives would have to treat and reach conclusions. The commissioners were still talking, lured ever onwards by hints that if just one or two more points could be resolved the Spaniards would be ready to conclude an agreement, when the Armada entered the Channel.[12]

Moving with characteristic speed and decisiveness, Parma had concentrated an army of almost 20,000 men in Bruges by early June 1587, in preparation for an attack on either Ostend or Sluys. Ostend was partly garrisoned by English troops, Sluys defended by its own militia, strengthened by Walloons and Flemings exiled from their own cities. Both garrisons had made sniping, harassing raids against the Spanish troops around Bruges but neither appeared strong enough to withstand a siege. Seeing the danger, their commanders appealed for help and reinforcements to the Dutch States General and to England. Lord Buckhurst, the Queen's representative at the Hague, sent reinforcements and provisions to the garrison at Ostend and Sir William Russell, Governor of Flushing, sent enough supplies to Sluys, he believed, to enable the town to hold out under a siege of two or three months' duration. Parma had other ideas. He first staged a diversionary attack on Ostend and then surrounded Sluys. It was not itself a deep-water port, but its conquest would open the way to Flushing, providing Parma with the anchorage that he required. Russell responded by sending Sir Roger Williams and four companies of English foot soldiers to reinforce the garrison. They managed to fight their way through the Spanish lines but Parma then blockaded Sluys from the sea and brought up his siege guns to pound the defences.

Elizabeth was apprised of the threat to Sluys and, ignoring his previous failures, she ordered Leicester to return to The Netherlands to relieve the town. On 2 July Leicester and 5,000 troops were convoyed to Flushing. Lookouts on the walls of Sluys could see the banners and pennants of the fleet and greeted the sight with a storm of fire at the Spanish forces surrounding them, confident that the raising of the siege would not now be long delayed. Their confidence was wholly misplaced. Leicester's first attempt to relieve the town came when he landed near Ostend at the head of 4,000 infantry and 400 cavalry, but with an incompetence or cowardice that surprised no one on the Dutch side, when he saw the Spanish forces massing to repel the attack, he lost his nerve, re-embarked his troops and sailed back down the coast. Two weeks of such futile sorties, manoeuvres and landings left the English forces no nearer to reaching the embattled and desperate defenders of Sluys. One of them, Sir Roger Williams, had spent a large part of the previous fifteen years fighting in The Netherlands. He was a professional soldier, a Welshman who wore on his morion the tallest plume of feathers in either army, "so that his friends and his foes might know where he was." He now wrote to the Queen, "We doubt not Your Majesty will succour us for our honest mind and plain dealing towards your Royal Person and dear country . . . Our ground is great and our men not so many, but we must trust in God and our valour to defend it . . . We mean to let out every acre for a thousand of their lives besides our own."

As the Spaniards resumed the attack, the defenders once more showed their valour. "Since I followed the wars I never saw valianter captains or willinger soldiers . . . at eleven o'clock the enemy entered the ditch of our fort with trenches upon wheels [carts covered in shields, proof against musket-fire]. We sallied out, recovered their trenches . . . repulsed them into their artillery, kept the ditch until yesternight and will recover it with God's help this night, or else pay dearly for it." That night Williams wrote to Leicester urging him to enter the Channel of Sluys. "If your mariners will do a quarter of their duty . . . the Spanish cannot stop them. Before you enter the Channel, we will come out with our boats and fight with the enemy and show there is no such great danger. You may assure the world that here are [no traitors] but valiant captains and valiant soldiers such as had rather been buried in the place than be disgraced in any point that belongs to men of war."

Ten days passed without any sign of an attack and Williams again wrote to Leicester, in terms that came close to accusing him of cowardice. "You must consider that no wars may be made without danger. What you mean to do we beseech you to do with expedition." After another ten days, the last three of which saw the rescuing fleet motionless off Sluys, he wrote a final dispatch to Leicester. "We are slain and spoiled ten captains, six lieutenants, eighteen sergeants, of soldiers in all almost six hundred. Never were brave soldiers thus lost for want of easy succours . . . We have not now powder for three skirmishes. For myself I wish myself dead for [leading] so many brave men to their ruin. The old saying is true: wit is never good until it be dearly bought but I and the rest of my companions are like to pay too dear for it." The town held out for another eight days, losing another two hundred dead in the process. During that time Leicester's men at last attempted to force the channel, using the spring tide and a following north-westerly wind, while the Dutch launched a fireship to burn the floating bridge across the river, but Parma's forces held their nerve. Sections of the floating bridge were swung apart, allowing the fireship to pass through and burn out harmlessly on the shore, and the gap was closed again before Leicester's ships, following too far behind, could force the gap. As the tide slackened, Leicester once more withdrew.

Following that failure, the Commandant of Sluys, Groenenbelt, asked Parma for a parley and negotiated the terms of his surrender. In order to conclude the siege before fresh reinforcements could be sent from England, Parma granted unusually lenient terms, and on 5 August the remnants of the garrison—700 out of the original 1,700 men, most of them maimed or wounded—were allowed to march out with their arms and baggage and the full honours of war. Parma offered Sir Roger Williams, wounded in the arm, the chance of a command where he assured him he would never have to fight against his co-religionists or his fellow countrymen, but the fiercely Protestant Williams answered that if he ever served anyone other than his Queen it would be in the army of Henri of Navarre. Returning to England so poor that he could not even afford a horse, he said he was so "weary of the wars, if I can devise how to live, I will quit and follow my Lady Walsingham's counsel to marry a merchant's widow."

Leicester was recalled in November, almost his last act in The Netherlands having been to submit a claim for £24,000 in undocumented expenses. He and his thousands of troops had achieved virtually nothing save to empty Elizabeth's treasury of money that would have been far better spent in strengthening and supplying her fleet. And Parma had taken Sluys, albeit at a terrible cost of dead and wounded. "Never since I came to The Netherlands has any operation given me such trouble and anxiety as this siege of Sluys." The next obvious step for Parma was to take the town of Bergen-op-Zoom, cutting off the deep-water port of Flushing on the poorly defended island of Walcheren. If he could expel the English garrison, the Armada would have a safe haven in which to embark the invasion force. But Philip was too impatient to wait: the capture of Flushing would have to follow, not precede the Enterprise of England. At Philip's orders, Parma was now to devote all his energies to preparing for the invasion, and operations in Flanders were to be restricted to feints to distract the English and Dutch, while he mustered "the bulk of the army intended for the main business [the invasion of England] on the pretence of attacking Ostend."[13]

Parma's engineers at once began widening and deepening the existing drainage canals to enable barges to reach Dunkirk without facing the Dutch inshore fleet. If he still lacked a deep-water port in which the Armada could take refuge, he at least now had a base from where the invasion force could embark in its barges. However, the prevarications and delays in launching the Armada soon began to have a negative effect. A strong contingent of reinforcements arrived from Italy in September 1587, Parma's armouries were full of powder and shot, and he had 30,000 troops fit and ready to take the field against the enemy but, ordered to avoid any offensive manoeuvres that might have alarmed the English, he was forced to leave his troops idle in winter quarters. As disease and desertions took their toll, the strength of his great army was steadily depleted. By 21 December "the number of men of all nationalities has fallen so much through death, disease and desertion that one third of those we were to take are gone." The few replacements he now received were ill-trained and in poor physical condition. Raw recruits were normally garrisoned in Milan, Naples or the Spanish enclaves in North Africa while they received basic military training, but with Philip urging ever-greater haste, recruits were now sent straight to the fleet in Lisbon or to Parma in Flanders. A force of Castilians recruited specifically for the invasion of England arrived much depleted by deaths and desertions during the route march along "the Spanish Road."

On 31 January 1588, Parma complained to Philip about "both men and money having been delayed beyond the time your Majesty indicated and particularly the Spanish troops, who are the sinews of the whole business, the numbers moreover being less than those agreed upon. They have arrived after all, so dilapidated and maltreated that they do not look in the least fit for effectual service for some time. The Italians and Germans have dwindled very much in consequence of having marched so quickly in such bad weather; and in order to keep them near the points of embarkation, they are so badly housed that very many are missing." Three weeks later he again wrote to the King. "The munitions are on board, the transport boats are collected at Dunkirk and Sluys and the men are concentrated near the ports ready for embarkation," but the Armada did not appear. By March, "of the 28,000 or 30,000 I hoped to ship, in truth I cannot find now more than 17,000"—8,000 Germans and Walloons, 4,000 Spaniards, 3,000 Italians, 1,000 English exiles and 1,000 Burgundians. Even with the 6,000 reinforcements from the Armada, he warned that "I shall still have too few troops as the men here are dwindling daily." He levied more Flemings, Walloons and Germans, but the new recruits barely kept pace with the losses to disease and desertion and the situation had improved little, if any, by the time the Armada finally arrived. With heavy sarcasm, Parma berated the endless delays—"Since God has been pleased to defer for so long the sailing of the Armada from Lisbon, we are bound to conclude that it is for His greater glory"—and the lack of secrecy that had led even the common soldiery in The Netherlands to talk of the coming invasion of England as if it was as certain as the march of the seasons. "The enemy have been forewarned and acquainted with our plans and have made all preparations for their defence, so that it is manifest that the enterprise, which at one time was so easy and safe, can only now be carried out with infinitely greater difficulty and at a much larger expenditure of blood and trouble."[14]

Parma warned Philip that, "saving the favour of God, success mainly depends upon expenditure of money," and that unless more was found to pay his forces, "we shall be face to face with a mutiny of the men and irreparable disorders, since the troops are of many nationalities. It may be that God desires to punish us for our sins by some heavy disaster." By early June he was "almost in despair for want of money . . . without money we shall be ruined," after Philip used the 670,000 ducats previously earmarked for Parma to meet the ever-rising costs of the Armada. On 20 July, with the Armada preparing to sail from Corunna, Parma again wrote begging for money. "We are on the eve of the execution of the task and yet at the last moment we may have to break up from sheer necessity . . . I beseech your Majesty not to think that there is any exaggeration in this, for it is simply the naked truth." But the year's revenues had already been spent and Philip had no more money to send him until the treasure fleet arrived, for Sixtus's million ducats still remained out of reach. "His Holiness is firm in his determination not to disburse a crown until the news [of a successful landing] arrives." "Cardinal Carrafa addressed him in terms that would have moved any other heart, but the Pope only shrugged his shoulders, for when it comes to getting money out of him it is like squeezing his life-blood."[15]

Despite his money troubles, Parma had taken steps to secure Spain's flanks in Flanders during the invasion of England. Land campaigns against the Dutch rebels had severed or threatened the river routes by which they launched raids into the interior, and the Meuse and much of the Ijssel valley were now under his control. However, German Protestant troops led by Casimir of the Palatinate offered a potential threat to Parma's supply lines and the province of Brabant in the south of Flanders. The city of Bonn, in the Electorate of Cologne, no more than fifty miles from the frontier of Flanders, had been captured by Casimir's troops the previous winter, and Philip ordered Parma to commit part of his forces to prevent the Catholic Elector of Cologne from being deposed and to protect the Rhine crossings from any Protestant advance. Parma launched a campaign against Neuss (near modern Düsseldorf), dominating the Rhine and controlling access to Cologne a few miles upriver. Neuss was duly taken amid terrible slaughter and the Rhine and Brabant secured. Franche-Comté, the Habsburg territory bordering the Alps in south-east France, was also vulnerable to attack by forces loyal to Henri III, cutting Parma's lifeline from Italy and Spain. Yet more of Philip's gold was expended in paying retainers to a force of German mercenaries who were on standby to fight, if needed, to protect Franche-Comté against a French attack.

Parma had now taken all the steps he could in this vulnerable region. The Dutch rebels' raiding routes had been interdicted, fortifications on the French border had been strengthened, Franche-Comté protected and the northern Rhine secured, and even when the invasion force embarked for England, a garrison of 16,000 soldiers would remain in Flanders, supported by a mobile force of 10,000 foot and 1,000 cavalry, to guard against surprise attacks from any quarter. All he could do now was await the arrival of the Armada.

PART II

The Wall of England

CHAPTER EIGHT

The Army of 20000 Souldiers laid along ẏ Southern Coast of England.

Like Bears Tied to Stakes

Well before the end of 1587, the unprecedented scale of the huge fleet gathering in Lisbon had been impossible to conceal. Spanish disinformation hinted that an attack on England would only be a feint before an assault on the rebellious Dutch, but Englishmen such as Lord Henry Seymour, Admiral of the Narrow Seas, were not fooled. "As by the last year's experience, he [Parma] made show for Ostend, and yet went to Sluys, so likewise now, he would busy our heads sometimes for Scotland, at other times for Ireland, otherwise for Norfolk or Suffolk, the more to blind our eyes by bending our forces those ways."

As fears of the Armada grew, English booksellers found a growing market for titles such as *The Art of Shooting* and *The Most Excellent Method of Curing Wounds*.

Philip's grand stratagem was obvious to every interested observer, and in every capital of Europe there was gossip and conjecture about the Armada and the likely outcome of the impending battle. For all the logistical difficulties and the undoubted power of Elizabeth's fleet, most dispassionate observers could foresee only an English defeat. The relentless tide of Spanish successes across the globe, the brilliance of Parma as a military commander, the power and savagery of the forces he commanded and the huge fleet of ships that Spain had assembled would surely be too much for England's pirate navy and its semi-trained militia, commanded by an incompetent royal favourite. If Parma's armies with their siege train could only be landed in England, they would encounter—or so it was widely believed—no forces capable of obstructing their march on the capital.

Even loyal Englishmen were well aware that Elizabeth's troops "were of no such force to encounter an Army like . . . the Prince of Parma should have landed in England," and it was greatly feared "what the puissance and force of a gross army of trained soldiers can do against a number of raw men, unexperienced." There was no standing army except for the Yeomen of the Guard and a garrison at Berwick, and the only battle-hardened troops Elizabeth possessed were of questionable loyalty. The 4,000 men recalled from the Netherlands campaign to defend the capital included many Catholics, and many of them were of Irish origin. The English garrison of Aalst in The Netherlands had laid down their arms to Parma in return for 45,000 ducats, and the treachery of Sir William Stanley and Rowland York at Deventer and Zutphen was still fresh in English minds. Even the indomitable warrior Sir Roger Williams had fought for Parma for several years during the 1570s.[1]

Mercenaries had been widely used throughout the rest of Europe since the fifteenth century, but while Elizabeth had hired German troops to fight in The Netherlands and France, she had relied for her own defence, at least in part, on the creaking feudal system of summoning the nobles and gentlemen of each county with forces recruited from their retainers and tenants. The English militias had had some training during the 1560s and the scare of the Rising of the North in 1569 had prompted further efforts to create a defence force. In 1573 Elizabeth authorized training for some of the men at least notionally capable of taking arms. These "Trained Bands" were formed out of 182,929 men registered in musters held throughout England in 1575.

In all, 2,835 cavalry and 11,881 foot soldiers received training, weapons and equipment, while a further 62,462 received equipment but no training. All London citizens between the ages of eighteen and sixty were compelled to enrol in the Trained Bands and be ready to defend the Crown and the City, but musters there and elsewhere in the country were often patchily attended, despite payment for attendance and the carousing that often accompanied them. The training was also of questionable value. Sir George Carey in the Isle of Wight complained of "a band of men termed trained, who I find rather so in name than in deed." Efficiency was further impaired by the difficulty of persuading gentlemen to accept orders from those of higher military rank but equal or lesser social standing, and by the tendency of the commanders of greater nobility or status to accumulate the largest forces.

There were not enough weapons. Although English troops had first used cannon at the battle of Crécy in 1346, the great English victories, including Crécy, Agincourt in 1415 and Flodden Field in 1513, had been won primarily with the longbow, and it remained the preferred anti-personnel weapon well into the sixteenth century—the *Mary Rose* was carrying 250 bows and 4,000 armour-piercing arrows when it sank in 1545. Longbows had a pull of around 100 pounds, and archers, selected, nurtured and trained from an early age, developed a stature and upper-body strength far in excess of that of most of their peers. They formed a professional elite, hiring themselves out in bands as guards and garrisons in time of peace, and in combat they could maintain a rate of fire of six arrows a minute at a killing range of upwards of 200 yards.

Firearms such as the arquebus, musket and pistol were introduced in the early sixteenth century, but were treated with great suspicion. They were expensive and forced England to depend on supplies of gunpowder from overseas, rather than the yew and ash trees growing in every parish, and at first it was by no means proven that they were better weapons than longbows. The first experiments of the London Trained Bands with muskets in the reign of Mary Tudor led many to "brake their pieces," while others were wounded or suffered powder burns and the remainder were understandably inaccurate when firing them. "In times past the chief force of England consisted in their longbows. But now we have in manner generally given over that kind of artillery . . . the Frenchmen deriding our new archery . . . turn up their tails and cry 'Shoot English!' and all because our strong shooting is decayed and laid in bed." Reloading muskets and arquebuses was a slow process, causing their rate of fire to remain slower than longbows, and they could not be used in wet weather because damp black powder would not ignite, but they had twice the range, a more lethal impact, and the thunder and flame of their discharge had a powerful psychological effect on the enemy. Musketeers and arquebusiers also required far less training than archers, and their weapons soon became more reliable and accurate and, by adopting a co-ordinated firing sequence like the rolling broadside of a ship, a continuous fire could be maintained.

The longbow remained important during the first half of Elizabeth's reign—football was banned because it distracted her subjects from archery practice, and as late as 1586 any able-bodied man in Somerset who could not produce a bow and four arrows ready for military use was liable to a fine—but it was steadily superseded. The "company of bowmen" that the Earl of Leicester took to The Netherlands in 1585 was the last to be deployed overseas, and levies raised to defend Ireland were ordered to surrender their bows and arrows and were issued with muskets instead. By 1590 Sir Roger Williams was writing, "God forbid we should try our bows with their muskets and calivers [a standardized form of the arquebus] . . . 500 musketeers are more serviceable than 1500 bowmen." The tradition founded at Crécy and Agincourt had ended with the Armada.[2]

However, the acceptance of firearms did not mean that they were universally available, and many militiamen continued to be issued with bows and arrows for want of any other weapons to give them. Out of 1,800 men mustered in Surrey, 300 were armed only with bows. The Kent militia of less than 1,700 men also included almost 600 archers, and only 400 of the 1,000 men sent from the county for the defence of London had any arms at all. Other counties were even worse provided. Cornwall was a poor county and could supply only 1,500 bows and 2,000 bills or halberds to arm its militia. The rest marched with only axes, hayforks or reaping hooks as weapons against Spanish muskets and cannon, and in one area of the county only eight of the 575 men had any weapon other than a reaping hook or a bow. The authorities in Lancashire and Cheshire went so far as to cheat the system by calling their practice musters at different times and lending each other all their weapons and armour, so that both could "pass muster" without buying any more equipment. Devon was particularly vulnerable to attack since Drake's Western Fleet was based at Plymouth, and its militias were reasonably well armed, but as soon as the immediate crisis was past Plymouth recouped some of its expenses by selling its arms again; Sir Francis Drake and Sir John Norris "bought of the town calivers, muskets and pikes from the Island" (of St. Nicholas, now known as Drake's Island). Those militiamen who did have muskets or arquebuses often lacked the "powder, match, lead" to use them, and by a piece of cheese-paring accounting that was bizarre even by Elizabethan standards, troops in combat were charged for the powder they used: the more they fired their weapons, the greater the deductions from their pay.

The gunpowder weapons of the new age called for a matching revolution in logistics. In past times armies had marched to the wars carrying their swords, pikes, bows and arrows and foraging for food along the way, but now carts, heavy horses and oxen were needed to carry the guns, powder, shot and heavy equipment. Inventories were taken of every warlike supply in every county: powder and shot, pigeon cotes for saltpetre, an essential ingredient of gunpowder, cannons, muskets, pikes, swords and armour. The numbers of carts and beasts of burden and the names of blacksmiths and wheelwrights were also recorded, but there were few enough of them. On her royal progresses Elizabeth was often followed by a train of 400 six-horse wagons carrying the beds and furniture needed for herself and her retinue, but they moved at a snail's pace, making no more than ten or fifteen miles a day, and there were few other wheeled vehicles anywhere. Men travelled on foot or on horseback, women and children in horse-litters, and packhorses or packmules were the principal means of carrying goods, save for a few carters' wagons around London. The ability to move troops, guns, equipment and supplies to confront an invader was therefore very limited. The marshal of the Somerset militia complained that his men carried their armour in sacks or piled it in carts, "very hurtful to the armour by bruising or breaking thereof," and when they arrived at their destination there was often such a rush to put on the armour that "little men do put on great or tall men's armour and leave little men's armour unfit for great men to put on." In any event, armour offered no real protection against firearms, though it continued to be worn for psychological reasons.[3]

The equipment that the Trained Bands did possess was also constantly being depleted. Every time levies were raised to join the English forces in The Netherlands, the arsenals of the Trained Bands were raided to equip them, but shortages were caused as much by the venality of the officers and their men as by the poverty and stinginess of the Crown. They took every opportunity to enrich themselves, not only by the traditional false accounting and pocketing of others' pay, but also by selling equipment on the thriving black market. The scarcity was duly noted by Spanish agents. "One of the greatest peers of Spain did solemnly utter in no obscure place that it should be an easy matter in short time to conquer England because it wanted armour [i.e., arms]."

As the militias went through their rudimentary training, hasty repairs were begun to coastal fortifications. Beaches and other potential landing sites in England and Ireland, where the coast of Galway was surveyed in preparation for the construction of earthworks, were embanked and lined with sharpened stakes. Trenches were dug and earth banks thrown up as crude defenceworks—those on the Isle of Wight were eight feet wide and four feet high and were to be manned by musketeers to "give some terror to the enemy on landing." Gun platforms were also constructed, though not all could afford guns to mount on them. The Mayor of Weymouth complained, "to our very great charge we have built a platform for some defence of this town and country, at this instance not furnished with needful ordnance by reason of our poverty," and Sir George Carey, governor of the vital defences of the Isle of Wight, one of the most likely sites for a landing by the Armada, had just four mounted guns, no firing platform and only one day's gunpowder.

There were no guns to spare even though the foundries of the Weald of Kent and Sussex and the Forest of Dean were casting cannon and shot without cease, belching out columns of black smoke day and night and burning charcoal so fast that the once-dense forests around them were "marvellously wasted and decayed; and . . . will in short time be utterly consumed." Every cannon was reportedly taken out of the Tower of London, "even the pieces which were mounted on the White Tower," to equip the fleet or the coastal fortifications, and some were even bought or borrowed from private citizens. Richard Hawkins supplied Plymouth with "four demi-culverins and three sakers" and, after the Armada crisis was over, John Capelin of Southampton reclaimed from "Mr. Mayor and his brethren one piece of brass ordnance, which I lent . . . at such time the Spaniards were upon the coast."[4]

Preparations were made to demolish bridges and flood sections of road, and some of those not recruited into the militia were organized to drive off pack animals, cattle and other livestock, remove carts and waggons that might be used by the Spaniards, and destroy crops "that rather the corn may be burnt and spoiled than left to their use," "so as no victuals remain to them but such as they shall carry on their backs, which will be small." Detailed instructions were issued to each county commander specifying the strongpoints to be held, the bridges to be destroyed, the places where provisions were to be stored and livestock held, and what local landmarks would serve as rendezvous points for retreating English troops.

The old chains of beacons were re-established so that when the Armada was sighted, the news could be passed along the coast and far inland. The Romans had used line-of-sight signalling to communicate between their military headquarters at York and their forts on Hadrian's Wall, and beacons had long been constructed on the same vantage points to warn of the approach of border raiders from Scotland. A chain of thirty-one beacons had been used to protect the Isle of Wight since 1324, and Henry VIII's men had lit beacon fires to summon loyal troops to assist the crushing of the Pilgrimage of Grace in 1536. The same network of beacons—Devon alone had fifty—was now brought back into use once more. Braziers were erected on every prominent hill and crag, from Carn Brae within sight of Penzance to Berwick on the Scottish border, and each was supplied with stockpiles of brushwood, pitch, flint and match to light them, and paid watchers to man them. While men stalked the sea cliffs of Cornwall, seeking the first sight of the Armada, other watchers stood on Beachy Head, Dungeness, the chalk cliffs of Dover, the South and North Forelands and the wooded hills above the Medway, scanning the horizon for any sign that might herald an invasion fleet from Flanders. The Thames approaches were patrolled by coast watchers on land and by watermen threading their boats through the mudbanks and low grassy islands flanking the shores. The French ambassador reported that "no foreign vessel can show itself without the whole country being roused."[5]

As the threat of the Armada grew, a force was raised from the retainers of the nobility, bishops and privy counsellors to form a personal guard for Elizabeth herself, further depleting the Trained Bands, since many, probably the majority, were summoned from them to serve instead with their lord, but gentleman volunteers bringing with them their tenants and dependants were no longer sufficient to raise armies, and increasingly troops were also recruited through levies and forced conscription. The "tentacles of the press spread ever wider" and vagrants, the unemployed and convicts were swept into the land forces, until their desertion rate and dismal quality forced a rethink. In general the "enthusiasm for military service, never great, diminished in direct proportion to the demands made upon them." Desertion was frequent, with service in Ireland so dreaded that men would "venture any imprisonment" rather than serve there, but captains rarely recorded desertions, since they continued to draw the pay for those nominally on their muster roll. Many captains also profited from desertions in other ways: some at Tilbury were accused of charging men £5 to allow them to buy themselves out of service and many soldiers were willing accomplices. "They will either be hiring of men in their places or else bribing to get themselves released." Graft also led to frauds in pay, rations, powder and shot. Soldiers' nominal pay was around eightpence per day, but even when their captain had not appropriated all or part of it, paydays were erratic and most soldiers were in permanent arrears.

Apart from the 10,000 or so troops centred on London to protect the Queen, a theoretical total of 2,500 cavalry and 27,000 infantry were available to defend the South Coast. A further 12,500 would assemble at Tilbury in Essex, and smaller contingents from East Anglia and northern England would guard the coasts north of Harwich and stand ready to counter any invasion by the Scots. The actual number and quality of men who would appear when the beacons were lit was another question entirely; there were probably no more than a few thousand under arms at any point of the Armada campaign. A notional total of 6,000 Cornish men stood ready to march to the defence of Arwenack (Falmouth) or Plymouth at the lighting of the beacons, but, according to one observer, they were "the roughest and most mutinous men in England, and during hay-time and harvest in particular, the seasons when the Armada was most likely to appear off the coast, perhaps as many as half might have refused to answer a call to arms."[6]

With typical Elizabethan thrift, the counties were also required to bear the cost of their own defence. For understandable reasons, those counties with a sea coast were quicker to raise funds and forces than those inland. Lord North reported to the Privy Council that for "nice and curious reasons which might have been forborne in this time of special service," many Cambridgeshire JPs had refused to supply mounted troops and many of the members of the Trained Bands had failed to appear, though whether that was through death, disease or disinclination was not revealed. The old feudal obligations to serve under arms were invoked and at least one Lord Lieutenant, Sir Henry Cromwell, uncle of the future Lord Protector, was moved to remind copy-holders in his county that failure to comply would entail forfeiture of their land. Cromwell roused Huntingdonshire by the force of his own example, summoning strong young men "to supply the defects of the former Trained Bands and to take place of those less fit for the service." Once more, there were few weapons and some had only "rusty bills and bows." Cromwell at once appealed to the Lord Lieutenant, Lord St. John, to make good the deficiencies in weaponry and ordered all his men to prepare and man the warning beacons, silence and incarcerate all those spreading defeatist rumours, and be ready to march at an hour's notice.

Despite these attempts to improve England's defences, the country appeared to stand ripe for invasion. The key South Coast harbours were defended by castles and gun batteries, though in the case of

Portsmouth at least, half the gunners manning them were "by age and impotency by no ways serviceable," but beyond these questionable strongpoints were hundreds of miles of barely defended coastline in England and Wales, let alone the perennially troublesome Ireland and Scotland. There were many ports, harbours and beaches where an invasion force could disembark, much of the surrounding land was rich and fertile, and in summer troops could forage for their supplies easily enough. Kent in particular was "the key of all England . . . fertility, wood, pasture, cattle, fish, fowl, rivers, havens." Lanes and hollow ways wound between hay meadows, orchards heavy with fruit and fields of vegetables and ripening corn; pigs rooted for windfall acorns and beechmast in the cool shade of dense woodland, and cows and sheep grazed the downs and the sun-dappled pastures. The roads, often impassable because of mud and standing water in winter, were adequate in summer and although the new fashion of hedgerows to enclose land was beginning to spread, much of England was still open country and easy to traverse. There were few other barriers to an invader. Even supposing the inhabitants of London showed any stomach for a fight, the medieval city walls were crumbling and ruinous, and there were few fortifications, including the Tower, stout enough to repel or even delay a Spanish invasion force.[7]

Under the threat of Spanish invasion, attempts had been made to modernize and strengthen some of the medieval castles, and reinforce town defences as much as the limited time and funds allowed. Blocked and overgrown ditches were cleared and deepened, crumbling ramparts repaired and strengthened a little, and earthworks were thrown up around the principal forts and castles. The "wall" of Great Yarmouth—a bank of "earth and manure more than 40 feet in breadth" topped by a rampart—had been completed in 1587 and was claimed to be "resistable, by God's help, against any battery whatsoever," but Parma's engineers had years of experience in mining and reducing far more impressive fortifications and, despite the recent repairs and improvements, there were at most a handful of English castles capable of withstanding the Spanish siege artillery. The exiled Jesuit Robert Parsons did not speak from recent personal knowledge and his views were coloured by his intense desire to see England invaded and Elizabeth overthrown, but his assessment of the English defences was not a wild exaggeration: "In the whole realm there are but two fortresses which could stand a three days' siege. They have not a man who can command in the field. The people are enervated by a long peace, and except for a few who have served with the heretics in Flanders, cannot bear their arms." As the campaigns in The Netherlands had proved, the Army of Flanders was more than capable of advancing at a rate of ten miles a day, even against the far more organized opposition of the Dutch. Four years after the Armada, Parma invaded Normandy and marched a force of 22,000 men 65 miles in just six days. At such a rate, London would have been occupied within a week of a landing on the Kent coast, and Sir Walter Ralegh certainly believed that a Spanish advance on the capital would have been virtually unopposed.

There was also a fear in English hearts that a Catholic fifth column stood ready to rise if the Armada landed. "They stand very ill-affected to their prince . . . they deal secretly; they practise in the dark, they conspire in corners." Mendoza identified several dozen disaffected Catholic nobles who would support an invasion, including Sir Henry Benenfield, the guardian of Elizabeth during the reign of Mary Tudor; "I wish to God they had burnt her then as she deserved," Mendoza complained. "We should be living now in peace and quietness." It was widely believed that so many Englishmen were open or covert Catholics that the landing of a Spanish invasion force would lead to a wholesale uprising. The once-dissident Welsh had been won over to the Tudors, but parts of the North of England, Scotland and Ireland remained indifferent or openly hostile. English Catholic exiles claimed that "the King has more friends in England than the Queen's Majesty" and that as many as two-thirds of Englishmen would rise in support of a Spanish invasion.[8]

The exiles were inevitably prone to exaggeration in support of their cause, but even Protestants feared that as much as a third of England's population might support an invasion. The Puritans and Protestants of the south and east would surely fight, but the retainers of the Catholic families of the north and west might well flock to the Spanish standard. English officers in The Netherlands had betrayed their country for Spanish gold, English troops fought for and alongside Parma, English pilots served with the Armada, and English exiles in Paris, Madrid and Rome awaited the overthrow of Elizabeth and the restoration of the old faith. There had been eight rebellions under the Tudors, including the Pilgrimage of Grace in 1536, Sir Thomas Wyatt's revolt against Mary Tudor's Spanish marriage in 1554 and the Rising of the North in 1569. The only successful revolt had been the one that overthrew Lady Jane Grey and installed Mary Tudor as Queen in July 1553, but none had been supported by the might and power of Spain.

Despite the ever-present fear of rebellion and Burghley's warning of "the secret treasons of the mind and heart," Elizabeth had held back from a wholesale incarceration of her Catholic subjects. The majority were to be left undisturbed as long as they accepted the authority of the Crown and maintained at least an outward show of conformity to the Anglican religion. It was either a daring gamble, sheer hubris or a cold calculation that most Englishmen—even Catholic ones—would prefer the stability of the status quo to the uncertainty, disorders, purges and persecutions that would inevitably follow the overthrow of a moderate Protestant regime and its replacement by an evangelical Catholic monarchy.

Although she was shrewd enough to whip up religious fervour when it suited her ends—she ordered that every sea-captain should take a copy of *Foxe's Book of Martyrs* to sea and read it to his crew "to teach them the nature of the Papist enemies"—Elizabeth was at pains to avoid the doctrinal religious controversy that had riven Europe. The persecutions and burnings of Mary Tudor's reign had aroused genuine horror in England, but the purges and executions of Elizabeth's middle to later years aroused much less revulsion because they were carried out in the name of national security, not doctrinal purity; the victims were tortured and killed not because they were heretics but because they were traitors plotting against the Crown.

The Oath of Supremacy required every office holder, cleric, MP and lawyer to swear an oath of allegiance to Elizabeth, and the deeply ingrained belief that breaking or falsely swearing an oath was a mortal sin endangering the soul made it a potent weapon, even though the Pope attempted to ease the path for Catholics by granting a dispensation to those who swore a false oath under duress. English Catholics had always been urged to keep separate from the heretics—attendance at an Anglican service was a deadly sin—but if the faith was kept pure and strong as a result, it also forced Catholics to declare themselves openly, increasing their peril in the face of Protestant reprisals after the Rising of the North, the St. Bartholomew's Day Massacre and the plots against Elizabeth. Recusants were readily identified at first and subject to increasing harassment and state persecution, often triggered by their neighbours' reporting comings and goings in the night. The mere suspicion of holding a forbidden Mass was enough to bring arrest.

In 1580, recognizing this dilemma, Pope Gregory XIII amended the Bull of Excommunication, the "roaring bull" *Regnans in Excelsis* issued by Pope Pius V ten years before, which had proclaimed the excommunication of "Elizabeth, pretended Queen of England, the serpent of wickedness" (begging the question of how one who was not of the faith could be excommunicated from it), as a heretic and a persecutor of the true religion, her deposition from the throne, and the excommunication of all those who continued to recognize her as their sovereign. It was an open invitation to English Catholics to overthrow their Queen; Elizabeth had responded with the first penal legislation against Catholics of her reign, and a man who had nailed a copy of the Bull to the door of the Bishop of London's palace was tortured and executed.

Gregory authorized English Catholics to profess their loyalty in public while privately preparing to overthrow her at the first opportunity and gave advance absolution as an incitement to her murder. "There is no doubt whatsoever that who sends that guilty woman of England out of the world with the pious intention of doing God's service, not only does not sin but gains merit." His Secretary of State, the Cardinal of Coimo, gave written approval to an assassination attempt soon afterwards. In response, English persecution of Catholics increased. The fine for non-attendance at church, twelve pence a Sunday in 1559, had risen to twenty pounds a month by the 1580s and an Act of Parliament authorized the seizure of the land and goods of those who could not pay. Over the remainder of the decade, the Treasury collected a windfall of £45,000 from just 200 individuals. Those whose conscience brooked no compromise paid fines as long as they could raise the funds or went to prison—and Puritans as well as Catholics were imprisoned and persecuted for their beliefs—but the majority fell into acceptance of the religious status quo as much through habit as conviction. Few could afford the fines, and even the wealthiest Catholic gentry were worn down. Most became "schismatics," attending Anglican services even if privately adhering to the old faith. Lord Montagu's confessor reassured him that it was "expedient something to give to the time . . . they durst not determine such a fact to be sin," and many Catholics "did not discern any great fault, novelty or difference from the former religion . . . save only change of language . . . and so easily accommodated themselves thereto."

In the end the greatest blow to Catholic hopes was probably none of the dramatic events such as the crushing of the Rising of the North or the failure of the succession of plots against Elizabeth, but simply the numbing effect of the passing years. In 1558 Protestants were in the majority only in London and Kent, but by the time of the Armada thirty years later they formed the majority in every single county, even in the traditionally Catholic north. The sheer length of Elizabeth's reign and the short life expectancy of her subjects—an average of twenty-five years for the poor and thirty-five for the rich—meant that by the time of the Armada, there were few alive, even among Catholics, who could remember or had witnessed the rituals of the old Catholic faith, prompting one ageing English adherent to lament, "Dead cold is our age, there is blue ice in our churches."[9]

William Allen, a prominent English exile in Rome, was made a cardinal by Pope Sixtus "to please Your Majesty" (Philip, who was paying Allen a substantial retainer), with the express intention of installing him in England after the Spanish invasion. Allen had published "an admonition to the nobility and people of England concerning the present war . . . [and] the excommunication pronounced by Pius V against Elizabeth, as well concerning her illegitimation and usurpation and inability to the Crown of England as for her excommunication and deprivation in respect of her heresy, sacrilege and abominable life." Citing natural law, because Elizabeth was a tyrant, and divine law, because she was a heretic, Allen relayed Sixtus's command that no Englishmen must obey or defend Elizabeth and all were to be ready "at the arrival of his Catholic Majesty's forces . . . to join the said army . . . to help towards the restoring of the Catholic faith and deposing the usurper." Only by purging their country of Elizabeth and all her doings could Englishmen save their own and their children's souls. Allen urged all Englishmen at home or abroad "in the service of the Almighty and of the greatest and justest monarch in all the world [Philip] and under a General so peerless [Parma] . . . reduce our people to the obedience of Christ's Church and deliver our Catholic friends and brethren from the damnable and intolerable yoke of heresy." Some Englishmen welcomed the prospect. "If I heard that the entire destruction of England was for the greater glory of God and the welfare of Christianity, I should be glad of its being done."

In the face of this threat, Jesuits, itinerant "seminary priests" and their accomplices were seized by Walsingham's agents and tortured to extract information. Most were then executed, the remainder deported—60 per cent of those sent to England fell into the hands of the authorities—but English exiles believed that 300 priests were still living undetected in the houses of gentlemen and nobles, keeping alive the Catholic faith in England. The weapons of all known recusants had been confiscated in 1586, and after January 1588 some were taken into custody and others confined to their parishes or sometimes their houses, but only in late July, with the Armada at the gates, were a large number of the leading English Catholics interned in Wisbech Castle, "in the custody of Lord North." When Henry VIII had been threatened by a French invasion supported by the Papacy, he had put to death many of the leading Catholic nobles "whom he suspected to favour their enterprise . . . The Queen, disliking this as a cruel counsel, thought it sufficient to commit some of the Papists, and those not of the chief, to custody." Even then, the polite fiction was maintained that "for their own safety's sake, they ought not to be at large and at the mercy of their infuriated Protestant neighbours" in the event of a Spanish invasion.[10] It did not convince Philip's English secretary, Sir Francis Englefield. "Those Machiavellian scholars, the Queen's ministry were too cunning to put eighty Catholics openly to death at once, but sent them to Wisbech Castle, where the ill air would consume them privately."

There was more than a grain of truth in suggestions that Catholics would be at risk from hostile Englishmen. England was largely insulated from foreign influences and most travellers abroad were soldiers going to fight in The Netherlands or France. Others had to convince officials of their probity and ideological and doctrinal correctness, and give sureties as to their conduct. Only sixty "licences to pass beyond the seas" were granted to Englishmen between 1572 and 1578 and the travellers were closely watched by spies hoping to augment their income by denouncing them for meeting with papists or attending a Mass. Communities of Huguenots and Flemish weavers had settled in England and there were many foreign merchants, traders and diplomats and their retinues in London. "Because of the common danger, watch had to be kept on the great crowd of foreigners from the Low Countries, France and other places, who lived in London on their earnings as craftsmen. No more was known of some of them except that they had come on account of their religion; but the city was full of such as might be faithful or not under the cloak of the same religion . . . Every day these foreigners received insulting words from the prentices and the lower classes, people who are naturally the enemies of foreigners." The threat of the Armada tangled with fears buried in the psyche of every Protestant: the burning of the Marian martyrs, the St. Bartholomew's Day Massacre, the Spanish Fury in Antwerp and the "Black Legend" of the bestial cruelties of the Conquistadors and the Inquisition were all widely known and disseminated throughout England. Broadsheets sold on the streets of London recounted the deaths of Protestant martyrs, illustrated by woodcuts depicting tortures and mutilations in specific and horrific detail.

Rumours were spread, fuelled by black propaganda from the Crown, "that in the Spanish ships were many instruments of torture with which to afflict the English people," and pamphleteers produced ever more graphic descriptions of Armada ships laden with pox-ridden prostitutes, thousands of wet-nurses to suckle all the infants who were to be orphaned, "strange and most cruel whips" and scourges "to whip and torment English men and women" and nooses to hang them. "All men and women who would not have bowed the knee to Baal, had then been put to the sword; their children had been tossed at the pike's end or else their brains dashed out by some ill-faced Dons or other." All English males between the ages of seven and seventy would be put to death, and younger children branded with a mark of shame that they would carry for the rest of their lives—"certain irons graven with marks, to be heated for the marking of all children in their faces, being under seven years of age, that they might be known hereafter to have been the children of the conquered nation." "We know that the only object of this is to incense the people against the Spaniards," but "these things being easily believed, the whole of the lowest and most credulous part of the people were moved to a mortal and dangerous hatred of all foreigners."[11]

Such a tide of popular fear and hatred made it inconceivable that up to two-thirds of the English population would rise in support of a Spanish invasion or that it would have been as easy as many have suggested. The Dutch had demonstrated how counter-productive the Spanish atrocities were—the inhabitants of Leiden burned their own town to the ground rather than allow it to fall into Spanish hands—and even though Parma had introduced greater discipline and shown restraint as well as ruthlessness, the stories of Spanish atrocities were too well engraved on Protestant minds. There would have been no willing surrenders, no easy victories on the march to London.

The English militias were woefully under-trained and under-armed, but people, both soldiers and civilians, facing an enemy they believe is intent on their extermination, will fight to the death rather than surrender, even if it means matching pitchforks against muskets and pikes, and Englishmen went armed at all times. "Seldom shall you see any of my countrymen above eighteen or twenty years old to go without a dagger at the least at his back or by his side although they be aged burgesses or magistrates of any city who in appearance are most exempt from brawling and contention. Our nobility wear commonly swords or rapiers with their daggers, as does every common serving man also that follows his lord and master. Finally, no man travels by the way without his sword or some such weapon." And even if the militias were poorly equipped with firearms, there was no lack of martial spirit in Elizabeth's subjects. George Owen of Henllys, commenting on a game of knappan, a Welsh form of football that pitted whole villages against each other in a rowdy and often brutal ritualized conflict, reported the comment of a stranger witnessing the game in 1588. "If this be but play, I could wish the Spaniards were here to see our plays in England. Certainly they would be in bodily fear of our war."

The belated preparations against the Armada were feeble enough in the face of the forces ranged against them, but England's primary defence did not rest on fortifications and land forces. Ever since the battle of Sluys in 1344 under Edward III, English gold coinage had included a representation of a warship, a recognition of the vital importance of the navy in the nation's defence and the national wealth. There was no royal navy in Spain beyond that annexed from Portugal, no state dockyards or shipyards, and all ships were hired or impounded in time of war. England had a navy of fine ships, augmented by scores of armed merchantmen, and dockyards at Chatham, Deptford and Woolwich, Portsmouth (albeit almost moribund) and Plymouth. There had been no Royal Navy until 1535; by "ancient custom" the Crown created and dissolved armies and navies at will, and merchant ships were simply requisitioned from their owners, with or without compensation, and returned to them when the crisis was past. The first permanent navy, established by Henry VIII at ruinous expense and largely paid for out of the revenues confiscated from the Church of Rome at the Dissolution, had laid the foundations of the Grand Fleet that Elizabeth could now command. On acceding to the throne, she could draw on only 27 active fighting ships from her father's great navy, many already in a dilapidated condition, plus a further seven in dry dock in varying stages of disrepair, and seven armed merchantmen. A few new ships were built over the following decade, but they merely replaced the older ones taken out of service, and by 1575 she could still draw on only 23 men-of-war. By 1588, she had 34 galleons in her fleet, only a modest increase in numbers, but while six of them still dated back to Henry's reign, under the inspired leadership of John Hawkins the majority of the Queen's galleons had recently been redesigned on revolutionary lines.

Overshadowed by Drake in his own lifetime and "denied the high position to which his talents and his character entitled him," Hawkins was a man of great wealth and a seaman of unparalleled experience. He had married the daughter of Benjamin Gonson, Treasurer of Marine Causes, and succeeded him in the post, and at once set about the modernization of the fleet. Eleven new galleons had been built in the five years preceding the Armada alone and another dozen had been rebuilt to the same specifications. Elizabeth could also draw on an ever-growing fleet of armed merchantmen, a product of the profits to be made from privateering and from England's burgeoning overseas trade in legitimate goods; the Privy Council estimated that 135 merchantmen of over 100 tons and 656 of less than that burthen could be added to the fleet from the merchant marine. For the most part, such ships had seen considerably more action than the Queen's galleons. A dozen merchantmen had taken part in Drake's raids on the Spanish Main in 1585, and seventeen were in the fleet that attacked Cadiz in 1587. Only half a dozen of the Queen's galleons had been involved in either voyage.[12]

Until Hawkins's era, English warships had been built like their continental counterparts, with high forecastles and top-gallant forecastles at the prow of the ship and a series of poop-decks rising from the stern, often capped with a final roofed deck resembling a garden shed overhanging the stern at a precarious angle. No "great ship" ever had less than a poop and top-gallant poop, and three poop-decks were commonplace. Small, round wooden towers were also often carried where the fore- and sterncastles rose from the waist of the ship, in addition to the "fighting tops"—enlarged versions of crow's nests capable of housing up to a score of snipers or archers—mounted high on all four masts. As a result of carrying these massive upperworks, the ships were ponderous and very top-heavy, prone to excessive rolling and pitching, and even to overturning and sinking, like Henry VIII's *Mary Rose*, or the Swedish ship *Vasa*, which sank on its maiden voyage.

However, the innovations of Henry VIII and the continuing improvements during the reign of his daughter had put English shipbuilders and gun-founders years in advance of their European counterparts and Hawkins exploited this technological advantage to the full. His ship designer, Matthew Baker, the first man to be designated a master shipwright, was the son of a shipbuilder but he had also studied mathematics and brought the disciplines of that science to his craft. Rather than working by hand and eye alone, he was the first shipbuilder to make accurate blueprints, enabling successful designs to be replicated exactly. In total, eighteen great galleons and seven smaller ones were constructed on clean, "race-built" lines (the word derives from "raze," not "race," and denotes the razing—lowering—of the upperworks, particularly the fore- and sterncastles). They were longer in keel—a proportion of length to breadth of three to one was thought ideal—narrower in beam and lower in the water than their predecessors. The forecastle was reduced to a single deck and the sterncastle to a poop accommodating the officers and the helmsman. The massive oak ribs of the hulls were clad in a double layer of four-inch oak planks, and the cavity between them filled with a layer of tar mixed with animal hair, like the wattle and daub used in house-building, to preserve the hull from rot. Recent improvements in rigging, such as the bowline, were also adopted; once more the Spaniards failed to follow suit. Hawkins also commissioned even sleeker and faster pinnaces for use as fighting ships in shallow waters and against weaker targets, and scouting vessels for the main fleet.

He outlawed the short cuts and sharp practice traditionally tolerated in shipbuilding, ensured that used timber and green or summer-
felled wood—prone to rotting and warping—was rejected, and built up
a store of seasoned, winter-felled oak for the construction and repair of
his ships. He also eliminated much, though not all, of the traditional
graft and corruption by introducing a system of building on contract,
and reduced the annual cost of the upkeep of the fleet from £10,000 to
£6,000. His economies made enemies of those who had previously
profited from graft, and some misrepresented his actions and accused
him of lining his own pockets. He was said to have "laid the foundation
of a large fortune by cheating the Spaniards, and increased it, it was
suspected, by cheating his own countrymen." Hawkins's rival, Sir
William Wynter, sent an unsigned and highly hypocritical letter to
Burghley, accusing Hawkins of pocketing money that should have been
spent on "repairing, trimming and ransacking of Her Majesty's ships
in this later time. [It] has bred a far greater charge to Her Highness . . . besides the clouterly [clumsy] patching and doing of the same,
very discommodious in the use of the ships." "This commission has
been very beneficial to him, not only in furnishing Her Majesty's yard
with planks, timber, boards, etc., but also of one other yard in Deptford, which he reaps benefit as a partner, which yard has and does consume   more   than   Her   Majesty's   yard   has   done   within   two
years . . . which breeds ill speeches in the country and may hinder the
service to come . . . He spared himself and charged Her Majesty."
Hawkins reacted angrily to the accusations. "The navy is in good and
strong estate, contrary to their hypocritical practice and vile reports."
He amply fulfilled his duties to the Crown and if he did also profit from
his office it was much less than his predecessors had done, including his
principal critic, Wynter.[13]

Hawkins's innovations were distrusted in some quarters, where
sea-captains bred in an earlier era complained that he was abolishing
the fighting castles, valued "for their majesty and terror," but Sir Walter Ralegh was quick to dismiss their complaints. "The greatest ships
are the least serviceable . . . less nimble, less mainable [easy to handle]
and very seldom employed. A ship of 600 tons will carry as good ordnance as a ship of 1,200 tons; and though the greater have double her
number, the less will turn her broadsides twice before the greater can
wind once. The high charging of ships brings them ill qualities, makes
them extreme leeward, makes them sink deep in the water, makes them
labour and makes them overset. Men of better sort and better breeding
would be glad to find more steadiness and less tottering cage-work."

Hawkins had spent his life at sea, and knew exactly what he wanted from his galleons. They mounted more guns, yet were lighter, stronger, faster, more manoeuvrable and could sail much closer to the wind—"four points off" or 45 degrees to the wind—than their predecessors. Even the larger and older ships such as the 1,100-ton *Triumph*, unaltered since it was built in 1561, were significantly faster and much more heavily gunned than the Spanish ships they would face. "There is no prince in Europe that has a more beautiful or gallant sort of ships than the Queen's Majesty of England at this present and those generally are of such exceeding force that two of them being well appointed and furnished as they ought, will not let to encounter with three or four of those of other countries and either budge them or put them to flight, if they may not bring them home . . . The common report that strangers make of our ships amongst themselves is daily confirmed to be true, which is that for strength, assurance, nimbleness and swiftness of sailing, there are no vessels in the world to be compared with ours."[14]

Their armament was also revolutionary. Guns had been carried on English ships since at least 1410 when the *Christopher of the Tower* mounted three cannon, but it was to be another 150 years after that before ship-mounted cannons ceased to be primarily anti-personnel weapons used in the prelude to boarding, and became decisive weapons in their own right. Early cannon were manufactured from strips of wrought iron, formed into a barrel by hammer-welding around a core. The welds were reinforced with lead and the barrel held together by ropes wound around the barrel or rings of wrought iron. Wooden wedges were driven into the breech to secure the removable chamber containing the powder, and the weapon was fired by applying a smouldering match-cord to a trail of powder in the touch-hole. The lighter "murthering pieces"—breech-loading weapons, using pre-loaded chambers—could achieve rates of fire of twenty to thirty shots per hour and wreak havoc among enemy personnel during boarding attacks, but the heavier cannon were far less effective. They had to be lashed down with ropes, making no allowance for the recoil, and they sometimes broke free when fired, to the devastation of those gathered around them. Flaws and impurities in the iron and the weakness of the welds also made the barrels liable to burst under the stresses of firing, and the wedges and powder chambers were often blown out of the breech, killing any gunner careless enough to be standing nearby.

The design of cannons and the techniques of manufacture were continuously being improved during the Tudor era. The principal English arms foundry was in Calais—English territory until 1558—but Henry VIII also set up a foundry in the Weald of Kent for Hans Poppenruyter of Mechlin, a gunmaker who had successfully produced muzzle-loading heavy cannon that were cast upright, in a single piece, ensuring that the most dense and flawless metal was concentrated around the powder chamber at the base. This introduction of muzzle-loading weapons that could withstand much higher firing pressures was a significant development, and Poppenruyter demonstrated their efficiency by demolishing a ramshackle row of houses in Houndsditch with a single shot. Bronze cannon were still preferred—the metal was less prone to casting flaws and more resistant to corrosion, and a faulty or overloaded bronze cannon would bulge before disintegrating, whereas an iron one would simply explode into fragments, killing the guncrew and anyone else within range—but English iron cannon grew increasingly reliable as techniques to remove air bubbles, sulphur and phosphorus improved, and they were a fraction of the price—only 15 per cent of the cost of the cannon produced by the seven bronze foundries in Lisbon. The price of iron guns actually fell by a quarter during the last three decades of the century at a time when rocketing inflation was more than doubling the price of almost every other commodity.

As a result of these developments, Henry VIII soon had "cannon enough to conquer hell"; his artillery fired 100,000 shots into Boulogne during a siege in 1544, and by the later years of his reign English bronze and iron cannon were eagerly sought throughout Europe, forcing Henry to ban their export. But Calais remained the principal focus of English arms production, and its loss during Mary Tudor's disastrous war on France cost England over a thousand cannon and its principal arms foundries. It was said at the time that the country would never recover from the loss, and at the start of Elizabeth's reign England was heavily dependent on imports, primarily from Flanders. However, as the likelihood of hostilities with Spain increased, the rapid further development of iron-working and gun-casting in the Weald and the Forest of Dean, and the immigration of skilled metal workers fleeing persecution in the Low Countries and Germany, enabled England once again to become a substantial manufacturer and exporter of weapons.

Naval cannons had previously tended to be of small size—the weight of heavy guns carried at deck level affected the stability of the ship—but, at Henry VIII's insistence, ways had been found to solve this problem. The short-ranged cannons and batteries of anti-personnel weapons carried on older ships were replaced by culverins and cannons of far superior range and quality. The development of gunports in the early years of the sixteenth century, adapted from the earlier ports cut into the hull to facilitate the loading of cargo, and the subsequent introduction of gundecks also allowed the relocation of heavy weapons nearer to the waterline, where their weight was less likely to destabilize the ship.

Under John Hawkins, a continuous gundeck was introduced and the traditional low waist of the ships was also raised, allowing an additional row of lighter guns at deck level. Despite the galleons' slender construction, these longer gundecks enabled them to carry a far greater weight of great ordnance than the Spanish ships they were to face, as much as 10 per cent of the total weight of the ship. The *Revenge*, built in 1575, carried 43 guns, 20 on the lower deck of 4,000 to 6,000 pounds in weight and 23 on the upper deck of 2,000 to 3,000 pounds. These great guns fired projectiles of from nine to 60 pounds in weight. By contrast, the galleass *San Lorenzo*, one of the most heavily armed ships of the Armada, had 40 guns, but 16 of those were sakers or minions, firing only four- or six-pound shot.

English seamen had also solved the intractable problems of manoeuvring and reloading heavy cannons in the cramped, dangerous confines of the gundeck. The two-wheeled gun-carriages used on land were replaced by four-wheeled "truck-carriages" that occupied less space and were far easier to handle, allowing them to be pulled back from the gunport for reloading, and withdrawn towards the centre of the ship when not in use, further improving stability. In addition, the preferred weapon of the English navy, the culverin, was cast much heavier than strictly necessary, allowing for casting flaws that might otherwise have caused the weapon to explode and absorbing much of the energy of the recoil that would have stressed the ship's frame or sent the weapon careering backwards, mowing down the guncrew. In compensation for this increased weight, the barrel length of the cannons and culverins was reduced by a third compared to the guns used by land forces—from fourteen to nine feet—with no loss of muzzle velocity, since black powder combusts so rapidly that a shot reaches its maximum velocity after travelling less than ten feet. A longer barrel tends to reduce rather than increase the range and, given the inherent inaccuracy of the weapons, firing at long range was in any case a pointless exercise. "He that shoots far off at sea had as good not shoot at all." The English naval culverins had a theoretical range of well over a mile, but the range at which they could cause significant damage to an enemy ship was much shorter, as little as 100 yards against the stout oak hulls of warships. However, at such a distance they could be devastating; one artillery expert claimed that a 24-pound shot fired at that range could penetrate four and a half feet of "sound and hard oak."

The standardization and more precise calibration of the bore of cannons and the diameter of the "great shot" they fired was of equal importance, allowing much greater accuracy than had previously been possible, when variations in the size of cannonballs and in the quality and quantity of black powder used to fire them, coupled with the inevitable delays between the gunner's decision to fire and the actual ignition of the firing charge after he put the matchcord to the touch-hole, made gunnery more a lottery than an exact science. Naval guns were now manned by specialist crews whose firing rate and accuracy was three or four times that of their European counterparts, and gunnery had become an honoured and sought-after profession within the ship's company. So proficient and widely admired were English gunners that "a register of all the gunners, both serving Her Majesty in the ships and in forts and of others serving merchants" was kept, "that none depart the realm" to take the high wages offered to fight for England's enemies.[15]

Gunpowder also underwent a quantum leap in quality with the introduction of "corned" powder. The earlier "serpentine" powder was prone to deterioration through damp or separation into its individual constituents, and was highly unstable. A gunner using his ramrod with too much vigour might blow himself to pieces, but if he was too tentative the gun would either discharge feebly or not fire at all. In the new process, small fragments of powder were glazed so that they remained stable and relatively impervious to moisture and burned at a more predictable and constant rate. However, securing adequate supplies of gunpowder remained a serious problem. As early as 1562, Elizabeth had been warned of the danger of not maintaining a strategic reserve of powder. "It will be only that thing she shall lack if wars should chance, which should be foreseen in time, because our forces and ships be nothing without powder." The warnings had gone unheeded and despite occasional attempts to boost domestic production, nearly all of England's saltpetre (nitre or potassium nitrate, the chief constituent of black powder) was imported. Saltpetre was primarily extracted from processed urine or manure. So desperate was the need that laws were passed encouraging the establishment of pigeon cotes—pigeon droppings were particularly rich in nitre—and "saltpetre men" also periodically dug up the floors of earth closets, stables, pigsties, henhuts and sheep pens to obtain the precious commodity "black earth." "Urine from people who drink strong drink" was particularly recommended, along with fresh dung from horses "who like to eat oats." The process of extracting saltpetre was lengthy, complex and foul. A trench was dug and filled with quicklime and straw. Quantities of manure and urine were added daily for three weeks, and the uric acid in the urine oxidized to nitrate. The resulting mixture was then dug up again and boiled in lead or copper vats to evaporate the liquid. The crystallized saltpetre produced in this way was of variable strength and quality, making the charging of weapons an inexact science.

In the early 1570s English traders had found a more reliable source in Fez on the Barbary Coast (in modern-day Morocco). Islamic and Christian states were implacably opposed but there was a commonality of interest—the Sheriff of Fez granted a monopoly of the trade in saltpetre in return for English iron cannon and cannonballs, pikes, helmets and small arms. It was an unlooked-for but welcome bonus for English diplomacy that these weapons were then used against Spanish shipping in the Mediterranean. For the first time, England now had a dependable supply of gunpowder of consistent quality, enabling the charge of a weapon and therefore its range and trajectory to be calculated with greater accuracy, but persuading the Queen to purchase sufficient stocks of this expensive commodity—black powder cost around £100 a ton—and prising it from her magazines at the Tower of London when required remained problems that English naval commanders had yet to solve. Only when the Armada was actually off the coast were attempts made to obtain additional supplies and by then it was too late.

Sheer weight of numbers was on the Spanish side, but the massed troops and their mountains of equipment and supplies made their ships slow and unwieldy, and they were overmanned with soldiers and undermanned with seamen. While Howard's 800-ton flagship, the *Ark*, had 300 seamen and only 125 soldiers aboard, Medina-Sidonia's 1,000-ton *San Martin* carried 300 soldiers and only 177 seamen. The English crewmen also tended to be more skilled and experienced, particularly in Atlantic conditions. Some Spanish sailors were not unused to rough seas; the Bay of Biscay and the Atlantic, where the sailors of the west and north coasts plied their trades, can be as wild and rough as any but the southern oceans. But the experience of most Spanish, Venetian and Neapolitan sailors was largely confined to the Mediterranean, and with the exception of the Basque fishermen working the Grand Banks off Newfoundland, those who had sailed the Atlantic had rarely ventured much beyond the run with the trade winds to and from the Caribbean. Philip described "the enemy's crews" as consisting of "novices, drawn from the common people, a tumultuous crowd, lacking military discipline," but he grossly underestimated their experience and ability. It was true that pressing men for the Queen's galleons—though not for privateers—remained a necessity, for "their usage has been so ill that it is no marvel they show their unwillingness to serve the Queen. For if they arrive sick from any voyage, such is the charity of the people ashore that they shall sooner die than find pity; unless they bring money with them." As a result, some English crewmen were still an undisciplined, unskilled rabble, the scourings of the seaports, but there was a solid core of well-trained and experienced seamen that the navy could draw on in time of war, and knowledge of the sea extended even beyond the coastal ports of England, for many younger sons from inland towns were apprenticed to ships' captains.[16]

Henry VIII's sailors never voyaged further than the Bay of Biscay and the North Sea; under Elizabeth, Durham and Newcastle colliers still sailed the North Sea, and grain and cargo ships crossed the Channel, but large numbers of her seamen had also sailed the stormy waters guarding the rich fisheries off Ireland, Iceland and Greenland, where East Coast ships were challenging the German and Scots fishing fleets, and Bristol and West Country ships had begun to fish the Grand Banks off Newfoundland, previously monopolized by the Basques. Still others had voyaged in search of the North-West Passage with Frobisher or John Davis, on raids across the Bay of Biscay to mainland Spain, or gone plundering in the Spanish colonies of the New World. Merchant adventurers in London, Bristol and the South West also made their own journeys to secure the goods once brought by Venetian and Hanseatic ships, and Turkey merchants of the Levant Company pursued the Mediterranean trade, "extremely profitable to them, as they take great quantities of tin and lead thither," as well as stockfish, corn and fine cloths. The Barbary Company carried on a brisk trade with Morocco, where English iron, cloth and timber were exchanged for sugar and saltpetre. The Eastland Company, established in 1579, traded finished cloth with the Baltic countries and Poland in return for timber and naval supplies, and the Muscovy Company traded the same commodities with Russia. Merchant explorers such as Gilbert, Hawkins, Wyndham, Willoughby and Chancellor were meanwhile pioneering trade with the New World, Africa and Asia.

Improvements in the design, seaworthiness and durability of sailing ships helped to encourage the new trades. The single-masted ships of medieval times were replaced by two-, three- and four-masters, lateen sails were introduced and hulls became longer and narrower, making ships faster and better able to sail close to the wind, and the introduction of topmasts and topsails increased the canvas they could carry and therefore the speed they could achieve. The Crown also introduced a bounty to encourage shipbuilding, and took steps to promote the fishing industry, the training ground for most of the nation's mariners, by imposing a statutory meatless day once a week—increased to two days a week by Elizabeth. Fast days also fulfilled religious duties but their prime purpose was secular: to conserve meat supplies, especially during Lent at the end of winter, when meat stocks were at their lowest; and, of equal or greater importance, to encourage the consumption of fish.

Unlike their counterparts in The Netherlands, France, Naples, Genoa, Venice or Portugal, few English mariners served foreign rulers. They made their voyages of exploration, trade or privateering in English ships, under English captains, and they were seasoned, honed and battle-hardened in sea fights by years of privateering. All English merchant ships, particularly those of the Levant Company, were armed against attacks by pirates and corsairs, and if the vessels used in the Baltic trade were often of modest size, the ships used in privateering or the Levant trade, such as the 400-ton *Merchant Royal*, were almost as large and heavily armed as the Queen's galleons. Many merchants found the speculative profits from using their vessels in privateering voyages even more attractive than legitimate trading, and some of the most enthusiastic were those who had previously traded with Spain. "The very men whose business was with Spain seemed fated to become her worst enemies." During the 1570s and 1580s, a substantial armed merchant fleet had been built up, together with a correspondingly large pool of men experienced in seamanship and naval warfare.

All this was of both immediate and long-term benefit to the Crown, for "the state may hereafter want such men, who commonly are the most daring and serviceable in war." Fear of Spanish land forces was universal, but English sailors had been fighting the Spaniards at sea for twenty years and had formed no high opinion of their fighting abilities. The primary role of English crewmen was to sail the ship, not fight battles, and they were normally armed only with a "kidney dagger"—after the place in the belt where it was kept—but those who worked on privateers soon acquired expertise with musket, pike, sword and axe, and would take them up as required either in defence of their own ship or, more usually, to attack a prize. English seamen saw nothing in Spanish ships and sailors to cause them fear. They "had already taken the measure of Spain and, unlike the politicians in London, regarded her much as a prize-fighter regards a fat citizen with a full purse."[17]

English captains and admirals were also superior to their Spanish opponents. English ships had their share of lords and gentlemen in command—Lord Howard owed his position as Admiral of the Fleet to his ancestry, not his naval skills—but there were powerful reasons why a lord would be preferred as overall commander even by the lowliest of his men. A man of power, influence and connections at Court was far more likely to secure improvements in pay and conditions, or obtain supplies of food or munitions in a crisis, than any commoner. But that special case aside, the vast majority of captains in the English fleet had won their commands on merit. The very discomforts and dangers of life at sea ensured that only the most dedicated—or desperate—would seek his fortune in that way. Of the commanders of the thirty-four prime fighting ships in the English Grand Fleet, only five were lords, and one of those, the debt-ridden Earl of Cumberland, was a very experienced if not conspicuously successful privateer. Several others, including Drake, were knights but they had been honoured for their expertise at sea, not promoted because of their titles, and the remaining captains of the fleet were all commoners. It was inconceivable that Spanish galleons would have been commanded by common men.

On Spanish ships, the sea-captains were subordinate to the army officers on board; on English ships the reverse was true, and if the captain of a ship was every bit as much the absolute ruler of his kingdom as his monarch on land, there was a democracy of effort and shared risk aboard English ships that was utterly foreign to Spaniards. Drake famously insisted that "I must have the gentleman to haul and draw with the mariner, and the mariner with the gentleman . . . let us show ourselves to be of a company. I would know him that would refuse to set his hand to a rope, but I know there is not any such here." Drake did his share of hauling and drawing with his men, but to partake of such menial activity was anathema to Spanish officers and gentlemen, and morale aboard their ships was further hampered by the unending hostility, sometimes to the point of blows and bloodshed, between the crewmen and the soldiers. Englishmen were not immune to such disputes, but Drake stamped out any show of disunity. "Such controversy between the sailors and the gentlemen and such stomaching between the gentlemen and the sailors . . . does make me mad to hear it."

There was still a marked inequality of rates of pay and the remuneration of an admiral depended more on his social rank than his skill. As Lord High Admiral of England, and one of the most prominent peers of the realm, Charles Howard was paid £3 6s 8d per day. Lord Henry Seymour, Admiral of the Narrow Seas and second son of the Earl of Hertford, received £2 a day, comfortably more than the lowly born Drake's 30 shillings. Wynter and Frobisher had to be content with £1, captains received half a crown (12½p) and the "common man" 10 shillings a month—4d a day, at a time when 1½d to 2d per day was judged the minimum necessary to keep Spanish prisoners of war from starving to death. The "allowance for a diet for the Lord

Thomas Howard and Lord Sheffield" was a generous one, however, amounting to £433 during the period of their service. Captains and officers also profited from "dead-shares": the wages paid to dead or non-existent mariners on the ship's books, but little if any of this money filtered down to their living crewmen.

In 1585, John Hawkins had performed the near miraculous feat of persuading the Queen and Burghley to raise seamen's pay by a third, so that "the common man, that had but 6s 8d by the month, shall have 10s." After strident protests from Elizabeth, Hawkins pointed out, with an eye to the Queen's customary priorities, that it could actually be a means of saving money as well as improving the service, since a few well-trained and experienced men were worth more to a ship's captain than twice as many members of an ill-disciplined rabble. "By this means, Her Majesty's ships will be furnished with able men, such as can make shift for themselves, [and] keep themselves clean without vermin and noisomeness which breeds sickness and mortality . . . The ships would be able to continue longer in the service . . . There is no captain or master but would undertake with more courage any enterprise with 250 able men than with 300 of tag and rag, and assure himself of better success. The wages being so small, cause the best men to run away, to bribe and make means to be cleared from the service, and insufficient, unable and unskilful persons supply the place." His argument was undoubtedly true; there was a general complaint that "the muster masters do carry the best men in their pockets" and the Weymouth press-masters were accepting bribes of £1 a head to let seafarers avoid the press gang, with unqualified "men of all occupations, some of whom did not know a rope and were never at sea," being taken in their place. It was unsurprising that the press-masters were susceptible to bribes since, like her soldiers and seamen, they often went unpaid by Elizabeth.[18]

Hawkins continued to petition her to improve seamen's wages—"If it shall please Her Majesty to yield unto this increase, Her Highness's service would be far safer and much bettered, and yet the charge nothing increased"—and the pay was eventually raised, but the rise did not even compensate for the effects of inflation. Wages were still so meagre that the only means of filling the ships with men frequently remained the forced recruitment of the press gang, though even on the Queen's ships many crewmen, often the majority, were volunteers drawn by the promise of a share in rich prizes from pillage and plunder. "We find it in daily experience that all discourse of magnanimity, of national virtue, of religion, of liberty and whatsoever else has been wont to move and encourage virtuous men, has no force at all with the common soldier [or sailor] in comparison of spoil or riches," and English seamen were notorious throughout Europe as "the most infamous for outrageous, common and daily piracies."

Aboard ship was no place for faint hearts. One jaundiced mariner wrote of "continual destruction in the foretop, the pox above board, the plague between decks, Hell in the forecastle and the Devil at the helm." Discipline was enforced by the personality of the captain or the brawn of his underlings as much as by regulation, and privateers were notoriously undisciplined, but a code of punishment serving the interests of the crews as well as their captains was enforced with more or less rigour. Falling asleep on watch, leaving the ship vulnerable to attack and capture, was a serious offence. The punishment increased with each of the first three infractions, the guilty watchman being lashed to the capstan or the mast with progressively heavier weights attached to his limbs, causing "much pain to his body at the will of the captain." If he fell asleep a fourth time, he was effectively sentenced to death, suspended from the bowsprit "in a basket with a can of beer and a loaf of bread and a sharp knife." He was left to "hang there until he starve or cut himself into the sea." Thieves were hauled behind the ship on a rope into the next port of call and thrown ashore; seamen drawing a weapon during a dispute or brawl had their right hands nailed to the mainmast or cut off, and murderers were bound to the bodies of their victims and thrown overboard to drown. "If the offence be very foul," keelhauling was also practised, in which men were dragged under water from one side of the ship to the other by a rope passed right under the keel. "Whilst he is thus under water, a great gun is fired right over his head, which is done as well to astonish him as to give warning to all others of the fleet." It was a punishment of such brutality that many died from it, but discipline was maintained by such rough justice long after the Elizabethan era.[19]

In parallel with the improvements to English ships, crews and armaments, the traditional tactics of naval warfare, in which ships were merely an augmentation of the land forces or the means of transport by which troops were delivered to a hand-to-hand fight with the enemy aboard their own or the enemy's ships, were also revolutionized. When France tried to invade in 1545, Henry VIII's fleet was drawn up close to the shore batteries of Spithead so that together they could defend the land, but the privateering raids of Drake had showed that ships could be decisive in their own right. The troops that his ships carried were used primarily for sorties on shore, not for ship-to-ship fighting, and such warfare required a completely different strategy and tactics, aggressive instead of passive, defending the country by waging war on the high seas or in the enemy's ports and strongholds, and destroying his ships in his own territorial waters. In this new form of warfare, economic blows against the enemy were as vital as military ones; every treasure ship that was intercepted by English privateers was one less hoard of silver that Philip could use to pay his troops or crew his ships. Sea power therefore offered the prospect of achieving foreign policy ends without recourse to the damaging, financially draining continental wars that had emptied England's treasury for centuries. The Fighting Instructions issued by William Wynter, Surveyor of the Navy, in 1558 showed that cannon were then still intended to be used in conjunction with boarding and hand-to-hand fighting, rather than as a substitute for it, but by the 1570s, under Wynter's successor and bitter rival, John Hawkins, the emphasis had shifted. English galleons would now aim to outsail and outmanoeuvre their enemies and defeat them with the power and accuracy of their gunnery alone.

English crewmen were inured to hardships such as "a hard cabin, cold and salty meat, broken sleeps, mouldy bread, dead beer, wet clothes, want of fire," but their commanders had cause for concern about the physical state of their men and the availability of the provisions and munitions upon which they depended. Baking or salting were then the only available methods of preserving food and the lack of knowledge of basic nutrition, medicine and hygiene was reflected in the widespread ill-health of seamen. They were often malnourished even before they joined their ships and the shipboard diet was a virtual guarantee of sickness. When the rush floor-coverings of houses routinely harboured "spittle, vomit, the urine of dogs and men, the dregs of beer, the remains of fish and other nameless filth," the decks and ballast of ships at sea would scarcely be cleaner. All this left the crews especially vulnerable to the plagues that infected every fleet: dysentery, typhus and scurvy.

The early symptoms of scurvy—progressive weakness, tiredness and depression—take five to six weeks to develop, but the diet of most Englishmen, especially in the winter months, was so lacking in fruit and vegetables that seamen were often suffering from a deficiency of vitamin C before they even put to sea. The Mediterranean seaman's diet, based on dried or salt tunny, cod, sardines or squid, pulses, olive oil and ship's biscuit, was only marginally better. Seamen who had been kept on board for weeks or months to prevent desertions before the fleet sailed were also at increased risk. "Feeding them on salt-meat with only the diet of the ship two or three months sometimes before their going out to sea, must needs prostitute them to much sickness and infection and I believe has been the main occasion of those so extraordinary losses of men . . . in our sea expeditions." With the men already debilitated, scurvy could rapidly progress to its terrible later stages. Men's limbs became swollen and black, scars that had healed years before opened up again and old fractures of the bones broke once more. Teeth fell out in handfuls and blood trickled constantly from nostrils and eye-sockets. If fresh fruit was eaten, the recovery from the disease was near-miraculous, but without it death was inevitable. Despite halts in the New World and Asia to take on fresh supplies, Drake lost a quarter of his men to scurvy during his circumnavigation and there were recorded instances of every single member of a ship's crew perishing from the disease, leaving a ghost ship drifting over the seas.[20]

Within five years of the Armada, John Hawkins's son Richard—"the compleat seaman," who also designed a warm "gown" that seamen could wear over their other clothes in cold and wet conditions—was writing that "most fruitful for this sickness is sour oranges and lemons . . . a certain remedy for this infirmity," but even when they could be supplied, fruits and "roots" (vegetables) were considered very inferior foodstuffs. The standard diet of the poor was heavily dependent on black bread, made from barley, wheat, rye or oats, and in times of shortage or poor harvests they ate bread made from "horse-corn" (beans, lentils and even acorns), but rich and poor alike believed that the only proper food for man was meat. English seamen were "so besotted in their beef and pork that they had rather adventure all the calentures [fevers] and scurvies in the world than to be weaned from their customary diet." Coupled with the complacency, indifference and incompetence of the officers and administrators of the navy, this attitude ensured that the disease continued to claim lives for a further 250 years. Richard Hawkins also devised a "water still" capable of distilling potable water from seawater but, like the observation made by a merchant captain in 1572 that mosquito bites and malaria were connected, his discovery was ignored for centuries. Seamen continued to suffer and die from disease in far greater numbers than ever fell prey to enemy guns. Some 750 men, including some of Drake's best captains, died of scurvy, yellow fever, dysentery and typhus on the voyage to the Spanish Main in 1585.

Malnutrition and even starvation were also frequent. The conditions on board ship, bad enough when at sea, were actually worse when men were confined to the ships in port. While beer in cask, often sour and fetid, was preferred when available—and large quantities of fluids were required with a diet of dry biscuit and salt-meat—water for drinking and all other purposes was often drawn from the harbour, polluted with all the filth and excrement garnered by the rivers that emptied into it and the towns that surrounded it. Voyages lasting months, or even years in the case of Drake's circumnavigation, required seaworthy ships with powerful armaments, but they also had to be capable of sustaining their crews in good enough health to sail them. The narrow construction of the ships that made them fast and weatherly meant that they had little room for stores. Each man at sea was supposed to receive "for one flesh day [one of the four days per week when salt meat rather than fish was served], Biscuit 1 lb., Beer 1 gallon, Beef 2 lb. . . . On the fish day: Biscuit 1 lb., Beer 1 gallon, Butter/lb., Cheese/lb., Stockfish/fish," but on every long voyage the men were routinely put on short rations to conserve supplies, six sharing the food of four.

Soldiers were able to plunder what they could "on the country" to augment their diet, but sailors remained on short rations or starved until fresh provisions were supplied. Despite being reprovisioned from the stores of captured ships and by food seized when ashore, seamen of one of the ships of Drake's 1587 raid on Cadiz complained of "weak victualling and filthy drink . . . what is a piece of beef of half a pound among four men . . . or half a dry stockfish [and] a little beverage worse than the pump water?" The few victualling yards, breweries and naval stores that existed in England were incapable of producing huge quantities of supplies at short notice and, allied to the familiar combination of Crown parsimony and unpreparedness, it ensured that even the limited hold space in the English galleons remained unfilled. Elizabeth's penny-pinching extended to the most trivial of items; "no oakum [the soft hemp fibres, like modern cotton waste, that had a multitude of uses aboard ships: cleaning, staunching leaks, protecting ropes from wear, etc.] is to be had but at the hands of such as [make] it of rotten ropes."[21]

If the quantities of provisions were inadequate, the quality was even worse. Elizabeth's officials had forced down the price in real terms paid to contractors. A daily allowance of 4¹/₂d per man in harbour and 5d a day at sea in 1565 had been increased only to 6¹/₂d and 7d by the Armada year, during which time rampant inflation throughout Europe had caused the price of victuals to rise steeply. Beer and salt-beef had gone up by 50 per cent in a decade and stockfish had almost doubled in price. Even the new allowances were to be maintained only "until it shall please Almighty God to send such plenty as the high prices and rates of victual shall be diminished." Contractors responded by salting the very cheapest cuts of meat, not necessarily beef, and including pieces of offal, bone and hoof, or meat that was already rotting before it was put into the cask. As the beer went sour, the biscuit became worm-eaten and the beef, fish and cheese rancid, food poisoning and dysentery joined ship's fever in reaping a continual harvest of seamen. When even this food ran out, the men were reduced to eating rats, gnawing pieces of leather from belts and jerkins, or boiling straw in seawater for whatever nutrients it might contain.

The shorter supply lines of the English fleet when fighting in home waters should have conferred a considerable advantage, but, to save money, provisions were only issued a month at a time, greatly heightening the risk that commanders confronting the Armada might be forced to choose between starvation for their men and flight in the face of the enemy. Even worse, the orders for supplies of provisions were never issued more than one month ahead of time, even though it could take two months to assemble the victuals and then deliver them to the waiting ships. In April 1588, the Lord High Admiral, Charles Howard, had warned "how necessary it is to have a better proportion of victual than for one month, considering the time and the service that is likely to fall out; and what danger it might breed if our want of victual should be at the time of service. We shall now be victualled, beginning the 20th of this April unto the 18th May . . . the likeliest time for the coming out of the Spanish forces is the midst of May, being the 15th, then we have three days victual. If it be fit to be so, it passes my reason." The situation was not remedied, with the result that the fleet was again effectively immobilized from 26 June to 2 July and from 24 to 29 July. Had the Spaniards arrived off Plymouth during those periods, the English fleet would have been unable to pursue them for lack of provisions.

Gunpowder was also in desperately short supply, so scarce that musketeers for the militia were trained with "false fires" in which only the priming pan of the weapon was filled with powder; there would be a flash as it was ignited but the weapon would not fire. Attempts were made to reduce the naval custom of firing guns in salute of forts and other galleons and Elizabeth even criticized Drake for allowing his seamen to "waste" powder and shot in target practice, and cut back his supplies still further, leaving him with no more than enough for a day and a half's fighting. "Powder and shot for our great ordnance in Her Majesty's ships is but for one day and a half's service . . . and but five lasts of powder [equivalent to six tons; one last was 2,400 pounds] for 24 sail of the merchant ships which will scant be sufficient for one day's service . . . I beseech you to consider deeply of this, for it imports but the loss of all . . . such powder and munition as are delivered unto us for this great service, [are] just a third part of that which is needful; for if we should want it when we shall have most need thereof, it will be too late to send to the Tower for it." Given that each cartridge for a cannon contained over twenty pounds of powder, it is easy to see why Drake was so concerned. In any event, the arsenal in the Tower had little powder available as its stocks had been allowed to deplete as yet another of Elizabeth's cost-cutting measures.[22]

Throughout the winter Elizabeth's commanders had urged her to order them to sea to strike another preventive blow against the Armada, just as Drake had done at Cadiz the previous summer. She did not respond, though in her defence it must be said that such an attack was not certain to succeed and the damage done to her ships and crews by storms, poor provisions and disease might have outweighed any advantage gained by a swift strike against the enemy. There was also the terrible fear that the Armada might already be at sea and could slip past her fleet unseen to arrive off the coast of an undefended England. However, on the strength of her delusion that peace might yet be at hand, Elizabeth ordered her fleet to be laid up at Chatham and the crews to be discharged.

Howard's horrified warnings to her of the potential consequences grew less and less guarded as his frustration mounted. "I do warrant you our state is well enough known to them in Flanders, and as we were a terror to them at first coming out, so do they now make little reckoning of us; for they know that we are like bears tied to stakes, and they may come as dogs to offend us and we cannot go to hurt them. I have a good company here with me, so that if the Queen's Majesty will not spare her purse, they will not spare their lives." "Before these ships can have their full number of men again it will be a month to gather them, do what we can. And I pray to God we shall have them when we shall need." "If the forces of Spain do come before the midst of April, there will be as much ado to have men to furnish us, as ever was; but men we must have or else the ships will do no good." Howard's complaints fell on deaf ears and some of Elizabeth's finest ships continued to lie idle, uncanvassed and unsupplied. The cost of keeping a Queen's galleon at sea was under £400 per month; a fleet of half a dozen galleons and their attendant pinnaces could therefore be kept at sea for less than £3,000 a month, but despite warnings that "the King of Spain does not keep any ship at home . . . sparing and war have no affinity together," the Queen's ships "shall be to keep Chatham Church [kept in reserve], when they should serve their turn abroad."[23]

CHAPTER NINE

The twelve Spanish Shipps
Caled the 12 Apostles

The Advantage of Time and Place

With varying degrees of foreboding—for even Catholic govern-
ments had no appetite for further Spanish aggrandizement, and
there were those in Prague, Venice and the Vatican praying that Philip
might fail—Europe waited for the inevitable battle and the seemingly
inevitable Spanish victory. And England was only the first link in the
chain. If Elizabeth fell, the English fleet could then be used to blockade
the Channel and North Sea approaches to The Netherlands, starving
the Dutch rebels into submission. Encircled, Henri III of France would
either have to submit entirely to Philip's will or be crushed, and with

the whole of western Europe under his control there would then be nothing to stop Philip's forces moving eastwards and northwards, rolling up the Protestant princedoms, palatinates and cantons of Germany, Switzerland and Scandinavia one by one.

Yet a moment's rational thought should have shown that the idea of a successful Spanish conquest of England was a chimera. For thirty years Philip had been trying and failing to subdue a revolt in The Netherlands. How then, when even his fabulous wealth was already so mortgaged and over-committed, could he ever hope to subdue a country that if no more populous, was far larger, more powerful and, away from the South East, of far more difficult terrain? The Army of Flanders might fulfil the expectations of Catholic Europe and sweep into London, and Elizabeth might be deposed and her Council captured and killed, but much of England would remain unconquered, new leaders would emerge, and as summer faded into winter Spain would inevitably find itself mired in another protracted and probably unwinnable campaign.

Much of the western, eastern and northern fringes of Elizabeth's realm remained wild and lawless territory. Armies of reavers and moss-troopers raided north and south of the Scottish border with virtual impunity, the moors and mountains of the North, Wales and the South West were populated by people of ferocious independence and tribal cohesion, and in the Fens men of "brutish, uncivilised tempers" still used stilts to traverse their near-impenetrable kingdom of meres and marshes. Such territories were ideal for guerrilla warfare and it is unlikely that Spain could ever have entirely eliminated English resistance. Any attempt to reduce or withdraw the Spanish garrison in England would have invited insurrection, but without reinforcement the massively reduced Army of Flanders would also have come under renewed Dutch assaults. Secure in the certainty of his divine mission, Philip seems never to have considered this catastrophic possibility. Yet neither do there seem to have been any English contingency plans for a strategic withdrawal from London in the event of a successful Spanish invasion. Whether Elizabeth intended to stand or fall with her troops as her later rhetoric at Tilbury claimed, or had a secret plan of staged retreats to redoubts in the Midlands, Wales or the North, or whether the idea of defeat was as inconceivable to her as it was to Philip, will never be known, but the die was now cast and all Europe awaited the outcome.

The year 1588 was already being heralded as a momentous "year of wonders," as a result of an arcane prophecy based on the numerology of the Revelation of St. John. It identified the years 1588 and 1593 as the 5550th and 5555th since the Creation and claimed that there had been seven great cycles since the time of Christ. The previous cycle, the sixth, had ended in 1518, the year after Martin Luther had begun the great schism with the Catholic Church by nailing his Ninety-five Theses to a church door in Wittenberg. The final cycle was to culminate in 1588, heralded by an eclipse of the sun in February and two eclipses of the moon, one in March and one in August, presaging the opening of the seventh seal, the overthrow of the AntiChrist and the onset of the Last Judgement. Comets, tempests, floods and earthquakes, snow and hailstorms in summer, darkness at noon, monstrous births, even skies raining blood, were all proclaimed as portents of the terrible events to come. Some warned that "an utter and final overthrow, and destruction of the whole world shall ensue." "If this year, total catastrophe does not befall, if land and sea do not collapse in total ruin, yet will the whole world suffer upheavals, empires will dwindle and great lamentations will ensue."

The prophecy by Cyprianus Leovitius, often incorrectly attributed to the fifteenth-century mathematician Johan Muller, known as Regiomontanus, was greatly feared throughout Europe, and most regarded the impending confrontation between the champions of the Catholic and Protestant religions as the portended conflict. Pope Sixtus received a report from England claiming that an earthquake had struck the ruins of Glastonbury Abbey, exposing a marble slab on which the prophecy had been incised. The papal informant took this as proof that the English Crown was the one threatened by the prophecy, but there was no shortage of others willing to believe that the Spanish, French or other thrones could be at risk. In Prague, the Emperor Rudolf II, an obsessive astrologer who claimed lineal descent from the Roman Empire at the time of Christ, felt himself particularly threatened and was so distracted by the prophecy that Venetian spies reported that vital dispatches lay unread for weeks on his table and even Philip's ambassador could not gain access to him. It was also reported that recruiting in the Basque region of Spain was becoming impossible "because of many strange and frightening portents that are rumoured," and belief in the prophecy persisted despite denunciations of astrology and other superstitions from the pulpits of Spanish churches. As 1588 approached, desertions from the Armada fleet in Lisbon increased dramatically.[1]

In the Protestant countries too, particularly the rebel provinces of The Netherlands, the prophecy was reprinted and endlessly discussed. Some felt it portended doom for the "papist antichrist," and the Protestant mystic James Lea saw a vision of the destruction of a giant born of a union between the devil and its mother, Pope Sixtus. The body was a swarm of priests, monks and Jesuits, the tail a rabble seeking spoil. "His arms thoroughly imbued with blood, his sword dyed red in the same, as though he had lately come from the slaughter of an infinite number of seely lambs and sheep . . . in the latter end of the year 1588, I found him dismembered, wounded, and humbled."

Others were less sanguine, fearing that their own Protestant state and religion was the most threatened. Only in England were the almanacs relatively silent about the fateful prophecies. Elizabeth's horoscope had been cast by the celebrated astrologer Dr. Dee, who discovered that the second of the year's eclipses of the moon coincided with her ruling sign in the ascendant and came just twelve days before her birthday. The implications of such a portentous conjunction were obvious, but almanac writers were well aware that any attempt to suggest, even by the most indirect means, that the Queen herself or her throne was in peril was high treason punishable by death. Even so, the prophecies were the common currency of tavern conversations, and every strange occurrence, from "a vast number of fleas collected together" on a window of the Queen's Presence Chamber to "30 great fish commonly called porpoises" swimming up the Thames to the watergate of the Queen's palace, was scrutinized for its significance. One of Mendoza's English spies wrote to tell him that in the eastern counties there was talk that an old prophecy about soldiers conquering England with snow on their helmets would soon be fulfilled. In August 1587, rumours of a Spanish fleet of two hundred ships off the coast had sent people fleeing in droves and many of the rich decamped to London to escape the immediate danger. Elizabeth issued a proclamation compelling them to return to their country homes, but a further rumour in December that the Spanish fleet was already in the Channel again sent many of the inhabitants of coastal towns scurrying for safety inland, to her undisguised fury.[2]

Reports from English spies in Spain, Lisbon and The Netherlands confirmed that the Armada was about to be launched against England, but though most of the Queen's ships lay idle at their moorings throughout the winter, unarmed, unprovisioned, unrigged and carrying only skeleton crews, their apparent lack of readiness was a little misleading. When Walsingham warned Elizabeth in December 1587 that Santa Cruz might sail with the Armada even before Christmas, the fleet and most of the armed merchantmen were crewed, provisioned, armed and ready to put to sea within a fortnight. After contradictory reports were received, most of the ships were stood down again and rode at anchor in the Medway or Plymouth, where "the harbour is badly defended at present, as the men have been landed to save the victual in the ships." Only four galleons and a few pinnaces maintained a patrol off the coast of Flanders. The crews of the other ships were once more reduced to a minimum, saving the Queen, by Burghley's calculations, almost £2,500 a month—a tiny fraction of what Elizabeth had squandered on futile expeditions to The Netherlands by her land forces and the hire of ineffective Swiss and German mercenaries.

Her finances were sorely stretched. Her military adventures in Europe had drained the Treasury and the interdiction of English trade had reduced it to a fraction of its former value, and Elizabeth made England's trading performance even worse by granting monopolies to favoured courtiers or selling them to boost her revenues. The export of wool and finished cloth by the merchant adventurers was England's principal source of wealth, accounting for 80 per cent of exports at the start of her reign, the vast majority of which was sold through the great market of Antwerp. The blockade of Antwerp and hostilities with Spain severely damaged English exports, and although new "vents" (markets) were found in Hamburg, Middelburg, Emden and Stade, the trade was far below its levels of the 1560s. In December 1586, the Privy Council had even tried, without success, to compel the merchant adventurers to continue purchasing cloth for which they had no market. The lucrative markets of Spain and Portugal were closed to Englishmen, though many carried on trading "under cover of Scottish merchants," and Spanish hostility made trade with the Mediterranean fraught with difficulties.

Elizabeth's weak financial position was not unique. The whole European trading economy was close to collapse and even countries striving to remain neutral found their markets restricted. If there was money to buy their goods, ports were blockaded, and their ships were liable to be embargoed, impounded or seized upon the high seas, for privateers unable to find legitimate targets were more likely to take neutral ships as prizes than return home empty-handed. Even Spain was suffering from the disruption to trade. Before the Dutch revolt, the tax revenues from the Spanish Netherlands had contributed more to Philip's Treasury than even the plate fleets from the New World. Now Antwerp, once the most densely populated and prosperous mercantile centre in Europe, self-proclaimed "for the uses of all merchants of whatever land or language," was virtually deserted, and ships rotted at their berths in the ports, unable to run the blockade imposed by the Dutch Sea Beggars. Philip's trade and tax revenues had disappeared and his sea communications with Flanders were vulnerable to interdiction by English ships; he was reduced to smuggling gold to Parma by "ordinary passenger barks freight with oranges, which under that small show do often carry the Spanish pay into Flanders."[3]

As winter passed into the spring of 1588, Elizabeth continued her lifetime habit when faced with difficult or unpleasant realities: to prevaricate, vacillate, obfuscate and then to reach abrupt decisions only to retract them at once. Howard expressed his fears that the time for action was almost past and that Elizabeth's indecision and tight-fistedness would be the cause of her downfall. "I fear me much and with grief I think it, that Her Majesty relies upon a hope that will deceive her and greatly endanger her; and then will it not be her money nor her jewels that will help; for as they will do good in time, so will they help nothing for the redeeming of time being lost."

While they awaited Her Majesty's permission to set sail, her captains worked to bring their ships to a pitch of battle readiness. They had taken a battering in the winter storms and needed repairs and refitting. "This winter's weather, although we have been but a while abroad, has so stretched our sails and tackle, torn many of our blocks and pulleys and sheevers, stretched our boats and destroyed some of our pinnaces . . . as a man would never believe it unless he does see it; these be the fruits that the seas bring forth, especially in this time of the year." During January and February, William Hawkins, elder brother of John and Lord Mayor of Plymouth, had each of the great galleons of the Western Squadron careened in turn on the Plymouth shore. One side was scraped and tallowed by day and the other side that night "by torchlight and cressets [metal containers filled with blazing pitch or oil], and in an extreme gale of wind, which consumes pitch, tallow and firs abundantly," before being refloated on the spring tide.

He also made every effort to purify the ships and remove the reek of corruption and disease. Half-hearted attempts were often made to sterilize the lower decks by having a man carry a shovelful of smouldering pitch, sulphur or other pungent or aromatic substances through the ship. Hawkins preferred to send men up into the hills around Plymouth for cartloads of broom branches. Fires were built on the galley hearths in the bilges of the ships, and when well alight they were smothered in armfuls of wet broom. Clouds of dense, choking smoke filled the air as the men retreated and closed the hatches. The fires were left to burn themselves out overnight and the ashes were then removed, having destroyed, or so it was hoped, rats, lice, fleas and the taint of ship's fever, flux and scurvy that hung over any ship long at sea.

His work complete, Hawkins declared that the ships were "so staunch as if they were made of a whole tree," and Lord Howard shared his confidence. "I have been aboard of every ship that goes out with me, and in every place where any may creep and I do thank God that they be in the estate they be in; and there is never a one of them that knows what a leak means. There is none that goes out now but I durst go to the Rio de la Plata in her." "I protest before God and as my soul shall answer for it that I think there are never in any place in the world worthier ships than these are, I had rather live in the company of these noble ships than in any place."[4]

When Drake's former flagship, the *Elizabeth Bonaventure*, went aground near Flushing, Howard went aboard her. Though she remained grounded for two tides before she could be refloated, "in all this time there never came a spoonful of water into her . . . Except the ship had been made of iron it were to be thought impossible to do as she had done and it may be well and truly said there never was nor is in the world a stronger ship than she is." He became even more effusive about his own flagship, the *Ark*. Commissioned by Sir Walter Ralegh, the *Ark Ralegh* had been "purchased" by Queen Elizabeth in January 1587 while still under construction. Ralegh waited five years to be compensated and was then told that the value of the ship, £5,000, was being struck from his debts to the Crown. The 800-ton ship, later renamed *Ark Royal*, carried 55 heavy guns, including four 60-pounders, four 30-pounders and twelve 18-pounders. Howard had originally taken the *Bear* as his flagship, with his cousin Lord Thomas Howard in the *Ark*, but he made the change in mid-January 1588, as soon as he had inspected the ship. "I pray you tell Her Majesty for me that her money was well given for the *Ark Ralegh* for I think her the odd ship in the world for all conditions . . . We can see no sail great or small but how far soever they be off, we fetch them and speak with them." Even Sir William Wynter was forced to admit that "our ships do show themselves like gallants here. I assure you it would do a man's heart good to behold them, and would to God the Prince of Parma were upon the seas with all his forces . . . we would make his enterprise very unpleasant to him."

Reports of the death of Santa Cruz had reached Elizabeth in late February or early March and allowed her to again delay putting her fleet to sea, but Howard continued to press her for greater urgency in the defence of her realm and eventually persuaded her to send another eight ships to join the squadron cruising off the Dutch coast. Drake was meanwhile champing at the bit to be off for the coast of Spain. Even though there were reports of as many as 400 to 500 ships manned by 80,000 men in Lisbon, he asked only for four more of the Queen's galleons and some London ships to bring his own squadron up to 50 ships. "The advantage and gain of time and place will be the only and chief means for our good . . . with fifty sail of shipping we shall do more good upon their coast, than a great many more will do here at home; and the sooner we are gone, the better we shall be able to impeach them." He was ready to mount a blockade, "attacking several different places along the coast," and by so doing deter the Armada from setting sail, for "he knew (without self-flattery) what great fear his name inspired all along the coast of Spain." The mere rumour of El Draque's presence, "the dragon upon the coast," was enough to keep Spanish ships cowering in port.[5]

Drake argued as forcibly as he dared for an easing of Elizabeth's purse-strings to enable the fleet to be properly armed and provisioned, and for her to show the urgency and speed of decision that her perilous situation required. "I assure Your Majesty, I have not in my lifetime known better men, and possessed with gallanter minds . . . We are all persuaded that God, the giver of all victories, will in mercy look upon your most excellent Majesty and us your poor subjects, who for the defence of Your Majesty, our religion and native country, have resolutely vowed the hazard of our lives. The advantage of time and place in all martial actions is half a victory, which being lost is irrecoverable. Wherefore if Your Majesty will command me away with those ships which are here already and the rest to follow with all possible expedition, I hold it in my poor opinion the surest and best course; and that they bring with them victuals sufficient for themselves and us to the intent the service be not utterly lost for the want thereof . . . for an Englishman being far from his country and seeing a present want of victuals to ensue and perceiving no benefits to be looked for, but only blows, will hardly be brought to stay. I have order but for two months' victuals . . . whereof one whole month may be spent before we come there; the other month's victuals will be thought with the least to bring us back again. Here may the whole service and honour be lost for the sparing of a few crowns. Touching my poor opinion how strong Your Majesty's fleet should be to encounter this great force of the enemy, God increase your most excellent Majesty's forces both by sea and land daily, for this I surely think, there was never any force so strong as there is now ready or making ready against Your Majesty and true religion."

John Hawkins argued equally forcibly for action on the coast of Spain and, showing his usual keen awareness of the best way to the Queen's favour, urged "that there be always six principal good ships of Her Majesty's . . . which shall haunt the coast of Spain and the islands and be a sufficient company to distress anything that goes through those seas . . . The charge . . . may be £2,700 a month for wages and victuals and it will be a very bad and unlucky month that will not bring in treble that . . . For these six ships we shall not break the strength of the navy; for we shall leave a sufficient company always at home to front any violence that can be any way offered to us."[6]

A plan approved by the Privy Council on 25 February 1588 had called for the fleet to be divided in two, one half to patrol the Straits of Dover, the other "towards Ireland and Spain." Two further small squadrons were also to be separated from the main fleets, one to intercept the *flota* in the Azores and the other to exploit the absence of Spanish forces with the Armada by attempting to stir an insurrection in Portugal. Such a profusion of aims and divisions of the English fleet was liable to end in disaster and the attacks of the two squadrons were deferred, but Elizabeth and her Council continued to insist that the fleet should be divided between the eastern and western approaches to the Channel, with the bulk of it, including John Hawkins and Lord Howard and the Eastern Squadron, stationed in the Medway and the Downs off the coast of East Kent.

Drake was the first to understand that Philip's strategy would be to use the Armada to convoy Parma's troops to England, and in a stream of letters and a personal appearance at the Court, he argued that, given the prevailing westerly winds in the Channel, the traditional defensive strategy of massing a fleet in the Narrow Seas was fundamentally flawed, yielding the weather gauge to the enemy and allowing them the opportunity to make a landing anywhere along the South Coast. Instead the bulk of the fleet should be based at Plymouth, from where it would have the ability both to pre-empt any landing by the Armada and defend the Channel coast throughout its length, and to shadow and attack it from windward as it made its way towards Flanders. Ireland was perennially vulnerable to Spanish invasion but the English ships could not patrol the Irish coast without leaving their own shores vulnerable to attack. If the Spaniards landed in Ireland, forces could then be mustered and convoyed to attack them, as had happened when the Hispano-Papal force was landed at Smerwick in 1580, but meanwhile it could be left to its own defences.

Having argued for the correct defensive strategy, Drake continued to urge even more strongly the pressing need to make a pre-emptive attack on the Armada. The first line of England's defences was not the coastline of England but that of its enemy, and the first blow should be struck there. There was no shortage of precedents; many of Elizabeth's forerunners—King John in 1213, Edward III in 1340, Henry V in 1416 and 1417 and her own father in 1512—had waged defensive war on an enemy coast. When the Queen, more as a delaying tactic than through any sudden interest in naval strategies, asked for details of his plans of attack, he replied that though "Your Majesty would willingly be satisfied from me how the forces now in Lisbon might best be distressed, truly this point is hardly to be answered as yet for two special causes: the first that our intelligences are as yet uncertain; the second is the resolution of our own people, which I shall better understand when I have them at sea. The last example at Cadiz is not . . . yet forgotten, for one flying now as Borough did, will put the whole in peril, for the enemy strength is now so greatly gathered together and ready to invade. But if Your Majesty will give present order for our proceeding to the sea and send to the strengthening of this fleet here four more of Your Majesty's good ships, and those sixteen sail of ships with their pinnaces which are preparing in London, then shall Your Majesty stand assured, with God's assistance, that if the fleet come out of Lisbon, as long as we have victual to live upon that coast, they shall be fought with."

Drake had surveyed the outer defences of Lisbon while lying off the coast the previous summer, and later in 1587 an English pinnace had sailed undetected up the Tagus to "between the tower of St. Gian and that of Belém, where it remained one night," to spy on the Spanish preparations and evaluate the Armada, but if his intention was to penetrate the most secure harbour in Europe he was scarcely likely to reveal his proposed tactics to anyone, even the Queen, since they would then be the subject of Privy Council discussion and Court gossip, and details would inevitably be passed to Spain. It's equally possible that Drake simply did not know how he proposed to act—he had admitted at the start of his circumnavigation of the globe that "I have taken in hand that I know not in the world how to go through"—and he may well have been relying on his customary blend of guile, subterfuge, bold aggression and the fortune that attends the brave to carry the day. But even if he deemed the defences and the narrow twisting channels leading into the Tagus to be impregnable, he merely had to lie off shore and await the emergence of the Armada . . . assuming it was not already at sea.

Information on the state of the Armada remained sketchy, leading Howard to complain, "This I am sure of, if Her Majesty would have spent but 1,000 crowns to have had some intelligence, it would have saved her twenty times as much. Assure yourself he [Philip of Spain] knows what we do here." The information that was available was alarming in the extreme, for most reports greatly exaggerated the number of ships and men in the Armada. In April Frobisher informed Howard that a hundred pilots, including two Englishmen, had passed by Calais in a flyboat from Dunkirk, on their way to rendezvous with the Spanish fleet. A report brought from St. Malo by "a man of Dartmouth," and passed on to the Queen by Drake, claimed "that their fleet is in number between four and five hundred sail, ready furnished with seventy or eighty thousand sailors and mariners." Wildest of all, Nicholas Abraham and Johan Lambert, "being prisoners in Bilbao for the space of 12 months and 20 days . . . did understand by credible report that there was provided and should be 700 sails of ships, galleys, galleasses, pinnaces, and patches, and of men to the number of 280,000, said to be for England." A rather more reliable witness, "a Breton who thirteen days past departed from Cadiz," reported that all shipping was "stayed until such time as the Spanish fleet should be departed . . . for that no news should be carried to England," and a letter from a Spanish nobleman in Lisbon, intercepted by Walsingham's spies, confirmed that the Armada was ready to sail. "All things are embarked, even to the mules that must draw the artillery; and [it is] commanded here, upon pain of death, no man to go ashore; only we do tarry for a fair wind to go to sea."[7]

As usual, Drake's pleas for immediate action were backed by Walsingham and opposed by Burghley, who believed that Drake's voyages were "only profitable to himself and his companions, but an injury to the Queen as they only irritated foreign princes." As was her wont when faced with conflicting advice, Elizabeth first assented and then changed her mind, over and over again. Howard had originally preferred to marshal his forces close to England but by the spring of 1588 he had been convinced by Drake and his other commanders of the need for a pre-emptive strike. "I confess my error at that time . . . but I did and will yield ever unto them of greater experience," and from then on he argued strenuously for that course of action. "The opinion of Sir Francis Drake, Mr. Hawkins, Mr. Frobisher and others that be men of greatest judgement and experience, as also my own . . . is that the surest way to meet with the Spanish fleet is upon their own coast or in any harbour of their own, and there to defeat them." Howard also criticized the half-cock preparations for war that were all the Queen would authorize. It was one of the few areas where a nobleman with little naval experience was more effective than a low-born sea-fighter like Drake, for as the Queen's cousin and one of her oldest friends and allies Howard could write to her in terms that would not have been tolerated from any other source. "Surely this charge that Her Majesty is at is either too much or too little; and the stay that is made of Sir Francis Drake going out I am afraid will breed grave peril." "I am sorry Sir F.

Drake is not in more readiness than he is. I know the fault is not in him. I pray to God Her Majesty do not repent these slack dealings."

The Queen's other captains also urged action. Thomas Fenner wrote to Walsingham, "I would to God we had been now upon that coast [of Spain]; the impediments would have been great upon their army [i.e., the Armada] gathering together . . . We rest here a great number of valiant men, and to great charge upon my gracious mistress, and a great grief of mind to spend Her Majesty's treasure and do nothing upon the enemy." Lord Henry Seymour even managed to turn his account of running aground in the *Elizabeth Bonaventure* off Flushing into a plea for the restraints on the navy to be removed. "I wish that this honourable ship, being grounded 12 hours upon the sands, had been as long in fight and trial with the Spaniards in good sea-room." Walsingham took little persuading of the need for an end to cheese-paring and a start to decisive action. "I am sorry to see so great a danger hanging over this realm so slightly regarded and so carelessly provided for. I would to God the enemy were no more careful to assail than we to defend."[8]

When Elizabeth was at last persuaded of the wisdom of basing her main forces at Plymouth—she continued to prevaricate about allowing Drake to launch a pre-emptive attack on the Armada—she uncharacteristically granted even more than he had requested: fourteen of her strongest galleons and many of the armed merchantmen and volunteer ships, but a fleet of that size had to be commanded by the Lord Admiral himself, leaving Seymour's squadron to guard the Narrow Seas. Howard sailed for Plymouth on 31 May—"the wind serving exceedingly well, I cut sail at the Downs"—and he arrived at eight o'clock on the morning of 2 June, flying the royal standard and the flag of an admiral, and followed by the other thirty ships of his fleet in battle order. Drake sailed out to meet him with his ships in three files, "making a brave show of his skill and diligence, sending the pinnaces and other smaller craft ahead, making a show of reconnoitring the ships that were coming in." The "decks, tops, yards and shrouds" of Drake's ships were lined with men and he fired his guns in salute, had the drums and trumpets sounded, and lowered his own flag—until then he had been Admiral in the West—and hoisted the vice-admiral's flag that Howard had sent him to acknowledge the Lord Admiral's primacy. Drake's demotion was more than a matter of mere pride, for his share of the income from patronage and junior officers' appointments was correspondingly reduced, but Howard's fears of Drake's resentment proved unfounded. To the surprise of many, he accepted his position without apparent demur and, whatever his private feelings, in public he showed all the proper respect to his commander. "I must not omit to let you know how lovingly and kindly Sir Francis Drake bears himself and also how dutifully to Her Majesty's service and to me."

If Howard feared problems with his vice-admiral, Drake also had potential problems with his immediate subordinates. The vastly experienced John Hawkins had once been Drake's own captain and might resent taking orders from him, and Martin Frobisher had returned from his voyage with Drake in 1586 burning with resentment at Drake's arrogance and indifference to opinions other than his own. Time had in no way diminished his fierce hatred. The captains of the ships provided by the City of London took a different view. A Spanish agent claimed that they had refused to serve under the inexperienced Howard "and wish to be commanded by Drake." Their request was granted but Howard's position within the fleet was strengthened by his contribution of seven of his own ships, all of which were commanded by relatives or close associates. He also had a network of relatives commanding several of the Queen's ships: Lord Henry Seymour, Admiral of the Narrow Seas, was his brother-in-law, Sir Robert Southwell and Sir Richard Leveson were his sons-in-law, Lord Thomas Howard his cousin, and Lord Sheffield his nephew.[9]

Although one potential obstacle had been avoided, Howard had much else to occupy his thoughts. After shortages in the fleet and the absence of either supplies or funds from the Crown had forced Drake and Hawkins to use their own money to buy food for their crews, Howard appealed to the Privy Council for £5,000 or £6,000 to buy provisions, and even expressed the belief that the Armada's departure might be deliberately delayed to aggravate the supply problems of the English fleet. "I am verily persuaded they mean . . . to linger it out upon their own coast until they understand we have spent our victuals here." Victuallers bringing supplies from London were repeatedly delayed and Howard's orders from the Queen were countermanded, reinstated and then countermanded again. He wrote angrily to Burghley on 7 June to complain that he had been told that the victuals for the fleet, promised a week earlier, "would not be ready to depart in 12 or 14 days after . . . I judged it would be so, for when there is more care had of the merchants' traffic than there is of such matter of importance as this is, it is like it will be no better. My Lord we have here now but 18 days' victual and there is none to be gotten in all this country and what that is to go withal to sea, your Lordship may judge, and to tarry, that we must not . . . God send us a wind to put us out, for go we will, though we starve . . . for I believe surely if the wind hold here but six days, they will knock at our door."

Adding further point to Howard's protests about the preference being given to merchants, Burghley sent a letter ordering him to allow a ship from Hamburg laden with rice and other foodstuffs to depart for London. Howard replied that he had already "caused the said rice to be stayed and taken for Her Majesty's use," and once more appealed for further supplies. "There is here the gallantest company of captains, soldiers and mariners that I think was ever seen in England. It were pity that they should lack meat when they are so desirous to spend their lives in Her Majesty's service." "I will never go again to such a place of service but I will carry my victuals with me and not trust to careless men behind me. We came away with scarce a month's victuals; it had been little enough but to have gone to Flushing. We think it should be marvelled how we keep our men from running away, for the worst men in the fleet know for how long they are victualled, but I thank God as yet we are not troubled with mutinies, nor I hope shall not [be], for I see men kindly handled will run through the fire and water." Burghley ignored the complaints and continued to busy himself with attempts to balance the Crown accounts—a hard task for a man "unable to handle the simplest addition or subtraction sums in any but Roman figures, with the inevitable result of frequent mistakes and faulty account-keeping." There was, it is true, little enough money to go round, but the predicament was as much of Elizabeth's making as of outside factors such as the decline in trade. Had she reined in her more useless expenditures in previous years or summoned Parliament to meet the extraordinary situation with an extraordinary grant, more money might have been available, but as it was, her fleet remained starved of victuals and warlike supplies.[10]

Despite the concerted arguments of Howard, Drake, Hawkins and Frobisher that the place to defend the coast of England was on the coast of Spain, the Queen still directed Walsingham to veto any such plan, fearing that the Armada might outflank her fleet and "shoot over to this realm." Howard's reply pointed out the futility of trying to use his fleet to defend all the possible approaches and landing places that the Armada might choose along the entire coastline of Scotland, Ireland, Wales and England. He added, with heavy sarcasm, "I must and will obey, and am glad there be such there [at Court] as are able to judge what is fitter for us to do than we here." Having registered his protest, Howard was forced to patrol uselessly, "plying up and down" far out in the western approaches as the Queen required, despite bad weather and rough seas. By 23 June he was complaining that "here is such weather as never was seen at this time of the year . . . the wind has continued so bad these 15 days we could by no means send any pinnace into the Trade [the sea area between Brest and Ushant]."

Over the following days, alarming reports began to come in of sightings of Spanish ships near the Scilly Isles. On Thursday 30 June "a barque of Mousehole in Cornwall being bound for France to lade salt, encountered with nine sail of great ships between Scilly and Ushant, bearing in North-East with the coast of England . . . their sails were all crossed over with a red cross . . . The same morning . . . the English-man had speech with a flyboat who . . . willed him in any wise, as he loved his life, not to proceed, for said he, the Spanish fleet is on the coast." There were other reports of fleets of great ships with red crosses upon their sails, and on 1 July a Dublin barque was captured "some 15 leagues South-west of Lizard" by a group of Spanish ships and taken in tow. The cable parted in "foul weather" and three of the Irish crew made their escape. They reported that the ships were "eigh-teen sail in number, great hulks and very full of Spaniards, not less than ten thousand." A trader, Simons of Exeter, was chased by "fifteen Span-ish ships." He reached harbour in Cornwall and at once rode for Ply-mouth to bring a warning to Drake, but by then reports were coming in that the Armada had been scattered by storms, with many ships in harbour at Corunna.[11]

The Queen at once "swore by God's death, as she is accustomed to do, and with a great deal more brag, that she would send her fleet to disperse the Armada, even if it were in the interior of Spain," or so the Spaniards were informed by one of their agents. In fact the Queen rather more typically took the opportunity to tell Lord Howard that with the Armada scattered, at least for the moment, three of her galleons could be returned to their previous employment of "keeping Chatham Church," and their crews laid off. Only the most furious and desperate arguments from Howard persuaded her to change her mind. Meanwhile, restricted to port by the shortage of victuals, his fleet missed the chance to strike a damaging blow at the Armada, for while it remained in or near Plymouth, as the reports had indicated, eighteen Spanish ships blown off course by a gale were hovering around the Scillies, where they would have proved easy prey.

Plymouth was a town of only 2,000 citizens and the fleet assembled there had more than doubled its population, causing severe pressure on food supplies at a time of year when the ripening grain had yet to be gathered and the previous year's poor harvest had caused a tripling of the price of wheat. When the supplies promised from London failed to appear, Marmaduke Darell, responsible for victualling the Western Fleet, toured the countryside of Devon and Cornwall, one of the poorest regions of the country, buying what provisions he could find, "more like a mess steward with a market basket than the agent victualler of a great fleet." He managed to scrape together a fortnight's provisions, but the staple of the navy, salt-beef, was not to be had. Even if enough bullocks could be found and slaughtered, it took "at least eighteen days to barrel the salt meat." When the London victuallers still failed to appear and supplies again ran low, Darell was once more forced to cajole, bribe and threaten farmers, brewers, bakers and suppliers into producing a few more days' provisions. Howard was now beside himself with impatience to be provisioned and at sea, so that his fleet could either defend the coast if the Armada was upon them, or attack it in harbour if it was still at Corunna. On 29 June he wrote to Walsingham, pleading, "For the love of God, let not Her Majesty care now for charges, so as it be well used . . . I pray send to us with all speed, but I hope to be gone before I hear from you, for I will not tarry one hour after our victuals do come to us and if the wind will serve us, for there must be no time lost now and we must seek to cut off their time."[12]

Drake echoed his words. "Our staying here in this place shall but spend our victual, whereby our whole action is in peril." Three days later, on Saturday 2 July, Howard sent another desperate appeal. "Our victuals are not yet come . . . our extremity will be very great . . . Men have fallen sick and by thousands fain to be discharged [and] others pressed in their stead, which has been an infinite charge [and] great trouble to us . . . we have been more careful of Her Majesty's charges than of our own lives as may well appear by the scantyings [scrimpings and savings] which we have made." "I am very sorry that Her Majesty will not thoroughly awake in this perilous and most dangerous time." Around midnight that night, the victualling fleet at last arrived at Plymouth, together with fresh orders from the Queen to set sail for Spain. It was only just in time, for even on short rations the fleet was down to its last three days' supplies. After a sleepless night, Howard sent a message that was both an acknowledgement that the supplies had been received and a final exhortation to the Queen. "They were no sooner come in, though it were night, but we went all to work to get in our victuals which I hope shall be done in 24 hours, for no man shall sleep nor eat till it be dispatched so that, God willing, we shall be under sail tomorrow morning . . . For the love of Christ, Madam, awake thoroughly and see the villainous treasons round about you, against Your Majesty and your realm, and draw your forces round about you like a mighty prince, to defend you."[13]

By seven that Sunday evening Howard was writing to Walsingham, "God willing, I will cut sail within this three hours," and with the north-east wind behind them and fearing that at any moment the Queen would yet again countermand her orders, the fleet put to sea without even waiting to complete the loading of the stores. Almost a hundred armed ships set sail for Corunna in the early hours of Monday 4 July, a great arc of ships, with a screen of pinnaces extending for several miles ahead and to either flank. If the Armada was upon the seas, only the most foul ill luck would enable it to avoid detection, but ill luck with the weather they had in plenty. The wind backed southerly and was blowing a gale before they had passed out of the Channel approaches, between the Scillies and Ushant (the Île d'Ouessant), and for over a week they beat into the wind, making painfully slow progress towards Spain. On 17 July the wind came northerly again, but the fleet was once more short of provisions and Howard was stricken with fear that the Armada might have put to sea and be able to slip by the English screen in the vast reaches of the Bay of Biscay. Drake would have none of it; there were provisions for the taking on Spanish ships and the Spanish coast, and he argued vehemently—on no more than experience and instinct, and the lack of sightings of Spanish ships on the open seas—that the Armada still lay at anchor in harbour.

The Lord Admiral was duly persuaded to use the following wind to make a dash for Corunna, but within sixty miles of their target the wind betrayed them. It died to a flat calm and when it rose again it was blowing from the south-west and strengthening all the time. The difficulties of beating against the wind were compounded by the fear—now shared even by Drake—that the Spaniards might be using the same wind to put to sea. They had been in port for a month, ample time to refit and repair storm damage. It seemed inconceivable that they would not take advantage of this favourable wind to make for England, and if they passed the English fleet unseen they would arrive in the Channel to find it undefended. Howard and his commanders turned for home. Five days later they were back in Plymouth. In fact, they returned on the same day, 22 July, that the Armada once more set sail. The Queen's galleons had proved their worth; they were little damaged by the gales and rough seas they had encountered, but many of the armed merchantmen needed repairs, having been "dispersed and returned in great misery, as by sickness and foul weather much beaten and spoiled," and having lost spars and rigging or sprung leaks.

No sooner had Howard dropped anchor than he was in receipt of a complaint from the Queen that he was not making sufficient efforts to locate the Armada. His reply was heavily sarcastic. "We are here to small purpose for this great service if that had not been thought of . . . There has been no day but there have been pinnaces, Spanish caravels, flyboats and of all sorts sent out . . . The winds have been so southerly and such foul weather . . . I know not what weather you have had there, but there was never any such summer seen here on the sea." Seymour also bemoaned the weather as he rode the Straits of Dover but noted that though the south-westerly gales were the most favourable winds for the Armada, they would also batter its vessels. "Such summer season saw I never the like for storms and . . . westerly great gales . . . the same serve well many times for the Spaniards to come, yet shall they be as greatly dangered by the raging seas as with their enemies."

Howard had other worries than the weather, for even though the English crewmen had been on short rations throughout the voyage, some ships were already again short of food and water, and dysentery and ship's fever were breaking out among the crews. "God of his mercy keep us from sickness, for we fear that more than any hurt that the Spaniards will do. I would Her Majesty did know of the care and pains that is taken of all men for her service. We must now man ourselves again for we have cast many overboard and a number in great extremity which we discharged. I have sent with all expedition a prest [press gang] for more men." Appeals were sent out to the Justices of the Peace throughout the South West for new recruits. Having scoured the seaports, press gangs ranged further and further inland, seizing men from their labour in the fields and even as they emerged from Sunday service in church. They were brought to Plymouth with only the clothes they stood up in. Meanwhile provisions and more munitions and powder were loaded aboard the ships, though the niggardly amounts of money allocated by the Queen would buy precious little of either. As it rode at anchor in Plymouth that day, Howard's fleet had no more than ten days' provisions and two days' worth of gunpowder.[14]

The Bristol merchant Thomas Cely was employed "by my Lord Admiral and Sir Francis Drake" as a spy upon the coast of France and Spain and on 27 July he forwarded a report that the gales had caused some damage to the Armada. "There is two of their galleys left, and two of their galleasses have rolled their masts overboard and many of their fleet have broken their yards and other their tackling. Notwithstanding . . . they arm themselves as fast as they can to proceed in their wicked and malicious attempt . . . A sharp war and a short, although it be chargeable . . . is fit for England. The Queen's subjects desire it. If I might have been heard, it had been done before this day, with a great deal less charges . . . if it had pleased Her Majesty. The King of Spain will make our mistress wise within few years, if it be not prevented." He also complained that his earlier attempts to alert the Queen and her Privy Council to the threat from Spain had been spurned, one Counsellor telling him that if he "could do Her Majesty any service, so that it did cost money, or that if charges should arise upon it, never speak of it, for she will never consent to it. So I went my way with a flea in my ear."

The English commanders all knew well enough the threat they faced. The winds that had driven them home were from the right quarter to speed the Armada towards England, and they made frantic efforts to resupply their ships with provisions and fresh men. On 27 July Howard reported that "Four or five ships have been discharged [of their men, for the] sickness in some is very great," and bemoaned the shortages that had forced his fleet back into port at the most dangerous time of all. "If it had not been to water and that all the ships sent out by the coast towns wanted victuals, I would not have seen this town [Plymouth]." As if the shortages of men, munitions, food and beer were not bad enough, a fresh crisis was now brewing that threatened to cause a mutiny in the fleet. The seamen's wages, which were in any event barely above subsistence levels, had remained unpaid for between five and sixteen weeks. Thomas Fenner sent an impassioned appeal to Walsingham for the necessary funds and supplies to be made available at once: "Now is the time, I beseech God move your Honour, to further and hasten our departure." Similar appeals came from Howard, Hawkins and Seymour in the Narrow Seas. Hawkins complained that "the men have long been unpaid and need relief," and Seymour urged Walsingham "to move the Lord Treasurer [Burghley]. Sir, You shall do very well to help us with a pay for our men, who are almost sixteen weeks unpaid; for what with fair and foul means, I have enough to do to keep them from mutiny." Burghley replied the next day, complaining that the subject was causing him more distress than "purging" of his stomach, but professed a complete inability to pay the sums owed for wages and provisions, now totalling some £50,000. Even Mendoza and Parma could not have designed a more dangerous way to sabotage the English fleet.[15]

CHAPTER TEN

The Earle of Oxford Northumberland Cumberland, w^{th}
many more of the Nobility
and Gentry going to visit the
English Fleet.

ᴄⱯ Bad Place to Rest In

For four days after leaving Corunna, the Armada made good if slow progress, sailing northwards on a strengthening south-west wind, warmed by the sun shining from clear skies, and crossing calm seas that belied Biscay's fearsome reputation. Medina-Sidonia complained that had he not had to govern his speed by that of "the scurviest ship in the fleet" he would have been "at the mouth of the Channel" by 25 July instead of still struggling north across the Bay of Biscay. On that day Medina-Sidonia sent "the captain Don Rodrigo Tello to Dunkirk to advertise the Duke of Parma of his coming and to bring back word of what state Parma should be in and where it seemed to him best for them to join their forces," but the next morning the wind shifted into the north and grew steadily in strength. The Armada struggled on under a black and lowering sky, the wind screeching through the rigging and rain cascading from the sodden sails, flooding the decks. All that day and the next, the storm—the Spaniards called it a *tormenta*—battered the Armada, and many of its ships were again scattered.

In such heavy weather, conditions aboard the less weatherly of the Armada ships were almost intolerable. Many were "stiff boats"—slow to roll with the swell and quick to spring upright again—with a lurching motion that reduced even some of the experienced seamen to helpless seasickness. The huge Atlantic head-seas hit the broad bows of the lumbering hulks and merchantmen with a shock like an axe. The soldiers were discouraged from spending time on deck, where they might obstruct the work of the seamen handling the ship and cause yet more friction between them, but every inch of space on the crowded lower decks was contested. With the gunports and main hatches closed and caulked against the wild weather, the air was fetid and stifling, stinking of men's sweat, vomit and the sour stench of bilgewater. The planking glistened with condensation and beads of moisture dripped from the beams overhead. A handful of lanterns, swinging through pendulum arcs as the ship rolled, gave the only illumination and in the semi-darkness ships' rats made scuttling forays from nests and havens in the bilges and among the mountains of equipment in the holds. Men lay in their flea- and lice-ridden clothes, taking what rest they could among the jumble of great guns run in towards the centre line of the ship, the stacks of ramrods and powder scoops, armour, weapons and personal equipment. Anything not lashed down was thrown around as the ship pitched in the heavy seas and the ranks of whey-faced men must have prayed even for battle as a distraction from the woes of seasickness. The wild motion was greatly magnified in the towering sterncastle where the officers had their quarters, and even more in the rigging where men clinging to slippery yards fought to reef and furl the sails as spray and spume filled the air and the wind shrieked around them, cracking loose rigging like whips.

As the storm continued, "seas broke clean over the ships and the whole stern gallery of Diego Flores' flagship [the *San Cristobal*] was carried away," but the vice-admiral of the galleys, the *Diana*, "making so much water that she was unable to follow the Armada," was the first ship to separate from the fleet. The captain made a desperate attempt to reach a safe haven but the *Diana*, wallowing low in the water, with waves coursing over the bows and half drowning the slaves and convicts at the oars, ran aground near Bayonne. Her guns were salvaged and the crew, even down to the slaves, were rescued, but the ship broke up under the pounding of the waves. The remaining three galleys—built for the placid waters of the Mediterranean and, even after being strengthened, too low-waisted, long and narrow for Atlantic conditions—were also forced to run for the coast as the seas grew heavier. "After nightfall when the weather became thick with very heavy rain, they were lost sight of and we have seen them no more." They never rejoined the Armada. A Dublin merchant later reported that he had "found Spaniards upon the water and took them up and took off their clothes," and their vessels were "so sore beaten with weather that they had the carpenters ten days repairing of the galleys" when they reached harbour in France.[1]

The fifth loss to the Armada was even more serious. The *Santa Ana*, flagship of the Biscayan squadron, had already been damaged in the earlier storm off Corunna, and the captain now chose to run before the gale into the Channel, seeking shelter in the Bay of La Hogue. He made no subsequent attempt to rejoin the Armada and the loss of the 30-gun warship with its complement of 300 sailors and fighting men was a serious blow. The battering of the waves had also damaged Don Hugo de Moncada's flagship of the galleasses, the *San Lorenzo*, "her rudder being broken. These craft are really very fragile for heavy seas such as these." Even the most powerful Armada ships suffered storm damage. "Not only did the waves mount to the skies but some seas broke clean over the ships . . . It was the most cruel night ever seen," Medina-Sidonia complained with the hyperbole of a landsman experiencing his first major storm at sea. John Hawkins sailed through the same storm and described it as "a little flaw."

On Thursday, 28 July, "the day dawned clear and bright, the wind and sea more quiet," but in addition to the galleys, "forty ships were counted to be missing." Just before the sun rose, the navigators had calculated the Armada's position. When out of sight of land, they used a cross-staff or astrolabe to chart the position of the sun at noon or the Pole Star at dusk or dawn, and dead reckoning to calculate the distance sailed. When within sight of land, they navigated from headland to headland, using a rutter to help identify coasts that they did not know. The helmsman set his course from a compass mounted in a binnacle and lit by a lantern at night. But in unfamiliar waters, without a chart, a rutter or a local pilot, ships' captains did "but grope as a blind man does, and if that they do hit well [find the place they were seeking], it is but by chance and not by any cunning that is in them."

As the carpenters of the *San Lorenzo* and *San Cristobal* continued frantic repairs to their storm-damaged ships, Medina-Sidonia ordered soundings to be taken. The leadsman swung the heavy lead forward from the bows, hauled in the slack and took the reading as the line came to the vertical beneath him. Establishing the depth and comparing the sand, crushed shell or mud embedded in the cup-shaped, tallow-filled hollow in the lead's base with the known nature of the sea bottom in an area helped to confirm—or deny—the position calculated by the navigators. In deeper waters a lead of twice the weight was used, attached to up to 200 fathoms of line, but it could only be used from a stationary ship. The leadsman "found bottom at 68 fathoms," and fine white sand was embedded in the tallow, confirming that they were just outside the Channel approaches and still some distance from the Lizard. "One league off the Lizard the depth is forty fathom, coarse sand but clear, and the more to the westwards, the deeper the water and the finer the sand . . . the deepest water between Scilly and Ushant is 64 fathom, so unless there be 64 fathom when you ground, the Channel is not yet entered." Medina-Sidonia then sent off three pinnaces, one to make for the Lizard and "see if the missing ships were there . . . another should discover land and examine the same, and the third was to turn back and order all the ships [behind] to make more sail." Meanwhile the Armada departed under shortened sail.[2]

The next morning, Friday 29 July, the pinnace sent to the Lizard "returned with news that the missing ships were in front, under the charge of Don Pedro de Valdes, who had collected them," and the Armada was reunited soon afterwards. The long, slow swell of the Atlantic was now giving way to the shorter, steeper, tidal chop of the Channel and there were growing signs of the closeness of land. Seabirds increased in numbers, a line of land clouds was visible to the north, dimly hazed with smoke, and even some miles from shore the dark tint of the deep ocean became paler and the water was faintly discoloured with silt washed down from Cornish rivers. Scraps of kelp and flotsam drifted past on the current and, in the distance ahead, a flock of gulls wheeled and cried in the wake of a fishing boat scurrying for harbour at the dread sight of the advancing Armada.

At four o'clock that afternoon "the coast of England was seen, and was said to be the Lizard," for centuries the first landfall of ships entering the Channel. Even the stolid Medina-Sidonia must have been gripped by emotion at this, his first sight of the coastline of the country he had been sent to conquer, just visible as a dim, misted outline against the cloud-streaked sky before the weather again closed in and hid it from view. From this moment on, there could be no thought of retreat or return to Spain until the invasion was complete or the Armada vanquished. The sacred standard blessed by the Pope and carried in procession through Lisbon Cathedral before the Armada sailed was raised on the mainmast of the *San Martin* and the royal standard on the fore-mast, answered from all the other ships by a forest of flags bearing the dragons and shields of Portugal, the castles of Castile, and the flags of the other home provinces, together with the flags and pennants of the nobles and knights aboard, the emblem of the saint to whom each ship was dedicated and King Philip's flag—the Burgundian red cross. Three signal guns were fired, calling every man to a prayer of thanksgiving for the Armada's safe arrival and "beseeching Our Lord to give us victory against the enemies of His Holy Faith."

There were still several hours of daylight remaining, but rather than pressing on with all speed while the advantage of surprise was with him, Medina-Sidonia chose to heave-to, allowing the repairs to the *San Lorenzo* and *San Cristobal* to be completed and the slow-moving hulks and converted merchant ships straggling behind to close up to the main formation. "I will set sail as soon as the flag galleass has been put in order," he wrote to the King that night. With their sails furled, the ships of the Armada were rendered almost invisible below the horizon to any watchers scanning the seas from the Cornish coast, and the bea-cons on the cliffs and hilltops remained unlit. As the great ships rode the swell, Medina-Sidonia ordered a gun fired and a flag put out to sig-nal a council of war and once more his senior commanders were rowed across to the *San Martin*. Their deliberations produced only one clear decision: in defiance of Philip's specific orders issued before they sailed and repeated in the message he sent to Corunna, they determined "to proceed as far as the Isle of Wight and no further" until they had some indication of the state of readiness of Parma's forces. "All along the coast of Flanders there is no harbour or shelter for our ships," and if Parma's troops were not embarked and ready, the Armada would be in a hopelessly vulnerable position. "Our vessels might be driven on to the shoals where they would certainly be lost." It was an assessment shared by the English. "These huge ships that are in the Spanish army shall have but a bad place to rest in if they come to the eastward of Portsmouth." Recalde had argued instead for taking Falmouth, Ply-mouth or Dartmouth "especially as the highly necessary reinforce-ments of men and stores will have to be sent from Spain, and isolated vessels will be exposed to much danger from the enemy higher up the Channel," but Medina-Sidonia preferred, or was persuaded, to choose an anchorage closer to Flanders.[3]

Don Alonso de Leiva, supported by Recalde and Oquendo, two of the most experienced commanders, then urged an immediate attack on Plymouth, "where, by the report of a fisherman whom we took, we had understanding that the English fleet was at anchor. It was resolved we should make to the mouth of the haven and set upon the enemy if it might be done with any advantage, or otherwise keep our course directly for Dunkirk." The mention of Dunkirk rather than "the Cape of Margate" was significant; Medina-Sidonia had now either realized or been persuaded by his commanders of the folly of contemplating a rendezvous within sight of the English coast, leaving Parma to cross forty miles of open ocean in barely seaworthy and undefended barges. An attack on Plymouth was again contrary to Philip's explicit instructions, and Medina-Sidonia and others also feared the shore batteries guarding the narrow and difficult approaches to Cattewater, the mouth of the river Plym, where the English fleet lay at anchor. "The fleet was within the haven, whereof the mouth is so strait as not more than two or three ships could go in abreast, which was insufficient for that action."

It was the sort of opportunity with which Drake had been presented at Cadiz: a fleet at anchor, still reprovisioning and held captive by the prevailing wind and tide. He had not hesitated for a second. Ignoring the cautious William Borough, he had pressed ahead at once, leaving his fleet to follow him as swiftly as it might, and by sailing into the enemy lair he had secured a famous victory. Had the Armada ships arrived off Plymouth in time and run the gauntlet of the shore defences, they would have had Howard's fleet helpless. The English shore batteries might have given the Spaniards a pounding as they closed, but the Armada had troops enough to land a force to silence the guns and take the city—its population of barely two thousand could not have provided much resistance.

The English ships could not have escaped from the harbour against the south-westerly wind and flood tide that would have brought in the Spanish fighting ships, and in the tight confines of the upper Sound and the Cattewater, they could not have manoeuvred to avoid being boarded. Even if not silenced, the shore batteries could not have continued to fire for fear of hitting their own ships, and the Spanish troops, superior in numbers, equipment and close-combat experience, would then have made short work of their opponents. It would have been a gamble, for the hulks and merchantmen would have had to be left outside the Sound with only a modest force to protect them, but if the main English fleet was in harbour, the only other force that could have attacked the Armada's hulks was the Squadron of the Narrow Seas, and there was not the slightest possibility that Sir Henry Seymour would have risked deserting his station in the Straits of Dover with Parma's invasion force so close at hand.

Faced with such a dilemma, Santa Cruz might well have pressed ahead and attacked Plymouth. Hampered by his own cautious instincts and lack of naval experience, and bound by the rigid instructions of the King, Medina-Sidonia had chosen to heave to. Later that night the arguments about whether to attack or blockade Plymouth were rendered irrelevant when one of the Spanish pinnaces under the command of the Duke's ensign bearer, Alferez Juan Gil, returned with four captured men—the terrified crew of a Falmouth fishing boat. Under interrogation they revealed that an attack would be pointless for "they had that evening seen the English fleet go out of Plymouth under the charge of the Admiral of England and of Drake."[4]

At around four that afternoon, Friday, 29 July 1588, the same time that the Duke of Medina-Sidonia was taking his first sight of England, Thomas Fleming, captain of the 50-ton barque *Golden Hind*, "a pirate, who had been at sea pilfering," dropped anchor in Plymouth and raced ashore. Although he would certainly not have spurned any prize that came his way, Fleming, together with Robert Scarlett, "Hill the Fisherman" and several others, had been assigned to patrol the western approaches of the Channel, forming a screen of fast ships and pinnaces, some of them disguised as innocuous merchantmen, "for discovery" of the Armada. At dawn that day Fleming's lookout in his perch high on the mainmast had sighted a large flotilla of fifty Spanish ships near the Scilly Isles, their sails struck, "hovering in the wind, as it seemed to attend the rest of the fleet." Fleming had at once set course for Plymouth, over a hundred miles away, piling on every scrap of sail, the masts and spars groaning and the stays taut as lute strings as the pinnace sped over the sea, its lines so sleek that it pierced the swell like a knife.

The news that he brought to his squadron commander, Sir Francis Drake, that humid summer afternoon could hardly have been more ill-timed. The fleet had returned only seven days previously from the abortive attempt to destroy the Armada as it lay at anchor in Corunna. Even on that eighteen-day run, many crewmen had succumbed to dysentery and ship's fever, and only with great difficulty had new men been found or pressed to replace those discharged from the fleet; "the men may not well be spared, being a great number and many from home already with Sir Francis Drake." Repairs to the sails and rigging of the storm-battered ships had been carried out but, as usual, there had been delays with the victuals, and even supplies of fresh water were a problem in Plymouth. The sources within the town were often inadequate or foul and mariners were "many and often times driven by necessity to go a mile or more from the town and their ships to fetch fresh water." Fresh supplies were still being loaded aboard some of the ships when the news of the sighting of the Armada was received—low water at Plymouth, with the flood tide just beginning to run. It was impossible to leave harbour against the tide and the south-west wind, and for several more hours Drake and Howard could do little but watch and wait.

The legend of Drake's game of bowls on Plymouth Hoe may well be apocryphal—the first reference to it did not come until thirty-six years after the event—though the remark attributed to him, "We have time enough to finish the game and beat the Spaniards too," fits the "brag countenance" he liked to display. There was little further he could do aboard his ship until the tide began to turn around nine o'clock that night and, whether playing bowls or not, he would certainly have been on the Hoe at some time that afternoon. It was a natural lookout point above the town, from where he could scent the breeze for any change in the wind direction and gaze out past the green slopes of Mount Edgecumbe and St. Michael's Island, across the wind-ruffled waters of the Sound, flecked with the sails of fishermen returning with the day's catch. Their mean cottages huddled around the shores, "walls of earth, low thatched roofs, few partitions, no planchings or glass windows and scarcely any chimneys other than a hole in the wall to let out the smoke."[5]

The route back from the Hoe led past the decaying thirteenth-century Castle Quadrate and through the Barbican, a warren of cavernous cobbled streets, deeply shaded even at the height of the day, and lined with tall stone houses, their oak casements pierced by diamond-paned leaded windows. It would be surprising if Drake had not made the time to say his farewells to his wife Elizabeth, waiting at his town house in Looe Street. Seamen's wives grew used to such partings, the long absences that followed and the ever-present fear that their husbands might not return, but those emotions would have been multiplied tenfold by the thought of what awaited Drake this time when he put to sea. Perhaps they also spent a few moments in contemplation and prayer together in the walled garden, seated on the stone bench in the shade of a fig tree, the air heavy with the scent of roses, lavender and thyme, and drowsy with the buzzing of bees. It would be some time before he or his men would again have the luxury of such moments of repose.

In late afternoon or early evening, as the shadows lengthened over the water, Drake walked down through the maze of streets and alleys on the steep hillside above Sutton Harbour, avoiding the piles of horse dung and rubbish. The morning rain had swept some of the filth from the cobbles, washing it into the harbour where the tides would scour it clean, but refuse was piled high in some of the meaner courts and side alleys. Groups of ragged children picked over it like the mudlarks waiting on the shore for the tide to turn and expose a new harvest of flotsam from the sea. The chandlers, roperies and sail-lofts, and the warehouses of New Street, were all closing for the night, the last loads being hauled out on the beams and pulleys projecting overhead and lowered to the waiting carts in the street. The dockside taverns and whorehouses were almost deserted, for the vast majority of men of all ages were already aboard ship or had made themselves scarce lest they too be pressed to serve with the fleet, but a few boats still plied between the quays, slipways and gently sloping beaches, and the fleet anchored offshore.

Whenever ships were to sail, women and old people gathered in groups around the quayside. This time the talk would not have been the customary speculation about the plunder that their men might bring back but sombre discussion about the prospect of invasion and the likely fate of their sons, brothers and husbands. Drake's appearance on the quayside invariably caused a great stir. Even the children playing in the dust, indifferent to the concerns of their elders, would gaze open-mouthed as this most famous of Englishmen strode by. Many people would call out to him, bless him and jostle to touch his sleeve or scan his face, searching for some sign of hope, some clue to England's fate. Drake undoubtedly gave an outward show of confidence, and it would not have been assumed; an inner certainty of the rightness of his cause and the blessing of his God was as central to Drake's being as it was to Philip of Spain; the Protestant and Catholic champions were both driven by a faith that bordered upon fanaticism.

The smaller armed merchantmen and some of the Queen's great ships were clustered in the Cattewater, while the remainder rode at anchor in the rougher waters of the Sound. Drake was rowed out to his ship, the *Revenge*, the finest galleon in the fleet, anchored in the lee of St. Nicholas' Island. She was over a hundred feet long at the keel, but the bowsprit and the great wooden beak of her prow made her look much longer. Her forecastle, rails and poop deck were decorated in chevrons of green and white but the paintwork was faded and weather-stained. The jet-black hull had a dull gleam, for it was freshly tarred, and the familiar smell of pitch was strong in the air as Drake climbed aboard. He moved stiffly, his limp a permanent reminder of the injuries he had suffered at Spanish hands. The ship stood ready when the order was given; all the barrels of provisions that there had been time to load—"the haste of my Lord Admiral was such . . . that several of his ships had not leisure to receive the full of their last proportions [supplies]"—had already been stowed and secured and the gun tackles tautened and belayed.

Like the other commanders, Drake at once began his last inspection of his ship before sailing into battle. He stood for a moment looking over his domain, then began pacing the upper deck, the planking beneath his feet fresh-scoured with sharp sand and still warm from the last rays of the setting sun. Fore and aft the bilge pumps were already at work, their cylinders formed from single hollowed-out elm or alder trees, still covered with bark to prevent the wood from drying out and cracking or splitting. The pumps were caulked with pitch, and iron plungers flanged with leather washers rose and fell inside them, sending spurts of filthy bilgewater spewing out of the sides.

Groups of crewmen stood by the fore- and mainmasts, ready to spring aloft at his command. His keen eye ranged over the masts, banded every couple of yards with iron hoops, the rigging and the sails neatly furled at the yards, and scanned the pennant at the mast tip for the first stirrings of a land breeze that would help him out of harbour, but the wind was still from the south-west, carrying the salt tang of the open sea. If he saw anything out of place, a word from Drake would send crewmen scrambling to rectify the fault. Some of the men aboard were veterans of many voyages with him and they must have greeted him with a look that hinted at shared knowledge and experiences, and confidence in the outcome of the battle that they faced. An empty hogshead was chained to the rails on either side of the ship towards the forecastle "for the soldiers and mariners to piss into, that they may always be full of urine to quench fire with, and two or three pieces of old sail, ready to wet in the piss." The hogsheads were placed there on all the Queen's ships, in accordance with orders laid down years before, and none had apparently ever questioned why urine should prove any more effective in fighting fires than the limitless seawater available by dangling a bucket on the end of a rope over the side.

Guncrews tended the lighter weapons mounted on the upper deck, and others stood ready as Drake descended the companionway into the darkness of the gundecks where the great bronze and iron cannons and culverins were housed, closer to the waterline where their weight would not unbalance the ship. The master gunner, William Thomas, a veteran of many voyages with Drake, presided over the main gundeck with his apprentice, Russke. It was a single, low-ceilinged space, running almost from stem to stern. Gnarled oak beams close overhead spanned its full width, the marks of the shipwrights' adzes and axes still clearly visible in the surface of the wood, and the cavernous space was interrupted only by the great trunks of the masts rising like majestic trees in some dark forest clearing. Every timber and beam was blackened by spent powder and gunsmoke, and a faint brimstone smell still hung in the air, even though it was many weeks since the great guns had last been fired in anger. The open hatches and gunports spilled small pools of light into the gloom; the only other illumination came from a single lantern at either end of the deck.[6]

The great guns were decorated with coats of arms in bas relief and lifting handles in the shape of dolphins, wolves and lions, and their polished barrels shone dimly in the faint light. The gun-carriages that bore them were equally massive, stepped like ziggurats, with wheels cut from solid rounds of a tree trunk. The oak planking around them was worn and grooved where the guns had been run in and out, over and over again. Pyramids of great shot and piles of cloth and "paper royal" cartridges—stout paper cylinders each containing a measured charge of black powder—had been stacked in the lockers by the guns, with lengths of unlit match-cord coiled alongside them. Long-handled ramrods, powder scoops and "sponges"—lambskins to swab out the gun-barrels between shots—stood at the side of each gunport, held in place by leather straps. A failure to sponge the cannon properly before reloading could prove fatal; hot powder residue could ignite the fresh charge prematurely and kill the guncrew. Powder and shot were not brought to the guns until action was imminent—powder could rapidly become damp and unusable, and shot breaking loose from the lockers in heavy weather was almost as much of a menace to the guncrews as that fired from enemy ships—but none knew what awaited them as they cleared the Sound that evening and the crew was prepared for any eventuality. The main shot and powder stores were sited below the waterline on the ballast at the bow and stern, as safe as they could be made from enemy fire. The black powder contained there was so volatile that it could be detonated by a spark of static electricity, and artificial light was permitted in the stores only "upon special occasions"—emergencies—and then only "a candle . . . fixed in a close-glazed lanthorn." Cartridges were carried from the stores inside wooden cases "to avoid the peril of being fired by the way."

The light grew progressively more dim and the air more foul as Drake descended into the stifling confines of the lower deck. The cramped quarters of the ship's surgeon, one of only a handful in the fleet, contained a wooden table fitted with leather restraining straps, on which casualties would be laid. The surgeon's chest stood ready for use, filled with the savage tools of his trade: "incision knives, dismembering knives, razors, head-saws, cauterising irons, various types of forceps, probes and spatulas designed for drawing out splinters and shot," all wrapped in oily rags to protect them from rust. The "plaster box" next to it contained less extreme remedies: "Stitching quill and needles, splints, sponges and clouts [cloths], along with cupping glasses, blood porringers . . . and a range of plasters."

The ship was ballasted with gravel, laid on the seeling—the thick planking above the bilges in the bottom of the hull. Well compacted, the gravel was not overprone to shifting in heavy seas, but it was a harbour for filth and disease and had to be "rummaged"—removed and cleaned or replaced—every few weeks, if the exigencies of the service permitted such a luxury. Although this had been done while in Plymouth and the ship thoroughly cleaned and sluiced, the holds still reeked with the sour odour of bilgewater. The sail stores, rope and cable lockers, timbers and tools of the ship's carpenters, the caulkers' pitch, tallow and tow, and the hides, wooden plugs and lead sheets used by the divers and carpenters to repair shot-holes in the hull were stored in the holds or wherever space allowed. Spare masts and yards were usually lashed to the outside of the hull.

The huge water butts stood on the gravel in the bilges, adding their considerable weight to the ballast. Nearby were the provision stores and the galley fires on cast-iron hearths, from which smoke rose through a crude wooden chimney to the upper deck. The galley fires were sited on the ballast because it was the only fire-proof element in the ship, but the heat hastened the decay of the provisions stored nearby. Scraps of rotting food, bilgewater, the refuse of the boat and even human ordure also contaminated the ballast. Seamen usually defecated over the rails of the forecastle—the flukes of the anchors slung against the hull were often fouled as a result—but men racked with dysentery, scurvy or ship's fever inevitably fouled their quarters and the resultant waste, sluiced from the decks with buckets of seawater, found its way into the gravel in the bilges. Enlightened ship's surgeons argued that "close-stools" (portable commodes) should be provided so that a seaman suffering from dysentery might "find comfort in his most pitiful distress . . . a poor weak man in his extremities should not continually go to the shrouds or beak head to ease himself, nor be noisome to his fellows"—but they were deemed inessential and the ship's ballast continued to be fouled. The galley and food stores and the source of disease and infection were thus in the closest possible proximity to each other. On such wooden ships, fire was also a constant fear. The galley fires were extinguished at sundown and men were detailed to search the ship at night to make sure that no candles were in use. All the candles belowdecks were housed in lanterns glazed with wafer-thin horn and were allowed only for the most essential purposes, and the smoking of pipes was forbidden anywhere but on the upper deck.[7]

The men's quarters were spartan, cramped and minimally furnished. Those who had sailed to the New World had seen the natives of the Caribbean using hammocks, and John Hawkins had pioneered their use in English ships in 1586, but though the fashion had spread rapidly, there were still relatively few men striving "for a place to hang up their netting for to lie in." The majority of their crewmates still slept on the bare boards of the deck, with only a single coarse and frequently lice-infested blanket "of dogswain" (rough cloth), and "a good round log" or a folded jerkin for a pillow. Even the most well-equipped men had few clothes and fewer possessions aboard and the pressed men often had nothing but the clothes they stood up in. The experienced men had already staked out their portion of deck, leaving the lower ranks of the shipboard hierarchy—the pressed men and cabin-boys—with the least favoured areas, hard up against the bows where the pounding of the waves was loudest and where, in even the most well-found ship, water always leaked from around the base of the bowsprit as it flexed and twisted, rising from and burying itself in the swell.

Drake's own cabin and quarters beneath the poop deck at the stern were much more comfortably furnished, but far from large. In such a tight and narrow ship, no more than thirty-eight feet at its greatest breadth, there was little space to spare even for the Vice-Admiral of the Fleet. On his circumnavigation and his voyages to the New World, Drake had often dined in style with two or three musicians to serenade him as he ate. There would be no such luxuries on this voyage and precious few moments of repose. His charts and navigational instruments were stowed away. He had little need of them in the Channel waters, which were as familiar to him as the streets of Plymouth. Before sailing, as was his routine practice, he called his men together around the mainmast and led them in prayers for the safety of their loved ones and for victory in the battles to come, kneeling on a cushion at a table, while his crew chanted the responses. Then each man went to his post, alone with his thoughts as they prepared to make sail, the warm, familiar sounds and smells of the dockside drifting to them over the water.[8]

Just before nightfall, with the wind easing and the tide now on the ebb, a signal gun was fired and orders were shouted, the noise rolling over the water and echoing through the streets of the town. The royal galleons and the largest and best-armed of the other great ships weighed anchor, the capstans creaking and the decks resounding to the rhythmic tread of men straining at the bars. As the great cables wound around the capstans, seawater was squeezed from them like wrung washing and rivulets snaked across the deck, spilling into the scuppers. As each huge iron anchor broke surface, rust-stained, wet and glistening, and trailing mud and weed, it was caught and swung aboard one of the ship's boats, instead of being hauled up and lashed against the hull. The men bent to the oars and began warping their ships out of Cattewater and down Plymouth Sound, using the lee of Mount Edgecumbe to shield them as much as possible from the south-westerly wind. It was a slow, laborious process. Again and again a longboat would row out ahead of the *Revenge*, carrying the anchor and fathoms of sodden, weed-encrusted cable. Six inches in diameter, the cables weighed between one and two tons when dry, and their weight doubled when wet. When all the cable had been paid out behind the boat, the anchor was pitched overboard and the galleon winched up to it by the sweat of the crewmen manning the capstans. As one cable was hauled in, a second ship's boat was already rowing ahead with another.

Other galleons were towed out behind their ship's boats or winched by cables fixed at points along the shores of the harbour or St. Nicholas' Island. It was back-breaking toil for the men at the oars and those at the capstans, but none complained or slackened his efforts. If the Armada reached Plymouth while the English ships were still warping out, the battle would be over before it had begun. The men at the capstans trudged in an endless circle, heaving at the wooden levers as the leathery soles of their bare feet strained for purchase on the planking, and the only mark of their progress was the rhythmic dry click of the capstan's ratchets. The sound echoed across the water to the crowds lining the quays. Like seamen's families and friends down the centuries, they had come to see their loved ones sail, a smile set like a rictus on every face, knowing in their hearts that many of these men would never return.

As each ship in turn emerged into open water with searoom to use the breeze, men sprang to the rigging, climbing aloft to unfurl the sails while the deckhands stood ready at the braces, sheets and falls. The great galleons were living things, constantly in motion and full of sound: the hollow, echoing thud of waves against the bows, the soft rush of water beneath the stem, the continual creaking and groaning of the timbers as the ship flexed with the swell, the faint hum of the rigging and the endless but ever-varying sound of the wind through the sails. The long "beak head" at the bow broke up head seas, and though the ships still pitched and rolled in the swell, their frames were flexible enough to withstand the effects of even the worst storms of the Atlantic and the North Sea. Yards and spars bent with the wind and, as the ship heeled before it, the mast swayed as much as a yard out of true. The rigging, stays and shrouds on the lee side slackened and hung loose, while those on the weather side were dragged as taut as bow strings. Ropes and rigging chafed and wore with every movement and had to be constantly renewed. The helmsman felt each tremor through the helm in his hands and was alive to every facet of the ship under his control, his gaze shifting constantly between the horizon on the weather side, the ocean ahead, and the spars, rigging and mastheads above him.

As the deckhands bent to their work, their leather jerkins gleaming with salt spray, the guncrews went below to check their weapons, stack further piles of shot and bring more powder and cartridges from the bow and stern stores. No one knew when the first encounter with the Armada might occur. It was now well over twelve hours since Thomas Fleming had first sighted it and, with the following wind to speed them, had the Spanish galleons come on under full sail they could easily have been bearing down on the English ships as they began to emerge from the Sound. However, the topmen peering into the darkness reported the night sea empty of hostile ships and one by one the fleet pulled clear of the Sound and anchored in the lee of Rame Head, all lanterns and torches extinguished, as the flood tide again began to run. The danger of at least a part of the fleet being trapped by a Spanish attack was far from past, particularly if the wind backed southerly, as a west wind often did on this coast, but the night passed without incident and the dawn light revealed no more than an empty sea.

During the morning, as the wind freshened and the tide again began to ebb, many more ships pulled clear of the Sound. At the head of a fleet of fifty-four ships, Howard was already beating out to sea, "very hardly, the wind being at south-west." Even with the help of the tide, progress to windward was painfully slow, barely three knots an hour, and it was not until around three o'clock that they passed the Eddystone Rock, thirteen miles south of Plymouth. Soon afterwards Howard's topmen caught their first tantalizing glimpses of the great Armada through the rain squalls sweeping up the Channel on the wind: "120 sail, whereof there are four galleasses and many ships of great burden." Seamen swarmed to scale the rigging and see for themselves the fabled and long-awaited enemy, but a few moments later it was lost to sight again as the cloud and rain closed in once more.[9]

The Armada had resumed its progress up the Channel at dawn that morning, Saturday 30 July. On that very day thirty-four years earlier, another Spanish armada had landed in England to deliver Philip II to his wedding with Mary Tudor at Winchester. Diego Flores de Valdes had been at his side then, and would have needed no reminding of the significance of the date. As at first light every morning, "men of quick sight" were at the mastheads scanning the horizon for enemy ships and counting the sails of the Armada. If they discovered "any in excess"— enemy ships that had infiltrated the formation during the night—they would shout for the topsail to be dipped twice and a gun fired and the nearest ships to the intruders would take up the pursuit.

Other eyes were also scanning those dawn seas for enemies. Throughout the night, a watchman had been huddled on Pen Olver, a jumble of rough granite knuckles of rock rising above the sheer cliffs of the Lizard like the ruins of some ancient fortification. Even before the first faint hint of light in the eastern sky, the rising chorus of birdsong had given warning of the approaching dawn. There had been no other sounds to break the stillness of the night, no creak of timbers, no oars working in their rowlocks, no muttered voices. For months he and his fellows had kept watch here. Each time a sail appeared there was a frisson of doubt—was this the forerunner of the dread Armada, or just another of the traders or fishermen endlessly plying the Channel? Each time it had been no more than a false alarm but now, as dawn broke, he saw the mast tip and pennant of a ship heading up the Channel on the strong south-westerly breeze. He crept stiffly from his crude shelter, a gap between two boulders, roughly roofed with driftwood spars and turf. The dew glistened on the coarse serge of his coat as he leaned on the wind, a hand braced against a lichen-encrusted boulder, straining his keen eyes into the haze. He glanced away, then looked again as the ship inched into view with painful slowness. Another speck appeared behind it, and then another and another. As he stared, transfixed, more and more dark shapes were visible, wraiths shifting and changing like the eddies in the mist, then slowly coalescing into sails like great grey clouds drifting over the water. Beneath were the dark shapes of upperworks and hulls. He waited, his heart pounding, wanting to be sure.

All that year and the last there had been enough false alarms. The Hampshire militia had been called out as a result of a fire lit to smoke a badger out of its sett, and bored, disaffected or malicious people had ignited hilltop fires on a number of occasions, causing widespread panic. Coastal watchers had also caused the beacons to be lit at the approach of strange ships that proved to be only English galleons or merchantmen: "The country . . . up in arms and beacons lit in consequence of certain hulks having been sighted in formation." One of Sir Walter Ralegh's captains had sighted "more than 60 sail off the point of Cornwall" and sparked a frenzied embarkation of the fleet and embargoing of merchant ships. That fleet had proved to be only "a flotilla of

60 hulks belonging to Hamburg," but this time the watchman was certain that these were no hulks or English men-of-war. He could now discern masts, crow's-nests, even the tracery of rigging on the leading ships, and with every passing minute more and more came into view, until the sea seemed black with galleons, their fighting castles towering above the waves, the cream canvas of their billowing sails tinged orange in the low rays of the rising sun, but emblazoned on each one was a great blood-red cross, the symbol of the crusades.

There was no longer the slightest room for doubt. The watchman shouted to his fellow, no doubt dozing inside the shelter, despite the regulations forbidding it. He emerged bleary-eyed, then snapped to attention as he saw the great ships riding the sea. The other watchman reached into his shelter, snatched up a brushwood torch and his length of smouldering match—a thumb-thick length of soft oakum, loosely woven into a cord. As he straightened up, he must have hesitated, not because he doubted what his eyes were telling him but because of the orders they had been given. Few of the watchmen could read, but the orders issued from Elizabeth's Court—a modification of the system introduced by Henry VIII to guard against a French invasion in the summer of 1545—had been drummed into them until there was no possibility of a mistake. A single beacon fire meant that the Armada had been sighted. A second called the local militia to their assembly point. Three simultaneous fires meant that the Spaniards had landed or were about to land and commanded all militia and able-bodied men to make at once for the coast to repel them. But false alarms irritated both the men called needlessly from their work in the fields and the Queen and her Treasurer Burghley, who begrudged every penny legitimately spent, let alone those wasted to no purpose. As a result, only a Justice of the Peace could authorize the lighting of the beacons, having verified the threat with his own eyes. The watchman knew that it would take up to an hour for word to be carried to the justice, who would have to be roused from his bed and hurried to Pen Olver to see for himself. By the time the alarm was raised and the militias assembled, the Spaniards might already be ashore at Helford or Falmouth.[10]

He hesitated no longer. He held the match-cord in the wind to fan it into flame, kindled the torch and then stumbled over the granite boulders, climbed a crude ladder propped against the beacon and thrust the blazing torch into one of the three iron baskets of pitch-soaked gorse, driftwood, timber and lumps of animal fat set on poles high above his head. There was a thin trickle of smoke and then the fire ignited with a roar, spitting and crackling as flames rose into the sky and a plume of black, oily smoke was driven to the north-east on the wind. As soon as it was alight, he left his fellow to maintain the watch and ran along the path winding through the dew-sodden grass towards the cluster of cottages above Housel Bay. Within minutes a messenger was riding hard inland while a knot of men hurried back to Pen Olver with the watchman to see for themselves the appearance of the long-dreaded Armada.

Twenty miles to the north of Pen Olver, two more watchmen were huddled on a hilltop above the hamlet of Higher Manhay. Almost the whole of Cornwall was visible from this isolated vantage point. On this bleak and lonely summit, the wind soughing through the grass had a cutting edge even in high summer, and they were glad of the protection afforded by the crude stone shelter. A massive granite slab, twelve feet in length and nine across—a dolmen from the Celtic past—formed the roof, supported on a single huge boulder at the rear and by rough dry-stone walling at either side. The south side was also walled to chest height, leaving a broad slit commanding the views down the Lizard and of the coasts to the south-east and south-west.

In maritime counties a watch for hostile ships had been maintained throughout much of Elizabeth's reign. Watchmen were at their posts day and night between the spring and autumn equinoxes when attack was more probable, and by day in winter. With the Armada at hand, the watch was strengthened. Four watchmen were designated to each beacon site, with two always on duty. They were paid eightpence a day, raised by a levy on the parish, and provided with the wood from three trees as fuel for their beacons. To ensure their alertness, they were forbidden to have dogs with them, lest they prove a distraction from their duties, and their huts contained no "seat or place of ease lest they fall asleep." "Scoutmasters" were appointed to ensure that the watchmen were alert and at their posts; one in Essex reported that he found the Stanway beacon deserted and the watchmen poaching partridges in a nearby field. In particularly vulnerable areas such as the Isle of Wight, the watchmen had to sign in and out for their spells of duty, were subject to at least three unscheduled inspections during each duty period and "had to blow whistles or horns at least every fifteen minutes to indicate that they were still awake." The watch was maintained with much less rigour away from the South Coast; in Lancashire, even in the Armada year of 1588, watchmen were paid only from 10 July to 30 September.[11]

The ground inside the shelter at Higher Manhay was thickly lined with soft moss and ferns sprouting from every crevice and it was dry enough for the watchmen to sit cross-legged by the flat rock that served as their table. On it lay the remains of their food, perhaps a hunk of stale black bread, a piece of cheese wrapped in fern leaves and a jug or leather bottle of ale, and a pouch of dry kindling, flint and match-cord. Half a dozen torches were stacked against the wall, the smell of pitch mingling with the musty scent of ferns. As they and their brethren had done throughout that long summer, each watchman stood up every few minutes, easing the stiffness from his limbs as he scanned the horizon from west to east before resuming his seat. Now, as he gazed south towards Pen Olver, his eyes were caught by a smudge of smoke. He continued to stare, shielding his eyes from the glare of the sun, as his pulse beat a rising tattoo in his temple. The smoke strengthened and darkened and a single bright spark of flame was visible at its heart.

Either less brave or more prudent than the men who kept the watch on Pen Olver, they left the beacon fire unlit, and one of them hurried away down the hillside towards Manhay. Ten minutes later a hastily saddled horse was being ridden hard for Helston three miles away. Even when the Helston Justice of the Peace had been alerted, the beacon at Manhay remained unlit, for the justice could not authorize its firing until he had confirmed that the threat was genuine and not another false alarm. The justice at the Lizard merely had to ride the short distance to the coast to see the Armada for himself, but the Helston man had to send a messenger down the Lizard for confirmation. Even if he met a messenger riding up from the coast with a report, a minimum of two or three hours must have elapsed before word was at last brought to the Manhay watchmen to fire the beacon. By then two lights were burning at Pen Olver.

When authorization was at last given, one of the Manhay watchmen took a torch, struck a spark to kindle it into life, and, shielding it from the draught until the flame strengthened, he hurried outside. To the front of the great roof-stone and to the rear at either side, an iron-ringed spike had been driven into the granite. In each was a conical iron basket of pitch-drenched wood. He thrust his blazing torch into the heart of the central one and then the right, and stood back as they flared into flame, while droplets of burning pitch ran down the iron stems of the baskets and fell to the ground. Now well alight, the fires belched flame and black smoke into the sky, streaming away on the wind, visible almost from Penzance in the west to Bodmin in the east. The fires both summoned the local militias to their mustering points and relayed the alert to the adjoining county. As the warning of the beacon was read in the surrounding towns and villages, men began ringing out a discordant reverse peal of the church bells, sounding the warning to all within earshot. Men of Constantine and a score of other villages ran to the churches where the local weapons and armoury were housed.

The same pattern of delay was repeated from beacon to beacon across the county and the country. Since most were sited on isolated cliffs and hilltops—only in the flatlands of the Midlands and East Anglia were they sited on church towers in the heart of villages—there was an inevitable delay, often of hours, between the sight of a beacon flaring on one hill and the ignition of the next link in the chain. Most later accounts have claimed that, within minutes of the first sighting, beacons were ablaze along the chain of hilltops to the north and east, spreading the news of the Armada from Penzance to Dover and from Southampton to the Scottish border. It is an arresting image but not one borne out by the facts. The reality was that it was not hours but days before word of the coming of the Armada had spread across the country, and pinnaces travelling by sea and couriers riding "post" carried the news as fast or faster than the beacon fires. Had the Armada made a dash for the nearest landing site, Spanish troops might well have been arriving at the door of the local Justice of the Peace at the same time as the panting messenger was bringing news that the Armada had been sighted.

The Spaniards also saw the beacons—"The Armada was near with the land, so as we were seen therefrom, whereupon they made fire and smokes"—and Medina-Sidonia knew that attack could now come at any time. Many ships were glimpsed through the mist and rain, but the first clear sighting of an English warship came as a pinnace flashed across their bows, firing an insolent round from its puny cannon. The heavy guns of de Leiva's *La Rata Santa Maria Encoronada* thundered in reply but failed to find their mark, and the pinnace skimmed away so fast over the grey-green swell that the Armada might have been at anchor. It continued its slow advance up the Channel for the remainder of that day, the Levant squadron and the galleasses leading the way, followed by Medina-Sidonia with a squadron of galleons. Then came the Guipuzcoans and the Andalusians guarding the flanks. The hulks were in the centre of the fleet, while the Biscayans and the remaining galleons protected the rear. The coast lay within sight for much of the day, as the gaunt sea cliffs, crags and tors of the far west gave way to a softer country of rolling, thickly wooded hills, neat villages, rich pastures, hay meadows and cornfields studded with wildflowers, a sight to make the Armada's conscripts nostalgic for their own homes and fields. Silent, watchful men stared back at them from every headland and hill-top, drawn partly by fear, partly by curiosity, to see the long-threatened Armada. As the weather began to clear towards nightfall, in the distance to the east near the black, glistening rocks of the Eddystone the lookouts glimpsed the sails of English ships, shining with an eerie light as they caught the last rays of the setting sun. To the English topmen the Armada was a spiked black mass dimly outlined against the sky; so many ships, so close together, that they looked like some vast, floating fortress, bristling with menace.

The sight of the English fleet would not have troubled Medina-Sidonia and his commanders unduly, for the Armada had the weather gauge, the position that all captains strove to obtain. To ensure that they were not carried past the English by wind and tide during the hours of darkness, they came to anchor near Dodman Point, holding station there through the night, intending to engage the enemy at dawn. The men of both fleets used the evening hours to prepare themselves for battle. Soldiers cleaned their armour and weapons, and checked their cartridges, shot and powder flasks. The gunners filled their shot-lockers, checked the lashings on their cannons, each already "loaded with ball," and filled buckets to swab the weapons. "Half-butts and hogsheads of water" were made fast in several places upon the decks and "old rags and blankets" were soaked and stacked nearby to stifle fires and burning powder remnants. Buckets of "fighting water" were also slung from hooks in the overhead beams at intervals along the gundecks. The water they contained was often rank and as battle raged and the guns thundered it was contaminated with gunpowder and even blood, but it was still drunk by the men toiling in the furnace heat of the gundeck.

The sides of the holds were cleared, with all the stores stacked near the centreline of the ship, aiding stability, but also so that "the carpenters may the sooner and surer find the enemy's shot and stop the leaks." As protection against "the spoil of the enemy's cannon," a double row of "elm planks or the like wood that will not splinter" four or five inches in thickness had been erected right along "the midships part" on each deck. Held in place by stanchions, the planks were set four feet apart and the void was stuffed with "junks of cables, old ropes, sea-gowns, beds or the like, and so made cannon-proof." All seamen who could be spared from manning the guns or trimming the sails could "withdraw themselves to that side of the barricade . . . most remote from the enemy, and hereby safeguard themselves from the violence of their great shot in general, and especially from cross-bar and chain shot which is the chief spoil of men." The bombardiers on the upper deck also prepared "the usual buckets and tubs full of vinegar and water, and all the customary preparations of old sails and wet blankets, to protect the ships against fire thrown upon them." Screens and waistcloths were erected to conceal the gunners and musketeers on the deck from the enemy gunners and snipers, and anti-boarding nets were rigged to make it more difficult for boarding parties to clamber aboard. Other crewmen carried "fire-pots"—incendiary devices thrown onto the decks of an enemy ship—and "casting stones to be made use of during a fight" to the deck and the poop, and hauled more of them up to the fighting tops in rope nets and buckets.

The men of both fleets must have spent a troubled night, knowing that the morning would bring the start of a battle in which many would inevitably die. In muttered conversations in their cramped quarters or in the night watches on deck, like all warriors, in all eras, men spent some of the night hours making dispositions of their keepsakes and personal belongings. Some wrote letters of farewell with the help of the few literate men among them, and all sought pledges from their fellows that, if they should fall in battle, their last words and what money they had would be carried to their wives and children. But all knew that if they died or were maimed, their families would face destitution. Many men must have passed the night in thought and prayer, recollection and regret. Away to the north-east, the faint glow cast into the night sky by torches and lanterns burning in Plymouth's lanes and around the harbour showed that in the city, too, few were sleeping. Ships were still warping out through the hours of darkness and a few supplies were still being loaded aboard the last stragglers.

Medina-Sidonia spent much of the night praying and pacing the deck of his flagship. The moon rose at two in the morning and the top-men strained their eyes in its faint light. Dim shapes might have been moving in the darkness to seaward, grey against grey, or it might only have been the roiling and eddying of the mist over the water. During that short summer's night the wind had backed to west-north-west and should have improved the Armada's position still more, but when the dawn light began to strengthen on that Sunday morning, 31 July, "80 ships were discovered in the weather." Far from the Armada holding the weather gauge, the main body of the English fleet was already upwind. Howard and his commanders had not waited, passive victims of the Armada. During the night, "leaving five ships cruising in the sight of us to make us think that the rest of his fleet was there," the English fleet did what it could "to work for the wind," tacking close-hauled into the wind across Whitsand Bay, beating its way slowly abreast of and then beyond the Armada. Many of the English captains had been sailing these waters all their lives. They knew every shoal and shifting sandbank from the Thames to the Lizard, and the contours of the coasts and seabed. They had learned to read the tides, clouds and changing winds, and the surface signs that showed the complex pattern of currents in the depths, and they steered their ships to where the tidal stream flowing westwards on the ebb was at its strongest.[12]

As day broke, a further squadron of eleven English ships (Medina-Sidonia's figure; a Spanish soldier on the *San Marcos*, Pedro Estrade, recorded only seven) was still beating its way west, making a series of six short, steep tacks between the Armada and the Eddystone just off-shore, using the back eddy that runs when the flood tide is at its peak. A signal flag was raised on the mizzen-mast of the leading vessel and at once there was a flurry of activity. Orders were bellowed, the gunports hauled upwards, thudding against the oak flanks of the ships, and the cannon were run out. At the limit of the seaward reach of each tack, within long gun range of Recalde's Biscayan ships, there was a series of explosions like the low, rolling thunder of a distant summer storm, as each galleon in turn loosed a burst of cannon fire, then swung away onto the landward tack. Even as Medina-Sidonia watched, powerless to intervene, the squadron turned onto its final tack to rejoin its admiral. Many of the Spanish commanders were already aware of what formida-ble opponents they faced. The rest now could see for themselves the speed and manoeuvrability of the English "race-built" galleons.

None of the Spanish great ships could sail anywhere near as fast or as close to the wind. Unless the wind changed, the nature of the ensu-ing battle and the range at which it was fought would now be entirely in the hands of the English. Holding the weather gauge also conferred one other vital advantage. All sailing ships heel over before the wind. For the English ships upwind this would have the effect of depressing the elevation of their guns, making it easier to target the upperworks and particularly the hulls of the enemy ships. For the Spaniards down-wind, heeling over would cause the elevation of their guns to be pushed skywards, making it harder to bring them to bear on the target, and also expose the most vulnerable portion of the hull to enemy fire. "Any stiff gale making them to slope, turns up their keels towards us while we shoot them between wind and water, and their sloping to the lee side so turns up the mouths of their ordnance on the weatherside which is towards us, that they are found to shoot clean over our ships that lie low and snug as the mariners term it." Some even claimed "that it is impossible to receive any great shot from an enemy to the leewards that can endanger the sinking of the ship, for . . . by letting fly only the sheets and thereby righting the ship . . . the hole or piercing of the shot is brought so far above the water that no peril can ensue and . . . it may easefully and speedily be stopped."[13]

The Galleon of Don Pedro taken Prifoner by St Francis Drake, and fent to Dartmouth.

The Greatest Navy that Ever Swam upon the Sea

For much of Elizabeth's reign, a hermit living in the ruins of the medieval St. Michael's Chapel at the lonely outpost of Rame Head on the foreland south-west of Plymouth had been paid to keep watch for enemy fleets. In these troubled times the watch had been augmented, no doubt to the hermit's impotent fury as his cherished solitude was violated, and two local men, John Gibbons and Henry Wood, were also paid "for watching at Rame Head . . . when the Spaniards were upon the coast." A single beacon had been lit at the first sight of the Spanish fleet, but that and the presence of the local Justice of the

Peace to confirm the sighting and order the firing of all three beacons to summon the armed militias to the coast were superfluous; Plymouth and the surrounding country had been alive with reports of the coming of the Armada since the previous afternoon. Commanding the seas west past Whitsand Bay and across the Sound to Wembury Point in the east, and out beyond the sunken menace of the Eddystone Rocks, Rame Head offered an unrivalled view of the great fleets as they prepared to do battle. As the daylight strengthened, a steady procession of men from the village of Rame, a mile inland, made their way over the rabbit-cropped turf and along the footpath between tufts of sea-pinks and clumps of bracken. They crossed a narrow land-bridge flanked by rocky cliffs dropping sheer to the sea, and, as they completed the stiff climb to the chapel on the summit, they looked out on an ocean that seemed black with ships from horizon to horizon.[1]

Medina-Sidonia at once fired the signal gun to bring his fleet into its battle order. As the ships manoeuvred into their prearranged positions, their guns were run out and lashed into place. The sheer size of the Armada made it intimidating, but many of the ships within it were useless in a fight, hulks and transports that were virtually unarmed and defenceless without the great galleons, galleasses and carracks to protect them. While anchored at Corunna, the senior Spanish commanders had discussed their fighting tactics to meet the threat of the faster and better-gunned English ships. There was no dispute about the formation when out of sight of the enemy. They would advance in a single broad column, like an army in line of march, with the fighting strength divided between the vanguard and the rearguard and the weaker vessels shielded in the centre.

In battle, nine of the ten members of Medina-Sidonia's war council had argued for a formation adapted from that routinely used by galley fleets in the Mediterranean and successfully employed at Lepanto and Terceira. Perhaps unsurprisingly, given the preponderance of army officers in the Armada and the precedence given to them in the overall chain of command, it was also remarkably similar to the formation used by Spanish troops in land battles. Three fighting units, vanguard, centre and rearguard in the routine order of march, would deploy in line abreast in battle, with the rearguard advancing and the vanguard withdrawing to present a broad front to the enemy, and shielding behind it the vulnerable transport sections—the siege train on land, the hulks at sea. The tenth commander, Pedro de Valdes, once more in a minority of one, proposed a more fluid and flexible formation with the "weak and slow vessels in the centre [and] the fighting ships divided equally into a rearguard and vanguard . . . thus the vanguard can support the rearguard, or should the attack come from ahead, the rearguard can reinforce the van." He was overruled.

When they first sighted it, most English observers called the Spanish formation a "half-moon" or "crescent," like the curved blade of a headsman's axe. In fact it was more the shape of a bird of prey in flight, with a small group of fighting ships including the flagship and the galleasses at the head, flanked by the squadrons of Portugal and Castile, and then extending out in two great trailing wings, the squadrons of Biscay and Andalusia on one side and those of Guipuzcoa and the Levant on the other. At the heart, encircled by the fighting ships, were the storeships and hulks, and the pinnaces and ships of the second line. The individual squadrons were deployed in line abreast, just like a galley fleet with its preponderance of forward-firing armaments would do. Indeed, the formation was not substantially different from that adopted at Lepanto, even down to the screen of galleasses operating in front of the fleet. The importance that the Armada's commanders attached to maintaining this solid defensive formation is indicated by the punishment for any captain breaking it without good cause: "forfeiture and death with disgrace," though a dozen or so of the most formidable galleons and galleasses were given roving commissions, with the freedom to break ranks in reaction to a threat from the enemy.

Manoeuvring with remarkable precision, the Armada now adopted its chosen formation, several miles across. Accustomed only to the loose formations required in rough Atlantic waters, no English fleet could have matched the discipline of such manoeuvres, routine to the Spanish after so many years of Mediterranean sea battles against the Turks. The weaker ships of the Armada now lay protected in the centre of the formation and any ship damaged in the fighting could also be "recovered into the midst of the fleet." Any English ship foolish enough to attack there would find itself encircled and the wind taken from its sails, leaving it helpless to resist grappling and boarding, as the Spaniards desired. In those circumstances, the huge numerical superiority of the Spanish marines would be certain to prevail. As long as the formation held, attacks could be launched in relative safety only against the wings, one commanded by de Leiva, the other by Recalde, where the most powerful fighting ships held station. Medina-Sidonia believed that "either of the two horns of our formation, with their supports and the two galleasses which accompany the first four ships, would be able to cope with one of the enemy's fleets." He was now to be given the opportunity to test that belief.

The Armada made an awesome spectacle as it rode the swell that morning, "the greatest navy that ever swam upon the sea." Even though their tonnage was actually very similar, the towering fore- and sterncastles made the Spanish ships appear much bigger than the English galleons. "The Spanish fleet with lofty turrets like castles, in front like a half moon, the wings thereof spreading out about the length of seven miles, sailing very slowly through with full sails, the winds being as it were tired of carrying them and the ocean groaning under the weight of them." Flags and pennants fluttered from every mast-top and yard, and the upperworks of the warships were richly decorated and gilded. The galleasses were particularly vivid, painted in scarlet and gold, and the crews at their bronze guns were protected by highly decorated shields; "the oars all red, the sails had upon them the bloody sword." The officers and men aboard were as richly attired as their ships, their dress maintaining strict gradations of class and rank. The Spaniards regarded uniforms as bad for morale and a soldier's or seaman's dress was a matter of individual taste and financial circumstances, provided he did not dress above his station. Beneath their armour, itself often chased in gold, the nobles, officers and gentlemen of the Armada wore jewels, gold insignia and silks and velvets of crimson, royal blue, gold and purple, embroidered with gold thread. Violet was particularly favoured, as the dyes to produce it were so expensive that they were beyond the reach of all but the very rich. The "principal men" of the Armada also "had crosses upon their suits," emphasizing the crusade on which they were embarked.[2]

Officers, ensigns, soldiers and mariners of long standing wore outfits that in colour and decoration, if not in opulence, competed with those worn by the gentlemen volunteers. The clothing taken from a group of Spanish prisoners in London's Bridewell, by no means the most exalted men of the Armada, included "a blue cloak of rash [a type of smooth cloth] with a gold lace round about it, a pair of breeches of murrey [mulberry, i.e. purple] tinsel of silk with a gold lace, and a buff jerkin laid over likewise with gold lace. Of the sergeant Pelegrin, a pair of blue velvet hose with a gold and silver lace and a jerkin of wrought velvet, lined with taffeta . . . Of the ancient bearer Cristobal de Leon, a leather jerkin perfumed with amber and laid over with a gold and silver lace." The musketeers, a self-elected elite, distinguished themselves from the common soldiery by wearing a crimson sash around one arm, broad-brimmed hats, banded and richly decorated with plumes—even the morions they wore in battle were plumed—and a bandoleer across their chest, hung with a string of ornate small powder flasks, each holding a single charge. The arquebusiers occupying the next rung of the military hierarchy wore plainer outfits but still trimmed them with lace and tassels, and even the slaves at the oars of the galleasses were dressed in red jackets, though in the heat and terrible exertion of battle they often rowed naked.

The English fleet and its men looked drab and tawdry by comparison. Lord Howard and other nobles wore the fine clothes, ruffs, lace and jewels befitting their station, but commanders such as Drake and Frobisher dressed in plain utilitarian fashion at sea. Deckhands wore wool shirts and long breeches, woollen hats and long coats or leather jerkins, and the fabrics were either self-coloured or dyed in dull, natural shades of brown and green. The sleeveless jerkins were wind- and weatherproof when new, but wild weather, baking sun, salt air and frequent soakings in spray and seawater soon left the leather cracked and brittle. Among the crewmen, only the master gunners stood out. It was an exalted profession and those who followed it were dressed accordingly, in banded hats and robes of red velvet trimmed with gold embroidery. The red cross motif on the sails and some of the flags of the Armada provoked fury among the English, who thought it an attempt to deceive them about the nationality of the ships by mimicking the cross of St. George, but it was in fact the Burgundian emblem: a white ground, emblazoned with a saltire raguled red—a diagonal red cross resembling two crossed branches, inspired by the rugged cross on which St. Andrew was crucified. It had been adopted as the Spanish flag by Philip's father, Charles V.

The English fleet was decked with flags and pennants "by way of trim and bravery . . . hung out at every yardarm and at the heads of the masts." Pennants also served to identify the ships of different squadrons. The "ships of the Admiral's squadron are to hang them out in their maintops, those of the Vice-admiral's squadron in their foretops, those of the Rear-admiral's [Hawkins] in their mizzen tops." In all, 32 flags of St. George had been purchased for the fleet, 15 ensigns, 110 pennants and 70 streamers, 46 of which were flown by Howard's flagship, the *Ark Ralegh*. The royal standard, the rose of the House of Tudor, was at the head of the *Ark*'s mainmast, and the cross of St. George flew from almost every English ship, along with "flags of the Queen's arms . . . ensigns of silk . . . and pennants great and small." The *Elizabeth Bonaventure* flew "a bloody flag"—the plain red flag used to signal "engage the enemy." The upper works of the Queen's galleons were decorated with geometric patterns in her colours of green and white, but the paintwork was cracked and sun-faded, and the hulls were tarred black from the deck to the waterline. The remaining ships were a motley collection; a handful lavishly decorated, but most as plain as a parson's coat. These were working ships and working men, and their worth would be proved in combat, not on parade.[3]

Those men now dispersed to their battle stations, "some of them to the Master for the management of the sails, some to assist the gunners in the traversing of the ordnance, others to the corporal to ply their smallshot, some to fill powder in the powder room, others to carry it from thence to the gunners in cartridges, and to the musketeers in bandoleers; the carpenters, some of them being ready in the hold with sheets of lead, plugs and the like necessaries for the stopping of such leaks as shall there be made by any great shot received from the enemy, others of them between the decks for the like purpose, the surgeons in the hold also with their chests and instruments to receive and dress all the hurt men, as likewise the Minister to comfort and exhort them, especially those who are most dangerously wounded; every man taking strict notice of his particular station and task, from whence he is not to budge without leave." Seamen scattered sawdust on the main and gundecks and even those facing their first battle at sea knew the significance of that action: to prevent the decks from becoming slippery with blood. The commanders took their stand on the poop deck, from where they could survey their ship and the battleground beyond, and communicate at once with the helmsman, even amid the thunder of battle.

The long-awaited battle began with actions harking back to the age of chivalry. Lord Charles Howard, Lord Admiral of England, sent his personal pinnace, the *Disdain*, captained by Jonas Bradbury, to "give the Duke of Medina defiance" by firing a token shot at the enemy, as if challenging the Spanish commander to a duel. The pinnace shook out its sails and raced ahead of the fleet, skimming over the waves, advancing towards the heart of the Spanish formation. There was a puff of grey smoke from its bow chaser and a moment later the sound of the explosion came rolling across the water. Even as the echoes were fading, the *Disdain* had come about and was tacking back into the wind. As it passed the Levant squadron on the Armada's starboard wing, cannons thundered a reply, but the shots fell short, merely raising white columns of water around the *Disdain*'s wake, and it returned unscathed to the English lines. In response to the pinnace's challenge, the Duke of Medina-Sidonia, Captain General of the Ocean Sea, "put abroad the royal standard at the foremast" and hoisted to the maintop his sacred banner, signalling his fleet to engage the enemy.

The formal courtesies observed, the battle could begin. Medina-Sidonia "made an appearance of attacking the port [Plymouth]" to draw the English fleet into combat as the Spanish infantry—the *San Martin* alone had 200 arquebusiers and 100 musketeers—lined the bulwarks of the fore- and sterncastles and the rails in the waist of their ships, concealed from the sight of the enemy by the wooden screens and waistcloths. Other marksmen scaled the masts and rigging to take up sharpshooting positions in the fighting tops, and pikemen stood ready to repel boarders. In the past, sea battles were effectively land battles at sea, fought as if the ships were really floating fortresses. The fore- and sterncastles were exactly that: fortified redoubts; some even had crenellated battlements, and trompe l'oeil stonework painted upon them. The enemy had to lay siege to them with artillery and then storm their battlements, and the result was almost invariably decided by hand-to-hand combat.[4]

As the oar-powered galleys and galleasses closed on their prey, a single, close-range fusillade would be fired from their guns—bronze cannon firing iron cannonballs and *pedreros* discharging stone projectiles, which shattered on impact to send a blizzard of rock fragments scything through the enemy troops. Smaller "murdering pieces" firing iron or lead hail-, scissor- and dice-shot—cubes of iron encased in lead which caused horrific damage to human flesh—and other anti-personnel ordnance helped "to beat his cagework and kill his men on the upper deck." Volleys of musket and arquebus fire caused further casualties and each galley then rammed its victim with its reinforced prow. Hand-thrown bombs and incendiary devices increased the panic and mortality among the defenders, and fire-pots—earthenware jars filled with gunpowder, spirit and resin—were hurled down to shatter on the enemy ship's deck. Ignited by the burning fuses attached to the outside of the fire-pot, the combustibles would explode with the force of a modern Molotov cocktail. *Bombas*—long-handled, hollow wooden tubes packed with alternating bands of gunpowder and shrapnel—were used like hand grenades. Grappling irons were thrown, locking the ships together, and a flood of soldiers then swarmed aboard from the *arrumbada*—the platform above the prow.

Great ships carried out the same form of attack, using their heavier armaments to smash the upperworks of the enemy and disable its anti-personnel weapons. As the two ships came together, the massive short-barrelled bombards carried in the waist of the ship were fired at point-blank range—no more than a handful of feet—so close that the solid combustion products of the black powder were often as devastating among the ranks of enemy troops as the shot being fired. The blast effect alone was often enough to maim and even kill, and the terror and disorientation induced by the concussive force of the blasts stunned even uninjured troops into immobility for a few crucial seconds. Musketeers and arquebusiers caused further carnage by unleashing a hail of small-arms fire from the towering fore- and sterncastles, and the enemy troops in the "fighting tops"—the firing platforms high on the masts, commanding the deck—were particularly targeted. The huge iron hooks attached to the ends of the yardarms would then "tangle with the sails and rigging of the enemy ship, holding him fast for the close-range gunners and preventing him from escaping."[5]

Men then poured aboard, clambering over the rails and swarming through open gunports. The most heavily armoured men were first aboard, followed by the rest, protected by no more than a leather jerkin. If the fusillades of fire had not swept the decks clean of defenders, the first troops aboard were met by a barrage of musket and arquebus fire and a forest of pikes and halberds. Vicious hand-to-hand fighting with pike, sword and axe would continue until the ship was captured or the attackers slaughtered. Spain had made successful use of these tactics when leading an alliance of "Christian states" to victory against the Ottoman Turks at Lepanto, and again off Terceira only half a dozen years before the Armada sailed, but those were the last great sea battles of a vanishing age. These tactics were now to be challenged in the first naval battle of a new era, by an English fleet reliant solely on its gunnery to defeat the enemy. It was an epochal moment; a system of warfare dating back to Roman times was now being supplanted by tactics forged in the dawning of the new industrial age.

Such was the Spanish dependence upon boarding and hand-to-hand combat that there was virtually no provision for reloading their heavier armaments during a battle. Only the breech-loading weapons used against human targets could be reloaded at speed, and only the lighter muzzle-loading guns could be readily swabbed clean and reloaded. The heavier cannon, all muzzle-loaded, were so large that they were difficult or impossible to haul inboards. A Dutch traveller aboard a Portuguese carrack of the same era noted that, after firing a cannon, "we had at least an hour's work to lade it in again, whereby we had so great a noise and cry aboard the ship as if we had all been cast away." Some even had to be reloaded from outside the ship by men straddling the barrels, a practice that could not be attempted in battle or heavy weather. Even the smaller cannon were difficult to haul inboards, since the Spanish two-wheeled gun-carriages were designed for use on land and were almost impossible to manoeuvre in the cramped, pitching confines of a ship's gundeck at sea. The largest weighed almost as much as the huge guns they carried and were so long that they occupied half the width of the deck. The guns were also lashed to the ship's hull before being fired and the strains that this imposed on the structure literally pulled some of the hulls apart.[6]

The Armada did not even use dedicated guncrews. The men

responsible—six or more to each gun—were soldiers drawn from the boarding force of marines as and when required. Under the direction of the gunner, they were summoned from their stations at the bow or waist of the ship to scour and sponge clean the barrel, and load it with black powder, shot and wadding. They would use blocks, tackles and handspikes to work the massive gun into its firing position, and wedges to bring it to the correct elevation. It was then lashed to the hull with ropes to prevent the recoil sending the gun careering back into the gundeck; the system of allowing the recoil to bring the weapon inboard for reloading was not developed until the middle of the seventeenth century. The guncrew would then return to its boarding stations, leaving the gunner to apply the match to fire the weapon. Even if it was capable of being reloaded in combat, the gunner would have to recall the men to do so amid the tumult of battle. As a result, the Spanish heavy guns were fired no more than an average of two or three times during the course of a day-long engagement. By contrast, the English design of narrow, four-wheeled gun-carriages allowed cannons and culverins to be rapidly hauled inboards after firing and swiftly reloaded by seasoned, specialist guncrews, and the rate and accuracy of their fire was far in excess of anything that the Spaniards could achieve. In practice, the only constraints on the English gunners were the size of their stores of powder and shot, and the need to allow the gun-barrels to cool during repeated firing to prevent premature detonation of the black-powder charges.

As much as the Duke of Medina-Sidonia, Lord Howard was reliant on the advice and opinions of his subordinates, and he and his senior commanders had already decided upon their strategy and tactics. With no experience of battle, he would neither have grasped the subtler significance of the manoeuvres nor been able to factor in the calculations of wind, tide and current that were second nature to seamen such as Drake and Recalde, but he had already shown his willingness to defer to the greater experience and sea wisdom of Drake, Hawkins and Frobisher, and it is certain that they took the leading part in deciding the battlefield tactics. They chose not an all or nothing, death or glory policy but a measured, cost-effective means of ensuring that the Armada would not succeed. No written record was made of their deliberations, for all preferred to keep the "secrets of the services" among themselves. Even Walsingham and Burghley were not notified, avoiding the risk of the chosen course of action being argued over by warring factions or leaked to Spanish agents, as Philip's gold lined too many English pockets for any secret to remain secure for long at Court. However, the subsequent events make abundantly clear both the tactics that the English commanders had chosen and the success with which they were put into practice.

Medina-Sidonia's battle plan was unknown, but the English commanders believed that he would try to secure a safe anchorage before moving on to a rendezvous with the Duke of Parma. Their aim was to keep the weather gauge on the Armada, in order to use their edge in speed, manoeuvrability and gunnery to maximum effect, but since the prevailing winds were westerly, by so doing they would be allowing the Spaniards to make an unopposed advance up the Channel. The English fleet would therefore "course" and harry the Armada from upwind as it sailed eastwards, and plans were also laid to use their superior knowledge of the local winds, tides and inshore waters to launch substantial attacks on the approaches to each bay or harbour that might serve the Armada as a base. Once driven to leeward of each one, the prevailing winds and the poor sailing qualities of the Spanish ships would prevent them from returning.

The sheer size of the Armada, and of its great ships, limited the possible havens. There were no more than half a dozen on the South Coast large and deep enough to accommodate it, secure against bad weather and defensible against an English counter-attack. As far back as the previous November, a council of war had established "the dangerous places for landing of the enemy." From west to east, they were Milford Haven, Helford, Falmouth, Plymouth, Torbay, Portland, and the Solent and the Isle of Wight. Milford, Helford and Falmouth were the least defensible, since they lay to the west—upwind—of Plymouth, but they were thinly populated, lacking in potential food supplies and poorly served by roads, "very noisome and tedious to travel in and dangerous to all passengers and carriages," and they were also hundreds of miles from London and from Parma's forces in Flanders. If the Spaniards did make a landing there, Elizabeth's commanders on land and sea would have ample time in which to plan and organize a defence against them. The remainder of the potential landing sites were surrounded by good agricultural land and had relatively good roads or easily traversed country linking them to the capital. Of all the potential havens, Plymouth, and the Solent and Spithead separating the Isle of Wight from the Hampshire coast were felt to be the most plausible. "It is unlikely the King of Spain will engage his fleet too far within the Sleeve [the western Channel] before he has mastered some one good harbour of which Plymouth is the nearest to Spain," while the Isle of Wight was the closest deep-water anchorage to Flanders and London. It was also "the only island off the English Channel coast large enough to accommodate an army and with the capacity to feed it, standing off far enough from the mainland to guard against a surprise attack, but within easy reach of a great extent of the English coastline." The English commanders were determined to defend these harbours at all costs.[7]

While the race-built galleons stood off and used their guns at long range, Frobisher was to deliberately place the *Triumph*—the largest vessel in either fleet and one of the few English ships with fighting castles close to the size of those of the Spanish great ships—in the most dangerous but crucial position, on the shoreward side of the Armada. He would be vulnerable to boarding and capture if the Spaniards could close with him, but he hoped to use the power of his armaments and his knowledge of the local currents, shoals and sea conditions to hold them at bay. Howard's squadron would maintain pressure upon the Spanish centre, preventing Medina-Sidonia from massing his warships against Frobisher, while the fast and weatherly squadrons of Drake and Hawkins would launch ferocious surprise attacks on the Armada's most vulnerable points. If the tactics were successful, the Spanish ships would be so harried and damaged that they would either scatter, be driven on to the rocks or, at worst, find themselves pushed by wind and tide past the havens they had hoped to secure. The great Falmouth anchorage of Carrick Roads was already well astern, but if Plymouth were taken by the Armada, the Western Squadron's own home base and shore defences could be turned against it. Accordingly, at nine o'clock that morning, "the Lord Admiral gave them fight within the view of Plymouth," leading his group of warships in an attack against the shoreward tip of the Armada's formation. As he was to do for the next few days, John Hawkins sailed in close proximity to the flagship, lending his vast experience and expertise to the untested Lord Admiral.

If the Spanish formation and discipline in manoeuvring were alien to British eyes, the English tactics were equally new to the Spaniards. Spanish and Portuguese manuals of naval warfare had always stressed that their galleys and warships with their forward-facing guns, reinforced metal rams and boarding troops should engage the enemy in line abreast, giving each ship's main armaments a clear field of fire. Commanders were warned never to expose their broadsides to the enemy, nor to attack in line astern "since only the ships in the van can fight." Insofar as they adopted a formation at all, the commanders of Howard's galleons preferred to make their attacks downwind in echelon or line astern, to maximize the impact of their broadside guns, but in this new kind of naval warfare, tactics were evolving and being refined as the battles were being fought.

Drake had earlier been censured by the Queen for allowing his men to practise rapid firing of their cannons, but the benefits of such drilling were soon apparent. As each gun was fired, it was hauled inboards and the barrel sponged and "wormed" clean of spent powder residue. The cartridge of black powder wrapped in cloth or paper royal was then rammed home and the barrel again sponged to remove spilt powder grains. The cannonball, wiped clean of dirt and debris, was inserted, rammed home and secured with hemp wadding, and the gun run out and lashed in place with ropes as thick as the crewmen's arms. The gunner checked the aim and adjusted the elevation by means of wooden wedges and his assistant poured a trail of priming powder into the touch-hole. On the master gunner's command, the assistant took his piece of smouldering match-cord gripped in the jaws of a linstock— a carved wooden holder that allowed the guncrew to keep at arm's length from the gun as it discharged—and put it to the touch-hole to fire the weapon. Skilled gunners could complete the whole process in as little as two minutes, though the problem of the barrel overheating through continuous firing reduced the achievable firing rate to something like ten or a dozen shots per hour.

In battle, the helmsman adjusted his course at the orders of the master gunner, and each gun was fired as it came to bear in a rolling, near-continuous broadside rather than a single massive fusillade of shot. The bow chasers were fired first, then the broadside guns on the lee side of the attacking ship, then the stern chasers as it came about, and the windward guns as it began to tack back into the wind, before turning for another pass. The broadside guns could be "bowed" or "quartered"—angled forwards or backwards—to enable them to be fired at an approaching target or one astern, as well as being fired broadside on, and a squadron attacking in line astern maintained an almost continuous bombardment of enemy ships that, having discharged their initial fusillade, were virtually powerless to repeat it, as only their bow and stern chasers could readily be reloaded. The musketeers kept up a harassing fire aimed primarily at the gunports, to "beat her men from the traverse and use of her ordnance." Fearing a musket ball more than the wrath of their officers, many guncrews would take no careful sights from a gunport rattled by musket shot and would often fire with the most cursory aim or simply abandon their station and retreat to a safer refuge. Much of the cannon fire was meanwhile aimed at the enemy's "yards, masts, sails and tackling . . . [to] disable her from tacking about to bring any fresh broadsides" to bear.[8]

The English cannons fired in a relentless drum roll. A flash and a gout of red flame lit up each gunport in turn, and powder residue spattered into the sea and was swept away in the wake. Dense, acrid clouds of black gunsmoke clung to the water, whipped into wraiths and tendrils by the wind, but constantly renewed by the next salvo from the guns. The screaming whine of shot through the air and the splash and hiss as some fell harmlessly into the sea was almost drowned in the splintering crash of iron on wood and the rending sound as sails and rigging were ripped apart. The screens and waistcloths hid the Spanish soldiers massed at the rails from sight, but the agonized cries of wounded men told their own tale, and the barrage of roaring, concussive noise from the guns held its own terrors. Not a man on either side, not even the most seasoned seamen and soldiers, had ever experienced the like, and for the conscripts—pressed men and raw recruits used to no louder noise than the church bells or the lowing of the oxen around their home villages—the barrage must have sounded as if the gates of Hell had been opened; many were unmanned by fear.

The gundecks were a bedlam of noise and confusion. The blasting of the guns was so loud that even orders bellowed through cupped hands into a man's ear remained unheard, and prolonged exposure to the detonations in that dark, confined space rendered every man of the sweat-soaked, near-naked guncrews temporarily, and often permanently, deaf. This deck of the deaf communicated as much by sign as speech. Crewmen ran to and from the shot-lockers carrying cannonballs and cartridges to the guns. They burned their hands and cursed as they hauled at their cannon, the barrels glowing a dull blood-red with the heat of repeated firing. As each gun was discharged, it was unroped, hauled in and swabbed out. The drenched sponges spat and hissed steam as they were rammed home to clean the powder residue from the bore, and the stink of scorching wool mingled with the sulphurous reek of powder smoke. In places the burned remnants of spent cartridges swabbed from the cannons littered the decks inches deep, and powder spills on the planking flared and ignited by stray sparks were frantically doused with water. The cannon was reloaded, run out and lashed back into place. The gunner adjusted his aim and then the deck shook beneath their feet as the great gun roared and the recoil tossed the three-ton monster back against the restraining ropes as if it were a toy.

Don Alonso de Leiva's *Rata Encoronada* was the outermost ship in the formation and as the *Ark* crossed astern de Leiva altered course, aligning himself broadside to broadside with the English flagship. Behind him came the great carrack, Martin de Bertendona's *Regazona*, the largest ship in the entire Armada, followed by the rest of the Levant squadron. Believing that the *Rata* was "the Admiral," the flagship "wherein the Duke was supposed to be," Howard exchanged fire "until she was rescued by several ships of the Spanish army." The lack of manoeuvrability of the Spanish great ships had at once been exposed; whenever the *Rata* attempted to come up into the wind to face its attackers, she lost steerage way and was pushed back by wind and tide, drifting helpless, broadside on to the English fleet, and making no headway at all.

De Leiva's wing had crumbled under the first assault of the English ships and "certain ships basely took to flight," crowding and disrupting the remaining ships of the Armada as they fled downwind and even becoming entangled with Recalde's Biscayans on the opposite wing, as much as two miles from their own designated position. In turn, many of the Biscayans fled before the cannonades from the other English ships, for at the same time as Howard's group was attacking the Levant squadron, a group led by Drake in the *Revenge* and Frobisher in the *Triumph*—at 1,100 tons larger even than the *Regazona*—attacked the far wing of the Armada commanded by the Vice-Admiral Juan Martinez de Recalde. His flagship, *San Juan de Portugal,* the largest of the galleons, swung to face the attack alone. "The enemy assailed him with great discharging of ordnance, without closing, whereby his ship suffered much in her rigging, her forestay was cut and her foremast had two great shot within," but Recalde "stood fast and abode the assault of the enemy, although he saw that he was being left unsupported, for the ships of the rearguard were shrouding themselves in the main body of the Armada."[9]

The motives of Recalde and the other captains at that moment remain unclear. Medina-Sidonia inclined to the belief that Recalde had either become separated from them by accident or had been deliberately deserted by them, yet both seem implausible. The Portuguese ships were manned by battle-hardened seamen who fought with great resolve and courage throughout the rest of the campaign and, famed for his skill and bravery, Recalde was too experienced to have made such a potentially fatal mistake. He had already seen enough to know that the English tactics were to lay off at long range and use their greater speed and the power, rate of fire and accuracy of their armaments to knock the Armada to pieces. He must have known that the only hope of drawing them in to close range was by offering them the target of an isolated and vulnerable enemy.

Never in the history of naval warfare had a single ship isolated by its enemies not been boarded. It was the only way to ensure that a valuable prize was captured intact and men like Drake, Hawkins and Frobisher had never been known to spurn the chance of a prize. Recalde's own ship would be in great peril against superior English numbers, but if he could attach his grappling hooks to one or two of his enemies the rest of his squadron could then return to the fray, tip the battle the other way and perhaps provoke a general mêlée in which more and more of the English would be forced into hand-to-hand combat. Yet if Recalde had adopted such a strategy, it was in defiance of a direct order from his commander and it is unsurprising that Medina-Sidonia was left to draw his own conclusions.

A second galleon, Don Diego Pimentel's *San Mateo*, "putting her head as close up to the wind as possible, did not reply to their fire but waited for them in the hope of bringing them to close quarters." The English ships were not drawn into the trap. They closed to within 300 yards but remained at that range, bombarding the *San Juan de Portugal* and the *San Mateo* with their long guns for almost an hour. When Medina-Sidonia saw his vice-admiral's ship surrounded he ordered his helm put hard over, "struck her fore-topsail and let fly the sheets." The fleeing ships from the vanguard and rearguard were also "peremptorily ordered to luff and face the enemy." They waited, sails hanging limp, as the fighting ships drifted slowly towards them on the wind, but as the range closed, the English fleet broke off the action and withdrew, leaving the Biscayan squadron to nurse the battered *San Juan* back into the midst of the Armada. Captain Vanegas, the gunnery officer on the *San Martin*, estimated that during this first battle the English fleet had fired 2,000 cannonballs, compared to 750 from the Armada. It was a fair reflection of the greater ease of handling of the English guns and of the greater skill of the English guncrews, and was to be repeated and even exceeded in all the subsequent battles.

Medina-Sidonia immediately re-formed his fleet from the purely defensive formation into attacking columns but, although they maintained a dogged pursuit for three hours, the English treated them with something bordering on contempt, closing or widening the range as they pleased, firing a salvo and then dancing out of range once more. Tiring of this profitless exercise, Medina-Sidonia eventually called off the chase and both fleets resumed their eastward progress, the Armada in the van, the English fleet a mile or two in trail. The official Spanish log reported that "the Duke collected the fleet, being unable to do anything more, because the enemy having recovered the wind, and their ships being very nimble and of such good steerage, they did with them whatsoever they desired."[10]

If not wholly unexpected—the Spanish commanders all knew by repute if not experience how fast and weatherly the English ships were—it was still a harsh lesson for them to absorb. Tied to its rigid formation, the Armada could proceed only at the speed of its slowest vessel, and that was wearisomely slow, barely faster than a rowing boat with a single oarsman. The pinnace dispatched by Drake after the opening battle off Plymouth reached Seymour in the Straits of Dover in well under two days. In the same wind conditions, the Armada travelled no further than the Isle of Wight—half the distance—in more than twice the time. Its heavy, square-rigged ships were awkward to manoeuvre and could not sail close to the wind. Many were not designed for the sea conditions they faced—hulks and transport ships routinely hugged the coasts and fled for the nearest port at the approach of a storm—or were so grossly overloaded with fighting castles, men and supplies that they were at constant risk of foundering in a heavy swell. But even the elite Spanish galleons used to escort the *flota* from the New World were at a marked disadvantage against the lightly crewed, streamlined English ships that, as a Spanish officer ruefully admitted, could sail away from even the fastest Armada ship, the *San Juan Bautista*, "as if we were standing still." The worst of the English fleet "without their maincourse or topsails, can beat the best sailers we have." If the English fleet was becalmed, then the oar-driven galleasses might be able to close with them and use their rams, grappling irons and fighting troops to overwhelm them, but while the winds blew, it seemed that the English ships would always be able to find enough searoom to keep the Armada at bay.

During this first battle the thunder of the guns had been clearly audible in Plymouth and for forty miles around. Anxious watchers crowding the shore opposite the Eddystone rocks, after sleeping out under the stars on the beaches and clifftops, had been able to catch glimpses of the fleets in action as they drifted eastwards with the wind and tide, but at such a distance, among the fogs of gunsmoke and the confusion of battle, they were unable to tell which side had gained an advantage. The participants in the fighting were little more certain. Pedro de Valdes dismissed the fighting as of small consequence. "Our ordnance played a long while on both sides, without coming to hand stroke [hand-to-hand fighting]. There was little harm done, because the fight was far off." Even Recalde's ship had not suffered irreparable damage. "His galleon had been sore beaten," the foremast damaged, some of the stays and rigging shot away and there were a number of casualties; one soldier cited fifteen dead and an unknown number of wounded—by the standard battlefield equation of ten wounded men for every fatality, around a further 150 of the ship's complement of 543 crew and soldiers would have been casualties—but the ship's hull was intact.[11]

In fact, the most serious damage to the Armada occurred around four o'clock in the afternoon, after the day's fighting was over. Having previously manoeuvred with such impressive cohesion in the face of the enemy, Pedro de Valdes' flagship of the Andalusians, the *Nuestra Señora del Rosario*, had collided with another of the ships of his squadron, the *Catalina*, as he went to the aid of Recalde, and "brake her spritsail and crossyard." Unable to maintain steerage way—such heavy vessels relied as much on the foresails as the rudder to maintain their course—the *Rosario* was helpless as "another ship fell foul with her likewise in the selfsame manner, and brake her bowsprit, halyards and forecourse."

A few minutes later there was a massive explosion from one of the Guipuzcoan ships, the *San Salvador*, clearly audible to the English ships following over a mile upwind. The stern powder store had been blown apart. Whatever the cause, a stray spark, a careless gunner trailing a length of smouldering match, or even sabotage—survivors spread a story that a Flemish or German gunner had deliberately "cast fire into the powder barrels" after being flogged by the captain—the effect was instantaneous. The iron-hard oak hull contained most of the force of the blast and channelled it upwards, sending it ripping through the afterdecks. The poop deck and two decks of the sterncastle were blasted apart, blowing blazing timbers as high as the mast tops and raining down debris on the surrounding ships. At least 120 men were killed instantly, though another witness who helped to take off the survivors put the total of dead at "more than 200," and the remnants of the decking were littered with burned and broken bodies and severed limbs. Blood-red flames and clouds of foul black smoke belched from the shattered decks and the smell of brimstone hung heavy in the air. Within moments the ship was ablaze from stem to stern, burning with such ferocity that many of the crewmen who had survived the initial blast threw themselves into the sea to escape the searing heat and were drowned.

Medina-Sidonia at once "discharged a piece of ordnance" signalling the Armada to halt, and steered back towards the *San Salvador*, "in which was the Paymaster General of this Armada, with part of the King's treasure." Smaller vessels secured lines to the burning ship and towed her round to face the wind so that the fire would not be driven towards the forecastle, where another huge store of powder was kept. Some of the burned and wounded were transferred to one of the two hospital ships in the Armada, and as the fires were brought under control, two galleasses began to tow the *San Salvador* back into the formation. Just as this was happening, the *Rosario*, almost impossible to steer without her headsails and pitching and tossing in the rising swell, was hit by a sudden squall. Most of the stays securing the foremast had snapped in the earlier collision and the unbraced foremast now "brake close by the hatches [at deck level] and fell upon the mainmast, so as it was impossible to repair that hurt but in some good space of time." Even with 422 men aboard to wield axes, saws and knives, the sheer mass of shattered masts, yards and spars, tangled rigging and torn sails obstructed any attempt to effect swift repairs, and Pedro de Valdes "discharged three or four great pieces, to the end all the fleet might know what distress I was in." One witness claimed that "there were none came to succour her for that the wind did blow much, the sea was grown and the English did follow us," but although the sea was growing increasingly choppy and the wind still freshening, Medina-Sidonia's official diary claimed that the *San Martin* had then approached the crippled ship and succeeded in passing a tow line to it. "Though great diligence was used, neither weather nor sea permitted of it," and no sooner had it been secured than it parted with a crack like a cannon shot. The strengthening wind and rising sea made it impossible to get another line to the ship, "and so she was left without sails" as night was coming on.[12]

At that point Diego Flores de Valdes, cousin of Pedro but still harbouring his long-standing grievance against him, appeared on the poop deck of the *San Martin*. His advice, backed by the full authority of his position as the King's official representative and Medina-Sidonia's Chief of Staff and principal adviser on all naval matters, was that Medina-Sidonia must at once retake his station at the head of the Armada and continue his eastward course. To heave to in such a sea and rising wind might lead to further accidents among the fleet and would certainly see it scattered. "Although Don Pedro de Valdes is of my blood and a friend," Flores de Valdes said, a statement that was at least half-correct, "without doubt, by the morning more than half the fleet would be missing . . . the enemy's fleet being so near, all the Armada should not be imperilled," he went on, "esteeming it certain that by shortening sail, the expedition would be ruined" for the sake of a single ship.

Medina-Sidonia claimed to have resisted at first, but then gave way, after ensuring that Ojeda's small galleon, four pinnaces, a galleass and the vice-flagship of the Andalusians, the *San Francisco*, were detached to go to the aid of the stranded ship "so as to take her in tow and remove her people, but neither the one nor the other was found possible, owing to the heavy seas, the darkness and the weather." By then the *San Martin* had already fired a signal gun, shaken out her sails and led the Armada on up the Channel, leaving Pedro de Valdes "comfortless in the sight of the whole fleet." As the *Rosario* dropped further and further astern and finally disappeared from sight, Medina-Sidonia remained on the deck of the *San Martin*, where he had been all day, eating nothing but a frugal supper of bread and cheese to the sporadic accompaniment of the sound of gunfire; "three or four shots were heard" in the gathering darkness behind him.[13]

It was the first of several crucial turning points in the campaign. Given that the chosen strategy was to engage the English fleet in hand-to-hand combat, the crippled *Rosario* could have been turned to the Armada's advantage, by using the ship as bait. If one of the English ships had been drawn in by greed for a fat prize or even a false promise of surrender, it could have been grappled and held for boarding, forcing the other English commanders either to relinquish one of their own great ships or to fight the close-quarter battle that the Spaniards were seeking. Instead, Medina-Sidonia's decision to abandon the *Rosario* dealt a body blow to morale within the whole Armada, by suggesting that any ship in difficulties or surrounded by the enemy might also be left to its fate. At least one officer of the Armada laid the blame for the subsequent defeat on this decision. "These misfortunes presaged our failure. The vile omen depressed the whole Armada."

It must also have been apparent that Medina-Sidonia's lumbering hybrid—neither a battle fleet nor a self-contained invasion force—would struggle to achieve its aims. Had he not been burdened with the requirement to meet the bulk of the invasion force off the coast of Flanders before proceeding to a predetermined landing place, he would have been free to choose the time and place of an invasion with a greater expectation of success. By the same token, had he not had the responsibility of keeping to the pace of the slowest hulk and protecting his vulnerable ships at all times from attack, he might have been able to pursue more aggressive tactics to force the English fleet to engage in a general mêlée that might have brought a Spanish victory. As it was, he could only sail on to the east, hoping that a change of wind or the miracle on which so many confident hopes had been predicated might bring a change of fortune.

Earlier that evening, Lord Howard had given orders for a blue flag to be raised, summoning his vice-admirals and commanders to a council of war, to pool and assess what had been learned from the day's encounters. They met in the Admiral's sumptuously appointed cabin, upholstered with green hides and green and yellow hangings, and were able to exult in "our swiftness in outsailing them, our nimbleness in getting into the weather of them, our little draught of water in comparison to theirs, our stout bearing up of our sides in all huge winds when theirs must stoop, to their great disadvantage many ways, our yawness in staying well and casting about twice for their once and so discharging our broadsides of ordnance double for their single, we carrying as good and great artillery as they do and to better proof, and having far better gunners." But his commanders also had some cause for alarm, not only at the size of the Armada and the skill and discipline that its captains and crews had shown in manoeuvres, but also at the lack of damage to the Spanish ships.

There was a curious suggestion from one quarter that not all the English commanders were eager to engage the Armada at all. Sir John Holles "was called to be present at all their councils of war, so great an opinion there was of him then. And particularly, he was present at that great debate whether they should fight the Spanish fleet or no: which was with difficulty carried upon the affirmative especially by the sound and resolute arguments of Sir Martin Frobisher." No other published account supports this intriguing version of events; had it indeed occurred, the advocates of inaction would no doubt have wished their views to remain undocumented, but it is harder to imagine the choleric Frobisher remaining silent. At least one English captain was also openly critical—albeit in a letter to Walsingham rather than in the council of war—of Howard's initial decision to engage the Armada at long range. "The majesty of the enemy's fleet, the good order they held and the private consideration of our wants did cause, in my opinion, our first onset to be more coldly done than became the value of our nation and the credit of the English navy." "In seafights you shall have some men, many times out of fear, some out of vain shows, that will discharge the broadsides upon an enemy ship when he is out of all reach . . . That is a very indiscreet wasting of shot and powder and but a bravado that discovers fear or folly to a wise and valiant enemy."[14]

A cannonball fired from one of the English great guns might travel a considerable distance—a mile or even two—but its kinetic energy was rapidly dissipated. Cannons and culverins had to be fired at no more than 200 yards' range to damage the upperworks, and the effective range at which they could do substantial harm to the stout hulls of the Armada's warships was 100 yards at most. The English cannon fire had been far more sustained and accurate than that of the Armada, but they had fought at such a range that some of the cannonballs had literally bounced off the undamaged oak flanks of the Spanish galleons. They were formidably well built to withstand gunnery attack, for their four-inch oak planking was mounted on oak ribs a foot in diameter and set so close together that they almost touched. However, unlike the less heavily armoured English galleons, that great strength of construction also made the Spanish warships too rigid to flex with the waves. Unable to absorb the stresses from the relentless pounding of the seas, many of them were prone to shedding the caulking between their seams and springing sections of their planking, causing leaks that could then be exacerbated by the effects of gunfire.

There had undoubtedly been many casualties among the densely packed soldiers massed on the decks of the Armada's great ships, but no ship had been crippled, let alone sunk, and Howard's commanders were well aware that a stand-off suited the Spaniards far more than it served them. On the evidence of the first day's fighting, if they kept the fight at long range, they might themselves suffer no harm but the Armada would proceed untroubled to its rendezvous with Parma. They drew consolation from the fact that they still held the advantage of the weather gauge and had prevented the Spaniards from entering Plymouth—if that had ever been their intention—but ahead lay Torbay, Portland, Poole and the Isle of Wight, all of which could provide the Armada with a safe anchorage and the possibility of replenishing their stores of food and water. It was essential that the English fleet be close enough at hand to prevent such a landfall.

After the council of war, Howard sent a message to Walsingham, a letter designed to put the best possible gloss on the day's events. "At nine of the clock we gave them fight, which continued until one . . . we made some of them to bear room to stop their leaks; notwithstanding, we durst not adventure to put in among them, their fleet being so strong. But there shall be nothing either neglected or unhazarded that may work their overthrow . . . For the love of God and our country, let us have with some speed some great shot sent us of all bigness; for this service will continue long; and some powder with it." Drake also sent a brief message to Lord Henry Seymour, Admiral in the Narrow Seas, warning of the advance of the Armada. "We had them in chase and so, coming up to them, there has passed some cannon shot between some of our fleet and some of them, and as far as we perceive, they are determined to sell their lives with blows . . . The fleet of Spaniards is somewhat above a hundred sails, many great ships, but truly I think not half of them men of war. Haste."[15]

As the fleets sailed eastwards, the Cornish militias stood down. The bulk returned home, pending another summons should a change of wind bring the Armada back to their coast. In theory at least, the pick of the troops began a slow march eastwards, ready to aid the neighbouring county if a Spanish landing was made: Cornishmen would march to the defence of Devon, Devon men to that of Dorset, and so on. In practice many men, seeing the immediate threat to their own homes removed, seized any chance to drift away or desert and return to their land to help gather in the hay or the harvest. With arms, armour, baggage and provisions to transport over roads that were still slathered in mud from the wet spring and summer, the remaining troops made a poor pace, slower even than the ponderous Armada off-shore, and they dropped further and further behind the fleets.

Pinnaces and Zabra's Com anded by Don Antonio de Mendoza wch were 22, and had in y.^{n} 479 Souldiers, 574 Mariners, and 193 Canons ez

The Heavens Thundered

At the end of the English council of war that evening, "dismissing each man to go aboard his own ship, His Lordship had appointed Sir Francis Drake to set the watch that night." Under battle conditions, ships showed no lights after dark, and the lantern on the poop deck of Drake's ship, *Revenge*, was to be the guiding light by which the rest would navigate. In the last of the evening light, the *Margaret and John* of London, a 200-ton privateer captained by John Fisher, came upon the crippled *Rosario*, still with her escort of ships. The *Margaret and John*'s officers claimed that "accompanied neither with ship, pinnace or boat of all our fleet" they went to the attack, and "the sudden approach of our ship" caused the other Spanish vessels to flee. By making that claim they were staking their right to a share in the spoils, but the captain of a galleass would hardly have been frightened by a privateer one-third the size of his own ship, and it must rather have been the fear of the rest of the English fleet bearing down out of the darkness that put the *Rosario*'s escort to flight.

As the crew of the *Margaret and John* looked over the apparently deserted ship, they kept to windward, "hard under sides of the ship . . . which by reason of her greatness and the sea being very much grown, we could not lay aboard without spoiling our own ship." The *Rosario*'s sails were furled, all lights were extinguished and she did not answer her helm. "Seeing not one man show himself nor any light appearing in her . . . we discharged 25 or 30 muskets into her cage-work, at one volley, with arrows and bullet." That fusillade provoked some return fire. "They gave us two great shot, whereupon we let fly our broadside through her, doing some hurt." The privateer drew off a little but remained close to the crippled Spanish ship until around midnight, when, "fearing his Lordship's displeasure if we should stay behind," the *Margaret and John* sailed away to rejoin the English fleet.[1]

A crescent moon silvered the waters and threw intermittent light on the scene, but it was often obscured by cloud, and visibility was poor enough that when the light on the poop deck of the *Revenge* was abruptly extinguished, the lookouts on the *Ark* could see no trace of Drake's ship. Lord Howard was called back on deck at once and eventually the lookouts caught sight of the glimmer of a light ahead, although at some distance from them. The *Ark* put on more sail to close the gap and, accompanied only by the *Bear* and the *Mary Rose*, resumed the silent pursuit. The remainder of the fleet "being disappointed of their light by reason that Sir Francis Drake left the watch to pursue certain hulks . . . lingered behind not knowing who to follow." Only when the eastern sky was lightening over the approaches to Torbay did Howard realize that he had been following the lantern of an enemy ship, and was so close, "within culverin shot," that he was at risk of being enfolded within the trailing wings of the Armada. The rest of his fleet was miles behind—"the nearest might scarce be seen half-mast high and very many out of sight." There was no trace at all of the *Revenge*.

The three English ships came about at once and used their greater speed and agility into the wind to pull clear of the Armada. There must have been at least a chance that the galleasses, powered by oars as well as sails, and able to make considerable speed directly into the wind over short distances, could have overhauled the *Ark*, and "Hugo de Moncada, Governor of the four galleasses, made humble suit unto the Duke of Medina that he might be licensed to encounter the Admiral of England." But, still adhering rigidly to Philip's orders, and perhaps also believing that honour required that he and not his subordinate should be the first to attack the English admiral, "this liberty the Duke thought not good to permit unto him."

When Drake was eventually reunited with his commander, his explanation of his nocturnal disappearance was that "late in the evening" he had seen the dim outlines of ships passing to seaward. Afraid that the enemy might be taking a leaf from the English book and seeking to beat into the wind and gain the weather gauge, Drake had turned to starboard to challenge them, extinguishing his poop lantern to avoid leading the fleet astray. With him was only the *Roebuck*, a Plymouth privateer under Captain Jacob Whiddon, and two of Drake's own pinnaces. The ships proved to be German merchantmen and Drake claimed that he had just set course to rejoin the fleet when dawn broke and he saw the crippled flagship of Don Pedro de Valdes no more than a cable length away.

The *Rosario*'s commander had at first attempted to bargain but was then told that he faced the legendary El Draque in person, who had not the "leisure to make any long parley." He was also reminded of the rules of war that commanders on land and sea routinely adopted: those, both officers and men, who surrendered at once, were accorded every civility and respect; those who fought, however briefly, before surrendering or being overpowered, were dispatched without mercy. Pedro de Valdes then surrendered on an undertaking that he would be fairly treated and the lives of his men spared. The Sheriff of Devon, George Cary, was later to complain that the men should have been "made water spaniels [drowned] when they were first taken," a practice that dated back at least to Chaucerian times. "What shall become of these people, our vowed enemies?" Cary said. "The charge of keeping them is great, the peril greater and the discontentment of our country greatest of all, that a nation so much disliking unto them should remain amongst them."[2]

The value of the *Rosario* was not only the 55,000 gold ducats it carried as wages for the invasion force and its treasure, including a box of Toledo swords with jewelled hilts that Philip had sent as presents for the English Catholic lords, nor even its forty-six cannon and "great store of powder and shot." Its capture also gave Drake and the other English commanders the opportunity to discover the nature and limitations of its armaments, particularly the difficulties in reloading them when in combat or heavy seas. Under interrogation, one of the ship's company, Gregorio de Sotomayor, one of 2,000 Portuguese who had been forcibly conscripted for the Armada "on pain of death," also revealed the parlous state of the Armada's provisions. When George Cary took charge of the *Rosario*, he reported to Walsingham that "their provision . . . is very little and nought, their fish savours [smells] so that it is not to be eaten, and their bread full of worms."

Having thoroughly inspected the *Rosario*, Drake took de Valdes aboard his own ship and then detached the *Roebuck* to escort the prize to Dartmouth, but the crippled ship could not make headway into the wind and it was taken into Torbay instead, where "for the better furnishing of Her Majesty's navy with munition," the powder and shot were at once removed and sent after the fleet. When news of the *Rosario's* capture was brought to London, "bonfires were lit all over the city and the bells were rung," and de Valdes and some of his fellow captives were later "taken in carts to London . . . so that the people might see that some prisoners had been captured." The ship's banners and flags, including a red damask standard of Philip's coat of arms flanked by twin angels, were also sent to London, where they were paraded through the streets and later hung in St. Paul's. Much of the *Rosario's* other stores and equipment was looted as self-interest dominated the national interest. Cary complained that "12 or 13 pieces of brass ordnance" had been stolen, "Jacob Whiddon, captain of the *Roebuck*, had ten, and likewise several muskets and calivers. A pinnace of Plymouth that came from my Lord Admiral for powder and shot had another two pieces, and the *Samaritan* of Dartmouth had the other, as also 10 muskets and 10 calivers. The *Roebuck* also had several pipes of wine and two of oil . . . Watch and look never so narrowly they will steal and pilfer." Howard also complained that the Earl of Huntingdon, the President of the Council of the North, had commandeered a load of powder aboard the *Roebuck*, intended for the fleet, and kept it to arm his own men in case of attack from Scotland.[3]

Like Drake's conduct the previous night, such actions were an example of "the uneasy balance between the national and the private interest" that the use of privateers entailed. "Privateering was not merely an incidental by-product of this war . . . it was the characteristic form of maritime warfare, the essential embodiment of the private initiative and enterprise that dominated the sea war," and it was all too easy for it to degenerate into an "indecorous scramble for private profits." The search for plunder and easy fortunes had hampered Ralegh's colonization attempts, while Frobisher's search for the North-West Passage was motivated (and supported by Elizabeth) because of the belief that a "black earth" found in the north-west territories could be converted by alchemists into pure gold. He made three expeditions in succeeding years, but abandoned the search when the black earth was revealed to be iron pyrites—"fool's gold"—useful only as the flints in wheel-lock muskets. Elizabeth's commanders also "went to places more for profit than for service" and, whatever the national interest or the requirements of the sovereign, in such "joint-stock" warfare the first priority was to capture prizes, goods and treasure, and the second to carry it home with all possible speed. "The one thing certain about the merchant officers was that they were not reliable when called upon to risk their vessels for any higher purpose than privateering." "We find it in daily experience that all discourse of magnanimity, or national virtue, or religion or liberty and whatsoever else has been wont to move and encourage virtuous men, has no force at all with the common soldier, in comparison with spoils and riches." Even Drake's reputation and success rate was not always enough to keep a fleet of privateers together. "The moment anything is undertaken other than robbery and plunder, they will abandon him."[4]

Drake was something of an exception to the general rule, in that his religious fervour and his burning hatred for Spain would sometimes lead him to acts that had limited commercial justification but, faced with a rich prize, his "piratical instincts again proved irresistible." The official account notes his breach of his orders without comment and, though the fiery Yorkshireman Martin Frobisher later made a stinging criticism of Drake, his complaint was mainly about the allocation of the spoils from the great prize. "After he had seen her in the evening, that she had spent her masts, then, like a coward, he kept by her all night, because he would have the spoil. He thinks to cozen [cheat] us of our shares of fifteen thousand ducats, but we will have our shares, or I will make him spend the best blood in his belly." Either because of his threats or simply because it was his due, Frobisher later received the not insubstantial sum of £4,979 as his share of prize money from the Armada campaign. Whatever they may have thought in private, no other captain, and certainly not Drake's admiral, Lord Howard, offered the slightest public complaint about his actions. He reported the capture in matter-of-fact terms. "There is a galleass [*sic*] of the enemy's taken with 450 men in her . . . there is an hundred gentlemen . . . who for the most part were noblemen's sons." If there was any general feeling in the fleet it was one of envy, tinged with resentment, that Drake and his crew had secured a prize that all must have coveted.

Pedro de Valdes's behaviour is harder to explain. His ship had not been so seriously damaged that, eighteen hours after the collision, it should still have been incapable of answering its helm or making head-way under a jury rig in place of its damaged masts and sails, yet no attempt seems to have been made to effect repairs. It was also a huge and powerful ship, one of the most heavily gunned in the entire Armada, carrying 300 soldiers in addition to its crew of 120, and with towering fore- and sterncastles that would have made it extremely haz-ardous for the smaller English ships to attempt to board. A robust defence would have held the English at bay for at least a day, but de Valdes's fury at being abandoned by the Armada may have made him disinclined to risk his own and his men's lives by resistance that might postpone but could not avert the inevitable capture or destruction of his ship. He himself claimed that after he had "resisted them and defended myself all that night . . . finding myself in so bad case, void of all hope to be relieved, out of sight of our fleet and beset with ene-mies . . . our last and best remedy" was to surrender.[5]

Whether de Valdes was bribed by Drake—during his later interro-gation he claimed that the King's Treasure aboard his ship was "near 20,000 ducats," understating its true value by 35,000 ducats, according to the interrogations of twelve other members of his crew—or was a coward, a realist, or still nursing his anger over the way the Armada had abandoned him, has never been revealed. He remained on the *Revenge* for a further week, witnessing the battles between the fleets from Drake's stern cabin, and was only sent ashore at the insistence of Wals-ingham and Burghley, alarmed that "the secrets of the services" might be revealed to one of the enemy's senior commanders. Drake was reluctant to hand over his valuable prisoners, losing the right to the ransom money that could be obtained, but realistic enough to know that if the Queen required them for her own gain, he could not refuse, though one can almost hear the grinding of his teeth in his words: "Don Pedro is a man of greatest estimation with the King of Spain and thought next in his army to the Duke of Medina-Sidonia. If they should be given from me unto any other, it would be some grief to my friends. If Her Majesty will have them, God defend but I should think it happy."

De Valdes and the other prisoners were closely questioned about the Armada's tactics and aims, but their interrogators also showed a particular and wholly understandable interest in the intended fate of Protestant nobles if an invasion took place, and in the identities of English exiles, traitors and collaborators. The list of questions pre-pared by the Privy Council to be put to Spanish prisoners included: "What they meant to do with the noblemen, gentlemen and other sub-jects of quality, as well of our religion as of the other? What the Englishmen should have done that came with them; and whether they had not especial direction whom they should spare and whom they should kill or where were they to receive it; and what it was? Whether the King of Spain would have retained this realm for himself or given it to any other, and who that is?" Whatever his motives in surrendering, de Valdes was enough of a patriot to mislead his interrogators about the fighting strength of the Armada and gave no worthwhile information about its proposed method of invasion, landing site, or the English collaborators aboard or ashore. Curiously, he came to be viewed as something of a hero both in England and in Spain, where he was widely regarded as an innocent victim of the callous decision to abandon him.[6]

The English fleet must have been planning to launch a further attack on the Armada that Monday morning, 1 August, as it approached its next possible refuge in Torbay; Frobisher referred to "the morning, when we should have dealt with them" in his diatribe against Drake. The disarray caused by the separation of Drake and Howard from the fleet ensured that no such attack occurred, but in the event the Armada did not deviate from its eastward course and sailed on past Torbay. At eleven that Monday morning, it lost a second crucial prize to the English fleet when the *San Salvador* was abandoned. The explosion that had destroyed her afterdecks had also sprung her seams and the few surviving members of the crew were unable to staunch the leaks; water was pouring in faster than the pumps could deal with it. Medina-Sidonia ordered "the King's money and the people to be taken out of her and the ship to be sunk," but the captain "was badly wounded and the men in a hurry to abandon the ship, so that there was no one to sink her; besides which, she had many wounded and burnt men on board, who could not be rescued as the enemy was approaching." The able-bodied crewmen, the money and some of the stores were taken off, but the injured men and the munitions were left aboard, and the ship was not scuttled but merely left to drift astern. For the second time in twenty-four hours, Medina-Sidonia had allowed one of his great ships to fall into the hands of the enemy and, like the *Rosario*, it was liberally supplied with powder and shot, for though the stern powder store had been destroyed in the explosion the store in the bows was intact.

The *San Salvador* was at once seized by the pursuing English ships "in sight of the Armada." Lord Thomas Howard, the twenty-seven-year-old nephew of the Lord High Admiral, and Sir John Hawkins went aboard, "where they beheld a very pitiful sight—the deck of the ship fallen down, the steerage broken, the stern blown out and about 50 poor creatures burnt with powder in most miserable sort. The stink in the ship was so unsavoury and the sight within board so ugly that the Lord Thomas Howard and Sir John Hawkins shortly departed." The *San Salvador* was in such a parlous state that the pumps had to be worked day and night to keep her afloat, but Thomas Fleming, captain of the *Golden Hind*, the pinnace that had brought the first warning of the Armada, managed to take the sinking hulk in tow and bring her safely into Weymouth harbour, "to the great joy of the beholders," though it prompted immediate complaints from the Town Council. "The burnt Spanish ship called Le *San Salvador* is much splitted and torn and the charge will be great in keeping her here for we are forced to keep therein ten persons continually to pump her for fear of sinking . . . We humbly beseech your Lordships to give some speedy direction what shall be done with them [the Spanish crew], for that they are here diseased, naked and chargeable."[7]

The 88 barrels of fine-corned black powder and 1,600 shot were removed as soon as the *San Salvador* came to anchor and sent to the fleet in "a bark of Dartmouth," and a further 600 shot, six of the ship's 14 cannon, "a ton of match" and 40 more barrels of powder were sent to the fleet the following day, "in Captain Fleming's pinnace." Even more could have been provided, but at least some Weymouth citizens had followed the example of England's naval hero and their fellows in Torbay, and ensured they were not out of pocket. "Surely in the stealing of her ropes and casks from her, and rotting and spoiling of sails and cables, etc, the disorder was very great. It is credibly thought that there were in her 200 Venetian barrels of powder . . . and yet but 141 [the inventory records only 132] were sent to the Lord Admiral." Even so, the powder retrieved from the *Rosario* and the *San Salvador* represented around a third of the total supplied to the English fleet, and it is far from fanciful to suggest that the final defeat of the Armada could not have been achieved without that Spanish powder and shot. An attempt was later made to move the *San Salvador* to Portsmouth for repairs, but the battered hulk sank during the voyage. "The great Spaniard, she was lost at Studland, but God be praised, there is saved 34 of our best men and there was lost 23 men, whereof six were Flemings and Frenchmen that came in the same ship out of Spain." A merchant from Portland was blamed for the sinking, having failed to provide the foresail he had promised, leaving the ship dangerously unmanageable. "All those who are saved will depose that he was the casting away of the ship and the death of the men."

Late on the Monday afternoon, Medina-Sidonia raised a flag to signal another council of war with his commanders. All that day fresh sails had been appearing over the horizon as more and more ships joined the English fleet and it appeared that Howard was calling for every reinforcement available. In response, Medina-Sidonia now divided his fighting ships into the "two squadrons, vanguard and rearguard" that Pedro de Valdes had earlier unavailingly proposed as the most efficient formation. The larger and more powerful grouping, "the best ships of the fleet," were to guard the rear, under the temporary command of Don Alonso de Leiva. He would cede control to Recalde when repairs to the *San Juan* were completed. A smaller group of fighting ships led by Medina-Sidonia himself took up position in the vanguard of the Armada. To stress his determination that the fleet should maintain its formation whatever the circumstances, preventing a recurrence of the previous day's incident when several ships had fled and left Recalde's ship to fight the enemy alone, Medina-Sidonia sent pinnaces through the Armada bearing written orders for each captain "that any ship which did not keep that order, or left her appointed place, that without further stay they should hang the captain of the said ship." In order to emphasize the threat, "the Provosts Marshal and hangmen necessary for carrying out this order," dressed in the robes of their calling, accompanied the messengers.[8]

Medina-Sidonia expected at any time to meet the remainder of the English Grand Fleet (as he thought under the command of John Hawkins, but actually commanded by Lord Henry Seymour), and hoped that this formation would enable him to repel an attack even if it came simultaneously from ahead and the rear. In fact, at the orders of his Queen, Seymour was maintaining a blockade of the Flanders coast, despite the dangers to his squadron in those waters. "How uneasily the lying of our ships against Gravelines, much more Dunkirk, I can say no more than I have many times written. But seeing it is Her Majesty's pleasure, we will endeavour to perform it as near as wind and weather will give us leave." Sir William Wynter, commanding the *Vanguard* in the same squadron, was even less sanguine about the task. "I humbly pray you that . . . you do not danger us here . . . I know there has been such as has promised . . . that he would ride athwart of Dunkirk all weathers . . . but I assure your Honours, his judgement and skill for that matter is neither grounded upon skill or reason." Seymour also complained at the lack of ships and—inevitably—supplies allocated to him. "Send us powder and shot forthwith, whereof we have want in our fleet and which I have several times given knowledge thereof . . . Our victuals do end the last of this month, yet upon extremity, now we know the enemy at hand, we will prolong that little we have as long as we can." Six vessels of his fleet had already been discharged for want of the provisions to feed the crews and a further four had been detached to escort the cloth fleet to Stade, near Hamburg. It was a further example of the uneasy balance of public and private concerns; the protection of powerful vested interests was to take precedence over the needs of the fleet. "Our fleet being from the first promised to be 78 ships . . . we have not above 20," Seymour complained. "If the wind come without the land, our merchant ships are enforced to forsake us as not able to ride, so that our trust for this service is only upon Her Majesty's ships, in number eight."[9]

Much was riding on them, in English eyes at least. "The only hope I can contain of this country is if my Lord Harry is always in their face when they shall attempt to come out of haven. They have just 37 ships with tops [sails] and such as common port ships are, not able to stand against Her Majesty's." As if to prove the truth of that assertion, while maintaining his blockade of the coast Seymour had chased, intercepted and fired on two ships emerging from Dunkirk after they refused to strike their sails when challenged. The crew of one vessel abandoned ship and waded ashore over the sandbanks, carrying their sails in their arms. The other struck its sails after a shot fired by one of Seymour's pinnaces brought down the mainmast. It was a French ship operating by permit from the Governor of Calais, but the ease and alacrity with which both vessels had been hunted down must have given Parma further pause for thought about the advisability of exposing his troop barges to the mercies of either the Dutch or the English fleets.

Philip's only reference to the means by which Medina-Sidonia could communicate with Parma as the Armada approached was to state that either a *zabra*—a pinnace—carrying dispatches could sail to and from Dunkirk, Nieuport or Gravelines, or a rowing boat could land a messenger "by night . . . on a beach in Normandy." Late that evening, Medina-Sidonia again dispatched a pinnace, commanded by Juan Gil, with a further message for Parma. "I beseech your Excellency to send with the utmost speed some person with a reply . . . and supply me with pilots for the Coast of Flanders." Pending a reply, he could only hope and pray that the invasion force was indeed assembled.

During the evening the wind died away, the sea abated and the skies cleared. The sea glittered in the starlight and the sails of the English ships, grit-grey against the night sky, were faintly visible a mile or so to windward. When the three-quarter moon rose towards midnight, it cast sufficient light to delineate the enemy's ships and enable friend to be distinguished from foe. At one o'clock that morning, de Leiva, Recalde and Oquendo were rowed across to the *San Martin* and persuaded their Captain General to order Hugo de Moncada's galleasses to attack the nearest English ships. This, it was hoped, would force the other English ships to come to their support and provoke the general mêlée that the Spaniards sought. To seek a battle was counter to Philip's orders, but the avoidance of the enemy over the preceding days must have irked Medina-Sidonia's pride and sense of honour as much as it did his commanders'. To salve Moncada's pride over the earlier refusal of permission to engage Howard's flagship, Medina-Sidonia reinforced his orders with the offer of an estate worth 3,000 ducats in the event of a successful action. Moncada, who considered himself the master of galley warfare and was still nursing his grievance, retorted that his honour required him to engage no lesser opponent than the admiral of the enemy. Such was his right and his duty and he would not demean himself by fighting some lesser opponent. He may or may not have made an outright refusal, but the galleasses did not row to the attack, as Lord Howard noted from the bridge of the *Ark*. "They might have distressed some of our small ships which were short of our fleet, but their courage failed them, for they attempted nothing." The moon set, the wind began to stir again and the chance was lost.[10]

By the time dawn broke on Tuesday 2 August, the wind had reversed its direction and was blowing stiffly from the north-east—the land breeze that could be expected at that hour. For the moment at least the Armada now had the weather gauge, but its topmen could see by the first light that the English fleet was already reacting to the change in the wind. Frobisher led a group of ships, close-hauled to the north-north-east "over against St. Albans, about five o'clock in the morning," sailing between the Armada and the shore in an attempt to forestall any attempted landing at Weymouth. But unlike off the Eddy-stone three days earlier, the Spaniards were now sufficiently alert to the manoeuvre and close enough to shore to try to cut him off. Howard and Hawkins led their group eastwards, tacking against the wind, to engage and "fix" Medina-Sidonia and the Spanish centre, while Drake's squadron set a course downwind, racing past the seaward wing of the Armada. Heartened by the wind in his favour, Medina-Sidonia ordered his fleet to the attack. The distance between the fighting ships narrowed to cannon and even small-arms range and great volleys of gunfire broke out from both sides. A pall of smoke from the guns hung like fog over the water and the cannon roar was a relentless assault on the eardrums, so continuous and so deafening that voices and signal guns were drowned, indistinguishable from the general din, and even on deck or high in the rigging the men were so deafened that a shouted order or the shrill blast of a whistle was inaudible from a few paces away. Amid the chaos and thunder of battle, signal flags often went unseen, lost in the swirling clouds of gunsmoke. "There was never seen so vehement a fight, either side endeavouring, through a headstrong and deadly hatred, the other's spoil and destruction. Although the musketeers and arquebusiers were in either fleet many in number, yet could they not be discerned or heard . . . by reason of the more violent and roaring shot of the greater ordnance, that followed so thick one upon another."

Not a man on either side had ever witnessed such a ferocious cannonade: "Blaze of burning darts flying to and fro, leams of stars coruscant, streams and hails of fiery sparks, lightnings of wild fire on water and land. Flight and shoot of thunderbolts, all with such countenance, terror and vehemence that the heavens thundered, the waters surged, the earth shook." The gunners' view of the battle was confined to snatches of the action glimpsed through the gunports, but in any event they had no time to assess the effects of their work; each cannon was no sooner fired than it was being hauled back and swabbed ready for reloading. From the upper decks men could see the flashes and puffs of smoke from enemy gunports and the plumes of water as cannonballs fell short. Their ears told them where a successful shot had found its mark: the dull bass thud of a ball striking the hull, the rending crash as a shot ripped through the upperworks, the whipcrack of a severed stay, the sound like a dry cough as a shot punched a hole through a sail, and the rattle of small-shot ripping through canvas, like hail drumming on a tile roof. Running beneath it was the constant sound of human voices, the cadence of shouted orders relayed through the ship, grunts of effort, curses and imprecations, and groans of pain, all drowned in the boom of outgoing shots as the guns came to bear, each detonation sending a physical tremor right through the ship. A deaf man gripping the rail could have timed each broadside through the vibrations under his fingers.[11]

If the intensity of the gun battle was ferocious, the speed was pedestrian. Unless a strong breeze was blowing, ships reliant for their motive power on the wind or on men straining at the oars moved with agonizing slowness. Captains sparred for position with the deliberation of chess masters, and five or ten minutes might elapse before it was apparent who had gained an advantage. A commander might see one of his ships under attack less than a mile from his own position and set a course to go to its aid, but if he was downwind, it might take him half an hour or more to cover that small distance—if he was able to make ground towards it at all. If his ship was poor at sailing into the wind, as most of the Armada vessels were, he might even be compelled to drop

an anchor or lie to with his sails furled or flapping loose, until the set of
the wind and tide brought the other ships drifting to him.

Again and again the Spaniards tried to close, grapple and board
their enemies, but once more the English ships were able to evade their
lumbering opponents while still maintaining the ferocious assault with
their guns. The Spanish soldiers, armoured and armed with musket,
arquebus, pike, axe or sword, remained at their boarding stations
throughout the battle, waiting for the close-quarter, kill-or-be-killed
combat that never came.

As the battle raged, the sun rose higher in the sky and the land
breeze began to abate and back southerly. As it swung first into the
south-east, it set both fleets drifting slowly into Lyme Bay, while a separate, much smaller battle was taking place right in the lee of Portland
Bill, a talon of rock extending into the Channel four miles beyond the
coast. There Martin Frobisher had brought his ship to anchor, flanked
by five armed merchantmen: the *Merchant Royal, Centurion, Margaret
and John, Mary Rose* and *Golden Lion.* The *Triumph* was better placed
than any other English vessel to resist boarding, for it had the high
fore- and sterncastles of the Armada's fighting ships, but seeing his four
huge galleasses "being carried by the current almost within culverin
shot, [Medina-Sidonia] sent them order that by oar and sail they should
endeavour to close with the enemy." In case Moncada should deem this
too a prize unworthy of his talents, Medina-Sidonia's messenger, Captain Gomez Perez, passed on a few further words to Moncada that
"were not to his honour." The galleasses duly rowed to the attack.

It was unclear to the watchers on the Bill whether Frobisher had
been unable to manoeuvre and had dropped anchor to wait for the
westward drift of the battle to again give him the weather gauge and
the leeway to escape, or whether the master mariner was trying to lure
the Spaniards into a trap. Frobisher had haunted these waters for ten
years, often basing himself on the Isle of Wight and preying on shipping sailing between the Baltic and North Sea ports and Spain and the
Mediterranean, though he was not above seizing merchantmen
inbound for Southampton as well. The goods and cargoes he stole
were unloaded and sold at Mead Holes before his victims had disappeared over the horizon. He knew every inch of the coast, every cove
and headland, every rock and shoal, and every quirk of the tides and
currents.

Portland Bill divides two large bays and the configuration of the
coast creates strong eddies on both the flood and ebb tides. The steep
slopes of the Bill continue beneath the sea, but just to the east the

Shambles, a long bank of sand and broken shell, creates a dangerous shallows. A tidal rip, the Portland Race, the fiercest on the South Coast, runs from the tip of the Bill towards this bank, reaching as much as seven knots at peak tide, while the eddy moves at one knot in the opposite direction. The division between these opposing flows is abrupt; one minute the current pulls one way, the next the opposite, and the surface water gives little sign of the turbulence immediately below it. The force of the current alone was dangerously destabilizing to low-waisted craft like the galleasses, but they faced the additional peril of the vortexes arising in the water where the energies generated by the clashing currents of the Race and its eddy are dissipated. The proximity of the cliffs also suggests the dangers of shallow waters and submerged rocks. In fact, there is deep water just offshore, as Frobisher well knew, and it is possible to navigate the Race, but it would be a very brave or foolhardy commander who would attempt it without that knowledge.

Frobisher was able to position himself in the eddy and remain virtually motionless in apparently still water, but, in order to attack, the Spanish galleasses were forced to cross the ferocious current of the Race. Even modern ships with powerful diesel engines can make little or no headway against the Race at full flood, and the oar-driven galleasses were powerless to cross it. Each time they entered that churning water, they were thrown around, pitching and tossing until they were half swamped, and were swept away from their target. As the galleasses approached, Frobisher's guns unleashed a hail of fire, cutting swathes through the troops massed on deck and the slaves chained at the oars, while the cannon of the galleasses did little damage in reply. Deprived of much of the propulsive power of their oars and faced with that ferocious current, the galleasses made no further attempts to attack, but held off, just within gun range, fighting against the current. From the safe distance of the *San Martin* it appeared to Medina-Sidonia (and to many later historians) that Don Hugo de Moncada was simply refusing to engage the enemy. "A fine day this has been," Medina-Sidonia wrote to Moncada that night. "If the galleasses had come up as I expected, the enemy would have had his fill." But in fact Moncada simply could not attack Frobisher without putting his craft at risk of being swamped.

The galleasses had been "well entertained by the [English] ships for the space of an hour and a half," but the wind was still backing and as the tide began to ebb Lord Howard led a line of the Queen's galleons and fighting merchantmen back into the fray, ordering them "to set freshly upon the Spaniards and to go within musket-shot of the enemy before they should discharge any one piece of ordnance, thereby to succour the Triumph." The help was indirect, for they were once more attacking the Spanish great ships of the rearguard rather than making directly for the galleasses threatening the *Triumph*, and in fact such assistance was probably neither needed nor wanted by Frobisher, who had been able to hold them at bay with some ease, but, seeing the move, Medina-Sidonia began to lead his own group of sixteen ships to intercept. Once more Recalde found himself surrounded by a dozen enemy ships, fighting alone with "no assistance from any other ship in the fleet." The changing wind had left Medina-Sidonia's group as the only Spanish ships to windward of the *San Juan*, and he signalled the rest of his squadron to put about and go to her aid, before sailing on alone to confront the *Ark*.[12]

As the courses of the two flagships converged, the *San Martin* "turned towards her and lowered her topsails." Lying broadside to Howard's ship, Medina-Sidonia was issuing an unmistakable invitation to grapple, board and come to hand-to-hand combat, but those were the tactics of the old era of naval warfare and this was a newer, less chivalrous age. Howard once more spurned the invitation and poured in a broadside for good measure as he passed by "within two or three score [paces]." Each English ship, in line astern, did the same. Then the whole line came about and riddled the *San Martin* with a second and then a third broadside, while Medina-Sidonia's gunners made what reply they could. The English gunfire was a continuous drumroll; the *San Martin*'s reply came in brief staccato bursts. As the Spanish great ships began to reinforce the *San Juan*, the English galleons surrounding her pulled away and switched their attacks to the *San Martin*. Beset from all sides, the flagship fought alone for what was claimed to be at least an hour, so shrouded by enemy gunsmoke that she was almost invisible to the rest of the Armada, and the target of "at least 500 cannon balls, some of which struck his hull and others his rigging, carrying away his flagstaff and one of the stays of his mainmast." The sacred standard was shredded by gunfire, the masts damaged, the yards splintered and the torn rigging hanging in shrouds over the dead soldiers and crew littering its deck.

Previously obscured by the fogs of gunsmoke, Drake's group now reappeared from out to sea, using the sea breeze that had arisen as the heat of the day increased to launch a sudden and savage downwind attack on the Armada's seaward wing. "A troop of Her Majesty's ships and sundry merchants [ships] assailed the Spanish fleet so sharply to the westward that they were all forced to give way and bear room." As it had done off Plymouth, the wing buckled under the onslaught, adding to the chaos and confusion at the heart of the Armada. "They all seemed to want to take refuge one behind the others, so that they fled from the action and collided together. It is a disgrace to mention it." Even while the battle raged, men still had to scramble aloft as the wind shifted, scaling the rigging and spreadeagling themselves over the yardarm to furl the sails. It was a perilous task at the best of times, the height above deck level magnifying the ship's movement, the masts flexing, whipping and swinging through every point of the compass as the ship pitched and tossed in the swell, the timbers groaning and the canvas cracking like gunshots as wind filled the sails. In the heat of battle, with chain-, bar- and dice-shot slicing through the rigging, and musket and arquebus shot filling the air, there can have been no more terrifying experience.[13]

The wind had now swung firmly into the south-west, pushing the fleets further and further from Portland Bill and across Lyme Bay, but allowing Oquendo to lead a line of galleons to the rescue of the *San Martin*. As they approached, the English fleet was rejoined by Frobisher, who had used the outgoing flow of the Portland Race to pull effortlessly clear of his Spanish assailants. As he did so, the fleet drew back from the battle and stood out to sea, moving with such speed that it seemed to the despairing Spaniards as if "they were anchored and the English had wings to fly as and where they wished." The battle had raged for five hours, "from five of the clock until ten," but Howard and his commanders had achieved their objective, using their knowledge of the local winds and the pattern of tides and currents to drive the Armada past another potential landing site and safe haven.

There was nothing fortuitous or mystical about the English success, and no recourse was necessary to Drake's legendary "crystal ball." The summer winds off the South Coast form a repetitive and predictable pattern. On nine days out of ten, a land breeze will be blowing from the north-east at first light, fading to a brief calm as the rising sun begins to warm the land. The wind will then swing round through 180 degrees, until the prevailing south-westerlies are blowing from sea to land. Those winds will continue until towards evening, when the sea breeze will again give way, after a brief calm, to the land breeze that prevails during the night. All that the English commanders had done was to use their knowledge of those winds to maximum effect.

Plymouth, Torbay and Portland now lay astern, beyond the Spaniards' reach in the prevailing south-westerlies, but the most obvious and vulnerable targets, the Isle of Wight and the Solent, still lay ahead as the battle-scarred Armada resumed its formation and its steady eastward course. The carpenters on the *San Martin, San Juan* and *San Mateo* worked with frantic haste to repair the worst of the damage. The English ships, once more holding the weather gauge on their enemy, maintained their relentless pursuit and carried out further harrying, sniping raids on the trailing arms of the formation.

At the councils of war that afternoon both sides had more hard lessons to absorb. The Spaniards now had plain evidence that even with the wind at their backs they were unable to close with and board the English ships. Once more their attempts to do so had been "all to little effect, because the enemy seeing that we endeavoured to come to hand-stroke with them, bare room [pulled away], avoiding our attack by reason of the lightness of their vessels." As Medina-Sidonia complained in yet another dispatch to Parma, "Some of our vessels have been in the very midst of the enemy's fleet, to induce one of his ships to grapple and begin the fight, but all to no purpose." He must now have been painfully aware that there was no possibility of engaging and destroying or driving off the English fleet before he effected his rendezvous with Parma. The enemy would be there, that maddening mile or two in trail of the Armada, every inch of the way, and even if the wind swung through 180 degrees in the blink of an eye, they had shown that they were perfectly capable of outflanking the Armada and reclaiming the weather gauge whenever they chose.

The Spanish commanders had also had two forcible reminders of the greater range, power, accuracy and firing rate of the English guns—three times as fast in the opinion of men on both sides of the battle. Even that underestimates the difference: English rates of fire averaged one and a half rounds per gun per hour, while the heavy gunners of the Spanish ships achieved no more than that in an entire day. The Spaniards had also suffered heavy casualties, some of which were self-inflicted. During the day's battle, two gunners on the vice-flagship of the hulks, the *San Salvador* (a different ship from the one crippled by explosion and captured by the English on 1 August), inserted a powder cartridge into a cannon that still contained a residue of red-hot particles from its previous firing. The resulting explosion killed both of them. A similar incident on another of the hulks during the same battle left two more gunners badly burned.

Yet Lord Howard and his commanders also had no great reason for self-congratulation. If the battle so far had shown that, barring the miracle for which they had so confidently hoped, the Spaniards could not achieve victory over the English fleet, there was as yet no evidence that the English ships could do more than harass and worry the Spanish rearguard. Despite two prolonged and furious battles, only two Spanish ships had been claimed and neither of those prizes could be attributed to English gunfire. At the ranges from which they were firing, for all the pounding given to the *San Juan* and *San Martin* and the carnage on their upper decks, the English gunners had still been unable to inflict sufficient damage to prevent either ship from continuing with the Armada on its slow progress up the Channel. The decisive battle had yet to be fought and meanwhile each passing day was bringing the Armada's rendezvous with the Duke of Parma a little nearer.

That evening, Medina-Sidonia sent a further message ahead by fast pinnace, urging Parma to have his troops embarked and ready to sail. He held to the same course, sailing "with the direct Trade," in a straight line between Portland Bill and Dunnose Head (now St. Catherine's Point) on the Isle of Wight. The fossil-laden grey cliffs of Dorset were steep and rocky, and the chalk cliffs of the Isle of Wight, shining like bleached bone in the moonlight, were equally sheer. There was only one potential landing site in the forty miles between these points: the Hurst Narrows, the western entrance to the Solent, guarded by the Needles, but it was then thought by many to be too rocky, narrow and dangerous to afford safe passage to great ships. Philip himself had told Medina-Sidonia "you should enter by the east side which is wider than the west." In fact the size of the navigable channels was not significantly different, but the eastern approaches, St. Helen's Roads (Spithead), offered a secure anchorage for the largest fleet, sheltered against all weathers and with scores of potential landing sites where men might forage for food and water or establish a defensible bridgehead and base. An attacking French fleet had sailed into St. Helen's Roads in 1545, and Philip's peaceful armada had brought him there in 1554 for his marriage to Mary Tudor. Within forty-eight hours, the Duke of Medina-Sidonia would have to attempt to emulate them. His crews used the quiet hours of the evening to clear the debris of battle, sweeping the decks clear of blood, splintered wood and shards of shrapnel, mending torn sails and rigging, patching broken planking and rails, then all settled to their vigils and their brief hours of rest.[14]

The Admirall ý L.ᵈ Sheffeild St. Tho: Howard and others joyn with Drake and Fenez agᵗ ý Spanish Fleet & worst them.

ᴀ Terrible Value of Great Shot

At dawn on the following morning, Wednesday, 3 August, the English topmen spotted another Spanish straggler. The *Gran Grifon*, the flagship of the fleet of hulks, had been moved to strengthen the seaward wing of the Armada but, although armed with thirty-eight guns, the lumbering merchantman, with blunt bows and a beam that appeared almost as great as her length, was too slow to maintain the speed of the fighting ships and during the night she had dropped further and further behind. In the darkness her commander, Juan Gomez de Medina, had been unaware of the peril he faced. With the first light he realized his danger and made desperate efforts to rejoin the formation, but an English ship, probably the *Revenge*, was already bearing down. Drake passed along the *Grifon*'s flank, firing a broadside at much closer range than before and taking some shots in return, turned about and gave another broadside, and then riddled the stern with a third. The range was so close, "half-musket shot," that lead shot from muskets and arquebuses, flattened by impact, was embedded in the *Grifon*'s hull. More and more English ships joined the action, keeping up the bombardment and almost using the *Grifon* for target practice, until the whole of the Spanish starboard wing became embroiled in the battle.

Medina-Sidonia sent one of his galleasses to the rescue of the *Grifon*, by now so badly damaged that she was unable to steer or make way. Her rudder head was broken, several guns dismantled and she had sustained severe damage to her masts and rigging, and suffered heavy casualties, more than the entire fleet had lost in the previous day's fighting. In the thick of the battle, the galleass managed to get a rope aboard and began to tow the crippled *Gran Grifon* back into the formation, as the remaining Spanish warships exchanged gunfire with the *Revenge*. The galleasses and some of the galleons "discharged their sternpieces . . . without quitting their station, and so the enemy retired without any other success, the galleasses having spoiled their admiral's [Drake's] rigging and shot away his mainyard." Medina-Sidonia and the rest of the vanguard made their way back through the Armada and struck their sails to signal a general engagement, but again the English ships spurned the invitation and drew away, still keeping up a harassing fire from long range with their cannons and culverins. Ignoring these assaults as no more than a delaying tactic, Medina-Sidonia once more re-formed the Armada and sailed on. There was no more fighting that day and the Armada "had good opportunity to look to their leaks, whereof they had no doubt a great number, for they had carried away many shrewd stripes from their enemies."

Smudges of smoke rose into the still air from a score of beacons burning on the Isle of Wight to summon the local militia and some of the Hampshire levies to the defence of the island, and Spithead was alive with small boats ferrying troops across the water from the mainland. The wind had now abated to a faint westerly breeze, and if the lack of wind to fill the sails rendered the Armada's progress even more wearisome—so slow that a man strolling along the cliffs could easily have kept pace with it—it also deprived the English fleet of much of its advantage in speed and manoeuvrability. By afternoon, a few miles to the south-west of the Needles, the wind had dropped altogether and the two fleets drifted helpless, barely a mile apart. The only movement was the steady procession of smaller craft, coasters and pinnaces warping or rowing out from every English harbour within range of the fleets. Some were loaded with supplies of powder and shot, some were full of gentlemen volunteers—the Earls of Cumberland, Oxford and Northumberland, Robert and Thomas Cecil and Sir Walter Ralegh were among many nobles and gentlemen joining the fleet as it sailed up the Channel, but the enthusiasm of some for action overrode their common sense. Lord Howard's young brother-in-law, Robert Cary, was in such haste to join the English fleet that, having searched all night and discovered a great company of ships just before dawn, he was almost in their midst before he realized that he was about to join the Armada. With some good fortune, his frigate put about and made its escape.[1]

Sir Horatio Palavicino, a Genoese banker who had settled in England, made a vast fortune and become heavily involved in the financial affairs of Elizabeth's government, also rushed from London to join the fight, pausing only to ensure that those left behind were made aware of the sacrifice he was making. "The greatness of my zeal which desires to be among those who do fight for Her Majesty's service and for the defence of her kingdom, constrains me, with an honourable company, to depart this night toward Portsmouth there to embark and join the Lord Admiral where I hope to be present in the battle and thereby a partaker in the victory or to win an honourable death, thus to testify to the whole world my fidelity to her Majesty." Still other boats carried spectators. Sir George Carey, Captain of the Isle of Wight, Henry Ratcliffe, Earl of Sussex, who was "Constable of Portchester Castle, Warden and Captain of the town, castle and isle of Portsmouth," and the Lord Lieutenants of Hampshire and Dorset all put to sea in search of a grandstand view of the battle, and a trail of such small craft followed each English squadron, like shoals of small fish tracking a school of sharks.

Ammunition was sorely needed by the fleet, volunteers rather less so. Disease and ship fever were taking a steady toll of crewmen and though the scrupulously recorded casualty figures of both sides were only in the low hundreds, with English casualties well below those of the Armada, they seriously underestimated the actual position. Men were recorded as being wounded only when they were actually disabled or incapacitated, and all captains—Spanish and English—were reluctant to document fatalities, for as long as a man's name remained on the ship's muster roll his pay could continue to be drawn. Commanders of land and sea forces often took "dead pays" at the rate of one for every ten men under their command. "I marvel that where so many are dead on the seas, the pay is not dead with them," as Lord Burghley bitterly remarked. Fresh seamen were welcome to join the fleet, but Lord Howard needed no more soldiers aboard and sent back a contingent of 100 musketeers from Sir George Carey and "the best and choicest shot of the trained bands" from Kent that the Privy Council had dispatched "to double-man the ships." Their weapons were of little use at the range at which the fleet had chosen to fight, and the men would merely be an added drain on already scant rations and water.

While his fleet lay becalmed, Lord Howard signalled for another council of war. Less than half of each fleet had been engaged in the day's brief hostilities but the English had again closed the range a little more and both fleets had taken heavier punishment as a result. One Spanish cannonball had damaged the main yard of Drake's *Revenge*, while on the Spanish side, the *San Martin* and the *San Juan* were damaged and the *Gran Grifon* crippled and in tow. Yet despite the expenditure of a mountain of powder and shot, still no Armada ship had been captured or sunk as a result of English gunfire, and each lull in the fighting allowed the Spanish carpenters to make repairs. Nor had the Armada's formation been disrupted enough to halt its relentless eastward progress. Nonetheless, Drake's attack on the *Gran Grifon*—albeit at the cost of the damage to his own ship—had demonstrated the most effective range for the English guns, and Drake and his men had seen for themselves the damage their culverins had done to the *Grifon*'s stout oak hull. For the first time, an Armada ship's hull had repeatedly been penetrated by shot. Far from the cannonballs' embedding themselves in the outer planking or even bouncing off, as had happened in the previous days' fighting, some shots had pierced the enemy ship "from side to side," and the *Gran Grifon* had been disabled as a result.

The attack had shown beyond doubt that the key to victory would lie in breaking up the Armada's formidable defensive formation, isolating individual ships and then assailing them with overwhelming force at close range. The informal groupings of Howard's fleet—each captain choosing for himself the leader he wished to follow into battle—and the improvisational nature of its attacks had not proved sufficient to achieve that aim, and Howard and his commanders now re-formed the fleet into four squadrons, one under his own command, the others led by John Hawkins—released from his duty of watching over the Lord Admiral—Francis Drake and Martin Frobisher. All knew the vital importance of the battle that would be joined the next day. A document circulated to the Privy Council had given three reasons why the Spaniards would attempt to seize a port on the Isle of Wight rather than at any other point on the coast. "First where he may find least resistance, and most quiet landing. Secondly, where he may have best harbour for his galleys and speediest supplies out of Spain, France and Flanders. Thirdly, where he may most offend the realm by incursions, and force Her Majesty, by keeping many garrisons to stand upon a defensive war . . . He may keep in safe harbour his galleys to make daily invasions . . . where they shall perceive the standing of the wind will impeach Her Majesty's ships to come to their rescue. So that all the castles and sea towns of Hampshire, Sussex and Dorsetshire will be subject to be burnt, unless Her Majesty will keep garrisons in those places." The course set by the Armada showed Medina-Sidonia's intention to enter St. Helen's Roads, to the east of the Isle of Wight; the English Grand Fleet now had to prevent him from securing the anchorage that he sought.[2]

Through the afternoon and evening, the fleets drifted slowly eastwards towards St. Catherine's Point, observed by watchmen in the ruined tower where medieval monks had once kept a light burning for the safety of shipping. Men laboured in both fleets to prepare for the next day's battle, checking the sails, tuning the running ropes and rigging, filling the cartridges with powder, stacking shot in the lockers by every gun, and preparing their personal weapons, before settling down to whatever rest and sleep they could obtain. Knowing that the next day's battle might decide the outcome of the war, Howard and his senior commanders were meanwhile planning a desperate gamble. The Queen's galleons and a handful of the large armed merchantmen had done the bulk of the fighting so far. Lacking the weight of armament to outmatch the Spanish galleasses and great ships, the rest of the fleet was of scarcely more value than the spectator craft. "If you had seen what I have seen of the simple service that has been done by the merchant and coast ships, you would have said that we had been little helped by them, otherwise than that they did make a show."

However, the English commanders now planned to launch a night attack, using twenty-four of these armed—and expendable— merchantmen to harass and disrupt the Spanish formation, leaving it all the more vulnerable to a dawn assault by the main English force. Any damage or disruption they could cause, even at the price of being lost themselves, would make the task of the galleons at first light that much easier. It would have been another daring innovation; sea battles had never been fought at night because "the fogs of battle," made worse by the darkness, created too much confusion, and there was also the danger of collisions or of "friendly fire" from other ships of the attackers' own fleet. But on this occasion, the potential advantages outweighed the risks and the attack would have been launched had the dead calm not prevented it. As it was, the hours of darkness passed without incident.

Over 9,000 men had been mustered by Captain Dawtrey to defend Southampton and 3,000 were deployed around the cliffs and harbours of the Isle of Wight, where Sir George Carey had been riding all night, checking his watchmen and guards on the headlands, sea cliffs and beaches, and urging them to ever greater vigilance, ears tuned for the least sound of muffled oars in the darkness, eyes turned towards the point where the line of the breaking waves was marked by a dim phosphorescence, straining for a glimpse of any strange craft approaching the shore. The main camp at Carisbrooke remained on full alert and armed patrols moved constantly along the coastal paths. They watched as the new formation of the English fleet received its first test at daybreak the next morning, Thursday, 4 August, St. Dominic's Day, and of particular significance to Medina-Sidonia since St. Dominic— Domingo de Guzman—was one of his ancestors. As the sun rose, the entire Armada raised flags in honour of the saint and an air of anticipation gripped the crews and soldiers on both sides. If the Spaniards were to seize an English port as a base and a refuge, it had to be today, for by nightfall the eastward drift of the wind and tide would have pushed them past St. Helen's Roads and into the Narrows where there was no deep-water harbour that would accommodate them. The English were well aware of the danger, and Howard's intention was "so to course [chase] the enemy that they shall have no leisure to land."[3]

If Medina-Sidonia tried to enter St. Helen's Roads, the tide would be running in his favour from around seven in the morning to noon. After that the force of the outgoing tide would be against him, and within three days of the peak spring tide, it would be running faster than the speed that the Armada could manage, even with a wind at its back. Medina-Sidonia's pilots must have told him this, so he knew he had only a few hours to achieve his aim. Through his pilots and commanders, Howard was even better informed of the set and duration of the tides and, whatever the circumstances, his fleet would have attacked at first light in an attempt to delay or divert the Armada. In the event, they were offered an immediate opportunity, for once more two Spanish ships—the royal galleon *San Luis de Portugal* and the *Santa Ana*, a merchantman of the Andalusian squadron—had drifted away from the Armada during the night. Medina-Sidonia may even have deliberately offered them as bait, the kind of trap to bring the English to close quarters that he had failed to spring with the crippled *Rosario*.

The flat calm still prevailed but Hawkins, whose squadron was nearest to the two ships, at once ordered an attack. Without the wind to fill their sails, his galleons were towed into range by men at the oars of the ships' boats, but such calm conditions were ideal for the Spanish galleasses, and Medina-Sidonia at once sent them to counter-attack. Three of them bore down, towing behind them the carrack *La Rata Encoronada*, to bring extra fire-power to bear. On the English side, the *Ark* and Lord Thomas Howard's *Golden Lion* were also being towed into range. The unprotected, unarmed men at the oars of the longboats were tempting targets for the gunners and musketeers aboard the galleasses, but there was enough harassing fire from the English galleons' bow chasers and forward-angled cannons to give them some protection, and as the range closed they hauled the bows of their galleons around to bring the broadsides to bear on the enemy. "There were many good shots made by the *Ark* and the *Lion* at the galleasses, in the sight of both armies. One of them was fain to be carried away upon the careen [listing] and another, by a shot from the *Ark*, lost her lantern which came swimming by, and the third his nose." But Howard's claim that the galleasses "were never seen in fight any more" was demonstrably false; within half an hour, they were once more engaged in the battle. If one had indeed been listing, its carpenters had quickly repaired the damage and its pumps had righted the ship.

A westerly breeze now began to stir and the remainder of the warships at once joined the action, fighting in a way that was almost identical to the battle off Portland two days previously. Frobisher again took the perilous shoreward flank, the squadrons of Drake and Hawkins attacked the seaward wing, and Howard's squadron once more had the task of "fixing" the Spanish centre. "At the same time that this conflict was in our rear, the enemy's admiral and other great ships assailed our capitana [the *San Martin*]. They came closer than on the previous day firing off their heaviest guns from the lowest deck, cutting the trice [mainstay] of our mainmast and killing some of our soldiers." The fact that the English commanders were only now using the heavy guns on the lower deck suggests that the seas may have been too rough on the previous days to allow the gunports close to the waterline to be opened, though it is also possible that they simply did not have enough powder and shot to fire them until this crucial point was reached.[4]

The significance that the English accorded to the battle was shown by the urgency that they showed and the risks they were now prepared to take, not only in being towed into battle against the galleasses and in closing the range on the Spanish great ships before opening fire, but in exposing Frobisher to even greater potential danger than off Portland. Once more, no record of the fleet's tactical plan was kept—the "secrets of the services" were still to be maintained—and it is possible that even

Howard was not informed of the precise tactics his commanders were to adopt. He would not have been the first, nor certainly the last inexperienced senior officer on land or sea to be told only what his more seasoned subordinates felt was appropriate for him to know. Whether or not Howard knew what was in the minds of Drake, Frobisher and Hawkins, the nature and timing of their attacks demonstrate that they were again using their superior knowledge of the local coastlines, tides, currents and wind conditions to manoeuvre the Armada into a position from where it would be unable to gain the haven it sought.

The fleets were now closing on the eastern approaches to Spithead and the Solent. If the Armada were to reach Bembridge Foreland while the flood tide was still running, the prevailing wind and sea conditions would make it easy for the Spanish ships to sweep into St. Helen's Roads and the English fleet could not follow them in without risking a battle at close quarters that would bring the overwhelming Spanish superiority in battle troops into play. If they held off, the Spaniards would be free to put enough troops ashore to overwhelm the English militias assembled to repulse them. However, if the Armada could be harried, diverted and delayed by just a couple of hours, the set of the tide and currents would change. The waters penned by the flood tide into the broad, crescent-shaped channel to the west, north and east of the Isle of Wight are released as the tide eases, fuelling an outgoing south-easterly current of four knots—twice the speed that the slowest Armada ships could manage. In addition, just as off Portland, there was a clashing tidal race and eddy—the St. Catherine's Race, making as much as six or seven knots in full spate—that those who knew the waters could utilize and those who did not would enter at their peril. These coasts were even more dangerous than those around Portland Bill, for the Isle of Wight marks a clear divide between the rocky cliffs and deep waters of the West Country and the shoals and shallows that line the Hampshire and Sussex coasts. That area had been lost to the sea only recently, in the inundations of the thirteenth and fourteenth centuries, and, though there were deep channels following the lines of ancient river valleys incised into the seabed, the depth of most of these inshore waters at low tide varied from three fathoms to as little as two—considerably less than the draught of the Spanish great ships.

Frobisher's squadron kept close inshore as the tide swept both fleets steadily eastwards at around a knot. The current was faster both nearer to the shore, where it pushed the *Triumph* to the north and east of the Spanish vanguard, and in the main channel several miles out to sea, where the squadrons of Drake and Hawkins were also advancing around the seaward wing of the Armada. Once more, the *San Martin* found itself isolated on the shoreward flank, accompanied only by "the galleass *Patrona*," and Frobisher's squadron was soon giving the flagship another battering, but the wind began to strengthen, enabling a number of Spanish ships, led by Miguel de Oquendo, to come to the *San Martin*'s aid. So powerful was St. Catherine's Race that Oquendo was forced to station his ship directly in front of the *San Martin*'s bow, "as the current made it impossible for him to stand alongside." Seeing the danger, most of Frobisher's squadron had already found enough searoom and speed to manoeuvre around the Spanish attack and make their escape, but the *Triumph* appeared trapped to leeward, in an almost identical position to the earlier battle off Portland.

Medina-Sidonia was confident that this time he had his foe cornered, and the strange motion of Frobisher's ship, holding station in the troubled waters between the race and the eddy, convinced most Spanish observers that his ship was crippled, the rudder "injured and useless." According to Medina-Sidonia, the Triumph had been "so spoiled in the fight that she struck the standard and discharged pieces to show her need of succour," but if so, Frobisher was foxing, attempting to lure the *San Martin* into danger. Once more he knew these waters so intimately that, having achieved his aim of delaying the Armada's eastward course, he then used his knowledge to make his escape. He ordered his longboats to be lowered and other members of his squadron also sent him their ships' boats, until a total of eleven were towing the *Triumph* into the furious waters of the race, while two of Howard's biggest galleons, the *Elizabeth Jonas* and the *Bear,* attacked the Spaniards in the flanks.

Medina-Sidonia maintained his course, intent on closing with his prey. "It appeared certain that we would that day succeed in boarding them, wherein was the only way to victory," but with the wind freshening and veering a little and the *Triumph* now positioned to ride the current, Frobisher ordered the longboats cast off, piled on sail and "got out so swiftly that the galleon *San Juan* and another quick sailing ship—the fastest vessels in the Armada—although they gave chase, seemed in comparison to her to be standing still." By the race-built standards of the English fleet, the *Triumph* was an old, top-heavy and clumsy vessel, and the speed at which it sailed away from its pursuers shows how adeptly Frobisher was utilizing the fast-flowing currents and races swirling about the headlands.[5]

At exactly the same time as Frobisher's squadron had been attacking the shoreward wing of the Armada and Howard had been battering the centre, the squadrons of Drake and Hawkins had thrown their weight into the action with a brilliantly conceived, sudden and ferocious assault from the south-west on the Armada's rearguard. No account mentions Drake by name at this point and there have been suggestions that, having sustained some damage to his mainmast in the previous day's fighting, he had dropped behind to repair it and took no part in the battle. That is certainly possible, but the damage was not severe enough to require the mast to be replaced—it was described as "decayed with shot" when the fleet was surveyed after its return to port that autumn—and the attack on the seaward wing is very much in Drake's style. Such was his reputation and influence that it would have been a severe blow to the fleet's morale if he had been absent from such a crucial battle. Ships carried spare yards and spars, either in the holds or lashed to the side of the ship, and the job of replacing one was not so huge that it could not have been achieved inside twenty-four hours, even if his men had to labour all night. If that had not proved sufficient, it is hard to imagine that Drake would have sat out the battle rather than commandeering another ship of his squadron as a temporary flag-ship. It is surely more probable that his role in the fighting was either unobserved by Howard and those on the far wing of the battle, or that in boosting their own role in their personal accounts they downplayed that of others.

Whoever was leading the attack, the English ships succeeded at once in isolating and pounding one of the royal galleons of Portugal, the *San Mateo*. It was too small and lightly armed to sustain the assault for long and, though the *San Francisco* manoeuvred to protect it, the whole seaward wing of the Armada was being battered and driven back. "After wonderful sharp conflict, the Spaniards were forced to give way and to flock together like sheep" around the *San Martin*. "There was never seen a more terrible value of great shot, nor more hot fight than this was." "The shot continued so thick together that it might rather have been judged a skirmish with small shot on land than a fight with great shot on sea." The relentless attack on the seaward wing, aug-mented by the continuing assaults from the squadrons of Howard and Frobisher, was compressing the Armada's defensive formation to the point of collapse and pushing it into dangerous waters. Past Bembridge Foreland the Armada ships were now met by the ebb tide flowing out from St. Helen's Roads, and wind and tide were combining to drive them away from their objective and closer to the perilous rocks and shallows of the Owers Bank, stretching miles out to sea off Selsey Bill.

The English fleet had tried the same manoeuvre against the French in 1545 and only a change in the wind had saved the French from catas-trophe. Now the quick reactions of his pilots rescued Medina-Sidonia. The shoal water was clearly visible and the jagged tips of black rocks broke the surface like shark fins. If the battle had been sustained for a few more minutes the Armada might have been driven onto them, but, apprised by his pilots of the danger, Medina-Sidonia fired a signal gun to break off hostilities, then put on sail and headed south-south-east, with the rest of his fleet in pursuit. One eyewitness remarked that after seeing victory snatched from him by a hair's breadth when the *Triumph* slipped the noose being drawn around it, Medina-Sidonia had saved the Armada from disaster by no greater margin. "If the Duke had not gone about with his flagship, instead of conquerors that we were, we should have come out vanquished that day."[6]

However, by steering clear of the danger of the shoals, he was also sailing away from his last possible refuge on the English coast. He would find no safe anchorage at all among the shallows and sea cliffs of the Sussex and Kent coasts stretching away into the haze. The English attacks had forced him to abandon the plan agreed with his command-ers "to proceed as far as the Isle of Wight and no further" until word had been received that Parma's invasion troops were assembled and ready. The Armada was now left on the open seas, at the mercy of the elements and the English fleet, lacking a base, a bridgehead or even a haven, its water, provisions and munitions dwindling, and with no cer-tainty that when it reached its destination Parma's forces would be ready to embark.

There must have been cheers from the English troops and specta-tors lining the cliffs of the Isle of Wight and Selsey Bill as they saw the immediate danger receding and the Armada sailing on out of sight of shore. One of the militiamen watching at Selsey had even taken time to get married that day "in sight of the Armada," departing from his troop just before the service and returning immediately afterwards. The church bells were said to be still sounding as the Spaniards were sighted off the Brill Point.

As the Armada passed from his sight, Sir George Carey at once ordered the camp at Carisbrooke to be struck and the men stood down, while beacons flared further up the coast to summon the militias of Sussex to their mustering points. Meanwhile the English ships again took up their dogged pursuit but made no effort to re-engage the Armada, for they had now expended "a great part of our powder and shot, so as it was not thought good to deal with them any more till that was relieved." Elizabeth's continuing parsimony had ensured that Howard's desperate appeals for supplies of munitions were answered only in part, if at all, and Walsingham complained that "for want of powder and shot, he [Howard] shall be forced to forbear to assail and to stand upon his guard until he shall be furnished." The scarcity in the nation's chief arsenal, the Tower, was so severe at one point that there was "but five last of powder, and if I shall take out (as I must of force) so much as I have sent unto my Lord Admiral, there would none be left." Elizabeth's ministers were now instructed to make belated enquiries about obtaining additional supplies of powder from overseas, and Edward Burnham, one of Walsingham's agents in The Netherlands, reported to his master that "there is no great quantity [of powder] to be had here, but the greatest store . . . is in Amsterdam. By some of our merchants I do understand that there is good quantity at Hamburg and Stade and better cheap than in these parts," but if any was purchased, none reached the fleet in time.[7]

The garrisons and towns of the South Coast did their best to fill the gap—"men, powder, ships and victuals" issued from every port. "All this day and Saturday . . . the Spaniards were always before the English army like sheep, during which time the justices of peace near the sea coast, the Earl of Sussex, Sir George Carey, and the captains of the forts and castles along the coast, sent us men, powder, shot, victuals and ships to aid and assist us." "John Holford of Heeth from the town of Southampton" supplied sixteen barrels of powder and "twenty hundredweight of shot and one hundred of match." Two shillings were spent by the mayor "for carrying down to the quay of the powder and shot," and Holford was paid £3 19s 2d by the mayor "for his boat, himself & his men with their victuals and charges in going to my Lord Admiral at two several times." When the Earl of Sussex, the Governor of Portsmouth, received Howard's plea for powder and shot at six the next morning, he at once sent off his entire supply, earning himself a reprimand from the Queen and several months of disgrace at Court for his profligacy—but with the exception of the stores kept in the shore batteries guarding the harbours, there were precious few cannonballs to be had.

The towns sent what they could, even down to plough-chains and broken pieces of scrap iron. Fired from a cannon at point-blank range, this improvised ammunition could cause carnage among a ship's crew, but to operate at such close range was an invitation to boarding, the one thing the English were determined to avoid. Meanwhile, in the absence of adequate supplies of provisions and munitions, Elizabeth, like Philip, sought divine support. In early August, the Privy Council ordered bishops and pastors to say "public prayers to Almighty God, the giver of victories, to assist us against the malice of our enemies," and lest this was ignored, the Council also required the Archbishop of Canterbury "to order Parsons to get people to pray against the Spaniards" and to preach on the need for the nation to unite against the invaders. "Every man's particular state is in the highest degree to be touched, in respect of country, liberty, wife, children, lands, life and (that which is to be especially regarded) for the profession of the true and sincere religion." Church sermons were the prime means of communication with the population as a whole, and to ensure her message was heard by everyone Elizabeth issued orders that the laws requiring every citizen to attend church were to be rigidly enforced.[8]

Despite another apparently inconclusive battle, Howard was in jubilant mood, hailing the day's action as a great victory. His good humour would only have been improved by the news brought out of Le Havre by the captain of a French ship. The greatest English fear had been that France might be persuaded to join the Catholic crusade against England, but the captain assured his interrogators that the French fleet showed no sign of being readied for sea. As night fell, thunder rolled around the sky and flashes of lightning lit up the darkness. If it was an ill omen, the Spaniards had much greater cause for concern.

CHAPTER FOURTEEN

The L.ᵗ Admirall Howard
Knighting Thomas Howard,
the Lord Sheffeild, Rog: Townsend
Iohn Hawkins, and Martin
Forbisher for thãr good service

Resolved There to Live and Die

The following morning, 5 August, as the wind again dropped, becalming the fleet, Howard knighted John Hawkins, Martin Frobisher, the remarkable George Beeston—commanding the *Dreadnought* at the age of eighty-nine—and several of his own relatives, including Lord Thomas Howard and Lord Sheffield, on the deck of the *Ark*, "in reward for their good services in these former fights." It has often been suggested that this can only have been for public show, boosting the morale of his men before the great battle to come, rather than a realistic reflection of his mood; but that is to overlook the success of the strategy the English commanders had adopted. Their primary aim was to prevent Medina-Sidonia from securing a base or an anchorage on the English coast. They had dogged the Armada eastwards, merely tracking it past coastlines that were unsuitable for a landing but ready to launch attacks on the approaches to each potential haven—Plymouth, Torbay, Portland and the Isle of Wight. The Armada had now been driven beyond its last possible refuge. Most of the Spanish ships could not sail into the wind, and would not dare to attempt it with the English fleet holding the weather gauge, so that only an east wind, a great rarity in the Channel in summer, would now allow the Armada to return and threaten the South Coast. Howard still faced the problem of preventing the conjunction of the Armada with Parma's forces, but he would be strengthened in that battle by Seymour's Squadron of the Narrow Seas, giving him the advantage of numbers. He and his commanders were right to celebrate their success, but it was by no means the decisive point in the war and his private thoughts must have remained at least a little troubled. His fleet had now fought three major battles, each one more sustained in terms of powder and shot expended than any before them in the history of naval warfare, but still the Armada remained apparently impregnable.

Although many of the Englishmen had privateering experience on the Spanish coast and the Spanish Main, it had not fully prepared them for this kind of sustained sea battle, using tactics that were completely novel, and if their guns were more powerful and quick-firing, they were still struggling to achieve sufficient accuracy and impact. William Thomas, a master gunner of Flushing, argued that even the trained gunners were far from masters of their craft. If "Her Majesty's ships had been manned with a full supply of good gunners when the Spanish fleet came through the Narrow Seas . . . it would have been the woefullest time or enterprise that ever the Spaniard took in hand, and not otherwise to be thought or doubted of but that the most noblest victory by the sea that ever was heard of would have fallen to Her Majesty. What can be said but our sins was the cause that so much powder and shot spent and so long time in fight, and in comparison thereof, so little harm." There was no point, Thomas argued, "furnishing of them plentifully with great and forcible ordnance" if the gunners firing it were the product of "blind exercise and unskilful teaching." However, his criticisms would carry more weight had he not been promoting his claims to be employed as a gunnery instructor to the Queen's navy at the time.

The English had so far either been too afraid of the Spanish guns or had overestimated the power and impact of their own weapons. At the range of between 200 yards and half a mile at which much of the fighting had taken place, few guns could pierce the massive oak walls of a galleon or an armed merchantman, and the damage that did occur was quickly repaired by ship's divers and carpenters staunching the holes with timbers, ox hides, lead sheets, sailcloth, oakum, pitch and "tallow and coals mixed together, and in some cases (when the leak is very great) pieces of raw beef, oatmeal bags and the like stuff." The example of the attack on the *Gran Grifon* demonstrated the obvious solution: to close the range still more, to the point where the great shot of the English cannons, and particularly the lighter but much higher velocity shot from the culverins, would be able to batter and pierce the Spanish hulls beyond the ability of any diver or carpenter to repair them. The equally obvious risk of suffering equivalent damage to their own ships would now have to be taken if a final defeat was to be inflicted upon the Armada.[1]

Medina-Sidonia's state of mind must have been much less happy than that of Howard. There was now no harbour available to him without turning back to the west, into the prevailing wind, a situation painfully familiar to one of his commanders, Martin de Bertendona, who had led a fleet bringing troops and supplies to The Netherlands in 1572, only to find that the Dutch Sea Beggars had seized Flushing, leaving no deep-water port available to him. The harbours held by Parma in Flanders were too shallow for the Armada to enter and the governors of the French Channel ports were unlikely to risk the wrath of their king by making their harbours available to the ships of his arch-enemy.

There was one friendly haven that could have accommodated the Armada: the Scheldt river, below Antwerp, but to reach it the Spaniards would have needed Flemish pilots—the channel to the Scheldt, the Wielingen, was narrow and difficult and extended miles out to sea, between sprawling sandbanks—and they would also have had to run the gauntlet of the English and Dutch blockade and the guns of the garrison at Flushing. They might have done so without serious losses, though they would have had to enter in single or double file and the Dutch flyboats would have had free rein to attack the hulks and other vulnerable ships and then retreat out of gun range over the sandbanks where no Armada ships, perhaps not even the galleasses, could have followed. But once inside the Scheldt they would have been trapped, unable to emerge again without being picked off one by one by the waiting English and Dutch fleets. It is even arguable that if the English fleet had been defeated by the Armada, the Dutch on their own would still have been powerful enough to prevent Parma's invasion force from ever emerging from harbour. Had they done so, the Dutch would have cut them to pieces in the shallows, while the Armada waited impotently in the deep water miles offshore. However, one other intriguing possibility remains. Had the Armada made a feint towards England and then entered the Scheldt to reinforce Parma's troops, the Dutch land forces, without the support of the 3,000 English troops withdrawn to defend England, might well have been defeated. With The Netherlands subdued, the Sea Beggars would have had to surrender or disperse and the Enterprise of England could then have been relaunched from the Scheldt.

Medina-Sidonia had been guilty of exaggerating to his commanders—and perhaps to himself—the extent of the damage inflicted on the opposing fleet, but he must have known the truth in his heart. The Spanish guns and the men who operated them were far inferior to their English counterparts. Few Spanish gunners were trained to fight at sea, and their personal defects were matched by those of their equipment; poorly cast weapons, variably sized charges and cannonballs and poorly designed gun-carriages made both their accuracy and their rate of fire abysmal. Medina-Sidonia remained unable to close with and board the English ships, he had no safe haven, his manpower, powder, shot, food and water were sorely depleted and, unlike the English, he had no friendly coast from which he could obtain fresh supplies.

His only hope of succour was now Parma, and that night and again the following morning he sent messages to Dunkirk with Captain Pedro de Leon and the pilot Domingo Ochoa, urging Parma to be ready to join forces with him, and appealing for cannonballs of all sizes but especially four-, six- and ten-pound shot for the lighter guns that were capable of being reloaded under battle conditions. He also begged Parma to send him "40 flyboats to join with this Armada, so that we might be able to close with the enemy, because our ships being very heavy in comparison with the lightness of those of the enemy, it was impossible to come to hand-stroke with them." It was a bizarre reversal; the great Armada that was supposed to sweep the Channel clear of the English fleet and protect the invasion force as it made the crossing was now appealing to Parma for protection. Medina-Sidonia can have had little realistic hope that supplies would arrive in time; Don Rodrigo Tello had not returned, and no word of any sort had been received from Parma during the entire voyage up the Channel. He now had no option but to transfer supplies from the hulks to the fighting ships, refilling at least some of the stores of powder and shot, and "proceed cautiously" towards the rendezvous, but if the invasion force was not embarked and ready to sail when he arrived, the Armada would be in great peril.

At sunset on the Friday, "the wind rose, whereupon our Armada pursued its course," past Cap Gris-Nez, reaching Calais Roads late on the afternoon of the following day, Saturday 6 August. Medina-Sidonia's local pilots argued very strongly against sailing any closer to Dunkirk, for fear that the flood tide and freshening wind would sweep the fleet through the straits and into the North Sea, putting it in peril of the shallows and shoals that littered the coast. Calais Roads was far from an ideal anchorage but it was the best now available, and it was no more than seven leagues—twenty-one miles—from Dunkirk and the rendezvous with Parma. Some of Medina-Sidonia's officers had already decided that the Armada had failed and they urged him to set sail for Spain, taking the long route around Scotland and Ireland, but he dismissed such defeatism out of hand. "The two fleets were very near to each other, though without firing," and when Medina-Sidonia's signal gun thundered the entire Armada "came all upon a sudden to anchor," "purposing that our [English] ships, with the flood, should be driven to leeward of them," losing the weather gauge, but the response of the English commanders was immediate. They also struck sail and dropped anchor with commendable speed and discipline, and the two fleets rode the swell together "against Scales Cliffs" within long gun range of each other.[2]

Medina-Sidonia at once sent Captain Pedro Heredia, "a soldier of great experience," to Giraud de Mauleon, Seigneur de Gourdan and the Governor of Calais, to advise him of "the cause of our presence there and to offer him our friendship and good offices." He found him "on the shore in a coach with his wife, watching to see whether there would be a battle." Like his townspeople, scenting profit or the entertainment of a sea battle before their eyes, Gourdan had seen the fleets approaching and hurried to a vantage point. "Flemings, Walloons and Frenchmen came thick and threefold to behold it, admiring the exceeding greatness of the ships and their warlike order." The cliffs of Dover were also lined with spectators, peering into the afternoon haze in the hope of seeing the decisive battle.

Calais had been liberated from English rule only thirty years before and anti-English sentiment was still strong in the town. Gourdan, who had lost a leg fighting in that battle, showed his own private sympathy for the Spanish cause by sending his nephew "with a present of refreshments" for Medina-Sidonia. He also warned him that "the place wherein he had anchored was dangerous to remain, because the currents and counter-currents of that channel were very strong," but, reluctant to identify himself too closely with the Spanish cause when the destiny of the French throne still hung in the balance, Gourdan was less accommodating to requests for supplies than Medina-Sidonia might have hoped, or Howard must have feared. He refused him the articles of war he was seeking but offered him the chance to purchase whatever additional provisions he needed, and boats were soon plying between the shore and the Armada. "Fresh victuals straight were brought abroad; captains and cavaliers for their money might have what they would, and gave the French so liberally as within twelve hours an egg was worth fivepence"—more than twenty times what they had been fetching before the Armada dropped anchor. A Spanish provision party was also sent ashore with 6,000 ducats to buy food but there was not enough in the whole region, let alone the town, to feed so many thousands of men and, while the officers and gentlemen adventurers were able to dine for a while on fresh fish, meat, fruit and vegetables, most of their men continued to subsist on a meagre diet from their ships' dwindling stores of rotting provisions.[3]

Medina-Sidonia had also sent Secretary Geronimo de Arceo ashore with a further message for Parma, "to advertise him of the place where he now was, and that he could not tarry there without endangering the whole fleet." "I am anchored here two leagues from Calais with the enemy's fleet on my flank. They can cannonade me whenever they like and I shall be unable to do them much harm. If you can send me forty or fifty flyboats of your fleet I can, with their help, defend myself here until you are ready to come out." It was the same futile request that he had made twenty-four hours earlier and his misunderstanding of the strength of Parma's naval forces shows how poorly briefed he had been by his King. Philip had continued to give Medina-Sidonia specific instructions to rendezvous with Parma at sea or "off the Cape of Margate" as though Parma's fleet was capable of sailing there unaided, even though the King well knew the true state of affairs. Parma had reminded him in January: "Your Majesty is well aware that without the support of the fleet, I could not cross over to England with these boats." Dunkirk is separated from Margate by some forty sea miles. Had the invasion barges been able to cross those perilous waters, evading the Dutch flyboats in the coastal shallows and the English warships on the open ocean, they would scarcely have needed the assistance of the Armada to make a landing on English soil.

Had Medina-Sidonia brought more galleys with him, and had they been able to survive the storms in the Bay of Biscay and the Western Approaches, they might have tipped the balance off Flanders, where they would have been more than a match for the Dutch flyboats. But Philip chose to ignore the pleas of both Santa Cruz and Medina-Sidonia for a galley fleet to be added to the Armada strength and instead had retained his fleets in the Mediterranean to guard against a surprise attack by the Turks and ward off raids by Barbary corsairs. Only four galleys had sailed with the Armada and all had been driven to part from it by the storms that assailed them before they had even reached the Channel. Medina-Sidonia's galleasses might have made short work of the Dutch flyboats, but he dared not spare them from the defence of the Armada; he feared being overwhelmed if he divided his forces. Parma had hired 16 ships for use as transport craft and impounded almost 30 others, but claimed to have fewer than a dozen flyboats available. Seymour reported that Parma had rather more—"40 sails of flyboats"—but even if this were true, they were far outnumbered by those of the Dutch rebels, who mustered at least 400. Parma had made some attempts to remedy his shortage of such craft but he delegated the supervision of the task to others and the construction of new flyboats in the shipyards around Dunkirk was beset with problems. Among the shipwrights and carpenters were many sympathizers with the rebel cause intent on sabotage. So slow was the work and so poor the workmanship that some completed ships had to be dismantled to remove the green or rotten planks used in building them; one had no running rigging and another had no guns and its mast had been left unstepped. Yet another was so unseaworthy that it was left stranded and waterlogged on a mudbank as soon as it was launched.[4]

Many of the invasion barges were no better constructed. The seams of some were left uncaulked and sprang leaks as soon as they were lowered into the water. Others began to leak when they were loaded and one sank to the bottom of the canal with its full complement of soldiers during a practice embarkation. English spies were well aware of their deficiencies and Seymour dismissed any idea that they could be used for an invasion. "The flat-bottomed boats . . . be no boats to be hazarded to the sea, no more than wherries or cockleboats." The majority were "60–70 feet long and 15–20 feet wide, and draw no more than three feet of water. They can carry men on and below deck, 200 men each," but equipped with neither guns, masts nor sails, nor even oarlocks, the flat-bottomed barges were virtually incapable of being moved under their own power and were helpless against the fast, agile and heavily armed flyboats. Parma was also "short of good pilots and even of seamen . . . the reason for this is not that the few we have are not well-treated or that we have neglected to obtain more, but because the well-disposed ones are so few and the Hollanders and Zee-landers are forbidden under heavy penalties to serve us."

Parma had been the first to propose an invasion from Flanders but the repeated postponements of the Armada and the loss of secrecy and surprise had caused a rapid waning of his enthusiasm. He voiced so many criticisms of the Enterprise that, tiring of his nephew's complaints, the King eventually ordered him to silence and acquiescence. Despite this, Parma had urged in April that the Armada should be deferred long enough to give him the opportunity to take the deep-water port of Flushing and the island of Walcheren, and when Philip refused to consider this, Parma's emissary, Luis Cabrera de Cordoba, warned him that it was going to be impossible for Parma's barges ever to meet the Armada. "The Spanish galleons draw 25 or 30 feet, and around Dunkirk they will not find that much water for several leagues. The enemy [Dutch] ships draw so much less that they can safely place themselves to prevent anything coming out of Dunkirk. Since the junction of the barges from Flanders with the Armada is the whole point of the enterprise, then it is impossible—why not give it up now and save much time and money?"[5]

On 22 June Parma again wrote to the King, complaining that Medina-Sidonia "seems to have persuaded himself that I may be able to go out and meet him with these boats. These things cannot be . . . If I were to attempt going out to meet the Duke and we came across any armed English or rebel ships, they could destroy us with the greatest of ease. Neither the valour of our men nor any other human effort could save us. This was one of the principal reasons which moved your Majesty to lay down the precise and prudent orders you did." Philip wrote in the margin, "God grant that no embarrassment may come of this," but sent no reply. Martin de Bertendona, commander of the Levant squadron, also raised with the King the issue of the lack of a deep-water port in the Channel, but similarly failed to elicit a response.

However, in a later annotation he made on a dispatch from Medina-Sidonia, Philip showed that he was aware that the absolute, overriding requirement to rendezvous with Parma's forces off the Cape of Margate could not be achieved until Medina-Sidonia had cleared the seas of the English fleet. After receiving Medina-Sidonia's letter of 10 June asking for details of where they were to rendezvous, Parma had sent yet another furious dispatch to Philip, once more pointing out the impossibility of his landing craft putting out to sea to meet the Armada offshore. "These vessels cannot run the gauntlet of warships; they cannot even withstand large waves." Unfortunately for Medina-Sidonia,

the officer who left Flanders on 14 July to convey a similar message to
the Armada was delayed and diverted by storms, shipwreck and the
presence of the English fleet, and his message never arrived.

As long ago as 13 May, Parma had been "anxiously looking from
hour to hour for news of the Duke," and he complained again on
18 July that he was "greatly grieved at receiving no news." Medina-
Sidonia was no less disturbed that at nightfall on Saturday 6 August he
was still awaiting a reply from Parma. One dispatch had been lost, and
due allowance needs to be made for the difficulties in maintaining communications over long distances, especially when one of the parties was
aboard a fleet on the high seas, but they can easily be exaggerated. The
roads were undoubtedly terrible, and the threat from robbers, parti-
sans, religious opponents and gangs of deserters on land, and of privateers, pirates, Sea Beggars and the English navy off the coast was real
enough, but dispatches were sent in fast, armed and oared pinnaces,
often sailing under false colours in hostile waters. There is some evidence that Juan Gil used such a subterfuge. Two English couriers sailing out of Rye encountered some fishermen who told them that a
many-oared ship "full of Englishmen," and flying the Queen's flag as
well as the banner of Santiago, had passed them, claiming to be on the
way to bring news of the Armada to the Squadron of the Narrow Seas.[6]

Given the relative speed of a fast *zabra* or pinnace and the snail-like
pace of the Armada, at least one of the stream of messages that Medina-
Sidonia began sending as soon as the Armada reached the open sea
should certainly have been with Parma weeks before the arrival date
ascribed to it. He had showed himself willing to wait weeks and even
months before replying to urgent communications from his King, and
he was perfectly capable of delaying a response to Medina-Sidonia.
The one message he did send had not reached Medina-Sidonia, but
had another dispatch been sent while the Armada was at sea, only similarly atrocious bad luck or bad navigation would have prevented it from
reaching its destination. The course the Armada was to follow was
known and a fleet occupying several square miles of sea space was
almost impossible to miss in the close confines of the Channel. In the
event, the first dispatch from Parma did not arrive until the Armada
was already anchored beneath the cliffs of Calais. The "fatal misunderstanding" between the two men "which wrecked the campaign" had
continued to the end.

Communications between the English and Dutch fleets were as
bad as those between Medina-Sidonia and Parma, but had Elizabeth or
her commanders had greater faith in the ability of the Dutch to keep
Parma's troops pinned in harbour, Seymour's Squadron of the Narrow

Seas could have joined Howard from the start of the campaign. Seymour had seen no more of the Dutch navy than an occasional sloop patrolling the coast close inshore, but the Dutch were more than ready. Defeated again and again on land, the rebels would not have spurned the chance to attack Parma's forces in their cumbersome barges at sea. If there were few ships visible, it was because Justin of Nassau was hoping to lure Parma's forces out of harbour by giving them the impression that the Dutch navy was elsewhere or unprepared.

Each appearance of Seymour's blockading squadron over the horizon must have driven the Dutch to distraction, for they could not alert their English allies to their plan without risking its betrayal: had two commanders of the English land forces in The Netherlands not recently taken Parma's bribes to surrender their fortified positions without a shot being fired? Nor had they much reason to trust the English when Elizabeth and her commissioners displayed every sign of being willing to conclude a peace treaty that would deliver them into Philip's hands. However, the news that the Armada was in the Channel and that the English had so far failed to dent it, let alone defeat it, changed Dutch plans. They could not risk a confrontation with the powerful warships of the Armada by pursuing Parma's barges out to sea, and instead the flyboats emerged from their hiding places and took up positions blockading the inshore waters along the coast around Dunkirk, where Justin of Nassau "was resolved there to live and die."

Seymour's pleas to be relieved of his blockading duties were finally successful when the two fleets reached Calais and fresh orders arrived from Court. "Forasmuch as Her Majesty sees how it imports her service to have somewhat done to distress the Spanish navy before they shall join with the Duke of Parma's forces by sea, her pleasure is that you should join with the Lord Admiral to do your best endeavour." His squadron of "36 ships . . . whereof five were large galleons," including the *Rainbow* and the *Vanguard*, the newest and finest ships in the entire fleet, was now rapidly approaching Calais, tacking into the breeze. Unlike those of the rest of the fleet, their shot-lockers and powder stores had not been depleted by the fighting in the Channel and, fully armed, Seymour's men must have been thirsting for their share of the action as they took up station "off Scales Cliffs, about eight in the evening."[7]

Medina-Sidonia's mood must have grown even blacker as he saw this potent new addition to the already powerful English fleet, but his position was about to worsen still more. Parma had deliberately scattered his troops to confuse the Dutch and their English allies about his intentions and prevent them from massing their fleet and forces near

Dunkirk. In this he was successful; the Dutch remained uncertain of his true target—was it to be England or a sudden attack on one of their own strongholds?—and they held back many of their ships to maintain the blockades on Sluys, Antwerp and the northern coast. The obvious disadvantage in Parma's tactics was that, once he had definite news of the Armada's arrival, it would take him time to move his troops to the embarkation point. Medina-Sidonia's first indication of that came only as he rode at anchor off Calais at dawn the following morning, Sunday 7 August, when Don Rodrigo Tello, sent ahead by pinnace two weeks previously to tell Parma that the Armada had reached Ushant, at last returned to the flagship in Calais Roads. The news he brought must have been profoundly dispiriting to Medina-Sidonia. Tello had found Parma still in Bruges and "although he had shown great satisfaction at the news of the Armada being arrived" and promised that within six days everything would be ready, when Tello left Dunkirk the previous evening Parma had still not arrived there and "they were not embarking either the men or the munition."

Another of Medina-Sidonia's returning messengers, Juan Gil, reported that Parma kept state in his opulent apartments and showed little apparent urgency for the task at hand. One witness claimed that Parma acted "as if he did not believe that the news of the Armada's coming could be true," but after the number of times he had been told by his King to stand ready for the Armada, only to be then informed that its sailing had been postponed, Parma could have been forgiven that reaction. There is other evidence that the Armada's arrival came as something of a surprise to at least some of the Spaniards in The Netherlands. The English commissioners still engaged in the prolonged and meaningless peace negotiations with Parma's representatives at Bourbourg did not receive word from England that the first battle had been fought off Plymouth until 6 August. They at once broke off talks and left, to the surprise of their counterparts, who wrote to Parma claiming that this might be a negotiating ploy. However, the fact that they were not informed of the impending arrival of the Armada does not mean that Parma was equally unaware, and he was clearly taking steps to preserve what secrecy he could, for on 5 August it was reported that he had "suffered no stranger this seven or eight days to come to him, or to see his army and ships, but he has blindfolded them."[8]

Twenty-four hours after Rodrigo Tello reported back to Medina-Sidonia, Secretary Arceo sent word from Dunkirk that Parma had still not arrived there, "the munitions were not embarked, and that it seemed to him impossible that all things would be prepared within a fortnight." This was much too pessimistic an assessment, and Arceo may have misunderstood a comment by one of Parma's aides: "God give us fifteen days of calm weather to do what we must," which presumably included the time required to cross the Channel, make the landing and secure the bridgehead. Medina-Sidonia could only send yet another dispatch to Parma "to urge him to come out suddenly," and he also sent the Inspector-General of the Armada, Don Jorge Manrique, to give Parma a personal account of "the state of the Armada and to represent to you the urgent need of providing a port for it, without which it will doubtless be lost." How Parma was supposed to provide this was not specified, but his conversation with Manrique degenerated into a furious row. Manrique accused him of failing to prepare his forces and sabotaging the Enterprise of England and Parma had to be restrained from attacking him.

As soon as Manrique had been hustled out of his presence, Parma wrote to the King defending his preparations for the invasion. He had reacted with disbelief to the suggestion that he should send flyboats to aid the Armada and expressed his anger that, far from the Armada's having cleared the Channel of enemy shipping, it had arrived in Calais bringing with it the entire English fleet. The seven leagues that separated him from Medina-Sidonia might as well be seventy; if the Armada could secure the seas, Parma was ready and willing to embark his troops and proceed with the invasion, but he could not be expected to fight the Armada's naval battles for it, or to put to sea without the protection of a fleet. Contrary to the claims of Medina-Sidonia's emissaries, "the boats are, and have been for months, in a proper condition for the task" and though "the boats are so small that it is impossible to keep the troops on board of them for long—there is no room to turn round and they would certainly fall ill, rot and die—the putting of the men on board . . . is done in a very short time and I am confident that in this respect, there will be no shortcoming in Your Majesty's service."[9]

Parma had certainly made considerable preparations for the invasion, including the construction of defensive fortifications made from wooden beams and bristling with pikes, and portable bridges built from barrels and spars to bridge the Medway on the advance through Kent. He had even obtained bundles of faggots that were to be issued to each man as crude shields for their firing positions when the invasion force first went ashore. He did not add a word, though he must have been tempted to do so, about the impossibility of maintaining such a huge force in constant readiness to embark on an Enterprise that had been heralded and then postponed over and over again during the preceding twelve months. He had wasted an entire campaigning season in The Netherlands waiting for the Armada to arrive; had he used his invasion troops against the Dutch instead, the rebellion might have been as good as over. Even now, it must have occurred to him that if the invasion did not take place, his Army of Flanders, augmented by the 6,000 soldiers that the Armada carried as reinforcements for his invasion troops, would be powerful enough to complete the stalled reconquest of The Netherlands.

Having sent his dispatch to Philip, Parma made haste to move from Bruges to Dunkirk and commence the rapid embarkation of his troops, but whether that was in realistic expectation of sailing or merely to safeguard himself against the kingly wrath that would follow a failure of the Enterprise of England was known only to Parma and his conscience. He always insisted that "my statement that we needed no more than three days to embark and be ready to sail forth was not made without justification. On the evening of the 8th I arrived at Nieuport where the embarkation of the men was so forward as to be practically completed, 16,000 troops having been shipped that day," and at Dunkirk he "found the men on the quay and everything ready so by that evening matters would be completed there also." It was a view not shared by another correspondent of the King, who, while careful not to criticize Parma, claimed that "the day on which we came to embark we found the vessels still unfinished, not a pound of cannon on board and nothing to eat. This was not because the Duke of Parma failed to use every possible effort . . . but because both the seamen and those who had to carry out the details openly and undisguisedly directed their energies not to serve His Majesty, for that is not their aim, but to waste his substance and lengthen the duration of the war, besides which the common people threw obstacles in the way." Whichever version of events was true, the embarkation was in any event a pointless exercise, for a gale was blowing offshore, whipping the sea into waves that would have sunk the barges as soon as they had crossed the harbour bar, and the battle in the Channel had already taken a decisive turn.[10]

The Spaniards on sight of the Fireships weighing Ancors cutting Cables and betakeing themselves to flight w:th a hideous noise & in great Confusion.

The Hell-burners

E arly on the morning of Sunday 7 August, Englishmen took Communion aboard their ships, while Mass was celebrated aboard those of the Armada. At the conclusion of his prayers, Howard at once signalled another council of war. Whatever previous communication problems there may have been between Parma and Medina-Sidonia, Howard had to assume that they were now in frequent contact, and it was evident that Medina-Sidonia intended to remain at anchor until the invasion force was embarked. Howard could only guess when that would be, for he had no intelligence on the strength of Parma's forces or the state of his preparations. Parma was only "one tide away" from England, and the spring tide at Dunkirk would allow the great ships of the Armada to approach nearer to the shore than at any other time to embark troops or provide an armed escort for Parma's barges. The urgency of Howard's deliberations with his commanders was also heightened by the dangers of their precarious anchorage. The previous evening, "there did drive aboard my Lord's ship, Her Majesty's ship, the *Bear*, and three others, who were all tangled together, so as there was some hurt done by breaking of yards and spoil of tackle, but a great favour of God showed that it had not made a destruction of many [of] our ships."

Medina-Sidonia also had ample proof of the strength of the tides that his pilots and Gourdan had warned him about. During the night the spring tide had run so strongly that most of the Armada ships had had to drop a second anchor to enable them to hold station. They were still in great danger of dragging their anchors in the soft, shifting sands and running aground on the Calais shore, and their pilots counselled a constant watch on the Armada. The watch should also have been extended to the men, for "at dusk the previous evening, the master and pilot of the hulk *San Pedro el Menor* deserted to the enemy's fleet." Once more, seeing his fleet's hopelessly exposed position and the haven of Calais harbour so close, a more decisive commander than Medina-Sidonia might have forced the issue and given Gourdan an ultimatum: to allow the Armada to enter or be attacked. The mere threat might have been enough to allow Gourdan a face-saving surrender, and if not, even with the guns of the castle his town could not long have resisted an assault by the Armada's troops. Torn by civil war, France was in little condition to exact reprisals on Spain for this breach of her borders, and with the capture of the harbour Medina-Sidonia would have had a port in which Parma's soldiers—a two-day march away by land—could have embarked for the crossing to England. The harbour then was much too small for the whole fleet to have entered, but screened by the warships, the hulks and armed merchantmen could have taken the troops on board with ease and safety, and Howard's ships could only have maintained their blockade at the risk of leaving themselves exposed to the dangers of the lee shore. However, there is no sign that such a course of action ever occurred to Medina-Sidonia—it was not in his instructions from Philip, after all—and any such considerations were soon to be rendered academic.

As the Armada rode the swell beneath the Calais cliffs that morning, Philip sat down at his desk in the Escorial to compose a letter to Medina-Sidonia. Had the Duke ever received the dispatch, it might have provoked even that mild man to an outburst of rage, for Philip was now advocating the very thing that he had previously been at such pains to forbid: "taking one of the enemy's ports where the Armada may refit. I think well to . . . impress on you how important it would be for you to enter and make yourself safe in the Thames itself. The season is so far advanced that this course seems to be necessary." But even as a courier was riding out of the Escorial, the English were taking steps to put the Thames beyond Medina-Sidonia's reach. At their meeting that morning, Howard and his commanders had resolved to use fireships to break up the Armada and drive it from its anchorage. They would then isolate and attack individual ships or groups and push them towards the threatening shoals and sandbars littering the coast and stretching as much as fifteen miles out to sea from Gravelines to beyond the Scheldt estuary. The dangers had been increased still further by the Dutch, who had demolished or taken up all the marker posts, buoys and other navigation points that might have helped pilots unfamiliar with those treacherous waters.[1]

One of Seymour's newly arrived captains, Sir Henry Palmer, was at once dispatched in a pinnace to Dover to collect ships loaded with brushwood, pitch and combustible materials. Nineteen such ships had already been prepared there at the orders of Sir Francis Walsingham but, impatient for action and fearing the consequences of the delay while awaiting Palmer's return, Howard and his commanders decided to use the spring tide and the freshening wind to make the attack that very night. Drake may have been one of the prime movers in this change of plan, for it was typical of his boldness and impetuosity, and he was the first to offer one of his own vessels, the *Thomas*, a 200-ton merchantman, as a fireship. John Hawkins matched the offer and a further six ships were assembled from within the fleet, the least of which was 90 tons burthen and the majority between 140 and 200 tons, far heavier than the normal fireships, making it correspondingly difficult for Spanish defenders in longboats to divert them from their course. The offer of their ships was not necessarily a disinterested one; the use of fireships was a standard practice and compensation was routinely paid. The compensation could often exceed the true value of an old, sea-worn ship near the end of its useful life: "There were seven or eight ships fired by my Lord Admiral's appointment for the removing of the Spanish fleet out of the Calais road, for which the owners demand £5,000."

A Cornishman, Captain Prouse, and John Young, an old Devonian countryman of Drake's who had been serving at sea since the time of Mary Tudor, were put in charge of preparing the fireships. During that

Sunday afternoon, all eight were tethered in line abreast at the down-wind edge of the English fleet and stripped of their stores, though one owner, Henry Whyte, claimed that he had been ruined by volunteering the use of his craft, "the Bark *Talbot*. I rest like one that had his house burnt and one of these days I must come to your Honour for a commission to go a-begging."

All the sails, spars and riggings were kept in place, for the fireships would be sent downwind under full sail. Nor were the guns removed; instead they were double-shotted and "loaded to the mouth with bullets, old iron, and every sort of destructive implement that could be collected" in the hope that their detonations as the flames reached them would create fresh panic and damage within the Armada. Prouse and Young "dressed them with a wild-fire, pitch, and resin and filled them full of brimstone and some other matter fit for fire." Everything from the masts and rigging to the deck timbers and rails was coated with pitch, and tar barrels were also lashed to the bows. A dozen men were detailed to crew each fireship, hauling the sails, holding them to their course and, at the last minute, as they approached the Armada's defensive screen, igniting fires to engulf them.[2]

In his precarious anchorage downwind of the English fleet and hemmed in by a lee shore, the Duke of Medina-Sidonia was well aware of the danger. He and his men had all heard tales of the "hell-burners of Antwerp" that had been used three years previously against the great bridge built by Parma to block the Scheldt below the city. One and a half miles long, protected by siege-gun batteries, armed blockhouses and a bullet-proof palisade stretching from shore to shore, and with a central floating section of barges linked by massive chains, the bridge had appeared impregnable, but the Spaniards had reckoned without the ingenuity of an Italian engineer named Federico Giambelli. He converted two 70-ton ships—the *Hope* and the *Fortune*—and lined their holds with walls of dressed stone and brick. Within each of these floating stone keeps he placed 7,000 pounds of gunpowder, shot, chains, shards of broken iron and angular rocks, then roofed them with timbers fire-proofed with lead sheet and overlaid with paving stones and old gravestones. The decks above were piled with wood. The triggers for these floating hell-burners were clock-operated flintlocks supplied by an Antwerp watchmaker. At a pre-set time a lever would engage, starting a steel wheel grinding against a flint surrounded by a charge of priming powder.

On 4 April 1585, two normal fireships were lit and sent downstream towards the bridge. Spanish soldiers in barges easily caught and steered them aside to burn out harmlessly against the banks, but while they were thus engaged, the *Hope* and the *Fortune* were set alight and loosed on the current and they swept past and crashed into the bridge. The defenders leaped aboard to extinguish the flames and cut the slow fuses they found leading from the deck. As more Spanish troops crowded around to examine their smouldering but apparently defused prizes, the bombs detonated with a blast that was heard over fifty miles away. The shock wave blew Parma, watching nearby, off his feet, and the blast killed 800 Spaniards, raining down shrapnel and flaming debris for a mile around.

Giambelli was now known to be working for Queen Elizabeth in England. In fact he was attempting—unsuccessfully—to construct a boom to protect the Thames at Gravesend, but the Spaniards had no way of knowing that. Coupled with the unease already spreading through the fleet as rumours circulated about the state of Parma's preparations, the mere suggestion that hell-burners might be set loose among them was enough to fill many with terror. Their fears appeared to be confirmed on the Sunday afternoon, when the Armada's lookouts saw more vessels joining the English fleet. They were actually supply ships bringing food, water, powder and shot, but the Spaniards feared that these might indeed be the dreaded hell-burners. An air of foreboding settled over the Armada. The English had daily demonstrated the superior speed, handling and gunnery of their ships, and the knowledge of how the *Rosario* and the *San Salvador* had been abandoned to their fate, and their presence here on a lee shore, with the English fleet upwind and able to attack at will or release fireships on the flood tide, conspired to undermine Spanish morale. The soldiers and crews had been recruited or conscripted from a dozen different nations and many saw no reason to risk their lives in a hopeless cause for a foreign ruler. A few men had already gone over the side, either swimming ashore, bribing the supply boats to ferry them, or deserting to the English. If the tide of battle continued to run against the Armada, there might soon be many more.

During the remaining hours of daylight, Medina-Sidonia urged all his commanders to refill their ships' water casks and obtain whatever provisions they could. He also made further vain attempts to secure more cannonballs and sent another succession of messages to Parma, still harbouring hopes that Parma would provide him with the fast, light boats that might enable him to outmanoeuvre and destroy the English fleet, and urging him to greater speed: "I therefore beg you to hasten your coming out before the spring tides end." Meanwhile he made what preparations he could to defend the Armada against a fireship attack. Captain Antonio Serrano, the commander of the forecastle of the *San Martin* and a man of proven courage and competence, was sent upwind with a screen of pinnaces and ships' boats equipped with grapnels to catch and pull aside any fireships drifting towards the fleet. Medina-Sidonia sent a message to every vessel in the Armada, warning that such an attack was expected. Only if the screen failed and their boats could not divert the fireships were his captains to slip and buoy their cables and put out to sea, leaving the fireships to drift ashore on the current. At first light they would then pick up their cables and regain their former anchorage.

During the afternoon a pinnace ventured out of the English fleet, and with an insouciance that must have driven the watching Spanish officers to fury mingled with despair, it circled the *San Martin* and loosed off four shots from its bow and stern chasers before returning to the English fleet. Only Hugo de Moncada's galleass, the *San Lorenzo*, managed to fire in reply, and that was but two shots, one of which missed. The other passed through the pinnace's topsail but caused no other damage. It may have been another English taunt, but with the fireship attack pending it is more likely that the pinnace's officers were gathering further intelligence on the Armada's disposition and state of preparedness.

Lord Howard called a further council with his senior commanders that evening, laying down the tactics that they would follow at dawn, providing the fireships had done their work. The *San Martin* and the strongest Spanish galleons and galleasses would be attacked in succession by the squadrons of Howard, Drake, Seymour, Frobisher and Hawkins. If the great ships could be crippled or destroyed, the rest of the Armada would then be forced to surrender or be hunted to destruction. The commanders dispersed to their own ships, summoned their men to prayer and spoke of the coming battle and the fate of their families, homes and country if it should be lost. Then all moved to their stations, the gunners stacking cartridges of powder and mounds of shot, soaking blankets and filling the butts with water, the captains studying their charts and the surgeons laying out their instruments. Those charged with readying the fireships made their final preparations, then all was vigilant silence as they waited for darkness and the turn of the tide.

The early watches of the evening passed without incident, as the wind freshened a little and cloud often obscured the moon. The strengthening tide set the Armada ships straining against their cables but there was no sign of any danger until the stroke of midnight, when the English skeleton crews cut the cables tethering the fireships and they began to move downwind in darkness and silence, gathering speed as they advanced. The tide, now at the flood, was running towards shore at around three knots and the wind was almost dead astern. It took ten minutes at most for the fireships to reach the Armada. Handfuls of men crouched in the holds and around the decks of each ship, holding flints or lengths of smouldering match, while each helmsman aligned his ship with the heart of the Armada and then lashed the helm to hold it to its course. At first the Spanish lookouts straining their eyes towards the point where the massed English ships formed a dark, spiked outline against the night sky may not have glimpsed the shapes separating from the main body of the fleet. Then they saw sparks in the night and flickers of flame, and within moments pillars of fire were rising from all eight ships. As the flames took hold with a roar, the helmsmen and the crews who had ignited the fires scrambled into dinghies towed behind the fireships or threw themselves into the sea to be rescued by waiting boats. They had done their work with such skill and bravery that Howard gave them £5 to share among themselves.

The Spanish lookouts screamed the alarm as the fireships, "with sail set, and fair wind and tide . . . all burning fiercely," bore down on the Armada, sweeping on under full sail, their outlines etched in red against the night sky as fires raked them from stem to stern, climbing the tarred ropes of the rigging and beginning to devour the sails. Still gaining speed as they rode the incoming tide, they advanced in what seemed to the Spaniards a perfectly straight line, as tight and disciplined as the Armada in manoeuvre. Black against the fierce glow of the flames, Serrano's pinnaces and small boats moved to their task within sight and gunshot of the English fleet, but the fireships were sizeable vessels. It required great skill and timing to get grapnels aboard and divert them from their course, and they worked "fearing that they should be explosion-machines" that at any moment might detonate, scattering flames and burning debris to engulf their own craft and shrapnel to shred their bodies.[3]

The fireships at either end of the line were successfully intercepted and diverted harmlessly onto the shore, but as the next reached the screen, its guns began to explode in the searing heat and "flared up with such fierceness and great noise as were frightful." Shot blasted in all directions and flaming fragments were scattered among the pinnaces and small boats. The defensive screen disintegrated in panic as the crews of each boat fought to save themselves. As they did so, the remaining fireships swept past them on the tide, closing at terrible speed on the great ships of the Armada. The fireships were now engulfed in flame from the waterline to the very tips of their masts and there were deafening explosions as their guns detonated, "spurting fire and their ordnance shooting," blasting out fresh hails of shot and burning fragments, and adding to the terror that greeted them, "a horror to see in the night." Sparks and embers lodged in the rigging and sails of Spanish ships and drifted to the decks, and panic-stricken men scrambled to extinguish each one before fire could take hold. The signal gun from the flagship was superfluous: the ships of the Armada were already under way, manoeuvring to find space and searoom to escape the perilous confines of the bay for the open sea, or simply cutting and running north-east before the wind and tide.

However, the elation of the watching Englishmen must soon have given way to something close to despair, for, as the blazing fireships swept on through the close-packed Armada, there were no answering flames. Somehow each one contrived to burn its way through the heart of the Armada without igniting a single Spanish vessel, and one by one they came to a halt on the Calais shore, where they continued to burn, casting a hellish light over the sea. Outlined against the glow of the fires, more and more of the Spanish ships could be seen putting out to sea and disappearing into the darkness of the night. It was impossible to tell if they had left in confusion or in disciplined order; that would be discernible only in the light of dawn. The Englishmen must have gone to their brief night's rest uncertain whether the chance to destroy the Armada had slipped from their grasp but in fact, unseen in the darkness, many of the Armada commanders had come close to panic as the fireships bore down upon them. Petrified by fear that hell-burners were loose among them, "that forest of ships and vast galleons, tumultuously cutting their cables, ran away in a shameful confusion" and, instead of slipping and buoying them, "left their anchors in the sea." Even the King's own representative, Diego Flores de Valdes, had shouted orders to cut the arm-thick cables, and on ship after ship seamen with axes hacked at them. Already taut as bow-strings from the pull of the tide, they snapped with the sound of gunshots, causing the loss "by report of some of them that were afterwards taken, of 100 or 120 anchors and cables." Even that seems a considerable underestimate; since almost all the Armada ships had at least two anchors out to hold them in the shifting sands against the pull of the currents, as many as 200 may still lie rusting in the mud beneath the Calais cliffs.[4]

The crews worked with desperate haste to save their ships. They had all been lying head to wind, and they had to scramble aloft, set sails to bring the bows around, then endure what must have seemed an eternity as they slowly swung first broadside on to the tide and the onrushing fireships, and finally came around enough to put the wind astern. The crewmen once more leaped to the task of resetting the sails, as the helmsmen searched for a course clear of the mêlée of ships around them. As more and more ships shook out their sails and gathered speed downwind, fleeing into the night, Medina-Sidonia dispatched the Prince of Ascoli in a fast pinnace after them, to urge them to reform in the open water and await their Captain General. It was a near-impossibility without anchors, but in any event few heeded him; most minds were filled only with the thought of escape. By daylight Ascoli found himself abandoned and as the English fleet bore down he was forced to flee into Calais for safety, never to rejoin the Armada.

The panic and the impossibility of manoeuvring so many ships in such a confined space in a darkness broken only by the red glare of the burning fireships also "caused the Spaniards . . . confusedly to drive one upon another, whereby they were not only put from their road-stead and place where they meant to attend the coming of the Duke of Parma, but did much hurt one to another." In the general confusion, the *San Lorenzo*, the flagship of the galleasses, "came entangled with the *San Juan de Sicilia*," fouled its rudder and mainmast, "and so damaged herself that she had to remain near the shore." Drifting helpless, the rudder damaged beyond repair, the *San Lorenzo* was pushed by the tide and the ever-strengthening wind towards the cliffs. The majority of the Armada ships were swept clear of the straits and driven north-east towards the shoals and sandbanks of the coast of Flanders, but their flagship and a handful of galleons were not among them. The *San Martin* beat out to sea a short way but then sailed back almost at once, dropping a sheet anchor within a mile of the original anchorage. The *San Juan*, the *San Marcos*, the *San Felipe* and the *San Mateo* were alongside her but, as dawn broke, these five were the only Armada ships visible in the whole vast sweep of ocean, apart from the crippled *San Lorenzo*, still drifting closer and closer to the Calais cliffs. The foreshore was littered with the smouldering remnants of the fireships—"the fire continued until the hulls were reduced to embers." Although they had burned no Spanish ships, it was now evident that the eight fireships had done what the entire English fleet had previously been unable to achieve, for the once immaculate formation of the Armada had been scattered to the winds.[5]

As soon as there was light, Lord Howard ordered a signal gun fired and trumpets sounded across the water. As one, the English fleet hauled in anchors and piled on sail, 150 ships in hot pursuit of a suddenly vulnerable enemy, but with notable self-effacement—or calculation—Lord Howard ceded to Sir Francis Drake the honour of leading the attack. It had been "resolved the day before my Lord Admiral should give the first charge, Sir Francis Drake the next and myself

[Seymour] the third; it fell out that the galleass distressed, altered my Lord's former determination, as I suppose, by prosecuting the destruction of her," and instead of pursuing the Armada, Howard led a handful of ships in an assault on the rudderless *San Lorenzo*. Don Hugo de Moncada was at last to get his wish; he was to fight the English Admiral. The galleass made desperate attempts to reach the harbour but, struggling through heavy surf against an ebbing tide, she was driven aground under the ramparts of Calais Castle. The galley slaves screamed for help, pounding impotently at their chains and manacles as the ship heeled over under the assaults of the surf, burying her starboard cannons in the mud and drowning some of the slaves at their oars, while the guns on the port side pointed uselessly at the sky.

The galleass had a much shallower draught than the English galleons and they could not get within cannon range for fear of grounding themselves. Indeed, the *Margaret and John* "approached so near that we came on ground also, but afterwards came safely off again with the flood, being damaged by nothing but by the town of Calais, who off the bulwarks [of the castle], shot very much at us and shot our ship twice through." Howard sent his longboat to the attack, captained by his lieutenant, Amyas Preston, "with 50 or 60 men, amongst whom were many gentlemen as valiant in courage as gentle in birth" and eager for a taste of action. They were joined by a pinnace from the grounded *Margaret and John* and a number of other small boats, but they were met with a hail of small-arms fire from the decks of the stricken galleass. The Englishmen were in a perilous position, "they being ensconced within their ship and very high over us, we in our open pinnaces and far under them, having nothing to shroud and cover us; they being 300 soldiers besides 450 slaves and we not at the instant 100 persons," though one anonymous Spanish agent reported that so many of the crew jumped overboard and fled that "not more than fifty men stood by the captain to defend the ship." Several of Howard's men "were slain and my lieutenant sore hurt" and the firing continued until Moncada was "killed by a small shot of a musket that pierced both his eyes." At this, his men began to break and run. The surviving galley slaves also made frantic attempts to escape as the English seamen swarmed aboard, clambering up the ship's sides and entering through the gunports. "Many [Spaniards] were there slain by the sword," the remainder "leaped overboard by heaps on the other side and fled with the shore, swimming and wading. Some escaped with being wet, some, and that were many, were drowned," "but some were saved by swimming into the haven of Calais."[6]

Over the next two hours the victorious Englishmen set to work to strip the ship of everything of value, including the pay chests of gold and silver bullion. "Then was everything movable taken away, and such part of the King's treasure as was therein," "each man seeking his benefit of pillage," while awaiting the turn of the tide to retrieve the ship and its cannon as well. They made a rich haul—a total of 22,000 ducats in coin as well as 14 chests of other valuables. The inhabitants of Calais watched from the shore, making no attempt to intervene until Gourdan sent two noblemen in a boat to negotiate. His message, relayed to Richard Tomson, the lieutenant of the *Margaret and John* and one of the leaders of the boarding party, was that "our prowess and manhood showed . . . we had well deserved the spoil and pillage of the galleass," but the *San Lorenzo* had gone aground on French soil and by the rules of war both the ship and its cannon were now Gourdan's.

Tomson told the men that they would have to negotiate with Lord Howard, "who was here in person nearby, from whom they should have an honourable and friendly answer," but as they departed, "some of our rude men who make no account of friend or foe, fell to spoiling the Frenchmen, taking away their rings and jewels as from enemies, whereupon going ashore and complaining, all the bulwarks and ports were bent against us and shot so vehemently that we received sundry shot very dangerously through us . . . and made us relinquish the galleass . . . which we had gotten with bloody heads." The ship was left "without value, which our men would have burnt, if the governor of Calais had not prevented them," but they did at least ensure that it was so badly holed that it would never float again, and it rotted where it lay on the mud below the castle walls. The greatest and most powerful galleass of all had been lost to the Armada but the looting and destruction had kept the English flagship and its squadron out of the battle for several crucial hours. Like Drake in the early hours of the previous Monday, Howard had also put the chance of plunder above the strategic interests of his sovereign's fleet, and more Englishmen had died in this single engagement than in all the rest of the fighting during the Armada campaign, including around twenty drowned "on account of the hurry in which they regained their boats," as they abandoned the *San Lorenzo*.[7]

Howard's squadron now piled on sail and raced to join the main battle, but while the Admiral and his men had been filling their pockets—or losing their lives—his Vice-Admiral, "seizing the occasion by the forelock," had led the assault on the scattered Armada. Medina-Sidonia and his group of ships had sailed downwind after his errant vessels, hoping that the tide, now running in the opposite direction, would help to bring the fleet back together, while Drake's *Revenge*, driven by the still strengthening south-westerly, was already leading the English squadrons to the attack. They sped through the straits into the North Sea, "coming on under a press of sail" to assail the *San Martin* and the other great ships about seven miles off Gravelines. With the prospect before them of a glorious victory and plunder for all, the English captains were now prepared to risk engaging the enemy at a range where they could inflict—or suffer—serious damage. Medina-Sidonia, "who was in the rear, seeing that if he bare room with his fleet [sailed away from the English downwind], it would be to their destruction, for that it was already very near the banks of Dunkirk . . . chose rather to save it by abiding the enemy's fleet."

The battle commenced around nine in the morning. As the *Revenge* closed on the *San Martin*, both held their fire until they were no further than "half-musket shot" "or even arquebus shot" apart— well under a hundred yards and perhaps as close as fifty. At last the *Revenge* fired her bow guns and then her broadsides, and took the *San Martin*'s broadside in return, being "pierced through with cannonballs of all sizes which were flying everywhere between the two fleets, and was riddled with every kind of shot," but her own fire had wreaked far greater damage on her foe. The lighter weapons on the deck and upper gundeck pulverized the upperworks of the *San Martin*, chain- and bar- shot shredding rigging, sails, spars and yards, while dice- and hail-shot wreaked terrible havoc among the close-packed soldiers lining the rails to discharge their small arms. Meanwhile the heavier cannon on the *Revenge*'s lower gundeck, close to the waterline, battered the *San Martin*'s hull. Even its four-inch oak planking and close-packed timbers could not withstand such an onslaught from 30- and 60-pound shot, fired at a range so close that smouldering powder residue and spent wadding drifted over the enemy decks like snow. Already weakened by the previous battles, the hull was pierced by shot still glowing and smoking from the furnace of the cannon. Smashing through the planking, each ball unleashed a blizzard of arrow-sharp splinters and shards of oak, filling the air like a swarm of murderous hornets, ripping, stabbing, blinding, maiming and shredding flesh from bone, and driven with such force that some jagged shards embedded themselves in the planking of the opposite hull, quivering like thrown knives.[8]

The *Nonpareil*, commanded by Sena, came next and then in turn the remainder of Drake's squadron, each ship loosing its broadside into the *San Martin* and being answered by the increasingly ragged replies from the Spanish flagship. According to Captain Alonso Vanegas, 300 rounds were fired from the flagship's 48 guns during the course of the nine-hour battle, but even allowing for the time spent out of gun range of the enemy, that barely amounted to one round per gun per hour. In reply the English ships poured in fire at three, four and five times that rate. Having delivered his broadsides, Drake led his squadron north-east in pursuit of the other galleons of the Armada as they struggled to break clear of the coast and reform. Martin Frobisher, in the van of his squadron as it attacked the Spanish flagship and still smarting over the division of spoils from Drake's earlier prize, saw a different motive for his tactics. "Sir Francis Drake reports that no man has done any good service but he; but he shall well understand that others have done as good a service as he and better. He came bragging up at the first, indeed, and gave them his prow and his broadside; and then kept his luff and was glad that he was gone again, like a cowardly knave or traitor—I rest doubtful but the one I will swear."

Drake was many things, not all of them pleasant, but a coward he was not. The incident at San Juan de Ulua in 1568 was the only other occasion on which his courage had ever been called into question and his exploits over the twenty years since then had given the lie to any suggestion that he would fly in the face of danger. A coward would not have led a tiny force against Nombre de Dios and Cartagena, nor have sailed straight into one of the enemy's principal harbours at Cadiz, leaving the rest of his fleet to follow him in as best they could. Frobisher's criticism of his actions at Gravelines was an obscene denigration of Drake. He gave the *San Martin* a broadside at a range close enough to inflict heavy damage on the Spanish flagship, and in so doing laid his own ship open to the risk of destruction by the return fire, but he did so knowing from his observation of the previous battles that the *San Martin* would not be able to reload its great guns for some considerable time, if at all, and would meanwhile lie open and poorly defended against the assaults of the ships following behind his own.

Whatever his prejudices towards Drake, there was no doubting the choleric Frobisher's courage either, and he brought the *Triumph* to the attack, laying up at close range and pounding the San Martin with his great guns while the rest of his squadron riddled her bow, stern and landward flank. They pulled away only to allow Hawkins in the *Victory* to lead his squadron in for another attack. Meanwhile Lord Henry Seymour with "the *Vanguard*, *Antelope* and others, charged upon the tail, being somewhat broken, and distressed three of their great ships, among which, my ship shot one of them through six times, being within less than musket shot." Sir William Wynter in the *Vanguard* also chose to refrain from "shooting of any ordnance until we came within six score [paces] of them." "In the continued assaults which we gave on them without entering [boarding] we made them to feel our ordnance, and if any ship was beaten out of their fleet, she was surrounded and suddenly separated from the rest."[9]

More and more Armada ships now rallied to the defence of the flagship and somehow by remarkable seamanship amidst the heat of battle, the gale and the rough seas, they once more adopted their characteristic defensive formation. They "went into the proportion of a half moon, their Admiral and Vice-Admiral were in the midst and the greatest number of them, and there were on each side in the wings the galleasses, armadoes of Portugal and other good ships. In the whole to the number of sixteen in a wing which did seem to be of their principal shipping." All took a savage pounding from the English guns. Wynter's group attacked the starboard wing of the formation and "making haste to run into the body of their fleet, four of them did entangle themselves one aboard the other." It was a cruel irony; the grappling hooks at the ends of the yardarms that they had hoped in vain to use against the English fleet were now ensnaring their own vessels.

As the Spanish crews fought to free their ships, hacking at spars and rigging with axes, the English ships kept up a barrage of fire. Shot pierced the *San Martin* "enough to shatter a rock." "So tremendous was the fire that over 200 balls struck the sails and hull of the flagship on the starboard side, killing and wounding many men, disabling and dismounting three guns, and destroying much rigging. The holes made in the hull between wind and water caused so great a leakage that two divers, working all day, had as much as they could do to stop them with tow and lead plates. The galleon *San Felipe of Portugal* was also surrounded by 17 of the enemy's ships, which directed against her heavy fire on both sides and on her stern. The enemy approached so close that the muskets and the arquebuses of the galleon were brought into service, killing a large number of men on the enemy ships. They did not dare, however, to come to close quarters [boarding range] but kept up a hot artillery fire from a distance, disabling the rudder, breaking the foremast and killing over 200 men in the galleon. This being noticed by the captain of the *San Mateo*, he brought his galleon to the wind and bravely went to the rescue. Then some of the enemy's ships attacked him and inflicted much damage upon him. One of the enemy's ships came alongside the galleon and an Englishman jumped on board, but our men cut him to bits instantly." So completely had the old tactics of grapple and board been superseded that, excluding ships that had grounded or surrendered, the foolhardy Englishman was the only man on either side to board an enemy vessel during the entire campaign.

Each battle of the campaign had been described in turn as the greatest ever seen. "Some Spaniards that we have taken, that were in the fight at Lepanto, do say that the worst of our four fights . . . did exceed far the fight they had there . . . at some of our fights we had twenty times as much great shot there plied as they had there." But this battle far surpassed all the others together. Nothing had ever been seen or heard that approached this weight and intensity of fire. The relentless cannonade was accompanied by a barrage of noise that left many soldiers and seamen battle-shocked and was heard on every coast and for many miles inland. The sulphurous smell of gunpowder was thick in the air and the smoke from the guns, pierced by the brilliant flashes of cannon fire, cloaked the water like a shroud and reduced the ships to dark shadows looming and disappearing in the fogs of smoke.[10]

The English and Spanish ships could often be distinguished from each other only by the rhythm of their gunfire—the irregular, staccato explosions of the Armada guns against the metronomic booming of the English cannon. They fired not in unison but in rapid, rhythmic succession as each gun came to bear, a drumroll along the length of the ship. The *Revenge* was "letting fly every way from both her broadsides, so that she seemed to repeat the fire as rapidly as any arquebusier," and so swiftly did the English gunners reload and the seamen perform their tasks that barely had the echoes of the last gun on the starboard side died away than the ship had come about and begun a fresh broadside from its port flank. By the time that broadside, too, had ended, the starboard guns had been hauled in, reloaded, pushed out and readied to fire once more as the next target came into view.

English helmsmen and gunners co-ordinated the firing of their cannons and culverins so that they were discharged as the Spanish ships heeled over before the wind, exposing the timbers below the waterline. As the heavier guns blasted the hulls "between wind and water," the lighter weapons kept up a withering fire on the upperworks, reducing them to matchwood and causing terrible carnage among the Spanish crewmen and marines. Slaves in the galleasses perished in hundreds at their oars and crewmen on the gundecks were mown down as shot smashed through the lower decks. The fighting troops in the waists, stern- and forecastles were cut apart by "murthering shot"—cube-shot, hail-shot, dice-shot and chain-shot, and the fragments of scrap iron fired when all other munitions had been exhausted—and the nobles perished alongside their men. Don Pedro Enriquez "had a hand shot away" and "Don Felipe de Cordoba, son of Don Diego, His Majesty's Master of Horse, had his head shot off."

Damage and casualties among the English fleet were remarkably light and even some of the few recorded incidents have the ring, not of truth, but of sailors' yarns much embellished in the telling. A gentleman adventurer aboard Drake's ship was supposed to have had his bed shot from beneath him by a cannonball as he took his ease, and the dinner of the Earl of Northumberland and Sir Charles Blount was then interrupted by a cannonball smashing through the hull, "grazing their feet, but taking off the toes of one who was there with them." It is hard to imagine why the gentleman would be reclining belowdecks or the earl and his guest dining in their cabin when the great battle they had come to witness was raging over their heads.

As the fighting continued, more great guns of the Spanish ships fell silent, either damaged or impossible to reload because of the ferocity of the fighting and the severity of the sea conditions, but the musket and arquebus fire seemed to go on undiminished even though the death toll among the soldiers was steadily mounting. The firing was so intense that even now some English captains were reluctant to close to the most devastating range for their own guns. The *Santa Maria de Begona* and the *San Juan de Sicilia* "came near to boarding the enemy, yet could they not grapple with them, they fighting with their great ordnance and our men defending themselves with arquebus-fire and musketry, the distance being very small," but great shot was now regularly piercing the tough oak flanks of the Spanish galleons and galleasses. All of them were damaged and leaking, their sails and rigging in tatters, their decks torn, splintered and littered with the bodies of the dead and dying.[11]

They "sustained the assault of the enemy as stoutly as was possible, so as all these ships were very much spoiled, and almost unable to make further resistance, and the greater part of them without shot for their ordnance," yet still the Spanish spirit remained strong and their courage rarely failed them. These were men whose ships had been repeatedly hammered by English gunfire and who now knew beyond any doubt that they would continue to be pounded without any compensating hope of boarding, destroying or even damaging any English ship. Yet still they returned again and again to the fight, in acts of futile but monumental courage. The crew of one of the hulks saw a great carrack, de Bertendona's *Regazona*, still sailing to the rescue of a sister ship even though its guns had been silenced and the blood of its men was cascading in torrents from its scuppers as it heeled before the wind. The *Regazona's* musketeers continued to fire, and again and again the ship took its place in the fighting line.

"Lord Henry Seymour in the *Rainbow* and Sir William Wynter in the *Vanguard* . . . did so batter two of the greatest armados," the *San*

Mateo and the *San Felipe*, that they were close to sinking. More than half the crew and marines of Don Diego Pimentel's *San Mateo* were dead or disabled, her guns silent and she wallowed low in the waves. "She was a thing of pity to see, riddled with shot like a sieve . . . all her sails and rigging were torn and sorely destroyed; of her sailors many perished, and of her soldiers few were left." The remaining crew threw broken masts, guns, gratings and even the bodies of their dead comrades overboard—anything that would reduce the weight and keep the battered ship afloat.

The clouds of gunsmoke were now so dense that the *San Martin*'s lookouts were "unable to see from the top . . . except that two of our ships were surrounded by the enemy." Even Medina-Sidonia climbed the mast in an attempt to penetrate the fogs of battle and, although the flagship itself was "sorely distressed by great shot between wind and water, so as by no means could the leak be stopped," and "her rigging was almost cut to shreds," he ordered his boats to make for the crippled *San Mateo* and take off the officers and men. Don Diego de Pimentel, Captain General of the Forces of Sicily, refused to abandon ship, and at his request Medina-Sidonia sent him a pilot and a diver to inspect the damage, even though the *San Martin* was "in great risk without him" since her own leaks and shot-holes were so bad. The diver reported that nothing could be done to save the *San Mateo* and, wallowing deeper in the rising seas, she was carried beyond the reach of the other Spanish ships. Medina-Sidonia's final sight of her was "seeing her afar off, going towards Zeeland."[12]

Don Francisco de Toledo's *San Felipe* was also doomed, bludgeoned by English gunfire beyond hope of salvation. Five of the starboard guns had been dismounted, one of the great guns spiked, "his upper deck was destroyed, both his pumps broken, his rigging in shreds and his ship almost a wreck." Seymour's *Rainbow* came to within hailing distance and an officer stood in the bow calling out, "Good soldiers that you are, surrender to the fair terms we offer you. But the only answer he got was a gun, which brought him down in the sight of everyone." As more volleys of musket and arquebus shot rang out, the *Rainbow* pulled away, while the *San Felipe*'s crew jeered them, calling them "cowards" and "Lutheran hens." It was their last defiance. The hulk *Doncella* came alongside and took off the crew of 300, but de Toledo and the *San Felipe*'s captain, Juan Poza de Santiso, hearing a shout that the hulk was now sinking, "replied that if that were the case, they had better be drowned in the galleon than in the hulk, and they both went back to her." The *San Felipe* then drifted helpless away from the Armada towards the Dunkirk shore. Just like the *Rosario* and the

San Salvador, two more Spanish great ships had been abandoned and left to their fate. It was an affront to Spanish honour and a further blow to the Armada's already crumbling morale. The authority of Medina-Sidonia and Diego Flores de Valdes was now fatally undermined, and de Oquendo refused even to attend the council of war held after the battle, such was his contempt for their failings.

The battle had raged for nine hours, while the wind backed steadily into the north-west, increasing the English advantage and the peril of the Armada. It was now all but overwhelmed, its formation broken, its great ships besieged on all sides by cannon fire and able to offer little in reply beyond musket and arquebus shot. The blood of noblemen, soldiers and common seamen alike mingled on the shattered decks, and the surface of the sea surrounding the warring fleets was littered with fragments of broken wood, torn canvas and the other debris of battle. One witness saw "some ships broken into bits, others without masts or sails, from which they were throwing overboard artillery, trunks and many other things, whilst men were trying to save themselves by escaping in boats." Still the five English squadrons pressed the attack, pounding the Spanish ships and driving them inexorably towards the fifty-mile stretch of sands and shoals known as the Banks of Zeeland.[13]

Most of the English pilots and commanders knew these treacherous waters—so shallow that at low tide shrimp fishermen worked the offshore sandbanks from horseback. In the years of peace before the gathering storm, English ships had continually crossed and recrossed these seas with cargoes of woollen cloth for the great market at Antwerp. Sir Francis Drake had been apprenticed as a boy of eleven to a coaster sailing out of Gillingham Reach on the Medway, and, like his peers, had learned to navigate the sandbanks and the meandering muddy channels of the Scheldt, and find his course in sudden storms, fogs and sea frets, against the shifting winds and relentless, surging tides. Now the Englishmen used their knowledge to harry the Armada ships, like dogs round a flock of sheep, pushing them closer and closer to the sandbanks that would spell their doom.

The Armada as a whole could not sail any closer to the wind than at right angles to it. With the wind now northerly, it was impossible for even the most capable ships to pull clear of the shallows. They could not anchor, for few ships had any anchors; they could not even sail parallel to the coast, for its line runs north or north-east as far as the island of Terschelling some two hundred miles away. By four o'clock in the afternoon, with the tide again running onshore, the Armada's position appeared hopeless. The leadsman in the *San Martin* was reporting a depth of only eight fathoms, leaving a bare fifteen feet of water between the ship's keel and the sandbanks, and the depth was decreasing with every passing minute. Those ships not already crippled or sunk by English gunfire would be driven aground to be captured and looted or left to the doubtful mercies of the vengeful Dutch Sea Beggars. "We saw ourselves lost or taken by the enemy, or the whole Armada drowned upon the banks. It was the most fearful day in the world, for the whole company had lost all hope of success and looked only for death."

Then, out of nowhere, a violent south-westerly squall hit the two fleets and a curtain of rain swept across the sea, so intense that visibility shrank to a few yards. On both sides, all hands that were able were at once at work trimming the sails, while their officers were fully occupied in steering clear of collisions in the mêlée of ships around them. The squalls and rain continued for almost half an hour and by the time they passed and the skies cleared, the Armada ships could be seen crowding on sail and making away to the north, already out of cannon range. As the English captains watched in disbelief, the battered Armada once more resumed the familiar, hated formation. Led by Medina-Sidonia, they even shortened sail, inviting the English to resume the battle.

It was a bluff, for the Spaniards now had little but small-arms fire to offer in combat, "nearly all the best ships being spoiled and unable to resist longer, as well from the damage they had received as from not having shot for their ordnance." But for the moment Howard's men too had little stomach for the fight. Their shot-lockers were almost empty and their stores of powder gone. Even the Squadron of the Narrow Seas had fired off almost its entire hoarded supplies in that one savage engagement. Wynter claimed that "out of my ship there was shot 500 shot of demi-cannon, culverin and demi-culverin, and when I was furthest off in distance I was not out of the shot of the arquebus and most times within speech of one another . . . No doubt the slaughter and hurt they received was great, as time will discover it; and when every man was weary with labour and our cartridges spent and munitions wasted—I think in some altogether—we ceased and followed the enemy."[14]

The English were content to track the Armada, knowing that it was still not free of the danger from the menacing Zeeland banks and that each mile took it further from the hoped-for rendezvous with Parma. Meanwhile the first rations and beer since before daybreak were issued to the crews, while carpenters, sailmakers and riggers carried out emergency repairs, the surgeons went about their bloody tasks, and ships' chaplains gave what comfort they could to those already beyond even that crude help. The gundecks were swabbed clear of blood and debris and the guncrews on those few ships that still had powder and shot brought the last of their supplies to their weapons, ready for whatever further hostilities the next day might bring.

PART III

Aftermath

CHAPTER SIXTEEN

The Spaniards Consulting ~
and at last resolving to return
into Spain by the north Ocean ~
many of their Shipps being disabled

A Wonderful Fear

Englishmen, Dutchmen, Spaniards and Frenchmen, straining to catch sight or sound of the day's battle from the shores of Kent, Zeeland, Flanders and Calais, had heard the distant bass rumble of the guns fall silent at last: "the cannonade was heard with the same fury the whole of that day, until at last it died away in the distance." As evening approached, they crowded the harbours and quaysides, waiting for the first returning boats to bring news of the battle. As ships tied up, word was passed among the crowds on the quays and shouted to those leaning out of windows or lining the cliffs above them. None of those aboard the fishing boats and coasters that had been bystanders at the battle had seen more than brief glimpses of the action through the dense, swirling palls of gunsmoke and the mist, rain and cloud wind-driven over the water, but imagination, speculation and hearsay filled the gaps in knowledge.

More reliable information arrived in England with the pinnaces bearing dispatches from the fleet, and one thing on which all Englishmen, at least, were agreed was that their fleet had carried the day and the Armada was in retreat. The next day, news of its flight from Gravelines was brought to the Queen while she was out hunting in Epping Forest, and it was claimed that she was so overjoyed that she rode her horse up the steps of a hunting lodge. Her jubilation was understandable, if a trifle premature. If the English fleet could renew its stores and ammunition, it might yet have a further opportunity to complete the destruction of the Armada, but the commanders' satisfaction was tinged with disappointment that further rich prizes had eluded them, and fears that the battered Armada might even yet retain the strength to return to the attack. "God has given us so good a day in forcing the enemy so far to leeward and I hope to God that the Prince of Parma and the Duke of Medina-Sidonia shall not shake hands this few days," Drake wrote that night, "and whensoever they shall meet I believe neither of them will greatly rejoice at this day's service." But he added a rider. "There must be great care taken to send us munition and victual whithersoever the enemy goes."

In a letter to Walsingham that night, Lord Howard also renewed his pleas for fresh supplies of foodstuffs, water and munitions, and bemoaned the prevarication of Elizabeth and her Council; something that she took care to blame on her closest advisers, though the fault was hers alone. "All irresolution and lacks are thrown upon us two in all her speeches to everybody," Burghley complained to Walsingham. "The wrong is intolerable." Howard was also infuriated by the bureaucratic insistence that he produce an itemized list of the supplies he required. "I have received your letter wherein you desire a proportion of powder and shot to be set down by me and sent to you which, by the uncertainty of the service, no man can do. Therefore I pray you to send me with all speed as much as you can." He also expressed his own cautious confidence in the outcome of the day's battle. "We have chased them in fight until this evening late and distressed them much, but their fleet consists of mighty ships and great strength . . . their force is wonderful great and strong and yet we pluck their feathers little and little."[1]

The second-in-command of the *San Lorenzo*, "a proper gentleman of Salamanca," had been captured as he tried to flee the stricken galleass and his interrogation seemed to confirm Howard's belief that the Armada was not yet fatally damaged by the fighting. "As terrible as it was in appearance, there were few men hurt with any shot, nor any vessel sunk. For, as this man reports, they shoot very far off and for boarding, our men have not any reason." However, the Spaniard was speaking from his experience of the previous days' fighting, not of the battle off Gravelines which he had not seen, being trapped aboard the grounded *San Lorenzo* and then held belowdecks on Howard's flagship.

The gentleman adventurer Sir Horatio Palavicino, and Richard Tomson on the *Margaret and John*, formed a more accurate impression of the outcome of the great battle. "They lost in that fight, beside the galleass, five or six great ships, and were pursued ten or twelve leagues beyond Dunkirk, being sorely beaten by our ordnance." "Her Majesty by God's help, may little fear any invasion by these ships; their power being, by battle, mortality and other accidents so decayed, and those that are left alive so weak and hurtless that they could be well content to lose all charges to be at home, both rich and poor." Thomas Fenner confirmed that view, but, like Drake and Howard, he also bewailed the lack of supplies that had prevented the fleet from completing the destruction of the Armada. "Many of their ships wonderfully spoiled and beaten, to the utter ruin of three of the greatest sort, beside the cutting off of the galleass, the enemy thereby greatly weakened. A thing greatly to be regarded is that the Almighty has stricken them with a wonderful fear; in that I hardly have seen any of their companies succoured of their extremities which befell them after their fights, but left at utter ruin . . . The want of powder and shot, and victual, has hindered much service which might otherwise have been performed in continuance with them, to their utter subversion in keeping them from water. There were many ships in our fleet not possessed with three days' victuals."[2]

As Palavicino, Tomson and Fenner had claimed, the Armada was indeed now in desperate condition. The squall might have saved them from annihilation but they were "very much weakened and dispersed, so that of the 124 sail that they were in Calais Road, we cannot now find above 86 ships and pinnaces." All the front-line ships were holed and leaking, and broken spars, torn sails and rigging littered their blood-spattered decks. "The admiral [Medina-Sidonia's flagship] was many times shot through, and [was] shot in the mast and their deck at the prow spoiled . . . the admiral's mast is so weak by reason of the shot in it, as they dare not abide any storm, nor to bear such sail as otherwise he might do." Every single sail on the *San Juan de Sicilia* was so rent and torn by gunfire that it had to be replaced and the *Maria Juan* of the

Biscayan squadron was beyond help. The sails on her broken mizzen-mast and yard trailed in the water like a sea anchor, the rudder had been shattered by a cannonball and the hull pierced again and again by great shot. As water poured into the ship, she settled so low in the water that the waves lapped at the rails and flooded the decks, and men climbed the rigging and clung to the yardarms screaming for help. Only one boatload of survivors had been taken off before the *Maria Juan* foundered and went to the bottom, taking the remainder of her crew of 275 with her, "to the great sorrow of everyone."

Casualties were very high among the soldiers and crews of the other fighting ships. The Spaniards admitted to 600 dead and 800 "wounded," but the latter figure included only those completely disabled or maimed and the true total must have been much higher. Using the standard battlefield estimate of ten wounded for every fatality would put the casualty figures close to 6,000. The Armada was well provided with medical help: 85 surgeons and assistant-surgeons had sailed with the fleet, concentrated on two hospital ships, but they were overwhelmed, working by candle- and lantern-light far into the night, staunching wounds, setting fractured bones using nothing more than their physical strength, and amputating limbs without anaesthetic. They did what they could, drenched from head to foot in other men's blood, hacking and sawing at severed flesh and shattered bone, but in the press and chaos of the fighting many wounded men were left where they fell until the heat of battle was over, and by then many had bled to death. Many more would succumb to their wounds, blood loss, shock and sepsis over the following days and weeks.[3]

The English casualties were much lighter, but the fleet was far less well served by physicians and surgeons. In theory doctors were required by their charter to serve their sovereign on request, but in practice they either paid a bribe to avoid doing so or sent some semi-skilled or unskilled deputy in their place. Although the Frenchman Ambroise Paré and the English Surgeon of the Fleet, William Clowes, sailing aboard the *Ark* with Lord Howard, had pioneered more humane and effective treatments for shot and bullet wounds, many surgeons remained semi-trained and wedded to the old beliefs that bullet wounds were poisoned with gunpowder and had to be cauterized with boiling oil or a red-hot iron. For every seaman who was saved by their efforts, another dozen died.

The priests with the Armada were wholly occupied in comforting the dying and administering the last rites, and bodies were put over the side with minimal ceremony. Among them were many of the English exiles. "The prisoners do hold it for a miracle that amongst the slain . . . the English ordnance . . . has always struck down the principal traitors and amongst others, has slain the banished English lords." There were too many dead for the full funeral rites to be observed and none of the survivors could be long spared from the tasks of patching sails, repairing torn rigging, staunching leaks and manning the pumps that worked night and day, wheezing and coughing like consumptives as they struggled to hold back the relentless tide of seawater gushing into the bilges and holds.

On some ships, men already weak from wounds, fever, thirst and hunger laboured until they collapsed where they stood, for there were none fit to take their places. In others the galley fires had been extinguished by the leaks and the firewood soaked beyond use. Men settled miserably to their meagre cold rations, the darkness echoing to the groans of the maimed and dying, and the low threatening roar of breakers on the shoals to the south and east. "Hardly a man slept that night. We went along, all wondering when we should strike one of those banks." Some of those awake had no intention of passively awaiting their fate. Fourteen Dutchmen, pressed to the service of the Armada in Lisbon, chose to desert within sight of their native shores. "Having made sails for their cockboat with their shirts, they are now fled away from the Spanish fleet." Many more of the Armada's polyglot ships' complements followed their example, stealing away in the ships' boats, swimming and wading ashore or, in the case of a number of Portuguese deserters, swimming or rowing to the English fleet during the hours of darkness.[4]

Early the following morning another ship, an armed merchantman from Diego Flores de Valdes' squadron that was already trailing the Armada by some distance, sank "between Ostend and Blankenberg" as its captain was attempting to negotiate the terms of his surrender to Captain Robert Crosse of the *Hope*. Out of sight of the Armada, the two ships abandoned during the previous day's fighting also met their ends. The crippled *San Mateo* and the *San Felipe* both grounded on sandbanks off the Dutch coast, the *San Felipe* off "Flushing and the other athwart of Rammekens." Prince Justin of Nassau's flyboats quickly surrounded them. The *San Mateo* "fought with us two hours and hurt divers of our men but at the last yielded . . . The best sort [those nobles and gentlemen who could command a ransom fee] were saved, the rest were cast overboard and slain." It was a common practice for captured enemies to be treated in this way and was even specified in the orders issued to captains in the English fleet. "Take the captain with certain of the best men with him, the rest, commit them to the bottom of the sea, for else they will turn upon you to your confusion." Among the dead were two English traitors, one of whom, Lord Montagu, had paraded with 200 retainers before Queen Elizabeth as a demonstration of his loyalty only a few months before. The Dutch claimed the two ships as prizes and carried off the banner of the *San Mateo* and hung it in the choir of St. Peter's church at Leiden. (It now hangs in the Museum de Lakenhal, Leiden.) They also "received great spoil" from the ships—to Seymour's disgust, for his ships had disabled the vessels and had hopes of claiming them for themselves—as well as taking a number of prisoners including the commander of the *San Mateo*, Don Diego de Pimentel. A Dutch commander also claimed that he had set fire to a third Armada ship that had stranded near Blankenberg.[5]

Sir William Russell, the English Governor of Flushing, sent his own ships and men out to the wreck and they returned with 100 Spanish prisoners. The chance to give Parma a forceful reminder of the fate of the Armada was not to be missed, and many of the prisoners were "so mangled that presently the Governor sent 60 of them over into Flanders, to carry news to the Prince of Parma what was become of the rest." The Dutch seamen bearing them along the coast had to be bribed with "a great charge" not to toss them overboard like their comrades before them. Parma was already having troubles enough in maintaining discipline among the mass of disaffected and still unpaid troops and mariners he had assembled for the invasion. "The mariners, which he had got together to be employed at sea, refuse the service and are grown into a mutiny. The Duke has thereupon ordered to be slain ten or twelve of them, but the rest, notwithstanding, are retired and dispersed and refuse to serve."

Parma forwarded the news of the loss of the ships in Calais and on the Zeeland Banks to Philip, "in order that Your Majesty may adopt such measures as you consider advisable in Spain and elsewhere to prevent this misfortune and the presence intact of the enemy fleet from leading to further evils." He could give no more news of the rest of the Armada than that it had last been seen fleeing northwards pursued by the English fleet, but offered a few words of consolation. "This must come from the hand of the Lord, who knows well what He does and can redress it all, rewarding Your Majesty with many victories and the full fruition of your desires, in His own good time . . . This great army moreover, which Your Majesty has intact should with God's blessing banish all cause for fear, especially as it may be hoped that . . . the mass of the Armada may not have suffered any further loss." But he again warned Philip that without funds the "great army" might soon disintegrate into desertion and mutiny. "The soldiers who have so willingly

Above: Map of the Dorset coast showing the coastal defences around
Portland Bill and Weymouth. Watchmen scaled crude ladders to
ignite the warning beacons set in iron baskets on tall poles.

Below: A dolmen used as a beacon hut at Higher Manhay,
Cornwall. The three iron brackets that held the
beacon fires are still in place.

Four of the engravings depicting the progress of the battles from the first sighting of the Armada to its flight through the North Sea.

On the right, the English fleet warps out of Plymouth. The last few ships have to tack close inshore to gain the weather gauge on the Spaniards. To the left, Lord Howard's pinnace *Disdain* is advancing towards the Armada's curved formation "to give defiance" before battle begins.

The English in pursuit of the Armada east of Plymouth at daybreak on 1 August. Lord Howard's ships are shown close to the Spanish fleet, having mistakenly followed the light of an Armada ship during the night. Drake, who had extinguished his own guiding light in order to chase the crippled *Rosario*, is shown at the bottom taking possession of his prize.

The battle off Portland Bill. Martin Frobisher's *Triumph*, top left, is holding the Armada's galleasses at bay, while the remainder of the English fleet engages the main body of the Armada. To the right, the English fleet has re-formed into four squadrons and is driving the Armada away from its last potential refuge at Spithead and the Isle of Wight.

The decisive battle off Gravelines. Lord Howard's squadron is laying siege to the stricken galleass *San Lorenzo* at Calais, while the squadrons of Drake, Hawkins and Frobisher, reinforced by Seymour's Squadron of the Narrow Seas, attack the Armada. One ship is sinking, top right, as three others drift out of control towards the Dutch coast.

The fireship attack off Calais.

Left: A contemporary depiction of a battered Spanish galleon.

Framed insert: Sir Richard Bingham, "the flail of Connaught," whose troops slaughtered many of the Spanish survivors.

Left: The resolution signed by all the English commanders, including Howard, Drake and Hawkins, undertaking to pursue the Armada as far as the Firth of Forth, "with further protestation that if our wants of victuals and munitions were supplied, we would pursue them to the furthest that they durst have gone."

Opposite: A gold salamander pendant, set with rubies, found at the wreck site of the *Girona*.

Above: The course taken by those Armada ships that followed the Duke of Medina-Sidonia well to the west of the Irish coast. Most of those that did not were wrecked there.

Below: The basalt pillars overlooking the wreck site of the *Girona*, where Don Alonso de Leiva drowned, "with all the chivalry and flower of the Armada."

Above: The Armada portrait of Elizabeth I. Behind
her are two views of the Armada campaign: the fireship attack off Calais and the storms that drove many
Spanish ships to destruction on the Irish coast.

Right: A list of thirty-three Spanish officers and
gentlemen taken prisoner by Sir Richard Bingham
but then executed on the orders of Sir William
Fitzwilliam, the Lord Deputy of Ireland.

Below: A depiction of the plight of the Elizabethan
poor, many of whom were seamen and soldiers
discharged by Elizabeth without food, clothes or pay.

Barthelmew Brabo cap^en
pedro Ryvera anncientbearer
Soargiant Calderon
frammiĵco maria Senteno
Don Diego Martell
Don Alonĵo Ladron de Gavara
Don Faques de mires
Giotam Abauncyes m^of ÿ Rata
gaĵher de Les Reys m^r
Barthelmew de Arboleda
Anthonio Moreno
philippe Cornetes
francefco cortes anncientbearer
Diego Ayllon
Francifco Defpinofa anncient bearer
Juan Pfafrano
pedro Acuma
Diego del Roncon
Francefco de Leon
Don Diego de Santillana
Anthonio Bacan anncientbearer
Juan Gil
Alonco de Serua
Bernardo pinelo

and quietly put up with trouble and misery in the hope of this enterprise, might change their tone and lose respect, especially if we cannot
provide them with the ordinary pay and their ration of bread."[6]

Still tracked by the English fleet, the remainder of the Armada had
continued to run before the strengthening wind during the night, but
soon after dawn on Tuesday 9 August the wind again began to back into
the north-west, putting it once more in mortal peril from the shoals
and sandbanks. "Although our flagship was brought up as close into the
wind as possible, she began to fall off to leeward towards the Zeeland
coast." Howard's men reacted with their customary ease and alacrity,
manoeuvring to keep the weather gauge and trap the Armada between
their guns and the Zeeland shore. The increasingly choppy sea, the
white crests of breakers in the distance and the changing colour of the
waters stained with sand and mud showed Medina-Sidonia the peril
that once more confronted him. The *San Martin* and the rest of the
rearguard lay to and Medina-Sidonia ordered an anchor lowered to try
to hold his position, then sent out pinnaces carrying the message that
those ships able to beat upwind towards him should do so, while the
rest were to drop anchor and lie to. Scores of ships either ignored or
did not receive the order, or had left their anchors in the escape from
Calais, and they continued to sail on, as close to the wind as they were
able. In the first light of dawn they must have crossed the Wielingen,
the channel leading into the Scheldt, but they had no maps of that coast
and there was only one Flemish pilot in the entire fleet. In such circumstances it would have been madness even to attempt the narrow entry,
surrounded not only by shoals and sandbanks but also by whirlpools
caused by "the violent meeting of sundry currents and tides."

The expected onslaught from the English fleet did not materialize.
As Medina-Sidonia soon realized, Howard, Drake and the rest saw no
reason to risk the Spanish guns and expend the remainder of their own
shot and gunpowder—if they had any—when the wind and weather
would do their work for them. The Armada was "very near to the banks
of Zeeland, for which cause the enemy remained aloof, seeing that our
Armada must be lost, for the pilots . . . men of experience of that coast,
told the Duke at this time that it was not possible to save a single ship of
the Armada, for that with the wind as it was in the north-west, they
must all needs go on the banks of Zeeland; that God alone could prevent it." The anchors of those Spanish ships that still had them could
not hold for long in the shifting sands of the Zeeland banks and the
wind and sea were now pushing them relentlessly downwind, increas-

ing their peril with every passing moment. Whether the ships lay to or kept under way was of no real consequence. The only course they could make led onto the sandbanks.[7]

Some of Medina-Sidonia's officers urged him to flee in a pinnace for Dunkirk with the Armada's sacred banner; it was later claimed that Diego Flores de Valdes had suggested he should surrender and that Miguel de Oquendo had responded by threatening to throw de Valdes overboard for his cowardice. Another version had de Oquendo responding to Medina-Sidonia's pleas for advice with "Ask Diego Flores. As for me, I am going to fight and die like a man." Captain Alonso Vanegas, who was on the poop deck of the *San Martin*, claimed that "people appealed to his [Medina-Sidonia's] conscience not to allow so many souls to be lost by shipwreck, but he would not listen to such advice and told them to speak no more of the matter." No signal was given and the Armada continued to drift with the wind and current. The leadsman in the bows of the *San Martin* plumbed the depths and counted down the intervals to their doom: eight fathoms, seven, then six and a half. The draught of the *San Martin* was five fathoms. Denied even a glorious death in battle, Medina-Sidonia and his officers and men sank to their knees in prayer, made their confessions and were shriven by the priests, or simply waited with dumb fatalism for the grinding crash as they ran aground. Barely a handful in any ship could swim and, encumbered by armour, clothing and the gold coins sewn into it, few even of those would survive the surf. Any who did manage to stagger ashore would be confronted by Dutch rebels, seeking vengeance for the slaughter of their countrymen by the brutal Army of Flanders.

Yet at around eleven that morning, as the sandbanks loomed, "being in this peril, without any sort of remedy and in six and a half fathoms of water, God was pleased to change the wind." The sudden, fierce shift in the wind from northerly to south-westerly gave them just leeway enough to break free from the deadly trap. They hauled up their dragging anchors as the wind filled their sails, and "the fleet stood towards the north without hurt to any ship," clearing the shoals and sandbanks and finding deep water again. Even those less devout than the Duke of Medina-Sidonia could only hail their deliverance as a miraculous sign of God's grace, a Catholic wind to save them from their Protestant enemies, though prosaic meteorologists explain it by "the eastward passage of a very sharp ridge of high pressure" between two lows. Cheated once more of their victory, the English "set on a brag countenance and gave them chase," resuming their grim pursuit.[8]

The paintwork of the ships of both fleets was now blackened by powder burns and smoke stains, the flags and pennants were split and faded, the sails carried patches over the shot-holes and the once precise lines of rigging were frayed and disarrayed. The stress on the men of both sides of the weeks and months at sea, the short rations and foul food and water, and the brutal ten-day running battle is impossible to overestimate. Many, particularly the pressed men taken aboard in whatever they happened to be wearing, and endlessly whipped by the wind, burned by the sun and soaked by salt spray and water, were now dressed in no more than rags. When they lay down to rest it was on the bare boards or on bedding that, like their clothes, was mildewed and black with damp, and they were pestered by rats, starving like the seamen and grown ever bolder in their search for food. The men's wounds were dressed with filthy, bloodstained bandages, and their bodies were black with dirt and pitted with powder burns. Poorly clad, ill fed and watered, they laboured on through days and nights of grinding toil and unremitting tension, and bouts of savage warfare, snatching at most a few hours' rest from the back-breaking labour aloft, at the pumps or on the gundecks. They endured the thunder of cannonades louder and more prolonged than any that human ears had ever heard, the crash of explosions, the whistle of shot and the screams of maimed and dying men, with the smell of blood and brimstone always in their nostrils, and knowing that at any moment might come the crash of the fatal shot, a glowing, smoking cannonball shattering the ship's planking, smashing through anything in its path and sending a blizzard of knife-sharp splinters through the air, lacerating any within range.

About four that Tuesday afternoon, with the wind now blowing strongly out of the west, Howard fired a signal gun and raised the flag summoning a further council of war. English casualties had been light and the ships were largely undamaged, but they were desperately short of food and water, powder and shot. Given their previous difficulties in obtaining supplies, the official "Relation of Proceedings" uses something suspiciously like sarcasm in referring to the absence of "our supply which Her Majesty had most carefully provided and caused to be in readiness." They maintained their pursuit of the Armada partly in the hope that fresh supplies could be brought to them and partly because of the fear that the Spaniards might yet try to make landfall in northern England or Scotland. John Hawkins aboard the *Victory* still saw the Armada as "very forcible and must be waited upon with all our force, which is little enough." He also made yet another plea that munitions should be supplied and wages paid. "There should be an infinite quantity of powder and shot provided and continually sent abroad, without the which great hazard may grow to our country, for this is the greatest and strongest combination to my understanding that ever was gathered in Christendom."

Hawkins and the other senior commanders—Francis Drake, Thomas Howard, Thomas Fenner, the Earl of Cumberland, Edmund Sheffield and Edward Hoby—all joined the Lord Admiral in putting their signatures to a resolution agreeing "to follow and pursue the Spanish fleet until we have cleared our own coast and brought the Firth [of Forth] west of us; and then to return back again, as well to revictual our ships, which stand in extreme scarcity, as also to guard and defend our own coast at home; with further protestation that if our wants of victuals and munitions were supplied, we would pursue them to the furthest that they durst have gone."[9]

As the rest of the fleet tracked the Armada northwards, Seymour's squadron was once more detached and sent back to the Downs—the sea area between the East Kent coast and the Goodwin Sands—to maintain a patrol in case Parma might even yet put to sea with his invasion force. Feeling he had earned the right to see the battle through to its conclusion, Seymour made furious complaints at Howard's apparent determination to keep the glory and the prizes to himself. "His Lordship was altogether desirous at the first to have me strengthen him, so having done the uttermost of my good will (to the venture of my life) in prosecuting the distressing of the Spaniards . . . I find my Lord jealous and loth to have me take part of the honour that the rest is to win."

His protests were to no avail. The captured second-in-command of the *San Lorenzo* had suggested that Spanish aims might yet be achieved "if they could but draw our fleet to the northward . . . whereby without impeachment, the Duke of Parma's men might land here." Vigilance had to be maintained against this threat and, whether through greed, ignorance or mistrust of his allies, Howard continued to insist that "there is not a Hollander or a Zeelander at sea," despite the Dutch blockade of the coast and the alacrity with which they had seized the grounded *San Mateo* and *San Felipe*. Seymour's ships were ordered to delay their departure until nightfall so that they could "bear away in the twilight, [so] the enemy might not see our departing," but the deceit was unsuccessful, for Medina-Sidonia recorded that "this night Juan Acles [the name by which the Spaniards knew John Hawkins, still erroneously thought to be in charge of the Squadron of the Narrow Seas] turned back with his squadron."[10]

Meanwhile, a council of war aboard the *San Martin* was taking stock of the Armada's dismal condition. The great ships had taken such a battering and lost so many men that fighting and even sailing some of them was difficult, if not impossible. Some were also very short of powder and shot, though it was by no means a universal complaint; many Armada ships still had large stores of unused munitions on board, a reflection not only of the difficulties in reloading the great guns during combat, but also of the illogical distribution of powder and shot and the often-voiced grievance that a handful of ships had borne the brunt of the fighting while others kept aloof. Despite the condition of their ships and men, the spirit of their commanders apparently remained unbroken. "When the Duke had explained the state of the Armada and the lack of shot . . . he wished them to say whether it were best to turn back to the English Channel or to return to Spain by the North Sea, seeing that the Duke of Parma had not sent word that he was ready to come out."

Despite the astonishment of some officers that Parma had neither used warships to try to breach the Dutch blockade—even at the risk of their destruction—nor tried to send out to the Armada whatever forces he had ready, they voted without a single dissenting voice that if the wind changed they would return to the attack and either seize an English port where they could reprovision and repair their ships, or fight their way back into the straits for a final attempt at a rendezvous with Parma. However, if the wind remained in the south-west for four more days, they agreed that they would have no option but to take the long route home around the north of Scotland. It was a daunting prospect. "We should have to sail . . . 750 leagues through stormy seas almost unknown to us before we could reach Corunna," and supplies would then be so short that their crews would come close to starvation before they could hope to reach Spain.

So Medina-Sidonia's official diary reported his council's judgement, but Recalde had a different recollection. He claimed that he had argued fervently that honour required them to return at once to the attack but had been overruled and the decision to return to Spain made there and then without conditions. He was also writing a report that would in due course be put before the King and so, like the others who spoke at the council of war, he sought to put the best possible gloss on his actions. They knew that their opinions and arguments would be recorded and that they would have to answer for them to Philip. In those circumstances it is unsurprising that none was willing to be publicly identified with the decision to flee for home. For the moment at least, the disagreement was academic, for the wind stayed in the same quarter for three days and the Armada was driven further and further from the Channel. Appalled and humiliated by the defeat of the Armada, Medina-Sidonia, "being frightened and dismayed," took to his cabin and left Diego Flores de Valdes and Don Francisco de

Bobadilla in command. "Besides the ill success he [Medina-Sidonia] always had with the enemy . . . he had been told that the two galleons, *San Mateo* and *San Felipe,* had been destroyed and sunk, and almost all hands drowned. For this reason the Duke kept himself in his cabin."[11]

Over that day and the next, the Spanish ships held on to the north, "pursuing their course with a strong wind from the south-west and a high sea." For the most part, the English fleet was content simply to track them, knowing that each northward mile made the prospect of the Armada's return to the Channel more remote, but as the wind eased a little towards the evening of Wednesday 10 August the English ships "came on under all sail towards our rear," hoping to isolate one or two of the stragglers and seize a prize. Medina-Sidonia—or Flores de Valdes—at once struck his topsails and fired three signal guns, ordering the fleet to lie to and await the enemy. Many of the Armada ships continued to bear away northward, but the sight of "the galleasses of the rearguard and as many as twelve of our [the Armada's] best ships" apparently inviting a further battle was enough to deter Howard's fleet from pursuing its attack. They also "shortened sail without shooting of ordnance," and the game of bluff and counter-bluff having produced no decisive result, the two fleets resumed their northward course.

However, more than half of the Armada had ignored the signal to lie to and await the enemy, and as soon as the danger from the English fleet had been averted a summary court martial was held aboard the *San Martin.* Medina-Sidonia may or may not have been presiding in person—one of the condemned men claimed he remained incommunicado in his cabin, leaving de Valdes and de Bobadilla to pass sentence— but after it had been determined that the order had been deliberately disobeyed, twenty captains were sentenced to death. One of them, Don Cristobal de Avila, a neighbour of Medina-Sidonia's at San Lucar in Jerez, was at once hanged at the yardarm of a pinnace "with insult and cruelty, although he was a gentleman." The dangling body was then paraded around the fleet as a warning to the others. The remaining nineteen captains were removed from their commands and "condemned to the galleys . . . reducing some soldier-officers [to the ranks]." Another captain, Francisco de Cuellar of the *Don Pedro,* was also sentenced to death but after his furious protests, citing the casualties his ship had suffered as proof of his service where the action had been hottest, he was placed aboard the *Lavia,* the vice-flagship of the Levant squadron, in the custody of the Judge Advocate General, Martin de Aranda. Believing that de Cuellar had "served His Majesty as a good soldier," de Aranda refused to carry out the sentence of death without a direct order to do so from Medina-Sidonia, and since that was not forthcoming de Cuellar remained alive.[12]

The feints and counter-feints of the two fleets were repeated towards sunset of the following day, Thursday 11 August, once more without shots being fired, and they again sailed on to the north, the English a couple of miles in trail and keeping slightly to shoreward of the Armada, ready to prevent any Spanish attempt to make landfall or capture a port. Yarmouth, Hull, Newcastle and Berwick had already been left astern, but Howard still expected that the Spanish ships "would put into the Firth [of Forth], where his Lordship had devised stratagems to make an end of them," but about noon of Friday 12 August the Armada crossed the mouth of the Firth, still sailing north.

Several of the English captains, including Thomas Fenner, were now convinced that the only thoughts of Medina-Sidonia and his commanders were of flight for home. "I verily believe great extremity shall force them if they behold England in sight again. By all that I can gather they were weakened of eight of their best sorts of shipping, which contained many men, as also many wasted in sickness and slaughter, their masts and sails much spoiled, their pinnaces and boats, many cast off and wasted, wherein they shall find great wants when they come to land and water, which they must do shortly or die." Fenner also prophesied the fate that the Spaniards would meet. "I verily believe they will pass about Scotland and Ireland to draw themselves home; wherein, the season of the year considered with the long course they have to run, and their sundry distresses and—of necessity—the spending of time by watering, winter will so come on as it will be to their great ruin . . . Mine opinion is they are by this time so distressed . . . as many of them will never see Spain again."[13]

Howard was also sure that Medina-Sidonia had no intention of taking a port in England or Scotland but he remained worried that, resupplied and reprovisioned, the Armada might yet return to the attack. "I think they dare not return [to Spain] with this dishonour and shame to their King and overthrow of their Pope's credit. Sir, sure bind, sure find. A kingdom is a great wager." However, the English fleet's own supplies were almost exhausted, for they had received virtually no food, water or beer since the fleet sailed from Plymouth and, more ominous still, ship's fever—typhus—was now ravaging the fleet. With a north-west wind to speed them home, Howard gave up the pursuit on Saturday 13 August, "for the safety of men's lives and shipping," leaving only "a pinnace of Her Majesty's, the *Advice*, and a fine caravel of my own [Drake]" to "dog the fleet until they should be past the Isles of Scotland [the Orkneys and Shetlands]." Howard intended to take his fleet into the Firth of Forth to replenish victuals and put the most sick men ashore, "but the wind coming contrary . . . the Lord Admiral altered his course and returned back again for England with his whole army." The power of the Queen of England, Mendoza later observed, "may be easily gauged by this: that her fleet was in Plymouth on 30th July, and yet on 12th August it was obliged to return to port to victual."

Had the Armada commanders been serious about returning to the Channel to make the rendezvous with Parma, this would have been their chance; the English fleet turning for home and a north-westerly wind to speed them south again. But no voice, not even that of the sick and dying old warhorse Recalde, was raised to propose this, and the Armada sailed steadily on to the north, as close to the wind as was possible for those cumbersome galleons and hulks. It was a humiliating retreat, with all thoughts of invasion abandoned. "God be praised, the enemy had never power to land so much as one man upon any territory of ours." The "sea giant . . . having not so much as fired a cottage of ours at land, nor taken a cockboat of ours at sea, wandered through the wilderness of the northern seas," never to return.[14]

CHAPTER SEVENTEEN

The Spanish Ships loft
on the Coaft of Scotland
and 700 Souldiers and
Marriners caft a Shoare.

The Rags Which Yet Remain

When the Spanish commanders saw the English fleet at last abandon its pursuit and disappear below the horizon, they were able to pause and take stock of the Armada. Seven front-line great ships had been lost, either captured, sunk or grounded. None of the others had escaped unscathed and some were so badly damaged that they were floundering in the North Sea swell, barely able to make headway. On every ship, men laboured day and night at the pumps. Each pump could raise from four to twelve gallons a minute, depending on the number of men at the levers, but that was barely enough to keep pace with the water spurting into the holds as the damaged hulls twisted and flexed in the heavy ocean swell. The *San Martin* itself was riddled with holes, including a huge one just above the waterline blasted at close range by an English heavy gun. Despite the best efforts of divers and carpenters to patch the holes, the flagship continued to ship water at an alarming rate.

The timbers of the *San Marcos* were in even worse condition, so holed and sprung that the captain was forced to pass three massive cables right under her keel. Secured to each of her masts, the cables bound the ship together for fear that otherwise it would simply fall apart. The *San Juan* was also badly holed and leaking, and unable to hoist sail on her mainmast, which had been struck by two cannonballs during the fighting. The ships of the Levant squadron, battered both by battle and by seas far heavier than those they had been built to face, were floundering badly and dropping further and further behind even the snail's pace that the rest of the fleet was able to make. Many of the hulks were also wallowing in the Armada's wake.

The lack of supplies was equally critical and grew even more so when a Hamburg barque sank almost without warning. Its crew was saved but its precious stores went to the bottom. With virtually no opportunity to replenish their food and water, other than a modest amount of fish they obtained from some Dutch and Scottish fishing boats that crossed the Armada's path, the remaining stores had to be conserved. Rice stored aboard the *San Salvador* was divided among those capable of sending boats to receive their share, and Medina-Sidonia ordered every man in the fleet, without distinction of birth or rank, to be issued with a daily ration of eight ounces of biscuit, half a pint of wine and a pint of water—nothing more. Even with this miserable allowance, there was water for only three or at most four more weeks.

The Armada was so short of water that all the hundreds of animals that would have served the invasion force were thrown overboard. They "cast out all their horses and mules into the sea" and left them to drown. While saving the water that they would have drunk made every sense, the chronic shortage of food made it astonishing that they were not at least butchered for meat. The terrified horses swam to keep pace with the lumbering ships for a while, but then gradually dropped astern. After the Armada had disappeared over the horizon, the crew of a fishing boat sailing through those waters reported the extraordinary sight of a sea devoid of ships but black with horses and mules, their eyes bulging and their tongues protruding, still locked in a desperate struggle to stay afloat, until one by one they slipped beneath the waves for the last time.

The morale of the Armada's officers and men alike had collapsed. A few ships, like de Leiva's *Rata Encoronada*, maintained at least a semblance of discipline, keeping the watches, manning the pumps, and making what light they could of their hardships and shortages, but others fell easy prey to despair. Hunger, thirst, wounds and disease, incessant labour, the bludgeoning of the winds and seas and the numbing cold and damp of the fog-shrouded, rain-sodden days, combined with the knowledge that the great enterprise had ended in humiliation, reduced many in each ship's complement to a sullen indifference to their fate. Others railed at the perceived failings of their commanders and their comrades, and the always simmering hostility between landsmen and seamen, soldier and sailor, erupted in taunts, insults and brawls.

At the council of war that Saturday, 13 August, not one Spanish captain was willing even to continue to pay lip service to the idea of returning to the Channel in an attempt to unite with Parma. De Leiva argued that the Armada should make for Norway to take on water and supplies and Diego Flores urged a landing in Ireland, but, supported by the remainder of his commanders, Medina-Sidonia instead proposed that they sail on around the north of Scotland and Ireland and, when there was searoom enough, set a direct course for Corunna. A unanimous vote, saving only Recalde, who lay dying in his bunk, confirmed the decision. It was a journey of over two thousand miles "through stormy seas almost unknown to us," and Medina-Sidonia stressed that the Armada should keep well to the west of the Irish coast. "Take great heed lest you fall upon the island of Ireland, for fear of the harm that may happen to you upon that coast." The danger was not only from the rocks, reefs and shoals that littered the coast but also from the English forces stationed in Ireland.[1]

Divers and carpenters had laboured without cease to repair the worst of the battle damage, but as the Armada struggled on, holding its course a little to the east of north, with rising seas, fog and driving squalls of rain making it harder and harder to keep the fleet together, ships continued to disappear. Few of the captains had any charts of these northern coasts, sun-sights were impossible by day and the Pole Star was hidden by fog and cloud at night. Whenever the Armada was within sight of the rocky coasts of the mainland or the islands, men watched its progress from the clifftops. Some were loyal to Catholic lords such as Morton, Bruce and Huntly, still with fervent hopes that a

Spanish landing might inspire a rising among their countrymen; others were Protestants, reporting at some remove to James VI in Edinburgh or to Elizabeth in London; some were clan chieftains musing on the uses to which Spanish soldiers could be put in pursuit of their endless feuds with rival clans; and still others were poor crofters, fishermen, wreckers and pirates, assessing the chances of spoil to augment their meagre harvest from the land and sea. Some of these at least were not disappointed in their hopes.

On Sunday 14 August, "there arose a great storm, which continued forty hours." Three Levant carracks, trailing far behind the Armada and wallowing ever deeper in the water, turned aside in an attempt to reach a coast, any coast, no matter how hostile, but they had left it too late; none of them was ever seen again. Three days later, during the night of 17 August, a fierce squall again blew up. By dawn the next morning the *Trinidad Valencera*; the *Gran Grifon*, the flagship of the hulks; and two ships of its squadron, the *Barque of Hamburg* and the *Castillo Negro*, had disappeared. None would survive.

Later that day, 18 August, the wind swung north-easterly and the *San Martin*'s pilots estimated that the Armada ships had made enough ground to northward to allow them to change course to the west-south-west, clearing Fair Isle and the Orkneys, and steering clear of the ferocious tidal rips, whirlpools and boiling surf around the Western Isles that made these some of the most treacherous waters in the world. They could do nothing to avoid the mists and fogs that cloaked the sea for days on end, shrouding the black rocks that might at any moment send their ships to their doom. They saw the sun little by day, and the phosphorescence of the waves and the spectacle of the Northern Lights at night filled them as much with superstitious terror as awe, for fear that they too were harbingers of some dread fate awaiting them. Even with a strong wind at their sterns most of the way, it had taken them ten days to round the north of Scotland from the Banks of Zeeland. It was a pitiful rate of progress, barely fifty miles a day, their ships' poor sailing qualities made even worse by leaks and holes, damaged masts and missing sails, and the accumulations of weed and barnacles on their hulls after months at sea.

As they cleared the Scottish mainland, Medina-Sidonia summoned a council of war near an island "off the north part of Scotland, where they stayed not, nor had any relief," and called in Pedro Coco Calderon, an officer aboard the *San Salvador* and an expert navigator with experience of sailing these waters. His advice was to keep well to the west and make directly for Spain in order to avoid all risk of coming to grief on the treacherous Irish coast. Diego Flores de Valdes again disagreed, arguing that only by taking the most direct route—due south, close to the Irish coast—could they hope to reach Spain alive. The inhabitants of Ireland and the Western Isles of Scotland were Catholics who traded regularly with Spain and would provide food and fresh water. To make for Spain by the route Calderon had suggested would risk the death of everyone from starvation.

Backed by the pilots of the *San Martin*, Calderon's argument won the day and Medina-Sidonia ordered all his captains to take the western route, but "haste themselves to the first place they could get to of the coast of Spain or Portugal, for that they were in such great distress through the great want of victuals." He also sent off Don Balthasar de Zuniga in a fast pinnace, to give Philip the bitter news of the Armada's defeat; Medina-Sidonia did not attempt to disguise it as anything else. "This Armada was so completely crippled and scattered that my first duty to Your Majesty seemed to save it, even at the risk which we are running undertaking this voyage, which is long and in such high latitudes. Ammunition and the best of our vessels were lacking and experience had shown how little we could depend upon the ships that remained, the Queen's fleet being so superior to ours in this sort of fighting, in consequence of the strength of their artillery and the fast sailing of their ships . . . We have . . . over 3,000 sick without counting the wounded, who are numerous on the fleet." Medina-Sidonia also asked Philip to begin preparations to feed and house the returning men but in the end de Zuniga was so much delayed by storms that he arrived back in Spain no sooner than the first ships of the returning Armada.

Day after day, huge Atlantic seas pounded them, and their progress was now even slower as they tacked into the wind through frequent showers and rainstorms. The gales drove some ships so far north that they were within fifty miles of the coast of Iceland. As the famines following poor summer harvests and the "Frost Fairs" held for weeks on end on the frozen surface of the Thames clearly show, the climate during the "Little Ice Age" that lasted from the mid-sixteenth century to the eighteenth century was generally much colder than it is today, exacerbating severe weather conditions and storms. At those latitudes, even in late August, the Spaniards found themselves facing raw and bitterly cold conditions. The men of the Mediterranean squadrons in particular were suffering badly. Every labour was made harder by the cold, hunger, thirst and sickness, and the numbing knowledge of defeat.[2]

The seamen were malnourished and bone-weary from days of unceasing work and nights of gut-gnawing tension, their faces grey and lined and their calloused hands bruised, bloodied and torn by sea-cuts from hauling on sodden, fraying ropes. But still they were forced aloft, reefing and furling sails as the winds again strengthened, patching torn canvas and securing flying ropes. Salt caked the masts and rigging like hoar-frost and the wind keening over the sullen ocean sent skeins of spume and spray snaking through the air, drenching anyone above decks. The bows bucked and plunged in the heavy swell and great grey-green waves cascaded over them and swirled away through the scuppers.

Belowdecks the guncrews looked like creatures from hell, their faces blackened by powder smoke and their skin pitted with burns from particles of spent but still red-hot powder. The men's quarters were a reeking mess, among which sprawled the sick and wounded and the few able-bodied men who could be spared from manning the ship, their faces devilish in the flickering glare of torches. They lay in semi-darkness, wrapped in sodden, mildewing blankets, and surrounded by filth and the stench of decay and death. Damp and condensation penetrated every corner and no man, not even the greatest officer or the most noble lord, had dry clothes to wear. The firewood was sodden, the stoves extinguished by waves breaking over the hatches or water leaking through the planking, and the pitiful, tainted scraps of food that were all that remained were eaten cold. Men could barely sleep for the incessant dull pounding of the waves battering against the hull, counterpointed by the rheumy, phlegm-ridden wheeze, suck and cough of the pumps. Manned night and day, their endless, dirge-like rhythm as they spilled constant spurts of foul bilgewater over the side still barely kept pace with the seawater seeping through the battered hulls.

By Sunday, 21 August, the pilots estimated that the Armada had reached 58° N, some ninety leagues to the north-west of the Galway coast. As he prepared to alter course again to make the run for home, Medina-Sidonia made a final attempt to gather his Armada around him and take a muster of his men. Malnutrition and disease, exacerbated by the cold and damp, were taking a fearsome toll of his already depleted crews. More than 3,000 men were sick and the water situation had grown markedly worse; either the supplies were leaking away or the rations were not being enforced. His men grew fewer and weaker with every passing day. In the *San Juan de Portugal* alone, there were "200 dead, twenty slain in the fight with the Queen's ships, the rest dead of the sickness." "There died four or five every day of hunger and thirst, and yet this ship was one of the best furnished for victuals," so much so that some of the crewmen of other, less well-supplied ships were transferred to it. The *San Juan de Sicilia* was "so much damaged that not a span of her sails was serviceable," and Medina-Sidonia's flagship, the *San Martin*, was in an even more desperate plight. "The admiral's mast

[was] so weakened by the shot through it that they dare not bear the sails they might to take them to Spain. The best that be in the admiral's ship are scarce able to stand . . . if they tarry where they are any time, they will all perish."[3]

The Armada ships kept trying to battle towards the south-west, but the wind blew unrelentingly from that quarter, often reaching storm force, and the fleet was then "severed by a great storm which held from four of the clock in the afternoon of one day to ten in the morning of the next," and another "great storm with a mist" ten days after that further scattered the remnants of the Armada. By Saturday 3 September, the pilots were again estimating the *San Martin* to be at 58° N and a little to the east of the position of a fortnight before. Over those fourteen days another seventeen ships had disappeared, including the *San Juan*, two of the remaining galleasses, and de Leiva's great carrack, the *Rata Santa Maria Encoronada*. During that Saturday the wind at last veered, backing round to the north-east. Medina-Sidonia sent off another pinnace with an updated report for Philip as the remnants of the Armada sailed for home.

While the flagship led its diminishing retinue of ships on the long sweep through the Atlantic, other commanders found themselves much closer to the Irish coast. Calderon in the *San Salvador* was driven by gales near to land but followed his own advice to Medina-Sidonia by tacking away into deeper waters well to the west before making course for home. "It is believed the rest of the Armada will have done the same. If not they will certainly have lost some of the ships, as the coast is rough, the sea heavy and the winds strong from the seaward." Other captains were less prudent or less fortunate, their ships "sore bruised and the men much weakened and almost starved," and, as Calderon had predicted, many came to grief on the coast. Storms in August and September are rarely dangerous to seaworthy ships, and significantly, though the English fleet was pounded by gales severe enough to damage sails, rigging and yards, no ships were lost and there are no accounts of other ships being sunk in the North or Irish Seas or the North Atlantic during this period. The only corroboration, if such it is, of the extreme violence of the weather comes from a legend that the entire village of Singleton Thorp on the Fylde coast in Lancashire was swallowed by the sea in the summer of 1588, never to reappear.[4]

The Armada ships approaching the unforgiving coasts of Western Ireland had been rendered barely navigable by English gunfire, and their crews were so depleted and weakened by battlefield fatalities, casualties, starvation and disease that they could barely work them. They had few or no anchors, having cut them loose in the panic-stricken flight from the fireships at Gravelines, their maps were inaccurate, placing the Irish coast well to the east of its actual position, their navigation was poor, they lacked pilots familiar with the waters and most were driven towards the coasts by relentless westerly gales. Others sought the coast deliberately, disobeying Medina-Sidonia's orders in their desperate need for food and water, and one or two commanders may even have harboured ambitions of salvaging something from the defeat of the Armada by establishing a base on the Irish coast from which a fresh invasion of England could be attempted. Whatever the causes that brought them to the Irish coast "like flocks of starlings," for the vast majority of the officers and men those great grey cliffs and wind-lashed strands were the last lands they were ever to sight.

The gales drove them shorewards over boiling seas with salt spray hanging in the air and ropes of spume tangling with the rigging, then torn away by the shrieking wind. Somewhere ahead, where sea and sky seemed to merge into each other in a maelstrom of wind and water, were the black rocks on which the breakers thundered in a long sullen roar that grew in volume until it drowned every other sound. One by one, their ships were wrecked "with all the chivalry and flower of the Armada." Their bleached bones are buried beneath the sea-washed dunes and the sodden Irish turf, or lie at the bottom of the sea; even today, human bones are still sometimes exposed by storms. "God send that the reader may be able to imagine some small part of what it was like, for after all, there is a great gulf between those who suffer and those who observe suffering from afar."

There had been initial confusion in Ireland over the first sightings of ships off the north and west coasts. "News of strange ships; whether they be of the dispersed fleet which are fled from the supposed overthrow in the Narrow Seas or new forces come from Spain directly, no man is able to advertise otherwise than by guess." But by 14 September they had been identified as Armada ships and the first ones had been wrecked. It took four days for even the fastest messenger to carry news from the west coast to Dublin, and it was 20 September before reports were dispatched to London. "On Thursday last, and since that time, there arrived first a bark which wrecked at the Bay of Tralee, another great ship being also now near that place; after that, two great ships and one frigate at the Blaskets in the Sound there, seven other sail in the Shannon . . . at the Lupus [Loop] Head, four great ships, and toward the Bay of Galway, four great ships more. It is thought that the rest of that fleet wherein the Duke was, which were severed by a late tempest, are also about some other part of this land . . . The people in these parts are for the most part dangerously affected towards the Spaniards, but thanks be to God, that their power by Her Majesty's good means, is shorter than it has been and the Spaniards' forces are so much weakened . . . there is no great doubt had here of any hurt that may grow thereby."

Parted from the Armada by the winds and heavy seas, de Leiva's *Rata Encoronada* had led a group of ships, including the *San Juan de Portugal*, the *San Juan Bautista*, the *Santa Maria de la Rosa* and three hulks, towards the west coast seeking water, food and shelter to carry out repairs. De Leiva's ship then lost touch with the rest, but Recalde knew the coast from his voyage during the doomed attempt to initiate a rising at Smerwick. Roused from his sickbed one last time—"after such time as the fight was at Calais [he] came not out of his bed till . . . the morning that they came upon this shore in Ireland"—he helped to guide the *San Juan de Portugal* through a perilous narrow gap in the breakers, "an entrance between low rocks about as wide as the length of a ship," to an anchorage in the lee of Great Blasket Island in Dingle Bay. Marcos de Arambaru's *San Juan Bautista*, the vice-flagship of the squadron of Castile, and the hospital ship *San Pedro el Mayor* followed his lead and also reached the relative safety of the bay. There they aimed to take on water and food, if any were to be had, for their men were "sick, destitute of victual, and in great extremity . . . they are dying daily in great numbers and being thrown into the sea." "The ship had been shot through fourteen or fifteen times, her mainmast so beaten with shot as she durst not bear her full sail, and now not sixty mariners left in her, and many of them so sick that they lie down, and the residue so weak that they were not able to do any good service, and there are daily cast over the board out of that ship five or six of the company."[5]

They had a near-miraculous escape from wrecking when surprised by a ferocious storm, though Recalde's ship dragged its anchor and was driven into the *San Juan Bautista*, damaging her stern lantern and rigging. Another ship was driven into the bay by the same storm, "all her sails torn to ribbons except the foresail," but also dragged her anchor and was driven onto a rock "and in an instant we saw she was going to the bottom, with not a soul escaping." Yet another hulk arrived in the bay later, her masts bare as winter trees and so badly damaged that she was abandoned and the surviving crew transferred to the *San Juan Bautista*. Don Pedro Pacheco's *Santa Maria de la Rosa* went down in the same storm after striking Stromboli Rock, yet as the moment of their death approached, the soldiers and mariners aboard still found time to feud with each other. Francisco de Manona, pilot aboard the ship, was accused of trying to run aground "by treason," and even as the storm was driving them towards the rocks he was murdered by one of the military captains. Every man aboard was drowned, "not a soul escaping," except for a Genoese seaman who was captured and interrogated by the English soldiers "waiting like hoodie crows on the tops of the dark cliffs," and in his terror or desperation to please his captors, he gave increasingly wild accounts of the nobles aboard his ship. It availed him nothing; once his interrogation was complete, he was executed. A party of eight men sent out as scouts by Recalde suffered the same fate.

The other three ships remained in Dingle Bay for thirteen days, and every day the bodies of dead seamen were cast overboard and washed up on the shore by the surf. When the wind at last relented, they put to sea again. Recalde's *San Juan* eventually reached Corunna on 7 October, and de Arambaru sailed into Santander a week later, but the leaking hospital ship, *San Pedro el Mayor*, failed to return. Realizing that he would never make Spain, the captain set a course for the Channel, hoping to reach a French port. Instead he was driven aground on Bolt Tail on the Devon coast on 7 November 1588. Some of the crew and a few of the wounded were saved, but many more perished in the surf. To the disappointment of George Clifford, Earl of Cumberland, who hurried to the scene, the reports of great treasure aboard and noblemen who could command a huge ransom proved false. "Being at Plymouth to water, I heard of a hulk beaten by foul weather . . . She was one of the Spanish fleet and it was reported the Duke [of Medina-Sidonia] was in her and great store of treasure . . . we found no such thing."[6]

The galleass *Zuniga* had anchored near Liscannor Castle on the Irish coast to mend her damaged rudder. "We were in such dire need of food that nearly 80 of our soldiers and convicts died of hunger and thirst but . . . the inhabitants were rustic savages devoted to England" and refused to allow them "to obtain water; nor would they sell us food. By necessity, we took up arms and obtained supplies by force." Some of the crew were captured and executed and a copy of Medina-Sidonia's orders for the return voyage to Spain carried by one of them fell into English hands, but the galleass put to sea again on 23 September. Battered and leaking after another gale, and with the rudder once more broken, she was forced to limp into Le Havre, passing the grounded wreck of the *Santa Ana* that had parted from the Armada two months previously. Only a fortnight before the *Zuniga's* arrival, a group of four English ships had sailed into Le Havre to attack the *Santa Ana*, determined to destroy any Spanish ship that might yet be salvaged and used in a fresh assault upon England, but they had been driven off by the guns of the castle.

The *Zuniga* was "storm-beaten, with the rudder and spars broken and the ship in a sinking state . . . without a bit of food or a drop of water; a day later and they would all have perished of famine." "The stores on board were all damaged and rotten and being useless, have been thrown into the sea." As soon as the galleass came to anchor, the convicts at the oars seized their opportunity to make a dash for freedom. The Frenchmen among them found a sympathetic welcome from their compatriots and they were allowed to make good their escape, but "the rest were detained with great trouble and they are under strong guard." However, even "the best of guard" proved insufficient "for so many people come on board to see the galleass that they cannot all be watched and they give files to the convicts," who used them to cut through their fetters and escape. "The Governor himself is beating them off with a stick every day; and if it were not for this, not a galley slave would be left. The Governor has a pair of sentries night and day to prevent any Frenchman going on the ship. Two convicts escaped this morning and I reported to the Governor that the guard at the town gate had aided them to get away. He at once went in person and gave the corporal of the guard twenty blows with his crutch, and . . . sent the corporal to seek the convicts . . . He brought them both back this afternoon, finely tricked out in French clothes. The Governor then issued an order that . . . any person who sheltered or aided a convict should be chained in the place of the man who escaped. God grant that this may be effectual. I have had new fetters made and put them on double."

The *Zuniga* remained in port throughout the winter and then attempted to sail home but, caught by yet another storm, lost her mast, boom and yards and sprang her timbers so badly that twelve guns and all the shot, anchors, cables, barrels of water and victuals were thrown overboard to keep her afloat. Half the oars, "which the convicts were ready enough to throw overboard," were also jettisoned. The galleass limped back to Le Havre, where she again ran aground. After several more attempts, the *Zuniga* eventually reached Spain, but never put to sea again.

Almost every other ship that sought shelter in Irish waters was wrecked. Many drowned as their ships sank and though some Irish were sympathetic to their traditional allies against the hated English, their sympathy often did not extend to rescuing those drowning in the sea. In many coastal areas—of England and Scotland as well as Ireland—there was a long-established belief that "the sea must have its due." To save a man from drowning was to risk the sea claiming a member of your own family as its tribute instead. As a result, Irishmen sometimes stood impassively by as Spaniards weighed down with clothing, armour and the gold they carried drowned within sight and sometimes reach of the shore. Those who did manage to drag themselves ashore were far from safe. The Irish robbed and stripped them, and the English hunted them down and killed them.[7]

The worst losses of all occurred in the Levant squadron, including ten Ragusan ships, creating "300 widows in Ragusa [modern Dubrovnik]" alone. De Leiva's *Rata Santa Maria Encoronada* ran immovably aground in Tullaghan Bay, County Mayo, but almost all the crew were saved, together with most of their weapons, armour, plate and coin. De Leiva had the ship fired, took possession of a ruined hill fort and sent out scouts. They reported that inland lay a vast, featureless morass of peat bog and marsh, but that further up the coast on the far side of Blacksod Bay a hulk, the *Duquesa*, had anchored to make repairs. He then marched his men the twenty miles to the bay—a gruelling slog over rocky headlands and soft sand, and through rivers and quaking peat bogs—and they were taken on board the *Duquesa*. The hulk's casks were filled with fresh, peaty water, the sweetest its starving, thirsting men had ever tasted, and it then put to sea unmolested, but grossly overloaded. The sea crossing to Spain was thought too long and dangerous and instead they attempted to use the prevailing winds to reach neutral Scotland, but, battered by westerly gales, the *Duquesa* was pushed back towards the shore and wrecked at Loughros Mor 100 miles to the north.

Again the survivors struggled ashore, fortified a camp and sent out scouts. Eight days later came news that another Armada ship, the galleass *Girona*, had put in for repairs at Killibegs in Donegal Bay, twenty miles to the south. Once more de Leiva—lamed in the latest wreck and carried in a litter by relays of four soldiers—marched the surviving crews of the two ships there and went aboard. After a stay of almost three weeks, during which yet another wreck was stripped of its timbers to effect repairs to the *Girona*, the galleass set sail on 26 October, groaning under the weight of 1,300 men. De Leiva again hoped to reach Scotland but, as the creaking vessel crept north-eastwards, a storm wind began to blow from the north. The makeshift rudder of the galleass broke—the by now notorious weakness of the ships—and the oars were useless in the heavy seas. The crippled ship was driven south towards the Antrim coast and around midnight on 28 October she hit the reefs of the Giant's Causeway. The *Girona* was torn apart in the boiling surf and almost all hands were lost. "Out of 1,300 men on board the galleass, only nine sailors were saved." De Leiva and his retinue of young followers from almost every noble house in Spain were drowned. When the news of this disaster was communicated to Philip, he said that it meant more to him even than the loss of the Armada. For every noble who perished, scores of common soldiers and seamen also went to their deaths. Perhaps the most poignant memorial to them is the gold ring given to one of the ship's company by a wife or lover and engraved with the message "I have no more to give you."[8]

Almost every part of the north and west coasts of Ireland claimed its share of the harvest of wrecks. The battle-scarred *San Marcos*, sheltering in the Shannon, caught fire or was put to the torch and burned down to the waterline before capsizing and sinking. Three ships—the *Lavia*, *Juliana* and *Santa Maria de Vison*—came to grief together on Streedagh Strand. They had sought shelter in the bay with its broad, sweeping beaches of fine white sand fringed by the Dartry Mountains, but it lay open to westerly gales and when a storm blew up the ships' cables parted and they were pounded to pieces in the surf. "A great gale hit us broadside on, with the waves reaching the sky . . . Within the hour our three ships broke up completely with less than three hundred men surviving. Over a thousand drowned, among them many important people, captains, gentlemen and regular officers. Many were drowning in the ships, others, casting themselves into the water, sank to the bottom without returning to the surface; others on rafts and barrels, with gentlemen on pieces of timber; others cried out aloud in the ships, calling upon God; captains threw their jewelled chains and crown-pieces into the sea; the waves swept others away, washing them out of the ships . . . More than six hundred other corpses that the sea had cast up were left to be devoured by ravens and wolves with no one to give any of them burial." The sea gave up even more of its dead over the following days and weeks. "I numbered in one strand of less than five miles in length, above 1,100 dead corpses of men which the sea had driven upon the shore."

Don Diego de Enriquez, "The Hunchback," and three other nobles on the *Lavia* had themselves entombed beneath the deck of the ship's boat along with their useless wealth, "more than 16,000 ducats in jewels and gold coins." Sailors caulked the seams of the hatch and prepared to launch the boat, but over seventy crewmen then rushed it, seeking their own salvation. The grossly overloaded boat at once overturned. The crewmen drowned and the battered boat was washed up on the beach. The Irish peasants waiting on the beaches "were stripping any man who swam to shore," but only when they broke up the boat the next day in search of salvageable timber and nails did they discover the bodies of the nobles, including Don Diego, who "expired in their hands," and wealth beyond reckoning. More than one Connaught fortune was founded on Streedagh Strand that day.

Two ships anchored outside Ard Bay, south-west of Carna in Gal-

way, were said to have been lured onto the rocks by a signal fire lit
either by the McDonagh family or Teigue na Buile ("The Furious")
O'Flaherty, who then plundered the ships and stripped the clothes and
valuables from the dead bodies of the crew. Local legend claims that
the sole survivor returned to Ireland years afterwards to wreak his
revenge on the perpetrators. All along the coast, among the oyster-
catchers, terns and gulls scavenging the tideline, were the inhabitants
of every farm, village and crofter's hut, scouring the beaches and the
shallows for gold plate, coins, chains, rings and brooches, sacred
objects, fine clothes, swords and daggers. Corpses were robbed where
they lay and survivors who did manage to crawl ashore were stripped
naked of their valuables and clothes on the beaches. Many of them
remained alive for no more than days, hours or even minutes. Some
were murdered, and many others died of shock, exposure and starvation, but even that was a more merciful death than the one meted out
by the English soldiers and their Scots and Irish mercenaries hunting
down the survivors.[9]

Some thought the Irish were "more greedy of spoil than to harken
after other things," but the Deputy of Ireland, Sir William Fitzwilliam,
had every reason to fear the sudden appearance off the coast of Spanish
ships carrying troops and prominent Irish exiles. "The Irishry are
grown very proud . . . and call themselves the Pope's and King Philip's
men." Savage English repression following the defeat of the Spanish
and papal troops at Smerwick in November 1580, coupled with the
effects of a terrible famine, had doused the flames of Irish rebellion in
recent years, but Fitzwilliam feared that the landings could either be
part of some new invasion attempt or would provoke a fresh Irish
uprising. He reported a "diversity of rumours raised by the ill-affected
to trouble and lead astray the minds of the people thereby to distemper
the government . . . [by] those foreign designs . . . against this realm."
Rebel chieftains such as O'Doherty, O'Rourke and McSweeny
McDoe—"a man of great power . . . and other neighbours of like dis-
loyal minds . . . will join with them . . . great hurt will grow thereby."
His alarm communicated itself to Elizabeth, who issued orders to "the
Lieutenants of counties, for putting men in readiness to march for Ireland within an hour's warning."

Even if the Spanish soldiers were mere fugitives and survivors from
the wreck of the Armada seeking food and water, enough were coming
ashore to mount a serious challenge to the English garrison of this
perennially rebellious territory. It was even conceivable that "Her
Majesty [might] be dispossessed of Ireland." "There are not 750 foot in

bands in the whole realm . . . We look rather to be overrun by the Spaniards than otherwise." It was a slight exaggeration. Some 670 horsemen and 1,250 foot soldiers were "furnished within the English Pale . . . against the Spaniards," but even with mercenaries, Protestant settlers and Irish levies of dubious loyalty, Fitzwilliam could count on putting no more than 2,000 men in the field, and he never contemplated for a moment showing mercy to any survivors who came into his hands. "Such of the Spaniards as escaped the waves were cruelly butchered by order of the Lord Deputy." His men were ordered to "apprehend and execute all Spaniards found, of what quality soever. Torture may be used." Officers, seamen and soldiers who fell into English hands were slaughtered, cut down where they stood or hung like rotting fruit from the branches of every tree, "which so terrified the remainder that, though sick and half-famished, they chose sooner to trust to their shattered barks and the mercy of the waves, than to their more merciless enemies, in consequence of which multitudes of them perished."[10]

Those governing the western provinces in Fitzwilliam's name shared his grim determination. Sixty-four men, the only survivors of hundreds drowned in the wrecks of two hulks on the coast of Clare, were delivered to Boetius Clancy, the Sheriff of Clare, and at once hanged on the hill overlooking the town. Among the dead was Don Felipe de Cordoba, the son of Philip's chamberlain, who would have fetched a rich price at ransom. A battered and waterlogged Spanish pinnace also ran aground in Tralee Bay. The twenty-four men of its crew were captured as soon as they rowed ashore. Sir Edward Denny, an English plantation owner in that remote territory, could see "no safe keeping for them" and all were summarily executed. According to local legend, his wife Lady Denny rode out with him and helped to carry out the task with particular relish.

Another ship—*an lang maol*, the bare ship—with all its masts razed to deck level by gunfire and storms, ran aground in Broadhaven, County Mayo. There are no records of any survivors. *El Gran Grin*, the vice-flagship of the Biscayan squadron, carrying "50 pieces of brass, besides four great cannon," was also wrecked on an island off the coast of Mayo, and though around 100 men reached shore, "whereof sixteen of the company of that ship landed with chains of gold about their necks," most were slaughtered by Dowdarra Roe O'Malley. Edward Whyte, Clerk to the Council of Connaught, recorded the toll of ships along the Galway coast and the grim fate of survivors who reached land: "eighty were killed with his gallowglass [mercenary] axe by

Melaghlin McCabb." When news of his exploits was brought to London, a broadside was published celebrating "the valiant deeds of Mac-Cab an Irish man."[11]

The *Trinidad Valencera*, commanded by Don Alonso de Luzon, "sprang a leak forward and for two days and nights they were at the pumps," but the ship was driven ashore and wrecked on a reef in Kinnagoe Bay. Her complement numbered some 500 souls, "whereof many sick and weak, besides which 100 and upwards were drowned in coming to the shore, being common soldiers and mariners . . . They landed . . . as many of them as they could in a broken boat of their own, some swam to shore and the rest were landed in a boat of O'Doherty's country [Drogheda], for the use of which they gave in money and apparel 200 ducats . . . He [de Luzon] and five more of the best of his company landed first, only with their rapiers in their hands, where they found four or five savage people—as he terms them—who bade them welcome and well used them until some twenty more wild men came to them, after which time they took away a bag of money containing 1000 reals of plate and a cloak of blue rash, richly laid with gold lace. They were about two days in landing all their men, and being landed, had very ill entertainment, finding no other relief of victual in the country than of certain garrans [horses] which they bought of poor men for their money, which garrans they killed and did eat, and some small quantity of butter that the common people brought also to sell . . . None were slain by the savage people."

De Luzon was leading the 400 or so survivors on a march along the coast, in hopes of sighting another Armada ship to rescue them, when they were intercepted by 200 well-armed English horsemen. After some preliminary skirmishing, de Luzon realized the hopelessness of his position and agreed to surrender in return for an assurance of fair treatment and safe conduct to Dublin, from where they could be ransomed and returned to Spain. "Their promise was not kept with them and the soldiers and savage people spoiled them of all they had." Once disarmed, the Spanish officers were separated from their men, who were then slaughtered, some in a manner made notorious by the Army of Flanders. Stripped of their valuables and clothes, they were forced to run a gauntlet of English soldiers armed with swords, knives and clubs. Others were shot by arquebusiers or cut down by cavalry. Most were killed "with lance and bullet," but a few managed to escape, though a claim that as many as 150, over a third of them, had fled seems implausible.

They took refuge in the nearby castle of Duhort under the protection of Bishop Cornelius, "a most seditious papist and a man very likely to procure great aid to the Spaniards if he can," and eventually escaped to Scotland, with the help of an Irish chieftain, Sorley Boy Macdonnell, from his stronghold of Dunluce Castle. The sons of many of the Irish lords and clan chieftains were held hostage in Dublin Castle as guarantors of their fathers' conduct, and Macdonnell had prostrated himself before a portrait of Elizabeth in Dublin earlier that year, throwing down his sword and kissing Elizabeth's feet in the painting as he vowed his allegiance and offering up his eldest son as hostage to his loyalty, but back in his own domain he continued to defy the English and aid the Spaniards.[12]

Huge numbers of other Armada survivors perished, often at the hands of Sir Richard Bingham, the provincial governor of Connaught. A veteran soldier of fortune, Bingham had served with Don Juan of Austria at Cyprus and Lepanto, but had also fought alongside the Dutch rebels against the Army of Flanders, and commanded a ship, the *Swiftsure*, in the English counter-attack at Smerwick in 1580. Known as "the flail of Connaught," Bingham issued a proclamation threatening "any man who had or kept Spaniards" with death, and revelled in the subsequent slaughter of Armada survivors. "By this may appear the great handiwork of Almighty God, who has drowned the remain of that mighty army, for the most part, on the coasts of this province . . . 700 Spaniards in Ulster were despatched . . . in 15 or 16 ships cast away on the coast of this province . . . there have perished at least 6,000 or 7,000 men, of which there have been put to the sword, first and last, by my brother George, and in Mayo, Thomond and Galway, about 700 or 800 or upwards . . . So as now—God be thanked—this province stands clear and rid of all these foreign enemies, save a silly [few] poor prisoners." "Twelve ships that are known of and two or three more supposed to be sunk to the seaboard of the Out Isles. The men of these ships all perished save 1,100 or more who were put to the sword, amongst whom were officers and gentlemen of quality to the number of 50 . . . The Lord Deputy [Fitzwilliam] sent me special direction to see them executed as the rest were, only reserving alive one Don Luis de Cordoba and his nephew till Your Majesty's pleasure be known."

De Cordoba, who had received the Armada's sacred standard from Medina-Sidonia's own hand in Lisbon cathedral, was one of the few taken by the English to escape execution, and even the bloodthirsty Bingham made bold to complain of Fitzwilliam's determination to eradicate every single survivor of the Armada wrecks. "My brother George had one Don Graveillo de Swasso and another gentleman by licence and some five or six Dutch boys and young men who, coming after the fury and heat of justice was past, by entreaty I spared them, in respect they were pressed into the fleet against their wills . . . But the

Lord Deputy . . . caused both these Spaniards which my brother had to
be executed . . . and the Dutchmen and boys, reserving none but Don
Luis and his nephew." Estimates of the number of dead varied but all
witnesses were agreed on the scale of the tragedy that had overwhelmed the beaten Armada. "The miseries they sustain upon these
coasts are to be pitied in any but in Spaniards, for there have been
wrecked between Lough Foyle in Ulster, and the Dingle in Kerry, 16
sails, many of them great ships. Of those that came to the land by
swimming, or were enforced thereto by famine, very near
3,000 . . . slain, besides about 2,000 drowned; so that it is supposed that
there have perished of them in this land by sword and sea about 5,000
or 6,000."[13]

The few ships to have escaped the coasts were "now departed for
Spain, where, if they arrive not soon, they will die of famine. Her
Majesty has great cause to praise God, that has so miraculously delivered her most malicious enemies into her hands without loss of her
subjects, and broken the bond between them and this people, so that
their hope from Spain is now gone . . . There is no rebellion in the
whole realm, so much terror prevails." Bingham also showed a sharp
awareness of the quickest way to his monarch's affections. "Thus God
be praised, was all the province quickly rid of those distressed enemies
and the service done and ended without any other forces than the garrison bands or yet any extraordinary charge to Your Majesty." "Touching the ordnance and other munitions lost here, all diligence shall be
used to save as much as may for Her Majesty's use," though, as elsewhere, looting had already reduced the value of the potential haul.
"Treasure and great wealth has been taken no doubt . . . by unworthy
persons." Fitzwilliam issued orders that "Whereas . . . much treasure
[is] cast away, now subject to the spoil of the country people, but also
great store of ordnance, munitions, armours, and other goods of several kinds, which ought to be preserved for and to the use of Her
Majesty . . . we authorise you to make inquiry by all good means, both
by oaths and otherwise; to take all hulls of ships, stores, treasure, etc.,
into your hands; and to apprehend and execute all Spaniards found
there, of what quality soever. Torture may be used in prosecuting this
inquiry."

Fitzwilliam was still displaying his chilling determination to complete the wholesale slaughter of survivors to the last man. "God has
fought by shipwrecks, savages and famine for Her Majesty against
these proud Spaniards." "There cannot be gone above 300 of all the
men which landed, neither have they now any one vessel left to carry
the rest away; and since it has pleased God, by his hand, upon the rocks

to drown the greater and better sort of them, I will, with his favour, be his soldier for the despatching of those 'rags' which yet remain." "This sanguinary man" then made his own tour of the coastal provinces, inspecting the corpses and debris still littering Streedagh Strand and ordering the chieftains to "give hostages, disperse their forces, deliver up all the Spaniards and Portuguese to whom they had given refuge, pay fines and make amends for all spoils which they had taken. Fitzwilliam, while he remained in town [Galway], caused several of the Spaniards delivered up on this occasion to be beheaded near St. Augustin's monastery on the hill amidst the murmurs and lamentations of the people . . . Their dead bodies were carefully wrapped in fine linen by the townswomen and committed to burial . . . Having thus wreaked his vengeance on these unfortunate men, he departed for Dublin." His victims were buried in the grounds of the Augustinian Friary just outside the town walls.[14]

Transcripts of the interrogations of those few Spaniards made prisoner in Ireland were forwarded to London, but their reliability was suspect. The prisoners were "common seamen" without any knowledge of the strategies of their officers and their King, and "they were half-dead with cold and hunger and half-mad with terror, expecting that death which fell on most of them, and ready to say anything which they thought might be pleasant to their captors." The chief translator, David Gwynn, was also prone to lies and wild exaggerations, as his account of his own escape from the galleys accompanying the Armada confirmed. He was later arrested for his "lewd and undutiful behaviour" in claiming that in Spain he had been shown a letter from Walsingham stating that "he was wholly for them and he would deliver Her Majesty's person into their hands." That accusation alone was sufficient to ensure a painful death, but he also stood accused of "embezzling, impairing and concealing of such chains, gold and money as he took from the Spanish prisoners at Tredagh, to the value of £160."

A handful of Armada ships had also come to grief on the coast of Scotland and the Western Isles. The *San Juan de Sicilia* ran aground at Tobermory Bay on the island of Mull. The local clan chieftain, Lachlan MacLean of Duart, allowed them to make repairs and take on supplies in return for using some of the Spanish soldiers as unpaid mercenaries in his feud with another clan. Elizabeth could not afford to have a force of armed Spaniards loose in Scotland, where dissident Catholic lords were ever ready to conspire and rise in rebellion against her, and after an interval of several weeks one of Walsingham's agents, John Smollett, succeeded in infiltrating the merchants provisioning the ship. On 18 November he laid a fuse to the powder store. "The great ship which lay in the West Isles [was] blown in the air by device of John Smollett," killing most of its crew of over 300 and sending the ship to the bottom of Tobermory Bay.

The *Gran Grifon*, under Juan Gomez de Medina, was leaking so badly both from the English gunfire and the strains on her hull imposed by the recoil of her own armament that she could be kept afloat only by keeping the wind and waves at her stern and manning the pumps day and night. Driven far back to the north-east and battered by gales and storm seas, the crew eventually gave up the struggle and left the ship to sink. "Truly our one thought was that our lives were ended, and each of us reconciled himself to God as well as he could, and prepared for the long journey of death. To have forced that ship any more would only have ended it and our lives the sooner, so we gave up trying. The poor soldiers too, who had worked incessantly at the pumps and buckets, lost heart and let the waters rise." But soon afterwards they spotted Fair Isle dead ahead and, regaining their will to live, they steered towards it and wrecked on the rocks of Stroms Hellier on 27 September 1588. Seven men died, but most of the crew of 280 managed to scramble ashore, taking with them from the wreck only the pay-chest. At first the islanders, seventeen families of crofters described as "dirty savages" by the Spaniards, sold them food in exchange for gold, but Fair Isle could barely support its existing population, let alone these castaways. A further fifty men died over the following seven weeks and were buried in a place forever after known as Spanniarts' Graves. Many perished from their privations but some were murdered and thrown over the cliffs.

The remainder were eventually rescued by a Scottish boat and taken first to Shetland and then to the mainland, where they came ashore at Anstruther "not to give mercy, but to ask." The commander, Juan Gomez de Medina, "grey-haired and very humble like," forgot his pride and honour sufficiently to prostrate himself before the assembled local gentlemen. The Laird allowed them to come ashore, but de Medina and a handful of priests and expatriates who were certain to be executed if they fell into the hands of Elizabeth's men then escaped in a small barque. Despite being wrecked off Cape St. Vincent, they eventually made their way home. De Medina at once repaid some of the debt he owed to his rescuers by freeing the crew of an impounded Scottish ship.[15]

Another thirty Spaniards staged an equally remarkable escape, overpowering the crew of the pinnace taking them from Ireland to Chester and sailing it to Corunna, but the most astonishing escape story—if it is to be believed—was that of Francisco de Cuellar, captain of the *San Pedro*. Condemned to be hanged for disobeying orders as the Armada fled through the North Sea, he was reprieved and transferred to the *Lavia*, one of the three ships wrecked on Streedagh Strand. He helped his saviour, the Judge Advocate General, Martin de Aranda, onto "a scuttle-board from the wreck" but then saw him washed away by a breaker and drowned, "calling upon God," dragged down by the weight of gold coins sewed into the lining of his coat. Thrown ashore by the pounding surf, de Cuellar crawled up the beach, dragging his injured, bleeding leg, and hid among the reeds and sand dunes as his fellows were robbed, stripped and killed. He sought shelter in the roofless stone ruins of Staad Abbey—despite its name, little more than a chapel—and found twelve of his countrymen had been hanged from "the iron grilles of the church . . . by act of the Lutheran English who went about searching for us, to make an end of all who had escaped from the perils of the sea." He was stripped of his clothes and his valuables, beaten with staves by Irish peasants and slashed with a knife by an English soldier, but he was not killed and, dressed in "some bracken leaves and a piece of old matting," eventually reached the house of a friendly chieftain, O'Rourke. There he met nineteen other survivors and together they set out for a Spanish ship that had put in on the nearby coast. Hampered by his injured leg, de Cuellar was the only one not to reach the ship before it sailed, to his good fortune, since it was driven back onto the coast by a storm and all on board were drowned or captured and executed by the English.

De Cuellar next fell into the hands of an Irish blacksmith who treated him as slave labour until forced to release him on the intercession of the local priest, and he then joined eight other Spaniards at a castle belonging to another Irish chieftain, set in the middle of a lake, and reached by a secret, winding causeway hidden below the surface of the water. There, or so de Cuellar claimed, they successfully resisted an English expeditionary force of several hundred men while the Irish all fled into the mountains. "Dreadful storms and heavy falls of snow" forced the English to withdraw but the Irish chieftain was so enamoured of his prisoners' martial prowess that he showed no sign of ever being willing to let them go. De Cuellar and four of his countrymen then escaped in the dead of night and, after many further adventures, he eventually found a boat willing to take him to Scotland, even surviving as his ship almost foundered during its crossing of the Irish Sea. He later had yet another remarkable escape when he sailed for Flanders with other Spanish survivors. De Cuellar's tale has been accepted at face value by every historian, and it is a vivid and often moving account, yet one is forced to wonder if the incessant catalogue of disasters, near misses and miraculous escapes that he recounts can really all have happened to one person in so short a compass of time. Parts must undoubtedly be true, but de Cuellar would not be the first raconteur to embellish a story a little with each retelling, and the fact that every woman under forty that he met appears to have been a dazzling beauty should alone be enough to sound warning bells.

Despite Fitzwilliam's zeal, perhaps as many as 1,000 Spaniards escaped the English dragnet, going to ground in the wild and remote regions where Elizabeth's writ barely ran. Some were later killed or captured but several hundred reached Scotland with the help of Irish rebel chieftains, who aided them out of hatred for the English, self-interest or common humanity. Some were given safe conduct to France aboard Scottish ships, but the men de Medina had left behind, joined by Francisco de Cuellar and 300 survivors from two ships wrecked on the Norwegian coast, were much less fortunate.

In August 1589, they were among 600 Spaniards ransomed through the largesse of the Duke of Parma, who paid five ducats for every one of his countrymen brought to Flanders. They were being carried there by four Scottish ships under a safe conduct signed by Elizabeth, but she had informed the Dutch Sea Beggars and their fleet was waiting in ambush. One ship was captured at sea and every man aboard tossed over the side to his death. The remaining ships were driven aground and many more of the Spaniards slaughtered. Once more Francisco de Cuellar was one of the few to survive. He saw "before our eyes the Dutch making a thousand pieces of 270 Spaniards . . . without leaving more than three alive." Parma took swift and brutal revenge. "They are now being paid out as more than 400 Dutchmen who have been taken since then have been beheaded."[16]

In Ireland, even Fitzwilliam's appetite for slaughter was eventually sated and on 25 January 1589 he issued a formal pardon to all Spaniards still in hiding. Many must have doubted the word of the butcher of their countrymen, but some at least of those who gave themselves up or were handed over to the English authorities were treated with mercy and sent by way of England to Parma in Flanders, who had paid their ransoms. Some remained there, fighting for Parma's army in the Low Countries, others were eventually restored to their homeland, but still others had stayed in Ireland, becoming retainers of rebel chieftains such as O'Rourke, Sorley Boy Macdonnell and Hugh O'Neill, Earl of Tyrone. The following spring, twenty-four of them were reported to be training O'Rourke's *kerne* (foot soldiers) and some later took part in a terrible revenge for the killing of their countrymen, joining in a massacre of 500 of the Lord Deputy's English troops. Eight of those wrecked on Streedagh Strand were still in the service of O'Neill and Macdonnell in October 1596, when they wrote to Philip seeking money "the better to serve Your Majesty here as guides, interpreters and otherwise as will be needful when the Spanish force lands." A few Spaniards also chose to remain in Scotland, where they "sparkled abroad in noblemen's houses, choosing rather to lead a serving man's life at ease in this country than to follow the wars in Flanders in want and danger."

The persistent claim that Spanish survivors fathered many children in Ireland whose descendants can be recognized to this day is one of many Armada myths. The dark eyes and hair of many Irishmen are attributable more to Celtic than Spanish blood, and those few who are of genuine Spanish descent are more likely to owe their ancestry to the centuries of trade between the two countries and the presence from medieval times to the present day of a large Spanish fishing fleet off the west coast of Ireland than to the amorous exploits of the battle-shocked, half-starved and half-drowned survivors of Armada shipwrecks.[17]

Other Armada survivors were imprisoned in England and most fared little better than their fellows in Ireland and Scotland. Captured English traitors faced an inevitably cruel regime. There were two Englishmen on board Pedro de Valdes' ship when it surrendered to Drake. One of them, Tristram Winslade, was imprisoned in Newgate. "Their Lordships' pleasure is that he be conveyed to the Tower . . . for the examination of the said Winslade upon the rack, using torture to him at their pleasure." Even under the torments of the rack he maintained his innocence of the charge of treason, and managed to convince his interrogators that "he was brought hither against his will." He was later released and at once fled England for Spain, where he was given a pension by Philip in recognition of his "having endured much suffering," suggesting that even with the rack to aid them his interrogators had been fooled.

The survivors of the *San Pedro el Mayor* were captured after the ship went aground in Devon, though many of the local populace would have preferred to see them killed outright. The local clerk to the council passed on its "pleasure for the deferring of the execution" of the Spanish noblemen pending an assessment of their value at ransom, but requested a decision "touching . . . of the rest as soon as your Lordships shall think convenient, for avoiding of the charge of their diet." The decision of the Privy Council would not have pleased him, since he was told to keep them alive and, even worse, the costs of feeding them were transferred from the Crown to the county on the ingenious grounds that, since the ship was endeavouring to return home when it was wrecked, its men were merely shipwrecked mariners rather than prisoners of war. As many of the Spaniards were also "greatly diseased," they were "conveyed to certain barns and outhouses standing apart from other tenements and dwelling places" to avoid the contagion's being passed to the inhabitants. The Spanish Barn in the grounds of Torre Abbey served as a temporary prison for many Spaniards; the sick were treated at two "leper houses" at Bodmin and Plympton.[18]

Securing the valuables from captured ships was as urgent a priority for Elizabeth and her ministers as minimizing the cost of keeping prisoners, but the Sheriff of Devon, George Cary, bemoaned his inability to achieve either aim in his county, complaining of "the great pilfering and spoils that the country people made" from the *Rosario*. "There is such havoc made thereof that I am ashamed to write what spoils I see . . . and though I have written to Sir John Gilbert to know what is become of the wines I left in his custody, yet I can receive no direct answer from him, but this I know by others, that all the best wines are gone" and "the tackle of the ship so spoiled by his negligent looking unto that 200 pound in ropes and other necessaries will not suffice to set her to the seas again."

Cary also complained that Gilbert, having demanded fourpence a day to feed each prisoner in his charge, but "being unwilling to take any pains where no profit arises, would fain thrust the 226 prisoners which remain at the Bridewell, sixteen miles from my house, to my charge. And he would take unto him the charge of 160 of the said Spanish prisoners remaining a-shipboard hard by his house, and every day hardly labouring in his garden in the levelling of his grounds, so that he is too wise for me (as he thinks) to have their daily labour and yet allowance from Her Majesty of 4d per diem to each of them." A week later, with fifteen of the prisoners in the Bridewell dead in the interim, Cary again wrote to the Council that they were "in some distress for want of relief to sustain them . . . I have taken order . . . to relieve their misery in allowing to each of them 1fid per diem and to some of them 2d per diem, and have disbursed the money out of my purse to make provision for victuals at the best and cheapest hand, for otherwise they must needs have perished through hunger and possibly thereby bred some infection, which might be dangerous to our country." Such an allowance was miserable indeed compared to the 6½d per man, per day, in harbour and 7d at sea paid to contractors supplying English ships with their modest provisions.[19]

The sufferings of some of the 397 men of the *Rosario* were only just beginning. The ship had been "cast ashore in England on the land of

Sir William Courteney, where she was pillaged and her people imprisoned." Twelve of them—those more likely to attract a ransom payment—were separated at the orders of a commissioner from the Queen. "To each of these they gave 4d for his daily sustenance and to each of the rest they gave 1d," starvation rates. Over a year later, on 24 November 1589, the surviving prisoners were released "by the Queen's order, excepting twelve which the Queen gave to Sir William Courteney." They were thrown back into jail with a ransom of 5,000 ducats on their heads, "which sum was not paid, for that there were none save only poor men." In January 1590 other Spanish prisoners in Devon were wandering "up and down the country" begging for food and the Privy Council issued an order that in future anyone taking a prisoner would be responsible for his upkeep, effectively instructing privateers to kill captives outright or throw them overboard to drown. By 11 August 1590, Courteney had increased his ransom demands for the men he still held to 12,000 ducats, and in desperation the prisoners wrote a letter to the Queen begging for the same clemency that had been granted to the other Spanish prisoners.

"This letter falling into the hands of the said Courteney, he thrust us into a strong prison, giving us for our diet but bread, broth and water. We were in such straits that seeing ourselves dying, we resolved to break out of prison and appeal to the justices for a remedy, but they answered that they were unable to relieve us, because he was a powerful man with whom they could not meddle. So that we were sent back to our prison and remained therein seven months, suffering great hardship." By February 1591, Courteney had increased his ransom demands to 25,000 ducats. It was again refused, and the surviving prisoners were still incarcerated in March 1592. Nothing further was ever heard of them.[20]

Other captives were in similarly desperate straits, often escaping from ship fever only to fall prey to jail fever instead. Of the remaining men from the *Rosario*, "five of the chiefest of them" had been sent to the Earl of Bath to await ransom and 226 were locked in the Bridewell in London. Alderman Radcliffe, Sheriff of London, complained of the cost and proposed that "some three or four" of them might by some means be made liable for it. "If some help be not obtained towards their maintenance by this means, we shall be compelled, in respect of the great poverty of the said house to make a general collection through the city for the maintenance of those Spaniards, which will be very unwillingly assented to by the common sort." The prisoners were subjected to daily Protestant sermons on top of their other sufferings, and "a Sardinian and . . . an Andalusian" gave a sufficiently convincing proof of conversion to the faith to be released from jail, though their joy must have been rapidly tempered when they were sent to Ireland to assist in the interrogation and processing of prisoners there who had somehow escaped the sword and the rope. Those left behind in the Bridewell who stubbornly refused to convert and compounded their offence by refusing "to listen to the preaching . . . are not allowed any share in the alms." Without the alms donated as acts of charity by the public, prisoners had no money to bribe their jailers to ensure they were fed, and many died. "Last week there died one of the Spaniards in Bridewell, Alonso de la Serna, and there are many of them ill. They suffer much, especially as winter is coming on and they do not have enough clothes to cover their nakedness. My heart aches for them, but I have not the power to help them."

The rest of the *Rosario*'s men were in even worse case, incarcerated "aboard the Spanish ship to live upon such victuals as do remain." When those rotting scraps had been consumed, the Sheriff of Devon bemoaned the difficulty of feeding them and "conveying . . . their victuals unto them, which was very burdensome to our people in this time of harvest . . . The people's charity unto them (coming with so wicked an intent) is very cold; so that if there be not order forthwith taken by your Lordships, they must starve. They are many in number, and several of them already very weak, and some dead."[21]

Don Pedro de Valdes and the other captured nobles and gentlemen received far less brutal treatment. De Valdes and two "captains of footmen" were lodged at the house of Sir Francis Drake's brother, Richard, until their ransom could be arranged, and "forty of the better sort" were accommodated in various private houses around London. On being told that the Lords of the Council "intended to take some honourable course for the releasing of the soldiers and mariners taken in his ship by way of ransom," de Valdes said "it was a clemency sufficient to mollify the hardest heart of any enemy; the news was as joyful unto them as if it had been tidings of their own liberty, in respect that the said poor people were raised by them and were their neighbours and came in this employment for the love and zeal that they bare unto them, so that if they should perish by long imprisonment or other want, it would be more grievous to them than all other accidents that might happen to themselves."

De Valdes made a plea that the price of ransom would reflect the fact that his mariners and soldiers were "very poor men, serving the King for four, six and eight crowns a month." The Council's "pleasure was to let go of the inferior sort for a month's pay or something more in respect of their charges," while "such as were found to be of quality and well friended in Spain should be detained, and exchanged for others of Her Majesty's subjects in prison and in the galleys of Spain, or else released for sums answerable to their vocations." De Valdes was permitted to send the Duke of Parma "letters of credit, to deal for the said ransom and for shipping for transportation of the prisoners into Spain." Haggling and foot-dragging between the Crown and Parma over the ransom to be paid continued for a year, but after he was warned that the Privy Council would "dispose of the prisoners" if the ransom was not paid, their release was finally effected on 24 November 1589.[22]

Pedro de Valdes himself was held until 1593, but found means to send secret dispatches to Philip which may have helped to rehabilitate him after the feeble surrender of his ship to Drake. He was eventually ransomed for £1,500; only Don Alonso de Luzon and Don Diego Pimentel had fetched a higher price. Richard Drake had charge of de Valdes throughout his long period of house arrest and when the Spaniard fell ill, Drake became so "fearful that the said Don Pedro would die and . . . that he would lose all the charges that he was at in keeping him" that he made desperate pleas for the ransom to be arranged. He may have galvanized the Council into action, for de Valdes was released not long afterwards.

All the Portuguese prisoners in English hands had been released much earlier, given their freedom "on condition that they should embark in Dom Antonio's fleet," sailing with Drake to Lisbon in January 1589. Most would not have had a long life in which to enjoy their freedom, for 9,000 men perished from disease during the disastrous voyage, and many of the Portuguese, already debilitated from their incarceration in jail, must have been among them. There were still Spanish prisoners in England in 1596, eight years after the Armada, and in June of that year the Privy Council decreed that the few remaining captives should be put in a "prison of severe punishment," in retaliation for the treatment of Englishmen in Spanish jails after the sacking of Cadiz. The last prisoners in English hands, a few survivors of the wreck of the *San Pedro el Mayor*, were not returned to Spain until 1597.[23]

CHAPTER EIGHTEEN

Queene Eliz: Riding in Tri=
umph through London in a:
Chariot drawn by two Hor=
ses and all ỹ Companies_
attending her w.ᵗʰ their Baṅers

The Disease Uncured

On the morning of Thursday 18 August, ships of the English Grand Fleet, battered by a storm the previous day, bore down on a north-easterly wind and began dropping anchor in harbours all the way down the East Coast. "My Lord [of Cumberland] bare with a pinnace into Harwich, I bare with some of the ships into Margate, where the rest be gone I do not know, for we had a most violent storm as was ever seen at this time of the year that put us asunder athwart of Norfolk." The same day John Hawkins led nine of the Queen's ships and another twenty-five armed merchant ships into Harwich. The Grand Fleet had suffered some storm damage but was virtually untouched by enemy gunfire. In a survey taken of the Queen's ships after they returned to port, all the requisitions were for "cables, hawsers, rope, &c, anchors and grapnels," plus a few longboats "lost at sea" or "not serviceable with a shiver [splinter] of iron in the head and one in the davit." Towed behind the main ship or stowed on deck, the ships' boats were always very vulnerable to battle or storm damage. The inventory of the *Elizabeth Bonaventure* included "a bloody flag" and a silk ensign "spoiled with shot," but with the exception of the *Revenge*, whose mainmast was "decayed and perished with shot," the masts, yards and timbers had suffered little more than normal wear and tear. However, every ship was almost empty of victuals, powder and shot, and riddled with typhus and dysentery.

As soon as they came to anchor, final reports on the outcome of the battle with the Armada were dispatched. Sir Horatio Palavicino reported an emphatic victory. "The enemy, without having attempted anything, have lost eleven or twelve of their best ships, that we know of; four to five thousand men, three parts of the King's treasure, which was divided amongst five vessels; are reduced to great extremity, not having a drop of water nor much victual, and very many sick, as all the prisoners report; so there is every appearance that very few of either ships or men will return into Spain." But not all were convinced that the final victory had yet been won. Lord Howard wrote to Walsingham that day, "in haste and much occupied . . . Some made little account of the Spanish force by sea, but I do warrant you, all the world never saw such a force as theirs was," though he could not resist adding, "let Mendoza know that Her Majesty's rotten ships dare meet with his master's sound ships; and in buffeting with them, though they were three great ships to one of us, yet we have shortened them 16 or 17; whereof there is three of them a-fishing in the bottom of the seas."[1]

Drake expressed general satisfaction at the outcome, but believed that the Armada would try to take refuge in Denmark, and though its losses were severe, after resupplying and refitting it might return to the attack. "We understand by several prisoners which we have taken that generally through all their whole fleet, there was not one ship free of sick people. Secondly their ships, masts, sails and ropes were very much decayed and spoiled by our great shot. Thirdly at Calais, by fire, we forced them to cut many of their cables, whereby they lost many of their anchors, which of necessity they must seek to supply. Further, if they had none of these great causes of distress, yet the winds and storm, with the wind westerly, as it was, has forced them there . . . I assure myself that whensoever Her Majesty shall hear of their arrival in any of these coasts, that Her Highness shall be advertised both of their great distress and of no small loss among them . . . We had no wind whereby they were able to recover any place of the mainland of Scotland . . . Norway or the out isles of Scotland can relieve them but with water and a few cows or some bad beef, and some small quantities of goats and hens, which is to them as nothing. And yet these bad reliefs are to be had but in few places and their roads [harbours] dangerous. The only thing which is to be looked for is that if they should go to the King of Denmark . . . he is a prince of great shipping and can best supply . . . great anchors, cables, masts, ropes and victuals, and what the King of Spain's hot crowns will do in cold countries for mariners and men, I leave to your Lordship, which can best judge thereof."

Drake warned that Parma still remained a threat. "Being so great a soldier as he is . . . will presently, if he may, undertake some great matter . . . My poor opinion is that we should have a great eye unto him." And with the other eye on Elizabeth's invariable tendency to mothball her ships at the first opportunity, Drake also warned that, though some "will say that winter comes on apace, my poor opinion is that I dare not advise Her Majesty to hazard a kingdom with the saving [of] a little charge." Drake wrote direct to the Queen that night, couching his advice in his customary guile and flattery. "We were entertained with a great storm, considering the time of the year, the which . . . has not a little annoyed the enemy's army . . . Their ships, sails, ropes and masts need great reparations, for that they had all felt of Your Majesty's force . . . I have not written this whereby Your Majesty should diminish any of your forces. Your Highness's enemies are many."[2] Walsingham echoed his concerns. "It were not wisdom, until we see what will become of the Spanish fleet, to disarm too fast, seeing Her Majesty is to fight for a kingdom."[3]

Some, less diplomatic, were bold enough to berate the damaging effects of Elizabeth's close-fistedness in the face of even this potent threat to her throne. "Our parsimony at home has bereaved us of the famousest victory that ever our navy might have had at sea." "If we had once more offered them fight, the General [Medina-Sidonia], it was thought by persuasion of his confessor, was determined to yield, whose example it is very likely would have made the rest to have done like. But this opportunity was lost, not through the negligence of the Lord Admiral, but merely through the want of providence of those that had the charge of furnishing and providing for the fleet, for at the time of so great advantage, when they came to examine their provisions, they found a general scarcity of powder and shot, for want whereof they were forced to return home . . . If we had been so happy as to have followed this course, we had been absolutely victorious over this great and formidable navy, for they were brought to that necessity that they would willingly have yielded, as several of them confessed that were shipwrecked in Ireland."

Sir Thomas Heneage, Vice-Chamberlain of the Household, reported the furious complaints of the Earl of Cumberland that the fleet had "not received a corn of all [the powder] that was set down in paper by my Lord Treasurer." He also complained that "having left the Spanish fleet for lack both of powder and meat . . . they [were] driven to such extremity for lack of meat as it is reported (I know not how truly) that my Lord Admiral was driven to eat beans and some to drink their own water [urine]." After perusing the reports, Walsingham concurred. "I am sorry the Lord Admiral was forced to leave the prosecution of the enemy through the wants he sustained. Our half-doings do breed dishonour and leave the disease uncured."[4]

With the immediate threat to England lifted but the Armada's whereabouts off Scotland unknown, the troops under the Earl of Huntingdon, Lord President of the North, were reinforced and word was conveyed to James VI that these armies were at hand to aid him in fighting the Spaniards if they landed, with the implicit threat that if James reached an accommodation with the Spaniards the same troops would be used against him. James meanwhile sent a message to Elizabeth enquiring when her ambassador's pledges to him of the Duchy of Lancaster and a formal announcement that he was her chosen heir would come into effect. Elizabeth delayed her response until the fate of the Armada was known for certain and then "told him she knew nothing about such a thing and repudiated her ambassador's promise." The ambassador in question, William Ashley, also received a letter from Walsingham, rebuking him for exceeding his authority, but it seems likely that this was for public consumption rather than genuine. It is inconceivable that Ashley would have made such offers to James without Elizabeth's express authorization. Whether her back-tracking afterwards was Machiavellian or merely yet another of her wilful changes of mind was irrelevant. By Elizabeth's calculation or her good fortune, with Spain defeated and his own Catholic subjects intensely hostile to him, James had nowhere else to turn but to his perfidious English ally.

Elizabeth and her Privy Counsellors now turned their attention to proposals for completing the destruction of the Armada and striking at the source of Philip's wealth. There was "great activity" to prepare the fleet for a return to sea, and so great was the haste that "all the beef in the London slaughter-houses and butcher's shops was taken and salted, leaving the town without beef." Sir William Fitzwilliam wrote from Ireland requesting Walsingham to "hasten five or six ships from Bristol to the Irish coast to destroy the 40 sea-beaten vessels returning into Spain." Even Burghley uncharacteristically urged the expenditure of additional money on the fleet, suggesting that "four good ships, well manned and conducted, might follow them [the Armada] to their ports, where they might distress a great number of them, being weather-beaten and where the numbers of the gallants will not continue on shipboard." Walsingham, equally out of character, rejected the suggestion. "Touching your Lordship's opinion for the sending of four ships well appointed to follow the Spanish fleet, I think, if it had been thought of in time, they might have been very well employed, but I fear it will now be too late."[5]

Seymour, still patrolling the Narrow Seas, dismissed any suggestion that he might pursue the Spaniards. "My summer ship, always ordained for the Narrow Seas, will never be able to go through with the Northern, Irish or Spanish seas, without great harm and spoil of our own people by sickness." "I hardly believe we shall find [the enemy and] this ship is not for the purpose, except she be presently mended and repaired; for our men fall sick by reason of the cold nights and cold mornings we find, and I fear me they will drop away far faster then they did the last year with Sir Henry Palmer, which was thick enough." Having ruled himself out of contention, he then urged immediate action to intercept the treasure fleet from the New World. "I fear them not this year, nor the next, if Her Majesty will not still be entertained with peace, but rather do proceed to intercept the India fleet [the *flota*] which is shortly to return."

The Queen expressed interest as long, inevitably, as it could be done without charge, but that prospect was faint. Howard "sent presently for Sir Francis Drake and showed him the desire that Her Majesty had for the intercepting of the King's treasure from the Indies . . . neither of us finding any ships here in the fleet any ways able to go such a voyage before they have been aground, which cannot be done in any place but Chatham and . . . it will be fourteen days before they can be grounded." Howard added a sarcastic reminder of the distance to the Indies and the proximity of winter. "Belike it is thought the islands be but hereby; it is not thought how the year is spent." The ships undoubtedly needed careening and rummaging, but even if they had been ready to sail there were barely seamen enough to crew them, and virtually no powder or shot to munition them.

The Queen did not deign to comment on the criticisms made of her own conduct of the war against Spain—assuming that any were bold or foolish enough to bring them to her notice—but she was apparently far from satisfied with the performance of the Grand Fleet that had saved her throne and her neck. Undoubtedly annoyed that so few prizes had been taken to fill the royal coffers, she demanded to know, among a lengthy list of other questions forwarded to Drake's brother Richard: "What losses of men and ships have been on the Spanish side . . . and what powder, munition and any treasure have been taken from them? What causes are there why the Spanish navy has not been boarded by the Queen's ships? And though some of the ships of Spain may be thought too huge to be boarded by the English, yet some of the Queen's ships are thought very able to have boarded several of the meaner ships of the Spanish navy." She also wrote to the Governor of Calais demanding that the galleass *San Lorenzo*, or at least its guns, be yielded to her, but that demand was met by silence.[6]

It was evident that neither the Queen nor her ministers had the slightest comprehension of the tactics that had brought her fleet victory—Philip of Spain's fighting instructions to the Armada showed that he at least understood them—and that the Queen's hunger for prize money to fill her treasury and jewels and gold to adorn her was at least the equal of that of her most avaricious admirals. Elizabeth wanted her realm defended but she would lay out the bare minimum to do so, and then she wanted a return on her investment, just as she did from her privateers. The carping criticisms of the way the Armada had been fought led Sir Walter Ralegh to publish a strong defence of Howard's conduct of the campaign, albeit one that did not see the light of day until after Elizabeth's death.

"Certainly he that will happily perform a fight at sea must be skilful in making choice of vessels to fight in; must believe that there is more belonging to a good man of war upon the waters than great daring; and must know that there is a great deal of difference between fighting loose or at large, and grappling," Ralegh wrote. "The guns of a slow ship pierce as well, and make as great holes, as those in a swift. To clap ships together without considerations belongs rather to a madman than to a man of war; for by such an ignorant bravery was Peter Strozzi lost at the Azores when he fought against the Marquis of Santa Cruz. In like sort had the Lord Charles Howard, Admiral of England, been lost in the year 1588, if he had not been better advised than a great many malignant fools were, that found fault with his demeanour. The Spaniards had an army aboard them and he had none, they had more ships than he had and of higher building and charging; so that, had he entangled himself with those great and powerful vessels, he had greatly endangered this kingdom of England. For twenty men upon the defences are equal to an hundred that board and enter. Whereas then, contrariwise, the Spaniards had an hundred for twenty of ours, to defend themselves withal. But our admiral knew his advantage and held it, which had he not done, he had not been worthy to have held his head. Here to speak in general of sea-fights (for particulars are fitter for private hands than for the press) I say that a fleet of twenty ships, all good sailers and good ships, have the advantage on the open sea, of an hundred as good ships and of slower sailing."[7]

Ralegh's views were not universally accepted, and ill-informed critics, at the time of the Armada and right up to the present day, have berated the English fleet's failure to sink more ships, and it is true that a mere handful sank as a direct result of English gunfire, but those critics have misunderstood the nature of the battle, the ships, the weapons and the men doing the fighting. At no period in naval history, not even in modern times, when the destructive power of naval weaponry is far in excess of anything conceivable in Tudor times, has it been common for ships to be sunk by gunfire alone, and wooden ships are naturally buoyant and very hard to sink, even when pierced by shot. A French ship of the Trafalgar era, captured by the Royal Navy and used first as a ship of the line and later as a training ship, was kept in use for another 140 years. In 1949, at the end of its long life, the rotting hulk was towed out to sea to be scuttled. Powerful charges of modern explosive were laid and detonated but the ship remained stubbornly afloat. In the end they "practically had to blow the bottom out of her before she went down."

Even if they could have achieved it, the intention of the English was not to sink the Armada. Most of the English ships were privateers, and although subsequent generations have hailed their commanders as great military strategists, the Elizabethan seamen were "sea-wolves that live on the pillage of the world," driven not by patriotism or altruism but by the profit motive. They were at war in defence of England, but not at the expense of their own financial interests, as is amply demonstrated by the behaviour of Sir Francis Drake and Lord Charles Howard when faced with a choice between the tactical interests of their fleet and the chance of a rich prize. Their business was to capture Spanish ships and loot their valuables, ordnance and cargoes, and even the Queen's ships were avid seekers of prizes, as much for their ever-demanding royal mistress as for themselves.[8]

In such a context, sinkings were not a success but a failure, for a ship at the bottom of the sea could not be plundered. The aim was never to sink the enemy ships but to cripple them, holing the hull, pulverizing their upperworks, blasting away sails, rigging and spars and inflicting casualties to the point where a ship was unable to make headway and could be isolated and forced to surrender. Some ill luck with the shifting winds off Flanders, the heroism of the Spanish fighting men, who, with the exception of Pedro de Valdes and a few others, appeared to prefer honourable death to surrender to the English heretics, and, above all, the shortages of munitions combined to prevent this from happening. The English fleet was forced to cease fire on several occasions for want of powder and shot, and finally to abandon the pursuit of the Armada altogether at the very point where the battle damage it had sustained at last made it vulnerable to wholesale capture or destruction. Had Howard, Drake, Hawkins and Frobisher been able to secure even one more day's powder and shot to complete the work begun at Gravelines, they would undoubtedly have reaped a rich harvest of Spanish ships and swollen still more the numbers wrecked on the coasts of Scotland and Ireland.

While arguments about the performance of the English fleet continued at Court, the Dutch advanced their claims for a share of the credit for the defeat of the Armada. "Although he [Parma] was ready and his soldiers embarked, he has been and now is so closely locked in by our ships . . . that notwithstanding all his force, we hope by the grace of God that he will be unable to come out . . . Our service in keeping and locking in the forces of the said prince has been the chief cause of the overthrow of the said Armada." However, they also expressed the very real fear that, deprived of a victory in England, Parma would turn his venom against them. "Your Lordships will also see how sure and certain it is that the Duke of Parma, understanding of the ill success of his enterprise against England will, in his fury, turn the great power that he has brought together in Flanders against this country, to revenge himself . . . for the loss and shame his master and he have had at the sea. We beseech your Lordships to . . . continue your favours to this afflicted country in the great need that now is, assuring your Lordships that on our part, we shall not fail to do the uttermost of our ability for the safety of Her Majesty and for our own safety."

Seymour was still maintaining his patrols in the Narrow Seas, despite being "famished for lack of victuals. Although the same have been drawn at length [made to last as long as possible] yet by increase of soldiers the same is all wasted." "This long foul weather past" had also caused much damage to the masts and sails of his fleet. He sent for a new topmast from Sandwich and begged for fresh supplies and munitions. Sir William Wynter echoed his concerns. "It were very necessary that victuals were provided, [and] munitions, powder, shot, match, lead and canvas to make cartridges, which are greatly wasted." Seymour ended with a statement that, while expressing a required continued willingness to serve the Queen in the present crisis, also revealed his absolute determination that it would be the last time he would do so. "Spare me not while I am abroad; for when God shall return me, I will be kin to the bear, I will be hauled to the stake before I come abroad again."[9]

Perhaps hoping to hasten his own return to England, Seymour also relayed Justin of Nassau's comment that Parma's fleet at Dunkirk did not "exceed 30 sails, altogether unfurnished of mariners, which he could never procure; so in his opinion his flat-bottom boats should never have enterprised anything upon England" unless the Armada had already defeated the English fleet. But had even part of the Armada still been off Dunkirk to protect Parma's forces from the Dutch flyboats and Seymour's Narrow Seas squadron, they would have found few other English ships capable of opposing them and, once they had landed, very few troops to block their march on London. The beacon fires had summoned the Trained Bands of the South West and South to the defence of their coastlines, and each in turn had armed themselves and assembled at their mustering points, then dispersed again after watching the Armada and the pursuing English fleet disappear up the Channel to the east, but Elizabeth's main land forces in the counties further east, where a Spanish invasion was most likely to occur, had been woefully unprepared.

Logistics, tactics and sheer common sense pointed to Parma choosing the shortest possible sea crossing for the cramped shallow-draught barges that would carry his invasion force. That indicated a landing in East Kent, as had indeed been decided. By 9 August the English forces should have known exactly where the landing—if it came—was to be made, for captured Spanish officers from the *San Lorenzo* had divulged that information. "He [Parma] would be in readiness upon Tuesday following and come and join with them with intent to come over and land their forces in England about Margate in Kent as since I have thoroughly learned of the Spaniards that were taken in the chief galleass that the King had, hard under the jetty head at Calais."

Yet Elizabeth and her advisers chose to base one of her main defence forces on a hill overlooking the bleak foreshore at West Tilbury in Essex, separated by some fifty miles and the width of the Thames estuary from the "Cape of Margate," and the planned "bridge of boats" that would have enabled them to cross from Tilbury to Gravesend was incomplete. The reason for the choice may lie in the information supplied on 7 June 1588 by an agent at the Spanish Court, stating that the "King's resolution is that . . . the Armada enter the Thames, which heretofore was intended upon the Wight and Portsmouth." The intelligence was partially correct—once the English fleet had been defeated, the Armada was indeed to enter the Thames, but only after landing the invasion force at Margate. Had the plan succeeded, a great part of the English troops assembled to repel them would have found themselves on the wrong bank of the river.[10]

Giambelli's boom to bar the Thames, fitted with explosive devices designed to detonate if rammed by enemy ships, and constructed from 120 masts bound together with chains and tethered by heavy cables to twenty anchors ranging from 500 to 800 lbs, had been constructed at the stupendous cost of £2,000, but had broken under its own considerable weight on the day it was completed, 31 July. Even if successfully repaired, "if two or three ships made of purpose should come against it with a full tide and a good strong gale of wind, no doubt they would break all and pass through." The only other defence of the Thames was mounted by William Borough in a decrepit galley, who was ordered to keep station at "Land's End"—the mouth of the Medway—commanding the Thames approaches. He was to give warning of the sighting of Parma's invasion fleet by firing his guns and was then to row upriver to Gravesend, resist with his guns as long as possible and then block the channel by scuttling the galley in midstream.

The mobilization of the land forces mirrored these half-measures. Orders were not issued until mid-March to arm 10,000 citizens of London. "Hardly 10,000 were found fit" and many received only bows and arrows. Nothing further was done until high summer, with the Armada already at sea, when attempts were made to form a reserve army near London, but only by stripping the surrounding counties of some of their forces. Militia commanders were instructed that part of their force was "to repair to the sea coast . . . to impeach the landing, some other part of the said forces to join with such numbers as shall be convenient to make head to the enemy after he shall be landed." The remainder, the greater part, was to be sent away from its home area "to join with the Army that shall be appointed for the defence of Her Majesty's person."[11]

On 28 June the Queen wrote to Lord Cobham, Lord Warden of the Cinque Ports and Lieutenant of the County of Kent, ordering him, "as the foreign army is already put to sea, to summon the best sort of gentry within his lieutenancy," and on 8 July she issued a general proclamation calling on the lord lieutenants of every county to prepare to defend their country, their lives and liberty and their true religion.

Three days after the first sighting of the Armada, her troops were at last summoned to the defence of the realm. Yet even in the face of peril no great urgency was shown, and, reluctant as ever to bear any cost that others could be forced to meet, Elizabeth left many of the militias in their home areas where they would be fed and funded by their own counties, since the Crown took responsibility for them only when they actually joined the national forces. Had Medina-Sidonia chosen to sail up the French coast, it is conceivable that the call to summon the militia would have come too late, with the Armada already at the door.

When the Queen's Lieutenant and Captain General, the Earl of Leicester, arrived at Tilbury, there was no camp there and no soldiers beyond his own small retinue. Work on fortifying the site did not even begin until 3 August. There was no food or beer, and no arrangements to obtain supplies, and even the royal warrant giving Leicester his commission to command his phantom troops had not been sent. The Essex men who were to join his forces were sent first to Brentwood, and finally appeared at Tilbury five days later, to Leicester's impotent fury. "If it be five days to gather the very countrymen, what will it be and must be to look for those who are forty, fifty and sixty miles off?"

By the time the Armada was off Dunkirk and there was a spring tide to give Parma a favourable crossing if he should venture out, 4,000 foot and a few hundred horsemen from Essex had arrived at Tilbury, together with another 1,000 foot soldiers from London, and enough equipment to arm them with at least some sort of weapon. "An estimate of the several sort of weapons of Her Majesty's forces presently at the camp at West Tilbury" included "32 Targets, 1,070 Muskets, 861 Halberds, 2,917 Pikes, 1,581 Bows, and 4,169 Calivers." But provisions remained in short supply and Leicester was still complaining that "I am here cook, cater and hunt" for his entire army. Some "brought not so much as one meal's provision of victual with them, so that at their arrival here there was not a barrel of beer nor loaf of bread for them." The shortage of beer was a potentially crucial issue; British soldiers and sailors had refused to fight in the past when supplies ran low. An expeditionary force of 7,000 soldiers sent to Spain by Henry VIII mutinied when they found that beer was unobtainable there, and an invasion of Scotland in 1542 was twice postponed because the beer ships had not arrived from London. When they finally did, they brought only enough to sustain a four-day campaign. Despite meeting no resistance from the Scots, the English troops retreated as soon as the beer ran out. The Scots mistook the cause of the retreat, launched a premature invasion and were then slaughtered on Solway Moss.[12]

On 5 August orders had to be issued forbidding any more troops to arrive at Tilbury unless they carried their own provisions with them. The next day a force of 4,000 men stationed near Dover, who had been neither paid nor provisioned, began to desert in huge numbers. Meanwhile, their commanders could not even agree on a defensive strategy. Sir John Norris argued for concentrating all the forces at Canterbury, as defensible as any town in the South East, to "stay the enemy from speedy passage to London or the heart of the realm." But the local commander, Sir Thomas Scott, preferred to draw up all his forces along the Downs, within two miles of the shore in order to make "a show" within the sight of the Armada, and was in favour of scattering contingents right along the Kent coast, so as to be able to offer at least token resistance wherever a landing was made. How Parma would have relished such a prospect. It was the traditional defensive strategy, employed ever since Julius Caesar's invading armies had been forced to fight their way ashore through the surf, but it was dismissed by Sir Thomas Wiltord, who recalled how "upon the firing of the beacons . . . the country people forthwith ran down to the seaside, some with clubs, some with pikes, staves and pitchforks . . . so inflamed with heat and fury as they would kill and slay all before they came near them, but if men might without danger see . . . how a few orderly soldiers would chase and pursue great numbers of the furious, inflamed, savage flock and herd, they would have second thoughts."

The influence of seasoned commanders such as Norris eventually persuaded the Privy Council to concentrate such forces as were available at inland mustering points from which they could march en masse to defend key areas, particularly the great ports such as Plymouth and Portsmouth. Whether such crudely trained militia, stiffened by veterans from the Netherlands campaigns—many of whom had already deserted and taken refuge in the Cinque Ports—would have proved much obstacle to the Spanish invasion force was another matter, though Parma certainly did not underestimate the fighting qualities of English troops. "If I set foot on shore it will be necessary for us to fight battle after battle . . . my force will thus be so much reduced as to be quite inadequate to cope with the great multitude of enemies." However, his comments about English strength should be seen in the light of his attempts to persuade Philip to defer or abandon the Enterprise of England until The Netherlands had been reconquered.[13]

In 1545, Henry VIII had marshalled 90,000 troops to guard the coast from Lincolnshire to Cornwall against the French invasion expected that summer. The army of 22,000 that Elizabeth had raised to fight the Spanish invasion was smaller even than the 28,000 men that she sent to crush the Rising of the North in November 1569. The great reserve army that was supposed to be established near Westminster to defend the Queen did not exist on the ground at all. However, London had 10,000 men in its Trained Bands and though its defences, ditches and walls were ruinous in parts, defensive lines had been laid out within the City and the old chains last used to bar the streets to Wyatt's rebels fifty years before had again been brought into use. Every householder was also commanded to provide himself with a leather bucket to fight fires.

Suspicion and hatred of foreigners, always high in London, grew even more marked, and those whose speech, dress or manner marked them out as strangers—whether Catholic or Protestant, Spaniard or Swede—were harassed, arrested or beaten by armed patrols and street mobs of xenophobic apprentice boys. "They care little for foreigners, but scoff and laugh at them; and moreover one dare not oppose them, else the street-boys and apprentices collect together in immense crowds and strike to the right and left unmercifully without regard to person; and because they are the strongest, one is obliged to put up with insult as well as injury." Other factions fought among themselves. In Southwark an exchange of taunts between the servants of Henri III's ambassador and those of Henri of Navarre—his retainers were called heretics and the murderers of the Prince of Condé, the ambassador's men were labelled papists, Spaniards and enemies of the Queen's Majesty—developed into a pitched battle with swords and clubs. It was easier to find "flocks of white crows than one Englishman . . . who loves a foreigner," and Spaniards had been the object of particular venom ever since Mary Tudor's deeply unpopular marriage to Philip. "The English hate us Spaniards worse than they hate the Devil. They rob us in town and on the road . . . we Spaniards move among the English as if they were animals, trying not to notice them."

The fear of invasion, compounded by the threat that an assassin might seek to strike down Elizabeth, just as William the Silent had been murdered, had kept her from her customary lavish progress through the southern counties that summer. Instead she remained in or close to London and her contingents of Guards. However, as reports continued to arrive that the Armada had been put to flight, Elizabeth took the opportunity to mount a pageant that was extravagant even by her grandiose standards. On 17 August Seymour had written to Walsingham that "The Duke of Parma has withdrawn his sea forces to Bruges and Dixmude . . . also news came to Calais that Breda was revolted . . . the withdrawing of the Duke's forces was either for

Ostend, Bergen-op-Zoom or Breda . . . It seems the Duke is in a great chafe to find his ships no readier at Dunkirk, also to find such discomfiture of the Spanish fleet at his nose."[14]

The following morning, Thursday 18 August, the same day that the battered remnants of the Armada were struggling through mountainous seas near the Shetlands and her victorious ships were returning to port, Elizabeth rode to the covered quay at Whitehall and sailed downstream in her royal barge through the heart of the capital, preceded by a boatload of trumpeters to herald her coming, and accompanied by the peal of the church bells throughout London. Only the deaf would have been unaware that Her Majesty was going to review her troops. The yeomen of her guard and the gentlemen pensioners of her household in their plumed helmets and half-armour followed in a fleet of other barges, past citizens lining both banks of the river and leaning from the windows of the tall houses on London Bridge as they passed by on the ebb tide. The summer heat and the breeze would have made the latter stages of the journey less than fragrant for the Queen, carrying to her the stench of the sprawling slums that spread eastwards from the Tower, "a continual street or filthy straight passage with alleys of small tenements or cottages builded, inhabited by sailors' victuallers, along by the river of Thames, almost to Radcliffe."

The Earl of Leicester awaited her at the camp at West Tilbury, with a force that now numbered several thousand men, though whether he would actually have led them into battle against Parma is open to question. His record in The Netherlands showed that he was sufficiently in awe if not in fear of Parma to avoid a confrontation with him, and his apparent preference was simply to retreat in the face of an invasion, laying waste the country until the Spaniards' lack of provisions forced them to withdraw. However, lined up at West Tilbury in troops of foot and of horse, his army made a proud show. The camp had been embanked and palisaded, and pavilions decked with flags and pennants had been erected to house the nobles, while ranks of green booths accommodated the common soldiery.

The Queen arrived at noon. Accompanied by her "court-like stately troupe," she was led along a raised causeway across the marshes. As she reached the camp on the ridge overlooking the lower reaches of the Thames, she was greeted with dipped pikes, colours and lances and a royal salute fired from the blockhouse. The thudding of hooves on the earth and the crash of cannon were so loud that "the earth and air did sound like thunder." Mounted on a solid white gelding, she then rode through every area of the camp "like some Amazonian Empress . . . full fraught with manly spirit." She moved among her ranks of soldiers accompanied only by a modest escort of four nobles and two pages. The Earl of Ormonde went ahead, carrying the sword of state. Behind came two pages dressed in white velvet, one carrying the Queen's silver helmet on a velvet cushion, the other leading her horse. The Queen's Captain General rode at her right hand. Once the Queen's favourite, Leicester was now white-haired and white-bearded, and forced to vie for her affections with the man who rode on the other side of her, his own stepson and the Queen's cousin, Robert Devereux, Earl of Essex, the latest "golden boy" in the long line of Court favourites who owed their position to their looks and their ability to be dazzled by the Queen's radiance on demand. The handsome twenty-three-year-old had already shown his mastery of his craft, telling the fifty-six-year-old, bald, shrivelled and gap-toothed Queen, "I do confess that, as a man, I have been more subject to your natural beauty, than as a subject to the power of the king." He was amply rewarded for his flattery and was already her Master of Horse and a Knight of the Garter. The great warrior, the Lord Marshal, Sir John Norris, marched behind them, and a standard-bearer completed the small procession, carrying Norris's colours from the Flanders campaign "all rent and torn and burned with bullets."[15]

Elizabeth was bare-headed, but her auburn wig was richly dressed with pearls—the symbol of virginity—and diamonds, and over her white velvet gown she wore a shining silver cuirass embossed with a mythological design, and she carried a silver truncheon chased in gold in her right hand. The sight of their Queen attired in a simulacrum of battle armour inspired her soldiers to cheers and expressions of their undying resolution and devotion to her cause, and when she later dined in state in Leicester's pavilion all the captains of her army queued to kiss her hand. Driven away in a coach ornamented with wrought gold, "diamonds, emeralds and rubies in checkerwise," she retired for the night to the nearby manor house of "Master Rich," Ardern Hall.

Elizabeth preferred "crafting bellicose ceremonies . . . martial pageants and mock battles" to the dangers and uncertainties of actual warfare, not to mention its prodigious expense, and she returned to Tilbury the next day to watch a march-past of her forces and a series of cavalry exercises and "combats with spear and shield." She was preceded to her place of honour by three sergeants bearing golden maces, nine trumpeters "bareheaded in scarlet coats" and a herald carrying a standard bearing the arms of England embroidered in gold on blue and crimson velvet. She made her carefully scripted and rehearsed great speech that day, expressing her own burning desire to play a part in a battle that she must have known was already over.

"My loving people, we have been persuaded by some that are careful for our safety to heed how we commit ourselves to armed multitudes for fear of treachery, but I assure you I do not desire to live to distrust my faithful and loving people. Let tyrants fear. I have always so behaved myself that under God I have placed my chiefest strength and safeguard in the loyal hearts and goodwill of my subjects. Therefore I am come amongst you, as you see at this time, not for my recreation and disport but being resolved in the midst and heat of the battle to live or die amongst you all and to lay down for my God and for my Kingdom and for my People, my honour and my blood even in the dust. I know I have the body of a weak and feeble woman but I have the heart and stomach of a King, and of a King of England too, and think foul scorn that Parma or Spain or any Prince of Europe should dare to invade the borders of my realm; to which, rather than any dishonour shall grow by me, I myself will take up arms. I myself will be your general, judge and rewarder of every one of your virtues in the field. I know already for your forwardness you have deserved rewards and crowns and we do assure you, in the word of a Prince, they shall be duly paid you."

Elizabeth's fire-breathing address to her army was entirely superfluous—the defeated Armada was already long gone—and whether the speech she delivered was really the one that has been handed down to us and quoted time without number is also open to serious question. The only eyewitness account was written by James Aske. He certainly mentioned the speech, and quoted extensively from it, but none of the quotations bears any relation to the words she is alleged to have used. Aske quoted her flattery of her troops' "loyal hearts to us their lawful Queen" and their courage against "fierce and cruel foes," and said that she pledged herself to march into battle alongside them like the Roman goddess of war, Bellona. She also promised that "the meanest man who shall deserve a mite, a mountain shall for his deserts receive." Many of her audience would have bitter cause to remember those words. The great, almost Shakespearian speech credited to Elizabeth was clearly intended for a far wider audience than the ranks of soldiers at Tilbury, and it seems probable that it was written and polished by others in the days following her visit, to "comfort not only the thousands but many more who shall hear of it." Copies were at once printed and widely disseminated, stirring many English hearts and burnishing still more the image of "Gloriana," the Virgin Queen.[16]

As she dined at Tilbury, word reached her that Parma was ready to come out of harbour on the next spring tide. Even without knowledge of Seymour's dispatch to Walsingham, it was an implausible claim.

With no Armada to protect him, the English knew as well as Parma how vulnerable his flimsy craft would be against the Dutch flyboats and the Squadron of the Narrow Seas. With equal implausibility it was claimed that Elizabeth had refused to desert her army in the face of the enemy—she had "a conceit that in honour she could not return" to the capital—but she then allowed herself to be persuaded that, at the least, Parma would not come out until he had news of the Armada, and on the Friday evening she went back to St. James's in her barge. Like so many of Elizabeth's actions, the Tilbury appearance had been pure theatre, mere show, and the speech to her forces that has echoed down the ages was a sham, delivered after the danger from the Armada had passed. The demobilization of her forces that began while her words were still ringing in their ears shows that she knew that as well as any. Such cynical exercises suggest a very modern queen, more surface and style than substance.

Within two days of her great speech, the armies at Tilbury and throughout the South East were being sent home, confirming that, for all the stirring propaganda, neither Elizabeth nor her ministers really believed that a Spanish invasion was imminent. Some 6,000 troops were retained at Tilbury for a further week, but they were then reduced to a rump of 1,500, and the casting of guns in the foundries of the Weald and the Forest of Dean was terminated soon afterwards. The demobilization went ahead despite reports from The Netherlands on 22 August of "intelligence . . . of the return of the Spanish fleet." Howard at once wrote a further letter to Walsingham "praying you, with all possible speed, to send down all the shipping and mariners from London that you can . . . powder and shot . . . pitch and tar," but Drake took a more sceptical view. "The uncertainty of the reports . . . make me rather to rest upon mine own conjecture than upon any of them, they disagreeing so much as they do, the one affirming that the Duke of Medina-Sidonia, with his fleet, is coming back again . . . the other affirming that it is for certain that the fleet of Spain is passed without Scotland for their way homewards." Drake also stated that if the Armada did return through the North Sea, it would not be to resurrect the invasion plan but because "the wind will not permit them good passage to go about the other way at this time of the year." He added that, even to attempt the crossing to England, the Spaniards would need the conjunction of "fair weather, the highest of a spring [tide], good wind and the Duke of Parma embarking all in one day."

The prospect of any return of the Armada became even more remote after the receipt of a report from the crew of a fishing boat off the Shetlands. On 18 August they had seen "a very great fleet of monstrous great ships . . . their course was to run betwixt Orkneys and Fair Island." With the wind blowing from the south-east throughout the following week, the fishermen believed that the Armada "could fetch no part of Scotland except some of the out isles." Drake counselled keeping a watch on Parma for another twenty days; after that the winter weather would be all the defence that England would need, although "it were good we saw the coast of Flanders as often as we might." Edward Wynter brought further news from Flanders at the end of the month. "The Duke of Parma is retired in some haste with certain troops of horse from Bruges, up into Brabant as high as Brussels, fearing, as it was thought, some sudden revolt. He has commanded such victuals as were aboard his fleet in Dunkirk to be unshipped, which they are now performing and already they have taken from many ships the sails from their yards. His mariners run away daily, many of whom he has caught and imprisoned sharply. They are all generally ill affected towards this service . . . Young Norris, that was sent after the enemy's fleet to discover which way they meant to take their course, brings certain news that he left them to the westward of the Islands of Orkney, which is their course directly for Spain."

Rumours about the return of the Armada continued long after its ultimate fate was known. As late as March 1589 George Clifford, Earl of Cumberland, was summoned to action "upon a letter from Her Majesty, commanding me to repair with my fleet to the road of Calais and to bring with me all such ships as I should find fit to do her service there." But most shared the belief voiced by one Spanish prisoner about the prospect of the Armada's return. "Those in the ship that he is in do say that they will go into the ground sooner than they will come such a journey again."[17]

Secure in her victory, Elizabeth had been further entertained by a series of reviews, pageants and jousts mounted in London by "the forces which had been raised by private persons"—the nobles and their retainers. The most lavish was staged by the Earl of Essex, involving "60 musketeers, 60 arquebusiers on horseback and 200 light horse," jousting between two of the Queen's favourites, Cumberland and Essex himself, and a series of mock cavalry battles during which "the musketeers and arquebusiers fired off their pieces at the same time. It was a beautiful sight." The rest of the populace was also given a spectacle: a series of public executions of men, and one woman, "condemned for being traitors and Catholics. An enormous crowd of people who were exhibiting every sign of rejoicing" followed them to the gallows, and a gentlewoman present who "said some words expressive of pity" was immediately arrested and imprisoned.

Several commemorative medals were struck to celebrate the defeat of the Armada. One showed Elizabeth in a triumphal chariot, holding the *Book of Common Prayer* in one hand and the palm of victory in the other, while on the obverse, fledglings in a nest fought off a menacing eagle. The myth of a "Protestant wind" that had blown the Armada to destruction was aired on another medal carrying the inscription "*Flavit et dissipiati sunt*" ("God blew and they were scattered"), even though on five separate occasions a "Catholic wind" had blown in the Armada's favour, not least when a sudden shift in the wind direction saved it from the Banks of Zeeland. Many Spaniards, including Cervantes, also sought to see the defeat in terms of divine, not human intervention. "What turns them back is the irresistible storm of wind and sea and heaven itself, which allows the enemy for a little while to raise its head, hateful to Heaven and detestable to earth." But it was not the wind that had wrought the Armada's destruction. When Burghley received a list of ships wrecked on the coasts of Ireland and Scotland, he wrote in the margin "but in truth they were lost in Zeeland" (i.e., in the fighting off Gravelines). Spanish and Portuguese ships had been strong enough to round the Cape, sail through the Straits of Magellan and survive Caribbean storms and hurricanes in the past. What brought them low was not the weakness of their construction, or the wild and unseasonal weather, or divine intervention. The main factor was undoubtedly the assaults of the English guns. That was why the Armada lost so many of its vessels while the English fleet lost not a single ship. Indeed, so superior were English ships, guns and gunners that in thirty years of more or less open war between England and Spain not one was ever sunk by enemy fire.[18]

Victory was not achieved because the English and Dutch were braver than the Spaniards, or because God was on their side. Neither was the Spanish defeat attributable to poor strategy or tactics, nor even to the sheer hubris of Philip II; such problems were not insignificant, but they could have been overcome. At root, the difference between the two sides came down to technology. English warships were faster, more manoeuvrable and armed with weapons that were, by the standards of the day, precision engineered, delivering projectiles with greater frequency, velocity and accuracy, over a greater range.

In our own era, wars between Israel and the Arab nations have invariably ended in Israel's favour. Once more this is not because they are intrinsically braver than the Arabs, or because God is necessarily on their side—as is usual in wars their opponents would argue the opposite—but Israel is a U.S. client state and has been equipped with weapons that are decades ahead of those produced by the Arab world's principal suppliers, the states of the former Soviet Union. In just the same way, the design of the warships, heavy weapons, munitions and gun-carriages of the English Grand Fleet in 1588 was not just years but two full generations ahead of those used by the Spaniards, who were operating ships that had not changed in significant detail in fifty years. Barring some catastrophic human error—and Elizabeth and her counsellors certainly did their best to supply that, for had the *Rosario* and *San Salvador* not been captured her fleet would have run out of powder and shot before the decisive battle of Gravelines had even begun—the technological advantage that her ships enjoyed was alone enough to guarantee victory.

During the autumn of 1588, a series of thanksgiving services was held at cathedrals and churches throughout England. A sermon preached in St. Paul's on 30 August praised "our great victory by [God] given to our English nation by the overthrow of the Spanish fleet," and a further service of thanksgiving was held there on 18 September. In Norwich on 2 October, "the day of giving God thanks for the overthrow of the Spaniard," "the great guns were firing salvos in salute all day long from dawn to dusk," yet the Queen still complained that "there has as yet been no Public Prayer and General Thanksgiving ordained" for the victory. A National Day of Thanksgiving, "a general concurrence of all the people in the Realm in repairing to their Parish Churches and giving public thanks," was duly ordained on 29 November 1588, St. Elizabeth's Day, "celebrating the return of the English Navy, the defeat of the Spanish Navy, news of disorders in Flanders and quarrels between the Spanish soldiers, their allies and the Duke of Parma, wherein is remembered the great goodness of God towards England."[19]

Five days later, on 4 December 1588, the Queen attended a final, triumphalist service in St. Paul's Cathedral. Shortly beforehand she was presented with the Armada Jewel, commissioned for her by Sir Nicholas Heneage and designed by Nicholas Hilliard. It was a double celebration, also commemorating the thirtieth anniversary of her accession to the throne on 27 November. Arrayed in silks and velvets, richly dressed with gold, silver and pearls, the warrior queen was drawn by a team of white horses through streets lined with "fair blue cloth," in a canopied, mock-Roman chariot, decorated with golden lions and dragons, and topped with an imperial crown. The Earl of Essex rode immediately behind her, followed by her ladies of honour. The Lord

Mayor and Aldermen dressed in scarlet robes awaited her at the Temple, and she led them in procession through the streets of the City to St. Paul's, followed by her Privy Counsellors, noble lords, courtiers, magistrates, officers of the Livery Companies, and "those who had been the instruments of so noble a victory"—by which of course was meant the admirals and high officers, not the fighting men. She paused frequently to watch pageants and hear the declamation of verses praising her wisdom and courage, but such was the continuing fear of insurrection or assassination that all the taverns and alehouses were closed and each householder whose property overlooked the route had to "stake his life and goods" on the loyalty of any people watching the parade from his house.

After arriving at St. Paul's the Queen knelt in prayer on the steps of the cathedral, allowing the assembled multitude a full view of her devotions, before entering through the great west door. Captured Spanish flags, banners and other booty from the Armada were paraded down the aisle and draped around the altar. Some doggerel penned by the Queen herself was sung in celebration of the victory, allocating the victor's palms in equal measure to God and his handmaiden.

> He made the wind and waters rise
> To scatter all mine enemies . . .
> And hath preserved in tender love
> The spirit of his turtle dove.

Following the service, the Queen dined in state at the bishop's palace and was then conducted back to Somerset House by a torch-lit procession through the gloom of a December evening. In all the paeans of praise heaped upon "Gloriana, the Virgin Queen," during the course of the day, the mariners who had won her battle and saved her throne, as many as half of them already dead of their wounds, starvation or disease, rated barely a mention.

A National Day of Thanksgiving commemorating both the defeat of the Armada and the accession of Elizabeth was celebrated throughout the remainder of her reign, and a re-enactment of the lighting of the beacons became the centrepiece of festivities in each town and village. The Stuart dynasty that began with the accession of James VI of Scotland, crowned as James I of England, following Elizabeth's death on 24 March 1603, had less enthusiasm for the continued celebration of a Catholic humiliation, and after the "Gunpowder Plot" of 1605 the commemoration of the Armada was subsumed into a celebration of national deliverance held on 5 November, the anniversary of the plot.

Although few today are conscious of the link to the events of 1588, and the central figure in the celebrations is an effigy of Guy Fawkes, it is thrown into a bonfire that echoes those beacon fires that blazed to warn of the coming of the Armada.[20]

Demobilization of Elizabeth's troops continued through August and September 1588, but it did not proceed smoothly. The familiar complaint, a failure to pay the wages owing, led some soldiers to sell their arms to raise the money to return home. The Queen responded with a furious proclamation against those who had "most falsely and slanderously given out that they were compelled to make sale of [their arms] for that they received no pay, which is most untruly reported." However, the allegation was true, and the only dispute was whether it was the result of Crown parsimony or the dishonesty of the soldiers' commanders.

Elizabeth meanwhile demanded an accounting from everyone involved in supplying the fleet. Hawkins was forced to justify and then rejustify every item of expenditure on powder, shot and supplies, the Earl of Sussex was subject to scathing criticism and ostracized at Court for answering Howard's pleas for munitions without the Queen's authorization; had he not done so, the Armada would not have been defeated. Even more outrageously, the victualler Marmaduke Darell was imprisoned in the Tower after exceeding his orders and purchasing more victuals for the fleet than had been authorized by the Queen. By restricting their victuals, Elizabeth may have intended not only to save money but to force her fleet to remain close to its base, preventing any further adventures on the coast of Spain, but the true effect had been to put her fleet and her throne in peril. And the debilitating effects of the weeks and months on short rations before the Armada had even appeared off the coast undoubtedly made a substantial contribution to the subsequent death toll from starvation and disease.

A hard-headed appraisal had been made by the Queen and her Privy Council as soon as her ships returned to port, and an order went out on 30 August 1588 to discharge the entire fleet except the Squadron of the Narrow Seas. From that moment on, she and her most senior courtiers showed no interest whatsoever in how that would be managed or what the effects might be, and no money to feed or pay her seamen was forthcoming. The Controller of the Navy, William Borough, went to St. James's for more detailed instructions, but after waiting in Burghley's outer chamber for some time he was told that "most of the navy should be discharged," and dismissed with curt instructions to "husband things as well as I could." Seeking further elucidation, Borough went to Walsingham's chamber but found him surrounded by other nobles and watching a "show of horsemen"—a victory parade passing in the street outside. Borough was ignored and left to reach his own conclusions; he and Elizabeth's other officers performed their unpleasant duties with such efficiency that the total paid in "rewards to the injured" came to no more than £180.[21]

By 14 September the numbers of ships and men at the Queen's charge had been reduced from a peak of 197 ships and 15,925 men to 34 ships—many of them keeping Chatham Church—and 1,453 seamen. But many seamen would not or could not leave their ships until they were paid. Sir William Monson argued that "it were better for them and much more profit and honour to the Queen to discharge them upon their first landing than to continue them longer unpaid," but it was not done. To her anguish and undisguised fury, Elizabeth was caught in a double bind. If the seamen remained on board, they had to be fed at Crown expense; if they were discharged, the wages owing to them became due. Both prospects filled her with equal horror, and her solution was to discharge the men unpaid. The pay—not that the majority received it in any case—of sick and crippled seamen was also stopped as soon as they were put ashore. As parsimonious as a pawnbroker even in the moment of victory, Elizabeth displayed an attitude that chimed perfectly with that of her Lord Treasurer, Lord Burghley, whose only published comment on the reports of the wholesale death of English seamen from disease and starvation was to remark that it should serve to reduce the wage bill for the fleet. Hawkins rejected any such idea. "Your Lordship may think that by death, by discharging of sick men, and such like, that there may be spared something in the general pay. First, those that die, their friends require their pay. In place of those which are discharged sick and insufficient, which indeed are many, there are fresh men taken, which breeds a far greater charge." And even dead men had wives and children.

His letter provoked an angry retort from Burghley, implying that Hawkins was lining his own pockets at the Crown's expense. "I am sorry I do live so long to receive so sharp a letter from your Lordship," the aggrieved Hawkins replied, "considering how carefully I take care to do all for the best and to ease charge . . . I do stay any payments saving sick men, such of the gentlemen that can be spared with their retinues, and soldiers, and discharge all the merchant ships . . . Some [seamen] are discharged with fair words, some are so miserable and needy, that they are helped with tickets to the victuallers for some victual to help them home, and some with a portion of money, such as my Lord Admiral will appoint, to relieve their sick men and to relieve some of the needy sort, to avoid exclamation [protest and riot] . . . It is impossible for me to spare time to peruse them but when the officers put their hands [sign their names] to confirm the pay books . . . that Her Majesty is charged with and no more. And I never knew yet any penny profit by sea books, nor know what a dead pay means, as it has been most injuriously and falsely informed . . . I pray God I may end this account to Her Majesty's and your Lordship's liking and to avoid my own undoing, and I trust God will so provide for me as I shall never meddle with such intricate matters more; for they be unbearable . . . if I had any enemy, I would wish him no more harm than the course of my troublesome and painful life."[22]

The following day, Howard wrote to Walsingham in response to orders to transport soldiers under the command of Sir Thomas Morgan to Sandwich. "I doubt much the soldiers will march before they have money . . . It is no small trouble that I have here in the discharging of ships of sundry places . . . to the westwards as far as Bristol and Bridgwater. We are fain to help them with victuals to bring them [there]. There is not many of them that has one day's victuals and many have sent many sick men ashore here and not one penny to relieve them." The ships from the West Country were ordered home, the crews unpaid, sick and dying, barely able to man their vessels, and carrying precisely one day's rations for a voyage of over 200 miles against the prevailing winds.

Howard and the other senior commanders did what they could to help their men. "I am driven to make John Hawkins relieve them with money as he can. It were too pitiful to have men starve after such a service . . . Therefore I had rather open the Queen's Majesty's purse something to relieve them, than they should be in that extremity; for we are to look to have more of these services, and if men should not be cared for better than to let them starve and die miserably, we should very hardly get men to serve. Sir, I desire that there may be but double allowance of as much as I [give] out of my own purse, and yet I am not the ablest man in [the realm]; but before God, I had rather have never penny in the world than they should lack." Lack they did, despite Howard's efforts. The discharged seamen had nothing to eat, only rags to wear and no means of travelling to their homes. Those suffering from dysentery and typhus were sent ashore to reduce further infection on board but were then left to their fate.

Fatalities in battle had been remarkably few, "the least losses that ever have been heard of . . . I verily believe there is not three score lost of Her Majesty's forces," but English seamen were now dying in their hundreds and thousands from ship's fever, scurvy and the bloody flux, a death toll exacerbated by the effects of starvation. By mid-September mortality rates, even in the flagships of the fleet—the *Ark, Revenge* and *Triumph*—were in excess of one-third. The *Victory* had lost 40 per cent of its 400-man crew, and the *White Bear* half its complement of 500. The placing of "six upon four"—six men sharing the rations of four to conserve supplies—was a routine practice on long voyages, but it was unusual for mariners in home waters to be subjected to it, and it had undoubtedly played a part in weakening the seamen and making them a more ready prey to disease. Poor sanitation was also significant and one commentator pointed out that "the ships commanded by the experienced old salts escaped comparatively lightly." Those that were most badly affected by typhus were the *Elizabeth Jonas*, the *Lion* and the *White Bear*, all commanded by kinsmen of Lord Howard with "no experience in the very necessary art of keeping a ship clean and sweet."[23]

During her speech at Tilbury, Elizabeth had promised her cheering men: "You have deserved rewards and crowns, and we do assure you, in the word of a Prince, they shall be duly paid you." The hollowness of those words quickly became apparent to the discharged seamen who had saved her throne. She showed an indifference bordering on contempt for the plight of the sick, starving and destitute men landed daily at ports from Harwich in the east to Plymouth in the west. In response to pleas from Howard, Hawkins and Drake, even the notoriously careful Burghley wrote to Walsingham, "What shall now be determined by Her Majesty I cannot judge, yet I mind to provide some money in readiness to be carried down to the seaside to relieve the decayed men for a time . . . yet I will not send it from London before I shall hear from you what you or Her Majesty shall think meet. My Lord Admiral I think will discharge all sick men and the refuse of the small vessels but being absent here alone, I dare not direct anything to him." Walsingham replied the same day. "For the sending of some money to the fleet for the relief of the decayed men, I think the same may be deferred until Her Majesty's return." Meanwhile "the refuse" would just have to starve.

Lord Howard was a man of notorious venality, hungry for prize money in his own right and also garnering a rich harvest of "tenths" from the prizes of others and pocketing bribes from those seeking commissions and preferment, or chasing letters of marque. His relatives, promoted by him to high positions, shared his preoccupations. "The pernicious influence of the Howards was a manifestation of the disease inherent in the system of patronage, a manifestation worse than most because the opportunities for private gain at the public expense were greater here than elsewhere and because the normal restraints of law and morality were more easily overborne where the proper business of all concerned was robbery with violence." Yet in the aftermath of the Armada campaign, Howard's actions on behalf of his men were entirely without thought for his own personal profit, and indeed cost him very substantial sums.

In the absence of word or action from London, he had made yet more pleas for provisions—"I hear nothing of my victuals and munition this night here, I will gallop to Dover to see what may be there, or else we shall starve"—but they went unanswered, as did his requests for the seamen to be paid the wages owing to them so they could at least buy food for themselves. He reported "the great discontentments of men here . . . who well hoped after this so good service, to have received their whole pay, and find it to come but this scantly among them." "There is a number of poor men of the coast towns—I mean the mariners—that cry out for money, and they know not where to be paid. I have given them my word and honour that either the towns shall pay them or I will see them paid. If I had not done so, they had run away from Plymouth by thousands. I hope there will be care had of it." The only reply he provoked from Elizabeth or her Council was a memorandum from Burghley, his resolve now perhaps stiffened by the return of his royal mistress, that in its smug complacency in the face of human suffering must have driven Howard and his fellow commanders to helpless fury. "To spend in time convenient is wisdom. To continue charges without needful cause brings repentance. To hold on charges without knowledge of the certainty thereof, and of means how to support them is lack of wisdom."[24]

The crews of the merchant ships fared even more dismally than those of the Queen's galleons. "These unfortunate men were, in word as well as deed, deserted by everyone." While the seamen starved on the docksides, their captains and ship owners made desperate but unsuccessful pleas for payment of money owing. Anthony Potts, owner of two ships "lately employed in Her Majesty's service . . . with victuals and the wages" of 100 men employed in them, had been "a continual suitor unto your Honours the space of six weeks past for such money as is due unto him, as well his great cost and intolerable expenses as also to the utter undoing of him and his for ever, by reason of his great charge and absence." The captains of Sandwich and Dover also complained that for four months they and their men had "dutifully and faithfully served Her Majesty . . . at their own great and excessive cost and charges . . . It may therefore please your Honour to grant speedy order for pay to be made . . . the great outcries and pitiful complaints of the poor needy mariners and soldiers, daily made for want thereof, cannot otherwise be relieved and appeased." Thomas Fleming, the man who had brought the first news of the sighting of the Armada, also sought payment for himself and his thirty-six men for "victuals . . . wages . . . loss of cables, anchors and masts, amounts to the sum of £70 at the least." Compensation for the vessels used as fireships was paid rather more quickly, probably on the grounds that if the Armada returned, fireships might again be needed and none would provide them if they knew they would not be compensated. In October Drake collected £1,000 for his 200-ton ship, the *Thomas of Plymouth*, and Hawkins £600 for "the Bark *Bond* of the burden of 150 tons," though an attempt by Thomas Meldrun to claim additional sums for the cost of six tons of beer, biscuit, beef and other provisions allegedly left aboard his fireship, the *Elizabeth* of Lowestoft, proved less successful.

Elizabeth's Privy Council also bickered with the county and town councils throughout the country over who should bear the burden of seamen's wages. Every port and coastal town had been charged with the provision, manning and equipping of ships to join the Grand Fleet. Almost without exception, they pleaded poverty, argued that they had been more harshly treated than their neighbours and petitioned for part or all of the cost to be met by the Treasury rather than themselves. It was not a course of action that was ever likely to appeal to Elizabeth or her Lord Treasurer, but while the petty wrangles over money continued Howard could only make another desperate appeal for help in the face of the suffering he was daily witnessing.[25]

"Sickness and mortality begins wonderfully to grow amongst us, and it is a most pitiful sight to see, here at Margate, how the men, having no place to receive them, die in the streets. I am driven myself of force to come a-land, to see them bestowed in some lodging, and the best I can get is barns and such outhouses, and the relief is small that I can provide for them here. It would grieve any man's heart to see them that have served so valiantly to die so miserably. The *Elizabeth Jonas*, which has done as well ever any ship did in any service, has had a great infection in her from the beginning, so as of the 500 men which she carried out, by the time we had been in Plymouth three weeks or a month, there were dead of them 200 or above. So I was driven to take out her ballast and to make fires in her of wet broom, three or four days together, and so hoped thereby to have cleaned her of infection, and thereupon got new men, as tall and able as ever I saw and put them into her. Now the infection is broken out in greater extremity than ever it did before and [they] die and sicken faster than ever they did . . . Sir Roger Townshend, of all the men he brought out with him, has but one left alive, and my son Southwell likewise has many dead. It is like enough that the like infection will grow throughout the most part of our fleet; for they have been so long at sea and have so little shift of apparel . . . and no money wherewith to buy it, for some have been— yea the most part—these eight months at sea. My Lords, I would think it a marvellous good way that there were a thousand pounds worth . . . of hose, doublet, shirts, shoes and such like sent down . . . for else in very short time I look to see most of the mariners go naked. Good my Lord, let mariners be pressed and sent down as soon as may be and money to discharge those that be sick here."

His attempts to fumigate the ships were almost pointless. The filthy rags the men wore, in the majority of cases the only clothing they possessed, were riddled with lice and fleas, carriers of the typhus that was killing them in hundreds and thousands. Others were still falling victim to scurvy and dysentery, and sour beer was widely regarded as the most likely source of infection and disaffection among the men. "The mariners have a conceit (and I think it true, and so do all the captains here) that sour drink has been a great cause of this infection among us . . . I know not which way to deal with the mariners to make them rest contented with sour beer, for nothing does displease them more." The belief may have been correct, as far as dysentery was concerned, for the European habit of flavouring beer with hops, which also acted as a preservative, had not crossed the Channel at this time and beer rapidly deteriorated, especially in the heat of summer.

Howard's pleas to the Crown once more went unanswered, and he next called a council of war attended by Seymour, Wynter, Drake, Hawkins, Fenner and Sir Henry Palmer, to discuss how the fleet was to be maintained in the face of the epidemics of disease. As soon as the discussions were over, he wrote to the Queen and the council. "My most gracious Lady, with what grief I must write unto you in what state I find your fleet here. The infection is grown very great and in many ships . . . it requires speed, [and] the resolution of Your Majesty." "The most part of the fleet is grievously infected and [men] die daily, falling sick in the ships by numbers; and . . . the ships of themselves be so infectious and so corrupted as is thought to be a very plague; and we find that the fresh men that we draw into our ships are infected one day and die the next, so as many of the ships have hardly men enough to weigh their anchors . . . The extremity being so great, the one touching the service of the realm, the other concerning the mortality and sickness . . . [that] fittest to be done is to divide our fleet into two parts, the one to ride in the Downs, the other at Margate or Gore-End, to bring our men . . . ashore and there to relieve them with fresh victuals and to supply such other their wants as we can . . . We do not see

amongst us all by what other means to continue this service, for the loss
of mariners will be so great as . . . it will be greater offence to us than
the enemy was able to lay upon us."[26]

Howard's prediction proved correct. John Hawkins's report on ten
of the fleet's great ships, written on 14 September, showed that only
2,195 of the original 3,325 men aboard them remained alive. That loss
alone would be bad enough, but fresh men had already been pressed to
serve aboard those ships and the figures also concealed those already
dead for whom their officers were still drawing pay, and those so ill that
they would not recover. Over the course of that summer, the total loss
of men on those ten ships and throughout the fleet as a whole cannot
have been less than half its original complement and may well have
exceeded it. The needless loss of so many seamen of such irreplaceable
experience was keenly felt throughout the remainder of Elizabeth's
reign and must have contributed to the failure to achieve further successes against Spain in the wake of the Armada's defeat.

In theory a seaman wounded in action—by which was meant an
injury of such seriousness that the man was permanently disabled—was
the responsibility of his home parish. However, few were willing to
meet the expense of feeding and housing such men. Some were given a
dispensation to beg for a limited period; Lord Howard issued a permit
for William Browne, whose arm was severed in the Armada campaign,
to beg "in all churches" for a period of a year. Another man, who lost a
leg in the fighting, was paid £1 13s 4d in full and final settlement—just
over three months' wages. It is a shocking indictment of Elizabeth's
government that, in some ways, these crippled men were the lucky
ones. Starving, unpaid, disease-ridden seamen still littered the streets
of the east coast seaports where their ships had docked, and any soldiers or seamen who complained about the Crown's treatment of them
or agitated for reform were subject to draconian punishment. The
Queen "does straightly charge and command as well soldiers as
mariners upon pain of imprisonment and such further punishment as
shall be thought meet to be inflicted upon such disordered and undutiful subjects to forbear from henceforth to make any such disordered
assemblies . . . Her Majesty commands them to repair out of hand to
the counties and places where they were last abiding and there to
employ themselves in dutiful sort according to their several vocations
and callings."

In the continuing absence of any positive action from the Queen or
her counsellors, Howard, Hawkins and Drake all drew on their own
resources to pay their men a pittance. Hawkins wrote a bitter letter to
Walsingham. "I would to God I were delivered of the dealing for

money . . . my pain and misery in this service is infinite . . . God I trust will deliver me of it 'ere it be long, for there is no other hell." He was forced to resign his post as Treasurer to the Navy in order to concentrate on salvaging his finances and laid the blame on "the last extraordinary accidents and charges about the late sea services . . . many great and unlooked for charges are thereby grown." His son, Sir Richard Hawkins, who commanded the *Swallow* against the Armada, faced the same problems during his own long service with the navy and it was said that his anger at delays in paying his men caused his death.[27]

Having exhausted his own funds, Howard used the only money to hand, the loot from the *Rosario*, to ease the distress of his mariners, but Elizabeth expected her full measure of any booty from the Armada and he was then forced to defend himself against accusations of profiteering at Her Majesty's expense. "I send you here enclosed a note of the money that Sir Francis Drake had aboard *Don Pedro*. I did take . . . 3000 pistolets as I told you I would; for by Jesus, I had not three pounds besides in the world and had not anything could get money in London; and I do assure you my plate was gone before. But I will repay it within ten days after my coming home. And by the Lord God of Heaven I had not one crown more, and had it not been mere necessity, I would not have touched one; but if I had not some to have bestowed upon such poor and miserable men, I should have wished myself out of the world."

Howard continued to display a concern for the welfare of his men that was not matched by Elizabeth and her Privy Counsellors. In December he brought Burghley the unwelcome news of a fresh "surcharge unto Her Majesty of £623 10s 11d, by reason of certain extraordinary kinds of victuals, as wine, cider, sugar, oil and certain fish provided and distributed among the ships at Plymouth by my order, and Sir Francis Drake's . . . to relieve such men as by reason of sickness or being hurt in fight should not be able to digest the salt meats at sea . . . these provisions were used for the relief and encouragement of such upon whose forwardness and valours the good success of the service did much rest . . . There was also a further supply of beer and wine distributed amongst the fleet by my order, which I have now caused to be stricken out of the book and for which I will make myself satisfaction as well I may, so that Her Majesty shall not be charged withal."

There is no record of Howard, Hawkins or Drake ever being reimbursed by the Queen for the considerable sums of money they spent from their own pockets to keep their starving seamen alive; as ever, the Queen was happy to see them and others absorb part of the cost of the nation's defence. The Earl of Cumberland, another who had emptied his pockets on her behalf, was still trying to obtain some recompense eleven years later. Adopting the guise of "a pensive and discontented knight at one of those romantic spectacles so fashionable in the reign of Elizabeth," he made a speech to the Queen bemoaning his misfortunes. "Is it not, as I have often told you, that after he had thrown his land into the sea [i.e., bankrupted his estates by equipping ships and even squadrons for the battle against the Armada and for a series of disastrous privateering voyages], the sea would cast him on land for a wanderer? . . . Has he not taken his fall where others have taken their rising, he having the Spanish proverb at his back that should be sticked to his heart 'Adelante los Abenstados'—'Let them hold the purses with the mouth downward, that have filled them with mouth upwards.'"[28]

Howard had received little popular credit for the victory. "They are speaking rather ill of the Lord Admiral, who they say did not do his duty. All the credit is given to Drake and there is a considerable amount of ill-feeling between them." Perhaps as a result of the criticisms, Howard had fallen out with his Vice-Admiral soon after the defeat of the Armada and became a powerful enemy of Drake at the Court, but despite their differences they did co-operate with Hawkins in ameliorating the immediate plight of Elizabeth's seamen and in taking steps to provide better care in the future. Hospitals and almshouses to aid "sore vexed, troubled, diseased and distressed" mariners had existed from the thirteenth to the fifteenth centuries, but had disappeared at the Dissolution of the Monasteries. In addition to their individual acts of charity, Howard, Drake and Hawkins now set up a fund for the "perpetual relief of such mariners, shipwrights and seafaring men as by reason of hurts or maim received in the service, are driven to great distress and want."

Established in 1590, the "Chatham Chest," named after the locked iron chest in Chatham dockyard where its money was kept, became a rudimentary health insurance and pension scheme—the first in the world—funded by deducting a small proportion of the wages paid to serving seamen and disbursed as cash payments for the maimed or wounded, pensions and even burial expenses. It continued to operate until 1802, when its funds were merged with those of the Greenwich Hospital. Sir John Hawkins also built a "hospital" (almshouse) for destitute seamen; it still stands in Chatham High Street. The hospital and the Chatham Chest established by Hawkins, Howard and Drake are far more fitting memorials to the brave men who lost their lives in Elizabeth's service than her own shabby treatment of them; "there can be no doubt that very many of those who fought the Armada died in misery, or were thrown penniless upon the tender mercies of the contemporary vagrancy laws."[29]

Elizabeth's indifference to the fate of her soldiers and seamen continued well beyond the Armada year. In November 1589 the Queen authorized "Lord Lieutenants of the several shires" to appoint provost marshals "for the apprehension and punishment of soldiers, mariners, and other vagrant and masterless persons and sturdy vagabonds," "these ragged rabblements of rakehells, that under the pretence of great misery . . . do win great alms," and Richard Williams of Plymouth was soon claiming payment "for a man whipped and sent away." Those who failed to enforce Elizabeth's commands were themselves punished. E. Langridge, Constable of East Grinstead, and H. Browne, Bailiff of East Grinstead, were indicted for "allowing some rogues or idle wandering people to walk and wander up and down," and by 9 December it was reported from Hertfordshire that "the county being cleared of many idle and vagrant persons, the provost marshals need only ride together three days every fortnight. Special sessions to be held for the trial of disbanded soldiers and vagrants."

Gangs of beggars and vagabonds were a common feature of both the country and the city throughout the Tudor era. Legislation specifically referred to "discharged soldiers or sailors" and sought to confine them to their own parish and punish those who refused to seek honest work, usually by "whipping at the cart-arse" (a phrase changed to "the cart-tail" by sensitive Victorian historians). Under Elizabeth, such vagabonds were "to be grievously whipped and burned through the gristle of the right ear with a hot iron." In 1591 more provost marshals were appointed "for the arrest and punishment of wandering soldiers, mariners, and other vagrant persons," and the Manor of Richmond issued a proclamation that "there is a wandering abroad of a multitude of people, the most part pretending that they have served in the wars, though many have not served at all, or have run away, and therefore ought to be punished instead of relieved. All such vagrants as have not been brought to sickness or lameness in the service, and cannot show sufficient passports, are to be apprehended and punished as vagabonds, and if they shall allege that they have been in Her Majesty's pay, and cannot show a passport from the Lord General or some officer, they are to be committed to prison, and indicted as runaways. Those that have served as soldiers, and can show their passports, ought to be relieved by some charitable means; but if they be found wandering abroad out of the ordinary ways mentioned in their passports, they are to be punished as vagabonds."[30]

Not until 1593 was any form of state aid proposed for those who had "adventured their lives and lost their limbs or disabled their bodies" in fighting for their country, with a bill "for relieving of poor soldiers and maimed mariners," but it had a difficult passage through Parliament. Robert Cecil reported on 28 March that no conclusions had been reached about how to proceed with the bill and it had been committed "to prison" rather than returned to the House, and he made an impassioned plea for its resurrection.

"I do not greatly marvel, though I am not a little grieved, that the good and Christian motion which has been made for the relief of poor, maimed soldiers has not taken such good effect as was both wished and expected . . . when we hear round about us so great a rumour of wars at home and are told of so great a preparation for war abroad, can there be a more seasonable time . . . for the maintenance and relief of such as, by the event of the wars, are deprived of means to relieve themselves? You have already and very dutifully yielded three subsidies for the maintenance of the wars. I pray and beseech you do not forget, nor neglect to make some kind of provision for the poor soldiers that shall return maimed out of the wars. Consider, I pray you, that we shall not provide for such as lose their limbs, for such as ventured their lives for their prince and country; for such as shall fare hard and lie hardly upon the boards or bare ground, whilst we, drinking wine, lying upon beds of down, sleep soundly and safely in whole skins . . . The poor soldiers you hear cry upon us daily in the street for relief. Assure yourselves they will cry out upon us, yea curse us, if we do nothing for them . . . It is to be feared if we give them no better encouragement, they will hide themselves hereafter when they shall be pressed or when they are pressed, slip or run away from their captains and leaders."

This last concern may have weighed more heavily on the legislators than previous appeals to their compassion, for within a week a new bill had been produced. "An Act for the Necessary Relief of Soldiers and Mariners" was voted into law on 3 April 1593. "A new bill for maimed soldiers came in this day . . . Every soldier maimed to repair into the county where he was pressed and to bring with him a certificate of his hurts and services, and every of these certificates to be first allowed by the General Mustermaster of England."[31] Every parish was charged with a sum weekly for the relief of sick, "maimed and sore hurt" soldiers and seamen, "which act is the first of its kind for this charitable and necessary purpose."[32]

Veterans of the battle against the Armada had waited over five years for some Crown relief from their misery, and many already lay dead. One of the beneficiaries of the new act, Robert Mackey, had been press-ganged into the navy at Wells in Norfolk, in early 1588. "During service against the Spaniards as a quarter gunner on the *Elizabeth Jonas* under the charge of Sir Robert Southwell, he was grievously maimed of both his hands, most apparent to be seen." Sir John Hawkins and William Borough, respectively the Treasurer and Comptroller of the Navy at the time of the Armada, had to present a signed "Certificate for the Relief of a Disabled Mariner" to the county treasurers in Norfolk, certifying that Mackey had indeed been maimed in the service of his country and not from some other cause. Upon receipt of this, on 9 October 1593, "Nathaniel Bacon, esquire, one of the treasurers in Norfolk for relief," was then moved of his charity to pay Robert Mackey 33 shillings and fourpence. Since the cost of feeding a seaman for a single day was estimated at between sixpence and ninepence, Mackey's windfall would have lasted him no more than two months. He made a ragged mark to acknowledge receipt of his money, presumably holding the quill pen between the stumps of his wrists.

Many counties showed a great reluctance to implement the new act. A "Memorial of an order taken for poor soldiers" complained that "the late statute for their maintenance is not performed in most counties, that the justices send them from the place where they were impressed to the place where they were born and vice versa, and refuse to sign their certificates so that they become vagabonds and the Queen is troubled, whenever she takes the air, with these miserable creatures." Not all were so callous and indifferent. The Commissioners of Charities enquired into the "abuse and perversion of charitable funds in the North Riding of Yorkshire. Know you that we, being moved with a most godly zeal to have all such poor, aged and impotent people, and specially soldiers and mariners . . . which have been or may be hurt or maimed in the wars for maintenance of God's true religion, and for the defence of us and their native country, to be godly and charitably provided for, relieved and maintained."

In 1595 the Mayor of Bristol was reminded that a hospital for seamen had once existed in the city and was ordered to re-establish it to accommodate seamen maimed in the Queen's service. It was funded by a levy on the Newfoundland fishing fleet operating out of the port. Further Acts in 1597 and 1601—the "Poor Laws"—amended the laws dealing with vagabonds and "wounded and impotent soldiers," and strengthened the duty of parishes to provide Poor Relief; parishioners who refused to pay could now be imprisoned. Vagabonds were still punished by whipping, with persistent offenders subject to banishment, but the death penalty was abolished for most vagabonds, though it was specifically retained for discharged soldiers wandering the country.[33]

The sufferings of Elizabeth's former seamen and soldiers had at last been addressed and some—very modest—relief introduced. They had to wait so long because there was no political will, on the part of their sovereign at least, to acknowledge the contribution they had made, or to alleviate their distress. The entire Armada campaign had lasted less than three weeks and the English fleet was rarely more than a few miles from its own coast. Even when at anchor off Calais or when pursuing the Armada through the North Sea, it was always in a position to be supplied from the nearest English harbours. In August and early September there was fresh food—meat, fish, grain, fruit and vegetables— in abundance; all that was needed was the will to provide it. If the Exchequer was bare, promissory notes could have been issued or Parliament summoned to vote an extraordinary grant in aid, and with the Armada defeated, credit was far easier for Elizabeth to obtain. There was no permanent infrastructure to handle the huge quantities of supplies that were required, but Marmaduke Darell and the Earl of Sussex had both demonstrated what determined individuals could achieve when faced with a shortfall in supplies for the fleet—and both men earned only brickbats from the Queen for their efforts.

The greatest English failing was not in the availability of provisions and munitions and money to pay for them, or of the means to collect and deliver them to the fleet. It lay in Elizabeth's wretched determination to pay not a penny more than she deemed appropriate. The result was that many of her seamen were either poisoned by their rank food, starved or fell easy prey to disease, and the fleet was deprived of the powder and shot with which it might have concluded the Enterprise of England in an even more emphatic manner. Her admirals, particularly Howard, were then subjected to endless sniping criticisms for failures that were not of their making.

In justification of her cheese-paring and parsimonious conduct, Elizabeth's supporters have argued that the poverty of the English Crown allowed no other course; it was a necessary and inevitable consequence of her lack of income. It is true that the Treasury was almost bare and foreign credit difficult to obtain at crucial periods, but she lavished money on herself—she had 3,000 gowns and 628 pieces of jewellery—royal progresses, extravagant shows and ceremonials, and futile military adventures for her favourites, while denying her fleet, her only real defence against the might of imperial Spain, the provisions and munitions it desperately needed. She also ignored the easiest way of raising additional funds—Parliament—because it would have insisted on a voice in how the money was spent. Since Elizabeth considered foreign policy to be the sole prerogative of "princes," she preferred to rule through her Privy Council and to exact "voluntary" donations from her wealthier citizens and "ship money" from her towns to offset some of the costs. The towns were told how many fully fitted-out ships they were required to contribute to the war effort; the gentlemen, merchants, traders and other solid and prosperous citizens were notified of the size of their voluntary donation and assured that Her Majesty's intention was to repay it at some unspecified time in the future. Few would have been so naive as to seek reimbursement.

Elizabeth's conduct before, during and after the campaign against the Armada has left a stain on her character that can never be erased. One choleric military historian has been savaged for his comments that "the woman who, in her imbecile parsimony, starved the fleet that went forth to fight the Armada, could not be expected to show better feelings towards the army. It was no thanks to the Queen that the Spanish invasion was repelled," but his intemperate and probably misogynistic criticisms nonetheless concealed much more than a kernel of truth. Elizabeth's vacillation and indecision before the Armada was launched left her country unprepared and stopped her navy from averting the looming catastrophe, and her parsimony even while the Spaniards were at her door so hamstrung her fleet that it was deprived of the chance to complete the Armada's destruction; but her actions in the aftermath of the battle were the most despicable of all. While her favourites and courtiers fawned upon her, lauding her courage and martial prowess, the naval commanders and officials who had done most to secure her throne were shunned and criticized, and the seamen who had risked their lives on her behalf were abandoned to their fate. Those few who died in battle or the thousands who succumbed swiftly to dysentery, typhus and scurvy must sometimes have seemed the fortunate ones to those who survived, unfed and unpaid, crippled, disease-ridden or starving.[34]

Philip of Spain insisted that his defeated mariners and soldiers should be fed, clothed, housed, and paid in full and more for their service to his Crown. Elizabeth and her ministers allowed the British seamen to die of disease or starvation aboard their ships, on the docksides or in ditches and hedgerows as they struggled to make their way home, hungry and dressed only in rags. Had her commanders such as Howard, Drake and Hawkins not used their own funds and, without Crown authorization, diverted prize money from captured ships to feed their starving sailors, the death toll would have been even higher. Elizabeth showed neither interest nor regret at the fate of her servicemen, and berated and even imprisoned those who exceeded their authority in attempting to care for them. Her callous indifference to those who had risked their lives to save her throne remains the most disgraceful episode in the life of Elizabeth I. That the English losses of personnel from ships that came through the battles virtually unscathed were every bit as heavy as those of the battered and shipwrecked Armada tells its own terrible story.

CHAPTER NINETEEN

The Spaniards bewailing
y misfortune of their friends

ＶＡＮＩＳＨＥＤ ＩＮＴＯ ＳＭＯＫＥ

Vanished into Smoke

Reports on the progress of the Armada had been received in London from the day of the first sighting off Cornwall. As it followed the normal track of ships heading east up the Channel, it had been in continuous sight of the English coast from the Lizard as far as the Isle of Wight, and every clifftop and headland was crowded with watchers. Supply ships and messengers passed daily between the south coast ports and the English Grand Fleet, and boatloads of volunteers and gentlemen spectators seeking a close-up view of the sea battles were continually heading out into the Channel by day and returning at night. East coast fishermen and traders brought further news of the later stages of the fighting off Gravelines and the pursuit of the Armada across the North Sea, until it disappeared over the horizon north of the Firth of Forth. Reports were slower to arrive from the north of Scotland and Ireland—it was late September before the first news of the disasters that had befallen the Armada on the Irish coast reached London—but Elizabeth and her Privy Council were far better informed than anyone else in Europe.

While this steady flow of news had been received in England, there was complete silence and ignorance on the other side of the Channel, broken only by the arrival of the *Santa Ana* in La Hogue and the news gleaned from the Armada's brief halt off Calais. It was known that the *San Lorenzo* had grounded and that fireships had been used against the Armada but the results of that were unknown, and all that anyone could say with confidence was that the English fleet had last been seen pursuing the Armada towards the North Sea. Parma had sent out pinnaces to scour the seas as far as Scotland in the north and Devon in the west, seeking the whereabouts of the Armada and bearing a letter urging Medina-Sidonia to return to Dunkirk where the invasion force was still assembled and waiting, but when the pinnaces eventually returned they reported that the great fleet had "vanished into smoke." Medina-Sidonia had kept Parma informed by dispatches about the Armada's progress as far as Calais but neither man had sent word direct to Philip, or to his ambassador in Paris. Isolated in the Escorial, Philip could only wait and pray for news. He ignored all state business except the procurement of supplies to be sent after the Armada, spent hours daily in prayer and ordered the Litany of the Forty Hours to be recited at every altar. His sentries watched the winding road descending to the plain 3,000 feet below, but the white, dust-laden surface shimmering in the fierce late summer heat was untroubled by any messenger bringing news of the fate of the Armada.

In Paris, Don Bernardino de Mendoza was equally desperate for word, and in the absence of hard news contradictory rumours grew and multiplied. Even intercepted communications and documents copied or stolen by his spies and agents could not be relied upon. Knowing that all communications were at risk of interception and that even their most closely guarded ciphers might be penetrated, both sides routinely issued a flurry of bogus orders and disinformation alongside their true communications, and Walsingham and Mendoza were both past masters of the art of laying false trails. Various sources reported that the Armada had achieved a great victory and was moving on unopposed towards its rendezvous with Parma, but others claimed that it had been destroyed and the remnants were fleeing with Drake in hot pursuit. Still others said that the Spaniards had already landed in England. Mendoza, who declared that he would forward his master's interests "even though I had to suffer a hundred waggons and cannons passing over my body," dutifully relayed the reports, adding always the rider that the stories were unconfirmed. He also remarked that the attitude of Henri III was notably more conciliatory and more respectful of Philip than had previously been the case, suggesting that the French king had also heard reports of English failure. Philip replied at once, "as you consider the news to be true I am hopeful that it will prove to be so . . . I am looking anxiously for the confirmation."[1]

On Sunday 7 August Mendoza received apparently more substantial news when one of his agents sent reports from several fishing barques that had passed through the warring fleets. It was said that Drake had fought the Armada on the previous Tuesday off the Isle of Wight. The battle had raged for a day and a night and the Spanish had sunk fifteen English galleons and captured several more, scuttling them after taking their guns. A large number of Englishmen had been taken prisoner after being rescued from the water. These reports were apparently confirmed by dispatches from Dieppe, where more of the Newfoundland fishing boats had landed. A Breton captain claimed to have been close to Drake's flagship during the battle and to have seen one of the galleasses bring down all the *Revenge*'s masts with the first salvo and sink her with the second. Drake had last been seen fleeing in a small boat. A broadside was being printed in Rouen to celebrate the great Spanish victory.

This time Mendoza passed on the reports without any cautionary footnote. He began talking openly of victory and had a huge bonfire prepared in the courtyard of his embassy, but delayed lighting it pending further confirmation. Similar reports came in from other Channel ports over the next few days, and Mendoza then left Paris to seek an audience with Henri III and demand his final submission to the demands of de Guise. While on the road to Chartres, Mendoza was overtaken by another messenger bringing reports that the Armada had reached Calais and achieved the rendezvous with Parma. It was said to be certain that by the time he received the message, Spanish troops would already have landed in England.

He forwarded the letter to Count Olivares in Rome, who sought an immediate audience with the Pope, claiming that Sixtus's pledge of one million ducats in gold, promised as soon as Spanish soldiers set foot on English soil, had now fallen due. Sixtus begged to differ. "When the terms of the agreement were fulfilled, he would give all he had promised and more," but until then, nothing would be forthcoming. "It becomes daily more evident that when he promised the million he did so in the belief . . . that the undertaking would never be carried through, and that it would serve him as an excuse for the collection and hoarding of money in all sorts of oppressive ways."

Mendoza met Henri III in Chartres on Friday 12 August, the day the Armada passed the Firth of Forth and the English fleet abandoned its pursuit. Under incessant pressure from de Guise and the Catholic League, the King had been forced into concession after concession and had signed the Edict of Alençon, pledging that "no heretic or supporter of heretics" would ever accede to the throne of France, but as yet he had made no further attempts to confront his Protestant heir apparent, Navarre, and yielded his ground grudgingly, perhaps still hoping for an English victory to lift the Spanish siege on his throne. Mendoza now presented him with a summary of the reports he had received and asked the King to order a Te Deum, a special service of thanksgiving for the Catholic victory, in the great cathedral of Chartres. He also suggested that now was the appropriate moment for Henri to return to Paris, putting himself even more at the mercy of de Guise.

The King demurred. "Your news, if it was certain, would be most welcome, but we too have news from Calais which you may wish to see." He then handed Mendoza a letter dated 8 August from the Governor of Calais, stating that the Armada had appeared in Calais Roads, hotly pursued by the English. The state of the rigging and upperworks of the Spanish galleons showed the damage that they had suffered from English guns. Gourdan reported that the Duke of Medina-Sidonia had asked for powder and cannonballs, which had been refused, but that provisions had been supplied. On the Sunday night the Armada had been scattered by fireships and had fled into the North Sea, save for one galleass which had grounded under the castle walls. The last sight of the English fleet had been as it sailed once more in hot pursuit. The only comment that Mendoza could muster was "Obviously our reports differ." He returned to Paris at once, where word reached him that both the English and the Dutch had captured two of the Armada's front-line ships. He sent another message to Philip warning that his previous reports might have been too optimistic, and the bonfire in the courtyard remained unlit.

During the next week the only further news was the curious claim of a skipper of a ship of the Hanseatic League that, while sailing south through the North Sea, he had entered an area devoid of ships and yet black with horses and mules, but the next group of reports once more raised Mendoza's spirits. Seamen in Dieppe were talking of a great sea battle off the Scottish coast that had resulted in over twenty English ships being captured or sunk. From Antwerp there were claims that Drake had had a leg blown off, Hawkins had been killed and Howard's flagship, the *Ark*, taken, one of 30 English ships captured, and that "four shiploads of killed and wounded have arrived at Dover." From Lille there were reports of 40 English ships sunk. "The great sailor John Hawkins has also gone to the bottom, not a soul having been saved from his ship." "The rest of the English fleet, seeing only ruin before them, escaped with great damage and their ships are now all in bits and without crews." A Danish ship's master claimed to have seen an English ship sinking, and one of the pinnaces Parma had sent to search for traces of the Armada reported a small group of English ships fleeing in disarray towards the coast. That was apparently confirmed by one of Mendoza's agents in England, who reported that 25 ships had been seen taking refuge near the mouth of the Thames. It was believed that this was all that remained of the Grand Fleet after a battle off Scotland on 13 August, in which no fewer than 15 English galleons had been sunk. Many others had been captured or so badly damaged that they had sunk in the storm that followed the battle, and the weather was all that had saved even the remnants of the English fleet from total destruction.[2]

Similar reports reached Mendoza from various different ports and cities and it is easy to see how the arrival of handfuls of English ships driven before the north-easterly wind that had brought them into port from Harwich to Margate around 18 August could have fed these rumours, particularly when the crews were then confined to their ships and refused permission to go ashore. Mendoza's informants went on to claim that the Duke of Medina-Sidonia had taken a Scottish harbour "in the territory of the Earl of Huntly and as most of the people are Catholics, it may be concluded that they will give all they have to Your Majesty's Armada." The Armada was refitting and taking on supplies while awaiting a north-easterly wind to carry it back to a triumphant rendezvous with Parma. The English Court was said to be in a state of panic. Talking or writing about the fate of the fleet was forbidden: "under pain of loss of life and property, no person is to write news to any part," and "a woman had been flogged for talking about it." The Queen had placed herself under the protection of her army and "the people of London were in such fear that though the officers of the law ordered them to open their shops, they refused to do so."

The version of events that Mendoza reported to Philip and then publicly announced in Paris as a torch was at last put to the great bonfire in the courtyard of his embassy was that Drake had been taken in the act of boarding the *San Martin* and was now a prisoner of the Duke of Medina-Sidonia. "Drake is captured. As yet the story wants confirmation from the Duke himself but it is widely believed and seems highly probable." It was certainly believed by the Count of Orgaz, who ordered Medina-Sidonia's administrator to organize a victory celebration. He lit torches and placed them in the galleries and windows of Medina-Sidonia's house and hired musicians to play for revellers dancing in the streets outside throughout the night. Mendoza's claim was circulated to every court in Europe and broadsides were produced in Madrid and Seville, embellishing and embroidering the stories. The legendary El Draque always featured prominently in them, sometimes wounded, sometimes fleeing, sometimes captured, sometimes killed, but still no official celebration was prepared. Spanish congregations were urged to continue offering prayers for the success of the Armada, and in one of the two poems he wrote about the Armada Cervantes referred to "the confused murmur of bad news" that was also filtering back to Spain.[3]

Brooding in the Escorial, Philip remained cautious, awaiting confirmation from Medina-Sidonia's own hand, but the Spanish ambassador in Prague, Don Guillen de San Clemente, was more easily convinced and ordered a Te Deum in St. Wenceslaus' Cathedral. Count Olivares returned to the Pope with Mendoza's further reports, urging a Te Deum in St. Peter's and in churches throughout Rome, the issuing of Legatine Bulls to the Cardinal of England, and the payment of the promised one million gold ducats, but Sixtus remained immovable. He heard Olivares out "without interruption, though he writhed about a good deal with inward impatience; but when I finished, his anger leapt out and he replied that he told me now, as he had told me before, that he would more than fulfil all he had promised, but I was not to worry him any more about the matter until positive news of the Armada was received."

Sixtus's own agents were offering contrary reports, and although on 17 August the Doge of Venice and his Senate had voted to instruct their ambassadors in Spanish provinces to convey their congratulations on the Armada's victory, Venetian informants were now hearing a very different version of events. Parma had swift evidence of the rapid change in European perceptions. He had to borrow yet more money in Philip's name to pay the Army of Flanders and interest rates climbed to extortionate levels as rumours strengthened about the Armada's fate;

Genoese bankers insisted on charging him 25 per cent interest on a four-month loan of "a million of gold."

The first substantial reports on the true course of events came when the Papal Nuncio, Morosini, obtained a copy of an English document, "Journal of all that passed between the armies of Spain and England . . . according to news from divers places." He at once forwarded it to the Pope. The document, closely resembling the "Abstract of Accidents Between the Two Fleets" that formed Lord Howard's report to the Privy Council in London, told a very different story from that promoted by Mendoza. If it grossly exaggerated the number of English soldiers under arms and the number of English Catholics flocking to support the Queen, its account of the battles in the Channel was relatively dispassionate.

Still the confusion persisted, and even in September, reports were still coming in of a Spanish victory. On the 4th the Governor of Calais relayed a fisherman's report that "Drake's death is confirmed from Holland," but as the days and weeks passed, the balance of reports shifted still more. "Certain Advertisements out of Ireland" recorded the shipwreck of many Armada ships and the massacre of their crews; news that was celebrated in every Protestant city. Another document, "A Pack of Spanish Lies," a detailed rebuttal of the broadsides published in Spain, was translated into every European language. By then confirmation of the real course of events was widespread. The Dutch published the interrogations of Don Diego de Pimentel and other Spanish captives from the *San Felipe* and *San Mateo*, and captured Spanish banners were hanging in St. Paul's Cathedral on 18 September. "There was openly showed eleven ensigns, being the banners taken in the Spanish navy, and particularly one streamer wherein was an image of Our Lady with her Son in her arms, which was held in a man's hand over the pulpit. The same banners the next day were hanged on London Bridge towards Southwark."[4]

In his darker moments Mendoza must have come to suspect the truth, and he was increasingly ridiculed on the streets of Paris by sarcastic requests for grants of the conquered English lands, but he still clung to his outward belief that the Armada had triumphed, hard though it was to reconcile with the reports that he also forwarded to Philip, warning that the English ships were regrouping and might launch a reprisal raid against the Spanish coast. The King took the warning sufficiently seriously to send out orders that any returning ships were not to disembark their men but remain at battle readiness to repel an English attack. However, Mendoza's optimism was once more to the fore as he sent a further report that the Armada had now completed refitting and reprovisioning in the Scottish islands and was making its way southwards, bringing with it a dozen captured English men-of-war. But on 24 September the dispatch that Medina-Sidonia had sent ahead of the fleet at last reached Philip's Court and the King received his Captain General's own report on the fate of the Armada. Even as a messenger was riding hard for the Escorial with Mendoza's dispatch, a further report reached Philip that the first battered remnants of his fleet had made harbour in Santander. When Mendoza's letter was delivered to him, Philip wrote in the margin, "Nothing of this is true. It will be well to tell him so," and on 13 October he commanded that prayers for the Armada should come to an end with a final solemn Mass.

Philip and his men had no desire to broadcast the true fate of the Armada, but news continued to spread, circulated by Venetian and Vatican agents and the triumphant Dutch and English. The final confirmation came from Ireland. All shipping had been embargoed in Irish ports from the moment when news of the sighting of the Armada off the Lizard had been received, but towards the end of October the Dutch, French and Baltic ships were allowed to leave on sureties that they would not trade with Spain, and they carried details of the catastrophe that had befallen the Armada on the Irish coast to every European port. The news was spread through Lisbon by a street cry:

> Which ships got home?
> The ones the English missed.
> And where are the rest?
> The waves will tell you.
> What happened to them?
> It is said they are lost.
> Do we know their names?
> They know them in London.

Those Portuguese street vendors must have recited the litany of Spanish catastrophe with particular relish.

Pope Sixtus found consolations for the failure of the holy crusade in the one million ducats he had been spared from paying Philip and in the humiliation of a king who was as much a rival as an ally. One can imagine the malevolent spark in his eye as he made his widely reported remark that it was "curious that the emperor of half the world should be defied by a woman who was queen of half an island." He had also avoided sending a Papal Legate to "openly avow the share he had in the enterprise," and when Count de Olivares pointed out how much he would have regretted not sending the legate if the Armada had been successful, "he replied that if the enterprise was ordained to succeed, the Legate would have been sent. He said this with great profundity and although I replied that it would have required a very prophetic soul to guess it, he only cast his eyes up to heaven and said no more."[5]

CHAPTER TWENTY

The Spanish fleet that remained, returned home disabled & with much dishonour

God Will Tire of Working Miracles

Riddled with fever and dysentery and weighed down with black depression, Medina-Sidonia had lain in his bunk ever since he had set course for home and he was too weak and dispirited to sit upright when his battered, listing flagship at last reached Santander on the morning of 21 September. As the current carried the *San Martin* towards the shore, her remaining powder was expended in a barrage of shots signalling her distress. Fishing boats at once put out from the port to take her in tow. A pathetic sight greeted them. The immaculate flagship of the Armada that had set sail four months earlier, her gilding and paintwork gleaming in the sunlight, banners, ensigns and pennants fluttering at the mastheads and the crimson cross of the Crusades emblazoned on her pristine cream sails, was now a wreck, weather-beaten, stained and befouled, the sails patched and torn, the rigging in tatters and the hull and upperworks pierced and splintered by shot.

The stench of death and corruption hung over the entire ship. Bodies in their hundreds had been thrown overboard during the long voyage home, but others still lay between the decks for want of men to move them, and those who remained alive were like living dead, gaunt, skeletal and fever-racked. Few could stand, let alone work the ship, and most were huddled in the reeking gloom belowdecks. The stench was so foul and the risk of infection so great that few of their rescuers could be persuaded to go down there, and such was his haste to be gone from the scene of his humiliation that Medina-Sidonia did not wait to see his men brought ashore. Even before the *San Martin* had been towed into harbour, he had clambered into a small boat and been rowed to the quayside. Head bowed, cloak drawn around him, he hurried away to find refuge without a backward glance.

Out at sea, the hulk *San Salvador* was in an even more parlous state. "There was not one drop of [drinking] water in the hulk and though both pumps had to be kept going day and night, they were unable to gain upon the leaks." Yet when four merchant ships were sighted, the *San Salvador*'s officers were unable to bear the exposure of their humil-iation and "wished to avoid them," letting them pass without signalling their distress. Twenty-four hours later they themselves sighted a dis-masted ship, "one of the best ships of the Armada, with three captains of infantry aboard," which fired a gun to signal for aid, but the men of the *San Salvador* maintained their course and passed by, unable to help themselves, let alone another ship. When they eventually made port in Santander, the holds were awash and the few survivors were more dead than alive.

Just eight ships had followed the flagship into Santander. Miguel de Oquendo landed at Guipuzcoa with five others and Diego Flores de Valdes had 22 ships with him when he reached Laredo. All were in a parlous state. Many had no anchors after abandoning them off Calais, and some had so few able-bodied crewmen that they could no longer be sailed. One of de Valdes's flotilla ran aground because there were not enough men to lower the sails, another grounded for want of the men to bring her to berth, and another capsized and sank in the harbour. The *San Pedro el Menor* ran aground and sank, and after anchoring safely, Miguel de Oquendo's flagship caught fire and blew up, killing 100 crew. Some of the great fighting ships, including the *San Marcos* and the *San Francisco*, were so badly damaged that they never put to sea again. Their guns and usable timber were salvaged and the rest was left to rot on the foreshore. Captain Bartoli, the commander of the *San Francisco*, died the day after the ship made port. The senior soldier aboard, Captain Gaspar da Sousa, stated that no ship in the Armada had done better service or been more frequently in the thick of the fighting and Medina-Sidonia confirmed as much in a letter to the ambassador of Florence. It was small consolation to the Grand Duke of Tuscany for the loss of his handsome galleon, once the pride of his navy.

Two dozen other ships of the Armada limped into port over the following days, weeks and months. Of the rest, over half the original fleet, there was no sign and no word. As time passed, news began to filter through to Spain of the fate of some of the missing ships. Some had "headed for Germany, others were driven onto the islands of Holland and Zeeland into the enemy's hands; others went up to Shetland; others to Scotland where they were lost and burned," and two of the Armada ships even reached Norway. But most of the missing ships had wrecked upon the west coast of Ireland. No fewer than 26 Armada ships were lost there, one on the English coast, two each on the coasts of Scotland, The Netherlands, France and Norway, two were taken as prizes by the English and an unknown number foundered or sank at sea. No precise figure for the total losses has ever been established, but a minimum of 40 never returned to Spain, and many of those that did were beyond repair and were broken up or left to rot. It is safe to say that, at the very least, half the Armada's 130 ships had been put beyond use by one means or another. English losses in the same campaign were nil.[1]

The losses of crewmen and soldiers were equally severe—"half the number of people do not return that came out in this army"—and thousands more must have died in the months following their return. "The like lamentation was never heard in Biscay and Asturia," and for months families of missing seamen and soldiers wandered from port to port along the northern coast, seeking any word of their whereabouts. Many families had lost every child, and some villages almost every one of their sons. In the end as many as two-thirds of the Armada's original complement of 30,000 men may have died, and for every one killed in battle or perishing later of their wounds, another six or eight died by execution, drowning, sepsis, disease, starvation or thirst.

Many of the able-bodied survivors took the first opportunity to desert their ships and flee for their homes, but the majority were too debilitated or diseased to follow their example. Still racked with fever and so weak that his spidery signature was almost illegible, Medina-

Sidonia sent appeals for food, clothing, bedding and medicines to all the surrounding towns and wrote a series of letters to the King, the Governor and the Archbishop of Santiago, begging for help for his starving men who were continuing to die in droves from ship's fever, scurvy and dysentery. "The troubles and miseries we have suffered . . . have been greater than have ever been seen in any voyage before, and on board some of the ships . . . there was not one single drop of water to drink for a fortnight." Many remained on board, unable to go ashore because there was nowhere for them to be housed and no money to pay them, and some ships were so destitute of supplies that men died of starvation even as they rode at anchor in their home ports. One had been without water for twelve days and its men were reduced to squeezing rainwater from their sodden clothes to ease their raging thirst. On Medina-Sidonia's own flagship, in addition to the hundreds killed or wounded during the battles, 180 men died of disease before the ship had even made port, and many more died as it lay at anchor. His servants "who once numbered 60, have died and sickened so fast that I have only two left." He ended his letter with a comment that from another hand could only have been blackly ironic: "God be praised for all He has ordained."[2]

In stark contrast to Elizabeth in England, Philip made every effort to ensure that the surviving seamen and soldiers from the Armada were well looked after. On learning that some were being discharged without full payment of their wages, he sent a furious letter warning that this was "contrary to Christian charity and also very much alien to my will . . . Those who have served, and are serving me, should not only be paid what they are owed, but rewarded as far as our resources permit." His envoy, Garcia de Villejo, was dispatched to Santander at once to supervise the provision of pay, lodging and clothing for the able-bodied survivors, medical care for the sick, and pensions for maimed soldiers and sailors, and for the widows and orphans of those who had not returned. Two ships laden with supplies were sent out to search for other ships of the Armada that might yet be struggling home.

The King's generosity was helped by the arrival of the *flota* in November, with a cargo worth one and a half million ducats in gold, but that barely began to repay the debts that the Enterprise of England had accumulated, and it is to Philip's lasting credit that he did not begrudge the cost of feeding, clothing and housing those who had served him. He and the survivors were also fortunate that the man deputed to help them, Villejo, was not only efficient but profoundly honest and decent too. His reports show the miasma of corruption, graft and double-dealing that surrounded government contracting in

Spain as in England, and his determination that the men should not suffer by it. The King also ordered several of the provisioning officers of the Armada to be executed as punishment for their corruption and their failings; the main supplier of ship's biscuit to the fleet, who was found guilty of adulterating the flour with lime, was hanged in Lisbon the following spring.

As soon as he had landed in Spain, the Duke of Medina-Sidonia, whose hair had reportedly gone grey during his time at sea, sent a plea to the King to be relieved of his command, so that he could return home to his orange groves at San Lucar. "Truly I have come back almost at my last gasp . . . I neither understand anything, nor want to." He also sent a plea to Secretary Idiaquez: "in his [Philip's] spirit of clemency, I hope that he will want only to be done with me . . . Insofar as naval matters go, for no reason and in no manner will I ever take them up [again], though it cost me my head." As Medina-Sidonia had hoped, Philip had no wish to be given further reminders of the humiliating failure of his great crusade by interviewing its commander—"I have read it all, although I would rather not have done, because it hurts so much"—and readily acceded to the request, even excusing Medina-Sidonia from the duty of appearing at Court to kiss hands.[3]

Medina-Sidonia had so thoroughly abdicated from his responsibilities with the Armada that he wrote to Villejo "that he had no instructions to give me . . . he leaves affairs in such a condition that I feel it my duty to say what I think about it. There are over a thousand sick and if the men be all disembarked at once, the hospital would be so overcrowded that, although there has been nothing contagious yet, I greatly fear that something of the sort will appear. It is impossible to attend to so many sick and the men are bound to fall ill if they sleep in the ships full of stench and wretchedness . . . we have 7,000 mouths to feed—2,000 seamen and 5,000 men-at-arms—and it is pitiable to see them. No one can believe that the arrival of this letter will cause matters to be remedied; but I write it, even if it is to be put into the fire . . . Pray do not think I am saying this to urge my own claims or anything of the sort. I know all about armadas and the expenses and wages attached to them; and until something serious is to be done, I would rather serve in the accountant's department, where if they do no favours, at least they deceive nobody with promises . . . I understand that there is a great deal of rotten foodstuff in the ships and I beg you to order it to be thrown overboard. If this is not done, someone will be sure to buy it to grind up and mix it with the new biscuit, which will be enough to poison all the armadas afloat . . . It would be very advisable to have a secret investigation of the notaries' books, taking them by surprise before they have time to ascertain what they have on board the ships, I think there has been a good deal of laxity in this matter . . . It would be advisable for the Alcalde of the Court, or of the criminal tribunal of Valladolid to be sent . . . This would avoid all the machinery of auditors, audiences, etc, and the mere presence of the Alcalde to look after people here . . . would make them all walk with their chins over their shoulders."

Despite the difficulties he faced, Villejo carried out his work with such efficiency that by 13 November, less than two months after the first ships had limped into port, every one of the returning soldiers and seamen had been treated for his wounds and ailments, fed, paid and found lodging. By then the Duke of Medina-Sidonia was gone. He had taken care to remain in Santander long enough to collect his own arrears of pay, the not insubstantial sum of almost 8,000 ducats in gold, and to make an unsuccessful attempt to claim an additional 20,000 ducats as a gift promised by the King, before departing for San Lucar on 5 October. Travelling by curtained horse-litter with a small escort and a mule-train to carry his baggage, Medina-Sidonia was taken home by a circuitous route, avoiding many towns for fear that the leader of the vanquished Armada might be abused and stoned by the angry citizens, as indeed happened at Valladolid. His cousin, the Constable of Castile, rode with him as far as Burgos, and Medina-Sidonia stayed with the Count of Oropesa when he reached the banks of the Tagus, but otherwise he seems to have avoided the houses of noble families, where he would scarcely have been a welcome guest; there were few in the whole of Spain who were not grieving over the loss of at least one son.

He eventually reached his home at San Lucar on 24 October and in time regained his health. He went on to serve Philip and his son, Philip III, for another twenty years but he never recovered from the blow to his honour and his good name; some of his critics even compared him to Sancho Panza. Nor had he seen the last of Spanish humiliations. In 1596 a huge Anglo-Dutch fleet of 110 ships attacked and captured Cadiz. The city was sacked and the treasure fleet burned by its own men before it could be captured. In all, 34 ships were destroyed and cargo worth four million ducats was taken, in addition to the value of the lost ships and guns. Medina-Sidonia, once more commanding the land forces of Andalusia, blamed the King's failure to supply money, guns or powder and shot, and the poor quality of the defending troops, but he did not enter the city until the attackers had sailed for home. Cervantes wrote a sardonic verse about the incident, ending:

Y al cabo en Cadiz, con muestra harta . . .
Triunfando entro el gran Duque de Medina.
And at last in Cadiz with a fierce display . . .
Triumphant, entered the great Duke of Medina.

As a result of this catastrophe, Philip was declared bankrupt for the second time in his reign and many financiers were ruined with him. But not even this humiliation could compare with that of the Armada. One French diplomat thought he could still detect the traces of the defeat in Medina-Sidonia's bearing and demeanour fifteen years after the event.[4]

Apart from the losses of men and materiel, the defeat of the Armada had eliminated Spain's officer class at a stroke. Santa Cruz had died before the Armada sailed, Moncada perished at Calais, de Leiva was missing, presumed drowned off Ireland, and Recalde and Oquendo both died soon after their return to Spain, the shame of defeat combining with disease and deprivation to hasten their end. After coming to harbour at Guipuzcoa, Oquendo remained in his cabin, refusing even to see his family, and died soon afterwards, on 2 October, probably of typhus. Recalde also stayed on board his ship, shutting himself away until death claimed him on 23 October, four days after his ship made port. Pedro de Valdes, de Luzon and de Pimentel were captives of the English and Dutch, and the Duke of Medina-Sidonia and Don Francisco de Bobadilla were destroyed and discredited by their experiences. "The flower of Spain's military perished in this Enterprise and through this disaster, God punished many sins committed by our people."

Martin de Bertendona was the only squadron commander still available for the King's service, for Diego Flores was in disgrace, incarcerated as soon as he landed, the penalty for the flawed advice that, as the King's chosen representative, he had offered to Medina-Sidonia. He had urged the abandonment of Pedro de Valdes and of other ships unable to maintain the Armada's pace, had issued the orders to cut cables off Calais that had certainly cost the fleet several other ships, and had been the first to argue for an immediate return to Spain following the battle of Gravelines. "It was known in Spain that Diego Flores de Valdes . . . persuaded the Duke to break the King's instructions, whereupon the King gave instruction to all ports where the said Diego Flores de Valdes might arrive to apprehend him." He was duly arrested and "carried to the Castle of Santander where he was not permitted to plead his excuse." His widespread unpopularity made him a convenient scapegoat, for none would spring to the defence of such a hated man, and he served three years in prison before being released, but he was the only one to face such public blame for the disaster.

Medina-Sidonia's attempts to lead by consensus and his unswerving adherence to the strategy laid down by Philip seriously hindered the Armada. A more resolute and self-confident commander would have known that, whatever their specific instructions, kings and princes have always abided by one overriding principle: they reward success and punish failure. Santa Cruz or Parma would have made their own tactical appreciation and then pursued the victory by the most appropriate means. If they had failed, they would have paid with their heads, but in victory they would have been garlanded with riches and honours. Medina-Sidonia's expertise lay in administration, not martial action, and with little personal experience to guide him he could only blindly follow the orders that his King had given him and the advice of the cabal of senior officers he had gathered around him. He also lacked the nerve—or hubris—that might have persuaded him to chance all on the sort of gamble that was second nature to Drake. As Medina-Sidonia's biographer concluded, "a reasonable man, he did not try his luck even when luck might have been his only chance."[5]

Despite bitter criticisms of Medina-Sidonia's conduct in dispatches sent by Recalde before his death, others, notably de Bobadilla, sprang to his defence and, perhaps mindful of his own role in forcing the office upon his unwilling subject, Philip offered no word of public criticism of the Captain General of the Armada, though some believed that only the intercession of Medina-Sidonia's wife spared her husband from further indignities. "It was not the want of experience in the Duke, or his laying the fault upon [Diego Flores de] Valdes that excused him at his return, but he had smarted bitterly for it, had it not been for his wife, who obtained the King's favour." Yet, whatever his failings as Captain General, Medina-Sidonia's conduct shows he was not lacking in personal courage and his flagship was always in the thickest of the action.

Although Philip sacked one of Parma's most persistent critics, Don Jorge Manrique, with whom he had almost come to blows when the Armada lay off Calais, it did not end the gossip and speculation about Parma, who remained under a cloud. Even allowing for the failure of communications with Medina-Sidonia, there were those—perhaps including Philip—who suspected that Parma, believing that the first priority should remain the defeat of the Dutch rebels, had deliberately allowed the Enterprise of England to fail. He could hardly be blamed if he felt resentment at his treatment by Philip. His years of service had brought him no present reward or future promise, his campaigns in The Netherlands had been disrupted and diverted by the requirements of the Armada, and its arrival had been postponed so often over the course of more than a year that his men had grown sick and mutinous and had deserted in huge numbers, while his constant battle for the funds to pay and arm them must have driven him to despair. Had he moved with less than his customary alacrity on this occasion, it would have been entirely understandable.

Drake, for one, was sure that Parma would bear the brunt of Spanish blame. "It is for certain that the Duke of Medina-Sidonia stands somewhat jealous of him and the Spaniards begin to hate him, their honour being touched so near; many of their lives spent—I assure your Honour not so little as 5,000 men less than when we first saw them near Plymouth—several of their ships sunk and taken, and they have nothing to say for themselves in excuse but that they came to the place appointed, which was at Calais, and there stayed the Duke of Parma's coming above 24 hours, yea, until they were fired from there." There was open speculation about Parma's fate in many European courts and Philip's son-in-law, the Duke of Savoy, at once volunteered to take over the command of the Army of Flanders, but Parma fought back with characteristic determination. He wrote to his uncle, a cardinal in Rome, urging him to defend his reputation, and sent Philip a detailed justification of his conduct, but as he awaited a response his thoughts must have turned often to his son Ranuccio, five years old when his father rode north for Flanders, whom he had not seen since then, and who lay at the mercy of Philip's garrison in Parma.

Ranuccio wrote to his father soon afterwards, warning him that his enemies were spreading rumours that he had betrayed Philip to Elizabeth and the Dutch rebels, and was to be made King of The Netherlands as reward for his treachery. In response, rapier in hand, Parma paraded his invasion troops through the streets and the Grande Place of Dunkirk and publicly challenged anyone to accuse him to his face—not as King Philip's commander but as Alexander Farnese—of sabotaging the Enterprise of England. None stepped forward, but the rumours continued. Seeking to widen the divide between Parma and his King, Walsingham sent word to him that letters taken from Pedro de Valdes showed that as soon as Parma had embarked for the invasion of England, he was to have been replaced as commander of the Army of Flanders by the Duke of Pastrana. Parma chose not to believe information from such a tainted source, but the claim was true. Once more Philip had offered no public criticism of Parma, but there was a widespread belief that privately he placed at least some of the blame on him. "In truth, neither his vessels nor his army were in readiness, which caused the King ever after to be jealous of him and, it is supposed, hastened his end."

Any criticism within Spain of Philip himself was inevitably muted; Spaniards knew well enough that voicing any complaints about their

King was treason punishable by death. It was left to foreigners, including a number of gloating Englishmen, to lay the blame for the failure of the Enterprise of England at the door of its supreme architect. Writing with the benefit of hindsight, Sir Walter Ralegh had no doubt where the fault lay. "To invade by sea upon a perilous coast, being neither in possession of any port, nor succoured by any party, may better fit a Prince presuming on his fortune, than enriched with understanding."[6]

Not since the Moors had conquered the Iberian peninsula had Spain suffered such a reverse and its aura of invincibility had taken a hammer blow. As Drake pointed out with understandable relish, "They did not, in all their sailing round about England, so much as sink or take one ship, bark, pinnace or cock-boat of ours, or even burn as much as one sheepcote in this land." Throughout Catholic Europe, critics of Philip found their voices and those he had opposed found renewed strength to fight back. On 29 August Parma had sent Philip a dispatch that was a formal acknowledgement that the Enterprise of England was over, at least for that year, and withdrew the troops gathered for the invasion of England from Dunkirk, but his attempts to use them to reconquer The Netherlands ended in another humiliation. They laid siege for six weeks to the town of Bergen-op-Zoom, the gateway to Flushing, but were comfortably held at bay and then forced to retreat by the onset of winter. It was, as Queen Elizabeth remarked with pardonable smugness, after rushing 2,000 troops under Sir John Norris to the defence of the town, "no less blemish" on Spain's martial reputation than the defeat of the Armada.

Philip's designs were also failing in Scotland and France. With masterly understatement, Mendoza passed on to the King a report from Scotland received in early September, that "the Earl of Bothwell killed Alexander Stuart, the man who had captured the Earl of Morton, and affairs were consequently becoming somewhat strained." Purportedly a Protestant and recently elevated to the title and made Lord Admiral of Scotland, Bothwell was secretly in Philip's pay. "The English faction in Scotland, knowing of the understanding" between the Catholic lords and Philip, were also "greatly oppressing the Catholics with the King's authority." Morton was in jail and Lord Claud Hamilton was "at Court, and has taken the Protestant oath, protesting that he did not do so voluntarily, but to escape further persecution." Robert Bruce and the Earl of Huntly sent bitter letters, reproaching Philip, Mendoza and Parma for their false promises. The Earl of Huntly could not "refrain from pointing out the long time that has passed since they first began to look for the reinforcements and the danger they are in . . . their King having embraced the English faction while they have declared themselves on the other side rather than violate their con-sciences, for which they have risked their lives."

Bruce and Huntly claimed that they "would have seized the King if they had means to resist the power of England or had any assurances that aid would be sent to them. Hopes were given to the Earl of Mor-ton . . . This is now more than three months since and there is no appearance of aid [from Philip] being sent . . . The country is in such a state that it cannot wait for the slow Spanish resolutions . . . In future it will be useless to write letters containing nothing but fair words, for these will never induce them to risk their homes and families. They wish to know first, for certain, whether the aid promised them is to be sent, and when." With 6,000 men and the promised money, they declared that "this postern of the island, which the Englishwoman fears to lose, would be assured to us and an entrance gained into England." Mendoza suggested that "as the Duke of Parma has so many troops, it would be well to relieve the country and provide winter quarters for them, which would prevent troublesome mutinies, by sending to the Scottish Catholic nobles the number of troops they request . . . It would compel the Queen to keep a standing army in the North, which would quite exhaust her, even if it only lasted two months," but no troops were sent and Philip's Scottish allies were left to their fate.[7]

In France, as Mendoza also glumly reported, Henri III was in high good humour and lauding the English success. "He said that what she [Elizabeth] had done lately would compare with the greatest feats of the most illustrious men of past times, for she had ventured, alone and unaided, to await the attack of so puissant a force as Spain, and to fight it while preventing the passage of the Duke of Parma's fleet . . . It had taken Your Majesty four years to gather these great fleets, which had been the wonder of the world, and yet it might be said that the Queen of England had triumphed over them." Henri also seized the chance to repay the Duc de Guise for his treachery; in December 1588, both he and his brother, the Cardinal de Guise, were murdered at Blois on Henri's orders, an eventuality about which Philip and Mendoza had been warning de Guise for months. Henri's action extricated him from the treacherous embrace of the Catholic League, and the death of his mother the following month also freed him from her scheming, but with Paris and most other French cities rising against him he was then forced into an alliance with Henri of Navarre. On 22 July 1589, Henri III was assassinated in revenge for de Guise's death, leaving the path to the throne open for Navarre, the close ally of Elizabeth of England.[8]

Throughout 1589, Parma's attempts to advance the reconquest of The Netherlands were hampered by a lack of funds and the Dutch naval blockade that prevented landings of Baltic grain. Coupled with harvest failures in the three previous years, it caused a famine in Flanders that affected Parma's troops as badly as the population. Then, in 1590, Philip ordered him to divert the majority of his forces to stem the military success of Navarre in France. In concert with English troops, Navarre had inflicted a crushing defeat on the armies of the Catholic League at the battle of Ivry and stood poised to take Paris. Philip was now willing to intervene openly, using Parma's army supported by papal troops and the forces of another Spanish client, the Duke of Savoy. Parma led his troops on a blood-soaked forced march through northern France notable even by the brutal standards of previous Spanish campaigns, and Paris was duly saved for the League, but a further intervention, in which Parma himself was seriously wounded, was necessary the following year to save Rouen from Navarre.

Philip's decision to intervene went against the hoary military dictum of never fighting simultaneous battles on two fronts and proved a fatal error, both weakening his effort in The Netherlands and failing to secure a Catholic victory in France. The depleted Army of Flanders mutinied every year from 1589 to 1602, and the Dutch recaptured lost territories and even had troops to spare to send to the aid of Navarre. Elizabeth also sent money, arms and forces to Navarre during the early 1590s. The Catholic League and their Spanish allies were defeated and Navarre duly claimed his inheritance, taking the throne as Henri IV and securing undisputed control of his kingdom by renouncing his Protestant faith; Paris was indeed "worth a mass."

Whatever trust had existed between Philip and Parma had long been shattered and at bottom Parma's continued loyalty was assured only by blackmail; his wife and children remained in his duchy a thousand miles away, at the mercy of a Spanish garrison. In June 1592 Philip summoned him to Madrid. As Parma well knew, it was a sentence of death. The Count of Fuentes was sent to succeed him in Flanders, with orders to ensure that the summons was obeyed but, campaigning in France and still suffering the effects of his wound from the previous year, Parma fell ill and was taken to Arras. There, like Don Juan of Austria before him, he cheated the fate that Philip had prepared for him, dying in December of that year at the age of forty-seven, almost fifteen years to the day since he had left Parma in the dead of night to ride to the Spanish Netherlands. In all those years Philip had constantly denied him permission to visit his home or see his sons, telling him that his elder son Ranuccio could manage the affairs of the duchy without him. As he died his lonely death, Parma's last thoughts must have been of his wife and the boys, now almost men, that he had left behind.

Spain's military success in The Netherlands died with Parma. The Dutch inexorably drove the Army of Flanders back on land, while at sea they remained the unchallenged masters of their coasts and also began to trade around the globe and launch raids on Spain's spice and treasure fleets and overseas possessions. A treaty of 1609 finally granted the Dutch their independence, bringing to an end forty-five years of war with Spain and with it the formal extinction of the dream of a "Catholic Atlantic empire" stretching from northern Europe to the New World.

As soon as it was clear that the Armada had been defeated, the thoughts of Elizabeth and her Council had turned to means by which they could further damage Spain. Their first success was to persuade the young King of Denmark to enter into an alliance with England and sign a pledge not to supply Spain with grain. Freed of their obligations to the defence of the realm, England's privateers also resumed business as usual, and in September Elizabeth issued orders to complete the destruction of the Armada in the harbours of Spain's north coast. However, frightened by the expense of using her own fleet, she first delayed its departure until the following spring and then insisted on sending Drake with a fleet of privateers. His orders were to destroy the Armada ships and then attack Lisbon in an attempt to install the Portuguese Pretender Dom Antonio as king, before embarking on the customary round of looting and prize-taking.

The voyage was a shambles, as one of Mendoza's spies in London had predicted. "These Englishmen, under cover of Dom Antonio, pretend to have great designs, but really will confine themselves to seizing ships and merchants." Drake did attack Corunna and destroyed three warships including the *San Juan de Portugal* and the *Regazona*, the flagship of the Levant squadron, but although the remainder of the Armada fleet lay virtually defenceless in Santander and Guipuzcoa (San Sebastian), Drake sailed at once for Lisbon. The attack was unsuccessful—he did not have the siege guns and engineers to breach its defences and there was no sign of a rising in support of Dom Antonio. Drake then set sail to the west to intercept the *flota*, but overcrowding and poor provisioning were already causing serious problems to the fleet. Food and water were very low and the crewmen were falling sick in great numbers, forcing the voyage to be abandoned without even reaching the Azores. Drake returned home empty-handed and with 9,000 men either dead or so racked with typhus, scurvy and dysentery that they had to be discharged.

The Privy Council was not slow to draw the obvious conclusion from the failure of the expedition: "This army was levied by merchants; whereas in matters of this kind, princes only ought to have employed themselves." Elizabeth ignored such oblique criticisms of her policy of "joint-stock warfare" but she had failed to reap her expected financial harvest from the voyage and showed her displeasure by banning the disgraced Drake from Court for four years. Nonetheless, English privateers continued to raid Spain's territory and shipping with considerable success throughout the remainder of Elizabeth's reign. Cadiz was sacked in 1596 and Puerto Rico put to the torch two years later.[9]

English interests might well have been best suited by an indefinite prolongation of the conflicts in The Netherlands and France, for defeat for Philip's forces in Flanders and his puppets in the Catholic League heralded an alarming resurgence of French power. Some modern analysts have claimed that Elizabeth's policy was to give the Dutch and the Huguenots enough support to guarantee their survival but less than enough to ensure a victory, demonstrating the sharpness of her analysis and the brilliance of her policy, but there is no evidence to suggest that she was doing anything of the sort. It would be far more in line with her conduct of other areas of policy to deduce that she was merely fire-fighting—reacting to events rather than seeking to shape them—with no overall strategy in mind.

There is no doubting the clarity of Philip's vision of his goals, or his willingness to expend his treasure to achieve them, and though his military strategy for the Armada was deeply flawed from the first, his parallel diplomatic strategy was brilliantly conceived. Potential opponents—the Turks, France, Denmark, Venice, the Palatinate—were neutralized or sidelined, potential supporters assiduously courted, and those who could bring military force to bear were recruited and mobilized. This wider strategy had only one flaw: its scale and ambition put it beyond even the financial capacity of imperial Spain. Had money been available, rebellions could and probably would have been fomented in Scotland and Ireland. The groundwork had been done and the Irish chieftains and Scots Catholic lords stood ready. Supplied with funds, arms and a stiffening of seasoned Spanish troops, they could at the least have proved an irritant and distraction to Elizabeth, diverting and dividing her forces, and it was far from inconceivable that Ireland would have fallen. The entire English garrison was fewer than 2,000 soldiers, aided by whatever additional men could be levied from the settlers in the Pale. Scotland was less easy to conquer, with a staunchly Protestant minority concentrated in the lowlands, but it was a state in name only, ruled by a king who exercised minimal control over his powerful and often lawless nobles. Once more, a rebellion required only the promised help from Philip, but the constant post-ponements of the Armada and the emptiness of the Spanish promises left the Scottish Catholic lords hopelessly exposed. Those who did rebel were isolated and hunted down, and the remainder nursed their grievances in private as the chance of successful rebellion passed.

The Armada itself was never equal to the task it had been set. There were insufficient warships and heavy guns to set against a far more technologically advanced opposing fleet, and the proposed ren-dezvous with the bulk of the invasion force broke every military rule and was quite simply unachievable. The crass omissions and contradic-tions in Philip's otherwise carefully thought out and crafted strategy have never been, and probably never will be, satisfactorily explained. Why did he repeatedly insist that the Armada should rendezvous with Parma's forces off the Cape of Margate when he knew that they could not put to sea without its protection? Why did he insist that the Armada was not to seek a confrontation with the English fleet when he knew that defeating it was "the essence of the business"? And why did he forbid Medina-Sidonia to capture the Isle of Wight or any other safe haven when it was the only means of safeguarding the Armada from destruction? The answers cannot be found in the realms of logic; they can only be attributed to Philip's frenzied haste to complete his ruinously expensive enterprise in the shortest possible time and his obsessive belief that God would produce the necessary miracles to guarantee the victory, no matter how flawed the strategy that his prin-cipal lieutenant, Philip of Spain, had laid down.

The failure of the Armada had dealt a blow to Philip's personal morale that at first seemed as terminal as the blow to his nation's pres-tige. Like most of his subjects, in the immediate aftermath of the return of the defeated Armada he gave himself up to grief and despair. Even those people who had not suffered the loss of a loved one went about their lives as if in mourning. On 10 November 1588, having heard the full extent of the disasters that had overtaken his Armada on the Irish coast, Philip was praying for death. "I hope to die and go to Him. That is what I pray for so as not to endure so much ill fortune." Yet just two days later he had decided to continue the war against Elizabeth and convinced himself that, despite the humiliation he had suffered, God remained firmly on his side.

As ever, Bernardino de Mendoza was urging him on, having set aside his own disappointment and restoked the fires of his hatred for a woman whose name he could not even bear to utter, calling her either "the daughter of the devil" or "the Englishwoman." "If it was impor-tant before to hold the Catholic nobles to their good resolve, it is doubly so now, and also to show the Queen of England that Your Majesty intends to assail her on all sides . . . She was so weak that her fleet which left port at the end of July was obliged to return on the 12th of August for want of victuals and stores. They had not even powder to fire after the combat off the Isle of Wight, until they took that which was on board Don Pedro de Valdes' ship. All this shows that the difficulty of reaching the place of combat in fit condition is much greater than that of fighting the enemy." His agents in England echoed his theme. "If the Armada had been conducted as it should have been and its commanders had taken advantage of the opportunities offered to them, the King of Spain would now be as much King of England as he is King of Spain."

The same source, the Genoese Marco Antonio Micea, reported that "the Queen is much aged and spent and is very melancholy. Her intimates say this is caused by the death of the Earl of Leicester, but it is very evident that it is rather the fear she underwent and the burden she has upon her. In order to send 1,500 men to Bergen she had to bleed at every pore and even then she could not get them together. Those that went had to be driven on board with cudgels." Micea also raised the possibility of invading Ireland. "If the King of Spain wishes to see the Queen of England dead, with the Treasurer, Walsingham and all the Council . . . if he wants to stop them from molesting them in the Indies or Portugal, let him send 3,000 or 4,000 men to Ireland . . . this is the only thing that the English fear and the real true way to take this country with little risk and trouble, and if a part of the Armada were to effect this, they would find it a very different matter from attacking this country." The King annotated this with his standard exclamation, "*Ojo!*" and added, "This would be a very important matter."[10]

Before the year was out, Philip was laying plans for a further armada to achieve the success that had eluded its predecessor and fulfil his destiny as the warrior of Christ. An English spy, Anthony Copley, reported that Philip had sworn "a great oath that he would waste and consume his Crown . . . but either he would utterly ruin Her Majesty and England, or else himself and all Spain become tributary to her." Others reported a more phlegmatic response to the manifestation of God's will, but Philip's repeated attempts to bring about the downfall of Elizabeth during the remaining decade of his life seem to bear out Copley's version of events. Each reverse only served to strengthen Philip's belief in his God-given destiny and further armadas were launched without apparent thought to the season, the weather or the prospects of success.

In late 1588 Philip entered discussions with one of his few surviving senior officers, Martin de Bertendona, on a better means of landing an invasion force in England. At the same time, the richest cities of his dominions were persuaded to pledge millions of ducats towards the cost of a fleet of a dozen new galleons, the "Twelve Apostles," constructed on the English race-built model and armed with powerful cannons and culverins. In the decade following the Armada year, a further sixty new warships were constructed. "Great thanks do I render unto Almighty God," Philip wrote, "by whose generous hand I am gifted with such power that I could easily, if I chose, place another fleet upon the seas. Nor is it of very great importance that a running stream should sometimes be intercepted, so long as the fountain from which it flows remains inexhaustible." The flow of gold and silver from the New World, and Catholic volunteers and pressed men, would continue throughout his reign. Many, many more would go to their deaths pursuing Philip's impossible dream.[11]

If Philip's European plans unravelled in the wake of the Armada, as he lost control of The Netherlands and France and saw his dreams of an empire stretching from the Baltic to the New World ended for ever, Spain grew more, not less, powerful at sea over the following decades, before finally ceding military supremacy to France in the mid-seventeenth century. But in economic terms the Armada defeat and the privateering "war" that both preceded it and continued long after 1588 was much more decisive. Although the English privateers never succeeded in capturing the treasure fleet or cutting off the supply of silver to Spain, the constant attrition of lost ships had a considerable cumulative impact on the Spanish economy. Well over a thousand ships—galleons, carracks, merchantmen, hulks and pinnaces—were captured or sunk during the period of hostilities and no economy, not even that of Imperial Spain, could sustain such losses indefinitely. Spain became "utterly without [merchant] shipping of regard . . . how many millions we have taken from the Spaniard is a thing notorious," and as more and more ships were diverted to the vital convoys to and from the New World, the control of first European and then international trade was effectively handed to Spain's competitors. The great Spanish and Portuguese merchant fleets had almost ceased to exist by the end of Philip's reign, at the same time as those of his European competitors were rapidly expanding. Before many years had elapsed, merchants from England, The Netherlands and France had established a near-complete dominance of trade, not only in Europe but in the New World, Africa and the Far East as well.

Four other Spanish armadas were launched. In 1596 the bizarre decision to sail in November was rewarded by the Second Armada's being wrecked by a winter storm before it had even left Spanish waters. In the following year the Third Armada was assembled to land a 6,000-strong invasion force at Falmouth, but yet again its departure was unaccountably delayed until 9 October, and though the first ships sailed to within twenty miles of the Lizard, a north-easterly gale battered and scattered the fleet, forcing the remnants to return home unsuccessful once more. The Fourth Armada sailed undetected the length of the Channel to reach the safety of Calais in February 1598, but though its arrival provoked panic in London, its target was not the invasion of England but the reinforcement of the Spanish Army in Flanders, to increase the pressure on Henri IV of France in peace negotiations. The Peace of Vervins was duly signed in April, leading Elizabeth to call Henri "the antichrist of ingratitude" for turning his back on her after she had supported him—albeit with great reluctance—for years.

Philip died the same year and was interred in a coffin made from the keel of a Spanish galleon—at least one Armada ship had arrived unscathed at its final resting place—but three years after his death his son, Philip III, continued his father's grand ambition by sending the Fifth Armada to support the revolt of the Earl of Tyrone in Ireland. Tyrone had cut a swathe through the English troops garrisoned there, but just as in both Scotland and Ireland at the time of the First Armada, the King of Spain had promised much and delivered nothing but useless blessings, letters of encouragement, small gifts and portraits of himself. Elizabeth so forgot herself that she poured in money and men on a scale that dwarfed any of her previous military adventures, even including the war in The Netherlands—she spent £1.8 million on the war in Ireland between 1595 and 1603, compared to an average annual cost of around £100,000 when the war in The Netherlands was at its peak. The tide of the conflict had turned and Philip, like his father, had delayed and prevaricated too long. Once more the Armada was a humiliating failure. The rebellion was already faltering and was brutally repressed, many Spaniards were killed and the remainder surrendered.[12]

The Duke of Parma had once warned Philip II that "God will tire of working miracles for us." His remark was prophetic; in 1588, and on each subsequent occasion when an armada was launched against England, the confident hope of a miracle proved to be nothing more than a foolish delusion.

$\mathcal{N}otes$

ABBREVIATIONS OF SOURCES CITED

CSPD Calendar of State Papers, Domestic
CSPF Calendar of State Papers, Foreign
CSPI Calendar of State Papers, Irish
CSPS Calendar of State Papers, Spanish
CSPV Calendar of State Papers, Venetian
PRO SP Public Record Office (now The National Archives), Special Papers
SPD State Papers, Domestic

CHAPTER ONE:

God's Obvious Design

1 M. M. Maxwell-Scott, *The Tragedy of Fotheringay*, appendices; Yelverton MSS.
2 Luis de Gongora, "Herman Perico," in *Obras Completas.*
3 Alison Weir, *The Life of Elizabeth I*, p. 32; Sir Robert Naunton, *Fragmenta Regalia;* H. R. Fox Bourne, *English Seamen under the Tudors*, vol. 2, p. 152.
4 Cecil to Walsingham, CSPD; Conyers Read, *Lord Burghley*, p. 87.
5 Sir Francis Englefield to the Queen of Scots, 9 October 1584, Lansdowne MS 96.12; Neville Williams, *All the Queen's Men*, p. 198; David Cressy, "Binding the Nation," pp. 217–34.
6 Folger Shakespeare Library, MS V.b.142, f. 26.
7 Cecil to Walsingham, CSPD.
8 Weir, op. cit., pp. 129, 195; Winston Graham, *The Spanish Armadas*, p. 55.
9 Ronald H. Fritze (ed.), *Historical Dictionary of Tudor England*, p. 43; Robert Dudley, *Correspondence*, p. 342.
10 PRO SP 12/194/30; Bernardino de Mendoza to the King, 7 February 1587, CSPS iv 15; Sir John E. Neale, *Elizabeth and Her Parliaments*, vol. 2, p. 129.
11 Bernardino de Mendoza to the King, 28 February 1587, CSPS iv 28; Neale, op. cit., p. 137; Read, op. cit., pp. 366–70.
12 Maxwell-Scott, op. cit., p. 239; Ashmole MS 830, f. 13.
13 Report to Lord Burghley, endorsed in his hand, 8 Feb. 1586 (o.s.). Printed in

Sir Henry Ellis, *Original Letters*, Second Series; Chantelauze, quoted in Maxwell-Scott, op. cit.

14 William Camden, *History*, vol. 2, p. 454; Report to Lord Burghley, 8 Feb. 1586 (o.s.), op. cit.

15 Report to Lord Burghley, 8 Feb. 1586 (o.s.), op. cit.

16 Ashmole MS 830, f. 13; Maxwell-Scott, op. cit., p. 236; Bernardino de Mendoza to the King, 28 February 1587, CSPS iv 28.

17 Bernardino de Mendoza to the King, 7 March 1587, CSPS iv 35; Bernardino de Mendoza to the King, 28 March 1587, CSPS iv 48.

18 Neale, op. cit., pp. 139–49; Thomas Fuller, *Worthies*, ii, p. 174.

19 "Advices from London," 12 February 1587, CSPS iv 18; James VI to Elizabeth I, 26 January 1588, in Anthony Bacon, *Memoirs of the Reign of Elizabeth*, vol. 2, p. 52; Bernardino de Mendoza to the King, 7 February 1587, CSPS iv 15; Letter written from England to a Councillor of the King of Scotland, 4 March 1587, CSPS iv 31; James VI to Robert Dudley, Earl of Leicester, quoted in Fritze (ed.), op. cit., p. 50.

20 The King to Bernardino de Mendoza, 31 March 1587, CSPS iv 57; Bernardino de Mendoza to the King, 6 March 1587, CSPS iv 32; Bernardino de Mendoza to Secretary Idiaquez, 18 February 1587, CSPS iv 24.

21 David A. Thomas, *The Illustrated Armada Handbook*, p. 9; Garrett Mattingly, *The Defeat of the Spanish Armada*, p. 47.

CHAPTER TWO:

In the Cause of God

1 David Howarth, *The Voyage of the Armada*, p. 33; Winston Graham, *The Spanish Armadas*, p. 26.

2 Bertrand T. Whitehead, *Brags and Boasts*, p. 3; Maura, *El Designio de Felipe II*; John C. Rule and John J. TePaske, *The Character of Philip II*.

3 J. M. Estal, "Felipe II y su Archivo hagiographico de El Escorial," pp. 207–9; Michael Apps, *The Four Ark Royals*, p. 26.

4 N.A.M. Rodger, *The Safeguard of the Sea*, p. 255.

5 Graham, op. cit., p. 23; Colin Martin and Geoffrey Parker, *The Spanish Armada*, pp. 258, 85; Spanish Advices, SPD cciii 33.

6 Painting by Sofonisba Anguisciola, c. 1579; Ronald Pollitt, "John Hawkins' Troublesome Voyages," pp. 26–40.

7 David B. Quinn and A. N. Ryan, *England's Sea Empire*; George D. Ramsay, *English Overseas Trade during the Centuries of Emergence*; George D. Ramsay, *The Smugglers' Trade*, pp. 131–57; Henry Kamen, *Spain's Road to Empire*; Kenneth R. Andrews, "Elizabethan Privateering," p. 11.

8 Alison Weir, *The Life of Elizabeth I*, pp. 59, 167; E. Kouri, "England and the Attempts to Form a Protestant Alliance in the late 1560s," p. 3.

9 SPD Elizabeth, xlviii 60; Michael Oppenheim, *The Maritime History of Devon*, p. 45; Duro, *La Armada Invencible*, I, p. 241; Martin and Parker, op. cit., p. 63.

10 Calvar Gross, *La Batalla del Mar Oceano*, vol. I, pp. 57–64; Thomas Cely to Lord Burghley, 12 December 1579, SP Add. xxxvi. 35; Alfred O'Rahilly, "The Massacre at Smerwick."

11 A. L. Watson, "Attitudes in Spain towards Philip II's Imperialism," p. 16; John

Knox Laughton (ed.), *State Papers Relating to the Defeat of the Spanish Armada*, I, xxv.

12 Philippe de Commines, *Memoires*, vol. 1; David A. Thomas, *The Illustrated Armada Handbook;* Alexander McKee, *From Merciless Invaders*, p. 26.

13 Santa Cruz to Philip II, quoted in McKee, op. cit., p. 25.

14 Martin and Parker, op. cit., p. 108; CSPV 8, 128–32, 1 May 1586.

15 Garrett Mattingly, *The Defeat of the Spanish Armada*, p. 82; Geoffrey Parker and I.A.A. Thompson, "The Battle of Lepanto," pp. 13–22; Sir Roger Williams, quoted in Judith Richards, "Before the 'Mountaynes Mouse,' " p. 13.

16 Jean Bodin, *Response to the Paradoxes of Malestroit;* Mattingly, op. cit., p. 82; Lippomano to the Doge, CSPV, 24 August 1586; King to the Prince of Parma, 4 September 1587, CSPS iv 141.

17 Martin and Parker, op. cit., p. 108; Notes of Public Business, 25 December 1585, SPD clxxxv 32; CSPI p. 67.

18 C. Christopher Lloyd, *English Corsairs on the Barbary Coast;* King to Bernardino de Mendoza, 11 April 1587, CSPS iv 60; CSPS iii 516.

19 Bernardino de Mendoza to the King, 27 December 1587, CSPS iv 188; King to Bernardino de Mendoza, 28 February 1587, CSPS iv 26.

20 "Statement which Gorion, the Apothecary of the Queen of Scotland was ordered to make," 24 October 1587, CSPS iv 157; Bernardino de Mendoza to the King, 27 November 1587, CSPS iv 175; King to Count de Olivares, 31 March 1587, CSPS iv 58; Bernardino de Mendoza to the King, 28 November 1587, CSPS iv 178.

21 Draft of propositions to be submitted by Count de Olivares to the Pope, June 1587, CSPS iv 117; King to Count de Olivares, 11 February 1587, CSPS iv 17; Count de Olivares to the King, 30 July 1587, CSPS iv 133; Count de Olivares to the King, 16 March 1587, CSPS iv 39.

22 Count de Olivares to the King, 30 June 1587, CSPS iv 115; A. M. Hadfield, *Time to Finish the Game*, p. 47; McKee, op. cit., p. 40; The Pope to the King, 7 August 1587, CSPS iv 137.

23 The Pope to the King, 7 August 1587, CSPS iv 137; Count de Olivares to the King, 2 March 1587, CSPS iv 30; Hadfield, op. cit.

24 "Considerations why it is desirable to carry through the Enterprise of England," 18 March 1587, CSPS iv 42; Count de Olivares to the King, 30 July 1587, CSPS iv 133; Maurice of Nassau to Walsingham, 9 December 1587, CSPF xxi, part 3 448–9; Bernardino de Mendoza to the King, 5 April 1587, CSPS iv 62.

CHAPTER THREE:

The Master of the Sea

1 Alison Weir, *The Life of Elizabeth I*, pp. 227, 238, 255; John Guy, *Tudor England*, pp. 331–51; Bernardino de Mendoza to the King, 20 May 1587, CSPS iv 91; Paul Hentzner, *Travels in England.*

2 R. B. Wernham, *Before the Armada*, p. 359; Jasper Ridley, *The Tudor Age;* Michael Oppenheim, Introduction to William Monson, *Naval Tracts*, I, p. 40; Guy, op. cit.

3 Wallace T. MacCaffrey, *Queen Elizabeth and the Making of Policy*, p. 338;

"Names of the Heretics, Schismatics and neutrals in the Realm of England," 1587, CSPS iv 190; Salisbury MS, III, P 67–70, CSPF xix 95–8; Guy, op. cit.

4 Sir Thomas Smith, quoted in Guy, op. cit.; P. W. Hasler (ed.), *House of Commons 1558–1603*, vol. 3, p. 572; MacCaffrey, op. cit., pp. 353–6.

5 Advices from London, 17 July 1588, CSPS iv 345; CSPS iii 159; CSPF xv, 302; Secretary Idiaquez to Bernardino de Mendoza, 28 January 1587, CSPS iv 14; Gordon K. McBride, "Elizabethan Foreign Policy in Microcosm," pp. 203–4; Bernardino de Mendoza to the King, 24 January 1587, CSPS iv 9.

6 E. Kouri, "England and the Attempts to Form a Protestant Alliance in the late 1560s," p. 16; King to Medina-Sidonia, 1 July 1588, in C. Christopher Lloyd (ed.), *The Naval Miscellany*, vol. 4, p. 23.

7 Bernardino de Mendoza to the King, 26 June 1588, CSPS iv 322; Bernardino de Mendoza to the King, 2 June 1588, CSPS iv 306.

8 Regulation as to Letters of Marque, SPD clxxx 15; William Camden, *Annales*; Garrett Mattingly, *The Defeat of the Spanish Armada*, p. 85; Samuel Purchas, *Purchas his Pilgrimes*, vol. VI, p. 1185; SP 12/49/40.

9 Gordon Connell-Smith, *Forerunners of Drake*, pp. 199–203; N.A.M. Rodger, *The Safeguard of the Sea*, p. 239; Richard Hakluyt, *Principal Navigations*, XI, pp. 114–15.

10 Letter of Don Francisco Zarate to Don Martin Enriquez, Viceroy of New Spain, in Zelia Nuttall (ed.), *New Light on Drake*; Ada Haeseler Lewis, *A Study of Elizabethan Ship Money*; Dr. Julius Caesar to Lord Howard, 18 December 1590, Lansdowne MSS 157, p. 434; Kenneth R. Andrews, *Elizabethan Privateering*, p. 30; Agenda for the Council, 3 October 1587, SPD cciv 2; Peter Kemp, *The British Sailor*, p. 17.

11 Andrews, op. cit., pp. 22–30; David Mathew, "The Cornish and Welsh Pirates in the Reign of Elizabeth," pp. 337–48; CSPD Elizabeth xxxiv 65; xxxv 5; Request of the Merchant Adventurers, 15 June 1587, SPD ccii 27.

12 Michael Oppenheim, *The Maritime History of Devon*, p. 31; Douglas Bell, *Elizabethan Seamen*, pp. 219–20; J. L. Motley, *History of the United Netherlands*, pp. 173–4; Cecil Henry L'Estrange Ewen, "Organised Piracy Round England in the Sixteenth Century," p. 30; Edward P. A. Cheyney, "International Law under Queen Elizabeth," in *Law in History*.

13 Sybil Jack, "The Cinque Ports and the Spanish Armada," p. 148; John Hagthorpe, *England's Exchequer*, p. 25; Andrews, op. cit., pp. 32, 16, 43, 128; CSPV 1617–19, p. 146.

14 Charles A. LeGuin, "Sea Life in Seventeenth Century England," pp. 111–34; William Monson, *Naval Tracts*, II, p. 237; Sir Julian Stafford Corbett, *Papers Relating to the Navy during the Spanish War*, pp. 281–2; *Boteler's Dialogues*, p. 36; Captain John Smith, quoted in Kenneth R. Andrews, *The Elizabethan Seaman*, p. 247; quoted in Andrews, *Elizabethan Privateering*, p. 42.

15 Leland, *Itinerary*; BL Stowe MSS, 555, 147–9; Edmond Howes, *The Annales, or Generall Chronicle of England*; SPD ccliii 49.

16 CSPV 8, 128–32, 1 January 1586; Bell, op. cit., p. 188; CSPS iii 45–6; John Stow, *The Annales or Generall Chronicles of England*.

17 Irene A. Wright (ed.), *Further English Voyages to Spanish America 1583–1594*, doc. 28; Sir Geoffrey Callender, "The Naval Campaign of 1587," pp. 82–91; Leonard Digges, *Geometrica*; John W. Shirley, *Thomas Harriot, a Biography*.

18 David A. Thomas, *The Illustrated Armada Handbook*, p. 79; Purchas, op. cit.,

vol. VI, p. 1185; Bernardino de Mendoza to the King, 20 June 1587, CSPS iv 112; Elizabeth S. Donno, *An Elizabethan in 1582;* John Cummins, *Francis Drake,* p. 148; Nuttall (ed.), op. cit., pp. 193–210; Stow, op. cit.

19 Letter of Don Francisco Zarate to Don Martin Enriquez, Viceroy of New Spain, in Nuttall (ed.), op. cit.; Fuller, *Worthies,* vol. 2, p. 174.

20 W.S.W. Vaux (ed.), *The World Encompassed,* p. 213; Don Francisco Zarate to Don Martin Enriquez, in Nuttall (ed.), op. cit.; Sir Francis Drake to Burghley, 26 July 1586, Lansdowne MSS 51 Art. 14; Peter Pierson, *Commander of the Armada,* p. 61; Spanish Advertisements, SPD clxxxix 24.

21 Geoffrey Parker, "Why the Armada Failed," p. 27; Rodger, op. cit., p. 242; Bernardino de Escalante to Philip II, 2 May 1587, in Herrera y Oria, *Felipe II,* p. 98 (my translation).

CHAPTER FOUR:

Smoking the Wasps from Their Nests

1 Jasper Ridley, *The Tudor Age,* p. 22; Alexander McKee, *From Merciless Invaders,* p. 33; Sir Julian Stafford Corbett, *Papers Relating to the Navy during the Spanish War,* xliv; SP 25 March 1587.

2 Advices from London, 20 April 1587, CSPS iv 75; Ridley, op. cit., p. 46; Relation sent by the Duke of Medina-Sidonia, 12 April 1588, CSPS iv 266; True Advices from England, CSPS iv 66; Sampson's Advices from England, 26 February 1587, CSPS iv 19.

3 Bernardino de Mendoza to the King, 9 April 1587, CSPS iv 65; Bernardino de Mendoza to the King, 19 April 1587, CSPS iv 71; King to Bernardino de Mendoza, 13 May 1587, CSPS iv 86; Drake to Walsingham, 2 April 1587, SPD cc 2.

4 Bernardino de Mendoza to the King, 19 April 1587, CSPS iv 72; Walsingham to Stafford, SP Foreign, France, vol. 88; Council to Sir Francis Drake, SPD cc 17; Burghley to Andreas de Looe, 28 July 1587, SP Flanders 32.

5 Henry Haslop, *Newes out of the Coast of Spaine;* Corbett, op. cit., p. 296; Garrett Mattingly, *The Defeat of the Spanish Armada,* p. 96; Agustin de Horozco, BL, Royal MS, 14.A.III.

6 Thomas Fenner to Walsingham, 17 May 1587, SPD cci 34; Sir Geoffrey Callender, "The Naval Campaign of 1587," p. 89; Letter from Drake in E. Edwards, *The Life of Sir Walter Raleigh.*

7 Sir Francis Drake to John Foxe, Harleian MSS clxvii, 104; A. M. Hadfield, *Time to Finish the Game,* p. 70.

8 The King to Bernardino de Mendoza, 13 May 1587, CSPS iv 86; Sir Francis Drake to Walsingham, 27 April 1587, SPD cc 46; Bernardino de Mendoza to the King, 9 June 1587, CSPS iv 100.

9 Robert Leng, "The True Description"; William Borough to Sir Francis Drake, SPD cc 57, ccii 14 ii, Lansdowne MSS lii 39; Bernardino de Mendoza to the King, 5 April 1587, CSPS iv 61; Richard Hakluyt, "Sir Francis Drake Revived."

10 Thomas Fenner to Walsingham, 17 May 1587, SPD cci 34.

11 Corbett, op. cit., xxxi; CSPD cci 33; Sir Francis Drake to Walsingham, 17 May 1587, SPD cci 33; Thomas Fenner to Walsingham, 17 May 1587, SPD cci 34.

12 Corbett, op. cit., xliii; Thomas Fenner to Walsingham, 17 May 1587, SPD cci 34; Drake to Walsingham, 24 May 1587, SPD.

13 Belvoir Papers iv, 219; Bernardino de Mendoza to the King, 5 August 1587, CSPS iv 136; Leng, op. cit., pp. 21–2.

14 Leng, op. cit., pp. 21–2; Michael Apps, *The Four Ark Royals*, p. 23; Maura, *El Designio de Felipe II*, pp. 163–7.

15 Maura, op. cit., pp. 167–8; Peter Pierson, *Commander of the Armada*, p. 76; King to Bernardino de Mendoza, 28 July 1587, CSPS iv 130; R. N. Worth, *Calendar of the Plymouth Municipal Records*, p. 128; Bernardino de Mendoza to the King, 16 July 1587, CSPS iv 127.

16 Report of the Carrack Prize Commission, SPD ccii 53; Bernardino de Mendoza to the King, 8 January 1587, CSPS iv 2; Michael Oppenheim, Introduction to William Monson, *Naval Tracts*, I, p. 28; McKee, op. cit., p. 33; CSPF ix, 513–14; Clarke and Thursfield, *The Navy and the Nation*, p. 187; Oppenheim, op. cit., I, p. 11.

17 Howard to Walsingham, 27 January 1588, SP ccvii 30; Bertrand T. Whitehead, *Brags and Boasts*, p. 29; Advices from London, 28 March 1588, CSPS iv 246; Howard to Walsingham, 27 January 1588, SP ccvii 30; Edwards, op. cit., I, p. 245.

18 Bernardino de Mendoza to the King, 2 September 1587, CSPS iv 140; Bernardino de Mendoza to the King, 13 September 1587, CSPS iv 143; Duke of Parma to the King, 31 January 1588, CSPS iv 210; Hadfield, op. cit., p. 26.

19 Duke of Parma to the King, 20 March 1588, CSPS iv 241; King to the Duke of Parma, February 1588, quoted in David Howarth, *The Voyage of the Armada*, p. 153; Advices from London, 21 March 1588, CSPS iv 244; Drake to the Queen, 28 April 1588, SP ccix 112; Howard to Burghley, 29 February 1588, SP ccviii 87.

20 Bernardino de Mendoza to the King, 26 June 1588, CSPS iv 323; Burghley to Walsingham, 18 July 1588, SP ccxii 63; Conyers Read, *Lord Burghley*, pp. 425, 58 on; Bailiffs of Ipswich to Walsingham, 12 April 1588, SP ccix 98; Sir G. Carey to Walsingham, 6 April 1588, SP ccix 71.

21 Mayor and Citizens of Exeter to the Council, 11 April 1588, SP ccix 84; Mayor and Aldermen of Poole to the Council, 5 April 1588, SP ccix 70; Sir G. Carey to Walsingham, 6 April 1588, SP ccix 71; Mayor and Aldermen of Southampton to the Council, 17 April 1588, SP ccix 97; Mayor and Aldermen of Hull to the Council, 7 April 1588, SP ccix 75; Mayor of Lyme Regis to the Council, 9 April 1588, SP ccix 81; Mayor and Aldermen of King's Lynn to the Council, 12 April 1588, SP ccix 87; John Guy, *Tudor England*; Apps, op. cit., p. 27.

CHAPTER FIVE:

The Floating Forest

1 Jasper Ridley, *The Tudor Age*, p. 207; Philip II to Parma, 4 and 14 September 1587, in Calvar Gross, *La Batalla del Mar Oceano* III, pp. 1006–7, 1069–70; Duke of Parma to the King, 31 January 1588, CSPS iv 209; CSPV 14 November 1587, 320–3.

2 A. M. Hadfield, *Time to Finish the Game*, p. 84; John Knox Laughton, *State Papers Relating to the Defeat of the Spanish Armada*, I, xxviii; quoted in David A. Thomas, *The Illustrated Armada Handbook*, p. 46; King to Duke of Medina-Sidonia, 14 February 1588, in C. Christopher Lloyd (ed.), *The Naval Miscellany*, vol. 4, p. 11.

3 Much of the biographical information on Medina-Sidonia is drawn from Peter Pierson, *Commander of the Armada;* CSPV 1 587 273ff; William Monson, *Naval Tracts,* vol. 1, pp. 152–73.

4 Duke of Medina-Sidonia to the King, 16 February 1588, CSPS iv 219; King to Duke of Medina-Sidonia, 20 February 1588, in Lloyd (ed.), op. cit., vol. 4, p. 12; Pierson, op. cit., p. 82.

5 Geoffrey Parker, "Why the Armada Failed," p. 29; I.A.A. Thompson, "Spanish Armada Gun Policy and Procurement," pp. 70, 77; Ernest Straker, *Wealden Iron,* pp. 147, 58, 154; CSPD vc 16.

6 Thompson, op. cit., pp. 74, 83; R. Norton, *The Gunner,* pp. 67–8; Duro, *La Armada Invencible,* I, p. 77.

7 Bobadilla to Idiaquez, 20 August 1588, quoted in Colin Martin and Geoffrey Parker, *The Spanish Armada,* p. 129; Bernardino de Mendoza to the King, 16 January 1588, CSPS iv 202; Confession of Gregorio de Sotomayor, SP ccxiv 19.

8 See Colin Martin, *"La Trinidad Valencera:* An Armada Invasion Transport Lost off Donegal"; Narrative of Petruccio Ubaldini, in Lloyd (ed.), op. cit., vol. 4; Monson, op. cit., vol. 2, pp. 63–5; Summary Statement of the Vessels that Compose the Most Fortunate Armada . . . 9 May 1588, CSPS iv 288; Thomas, op. cit., p. 60.

9 Lord Burghley, quoted in William Cobbett (ed.), *Parliamentary History of England,* vol. 1, 1066–1625, pp. 865–6; Monson, op. cit., pp. 63–5; King to Medina-Sidonia, 1 April 1588, in Lloyd (ed.), op. cit., vol. 4, p. 18; Alexander McKee, *From Merciless Invaders,* p. 40; CSPV April 1588.

10 Lope de Vega, *La Hermosura de Angelica;* Extracts from the "General Orders" issued by the Duke of Medina-Sidonia, May 1588, CSPS iv 293.

11 Instructions to the Duke of Medina-Sidonia, 1 April 1588, CSPS iv 251; Extracts from the "General Orders" issued by the Duke of Medina-Sidonia, May 1588, CSPS iv 293; William Laird Clowes, *The Royal Navy,* quoting Duro, op. cit., doc. 171, p. 281; Martin and Parker, op. cit., p. 27.

12 Examination of Spanish Prisoners, 2 August 1588, SP ccxiv 17; Admiral Juan Martinez de Recalde to the King, 11 July 1588, CSPS iv 340; Hadfield, op. cit., p. 88; General Order from the Duke of Medina-Sidonia, 5 July 1588, CSPS iv 293n; Duke of Medina-Sidonia to the King, 11 July 1588, CSPS iv 341; Examination of Spanish Prisoners, 2 August 1588, SP ccxiv 17; CSPI cxxxvi 29.I.

13 Garrett Mattingly, *The Defeat of the Spanish Armada,* pp. 191–2.

CHAPTER SIX:

So Violent a Sea and Wind

1 Duke of Medina-Sidonia to the King, 14 May 1588, CSPS iv 295; Instructions to the Duke of Medina-Sidonia, 1 April 1588, CSPS iv 251; King to Medina-Sidonia, 1 April 1588, in C. Christopher Lloyd (ed.), *The Naval Miscellany,* vol. 4, pp. 15–17, 20; Duke of Medina-Sidonia to the King, 28 May 1588, CSPS iv 301; Philip II to Cardinal Albert, Simancas Papers, iv, p. 188; King to the Prince of Parma, 4 September 1587, CSPS iv 141.

2 Duke of Medina-Sidonia to the King, 1 June 1588, CSPS iv 301; Robert Milne-Tyte, *Armada,* p. 10; King to Andres de Alba, 9 July 1588, in Lloyd (ed.), op. cit., vol. 4, p. 27; Confession of Gregorio de Sotomayor, SP ccxiv 19; Duke

of Medina-Sidonia to the King, 28 May 1588, CSPS iv 301; Duke of Medina-Sidonia to the Duke of Parma, 10 June 1588, CSPS iv 310.

3 Peter Pierson, *Commander of the Armada*, p. 89; Sealed Document which the Duke of Medina-Sidonia was to deliver to the Duke of Parma, April 1588, CSPS iv 253; King to Medina-Sidonia, 1 April 1588, in Lloyd (ed.), op. cit., vol. 4, p. 20; Duke of Parma to the King, 20 March 1588, CSPS iv 241.

4 Extracts from the "General Orders" issued by the Duke of Medina-Sidonia, May 1588, CSPS iv 293; Duke of Medina-Sidonia to the King, 21 June 1588, CSPS iv 318; John Knox Laughton, *State Papers Relating to the Defeat of the Spanish Armada*, I, xxxiii.

5 Duke of Medina-Sidonia to the King, 24 June 1588, CSPS iv 321; Report of the Council called by the Duke of Medina-Sidonia, 27 June 1588, CSPS iv 326; King to Duke of Medina-Sidonia, 1 July 1588, in Lloyd (ed.), op. cit., vol. 4, pp. 22–5; Duke of Medina-Sidonia to the King, 6 July 1588, CSPS iv 334.

6 King to the Duke of Medina-Sidonia, 1 July 1588, in Lloyd (ed.), op. cit., vol. 4, p. 29; Duke of Medina-Sidonia to Duke of Parma, 10 June 1588, CSPS iv 310; King to the Duke of Medina-Sidonia, 1 April 1588, in Lloyd (ed.), op. cit., vol. 4, p. 15.

7 Colin Martin and Geoffrey Parker, *The Spanish Armada*, p. 144; Admiral Juan Martinez de Recalde to the King, 11 July 1588, CSPS iv 340; Confession of Gregorio de Sotomayor, SP ccxiv 19; Duke of Medina-Sidonia to the King, 19 July 1588, CSPS iv 343n, 341, 343.

CHAPTER SEVEN:

The Sea Beggars

1 Summary of divers letters to the Duke of Parma, 12 September 1588, CSPS iv 427; Ronald H. Fritze (ed.), *Historical Dictionary of Tudor England*, p. 276; Master of Gray to Archibald Douglas, 14 December 1588, CSPS iv xlii 127; William Asheby to Burghley, 13 November 1588, CSPS iv xlii 117; James Hudson to Sir Francis Walsingham, 10 December 1588, CSPS iv xlii 124; Bernardino de Mendoza to the King, 24 January 1587, CSPS iv 9; Duke of Parma to Bernardino de Mendoza, 13 April 1587, CSPS iv 70; points of letter from Robert Bruce to the Duke of Parma, 6 August 1588, CSPS iv 367.

2 King to Bernardino de Mendoza, 28 January 1587, CSPS iv 12; King to Bernardino de Mendoza, 31 March 1587, CSPS 57; Robert Bruce to Bernardino de Mendoza, 18 February 1588, CSPS iv 222; Bernardino de Mendoza to the King, 15 March 1588, CSPS iv 238; King to Bernardino de Mendoza, 24 April 1588, CSPS iv 276; J. D. Mackie, "Scotland and the Spanish Armada," pp. 1–23; King to Bernardino de Mendoza, 21 June 1588, CSPS iv 316.

3 Bernardino de Mendoza to the King, 7 July 1588, CSPS iv 337; Advices from London, 17 July 1588, CSPS iv 345; Bernardino de Mendoza to the King, 20 May 1587, CSPS iv 89.

4 Account September 1588, CSP Scotland xlii 116; Bertrand T. Whitehead, *Brags and Boasts*, pp. 129–31; Anthony Bacon, *Memoirs of the Reign of Elizabeth*, p. 55; William Asheby to Lord Burghley, 6 August 1588, CSP Scotland xlii 108; Howard to Walsingham, 15 June 1588, SP ccxi 26.

5 The definitive account of the French diplomatic background to the Armada is

to be found in Garrett Mattingly, *The Defeat of the Spanish Armada*, pp. 162–3, 204–24; Bernardino de Mendoza to the King, 28 February 1588, CSPS iv 230; Mattingly, op. cit.

6   Edmund H. Dickerman, "A Neglected Aspect of the Spanish Armada," pp. 19–23; Bernardino de Mendoza to the King, 5 April 1588, CSPS iv 260; Bernardino de Mendoza to the King, 14 April 1588, CSPS iv 269; Mattingly, op. cit., p. 211.

7   Mattingly, op. cit., pp. 220–4; Bernardino de Mendoza to the King, 21 May 1588, CSPS iv 299; Bernardino de Mendoza to the King, 14 June 1588, CSPS iv 312; Bernardino de Mendoza to the King, 24 July 1588, CSPS iv 353.

8   Owen Feltham, *A Brief Character of the Low Countries*, I, p. 5; A. F. Pollard (ed.), *Tudor Tracts, 1532–1588*, pp. 438, 443; Mattingly, op. cit., pp. 48–9; Leon van der Essen's mammoth biography remains the definitive account of Parma's life.

9   Sir Roger Williams, *The Art of Warre*; Paolo Rinaldi, quoted in Leon van der Essen, *Alexandre Farnese*, V, p. 295; Lord Willoughby to Cristobal de Mondragon, June 1586, Ancaster Muniments, X, f. 1.

10 Sir John Neale, "Elizabeth and the Netherlands," pp. 373–96; Advices from London, 13 September 1587, CSPS iv 144; Neville Williams, *All the Queen's Men*, p. 196.

11 Sir Robert Naunton, *Fragmenta Regalia*, 1641; "Reply of the Queen of England to the request of the States for greater aid," 5 February 1588, CSPS iv 213; Bernardino de Mendoza to the King, 5 April 1588, CSPS iv 261; Advices from London, 15 February 1588, CSPS iv 217.

12 Bernardino de Mendoza to the King, 28 November 1587, CSPS iv 178; Mattingly, op. cit., p. 56; Howard to Burghley, 29 February 1588, SP ccviii 87; Relation of Proceedings, BM Cotton, Julius F.x. 111–17.

13 Mattingly, op. cit., pp. 137–40; SP Holland, 34, 117; King to the Prince of Parma, 4 September 1587, CSPS iv 141.

14 H. O'Donnell, "The Requirements of the Duke of Parma," p. 95; Duke of Parma to the King, 31 January 1588, CSPS iv 209; Duke of Parma to the King, 22 February 1588, CSPS iv 223; Duke of Parma to the King, 20 March 1588, CSPS iv 242; Duke of Parma to the King, 5 April 1588, CSPS iv 264.

15 Duke of Parma to the King, 20 March 1588, CSPS iv 242; Duke of Parma to the King, 8 June 1588, CSPS iv 309; Duke of Parma to the King, 20 July 1588, CSPS iv 349; Count de Olivares to the King, 8 July 1588, CSPS iv 338; Count de Olivares to the King, 8 August 1588, CSPS iv 376.

CHAPTER EIGHT:

Like Bears Tied to Stakes

1   Seymour to Walsingham, 17 June 1588, SP ccxi 33; Bertrand T. Whitehead, *Brags and Boasts*, p. 19; Sir Walter Ralegh, *History of the World*; Wynter to Walsingham, 20 December 1588, SP ccxix 36.

2   C. G. Cruickshank, *Elizabeth's Army*, pp. 17–40; CSPD Elizabeth cc 40; William Harrison, *The Description of England*; A. H. Dodd, *Elizabethan England*, p. 204.

3   A. L. Rowse, *Tudor Cornwall*, p. 387; R. N. Worth, *Calendar of the Plymouth Municipal Records*, p. 128; Emmanuel Green, *Preparations in Somerset against the Spanish Armada*; Colin Elliott, *Discovering Armada Britain*, p. 123.

4 Harrison, op. cit.; Lindsay Boynton, *The Elizabethan Militia*, p. 131; Elliott, op. cit., pp. 103–4; Mayor of Rye, Rye MS, 1581; Bernardino de Mendoza to the King, 28 February 1588, CSPS iv 231; Worth, op. cit., p. 128; A. L. Merson (ed.), *The Third Book of Remembrance of Southampton*, Vol. III, p. 55.

5 John S. Nolan, "The Muster of 1588," pp. 397, 392; CSPD, 17 November 1587; Elliott, op. cit., p. 115.

6 G. V. Scammell, "The Sinews of War," pp. 351–67; Cruickshank, op. cit., p. 16; Robert Milne-Tyte, *Armada*, p. 115; Leland, *Itinerary*.

7 Sir Henry Cromwell, and Lord St. John to Sir Henry Cromwell, quoted in William Mackreth Noble (ed.), *Huntingdonshire and the Spanish Armada*; Boynton, op. cit., p. 128; Leland, op. cit.

8 Boynton, op. cit., p. 129; Alexander McKee, *From Merciless Invaders*, p. 26; Colin Martin and Geoffrey Parker, "If the Armada Had Landed," pp. 28–9; Whitehead, op. cit., p. 40; Names of the Heretics, Schismatics and Neutrals in the Realm of England, 1587, CSPS iv 190; William Melsam to the Council, SPD clxxxvi 54.

9 A. O. Meyer, *England and the Catholic Church*, p. 271; Ronald H. Fritze (ed.), *Historical Dictionary of Tudor England*, p. 412; Dodd, op. cit., p. 107; Harrison, op. cit.

10 The Pope to the King, 7 August 1587, CSPS iv 137; Sir Francis Englefield to Father Seth Forster, 19 August 1589, Harleian MS 296.3; Instructions given to Dr. Allen as to the Answers he is to give to his Holiness' Questions, CSPS 55; Dodd, op. cit., p. 16; Fritze (ed.), op. cit., p. 455; Nolan, op. cit., pp. 393–4; William Camden, *History*, p. 313; Advices from London, 29 July 1588, CSPS iv 357.

11 Narrative of Petruccio Ubaldini, in C. Christopher Lloyd (ed.), *The Naval Miscellany*, vol. 4; William S. Maltby, *The Black Legend in England*; Thomas Deloney, *The Works of Thomas Deloney*, pp. 468–82; A. F. Pollard (ed.), *Tudor Tracts, 1532–1588*, p. 498; *Copie of a Letter sent to Bernardin Mendoza*; Advices from England, 10 August 1588, CSPS iv 381.

12 Harrison, op. cit.; Dodd, op. cit., p. 149; CSPF 1559–60, cxxviii–ix; Philip Gosse, *Sir John Hawkins*, p. vi; Henry E. Huntingdon Library, Ellesmere MS 6206 B, f. 14–15, 18–19.

13 John Knox Laughton, *State Papers Relating to the Defeat of the Spanish Armada*, I, lxxiv; Comparison of Charges, 8 October 1588, SP ccxvii 12; SPD ccviii 18; Hawkins to Burghley, 3 March 1588, SP ccix 5.

14 McKee, op. cit., pp. 87–8; Harrison, op. cit.

15 Sir Julian Stafford Corbett, *Papers Relating to the Navy during the Spanish War*, pp. 27–32; William Monson, *Naval Tracts*, vol. 4, p. 43; Manucy, *Artillery*, p. 63; Notes of Public Business, 25 December 1585, SPD clxxxv 32.

16 Lawrence Stone, "The Armada Campaign of 1588," p. 133; E. W. Bovill, "Queen Elizabeth's Gunpowder," pp. 179–86; John Knox Laughton, *State Papers Relating to the Defeat of the Spanish Armada*, I, xliv; King to the Duke of Medina-Sidonia, 1 July 1588, in Lloyd (ed.), op. cit., vol. 4, p. 23; Monson, op. cit., vol. 2, p. 244.

17 Mendoza to the King, 15 May 1582, CSPS; Kenneth R. Andrews, "Elizabethan Privateering," p. 15; G. E. Mainwaring and W. G. Perrin (eds.), *The Life and Works of Sir Henry Mainwaring*, II, pp. 14–15; Michael Oppenheim, *The Maritime History of Devon*, p. 34.

18 *The World Encompassed*, p. 213; Scale of Pay, SP ccxxxvii 62; Proposed increase of wages, 28 December 1585, SP clxxxv 33 II; Kenneth R. Andrews, *The Eliza-bethan Seaman*, p. 247; CSPD, 8 July, 10 July 1597; C. Christopher Lloyd, *The British Seaman*, p. 39.

19 Proposed increase of wages, 28 December 1585, SP clxxxv 33 II; Ralegh, op. cit., iv, ch 2, sect 4; Lloyd, *Seaman*, p. 27; Neil Hanson, *The Custom of the Sea*, p. 40; James Humphries, *Orders to be Used in King's or Queen's Majesties Ships*; Nathaniel Boteler, *Boteler's Dialogues*, pp. 17–18.

20 M. Christy (ed.), *The Voyages of Captain Luke Foxe and Captain Thomas James*, vol. I, p. 11; Boteler, op. cit., p. 43; Joan Druett, *Rough Medicine*, pp. 142–3.

21 Boteler, op. cit., p. 65; Lloyd, *Seaman*, p. 43; SP cviii 35; BL ADD MSS 12, 505, f. 241; SP ccviii 18.

22 Peter Kemp, *The British Sailor*, p. 4; Howard to Burghley, 8 April 1588, SP ccix 78; Drake to the Council, 30 March 1588, SP ccix 40.

23 Howard to Walsingham, 1 February 1588, SP ccviii 46; SPD ccviii 31; Howard to Walsingham, 7 April 1588, CSPD ccix 74; Howard to Walsingham, 10 March 1588, CSPD ccix 15 and I.

CHAPTER NINE:

The Advantage of Time and Place

1 William Camden, *Annales*; Richard Harvey, *An Astrological Discourse*; Garrett Mattingly, *The Defeat of the Spanish Armada*, p. 167; Bertrand T. Whitehead, *Brags and Boasts*, pp. 17–18.

2 James Lea, *A True and Perfect Description of a Strange Monster Born in the City of Rome in Italy*, pp. 6–9; Advices from London, 1 April 1588, CSPS iv 254; Bernardino de Mendoza to the King, 25 February 1588, CSPS iv 226; Bernardino de Mendoza to the King, 19 December 1587, CSPS iv 184.

3 Advices from London, 28 March 1588, CSPS iv 246; Advice sent to Don Martin de Idiaquez, 1588, CSPS iv 191; Sir George Carey to Walsingham, SPD clxxix 36.

4 Howard to Walsingham, 7 April 1588, SP ccix 74; Sir William Wynter to the Principal Officers, 28 February 1588, SP ccviii 85; William Hawkins to John Hawkins, 17 February 1588, SP ccviii 72; Howard to Burghley, 21 February 1588, SP ccviii 79; Howard to Burghley, 29 February 1588, SP ccviii 87.

5 Howard to Burghley, 9 March 1588, SP ccix 9; CSPD ccxlii 21; SPD ccviii 6; Howard to Burghley, 29 February 1588, SP ccvii 87; Drake to the Council, 30 March 1588, SP ccix 40; Narrative of Petruccio Ubaldini, in C. Christopher Lloyd (ed.), *The Naval Miscellany*, vol. 4; Extract from intercepted letter, SPD clxxxiii 28.

6 Drake to the Queen, 13 April 1588, SP ccix 89; John Hawkins to Walsingham, 1 February 1588, SP ccviii 47.

7 Drake to the Queen, 13 April 1588, CSPD ccix 89; Advices from London, 17 October 1587, CSPS iv 155; William Monson, *Naval Tracts*, vol. 1, 161; SPD ccviii 22; Howard to Burghley, 13 April 1588, BM Harl. MS 6994, 120; Drake to the Queen, 28 April 1588, SP ccix 112; RCHM 5th Report p. 578 (papers of Weymouth & Melcombe Regis Corporation); Advertisements from Rouen, SP ccix 127; extracts of letters written from Lisbon, SP ccx 20.

8 Bernardino de Mendoza to the King, 25 February 1588, CSPS iv 225; Howard to Walsingham, 15 June 1588, SP ccxi 26; Howard to Walsingham, 14 June 1588, CSPD ccxi 18; Howard to Walsingham, 9 March 1588, SP ccix 12; Howard to Walsingham, 10 March 1588, SP ccix and I; Thomas Fenner to Walsingham, 3 March 1588, SP ccix 6; Seymour to Walsingham, 10 March 1588, SP ccix 18; Lindsay Boynton, *The Elizabethan Militia*, p. 153.

9 Howard to Burghley, 23 May 1588, SP ccx 28; A. M. Hadfield, *Time to Finish the Game*, p. 95; Howard to Walsingham, 14 June 1588, SP ccxi 18; Advices from London, 21 May 1588, CSPS iv 300.

10 Howard to the Council, 22 June 1588, SP ccxi 45; Howard to Walsingham, 14 June 1588, SP ccxi 18; Howard to Burghley, 28 May 1588, SP ccx 35; Howard to Burghley, 28 May 1588, SP ccx 36; Howard to Walsingham, 13 June 1588, SP ccxi 17; Lawrence Stone, "The Armada Campaign of 1588," p. 123.

11 Walsingham to Howard, 9 June 1588, SP ccxi 8; Howard to Walsingham, 15 June 1588, SP ccxi 26; Advertisement of the Spanish fleet, 23 June 1588, SP ccxi 47; Considerations by Fenner, 14 July 1588, SP ccxii 10.

12 Bernardino de Mendoza to the King, 24 July 1588, CSPS iv 353; John Knox Laughton, *State Papers Relating to the Defeat of the Spanish Armada*, I, lxi; Bernardino de Mendoza to the King, 5 April 1587, CSPS iv 61; Howard to Walsingham, 19 June 1588, SP ccxi 37.

13 Memorandum by Drake, 4 July 1588, SP ccxii 9; Howard to the Council, 22 June 1588, SP ccxi 45; Howard to Walsingham, 22 June 1588, SP ccxi 46; Howard to Walsingham, 22 June 1588, SP ccxi 46; Howard to the Queen, 23 June 1588, SP ccxi 50.

14 Considerations by Fenner, 14 July 1588, SP ccxii 10; Seymour to Walsingham, 12 July 1588, SP ccxii 34; Howard to Walsingham, 13 July 1588, SP ccxii 42.

15 Thomas Cely to Burghley, 17 July 1588, SP ccxii 57; Howard to Walsingham, 17 July 1588, SP ccxii 60; Estimate of Charges, CSPD ccxii 61 I; Thomas Fenner to Walsingham, 17 July 1588, SP ccxii 62; Hawkins to Walsingham, 31 July 1588, SP ccxiii 71; Seymour to Walsingham, 18 July 1588, SP ccxii 64; Burghley to Walsingham, 19 July 1588, SP ccxii 66.

CHAPTER 10:

A Bad Place to Rest In

1 Relation of Medina-Sidonia, in John Knox Laughton, *State Papers Relating to the Defeat of the Spanish Armada*, II, 354–70; Duke of Medina-Sidonia to the King, 30 July 1588, CSPS iv 358; News out of France, 18 August 1588, SP ccxv 30, L.

2 Duke of Medina-Sidonia to the King, 30 July 1588, CSPS iv 358; Relation of Medina-Sidonia, in Laughton, op. cit., II, 354–70; William Bourne, quoted in Kenneth R. Andrews, *The Elizabethan Seaman*, p. 259; Nathaniel Boteler, *Boteler's Dialogues*, p. 30.

3 Relation of Medina-Sidonia, in Laughton, op. cit., II, 354–70; Duke of Medina-Sidonia to the King, 30 July 1588, CSPS iv 359; Wynter to Walsingham, 27 July 1588, SP ccxiii 49; Admiral Juan Martinez de Recalde to the King, 11 July 1588, CSPS iv 340.

4 Don Pedro de Valdes to the King, 21 August 1588, SP ccxv 36; Examination of Don Pedro de Valdes, 4 August 1588, SP ccxiv 22; Laughton, op. cit., II, 302n; Relation of Medina-Sidonia, in Laughton, op. cit., II, 354–70.

5 William Monson, *Naval Tracts*, vol. 1, pp. 152–73; R. N. Worth, *Calendar of the Plymouth Municipal Records*, pp. 128, 135, 214; A Brief Abstract of Accidents, SP ccxiv 42; Worth, op. cit., p. 214; Richard Carew, *Survey of Cornwall*.

6 Darell to Burghley, 22 July 1588, SP ccxiii 2; James Humphries, *Orders to be Used in King's or Queen's Majesties Ships*; H. J. Moule, *Descriptive Catalogue of the Charters . . . of Weymouth*, vi. 39, pp. 157–8.

7 Boteler, op. cit., p. 24; Joan Druett, *Rough Medicine*, pp. 18–19.

8 Alexander McKee, *From Merciless Invaders*, p. 49; Zelia Nuttall (ed.), "New Light on Drake," pp. 323–39.

9 Howard to Walsingham, 21 July 1588 (o.s.), SP ccxii 80.

10 Sampson's Advices from England, 14 February 1587, CSPS iv 19; The new confidant's advices from England, 28 July 1587, CSPS iv 132.

11 G. S. Thompson, "Twysden Papers," p. 78; Jack Davies Jones, "The Isle of Wight and the Armada," p. 11; Lindsay Boynton, *The Elizabethan Militia*, p. 133.

12 Relation of Medina-Sidonia, in Laughton, op. cit., II, 354–70; Boteler, op. cit., pp. 292–3, 304; extracts from the "General Orders" issued by the Duke of Medina-Sidonia, May 1588, CSPS iv 293; Statement made by the Purser Pedro Coco Calderon, 24 September 1588, CSPS iv 439; Howard to Walsingham, 21 July 1588, SP ccxii 80.

13 Colin Elliott, *Discovering Armada Britain*, p. 47; McKee, op. cit., pp. 88–9; Boteler, op. cit., pp. 293–4.

CHAPTER ELEVEN:

The Greatest Navy that Ever Swam upon the Sea

1 R. N. Worth, *Calendar of the Plymouth Municipal Records*, p. 128.

2 Pedro de Valdes to the King, 15 and 19 July 1588, AGS GA 225/55–6; Duke of Medina-Sidonia to the King, 28 May 1588, CSPS iv 301; *Considerations Touching a War with Spain*, p. 90; William Camden, *Annales*, vol. iii, p. 411; BL Sloane MS 262/66; "Emanuel Fremoso, a Portingal," Examinations of Spanish Prisoners, 12 September 1588, SP ccxvi 17.

3 Note of Certain Plunder, SP ccxv 78; Nathaniel Boteler, *Boteler's Dialogues*, pp. 274–5; Pipe Roll Declared Accounts [1588] 2225; SP Reports of Survey, 25 September 1588.

4 Boteler, op. cit., pp. 292–3; Relation of Proceedings, BM Cotton, Julius F.x. 111–17; Relation of Medina-Sidonia, in John Knox Laughton, *State Papers Relating to the Defeat of the Spanish Armada*, II, 354–70; Statement made by the Purser Pedro Coco Calderon, 24 September 1588, CSPS iv 439.

5 James Humphries, *Orders to be Used in King's or Queen's Majesties Ships*; Colin Martin, "Incendiary Weapons from the Spanish Armada Wreck *La Trinidad Valencera*, 1588"; N.A.M. Rodger, *The Safeguard of the Sea*, p. 205; Michael Apps, *The Four Ark Royals*, p. 21.

6 A. D. Burnell (ed.), *The Voyage of John Huyghen van Linschoten*, pp. 268–9.

7 H. J. Moule, *Descriptive Catalogue of the Charters . . . of Weymouth*, vi. 48, p. 162;

Acts of the Privy Council xv, 288; A. H. Dodd, *Elizabethan England;* SP 12/209, 49; Jack Davies Jones, "The Isle of Wight and the Armada," p. 7.

8 A Brief Abstract of Accidents, SP ccxiv 42; Colin Martin and Geoffrey Parker, *The Spanish Armada,* p. 148; Boteler, op. cit., p. 298.

9 Relation of Proceedings, BM Cotton, Julius F.x. 111–17; Statement made by the Purser Pedro Coco Calderon, 24 September 1588, CSPS iv 439; Relation of Medina-Sidonia, in Laughton, op. cit., II, 354–70.

10 Statement made by the Purser Pedro Coco Calderon, 24 September 1588, CSPS iv 439; Relation of Medina-Sidonia, in Laughton, op. cit., II, 354–70.

11 Statement made by the Purser Pedro Coco Calderon, 24 September 1588, CSPS iv 439; David A. Thomas, *The Illustrated Armada Handbook,* p. 136; Pedro de Valdes to the King, 21 August 1588, SP ccxv 36; information supplied by Warrant Officer Ken Connor.

12 Pedro de Valdes to the King, 21 August 1588, SP ccxv 36; A Brief Abstract of Accidents, SP ccxiv 42; Statement made by the Purser Pedro Coco Calderon, 24 September 1588, CSPS iv 439; Relation of Medina-Sidonia, in Laughton, op. cit., II, 354–70; William Monson, *Naval Tracts,* vol. 2, p. 303.

13 Relation of Medina-Sidonia, in Laughton, op. cit., II, 354–70; Pedro de Valdes to the King, 21 August 1588, SP ccxv 36; Statement made by the Purser Pedro Coco Calderon, 24 September 1588, CSPS iv 439.

14 William Laird Clowes, *The Royal Navy,* p. 569; G. Holles and A. C. Wood, *Memorials of the Holles Family 1493–1656,* p. 89; Alexander McKee, *From Merciless Invaders,* p. 61.

15 Howard to Walsingham, 21 July 1588, SP ccxii 80; Drake to Seymour, 21 July 1588, SP ccxiii 82.

CHAPTER TWELVE:

The Heavens Thundered

1 Relation of Proceedings, BM Cotton, Julius F.x. 111–17; Petition of the Captain, Master and Lieutenant of the *Margaret and John* of London, (?) 11 August 1588, SP ccxiii 89.

2 Relation of Proceedings, BM Cotton, Julius F.x. 111–17; Richard Hakluyt, *Principal Navigations;* Pedro de Valdes to the King, 21 August 1588, SP ccxv 36; George Cary to Walsingham, 29 August 1588, SP ccxv 67; Sir John Gilberte and George Cary to the Council, 27 July 1588, SP ccxiii 42.

3 Requisition for powder and shot, 24 July 1588, SP ccxii 59 I; Cary to Walsingham, 29 August 1588, SP ccxv 67; Sir John Gilberte and George Cary to Walsingham, 26 July 1588, SP ccxiii 42; Advices from London, 21 August 1588, CSPS iv 400; Bernardino de Mendoza to the King, 20 August 1588, CSPS iv 396; Cary to Walsingham, 27 August 1588, SP ccxv 69.

4 Kenneth R. Andrews, *Elizabethan Privateering,* p. 6; Eugene L. Rasor, *The Spanish Armada of 1588;* R. B. Wernham, *After the Armada,* p. 114; Michael Oppenheim, Introduction to William Monson, *Naval Tracts,* vol. 1, p. 35; Sir Walter Ralegh, *History of the World,* IV, 2, 4; Bernardino de Mendoza to the King, 19 April 1587, CSPS iv 72.

5 John Cummins, *Francis Drake,* p. 186; Matthew Starke's Deposition, 11 August 1588, SP ccxiv 63–4; Douglas Bell, *Elizabethan Seamen,* p. 219; Howard to Sus-

sex, (?) 22 July 1588, BM Cott MS Otho E. ix, 185; Pedro de Valdes to the King, 21 August 1588, SP ccxv 36.

6 Drake to Walsingham, 31 July 1588, SP ccxiii 73; Articles for Examination of Prisoners, SP ccxiv 16.

7 Matthew Starke's Deposition, 11 August 1588, SP ccxiv 63–4; Relation of Medina-Sidonia, in John Knox Laughton, *State Papers Relating to the Defeat of the Spanish Armada*, II, 354–70; Statement made by the Purser Pedro Coco Calderon, 24 September 1588, CSPS iv 439; Relation of as much as can be ascertained of the occurrences on the Spanish armada, 4 October 1588, CSPS iv 449; Relation of Proceedings, BM Cotton, Julius F.x. 111–17; William Camden, *Annales*, vol. iii, p. 412; Trenchard and Hawley to the Council, 24 August 1588, SP ccxv 49.

8 Gilberte to the Council, 29 July 1588, SP ccxiii 59; Inventory of the *San Salvador*, SP ccxv 49, III; Trenchard and Hawley to the Council, 24 August 1588, SP ccxv 49; Lawrence Stone, "The Armada Campaign of 1588," p. 135; John Thoms to Howard, 15 November 1588, SP ccxviii 24; Relation of Medina-Sidonia, in Laughton, op. cit., II, 354–70.

9 Seymour to the Council, 27 July 1588, SP ccxiii 50; Wynter to Walsingham, 27 July 1588, SP ccxiii 49; Seymour to the Council, 23 July 1588, SP ccxiii 12; Seymour to the Council, 27 July 1588, SP ccxiii 50.

10 Valentine Dale to the Earl of Leicester, 17 June 1588, CSPS iv 314; King to the Duke of Medina-Sidonia, 1 April 1588, in C. Christopher Lloyd (ed.), *The Naval Miscellany*, vol. 4, p. 15; Duke of Medina-Sidonia to the Duke of Parma, 1 August 1588, CSPS iv 360; Relation of Proceedings, BM Cotton, Julius F.x. 111–17.

11 A Brief Abstract of Accidents, SP ccxiv 42; Narrative of Petruccio Ubaldini, in Lloyd (ed.), op. cit., vol. 4; F. J. Furnivall (ed.), *Robert Laneham's Letters*.

12 Relation of Medina-Sidonia, in Laughton, op. cit., II, 354–70; Duke of Medina-Sidonia to Hugo Moncada, 2 August 1588, CSPS iv 362; Narrative of Petruccio Ubaldini, op. cit., vol. 4; Relation of Proceedings, BM Cotton, Julius F.x. 111–17.

13 Relation of Medina-Sidonia, in Laughton, op. cit., II, 354–70; A Brief Abstract of Accidents, SP ccxiv 42; Statement made by the Purser Pedro Coco Calderon, 24 September 1588, CSPS iv 439; Colin Martin and Geoffrey Parker, *The Spanish Armada*, p. 155.

14 A. M. Hadfield, *Time to Finish the Game*, p. 125; Sir George Carey to the Earl of Sussex, 25 July 1588, SP ccxiii 40; Relation of Medina-Sidonia, in Laughton, op. cit., II, 354–70; Duke of Medina-Sidonia to the Duke of Parma, 4 August 1588, CSPS iv 364; N.A.M. Rodger, "Broadside Gunnery," pp. 310–14; Supplementary Secret Instructions to the Duke of Medina-Sidonia, 1 April 1588, CSPS iv 252.

CHAPTER THIRTEEN:

A Terrible Value of Great Shot

1 Colin Martin, *Shipwrecks of the Spanish Armada*; Arthur Nelson, *The Tudor Navy*, pp. 148–9; Relation of Medina-Sidonia, in John Knox Laughton, *State Papers Relating to the Defeat of the Spanish Armada*, II, 354–70; Robert Milne-Tyte, *Armada*, p. 72.

2 Palavicino to Walsingham, 24 July 1588, SP ccxiii 19; Burghley to Walsingham, 19 July 1588, SP ccxii 66; Reasons why the Spaniards should attempt the Isle of Wight, SP ccx 47.

3 Wynter to Walsingham, 1 August 1588, SP ccxiv 7; Howard to (?) Sussex, 22 July 1588, BM Cotton, MS Otho E. ix, f. 185b.

4 Relation of Proceedings, BM Cotton, Julius F.x. 111–17; Relation of Medina-Sidonia, in Laughton, op. cit., II, 354–70; Diary of the Expedition to England, 21 August 1588, CSPS iv 402.

5 Relation of Medina-Sidonia, in Laughton, op. cit., II, 354–70; Statement made by the Purser Pedro Coco Calderon, 24 September 1588, CSPS iv 439.

6 Relation of Proceedings, BM Cotton, Julius F.x. 111–17; Sir George Carey to the Earl of Sussex, 25 July 1588, SP ccxiii 40; Sir George Carey to the Earl of Sussex, 25 July 1588, SP ccxiii 40.

7 Alfred Rusbridge, *Legend of "The Mound" at Selsey;* Hawkins to Walsingham, 31 July 1588, SP ccxiii 71; Walsingham to Burghley, 26 July 1588, SP Otho E. ix f. 214; Sussex to Walsingham, 26 July 1588, SP ccxiii 40; Ed. Burnham to Walsingham, 25 July 1588, SP Holland, lv.

8 Relation of Proceedings, BM Cotton, Julius F.x. 111–17; A. L. Merson (ed.), *The Third Book of Remembrance of Southampton 1514–1602,* Vol. III, p. 54; David Cressy, "The Spanish Armada: Celebration, Myth and Memory," p. 157; Extract from Papers of Sir A. Malet; Queen Elizabeth to the Lord Lieutenants, SP 12/212/64; John S. Nolan, "The Muster of 1588," p. 394.

CHAPTER FOURTEEN:

Resolved There to Live and Die

1 Relation of Proceedings, BM Cotton, Julius F.x. 111–17; Wm Thomas to Burghley, 30 September 1588, SP Holland lvii; Nathaniel Boteler, *Boteler's Dialogues,* p. 23.

2 Relation of Medina-Sidonia, in John Knox Laughton, *State Papers Relating to the Defeat of the Spanish Armada,* II, 354–70; Peter Pierson, *Commander of the Armada,* p. 159; Richard Tomson to Walsingham, 30 July 1588, SP ccxiii 67; Borough to Walsingham, 28 July 1588, SP ccxiii 57.

3 Duro, *La Armada Invencible,* ii, 46; Relation of Medina-Sidonia, in Laughton, op. cit., II, 354–70; John Stow, *The Annales or Generall Chronicles of England,* p. 748.

4 Relation of Medina-Sidonia, in Laughton, op. cit., II, 354–70; Duke of Medina-Sidonia to the Duke of Parma, 6 August 1588, CSPS iv 368; Duke of Parma to the King, 31 January 1588, CSPS iv 209; J.C.A. Schokkenbroek, "Wherefore Serveth Justin," p. 107.

5 Seymour to Walsingham, 20 July 1588, SP ccxii 69; H. O'Donnell, "The Requirements of the Duke of Parma," p. 97; Duke of Parma to the King, 13 May 1588, CSPS iv 292; Garrett Mattingly, *The Defeat of the Spanish Armada,* p. 290.

6 Duke of Parma to the King, 22 June 1588, CSPS iv 319; Colin Martin and Geoffrey Parker, *The Spanish Armada,* p. 170; Duke of Parma to the King, 18 July 1588, CSPS iv 348; David Howarth, *The Voyage of the Armada,* p. 126.

7 Mattingly, op. cit.; Killigrew to Walsingham, 3 August 1588, SP Holland lviv;

Council to Seymour, 28 July 1588, SP ccxiii 53; Relation of Medina-Sidonia, in Laughton, op. cit., II, 354–70; Lord H. Seymour to the Queen, 1 August 1588, SP ccxiv 2.

8 Relation of Medina-Sidonia, in Laughton, op. cit., II, 354–70; Mattingly, op. cit., p. 290; BL Sloane MS 262/62; Leicester to Walsingham, 26 July 1588, SP ccxiii 39.

9 Relation of Medina-Sidonia, in Laughton, op. cit., II, 354–70; Pierson, op. cit., p. 161; Duke of Medina-Sidonia to the Duke of Parma, 7 August 1588, CSPS iv 372 and 372n; Duke of Parma to the King, 8 August 1588, CSPS iv 374.

10 Robert Milne-Tyte, *Armada*, p. 74; Martin and Parker, op. cit.; Duke of Parma to the King, 10 August 1588, CSPS iv 380; Juan Manrique to Juan de Idiaquez, 11 August 1588, CSPS iv 384.

CHAPTER FIFTEEN:

The Hell-burners

1 Wynter to Walsingham, 1 August 1588, SP ccxiv 7; Statement made by the Purser Pedro Coco Calderon, 24 September 1588, CSPS iv 439; King to the Duke of Medina-Sidonia, 7 August 1588, CSPS iv 370.

2 Hawkins to Burghley, 12 September 1588, SP ccxvi 18; Henry Whyte to Walsingham, 8 August 1588, SP ccxiv 43; Sir Julian Stafford Corbett, *Drake and the Tudor Navy*, ii, p. 234; *Certain Advertisements out of Ireland*, p. 132.

3 Duke of Medina-Sidonia to the Duke of Parma, 7 August 1588, CSPS iv 371; PRO Pipe Office Accounts, 2223; Relation of Medina-Sidonia, in John Knox Laughton, *State Papers Relating to the Defeat of the Spanish Armada*, II, 354–70.

4 Advices of the Fleets sent from Rouen, 11 August 1588, CSPS iv 385; Alexander McKee, *From Merciless Invaders*, p. 168; Nathaniel Boteler, *Boteler's Dialogues*, p. 313; *Considerations Touching a War with Spain*, p. 92; Henry Whyte to Walsingham, 8 August 1588, SP ccxiv 43.

5 Richard Tomson to Walsingham, 30 July 1588, SP ccxiii 67; Relation of Medina-Sidonia, in Laughton, op. cit., II, 354–70; Advices of the Fleets sent from Rouen, 11 August 1588, CSPS iv 385v.

6 Lord H. Seymour to the Queen, 1 August 1588, SP ccxiv 2; Richard Tomson to Walsingham, 30 July 1588, SP ccxiii 67; Advices of the Fleets sent from Rouen, 11 August 1588, CSPS iv 385; Howard to Walsingham, 29 July 1588, SP ccxiii 64; Robert Cecil to Lord Burghley, 30 July 1588, SP ccxiii 66; Sir H. Palavicino's Relation, SP ccxv 77.

7 Sir H. Palavicino's Relation, SP ccxv 77; Richard Tomson to Walsingham, 30 July 1588, SP ccxiii 67; Narrative of Petruccio Ubaldini, in C. Christopher Lloyd (ed.), *The Naval Miscellany*, vol. 4.

8 McKee, op. cit., p. 173; Relation of Medina-Sidonia, in Laughton, op. cit., II, 354–70; Narrative of Petruccio Ubaldini, op. cit., vol. 4.

9 Matthew Starke's Deposition, 11 August 1588, SP ccxiv 63–4; Lord H. Seymour to the Queen, 1 August 1588, SP ccxiv 2; Wynter to Walsingham, 1 August 1588, SP ccxiv 7; Sir H. Palavicino's Relation, SP ccxv 77.

10 Wynter to Walsingham, 1 August 1588, SP ccxiv 7; Statement made by the Purser Pedro Coco Calderon, 24 September 1588, CSPS iv 439; Howard to Walsingham, 8 August 1588, SP ccxiv 50.

11 McKee, op. cit., p. 182; Statement made by the Purser Pedro Coco Calderon, 24 September 1588, CSPS iv 439; Narrative of Petruccio Ubaldini, op. cit., vol. 4; Relation of Medina-Sidonia, in Laughton, op. cit., II, pp. 354–70.

12 Relation of Medina-Sidonia, in Laughton, op. cit., II, pp. 354–70; Relation of Proceedings, BM Cotton, Julius F.x. 111–17; McKee, op. cit., p. 186; Diary of the Expedition to England, 21 August 1588, CSPS iv 402.

13 Statement made by the Purser Pedro Coco Calderon, 24 September 1588, CSPS iv 439; Advices of the Fleets sent from Rouen, 11 August 1588, CSPS iv 385.

14 David A. Thomas, *The Illustrated Armada Handbook*, p. 150; Relation of Medina-Sidonia, in Laughton, op. cit., II, pp. 354–70; Wynter to Walsingham, 1 August 1588, SP ccxiv 7.

CHAPTER SIXTEEN:

A Wonderful Fear

1 Advices of the Fleets sent from Rouen, 11 August 1588, CSPS iv 385; Drake to Walsingham, 29 July 1588, SP ccxiii 65; Howard to Walsingham, 29 July 1588, SP ccxiii 64.

2 Robert Cecil to Lord Burghley, 30 July 1588, SP ccxiii 66; Sir H. Palavicino's Relation, SP ccxv 77; Richard Tomson to Walsingham, 30 July 1588, SP ccxiii 67; Fenner to Walsingham, 4 August 1588, SP ccxiv 27.

3 Richard Tomson to Walsingham, 30 July 1588, SP ccxiii 67; Emanuel Francisco, Examinations of Spanish Prisoners, 12 September 1588, SP ccxvi 17; Statement made by the Purser Pedro Coco Calderon, 24 September 1588, CSPS iv 439; Joan Druett, *Rough Medicine*, p. 10.

4 The States of Zeeland to the Queen, SP Holland lvi; Alexander McKee, *From Merciless Invaders*, p. 193; Report of Deserters, 3 August 1588, SP Holland lvi.

5 The States of Zeeland to the Queen, 6 August 1588, SP Holland lvi; A Brief Abstract of Accidents, SP ccxiv 42; Borlas to Walsingham, 3 August 1588, SP Holland lvi; James Humphries, *Orders to be Used in King's or Queen's Majesties Ships*; Seymour to Walsingham, 4 August 1588, SP ccxiv 26; J.C.A. Schokkenbroek, "Wherefore Serveth Justin," p. 108.

6 A. M. Hadfield, *Time to Finish the Game*, p. 149; Willoughby to Walsingham, 3 August 1588, SP Holland lvi; Duke of Parma to the King, 10 August 1588, CSPS iv 380.

7 Diary of the Expedition to England, 21 August 1588, CSPS iv 402; David Howarth, *The Voyage of the Armada*, p. 186; Relation of Medina-Sidonia, in John Knox Laughton, *State Papers Relating to the Defeat of the Spanish Armada*, II, 354–70.

8 Statement made by the Purser Pedro Coco Calderon, 24 September 1588, CSPS iv 439; Robert Milne-Tyte, *Armada*, p. 102; Relation of Medina-Sidonia, in Laughton, op. cit., II, 354–70; Howard to Walsingham, 7 August 1588, SP ccxiv 42v; S. Daultrey, "The Weather of North-west Europe during the Summer and Autumn of 1588," p. 124.

9 Relation of Proceedings, BM Cotton, Julius F.x. 111–17; Hawkins to Walsingham, 31 July 1588, SP ccxiii 71; Resolution at a Council of War, 1 August 1588, BM Addl MS. 33740 f. 6.

10 Seymour to Walsingham, 1 August 1588, SP ccxiv 3; Robert Cecil to Lord Burghley, 30 July 1588, SP ccxiii 66; Wynter to Walsingham, 1 August 1588, SP ccxiv 7; Relation of Medina-Sidonia, in Laughton, op. cit., II, 354–70.

11 Relation of Medina-Sidonia, in Laughton, op. cit., II, pp. 354–70; Statement made by the Purser Pedro Coco Calderon, 24 September 1588, CSPS iv 439; Colin Martin and Geoffrey Parker, *The Spanish Armada*, pp. 209–10; Interrogation of Peter O'Carr, CSPI, 226–9; Francisco de Cuellar, *A Story of the Spanish Armada*, p. 19.

12 Relation of Medina-Sidonia, in Laughton, op. cit., II, 354–70; Francisco de Cuellar's account, p. 19; Statement made by the Purser Pedro Coco Calderon, 24 September 1588, CSPS iv 439.

13 Relation of Proceedings, BM Cotton, Julius F.x. 111–17; Fenner to Walsingham, 4 August 1588, SP ccxiv 27.

14 Howard to Walsingham, 8 August 1588, SP ccxiv 50; Fenner to Walsingham, 4 August 1588, SP ccxiv 27; Drake to Walsingham, 10 August 1588, SP ccxiv 65; Howard to Walsingham, 7 August 1588, SP ccxiv 42; Relation of Proceedings, BM Cotton, Julius F.x. 111–17; Bernardino de Mendoza to the King, 4 September 1588, CSPS iv 419; R. N. Worth, *Calendar of Plymouth Municipal Records*, p. 19; *Considerations Touching a War with Spain*, p. 92.

CHAPTER SEVENTEEN:

The Rags Which Yet Remain

1 John de Licornio, Examinations of Spanish Prisoners, 12 September 1588, SP ccxvi 17; Statement made by the Purser Pedro Coco Calderon, 24 September 1588, CSPS iv 439; CSPI, cxxxvii, 1, II.

2 Sir H. Palavicino's Relation, SP ccxv 77; "Emanuel Fremoso, a Portingal," Examinations of Spanish Prisoners, 12 September 1588, SP ccxvi 17; Duke of Medina-Sidonia to the King, 21 August 1588, CSPS iv 401; J. L. Anderson, "Climatic Change, Sea-Power and Historical Discontinuity," pp. 13–23; S. Daultrey, "The Weather of North-west Europe during the Summer and Autumn of 1588," p. 116.

3 "Pier o Carr, A Fleming," Examinations of Spanish Prisoners, 12 September 1588, SP ccxvi 17; "Emanuel Fremoso, a Portingal," Examinations of Spanish Prisoners, 12 September 1588, SP ccxvi 17; Statement made by the Purser Pedro Coco Calderon, 24 September 1588, CSPS iv 439; "Emanuel Francisco," Examinations of Spanish Prisoners, 12 September 1588, SP ccxvi 17.

4 "Emanuel Fremoso, a Portingal," Examinations of Spanish Prisoners, 12 September 1588, SP ccxvi 17; Statement made by the Purser Pedro Coco Calderon, 24 September 1588, CSPS iv 439; G. Fenton to Burghley, 28 October 1588, CSPI cxxxvii 49; William Thornber, *Traditions of the Foreland of the Fylde*.

5 David Howarth, *The Voyage of the Armada*, p. 207; Lord Deputy and Council to the Privy Council, 10 September 1588, CSPI cxxxvi, 32; Sir J. Popham to Burghley, 10 September 1588, SP Ireland cxxxvi 34; Interrogation of Peter O'Carr, CSPI, 226–9; Account of Marcos de Arambaru, in W. Spotswood Green, "Armada Ships on the Kerry Coast," pp. 263–9; CSPI cxxxvi 24; Certain Advertisements out of Ireland, p. 134v.

6 Account of Marcos de Arambaru, in W. Spotswood Green, op. cit., pp. 263–9;

Evelyn Hardy, *Survivors of the Armada*, p. 147; George Cumberland to Walsingham, 29 October 1588, Clifford family papers, HMC 3rd Report, p. 37.

7 Juan de Saavedra to the King, 4 October 1588, CSPS iv 447; Pedro de Igueldo to the King, 4 October 1588, CSPS iv 448; Pedro de Igueldo to Bernardino de Mendoza, 7 October 1588, CSPS iv 453; Pedro de Igueldo to Bernardino de Mendoza, 8 October 1588, CSPS iv 454; Hardy, op. cit., p. 41.

8 John de Courcy Ireland, "Ragusa and the Spanish Armada," pp. 251–62; Marolin de Juan, Pilot General of the Armada, 27 December 1588, CSPS iv 494; Robert Stenuit, *Treasures of the Armada*.

9 Francisco de Cuellar, *A Story of the Spanish Armada*, pp. 20–1; G. Fenton to Burghley, 28 October 1588, CSPI cxxxvii 49; Sean Spellissy, *The History of Galway: City and County*, p. 229.

10 Secretary G. Fenton to Burghley, 19 September 1588, CSPI cxxxvi 48; Sir Richard Bingham to the Lord Deputy, quoted in Robert Milne-Tyte, *Armada*, p. 137; CSPI cxxxvi 27; CSPI cxxxvi; CSPI cxxxvi 38; CSP, Carew MSS, 1588, 675; James Hardiman, *History of Galway;* Norris to Walsingham, 18/19 September 1588, CSPI, 26, 28.

11 CSPI cxxxvi 29.I; Geo. Woodloke to Mr. Alexander Brywer, Mayor of Waterford, 13 September 1588, CSPI cxxxvi 37; CSPI 12 September 1588, p. 40; Alexander Brywer, Mayor [of Waterford], to Walsingham, 13 September 1588, CSPI cxxxvi, 37.

12 Statement of Juan de Nova, 21 January 1589, CSPS iv 502; Examination of Prisoners, 13 October 1588, SP Ireland cxxxvii 15; Pa. Fox to Walsingham, 26 September 1588, CSPI cxxxvi 51.

13 Sir R. Bingham to Fitzwilliam, 21 September 1588, SP Ireland, cxxxvii, 1, I; Sir R. Bingham to the Queen, 3 December 1588, CSPI cxxxix 2; CSPI cxxxvi 45; CSP, Carew MSS, 1588, 669.

14 CSP, Carew MSS, 1588, 18, 669; Sir R. Bingham to the Queen, 3 December 1588, CSPI cxxxix 2; Sir R. Bingham to Fitzwilliam, 21 September 1588, SP Ireland, cxxxvii, 1, I; Lord Deputy Fitzwilliam to Burghley, 16 September 1588, CSPI cxxxvi 39; Lord Deputy Fitzwilliam to Walsingham, 28 October 1588, CSPI cxxxvii 48; CSPI 1588–92, p. 93; Hardiman, op. cit.; Spellissy, op. cit., p. 46.

15 John Knox Laughton, *State Papers Relating to the Defeat of the Spanish Armada*, II, 219; Lord Deputy and Council to the Privy Council, 18 October 1588, SP Ireland cxxxvii 25; Milne-Tyte, op. cit., p. 124; James Melvill, *The Autobiography and Diary of James Melvill*.

16 De Cuellar, op. cit., pp. 23–39.

17 CSPS iv p. 641; Milne-Tyte, op. cit., p. 149; Dr. Charles Smith, *History of Kerry*.

18 APCE, xvi, 273; Paula Martin, *Spanish Armada Prisoners*, pp. 75–6; Anthony Ashley to the Council, 12 November 1588, SP ccxxviii 14; Acts of the Privy Council, XVI, 328–9, 357, 373–4; R. N. Worth, *Calendar of the Plymouth Municipal Records*, p. 129.

19 Cary to the Council, 5 November 1588, SP ccxxviii 4; Cary to the Council, 14 October 1588, SP ccxvii 22; Cary to the Council, 6 October 1588, SP ccxvii 10; Cary to the Council, 14 October 1588, SP ccxvii 21; David A. Thomas, *The Illustrated Armada Handbook*, p. 41.

20 Statement of Gonzalo Gonzales del Castillo, 9 March 1592, CSPS iv 609; Acts of the Privy Council, 18 January 1590.

21 Alderman Radcliff to Walsingham, 27 August 1588, SP ccxv 60; Letter from London, 24 September 1588, CSPS iv 437; Advices from London, 25 September 1588, CSPS iv 440; Cary to Walsingham, 29 August 1588, SP ccxv 67.

22 Pedro de Valdes to the King, 21 August 1588, SP ccxv 36; Tomson's Statement, 8 September 1588, SP ccxvi 9; Pedro de Valdes to Walsingham, 8 September 1588, SP ccxvi 10; CSPF 1589–90, 355; Statement of Gonzalo Gonzales del Castillo, 9 March 1592, CSPS iv 609.

23 Martin, op. cit., p. 85; Bernardino de Mendoza to the King, 21 January 1589, CSPS iv 501.

CHAPTER EIGHTEEN:

The Disease Uncured

1 Howard to Walsingham, 8 August 1588, SP ccxiv 50; Reports of Survey, September 1588, SP ccxx; A Survey of the Navy, 28 September 1588, SP ccxvi 40; Sir H. Palavicino's Relation, SP ccxv 77; Howard to Walsingham, 8 August 1588, SP ccxiv 50.

2 Sir F. Drake to the Queen, 8 August 1588, SP ccxiv 47.

3 Drake to Walsingham, 10 August 1588, SP ccxiv 65; Drake to Walsingham, 8 August 1588, SP ccxiv 48; Walsingham to Burghley, 9 August 1588, Harleian MS 6994, f. 140.

4 Henry Whyte to Walsingham, 8 August 1588, SP ccxiv 43; William Monson, *Naval Tracts*, vol. 1, 152–73; Sir Thomas Heneage to Walsingham, 9 August 1588, SP ccxiv 53; Walsingham to the Lord Chancellor, 8 August 1588, Harleian MS 6994, f. 138v.

5 Advices from England, 5 November 1588, CSPS iv 470; Intelligence from Calais, 31 August 1588, CSPS iv 412; Lord Deputy Fitzwilliam to Walsingham, 16 September 1588, CSPI cxxxvi 40; Walsingham to Burghley, 9 August 1588, Harleian MS 6994, f. 142.

6 Seymour to Walsingham, 17 August 1588, SP ccxv 24; Seymour to Walsingham, 19 August 1588, SP ccxv 34; Seymour to Walsingham, 20 July 1588, SP ccxii 69; Howard to Walsingham, 27 August 1588, SP ccxv 59.

7 Sir Walter Ralegh, *History of the World*, ii, p. 565 (1736 edn).

8 Arthur Nelson, *The Tudor Navy*, p. 148; Peter Kemp, *The British Sailor*, p. 1.

9 The States of Zeeland to the Queen, SP Holland lvi; Council of State of the United Provinces to the Lords of the Council, 8 August 1588, SP Holland lvi; Seymour to Walsingham, 1 August 1588, SP ccxiv 3; Seymour, Wynter and Palmer to the Council, 6 August 1588, SP ccxiv 59; Wynter to Walsingham, 1 August 1588, SP ccxiv 7.

10 Seymour to Walsingham, 17 August 1588, SP ccxv 24; Richard Tomson to Walsingham, 30 July 1588, SP ccxiii 67; Jack Davies Jones, "The Isle of Wight and the Armada," p. 12.

11 Felix Barker, "If Parma Had Landed," p. 37; Leicester to Walsingham, 22 July 1588, SP ccxiii 9; Advices from London, 1 April 1588, CSPS iv 254.

12 RCHM 5th Report, p. 138 (papers of the Dukes of Sutherland); Leicester to Walsingham, 26 July 1588, SP ccxiii 38; RCHM 3rd Report, p. 258 (papers of Whitehall Dodd); Leicester to Walsingham, 25 July 1588, SP ccxiii 27; Leicester to Walsingham, 26 July 1588, SP ccxiii 38.

13 David A. Thomas, *The Illustrated Armada Handbook*; Sir Thomas Wilford, *A Military Discourse*, pp. 23–4; R. B. Wernham, *Before the Armada*, p. 400; J. N. McGurk, "Armada Preparations in Kent," p. 75; Duke of Parma to the King, 20 March 1588, CSPS iv 242.

14 "The Journal of Frederick, Duke of Wurtemberg, 1592"; Narrative of Petruccio Ubaldini, in C. Christopher Lloyd (ed.), *The Naval Miscellany*, vol. 4; Jasper Ridley, *The Tudor Age*, p. 293; Seymour to Walsingham, 7 August 1588, SP ccxiv 40.

15 John Stow, *Survey of London*; A. F. Pollard (ed.), *Tudor Tracts, 1532–1588*, pp. 493–6; David Cressy, "The Spanish Armada: Celebration, Myth and Memory," p. 159; Alison Weir, *The Life of Elizabeth I*, p. 402.

16 Mary Hill Cole, *The Portable Queen*; Pollard (ed.), op. cit., p. 496; James Aske, *Elizabetha Triumphans*; Barker, op. cit., p. 39.

17 Ernest Straker, *Wealden Iron*, p. 59; Howard to Walsingham, 22 August 1588, SP ccxv 42–3; Drake to Walsingham, 22 August 1588, SP ccxv 46; Sir G. Carey to Lord Hunsdon, 22 August 1588, SP ccxv 37; Edward Wynter to Walsingham, 24 August 1588, SP ccxv 47; George Cumberland to Walsingham, 20 February 1589, in Thomas Dunham Whitaker, *The History and Antiquities of the Deanery of Craven*; Emanuel Francisco, Examinations of Spanish Prisoners, 12 September 1588, SP ccxvi 17.

18 Letter from London, 7 September 1588, CSPS iv 423; Cervantes, *Dos Canciones inéditas*; Secretary G. Fenton to Burghley, 18 September 1588, CSPI cxxxvi 47. I; Richard A. Gould (ed.), *Shipwreck Anthropology*, pp. 3–22.

19 Cressy, op. cit., p. 161; *Norfolk Archaeology*, 1847, pp. 9, 18; Bertrand T. Whitehead, *Brags and Boasts*, p. 151.

20 David Cressy, *Bonfires and Bells*, pp. 110–29.

21 Proclamation CSPD, 25 August 1588; Borough to Walsingham, 27 August 1588, SP cxxv 57; Harleian MS 168/180–5.

22 Monson, op. cit., vol. 2, p. 244; Hawkins to Burghley, 26 August 1588, SP ccxv 56; Hawkins to Burghley, 28 August 1588, SP ccxv 63v.

23 Howard to Walsingham, 29 August 1588, SP ccxv 66; Fenner to Walsingham, 4 August 1588, SP ccxiv 27; John Knox Laughton, *State Papers Relating to the Defeat of the Spanish Armada*, II, 212 and 324–5, I, lxiv.

24 Burghley to Walsingham, 9 August 1588, SP ccxiv 54; Walsingham to Burghley, 9 August 1588, Harleian MS 6994, f. 142; Kenneth R. Andrews, *The Elizabethan Privateers*, p. 237; Howard to Walsingham, 8 August 1588, SP ccxiv 50; Howard to the Council, 22 August 1588, SP ccxv 41; Howard to Walsingham, 9 August 1588, SP ccxiv 61; Memorandum by Burghley, 12 August 1588, SP ccxv 3.

25 Lawrence Stone, "The Armada Campaign of 1588," p. 125; Petition of Anthony Potts, SP ccxvi 66; The Petition of the Captains &c., of Sandwich and Dover, SP ccxvi 67; Thomas Fleming to Burghley, 27 December 1588, SP ccxix 40; Allowance for Ships Burned, October, SP ccxvii 71; SP ccxvi 27.

26 Howard to Burghley, 10 August 1588, SP ccxiv 66; Howard to Walsingham, 25 August 1588, SP ccxv 55; Howard to the Queen, 22 August 1588, SP ccxv 40; Howard to the Council, 22 August 1588, SP ccxv 41.

27 PRO Lands MSS 144, f. 53; 73, f. 161; Hawkins to Walsingham, 6 September 1588, SP ccxvi 4; Petition of Sir J. Hawkins, 14 December 1588, SP ccxix 28.

28 Howard to Walsingham, 27 August 1588, SP ccxv 59; Howard to Burghley, December 1588, SP ccxix 23; Whitaker, op. cit.

29 Intelligence from Calais, 31 August 1588, CSPS iv 412; C. Christopher Lloyd, *The British Seaman*, pp. 23–4; Stone, op. cit., p. 125.
30 CSPD ccxxviii 10; John Guy, *Tudor England;* Calendar of Assize Records for Sussex, p. 234; CSPD ccxxix 21; Ridley, op. cit., p. 284; CSPD ccxl 59; CSPD ccxl 60.
31 Anonymous journal, quoted in T. E. Hartley (ed.), *Proceedings in the Parliaments of Elizabeth I*, Vol. 3, 1593–1601, p. 156.
32 Hartley (ed.), op. cit., pp. 144, 58–60; William Cobbett (ed.), *Parliamentary History of England*, pp. 863–6.
33 A. Hassell Smith and G. M. Baker (eds.), *The Papers of Nathaniel Bacon;* CSPD ccxliv 125; Egerton Papers, p. 161; CSPD, 5 October 1595.
34 Sir John Fortescue, *History of the British Army*, p. 151.

CHAPTER NINETEEN:

Vanished into Smoke

1 Richard Hakluyt, *Principal Navigations*, p. 397; Bernardino de Mendoza to the King, 24 September 1588, CSPS iv 436; King to Bernardino de Mendoza, 18 August 1588, CSPS iv 393.
2 Count de Olivares to the King, 26 September 1588, CSPS iv 441; Advices from Antwerp, 24 August 1588, CSPS iv 404; Advices from Dunkirk via Lille, 30 August 1588, CSPS iv 409; extract from Letter from Juan de Gamarra, 31 August 1588, CSPS iv 413.
3 Bernardino de Mendoza to the King, 4 September 1588, CSPS iv 419; extract from Letter from Juan de Gamarra, 31 August 1588, CSPS iv 413; Bernardino de Mendoza to the King, 4 September 1588, CSPS iv 419; Intelligence from Calais, 31 August 1588, CSPS iv 412; The current Duchess of Medina-Sidonia interviewed in Alan Ereira, *Armada;* Cervantes, *Dos Canciones inéditas.*
4 Count Olivares to the King, 26 September 1588, CSPS iv 441; CSP Venetian, August 1588; Statement of as much as can be Learned of the Royal Armada, 3 September 1588, CSPS iv 416; John Nichol, *Progresses and Public Processions of Queen Elizabeth*, 1823, ii, p. 537.
5 Bernardino de Mendoza to the King, 29 September 1588, CSPS iv 442n; Ereira, op. cit.; Count de Olivares to the King, 29 October 1588, CSPS iv 463.

CHAPTER TWENTY:

God Will Tire of Working Miracles

1 Statement made by the Purser Pedro Coco Calderon, 24 September 1588, CSPS iv 439; Relation of Medina-Sidonia, in John Knox Laughton, *State Papers Relating to the Defeat of the Spanish Armada*, II, 354–70.
2 "Pier o Carr, A Fleming," Examinations of Spanish Prisoners, 12 September 1588, SP ccxvi 17; Evelyn Hardy, *Survivors of the Armada*, p. 168; Report of John Brown of Clontarf, recently escaped from Ribadeo, 6 February 1589, CSPI, 121; Duke of Medina-Sidonia to the King, 23 September 1588, CSPS iv 433.
3 The King to the Captain General of Guipuzcoa, 26 December 1588, Archivo de la Casa de Heredia Spinola, Madrid, 122/120, quoted in Colin Martin and

Geoffrey Parker, *The Spanish Armada*, p. 242; Duke of Medina-Sidonia to the King, 23 September 1588, CSPS iv 433; Peter Pierson, *Commander of the Armada*, p. 171; Martin and Parker, op. cit., p. 240.

4 Garcia de Villejo to Andres de Prajda, 10 October 1588, CSPS iv 456; Philip Gosse, *Sir John Hawkins;* Pierson, op. cit., p. 279n.

5 Ron Keightley, "An Armada Veteran Celebrates the Death of Drake," p. 405; William Monson, *Naval Tracts*, vol. 1, pp. 152–73; Pierson, op. cit., p. 233.

6 Monson, op. cit., vol. 1, pp. 152–73; Drake to Walsingham, 10 August 1588, SP ccxiv 65; Sir Walter Ralegh, *History of the World*, iii, 4, 2.

7 David A. Thomas, *The Illustrated Armada Handbook*, p. 210; Summary of divers letters to the Duke of Parma, 12 September, CSPS iv 427; Points of a Letter from the Earl of Huntly to the Duke of Parma, 12 September 1588, CSPS iv 428; Letter from London, 7 September 1588, CSPS iv 423; Bernardino de Mendoza to the King, 2 November 1588, CSPS iv 466.

8 Bernardino de Mendoza to the King, 13 October 1588, CSPS iv 458; King to Bernardino de Mendoza, 3 September 1588, CSPS iv 417.

9 Advices from London, 21 November 1588, CSPS iv 476; Kenneth R. Andrews, *Trade, Plunder and Settlement*, p. 238.

10 Bernardino de Mendoza to the King, 2 November 1588, CSPS iv 466; Sir Robert Naunton, *Fragmenta Regalia;* Advices from England, 5 November 1588, CSPS iv 470; Winston Graham, *The Spanish Armadas*, p. 166.

11 I.A.A. Thompson, *War and Government in Habsburg Spain;* J. L. Motley, *History of the United Netherlands*, ii, p. 535.

12 Monson, op. cit., vol. 2, p. 94; G. M. Trevelyan, *History of England*, pp. 356–7n; Ronald H. Fritze (ed.), *Historical Dictionary of Tudor England*, p. 33.

Bibliography

British Library (BL)
Additional MS 28,376/66–7; Cotton MS Caligula D.I f. 292; Harleian MS 168/166–174, 168/180–5, 296, 3; Lansdowne MS 51 f. 46, 73, f. 130, 96.12; Salisbury MS, III, P 67–70, CSPF, XIX, 95–8; Sloane MS 262/62 and 66–7; Yelverton MSS 31 f. 545

Bodleian Library, Oxford
James P. R. Lyell, "Commentary on Certain Aspects of the Spanish Armada," (unpublished MS); Bod. Ashmole 830 f. 13 and 830 f. 18; Tanner MS 78

Historic Manuscripts Commission
Bagot Papers HMSSC. IV; Salisbury MSS, vols 3 and 4; RCHM 3rd Report HMSO 1872 (Devonshire Papers); RCHM 3rd Report (papers of Whitehall Dodd); RCHM 3rd Report (papers of Rev. F. Hopkinson); RCHM 4th Report (House of Lords Supplementary Calendar); RCHM 5th Report (papers of the Dukes of Sutherland); RCHM 5th Report (papers of Weymouth and Melcombe Regis Corporation); RCHM 5th Report (extract from Papers of Sir A. Malet); HMC 15th Report: Appendix, Part V, pp. 20–62 (orders issued by the Privy Council for the defence of the realm)

Public Record Office
SP 12/174/1–11, 14–18; SP 12/194/30; SP 12/205/70; SP 12/211/15; SP 12/211/36; SP 12/212/64; SP 12/213/45

Lincoln Record Office
Ancaster Muniments, X, f. 1, Willoughby to Cristobal de Mondragon

West Country Studies Library, Exeter
Drake clippings files

Magdalene College Library, Cambridge
Pepys MS 2991

University of Southampton, Hartley Library
Cope Collection

Dudley Borough Archives
Dudley Papers

University of Bristol Library
Paget Papers

Folger Shakespeare Library, Washington, D.C.
MS V.b.142, f. 26; MS V.b.214, ff. 83–5; MS G.a.1; MS G.b.5

PRINTED BOOKS AND PAPERS

Unless otherwise indicated, the place of publication is London.

Adams, Simon, *The Armada Campaign of 1588*, Historical Association, 1988
Adams, Simon, "The Battle that Never Was: The Downs and the Armada Campaign," in M. J. Rodriguez-Salgado and S. Adams (eds.), *England, Spain and the Gran Armada 1585–89: Essays from the Anglo-Spanish Conferences London and Madrid 1988*, Edinburgh, 1991
Adams, Simon, "Eliza Enthroned? The Court and its Politics," in C. Haigh (ed.), *The Reign of Elizabeth*, 1984
Adams, Simon, "The Lurch into War: The Spanish Armada," *History Today*, 38, May 1988
Adams, Simon, "New Light on the 'Reformation' of Sir John Hawkins: The Ellesmere Naval Survey of January 1584," *English Historical Review*, 105, January 1990
Adams, Simon, "The Outbreak of the Elizabethan Naval War against the Spanish Empire: The Embargo of January 1584," in M. J. Rodriguez-Salgado and S. Adams (eds.), *England, Spain and the Gran Armada 1585–89: Essays from the Anglo-Spanish Conferences London and Madrid 1988*, Edinburgh, 1991
Adams, Simon, "Stanley, York and Elizabeth's Catholics," *History Today*, 37, July 1987
Addington, Larry, *The Patterns of War through the Eighteenth Century*, Indiana University Press, Bloomington, 1990
Allen, William, *Letters and Memorials of William Allen*, 1882
Allingham, Hugh (trans. Robert Crawford), *Captain Cuellar's Adventures in Connacht and Ulster 1588*, 1897
Alsop, J. D., "Sea Surgeons, Health and England's Maritime Expansion: The West African Trade 1553–1660," *Mariner's Mirror*, 76:3, August 1990
Alvarez de Toledo, L. I., Duchess of Medina-Sidonia, *Alonso Perez de Guzman, General de la Invencible*, 2 vols., Cadiz, 1995
Alvear y Ward, Sabina de, *Historio de D. Diego Alvear Ponce de Leon, Brigadier de la Armada*, Madrid, 1891
Anderson, J. L., "Climatic Change, Sea-Power and Historical Discontinuity: The Spanish Armada and the Glorious Revolution of 1688," *Great Circle* 5, n.m., 1983

Anderson, R. L., *Letters of the Fifteenth and Sixteenth Centuries*, Southampton, 1921

Andrews, J. H., "Post Armada Cartography in Galway," in *Journal of the Galway Archaeological and Historical Society*, 52, 2000

Andrews, Kenneth Raymond, *Drake's Voyages: A Reassessment of Their Place in Elizabethan Naval Expansion*, Scribners, New York, 1967

Andrews, Kenneth Raymond, "Elizabethan Privateering," in Joyce Youengs (ed.), *Raleigh in Exeter 1985, Privateering and Colonisation in the Reign of Elizabeth I*, Exeter Studies in History, 10, University of Exeter Press, 1985

Andrews, Kenneth Raymond, *Elizabethan Privateering: English Privateering during the Spanish War, 1585–1603*, Cambridge, 1964

Andrews, Kenneth Raymond, *The Elizabethan Seaman*, National Maritime Museum, 1981

Andrews, Kenneth Raymond, *Trade, Plunder and Settlement: Maritime Enterprise and the Genesis of the British Empire, 1480–1630*, Cambridge University Press, New York 1984

Apps, Michael, *The Four Ark Royals*, William Kimber, 1976

Arambaru, Marcos de, *Account of Marcos de Arambaru* (trans. W. Spotswood Green), in *Proceedings of the Royal Irish Academy*, vol. 27, section C, 12, Dublin and London, 1908–9

Arber, E., *A Transcript of the Registers of the Company of Stationers of London, 1554–1640*, 5 vols., vol. 2, 232b, 1875–94

Archdeacon, Daniel, *A True Discourse of the Armie which the King of Spaine Caused to bee Assembled in the Haven of Lisbon . . . in the Yeare 1588*, 1588

Archibald, E.H.H., *The Wooden Fighting Ships in the Royal Navy* (illustrations of *Ark Royal* and *San Martin* by Ray Woodward), Blandford Press, 1968

Armstrong, Edward, "Venetian Despatches on the Armada and its Results," *English Historical Review*, 12, October 1897

Aske, James, *Elizabetha Triumphans*, 1588

Aubrey, John, *Brief Lives*, Mandarin, 1992

Bacon, Anthony (Thomas Birch, ed.) *Memoirs of the Reign of Elizabeth*, 2 vols., 1754 (1970)

Bacon, Nathaniel (A. Hassell Smith, G. M. Baker and R. W. Kenny, eds.), *The Papers of Nathaniel Bacon of Stiffkey*, 2 vols., Norwich, 1979–83, vol. 2

Bagwell, Richard, *Ireland under the Tudors*, 3 vols., 1885–90

Baker, H. Kendra, *Elizabeth and Sixtus: A Seventeenth Century Sidelight on the Spanish Armada*, 1938

Baldwin-Smith, Lacey, *The Elizabethan Epic*, Cape, 1966

Barker, Felix, "If Parma had Landed," *History Today*, 38, May 1988

Barrow, John, *The Life, Voyages and Exploits of Admiral Sir Francis Drake, with Numerous Original Letters from him and the Lord High Admiral to the Queen and Great Officers*, 1843

Barrow, John, *Memoirs of the Naval Worthies of Queen Elizabeth's Reign*, 1845

Beckett, Ian F. W., *The Amateur Military Tradition, 1558–1945*, Manchester History of the British Army, Manchester University Press, 1992

Beier, A. L., *The Problem of the Poor in Tudor and Early Stuart England*, Methuen, 1983

Bell, Douglas H., *Elizabethan Seamen*, Philadelphia, 1936

Benson, E. F., "Drake's Duty: New Light on Armada Incident. A Slur Removed," *The Times*, 17 September 1926

Besant, Sir Walter, *London in the Time of the Tudors*, 1904
Bhanji, Sadru, and Rogers, Jan M. (illustrator), *Topsham Saga: Armada and Ship Owners, Book 6, AD 1580–1625*, Apsam Books, Topsham, 1995
Bindoff, S. T., *Tudor England*, Pelican History of England, vol. 5, 1950
Bindoff, S. T., Hurstfield, Joel, and Williams, C. H. (eds.), *Elizabethan Government and Society: Essays Presented to Sir John Neale*, Athlone Press, 1961
Black, John B., *The Reign of Elizabeth 1558–1603*, Oxford History of England, 1959
Blackman, D. J. (ed.), *Marine Archaeology: Proceedings of the 23rd Symposium of the Colston Research Society, held at the University of Bristol, 4–8 April 1971*, Butterworths, 1973
Bodin, Jean (R. W. Dyson and H. Tudor, eds. and trans.) *Response to the Paradoxes of Malestroit*, 1568, Thoemmes Press, 1997
Bossy, John, *Giordano Bruno and the Embassy Affair*, Yale University Press, 1991
Boteler, Nathaniel (W. G. Perrin, ed.), *Boteler's Dialogues*, Navy Records Society, 1929
Boulind, Richard, "Drake's Navigational Skills," *Mariner's Mirror*, 54, November 1968
Bourne, H. R. Fox, *English Seamen under the Tudors*, 2 vols., 1868
Bourne, W., *The Art of Shooting in Great Ordnance*, 1587
Bovill, E. W., "Queen Elizabeth's Gunpowder," *Mariner's Mirror*, 33, July 1947
Boxer, Charles Ralph, *The Church Militant and Iberian Expansion, 1440–1770*, Johns Hopkins University Press, 2002
Boynton, Lindsay, *The Elizabethan Militia, 1558–1638*, Routledge, 1967
Bracken, C. W., "Drake's Game of Bowls," *Western Morning News*, 30 November 1938
Brecht, Bertolt, *Poems, 1913–1956*, Methuen, 1976
Brewer, J. S., and Bullen, W. (eds.), *Calendar of the Carew Manuscripts 1575–1588*, 1868
Brewer, J. S., and Bullen, W. (eds.), *Calendar of the Carew Manuscripts 1589–1600*, 1868
Bridge, Sir Cyprian, *Sea Power and Other Studies*, 1910
Brigden, Susan, *New Worlds, Lost Worlds: The Rule of the Tudors, 1485–1603*, Penguin, 2002
Brooke, Charles Frederick Tucker, "Some Pre-Armada Propagandist Poetry in England, 1585–86," *Proceedings of the American Philosophical Society*, 85, n.m., 1942
Bruce, J. (ed.), *Letters and Papers of the Verney Family Down to the end of the Year 1639*, Camden Soc., 1853
Bruce, John, *Report on the Arrangements which Were Made for the Internal Defence of These Kingdoms When Spain, by its Armada, Projected the Invasion and Conquest of England*, 1798
Bull, S. B., "Gunpowder, Ordnance and Warfare: Britain c. 1580–1655," PhD dissertation, University of Wales, 1989
Burghley, Lord William, *The Spanish Invasion*, 1588
Burnell, A. D. (ed.), *The Voyage of John Huyghen van Linschoten to the East Indies*, 1885
Burrows, C. T., "Drake's Game of Bowls," *Western Morning News*, 24 November 1931
Busino, Orazio, "The Diary of Orazio Busino, Chaplain of Pietro Contarini,

Venetian Ambassador," in *The Journals of Two Travellers in Elizabethan and Early Stuart England*, Caliban Books, 1995
Calderon, Pedro Coco, Account of Pedro Coco Calderon, in Calendar of State Papers Relating to English Affairs Preserved . . . in the Archives of Simancas, Elizabeth, vol. 4, 1899
Calendar of State Papers Domestic Series Edward VI, Mary, Elizabeth (1581–90), 1865
Calendar of State Papers Domestic Series of the Reigns of Elizabeth and James I, Addenda, 1580–1625, 1872
Calendar of State Papers, Foreign Series, of the Reign of Elizabeth, 1558–91, 23 vols., 1863 (1969) XIX, XXI (4 parts) and XXII, 1916, 1927–31, 1936
Calendar of State Papers, Holland and Flanders, 1586–88
Calendar of State Papers and Manuscripts Relating to English Affairs Existing in the Archives and Collections of Venice and in other Libraries of Northern Italy, 1556–1603, VIII, IX, 1894
Calendar of State Papers Relating to the Defeat of the Spanish Armada, Anno 1588 (John Knox Laughton, ed.), Scolar Press, 1987/Navy Records Society I–II, 1895
Calendar of State Papers Relating to English Affairs Preserved . . . in the Archives of Simancas, Elizabeth, 4 vols., 1899
Calendar of State Papers Relating to Ireland in the Reign of Elizabeth (1588–92), IV, V, 1885
Calendar of State Papers Relating to Scotland and Mary Queen of Scots, 1547–1603, 1936, vols X and XI (IX, 1586–88, 1915)
Callender, Sir Geoffrey, "The Naval Campaign of 1587," *History*, 3, July 1918
Calvar Gross, Jorge, *La Batalla del Mar Oceano*, Madrid, 1988
Camden Miscellany, Vol. XIII, 1924 (Devereux Papers 1575–1601)
Camden, William, *Annales . . . regnante Elizabetha* (T. Hearne, ed.), 3 vols., 1717
Camden, William, *Britannia*, 1695
Camden, William (Wallace T. MacCaffrey, ed.), *The History of the Most Renowned and Victorious Princess Elizabeth*, Chicago, 1970
Caraman, P. (ed.), *The Other Face: Catholic Life under Elizabeth*, Longmans, 1960
Carew, Richard, *Survey of Cornwall*, c. 1580
Carleton, *A Thankfull Remembrance*, 1630
Carroll, Michael J., *The Second Spanish Armada*, Bantry Studio Publications, 1992
Carter, Charles H. (ed.), *From the Renaissance to the Counter-Reformation: Essays in Honour of Garrett Mattingly*, 1965
"Certaine Advertisements out of Ireland, Concerning the Losses and Distresses Happened to the Spanish Navie, Upon the West Coastes of Ireland, in their Voyage Intended from the Northern Isles beyond Scotland, Towards Spaine," in *Harleian Miscellany*, vol. 1, 1808, 40
Cervantes (Manuel Serrano y Sanz, ed.), *Dos Canciones inéditas de Cervantes*, Miguel de Cervantes Saavedra, Madrid, 1899
Chamberlin, Frederick, *The Sayings of Queen Elizabeth*, 1923
Cheyney, E.P.A., *A History of England from the Defeat of the Armada to the Death of Elizabeth*, 2 vols., 1914, 1918
Cheyney, Edward Potts, *Law in History and Other Essays*, New York, 1927
Christy, Miller, "Queen Elizabeth's Visit to Tilbury in 1588," *English Historical Review*, 33, January 1919

Christy, M. (ed.), *The Voyages of Captain Luke Foxe and Captain Thomas James*, 2 vols., 1894

Clark, Peter, *English Provincial Society from the Reformation to the Revolution*, Harvester Press, Sussex, 1977

Clarke, George Sydenham, and Thursfield, Sir James Richard, *The Navy and the Nation*, 1897

Clarke, Samuel, *England's Remembrancer: Containing a True and Full Narrative of . . . the Spanish Invasion of 1588*, 1657

Clowes, William, *Profitable and Necessarie Booke of Observations*, 1615

Clowes, Sir William Laird, *The Royal Navy: A History*, 7 vols., 1897–1903

Cobbett, William (ed.), *Parliamentary History of England, Volume 1, 1066–1625*, 1806

Cockburn, J. S. (ed.), *Calendars of Assize Records Sussex Indictments 1590–1592*, HMSO, 1975

Cogar, William B. (ed.), *New Interpretations in Naval History: Selected Papers from the Eighth Naval History Symposium*, Naval Institute Press, Annapolis, 1989

Cole, Mary Hill, *The Portable Queen: Elizabeth I and the Politics of Ceremony*, Massachusetts Studies in Early Modern Culture, University of Massachusetts, 2000

Collier, J. P. (ed.), *The Egerton Papers*, Camden Soc., 1840

Collinson, Patrick, *Elizabethan Essays*, Hambledon, 1994

Colvin, H., *The History of the King's Works*, vol. 4, HSMO, 1982

Commines, Philippe de, *Memoires* (trans. A. R. Scoble), 2 vols., 1855–56

Connell-Smith, Gordon, "Forerunners of Drake: Some Aspects of Privateering and Piracy during the Last French War of Henry VIII," *Bulletin of the Institute of Historical Research*, 24, 1951

Connell-Smith, Gordon, "Forerunners of Drake: A Study of English Trade with Spain in the Early Tudor Period," Royal Empire Society, *Imperial Studies*, 21, 1954

"Considerations Touching a Warre with Spaine," in *Harleian Miscellany*, vol. 5, 1808

Cooke, Judith, *Dr. Simon Forman*, Vintage, 2002

Copeman, W.S.C., *Doctors and Disease in Tudor Times*, Dawson, 1960

Copie of a Letter Sent from Sea by a Gentleman who was Employed in Discouerie on the Coast of Spaine by Appointment of the Generals of our English Fleete, to a Worshippful Friend of His, Da Capo Press, New York, 1972

"Copie of a Letter Sent out of England to Don Bernardin Mendoza, Ambassador in France for the King of Spaine, Declaring the State of England, Contrary to the Opinion of Don Bernardin, and of All His Partizans Spaniardes and Others. This Letter Although it was sent to Don Bernardin Mendoza, yet by Good Hap, the Copies thereof as well in English as in French, Were Found in the Chamber of one Richard Leigh, a Seminarie Priest, who was Lately Executed for High Treason Committed in the Time that the Spanish Armada was on the Seas," in *Harleian Miscellany*, vol. 1, 1808

Corbett, Sir Julian Stafford, *Addenda*, The Navy Records Society, XXXV, 1908

Corbett, Sir Julian Stafford, *Drake and the Tudor Navy: History of the Rise of England as a Maritime Power*, 2 vols., 1898–99

Corbett, Sir Julian Stafford, *Fighting Instructions, 1530–1816*, Navy Records Society, XXIX, 1905

Corbett, Sir Julian Stafford, *Papers Relating to the Navy during the Spanish War, 1585–87*, Navy Records Society, 11, 1898

Cordingly, David, *Heroines and Harlots: Women at Sea in the Great Age of Sail*, Pan, 2002

Cressy, David, "Binding the Nation: The Bonds of Association, 1584 and 1696," in D. J. Guth and J. W. McKenna (eds.), *Tudor Rule and Revolution*, Cambridge, 1982

Cressy, David, *Bonfires and Bells: National Memory and the Protestant Calendar in Elizabethan and Stuart England*, Weidenfeld & Nicolson, 1989

Cressy, David, "The Spanish Armada: Celebration, Myth and Memory," in Jeff Doyle and Bruce Moore (eds.), *England and the Spanish Armada: Papers Arising from the 1988 Conference, University College, University of New South Wales*, Australian Defence Force Academy, Canberra, 1990

Croft, J. Pauline, "Trading with the Enemy, 1585–1604," *Historical Journal*, 32, June 1989

Cruickshank, C. G., *Elizabeth's Army*, Oxford University Press, 1966

Cuellar, Francisco de (Brendan Clifford, ed.), *A Story of the Spanish Armada by Captain Francisco de Cuellar*, Athol Books, Belfast, 1988

Cummins, John, *Francis Drake: The Lives of a Hero*, Weidenfeld, 1995

Custance, Sir R., *Invasion Overseas*, 1905

Dasent, J. R. (ed.), *Acts of the Privy Council of England*, XVI, London, 1897

Daultrey, S., "The Weather of North-west Europe during the Summer and Autumn of 1588," in P. Gallagher and D. W. Cruickshank (eds.), *God's Obvious Design: Papers for the Spanish Armada Symposium, Sligo, 1988*, Tamesis Books, 1990

Davies, J., *The English Companies of Foot in 1588*, Pike and Shot Society, Farnham, 2000

Davis, Ralph, *The Rise of the English Shipping Industry*, Macmillan, 1962

Defourneaux, Marcelin, *Daily Life in Spain in the Golden Age*, Stanford University Press, 1990

Deloney, Thomas, "Three Old Ballads on the Overthrow of the Spanish Armada," in A. F. Pollard (ed.), *Tudor Tracts, 1532–1588*, 1903

Deloney, Thomas, *The Works of Thomas Deloney*, Oxford, 1912

Devereux, Robert, 2nd Earl of Essex, "Declaration of the Causes Moving the Queenes Majestie of England to Prepare and Send a Navy to the Seas," in J. Somers (ed.), *A Third Collection of Scarce Tracts*, vol. 1, 1751

Devereux, Robert, 2nd Earl of Essex, *The Life and Glorious Reign of Queen Elizabeth . . . Also an Account of the Destruction of . . . the Spanish Armada*, 1708

D'Ewes, Sir Simonds, *The Journals of All of the Parliaments during the Reign of Queen Elizabeth*, 1682

Dickerman, Edmund H., "A Neglected Aspect of the Spanish Armada: The Catholic League's Picardy Offensive of 1587," *Canadian Journal of History*, XI, 1976

Dietz, Brian, "The Royal Bounty and English Merchant Shipping in the Sixteenth and Seventeenth Centuries," *Mariner's Mirror*, 77, February 1991

Digges, Leonard, *Geometrica*, 1571

Dodd, A. H., *Elizabethan England*, Batsford, 1974

Dodsley, R., and Dodsley, J., *The History of the Spanish Armada . . . Containing Lists of Ships, Land Forces, Mariners, Guns, Ammunition and Military Stores of All Sorts . . . to which is Prefixed a Map of the Beacons then Erected in Kent,* 1759

Donno, Elizabeth S., *An Elizabethan in 1582: The Diary of Richard Madox,* Hakluyt Society, 1976

Dop, Jan Albert, *Eliza's Knights: Soldiers, Poets and Puritans in the Netherlands, 1572–1586,* Remak, Alblasserdam, Netherlands, 1981

Douglas, K. S., and Lamb, H. H., *Weather Observations and a Tentative Meteorological Analysis of the Period May to July 1588,* University of East Anglia Climatic Research Unit Publications, Norwich, 1979

Douglas, K. S., Lamb, H. H., and Loader, C., *A Meteorological Study of July to October 1588: The Spanish Armada Storms,* University of East Anglia Climatic Research Unit Publications, Norwich, 1978

Doyle, Jeff, and Moore, Bruce (eds.), *England and the Spanish Armada: Papers Arising from the 1988 Conference, University College, University of New South Wales,* Australian Defence Force Academy, Canberra, 1990

Drew, C. (ed.), *Lambeth Churchwardens' Accounts 1504–1645,* vol. I, Surrey Records Society

Druett, Joan, *Rough Medicine: Surgeons at Sea in the Age of Sail,* Routledge, New York, 2000

Drummond, J. C., and Wilbraham, Anne, *The Englishman's Food,* 1957

Dudley, Robert (J. Bruce, ed.), *Correspondence of Robert Dudley, Earl of Leicester, during his Government of the Low Countries in the Years 1585 and 1586,* Camden Society, OS 27, 1844

Duffy, Michael, "The Foundations of British Naval Power," in Michael Duffy (ed.), *The Military Revolution and the State, 1500–1800,* Exeter Studies in History, Exeter UP, 1980

Duffy, M. (ed.), *The New Maritime History of Devon,* Conway Maritime Press, 1992

Dunn, Richard S., *The Age of Religious Wars, 1559–1689,* Norton History of Modern Europe, vol. 2, Norton, New York, 1970

Duro, Captain Cesareo Fernandez, *Armada Española desde la Union de los Reinos de Castilla y Aragon,* 9 vols., Madrid, 1877

Duro, Captain Cesareo Fernandez, *La Armada Invencible,* 2 vols., Madrid, 1884–85

Dyer, Florence E., "Burghley's Notes on the Spanish Armada," *Mariner's Mirror,* 11, October 1925

Dyer, Florence E., "The Elizabethan Sailorman," *Mariner's Mirror,* 10, April 1924

Dyer, Florence E., "Reprisals in the Sixteenth Century," *Mariner's Mirror,* 21, April 1935

Edwards, Edward, *The Life of Sir Walter Ralegh based on Contemporary Documents,* 2 vols., 1868

Elder, John R., *Spanish Influences on Scottish History,* Glasgow, 1920

Elliott, Colin, *Discovering Armada Britain: A Journey in Search of the Sites, Relics and Remains which tell the Story of the Defeat of the Spanish Armada 400 Years Ago,* David & Charles, Newton Abbot, 1987

Elliott, John Huxtable, "The Decline of Spain," *Past & Present,* 20, November 1961

Elliott, John Huxtable, *England under the Tudors,* Methuen, 1991

Elliott, John Huxtable, *Europe Divided, 1559–1598,* 1977

Elliott, John Huxtable, *Imperial Spain, 1469–1716,* St. Martin's, New York, 1967

Ellis, Sir Henry, *Original Letters Illustrative of English History,* 4 vols., 1846

England, Sylvia, *The Massacre of St. Bartholomew*, 1938

Entwistle, W. J., *Bulletin of Spanish* (now *Hispanic*) *Studies*, 24, 1947

Erickson, Carolly, *The First Elizabeth*, Summit, New York, 1983

Erlanger, Philippe (trans. P. O'Brian), *St. Bartholomew's Night*, 1962

Essen, Leon van der, *Alexandre Farnese*, 5 vols., Brussels, 1933–37

Estal, J. M., "Felipe II y su Archivo hagiographico de El Escorial," *Hispania Sacra*, XXIII, 1970

Ewald, A. C., *The Invincible Armada*, 1882

Ewen, Cecil Henry L'Estrange, *The Golden Chalice: A Documented Narrative of an Elizabethan Pirate*, Paignton, 1939

Ewen, Cecil Henry L'Estrange, "Organised Piracy Round England in the Sixteenth Century," *Mariner's Mirror*, 35, January 1949

Fallon, Niall, *The Armada in Ireland*, Stanford Maritime, 1978

Falls, Cyril, *Elizabeth's Irish Wars*, Methuen, 1950

Feltham, Owen, *A Brief Character of the Low Countries*, 1652

Fenwick, Kenneth, *HMS Victory*, Cassell, 1959

Fernandez-Armesto, Felipe, "Armada Myths: The Formative Phase," in P. Gallagher and D. W. Cruickshank (eds.), *God's Obvious Design: Papers for the Spanish Armada Symposium, Sligo 1988*, Tamesis Books, 1990

Fernandez-Armesto, Felipe, "Exploding the Myths," *Apollo*, 128, July 1988

Fernandez-Armesto, Felipe, *The Spanish Armada: The Experience of War in 1588*, Oxford University Press, 1988

Fincham, J., *A History of Naval Architecture*, 1851

Fiske, J., *The Elizabethan Sea Kings*, 1895

Flanagan, Laurence, *Ireland's Armada Legacy*, Sutton, Gloucester, 1988

Flanagan, Laurence, *Irish Wrecks of the Spanish Armada*, Country House, Dublin, 1995

Fletcher, Anthony, *Tudor Rebellions*, 1968

Fletcher, Joseph Smith, *The Remarkable Adventure of Walter Trelawney, Parish 'Prentice of Plymouth in the Year of the Great Armada*, 1894

Flower-Smith, M. A., "'The Able and the Wyllinge': The Preparations of the English Land Forces to Meet the Armada," *British Army Review*, 95, August 1990

Fortescue, Sir John, *History of the British Army*, vol. 1, Macmillan, 1976

Franzen, Anders, *The Warship "Vasa": Deep Diving and Marine Archaeology in Stockholm*, Stockholm, 1974

Fritze, Ronald H. (ed.), *Historical Dictionary of Tudor England, 1485–1603*, Greenwood, Westport, Connecticut, 1991

Frobisher, Sir Martin, *Letters to Lord Burghley*, 1592

Froude, James Anthony, *English Seamen in the Sixteenth Century: Lectures Delivered at Oxford*, 1895

Froude, James Anthony, *History of England from the Fall of Wolsey to the Defeat of the Spanish Armada*, vols. 7–12, 1856–70

Froude, James Anthony (A. L. Rowse, ed.), *Froude's "Spanish Story of the Armada" and Other Essays*, 1971, Sutton, Stroud, 1988

Fry, A. (ed.), *Abstracts of Inquisitions post mortem for the City of London 1577–1603*, Index Library, 1908

Frye, Susan, "The Myth of Elizabeth at Tilbury," *Sixteenth Century Journal*, 23, Spring 1992

Fuller, John Frederick Charles, *The Decisive Battles of the Western World and Their*

Influence upon History: vol. 1, From the Earliest Times to the Battle of Lepanto, vol. 2, From the Defeat of the Spanish Armada to the Battle of Waterloo, Spa, Stevenage, 1993, 1994

Fuller, Thomas, *Worthies*, Folio Society, 1987

Furnivall, F. J., *Robert Laneham's Letter*, 1871

Gallagher, P. (ed.), and Cruickshank, D. W., "The Armada of 1588 Reflected in Serious and Popular Literature of the Period," in P. Gallagher and D. W. Cruickshank (eds.), *God's Obvious Design: Papers for the Spanish Armada Symposium, Sligo 1988*, Tamesis Books, 1990

Gamazo, Gabriel Maura, Duke of Maura, *El Designio de Felipe II*, Madrid, 1957

Gerson, A. J., "The English Recusants and the Spanish Armada," *American Historical Review*, XXII, 1917

Geyl, Peter, *The Revolt of the Netherlands, 1555–1609*, Benn, 1980

Glasgow, Tom, Jr., "Elizabethan Ships Pictured on Smerwick Map, 1580," *Mariner's Mirror*, 52, 1966

Glasgow, Tom, Jr., "List of Ships in the Royal Navy from 1539 to 1588," *Mariner's Mirror*, 56, August 1970

Glasgow, Tom, Jr., "The Navy in the French Wars of Mary and Elizabeth I," *Mariner's Mirror*, 53, 1967; LIV, 1968; LVI, 1970

Glasgow, Tom, Jr., "The Shape of Ships that Defeated the Spanish Armada," *Mariner's Mirror*, 50, August 1964

Glete, J., *Navies and Nations: Warships, Navies and State-building in Europe and America, 1500–1860*, 2 vols., Stockholm, 1993

Glover, Winifred, *Exploring the Spanish Armada*, O'Brien Press, 2001

Goldingham, C. S., *The Personnel of the Tudor Navy and the Internal Economy of Ships*, 1918

Gongora, Luis de, *Obras Completas*, Madrid, 2000

Goodman, David C., *Power and Penury: Government, Technology and Science in Philip II's Spain*, Cambridge University Press, 1988

Goodman, David C., *Spanish Naval Power, 1589–1665: Reconstruction and Defeat*, Cambridge Studies in Early Modern History, Cambridge University Press, 1997

Goring, Jeremy, "Social Change and Military Decline in Mid-Tudor England," in *History*, 60, 1975

Goring, Jeremy, *Sussex and the Spanish Armada*, Pastfinder Publications, 1988

Gosse, Philip, *Hawkins: Scourge of Spain*, also titled *Sir John Hawkins*, 1930

Gould, Richard A., "The Archaeology of War: Wrecks of the Spanish Armada of 1588 and the Battle of Britain, 1940," in Richard A. Gould (ed.), *Shipwreck Anthropology*, University of New Mexico Press, Albuquerque, 1983

Gracia Rivas, Manuel, "The Medical Services of the Gran Armada," in M. J. Rodriguez-Salgado and S. Adams (eds.), *England, Spain and the Gran Armada, 1585–89*, Edinburgh, 1991

Gracia Rivas, Manuel, "El Motin de la Diana y otras Vicisitudes de las Galeras Participantes en la Jornada de Inglaterra," *Revista de Historia Naval*, II.4, 1984

Gracia Rivas, Manuel, *La Sanidad en la Jornada de Inglaterra, 1587–88*, Madrid, 1988

Gracia Rivas, Manuel, *Los Tercios de la Gran Armada, 1587–88*, Madrid, 1989

Graham, Winston, *The Spanish Armadas*, Collins, 1972

Gray, W., *An Almanacke and a Prognostication for Dorchester*, 1588

Green, Emmanuel, *Preparations in Somerset against the Spanish Armada*, 1888

Green, Janet M., " 'I My Self': Queen Elizabeth's Oration at Tilbury Camp," *Sixteenth Century Journal*, XXVIII, 1997

Green, Rev. William Spotswood, "Armada Ships on the Kerry Coast: A Translation and Extract from 'Account of Marcos de Arambaru ,' " *Royal Irish Academy Proceedings*, vol. 27, section C, No. 12, 1837

Green, Rev. William Spotswood, "The Wrecks of the Spanish Armada on the Coast of Ireland," *Geographical Journal*, 27, 1906

Greenhill, Basil, *The Ship from 1550–1700*, vol. 3, HMSO, 1980–1

Grierson, Edward, *The Fatal Inheritance*, Gollancz, 1969

Gross, Jorge Calvar, *et al.*, *La Batalla del Mar Oceano: Corpus Documental de las Hostilidades entre España y Inglaterra, 1568–1604*, Madrid, 1988

Guilmartin, J. F., *Gunpowder and Galleys: Changing Technology and Mediterranean Warfare at Sea in the Sixteenth Century*, Cambridge University Press, 1975

Guy, John C., *Drake and the Elizabethan Explorers*, Ticktock in association with the National Maritime Museum, Tonbridge, 1988

Guy, John C., *Tudor England*, Oxford University Press, 1990

Guzman, Alonso Perez de, 7th Duke of Medina-Sidonia, *Orders Set Down by the Duke of Medina*, Lord General of the King's Fleet, 1588

Hadfield, A. M., *Time to Finish the Game: The English and the Armada*, Phoenix House, 1964

Hagthorpe, John, *England's Exchequer*, 1625

Hakluyt, Richard, *Documents concerning English Voyages to the Spanish Main, 1569–1580 II. English accounts: "Sir Francis Drake Revived" and others*, reprinted (ed. Irene Aloha Wright) 1932

Hakluyt, Richard, *The Principal Navigations, Voyages, Traffiques and Discoveries of the English Nation*, 12 vols., 1903–5

Hakluyt, Richard (Adrian S. Mott, ed.), *Hakluyt's Voyages*, Boston and New York, 1929

Hale, J. R., "Armies, Navies and the Art of War," in R. B. Wernham (ed.), *The Counter-Reformation and Price Revolution 1559–1610*, The New Cambridge Modern History, 3, Cambridge University Press, 1968

Hale, J. R., *Renaissance War Studies*, History series 11, Hambledon, 1983

Hale, John Richard, *The Story of the Great Armada*, 1913

Hale, Lamond (ed.), *Discourse of the Common Weal*, 1893

Hall, Bert S., *Weapons and Warfare in Renaissance Europe: Gunpowder, Technology and Tactics*, Johns Hopkins University Press, 2002

Halliday, Frank Ernest, *A Cornish Chronicle: The Carews of Antony from Armada to Civil War*, David & Charles, Newton Abbot, 1967

Hamilton, C. H. (ed.), *Books of Examinations and Depositions, 1570–1594*, Southampton, 1914

Hampden, John (ed.), *Francis Drake Privateer: Contemporary Narratives and Documents*, Methuen, 1972

Hannay, David, *Short History of the British Navy*, 2 vols., 1898, 1908

Hanson, Neil, *The Custom of the Sea*, Doubleday, 1999

Hardie, Robert Purves, *The Tobermory Argosy: A Problem of the Spanish Armada*, 1912

Hardiman, James, *The History of the Town and Country of Galway*, Dublin, 1820

Hardy, Evelyn, *Survivors of the Armada*, Constable, 1966

Haring, C. M., *The Spanish Empire*, 1914

Harland, John, and Myers, Mark, *Seamanship in the Age of Sail: An Account of the Shiphandling of the Sailing Man-of-War, 1600–1860*, Conway, 1984

Harleian Miscellany: Or, A Collection of Scarce, Curious and Entertaining Pamphlets and Tracts, as well in Manuscript as in Print, Found in the Late Earl of Oxford's Library, 8 vols., 1808–11

Harrison, C. B., *The Life and Death of Robert Devereux, Earl of Essex*, 1937

Harrison, D., *Tudor England*, vol. 2, 1953

Harrison, William (F. J. Furnivall, ed.), *The Description of England*, 1877

Hart, Roger, *Battle of the Spanish Armada*, Wayland, Hove, 1973

Hartley, T. E. (ed.), *Proceedings in the Parliaments of Elizabeth I, vol. 3, 1593–1601*, Leicester University Press, 1995

Harvey, Richard, *An Astrological Discourse*, 1583

Hasler, P. W., *The House of Commons, 1558–1603*, HMSO, 1981

Haslop, Henry, *Newes out of the Coast of Spaine*, The English Experience Series, 466, Da Capo, New York, 1972

Hassell Smith, A., and Baker, G. M. (eds.), *The Papers of Nathaniel Bacon, vol. III (1586–1595)*, Norfolk Record Society, vol. LIII, 1987–8

Hattendorf, John B., *et al.* (eds.), *British Naval Documents 1204–1960*, Scolar Press for the Navy Records Society, 1992

Hawkins, Mary Wise Savery, *Plymouth Armada Heroes: The Hawkins Family*, 1888

Hayward, Sir John, *With the Beginning of the Raigne of Queen Elizabeth*, 1636

Hentzner, Paul (trans. Richard Bentley, ed. Henry Morley), *Travels in England during the Reign of Queen Elizabeth*, Cassell, 1901

Herrera y Oria, Enrique, *Felipe II y el Marques de Santa Cruz en la Empresa de Inglaterra*, Madrid, 1946

Hibben, C. C., *Gouda in Revolt: Particularism and Pacifism in the Revolt of the Netherlands, 1572–1588*, Utrecht, 1983

Higham, Robert, *Security and Defence in South-West England Before 1800*, Exeter Studies in History 19, University of Exeter Press, 1987

Higueras, D., and San Pio, M. P., "Irish Wrecks of the Great Armada: The Testimony of the Survivors," in P. Gallagher and D. W. Cruickshank (eds.), *God's Obvious Design: Papers for the Spanish Armada Symposium, Sligo 1988*, Tamesis Books, 1990

Hilton, Ronald, "The Marriage of Queen Mary and Philip of Spain," in *Papers and Proceedings of the Hampshire Field Club and Archaeological Society*, XIV, Part 1, 1940

History of the Spanish Armada . . . for the Invasion and Conquest of England . . . 1588, 1759

Hoffmann, Ann, *Lives of the Tudor Age, 1485–1603*, 1977

Hogg, O.F.G., "England's War Effort against the Spanish Armada," *Journal of the Society for Army Historical Research*, 44, March 1966

Holford, Ingrid, *British Weather Disasters*, David & Charles, Newton Abbot, 1976

Holinshed, *Chronicles of England, Scotland and Irelande*, 1577 (new edn., under title *The Description of England*, ed. F. J. Furnival, 1877)

Holles, G., and Wood, A. C., *Memorials of the Holles Family 1493–1656*, Camden Society, 1937

Hollyband and Erondell (M. St. C. Byrne, ed.), *The Elizabethan Home Discovered in Two Dialogues*, 1930

Hopper, C., "Sir Francis Drake's Memorable Service against the Spaniards in 1587," *Camden Miscellany*, V, 1863

Hortop, Job, *The Rare Travails of Job Hortop*, 1591

Hotson, Leslie, *Shakespeare's Sonnets Dated*, New York, 1949

Howard, Charles, 1st Earl of Nottingham, "Relation of Proceedings," in John Knox Laughton, *The Defeat of the Spanish Armada*, Navy Records Society, 1894

Howarth, David, *The Men-of-War: The Seafarers Series*, Time-Life, Alexandria, Virginia, 1978

Howarth, David, *The Voyage of the Armada: The Spanish Story*, Cassell Military, 2001

Howes, Edmond, *The Annales, or Generall Chronicle of England*, 1615

Hughes, P. L., and Larkin, J. F., *Tudor Royal Proclamations*, 3 vols., New Haven, 1964–69

Hume, Martin Andrew Sharp, "The Defeat of the Armada: An Anniversary Object Lesson," *Fortnightly Review*, 368, August 1897

Hume, Martin Andrew Sharp, *Evolution of the Armada*, 1896

Hume, Martin Andrew Sharp, *Two English Queens and Philip*, 1908

Hume, Martin Andrew Sharp, "The Visit of Philip II, 1554," *English Historical Review*, vol. 7, April 1892

Hume, Martin Andrew Sharp, *The Year after the Armada and Other Historical Studies*, reprinted Kennikat, Port Washington, 1970

Hume, Martin Andrew Sharp (ed.), *Calendar of State Papers Relating to English Affairs preserved in or originally belonging to the Archives of Simancas*, vol. 4, 1899

Humphries, James, *Orders to be Used in King's or Queen's Majesties Ships*, 1568

Huntress, Keith, *Narratives of Shipwrecks and Disasters 1586–1860*, Iowa State University Press, 1974

Instituto de Historia y Cultura Naval, *Coleccion Gran Armada*, 7 vols., Editorial Naval, Madrid, 1988–9

Ireland, John de Courcy, "Note on the Spanish Armada," *Mariner's Mirror*, 76, May 1990

Ireland, John de Courcy, "Ragusa and the Spanish Armada," *Mariner's Mirror*, 64, August 1978

Jack, Sybil, "The Cinque Ports and the Spanish Armada," in Jeff Doyle and Bruce Moore (eds.), *England and the Spanish Armada: Papers Arising from the 1988 Conference, University College, University of New South Wales*, Australian Defence Force Academy, Canberra, 1990

Jameson, A. K., "Some Spanish Documents Dealing with Drake," *English Historical Review*, 49, January 1934

Jensen, J. de Lamar, "Bernardino de Mendoza and the League," unpublished dissertation, Columbia University, 1957

Jensen, J. de Lamar, "Franco-Spanish Diplomacy and the Armada," in C. H. Carter (ed.), *From the Renaissance to the Counter-Reformation: Essays in Honour of Garrett Mattingly*, 1965

Jensen, J. de Lamar, "The Phantom Will of Mary, Queen of Scots," *Scotia*, IV, 1980

Jensen, J. de Lamar, "The Spanish Armada: The Worst-Kept Secret in Europe," *Sixteenth Century Journal*, 19, Winter 1988

Jerdan, W., "Documents Relative to the Spanish Armada and the Defences of the Thames and Medway," *British Archaeological Association*, 9, 1853

Jones, Frank, *The Life of Sir M. Frobisher, Knight, Containing a Narrative of the Spanish Armada*, 1878

Jones, Jack Davies, "The Isle of Wight and the Armada," Isle of Wight County Council, 1988

Kain, R., and Ravenhill, W., *The Historical Atlas of South-West England*, 1999

Kamen, Henry, *Spain's Road to Empire*, Allen Lane, 2003

Karraker, Cyrus H., *Piracy Was a Business*, Smith, Rindge, New Hampshire, 1953

Keeler, M. F., *Sir Francis Drake's West Indian Voyage*, Hakluyt Society, 2nd Series, CXLVIII, 1981

Keevil, J. J., with Lloyd, Christopher, and Coulter, Jack L. S., *Medicine and the Navy 1200–1900*, 4 vols., E. & S. Livingston, Edinburgh, 1957–63

Keightley, Ron, "An Armada Veteran Celebrates the Death of Drake," in Jeff Doyle and Bruce Moore (eds.), *England and the Spanish Armada: Papers Arising from the 1988 Conference, University College, University of New South Wales*, Australian Defence Force Academy, Canberra, 1990

Kelsey, Harry, *Sir Francis Drake: The Queen's Pirate*, London and New Haven, 1998

Kemp, P., *The British Sailor: A Social History of the Lower Deck 1588–1905*, Dent, 1970

Kemp, Peter, *The Campaign of the Spanish Armada*, Phaidon, Oxford, 1988

Kempe, A. J., *Particulars of the Armada and Preparations against the Invasion*, 1835

Kennedy, Paul M. (ed.), "On Sea Power: Sea Power, Past and Present," *International Historical Review*, 10, February 1988

Kenny, Robert W., *Elizabeth's Admiral: The Political Career of Charles Howard, Earl of Nottingham, 1536–1624*, Johns Hopkins University Press, Baltimore, 1970

Kent, Joan, *The English Village Constable, 1580–1642*, Oxford, 1986

Ker, William Paton, "The Spanish Story of the Armada," *Scottish Historical Review*, 17, April 1920

Kesteven, J. R., *The Armada*, 1965

Kilfeather, T. P., *Ireland: Graveyard of the Spanish Armada*, Anvil, Tralee, 1967

Kingsford, C. L., "West Country Piracy: The School of English Seamen," in *Prejudice and Promise in Fifteenth Century England, Ford Lectures, 1923–24*, Cass, 1962

Knight, R.J.B. (ed.), *Guide to the Manuscripts in the National Maritime Museum*, 2 vols., 1977–80

Koenigsberger, H. G., "Western Europe and the Power of Spain," in R. B. Wernham (ed.), *The Counter-Reformation and Price Revolution 1559–1610*, The New Cambridge Modern History, 3, Cambridge University Press, 1968

Konstam, R. Angus, *The Armada Campaign 1588*, Osprey, 2001

Konstam, R. Angus, "Sixteenth Century Naval Tactics and Gunnery," *International Journal of Nautical Archaeology and Underwater Exploration*, 17, February 1988

Kostic, V., "Ragusa and the Spanish Armada," in R. Filipovic and M. Partridge (eds.), *Ragusa's Relations with England: A Symposium*, Zagreb, 1977

Kouri, Erkki I., *Elizabethan England and Europe: 40 Unprinted letters from Elizabeth I to Protestant Powers*, University of London Institute of Historical Research, 1982

Kouri, Erkki I., "England and the Attempts to Form a Protestant Alliance in the late 1560s: A Case Study in Elizabethan Diplomacy," *Annales Academiae Scientarium Fennicae*, Series B, CXX, Helsinki, 1981

Kubler, George, *Building the Escorial*, Princeton University Press, 1982

Lace, William W., *Defeat of the Spanish Armada*, 1997

Lamb, Hubert, and Frydendahl, Knud, *Historic Storms of the North Sea, British Isles and Northwest Europe*, Cambridge University Press, 1991

Lander, R. J., "An Assessment of the Numbers, Sizes and Types of English and Spanish Ships Mobilised for the Armada Campaign," *Mariner's Mirror*, 63, November 1977

Laughton, Sir John Knox, *The Elizabethan Naval War with Spain*, 1904

Laughton, Sir John Knox, *The Invincible Armada: A Tercentenary Retrospect*, 1888

Laughton, Sir John Knox (ed.), *The Naval Miscellany*, Navy Records Society, 1987

Laughton, Sir John Knox (ed.), *State Papers Relating to the Defeat of the Spanish Armada*, 2 vols., Temple Smith for the Navy Records Society, Aldershot, 1987

Laughton, L. C., "English and Spanish Tonnage in 1588," *Mariner's Mirror*, 44, May 1958

Laughton, L.G.C., *The Navy, Ships and Sailors*, 1916

Lea, James, *A True and Perfect Description of a Strange Monster Born in the City of Rome in Italy, in the Year of our Salvation 1585*, 1590

LeGuin, Charles A., "Sea Life in Seventeenth Century England," *American Neptune*, 27, April 1967

Leimon, M., and Parker, G., "Treason and Plot in Elizabethan England: The Fame of Sir Edward Stafford Reconsidered," *English Historical Review*, CVI, 1996

Leland, John (L. Toulmin Smith, ed.), *The Itinerary*, 1906–10

Leng, Robert, "Sir Francis Drake's Memorable Service Done Against the Spaniards in 1587," *Camden Miscellany*, vol. V, 1864

Leng, Robert, "A True Description of the Last Voyage of that Worthy Captain, Sir Francis Drake, Knight, with his Service Done against the Spaniards, 1587," *Camden Miscellany*, vol. V, 1864

Leonard, E. M., *The Early History of English Poor Relief*, 1900

Leslie, J. H., "A Survey or Muster of the Armed and Trayned Companies in London, 1588 and 1599," *Journal of the Society for Army Historical Research*, 4, April 1925

Lewis, Ada Haeseler, *A Study of Elizabethan Ship Money, 1588–1603*, University of Pennsylvania, Philadelphia, 1928

Lewis, Michael Arthur, *Armada Guns: A Comparative Study of English and Spanish Armaments*, Allen & Unwin, 1961

Lewis, Michael Arthur, *The Hawkins Dynasty: Three Generations of a Tudor Family*, Allen & Unwin, 1969

Lewis, Michael Arthur, *The History of the British Navy*, Penguin, Baltimore, 1962

Lewis, Michael Arthur, *The Spanish Armada*, Batsford, 1960

Lindsay, Jack, *The Dons Sight Devon: A Story of the Defeat of the Invincible Armada*, Oxford University Press, London, 1941

Lloyd, C. Christopher, *The British Seaman 1200-1860*, A Social Survey, Collins, 1968

Lloyd, C. Christopher, *English Corsairs on the Barbary Coast*, Collins, 1981

Lloyd, C. Christopher, *The Nation and the Navy: A History of Naval Life and Policy*, Cresset Press, 1954

Lloyd, C. Christopher (ed.), *The Naval Miscellany*, vol. 4, Publications of the Navy Records Society, 92, 1952

Lloyd, C. Christopher, Carrington, C. E., and Waters, David W., "Drake's Game of Bowls: Series of Notes and Queries," *Mariner's Mirror*, 39, 40 and 41, 1953–55

Loades, D. M., *The Tudor Navy: An Administrative, Political and Military History*, Scolar Press, 1962

Longmate, Norman, *Defending the Island: Caesar to the Armada*, Hutchinson, 1989

Loomie, Albert J., "An Armada Pilot's Survey of the English Coastline, October 1597," *Mariner's Mirror*, 49, November 1963

Loomie, Albert J., "The Armadas and the Catholics of England," *Catholic Historical Review*, 59, October 1973

Loomie, Albert J., *The Spanish Elizabethans: The English Exiles at the Court of Philip II*, Fordham University Press, New York, 1963

Lozano, Fernando Riano, *Los Medios Navales de Alejandro Farnesio, 1587–88*, Instituto de Historia y Cultura Naval, vol. 7, Madrid, 1989

Lynch, John, "Philip II and the Papacy," *Transactions of the Royal Historical Society*, 5th series, 2, 1961

Lynch, John, *Spain, 1516–1598: From Nation State to World Empire*, A History of Spain, Blackwell, Oxford, 1992

Lynch, John, *Spain under the Habsburgs, vol. 1, Empire and Absolutism, 1516–1598*, New York University Press, 1981

Lynch, John A., *Tools of War: Instruments, Ideas and Institutions of Warfare, 1445–1871*, University of Illinois Press, Baltimore, 1990

Lynch, Michael (ed.), *Mary Stewart: Queen of Three Kingdoms*, Blackwell, Oxford, 1988

Macaulay, Thomas Babington, *The Armada and Other Poems*, 1880

McBride, Gordon K., "Elizabethan Foreign Policy in Microcosm: The Portuguese Pretender, 1580-89," *Albion*, V, 1973

MacCaffrey, Wallace T., "The Armada in its Context," *Historical Journal*, 32, September 1989

MacCaffrey, Wallace T., *Elizabeth I: vol. 3, War and Politics, 1588–1603*, Princeton University Press, 1992

MacCaffrey, Wallace T., *Queen Elizabeth and the Making of Policy, 1572–88*, Princeton University Press, 1981

McFee, William, *Sir Martin Frobisher*, 1928

McGurk, J. N., "Armada Preparations in Kent and Arrangements made after the Defeat (1587-89)," *Archaeologia Cantiana*, 85, 1970

McKee, Alexander, *From Merciless Invaders: The Defeat of the Spanish Armada*, Souvenir Press, 1988

McKendrik, Melveena, *Cervantes*, Boston, 1980

McKenzie, Kendall, *Wreck Detectives*, Harrap, 1972

Mackie, J. D., "Scotland and the Spanish Armada," *Scottish Historical Review*, 12, October 1914

Mainwaring, G. E., and Perrin, W. G. (eds.), *The Life and Works of Sir Henry Mainwaring*, 2 vols., 1920–22

McLeay, Alison, *The Tobermory Treasure: The True Story of a Fabulous Armada Galleon*, Conway Maritime Press, 1986

McNeill, C., "Report on the Rawlinson Collection of Manuscripts," *Analecta Hibernica*, I, 1930

Malfatti, Cesare V., *Cuatro Documentos Italianos en Materia del Expedicion de la Armada Invencible*, Barcelona, 1972

Maltby, William S., *The Black Legend in England: The Development of Anti-Spanish Sentiment, 1558–1660*, Duke Historical Publications, Duke University Press, Durham, North Carolina, 1971

Manucy, Albert C., *Artillery Through the Ages*, Washington, 1949

Mariana, Dr. Juan de, *Obras del Padre Juan de Mariana*, Madrid, 1950

Mariejol, Jean H. (trans. W. B. Wells), *Master of the Armada*, 1933

Marine Research Society, *The Sea, the Ship and the Sailor: Tales of Adventure from Log Books and Original Narratives*, Salem, Massachusetts, 1925

Markham, Sir C. (ed.), *The Hawkins Voyages*, Hakluyt Society, 1878

Martin, Colin J. M., *Full Fathom Five: Wrecks of the Spanish Armada*, Chatto & Windus, 1975

Martin, Colin J. M., "Incendiary Weapons from the Spanish Armada Wreck 'La Trinidad Valencera,' 1588," *International Journal of Nautical Archaeology*, 23.3, 1994

Martin, Colin J. M., "The Ships of the Spanish Armada," in P. Gallagher and D. W. Cruickshank (eds.), *God's Obvious Design: Papers for the Spanish Armada Symposium, Sligo 1988*, Tamesis Books, 1990

Martin, Colin J. M., *Shipwrecks of the Spanish Armada*, Tempus Publishing, 2001

Martin, Colin J. M., "A Sixteenth Century Siege Train: The Battery Ordnance of the Spanish Armada," *International Journal of Nautical Archaeology*, 17.1, February 1988

Martin, Colin J. M., "Spanish Armada Tonnages," *Mariner's Mirror*, LXIII, 1977

Martin, Colin J. M., "'La Trinidad Valencera': An Armada Invasion Transport Lost off Donegal," *International Journal of Nautical Archaeology*, 8.1, 1979

Martin, Colin J. M., and Parker, Geoffrey, "If the Armada Had Landed," *Modern History Quarterly*, 1, Autumn 1988

Martin, Colin J. M., and Parker, Geoffrey, *The Spanish Armada*, Mandolin, 1999

Martin, Paula, *Spanish Armada Prisoners: The Story of the "Nuestra Señora del Rosario" and her Crew and of Other Prisoners in England, 1587–97*, Exeter Maritime Studies, Series 1, University of Exeter, 1988

Masterson, Daniel M. (ed.), *Naval History: The Sixth Symposium of the U.S. Naval Academy*, Scholarly Resources, Wilmington, Delaware, 1987

Mathew, David, "The Cornish and Welsh Pirates in the Reign of Elizabeth," *English Historical Review*, 39, July 1924

Mattingly, Garrett, *The Defeat of the Spanish Armada*, Pimlico, 2000

Mattingly, Garrett, *The "Invincible" Armada and Elizabethan England*, Cornell University Press, Ithaca, New York, 1963

Maura, Gamazo, *El Designio de Felipe II*, Madrid, 1957

Maxwell-Scott, M. M., *The Tragedy of Fotheringay*, A. & C. Black, 1895

Mayer, Joseph, *On the Preparations of the County of Kent to Resist the Spanish Armada, from the MS Papers of R. Twisden*, Liverpool, 1868

Melvill, James (R. Pitcairn, ed.), *The Autobiography and Diary of James Melvill*, Edinburgh, 1842

Merriman, Roger Bigelow, *The Rise of the Spanish Empire in the Old World and in the New*, vol. 4, *Philip the Prudent*, Cooper Square, New York, 1962

Merson, A. L. (ed.), *The Third Book of Remembrance of Southampton 1514–1602*, vol. III (1573–1589), Southampton University Press, 1965

Meyer, Arnold O., *England and the Catholic Church under Queen Elizabeth*, Routledge, 1967

Miller, Amos C., *Sir Henry Killigrew*, Leicester University Press, 1963

Milne-Tyte, Robert, *Armada: The Planning, the Battle and After*, Robert Hale, 1988

Monson, Sir William, *Naval Tracts*, 6 vols., Navy Records Society, 1703

Motley, J. L., *History of the United Netherlands*, vols. I and II, 1860
Motley, J. L., *The Rise of the Dutch Republic*, 3 vols., 1855
Moule, H. J., *Descriptive Catalogue of the Charters, Minute Books and Other Documents of the Borough of Weymouth and Melcombe Regis*, Weymouth, 1883
Mullins, E.L.C. (ed.), *Text and Calendars II: An Analytical Guide to Serial Publications*, Royal Historical Society, 1958
Mumby, Frank A., *The Girlhood of Queen Elizabeth: A Narrative in Contemporary Letters*, 1909
Mutschmann, Heinrich, *Further Studies Concerning the Origin of Paradise Lost (The Matter of the Armada)*, Tartu, 1934
Naish, George Prideaux Brabant, "Documents Illustrating the History of the Armada," in Lloyd, C. Christopher (ed.), *The Naval Miscellany*, vol. 4, Publications of the Navy Records Society, 92, 1952
Naunton, Sir Robert, *Fragmenta Regalia*, 1641
Neale, Sir John, *Elizabeth I and her Parliaments*, 2 vols., 1953–7
Neale, Sir John, "Elizabeth and the Netherlands, 1586–1587," *English Historical Review*, 45, July 1930
Neale, Sir John, "The Elizabethan Political Scene: Raleigh Lecture," *Proceedings of the British Academy*, 34, 1948
Neale, Sir John E., *Queen Elizabeth I: A Biography*, Anchor, New York, 1957
Nelson, Arthur, *The Tudor Navy: The Ships, Men and Organisation, 1485–1603*, Conway Maritime Press, 2001
Nichol, John, *Progresses and Public Processions of Queen Elizabeth*, 1823
Nicholas, N. H., *Life of William Davison*, 1823
Nicholl, Charles, *The Reckoning: The Murder of Christopher Marlowe*, University of Chicago Press, 1995
Noble, Theophilus Charles, *A Collection of Papers Relating to the History of the Spanish Armada 1588*, 1888
Noble, Theophilus Charles, *An Historical Essay on the Rise and Fall of the Spanish Armada, A.D. 1588*, 1886
Noble, Theophilus Charles, and Tincey, John, *Armada Contributions*, Partizan Press, Leigh-on-Sea, U.K., 1988
Noble, William Mackreth (ed.), *Huntingdonshire and the Spanish Armada*, 1896
Nolan, John S., "The Muster of 1588," *Albion*, 23, Autumn 1991
Nolan, John S., *Sir John Norris and the Elizabethan Military World*, Exeter, 1997
Norfolk Archaeology, Norfolk and Norwich Archaeological Society, Norwich, 1847
Norton, R., *The Gunner*, 1628
A Notable and Wonderfull Sea-fight betweene Two Great and Wel-mounted Spanish Shipps, and a Small and Not Very Well Provyded English Shipp, Amsterdam, 1621
Nuttall, Zelia (ed.), *New Light on Drake: A Collection of Documents relating to his Voyage of Circumnavigation, 1577–80*, Hakluyt Society Series II, vol. XXXIV
O'Donnell, Hugo, "The Requirements of the Duke of Parma for the Conquest of England," in P. Gallagher and D. W. Cruickshank (eds.), *God's Obvious Design: Papers for the Spanish Armada Symposium, Sligo 1988*, Tamesis Books, 1990
O'Donnell, Hugo, y Duque de Estrada, *La Fuerza de Desembarco de la Gran Armada contra Inglaterra, 1588*, Instituto de Historia y Cultura Naval, vol. 5, Madrid, 1989
O'Donovan, J. (ed.), *The Four Masters*, Annals of Ireland, Dublin, 1851
Ohrelius, Bengt (trans. Maurice Michael), *Vasa—The King's Ship*, Cassell, 1962

Oman, Sir Charles, *A History of the Art of War in the Sixteenth Century*, 1937

Oppenheim, Michael, *History of the Administrations of the Navy*, 1896

Oppenheim, Michael, *The Maritime History of Devon*, Exeter University Press, 1968

O'Rahilly, A., *The Massacre at Smerwick (1580)*, Cork Historical and Archaeological Papers, I, Cork University Press, 1938

"Orders set Downe by the Duke of Medina, Lord General of the King's Fleet, to be Observed in the Voyage toward England," in *Harleian Miscellany*, vol. I, 1808

Orlin, Lena Cowen, *Material London ca. 1600*, University of Pennsylvania Press, Philadelphia, 2000

Overeem, J. B. van, "Justinus von Nassau en de Armada (1588)," *Marineblad*, LIII, 1938

Owen, D., *Calendar of the Manuscripts of the Marquess of Bath*, V, 1980

"A Pack of Spanish Lies: Sent Abroad in the World," *The English Experience*, Da Capo, New York, 1972

Palacio, Diego Garcia de (trans. J. Bankston), *Instruccion*, privately published, Bisbee, Arizona, 1986

Palliser, David M., *The Age of Elizabeth: England under the Later Tudors, 1547–1603, A Social and Economic History of Britain*, Longmans, 1992

Parente, Gonzalo, *et al.*, *Los Sucesos de Flandes de 1588 en Relacion con la Empresa de Inglaterra*, Instituto de Historia y Cultura Naval, vol. 3, Madrid, 1988

Parker, Geoffrey, *The Army of Flanders and the Spanish Road, 1567–1659: The Logistics of Spanish Victory and Defeat in the Low Countries' Wars*, Cambridge University Press, 1976

Parker, Geoffrey, "The Dreadnought Revolution of Tudor England," *Mariner's Mirror*, LXXXII, 1996

Parker, Geoffrey, *The Dutch Revolt*, Penguin, 1979

Parker, Geoffrey, *The Grand Strategy of Philip II*, London and New Haven, 1998

Parker, Geoffrey, *The Military Revolution: Military Innovation and the Rise of the West, 1500–1800*, Lees Knowles Lecture, 1984, Cambridge University Press, New York, 1989

Parker, Geoffrey, *Philip II*, Library of World Biography, Hutchinson, 1978

Parker, Geoffrey (ed.), *Spain and the Netherlands 1559–1659: Ten Studies*, Enslow, Short Hills, New Jersey, 1979

Parker, Geoffrey, *Success Is Never Final: Imperialism, War and Faith in Early Modern Europe*, Allen Lane, 2002

Parker, Geoffrey, "Why the Armada Failed," *History Today*, 38, May 1988

Parker, Geoffrey, and Thompson, I.A.A., "The Battle of Lepanto, 1571: The Costs of Victory," *Mariner's Mirror*, 64, February 1978

Pears, Edwin, "The Spanish Armada and the Ottoman Porte," *English Historical Review*, 31, July 1893

Penn, Christopher D., *The Navy under the Early Stuarts and its Influence on English History*, Manchester, 1913

Perry, Maria, *The Word of a Prince: A Life of Elizabeth from Contemporary Documents*, Boydell, Rochester, 1990

Petrie, Sir Charles, *Philip of Spain*, Eyre & Spottiswoode, 1963

Phillips, Miles, "A Discourse Written by one Miles Phillips, Englishman," in Richard Hakluyt, *The Principal Navigations, Voyages and Discoveries of the English Nation*, 1589

Pierson, Peter, *Commander of the Armada: The Seventh Duke of Medina Sidonia*, Yale University Press, 1989

Pierson, Peter, "Elizabeth's Pirate Admiral," *Journal of Military History*, 8, Summer 1996

Pine, John, *The Tapestry Hangings in the House of Lords: Representing the Several Engagements between the English and Spanish Fleets in the Ever-memorable Year 1588*, 1739

Plowden, Alison, *The Elizabethan Secret Service*, Harvester, Hemel Hempstead, 1991

Pollard, A. F. (ed.), *Tudor Tracts, 1532–1588*, 1903

Pollitt, Ronald, "Bureaucracy and the Armada: The Administrators' Battle," *Mariner's Mirror*, 60, May 1974

Pollitt, Ronald, "Contingency Planning and the Defeat of the Spanish Armada," in Daniel M. Masterson (ed.), *Naval History: The Sixth Symposium of the U.S. Naval Academy*, Scholarly Resources, Wilmington, Delaware, 1987 (also in *American Neptune*, 45, Winter 1984)

Pollitt, Ronald, "John Hawkins' Troublesome Voyages: Merchants, Bureaucrats and the Origins of the Slave Trade," *Journal of British Studies*, 12, May 1973

Pope Sixtus V, *A Declaration of the Sentence and Deposition of Elizabeth, the Usurper and Pretensed Quene of Englande*, Antwerp, 1588

Porter, Roy, *London: A Social History*, Hamish Hamilton, 1994

Powell, J. W. Damer, *The Bristol Privateers and Ships of War*, Bristol, 1930

Purchas, Samuel, *Purchas his Pilgrimes*, Hakluyt Society, Extra Series, vols. 14–33, Glasgow 1903–07

Quatrefages, Rene, *Los Tercios*, Madrid, 1983

Quinn, David B., *Drake's Circumnavigation of the Globe: A Review*, the Fifteenth Harte Lecture, University of Exeter, 14 November 1580, Exeter University Press, 1981

Quinn, David B., *Sir Francis Drake as Seen by his Contemporaries*, John Carter Brown Library, Providence, 1996

Quinn, David B., "Spaniards at Sea," in *The Times Literary Supplement*, 18 December 1981

Quinn, David B., "Spanish Armada Prisoners' Escape from Ireland: Notes," *Mariner's Mirror*, 70, May 1984

Quinn, David B., and Ryan, A. N., *England's Sea Empire, 1550–1642*, Early Modern Europe Today series, Allen & Unwin, 1983

Rait, R. S., and Cameron, I. A., *King James's Secret*, 1927

Ralegh, Sir Walter, *History of the World*, 1614

Ralegh, Sir Walter, "A Report of the Truth of the Fight . . . Betwixt the Revenge . . . and an Armada of the King of Spaine," in E. Arber, *English Reprints*, 1895

Ramsay, George Daniel, *English Overseas Trade*, Macmillan, 1957

Ramsay, George Daniel, "The Smugglers' Trade: A Neglected Aspect of English Commercial Development," *Transactions of the Royal Historical Society*, 5th series, 2, 1952

Ramsey, P., *Tudor Economic Problems*, Gollancz, 1963

Rasor, Eugene L., *The Spanish Armada of 1588: Historiography and Annotated Bibliography*, Greenwood Press, Westport, Connecticut, 1993

Rawlinson, H. G., "The Embassy of William Harborne to Constantinople, 1583–88," *Transactions of the Royal Historical Society*, 4th Series, V, 1922

Read, Conyers, *Mr. Secretary Walsingham and the Policy of Queen Elizabeth*, vol. III, Oxford, 1925

Read, Conyers, "Queen Elizabeth's Seizure of the Duke of Alva's Payships," *Journal of Modern History*, 5, December 1933

Read, Conyers, *William Cecil Burghley, vol. 2: Lord Burghley and Queen Elizabeth*, Cape, 1960

Rex, Richard, *The Tudor Dynasty*, Tempus, 2002

Richards, Judith, "Before the 'Mountaynes Mouse': Propaganda and Public Defence before the Spanish Armada," in Jeff Doyle and Bruce Moore (eds.), *England and the Spanish Armada: Papers Arising from the 1988 Conference, University College, University of New South Wales*, Australian Defence Force Academy, Canberra, 1990

Richmond, C. F., *The Invasion of Britain: An Account of Plans, Attempts, and Countermeasures from 1586 to 1918*, 1941

Richmond, Herbert, *The Navy as an Instrument of Policy, 1558–1727*, Methuen, 1953

Ridley, Jasper, *The Tudor Age*, Constable, 1988

Rivas, Manuel Garcia, *La Sanidad en la Jornada de Inglaterra, 1587–88*, Instituto de Historia y Cultura Naval, vol. 2, Madrid, 1988

"Robert, Earl of Essex's Ghost . . ." in *Harleian Miscellany*, vol. 5, 1808

Roberts, John C. de Villamar, *Devon and the Armada*, Gooday, East Wittering, West Sussex, 1988

Robinson, Gregory, *The Elizabethan Ship*, 1956

Robson-Scott, William D., *German Travellers in England 1400–1800*, Blackwell, Oxford, 1953

Rodger, N.A.M., *The Armada in the Public Records*, HMSO, 1988

Rodger, N.A.M., "The Development of Broadside Gunnery, 1450–1650," *Mariner's Mirror*, LXXXII, 1996

Rodger, N.A.M., "Elizabethan Naval Gunnery: Note," *Mariner's Mirror*, 61, November 1975

Rodger, N.A.M., *The Safeguard of the Sea: A Naval History of Britain, I; 660–1649*, 1997

Rodgers, William Ledyard, *Naval Warfare Under Oars, Fourth to Sixteenth Centuries: A Study of Strategy, Tactics and Ship Design*, Naval Institute Press, Annapolis, 1967

Rodriguez-Salgado, Mia J., "The Anglo-Spanish War: The Final Episode in the 'Wars of the Roses'?" in Mia J. Rodriguez-Salgado and Simon Adams (eds.), *England, Spain and the Gran Armada 1585–89: Essays from the Anglo-Spanish Conferences, London and Madrid 1988*, J. Donald, Edinburgh, 1991

Rodriguez-Salgado, Mia J., "Pilots, Navigation and Strategy in the Gran Armada," in Mia J. Rodriguez-Salgado and Simon Adams, (eds.), *England, Spain and the Gran Armada 1585–89: Essays from the Anglo-Spanish Conferences, London and Madrid 1988*, 1991

Rodriguez-Salgado, Mia J., and Staff of the National Maritime Museum, *Armada, 1588–1988: An International Exhibition to Commemorate the Spanish Armada*, Penguin, 1988

Rose, John Holland, "Was the Failure of the Spanish Armada due to Storms?" *Proceedings of the British Academy*, 22, 1936

Rose, Susan, *Medieval Naval Warfare, 1000–1500*, Routledge, 2002

Rowse, A. L., *The Elizabethan Age*, Macmillan, New York, 1978

Rowse, A. L., *The England of Elizabeth*, Macmillan, 1950

Rowse, A. L., *The Expansion of Elizabethan England*, Scribners, New York, 1972

Rowse, A. L., *Tudor Cornwall: Portrait of a Society*, 1941

Rule, John C., and TePaske, John J. (eds.), *The Character of Philip II: The Problem of Moral Judgements in History*, D. C. Heath, Boston, 1963

Rule, Margaret, *The Mary Rose: The Excavation and Raising of Henry VIII's Flagship*, Conway, 1982

Runyan, Timothy, J., "Ships and Mariners in Later Medieval England," *Journal of British Studies*, 16, Spring 1977

Rusbridge, Alfred, *Legend of "The Mound" at Selsey Old Church: An Incident of the Armada*, Chichester, 1900

Rye, W. B., *England as Seen by Foreigners in the Days of Elizabeth and James I*, 1865

Salgado, Gemini, *The Elizabethan Underworld*, Sutton, Stroud, 1995

Salzman, L. F., *England in Tudor Times*, 1926

Saunders, Roy, *The Raising of the "Vasa": The Rebirth of a Swedish Galleon*, Oldbourne, 1962

Savage, R., et al. (eds.), *Minutes & Accounts of Stratford-upon-Avon, vol. iv, 1586–1592*, Dugdale Society, 1929

Scammell, G. V., "European Seamanship in the Great Age of Discovery," *Mariner's Mirror*, 68, August 1982

Scammell, G. V., "Manning the English Merchant Service in the Sixteenth Century," *Mariner's Mirror*, 56, May 1970

Scammell, G. V., "Shipowning in England, c. 1450–1550," *Transactions of the Royal Historical Society*, 5th series, 12, 1962

Scammell, G. V., "The Sinews of War: Manning and Provisioning English Fighting Ships, c. 1550–1650," *Mariner's Mirror*, 73, November 1987

Schokkenbroek, J.C.A., "Wherefore Serveth Justin with his shipping of Zeeland? The Dutch and the Spanish Armada 1588," in P. Gallagher and D. W. Cruickshank (eds.), *God's Obvious Design: Papers for the Spanish Armada Symposium, Sligo 1988*, Tamesis Books, 1990

Scott, A. F., *Every One a Witness: The Tudor Age*, White Lion, 1975

Scott, W. (ed.), *The Somers Collection of Tracts*, vol. I, 1809

"The Scottish Queen's Burial at Peterborough, upon Tuesday, being Lammas Day, 1 August 1587," in A. F. Pollard (ed.), *Tudor Tracts, 1532–1588*, 1903

Shea, Michael, *Maritime England: The Nation's Heritage*, Country Life Books, 1981

Shepard, Alan, *Marlowe's Soldiers: Rhetorics of Masculinity in the Age of the Armada*, Ashgate, Aldershot, 2002

Shirley, John W., *Thomas Harriot, A Biography*, Oxford, 1983

A Short Admonition upon the Shameful Treason wherewith Sir William Stanley and Rowland York have Betrayed and Delivered for Money unto the Spaniards the town of Deventer and Scans of Zutphen, 1587

Sinclair, Peter, "Notes on the Spanish Armada," in Jeff Doyle and Bruce Moore (eds.), *England and the Spanish Armada: Papers Arising from the 1988 Conference, University College, University of New South Wales*, Australian Defence Force Academy, Canberra, 1990

Singman, Jeffrey L., and McLean, Will, *Daily Life in Elizabethan England*, Greenwood, Westport, Connecticut, 1995

Skilliter, S. A., "The Hispano-Ottoman Armistice of 1581," in C. E. Bosworth (ed.), *Iran and Islam*, Edinburgh, 1971

Slack, Paul, *Poverty and Policy in Tudor and Stuart England,* 1988
Sladen, D.B.W., *The Spanish Armada: A Ballad of 1588,* 1888
Smith, Bruce R., *The Acoustic World of Early Modern England,* University of Chicago Press, 1999
Smith, Dr. Charles, *History of Kerry,* 1756
Smith, David Bonner, "Drake's Prayer," *Mariner's Mirror,* 36, January 1950
Smith, W., *Particular Description of England: 1588,* 1879
Smyth, Admiral, *The Sailor's Wordbook,* 1867
Somers, John, *A Collection of Scarce Tracts,* 1809
Somerset, Anne, *Elizabeth I,* Weidenfeld & Nicolson, 1991
Soto, Jose Luis Casado, *Los Barcos Españoles del Sigle XVI y la Gran Armada de 1588,* Instituto Historia y Cultura Naval, vol. 4, Madrid, 1988
Southey, Robert, *English Seamen,* Chicago, 1895
Southey, Robert, *Lives of the British Admirals,* 5 vols., 1833–40
Speed, John, *The Counties of Britain, A Tudor Atlas,* Pavilion/British Library, 1988
Spellissy, Sean, *The History of Galway: City and County,* Celtic Bookshop, Limerick, 1999
Spence, Richard T., *The Privateering Earl,* Sutton, 1997
Spicer, Stanley, *The Age of Sail: The Master Shipbuilders of the Maritimes,* Formac, 2002
Spotswood-Green, William, "Armada Ships on the Kerry Coast," *Proceedings of the Royal Irish Academy,* section C, 1908–09
Steele, Robert (ed.), *Tudor and Stuart Proclamations,* Oxford, 1910
Stenuit, Robert, *Treasures of the Armada,* David & Charles, Newton Abbot, 1972
Stern, Virginia F., *Sir Stephen Powle of Court and Country,* Associated University Press, Cranbury, New Jersey, 1992
Stone, Lawrence, "The Armada Campaign of 1588," *History,* 29, September 1944
Stone, Lawrence, *The Crisis of the Aristocracy, 1558–1641,* 1965
Stow, John, *The Annales or Generall Chronicles of England,* 1615
Stow, John, *The Survey of London,* 1603, Everyman, 1970
Strachey, Lytton, *Elizabeth and Essex,* 1928
Stradling, R. A., *The Armada of Flanders: Spanish Maritime Policy and European War, 1568–1668,* Cambridge Studies in Early Modern History, Cambridge University Press, 1992
Straker, Ernest, *Wealden Iron,* 1931
Strype, John, *Annals of Queen Elizabeth's Reign,* 4 vols., 1725–31
Stuart, Elizabeth, *Lost Landscapes of Plymouth: Maps, Charts and Plans to 1800,* Sutton, Stroud, 1991
Sugden, John, *Sir Francis Drake,* Barrie & Jenkins, 1990
Taylor, A. H., "Galleon into Ship of the Line" (3 parts), *Mariner's Mirror,* 44–45
Tenison, E. M., *Elizabethan England,* 14 vols., Leamington Spa, 1933–60
Thomas, David A., *The Illustrated Armada Handbook,* Harrap, 1988
Thomas, R. (ed.), *Interesting and Authentic Narratives of the Most Remarkable Shipwrecks, Fires, Famines, Calamities, Providential Deliverances, and the Lamentable Disasters on the Seas, in Most Parts of the World,* Hartford, Connecticut, 1850
Thompson, G. S. (ed.), *The Twysden Lieutenancy Papers 1583–1668,* Kent Archaeological Society, 1926
Thompson, I.A.A., "The Appointment of the Duke of Medina Sidonia to the Command of the Spanish Armada," Historical Journal, 12, 1969

Thompson, I.A.A., "The Armada and Administrative Reform: The Spanish Council of War in the Reign of Philip II," in *English Historical Review*, 82, October 1967

Thompson, I.A.A., "Spanish Armada Gun Policy and Procurement," in P. Gallagher and D. W. Cruickshank (eds.), *God's Obvious Design: Spanish Armada Symposium, Sligo 1988*, Tamesis Books, 1990

Thompson, I.A.A., "Spanish Armada Guns," *Mariner's Mirror*, LXI, 1975

Thompson, I.A.A., *War and Government in Habsburg Spain, 1560–1620*, Athlone, 1976

Thomson, Alexander, "John Holles," *Journal of Military History*, 8, June 1936

Thomson, George Malcolm, *Sir Francis Drake*, 1972

Thornber, William, *Traditions of the Foreland of the Fylde, Elizabethan Era: Penny Stone; or, A Tradition of the Spanish Armada*, Preston, 1886

Thursfield, J. R., *The Spanish Armada*, 1895

Tillyard, E.M.W., *The Elizabethan World Picture*, Chatto, 1943

Tilton, William, "Lord Burghley on the Spanish Invasion," *American Historical Review*, 2, October 1896

Tincey, John, *Elizabeth's Army and the Armada*, Partizan Press, 1988

Tincey, John (illus. Richard Hook), *The Spanish Armada*, Osprey, 2000

Treece, Henry, *Wickham and the Armada*, Hulton Press, 1959

Trevelyan, George Macaulay, *English Social History*, Longman, 1978

Trevelyan Papers Pt 3, Camden Society, vol. 84

A True Relation of that which Lately Happened to the Great Spanish Fleet . . . and Many Strange Deliveries of Captaines and Souldiers in the Tempest, 1623

Twiss, Sir Travers, *Black Book of the Admiralty*, 1871

Two Famous Sea-Fights, Lately Made, betwixt the Fleetes of the King of Spain and the Fleetes of the Hollanders, the one in the West Indyes, the other . . . betwixt Callis and Gravelin, 1639

Tymme, Thos, *A Preparation against the Prognosticated Dangers of 1588*, 1587

Ubaldini, Petruccio, "A Discourse concerning the Spanish Fleet Invading England in the Year 1588," in *Harleian Miscellany*, vol. I, 1808

Ubaldini, Petruccio, *A Genuine and Most Impartial Narration of the Glorious Victory obtained by Her Majesty's Navy over the Falsely-Stiled Invincible Armada of Spain*, 1740

Ubaldini, Petruccio, *Lord Howard of Effingham and the Spanish Armada*, 1919

Unwin, Rayner, *The Defeat of Sir John Hawkins*, 1960

Usherwood, Stephen (ed.), *The Great Enterprise: The History of the Spanish Armada as Revealed in Contemporary Documents*, Bell & Hyman, 1982

Usherwood, Stephen, and Usherwood, Elizabeth, *The Counter-Armada, 1596: The Journall of the Mary Rose*, Bodley Head, 1983

Vanes, Jean, *Bristol at the Time of the Spanish Armada*, Bristol, 1988

Vaux, W.S.W. (ed.), *The World Encompassed*, Hakluyt Society, 1854

Vega, Lope de, *La Dragontea*, Madrid, 1598

Vega, Lope de, *Prosa*, Madrid, 1997

Versteeg, Dingman, *The Sea Beggars: Liberators of Holland from the Yoke of Spain*, New York, 1901

Wagenaer, L., *The Mariner's Mirror . . .* , 1590

Wake, J. (ed.), *A copy of papers relating to musters, beacons, subsidies, etc., in the county of Northampton, AD 1586–1623*, Northampton Record Society, Kettering, 1926

Waldman, Milton, *Elizabeth and Leicester,* 1946
Walker, Bryce S., *The Armada,* The Seafarers Series, Time-Life Books, 1981
Wallace, Willard M., *Sir Walter Ralegh,* 1959
Walsh, William T., *Philip II,* New York, 1937
Waters, David W., *The Art of Navigation in England in Elizabethan and Early Stuart Times,* Yale University Press, 1978
Waters, David W., "The Elizabethan Navy and the Armada Campaign," *Mariner's Mirror,* 35, April 1949
Waters, David W., "The Elizabethan Navy and the Armada of Spain," *National Maritime Museum Monographs,* 17, National Maritime Museum, Greenwich, 1975
Watson, A. I., "Attitudes in Spain towards Philip II's Imperialism," in P. Gallagher and D. W. Cruickshank (eds.), *God's Obvious Design: Papers for the Spanish Armada Symposium, Sligo 1988,* Tamesis Books, 1990
Watson, R., *The History of the Reign of Philip the Second, King of Spain,* 2 vols., 1777
Watt, James, "Surgeons of the 'Mary Rose': The Practice of Surgery in Tudor England," *Mariner's Mirror,* 69.1, February 1983
Weir, Alison, *The Life of Elizabeth I,* Cape, 1998
Wernham, Richard Bruce, *After the Armada: Elizabethan England and the Struggle for Western Europe, 1588–95,* Clarendon, Oxford, 1984
Wernham, Richard Bruce, *Before the Armada: The Growth of English Foreign Policy, 1485–1588,* Cape, 1966
Wernham, Richard Bruce, "Elizabethan War Aims and Strategy," in S. T. Bindoff, Joel Hurstfield and C. H. Williams (eds.), *Elizabethan Government and Society: Essays Presented to Sir John Neale,* Athlone Press, 1961
Wernham, Richard Bruce, *The Expedition of Sir John Norris and Sir Francis Drake to Spain and Portugal, 1589,* Navy Records Society, 127, 1988
Wernham, Richard Bruce, *The Making of Elizabethan Foreign Policy, 1558–1603,* Berkeley, 1980
Wernham, Richard Bruce, "Queen Elizabeth and the Portugal Expedition of 1589," *English Historical Review,* LXVI, 1951
Wernham, Richard Bruce (ed.), *The Counter-Reformation and Price Revolution 1559–1610,* New Cambridge Modern History, 3, Cambridge University Press, 1968
Whitaker, Thomas Dunham, *The History and Antiquities of the Deanery of Craven,* Leeds, 1878
White, Henry, *The Massacre of St. Bartholomew,* 1868
Whitehead, Bertrand T., *Brags and Boasts: Propaganda in the Year of the Armada,* Sutton, Stroud, 1994
Whiting, John Roger Scott, *The Enterprise of England: The Spanish Armada,* Sutton, Stroud, 1995
Wilford, Sir Thomas, *A Military Discourse,* 1734
Williams, Neville, *All the Queen's Men: Elizabeth I and Her Courtiers,* Weidenfeld & Nicolson, 1972
Williams, Neville, *Contraband Cargoes: Seven Centuries of Smuggling,* Longmans, 1959
Williams, Neville, *Francis Drake,* 1973
Williams, Neville, *The Life and Times of Elizabeth the First,* Cardinal, 1975
Williams, Neville, *The Sea Dogs: Privateers, Plunder and Piracy in the Elizabethan Age,* Weidenfeld & Nicolson, 1975

Williams, Penry, *Life in Tudor England*, English Life Series, Putnam, New York, 1964

Williams, Sir Roger, *The Art of Warre*, date unknown

Williamson, James A., *The Age of Drake*, 1970

Williamson, James A., *The English Channel: A History*, World, Cleveland, 1959

Williamson, James A., *Hawkins of Plymouth: A New History of Sir John Hawkins and of the Other Members of his Family Prominent in Tudor England*, 1969

Williamson, James A. *The Tudor Age*, A History of England, vol. 5, McKay, New York, 1964

Wilson, C., *Queen Elizabeth and the Revolt of the Netherlands*, 1970

Wilson, Derek, *The World Encompassed: Drake's Great Voyages 1577–1580*, Hamish Hamilton, 1977

Wilson, Derek A., *A Tudor Tapestry: Men, Women and Society in Reformation England*, University of Pittsburgh, 1972

Wilson, Thomas, *The State of England A.D. 1600*, Camden Society, 3rd series, vol. 52

Wingfield, Anthony, *A True Coppie of a Discourse written by a Gentleman Employed in the Late Voyage of Spaine and Portingale . . .* , 1589

Wood, Walter, *Survivors' Tales of Famous Shipwrecks*, Geoffrey Bles, 1932

Woodall, John, *The Surgions Mate*, 1617; facsimile with an introduction and appendix by John Kirkup, Kingsmead Press, Bath, 1978

Woodrooffe, Thomas, *The Enterprise of England*, 1958

Worth, R. N., *Calendar of the Plymouth Municipal Records*, Plymouth, 1893

Wright, Irene A. (ed.), *Documents Concerning English Voyages to the Spanish Main 1569–1580*, Hakluyt Society Series II, LXXI, 1932

Wright, Irene A. (ed.), *Further English Voyages to Spanish America 1583–1594*, Hakluyt Society Series II, XCIX, 1951

Wright, W.H.K., *The Spanish Armada*, 1887

Wurtemberg, Frederick, Duke of, "The Journal of Frederick, Duke of Wurtemberg, 1592," in William Rye (ed.), *England as Seen by Foreigners*, 1865

Wynkfielde, Robert, "The Execution of Mary, Queen of Scots," in H. Ellis (ed.), *Original Letters Illustrative of English History*, 1827

Youengs, Joyce, "Bowmen, Billmen and Hackbutters: The Elizabethan Militia in the South West," in *Security and Defence in the South-West of England before 1800*, Exeter Studies in History, 19, University of Exeter Press, 1987

Youengs, Joyce, "Ralegh's Country and the Sea," *Proceedings of the British Academy*, 75, 1989

Youengs, Joyce, *Ralegh's Country: The South-West of England in the Reign of Queen Elizabeth*, Raleigh, North Carolina, 1986

Youengs, Joyce, *Sixteenth Century England*, Pelican Social History of Britain, Allen Lane, 1984

Yturriaga, Jose Antonio de, "Attitudes in Ireland towards the Survivors of the Spanish Armada," *Irish Sword*, 17, Summer 1990

TELEVISION PROGRAMMES

Ereira, Alan, *Armada*, BBC, 1988

Wilson, David, "Armada," *Secret History*, Channel Four, 2001

Index

A NOTE ABOUT THE AUTHOR

Neil Hanson is a widely acclaimed journalist and speechwriter and the author of *The Custom of the Sea* and *The Great Fire of London*. He lives in the Yorkshire Dales in England.

A NOTE ON THE TYPE

This book was set in Janson, a typeface long thought to have been made by the Dutchman Anton Janson, who was a practicing typefounder in Leipzig during the years 1668–1687. However, it has been conclusively demonstrated that these types are actually the work of Nicholas Kis (1650–1702), a Hungarian who most probably learned his trade from the master Dutch typefounder Dirk Voskens. The type is an excellent example of the influential and sturdy Dutch types that prevailed in England up to the time William Caslon (1692–1766) developed his own incomparable designs from them.

Composed by North Market Street Graphics,
Lancaster, Pennsylvania

Printed and bound by Berryville Graphics,
Berryville, Virginia

Designed by Soonyoung Kwon